Athenian Law and Society

Athenian Law and Society focuses upon the intersection of law and society in classical Athens, in relation to topics like politics, class, ability, masculinity, femininity, gender studies, economics, citizenship, slavery, crime, and violence. The book explores the circumstances and broader context which led to the establishment of the laws of Athens, and how these laws influenced the lives and action of Athenian citizens, by examining a wide range of sources from classical and late antique history and literature. Kapparis also explores later literature on Athenian law from the Renaissance up to the 20th and 21st centuries, examining the long-lasting impact of the world's first democracy.

Athenian Law and Society is a study of the intersection between law and society in classical Athens that has a wide range of applications the study of the Athenian polis, as well as law, democracy, and politics in both classical and more modern settings.

Konstantinos A. Kapparis is UF Research Foundation Professor and Director of the Center for Greek Studies at the University of Florida, USA. He studied with D.M. MacDowell at the University of Glasgow. His research interests include the Attic Orators, Athenian Law, Greek and Roman Medical Authors, Women's History and Gender Studies, and the Social History of the Graeco-Roman World. He has published a commentary on Apollodoros *Against Neaira* (and also an expanded Modern Greek commentary of the same speech), a monograph on *Abortion in the Ancient World*, a large volume on *Prostitution in the Ancient Greek World*, a co-authored volume entitled *Legal Speeches of Democratic Athens*, and he has co-edited a collection of the articles of D.M. MacDowell. He has also published a number of articles on topics such as prostitution, citizenship and immigration, gender studies, history of medicine and science, and textual criticism.

Athenian Law and Society

Konstantinos A. Kapparis

Routledge
Taylor & Francis Group
LONDON AND NEW YORK

First published 2019 by Routledge

2 Park Square, Milton Park, Abingdon, Oxfordshire OX14 4RN
52 Vanderbilt Avenue, New York, NY 10017

Routledge is an imprint of the Taylor & Francis Group, an informa business

First issued in paperback 2020

British Library Cataloguing-in-Publication Data
A catalogue record for this book is available from the British Library

Library of Congress Cataloging-in-Publication Data
Names: Kapparis, K. A., author.
Title: Athenian law and society / Konstantinos A. Kapparis.
Description: New York : Routledge, 2018. | Includes bibliographical references and index.
Identifiers: LCCN 2018023497 (print) | LCCN 2018025945 (ebook) | ISBN 9781315568270 (ebook) | ISBN 9781317177524 (web pdf) | ISBN 9781317177517 (epub) | ISBN 9781317177500 (mobi/kindle) | ISBN 9781472449184 (hardback : alk. paper)
Subjects: LCSH: Law—Greece—Athens. | Athens (Greece)—Social life and customs. | Athens (Greece)—History.
Classification: LCC KL4115.A75 (ebook) | LCC KL4115.A75 K37 2018 (print) | DDC 340.5/385—dc23
LC record available at https://lccn.loc.gov/2018023497

ISBN: 978-1-4724-4918-4 (hbk)
ISBN: 978-0-367-66495-4 (pbk)

Typeset in Times New Roman
by Apex CoVantage, LLC

MIX
Paper from responsible sources
FSC™ C013985

Printed in the United Kingdom
by Henry Ling Limited

Contents

Foreword viii
Abbreviations x

Introduction 1

The development of Athenian law 1
Sources of Athenian law 4
Scholarship on Athenian law and society 9

1 **The administration of justice in the *polis*** 18

1.1 Sources 18
1.2 The division of powers in the Athenian Democracy 20
1.3 The question on the rule of law in the Athenian Democracy 22
1.4 Accountability of officials and individuals before the law 24
1.5 Protections of core human rights in Athenian law 30
1.6 Open government in the Athenian Democracy 36
1.7 Dispute resolution: processes and types of lawsuits 40
1.8 Blocking an improperly introduced lawsuit 46
1.9 The "amateurism" of Athenian law? 46
1.10 Rules of evidence and the rule of law 49
1.11 Executive officers of the Athenian state 54

2 **Citizens, metics and slaves in Athenian law and life** 70

2.1 Sources 70
2.2 Citizenship in the Greek polis *75*
2.3 Introduction into the citizen body 80
2.4 The rights, privileges and duties of Athenian citizen men 86

2.5 Metics 88
2.6 Slaves 96
2.7 Legal procedures for status disputes 101

3 The Athenian *oikos* 116
3.1 Sources 116
3.2 The oikos *and the* polis *117*
3.3 The oikos *and its members 119*

4 The formation and purposes of marriage: wives and concubines 138
4.1 Sources 138
4.2 The ever-shifting definition of marriage 140
4.3 Lawful marriage: types and purpose 147
4.4 Alternative unions and concubines 152
4.5 Conclusions 155

5 The continuation of the *oikos*: inheritance and succession 163
5.1 Sources 163
5.2 Succession by natural legitimate sons 166
5.3 Legitimate daughters and dowry 167
5.4 Epikleros *169*
5.5 Illegitimate children 171
5.6 Wills and succession by adopted children 172

6 The *oikos* in peril: divorce, adultery, prostitution 182
6.1 Sources 182
6.2 Divorce 185
6.3 Adultery 190
6.4 Prostitution 193

7 Criminal justice: violence and property crimes 207
7.1 Sources 207
7.2 Assault and slander: violence in Athenian law and life 214
7.3 Hybris *223*
7.4 Non-violent conflict resolution: arbitration 225
7.5 Sexual violence 227
7.6 Property crimes and disputes 229

8 Religion, the state and the law 241
8.1 Sources 241
8.2 The intersection of religion and the law 248

8.3 State religion, festivals and the law 252
8.4 Prosecutions on religious grounds 257
8.5 Homicide 268

9 The safety net: protecting those in need 280

9.1 Sources 280
9.2 Protecting legal minors and the elderly from abuse 283
9.3 Providing for disabled citizens 291
9.4 Caring for the elderly 292
9.5 Income support for the poor and the needy 294
9.6 The Athenian healthcare system: medical care and the law 298
9.7 Conclusions 302

Epilogue: Athenian law as the voice of the democratic *polis* 309

Bibliography 315
Index 352

Foreword

This volume began in 1998 with a series of lectures on Athenian law and society at the Queen's University of Belfast. In later years several versions of this course were taught as undergraduate, graduate and distance learning options at the University of Florida. While teaching these courses I came to the realization that there was no study adequately covering the intersection between law and society. We have a rich collection of good books and articles on Athenian law, and in more recent years an increasingly higher number of superb studies on Athenian society. However, there was no study exploring the intersection between the two, namely how and to what extent was Athenian law the product of peaceful or violent changes in 6th, 5th and 4th century Athens, and how and to what extent Athenian society as we understand it was influenced by the laws of the city. There were useful discussions on specific topics of law in historical studies, and sometimes there were useful discussions of the historical context in studies on Athenian law, but never a more thorough exploration of their interaction in public and private life from the time of Solon to the end of the Greek polis. This is the gap which this volume was meant to bridge. It was never meant to be another book on Athenian law or another book on Athenian society, but on the interaction between the two in the course of the classical period.

I was never under any illusion that I would be able to produce a fully comprehensive study in such a busy field. Only the titles in the bibliography of Athenian law maintained by Ilias Arnaoutoglou, David Mirhady and Mark Sundahl extend to almost 1000 pages, and the bibliographical references on Athenian society could just as easily be another 1000 pages. To this if one added a large number of original sources the task would appear daunting. The best one can hope for is to read enough to be well informed. With a project like this there was always an inherent danger of turning it into a review of the previous literature, and this decidedly was not my purpose here. My plan was to produce a synthesized account which could be useful to specialists, but which would not deter students and laypersons with limited understanding of the Athenian democracy and its institutions, or the fundamentals of Athenian society. The ultimate goal was to make sense out of Athenian law, to present it in context and explain how and why it was formed and formatted in the manner that it did, and how it affected the course of Athenian history. I am hoping that, in the end, what many a time appears to be strange and alien about Athenian law to the modern reader will seem less strange and awkward after reading this study. My overall conclusion, that the law of classical Athens was the voice of the Democratic Constitution, the avenue through which the abstract principles and ideals of the first democracy in history were translated into everyday rules regulating the life of the polis, the oikoi, and the people within them, might serve as a helpful guide for a better understanding of the principles and direction of Athenian law.

A Humanities Enchancement research grant from the University of Florida in the summer of 2015 allowed me to jump-start the final phase of this project, and a sabbatical in 2017–2018 allowed me to complete this volume. I'm grateful to the home institution for these opportunities, and especially to Victoria Pagan and Mary Ann Eaverly, our two successive Chairs in the Department of Classics for making sure that I had the necessary time to complete this project. I am also deeply grateful to Mrs Violet Wilson, who painstakingly typed all the recordings from the online lectures on Athenian law and society. And last but not least, I owe a big debt of gratitude to Michael Greenwood, the editor of Routledge who supported this project at its inception. Many more people would need to be thanked, especially my former students, who contributed with ideas, questions and insightful comments that have helped me to form cleared ideas, and reach better researched conclusions on many aspects of this vast topic.

Abbreviations

Abbreviations to Greek authors are as in the *LSJ*, and abbreviations to Roman authors are as in the *Lewis-Short*. Following the *TLG*, all references to Athenaios are by book and chapter of the edition of Kaibel. In general, when there are alternative reference systems, I tend to follow the one adopted by the *TLG*. I am not in favor of Latinizing the names of Greek authors, and I tend to keep them as close to their original form as possible, but for some commonly used names in English (like, for example, Plato or Epicurus) the Latinized spelling is standard, and I have kept it. Inevitably this creates an inconsistency, but since it is not likely to cause any confusion, I find it acceptable. Bibliographical references follow the Chicago style, and all abbreviations of journals are as in *L'Année philologique*.

Introduction

The development of Athenian law

The beginner in the study of Athenian Law may think that many of its provisions look strange, alien, the eccentric demands of a past society upon its citizens which often make no sense to the modern reader. After all, what kind of law was the one forcing a fourteen-year-old girl to marry the oldest male relative of her father, conceivably a nonagenarian, with no regard for her feelings over the matter and no avenue of escape? Bemusement and disbelief are the typical reactions of students when first presented with the law on the *epikleros*, before having the opportunity to read it in context, take into account the circumstances which led to the introduction of this law, the matters which it was meant to address, the wider social context within which it was meant to operate, and the long-term impact that it had on the stability and structures of the Athenian family. Once such matters are fleshed out what at first glance looked alien, temperamental or indefensible, starts to make sense, to be seen as a measured, even if coldly utilitarian, response to an issue within the socioeconomic parameters of Athenian society, and crafted with a clear purpose in mind. We may still feel that this was not a very good law, but we understand why it was introduced, and more importantly why it remained in force for hundreds of years without additions or modifications. It is precisely out of this need to flesh out Athenian Law, to make sense of it in its broader social, political, economic, cultural and ideological context that this book was born. Its twofold objective was to explore the circumstances and broader context which led to the establishment of the laws of Athens, and to study how these laws affected the lives and behaviors of the inhabitants of the *polis* in the course of the Athenian Democracy.

Athens was the first democracy in history, and one of few direct democracies, along with her allied city-states. Every single aspect of public and private life was part of this grand constitutional experiment that had never been tried before anywhere in the world, where the people governed themselves by coming together at regular intervals, to set up laws, elect or select magistrates, sit in court, and fully share the dangers of war and the benefits of community life. But what is even more striking about the Athenian Democracy is the appreciation for personal freedoms, individuality, openness of ideas, tolerance, acceptance of what was different, and diversity. The Athenians understood that their grand political experiment was only worth the effort if it guaranteed these precious rights and privileges, and proudly contrasted their constitution to that of totalitarian, secretive, closed-minded, intolerant, collectivized Sparta.[1] These core concepts of democratic political thought which consisted of political equality (ἰσοπολιτεία), equality before the law (ἰσονομία), the right of free speech (παρρησία), the rule of the people (δημοκρατία), and freedom from internal or external oppressors (ἐλευθερία) would remain carefully guarded ideals through the course of classical Athenian history, and even more so in the 4th century, after some misadventures which led to short-lived suspensions of the democratic constitution in the years of war and crisis of the late 5th century.

The laws of Athens were not the product of democratic political thought in their entirety. The homicide laws of Drakon, and the core corpus of the laws of Solon preceded the democratic constitution by approximately a century, and yet they were comfortably retrofitted into the new constitutional form. In fact, the laws of Solon became the iconic embodiment of democratic Athenian law, even though most of them reflected an older ideology of a troubled aristocratic society in acute crisis. The way the Athenians were able to integrate those older corpora into democratic law and ideology was through omission and reinterpretation. Irrelevant or incompatible statutes in time became obsolete, but often no one bothered to erase them from the Solonean corpus of laws. Other laws were given new meaning, and the basic Solonean core was augmented and enriched with several layers of democratic laws. When this happened, the entire edifice would be called a law of Solon, and often even laws which visibly had been introduced in much later times were still attributed to Solon, just as in Sparta every law, rule and custom, written or unwritten, was attributed to the quasi-mythical lawgiver Lycurgus. Eventually Solon came to represent the democratic rule of law, and for some the founder of democracy itself, even though the Athenians knew their history well enough to be fully aware of the fact that Kleisthenes was the true founder of their democracy.[2]

We know very little about the legislative processes through the course of the 6th century between the Solonean legislation and the establishment of democracy. Michael Gagarin has plausibly suggested that the *thesmothetai* had some form of legislative powers in those early years.[3] Although the Peisistratids retained the laws of Solon and Drakon, surely the wishes of the tyrants could override the law when it served their purposes.[4] After the establishment of the democratic constitution the Assembly took over the legislative process. We know little about legislative processes before the end of the 5th century, but it seems that for most of the 5th century the introduction of a new law required a *probouleuma* and then a simple majority in the Assembly. We know that quite a few laws were introduced in the 5th century, like for example the Periclean law on citizenship introduced in 451. They all seem to be disparate pieces introduced in response to specific pressures, needs or political imperatives. By the end of the 5th century, two centuries of scattered pieces of legislation augmenting the laws of Drakon and Solon must have created an impossible hotchpotch, a loose conglomeration of statutes, sometimes inconsistent, and certainly difficult to know, when we consider that each one of them was set up in some temple or public building around the city, and not in a central location, and some were not even written down, but were rules and customs broadly accepted by the community. This is why, after the short-lived oligarchic coup of 411 a need to put some order to the chaos led to a substantial undertaking to write down and clean up the body of Athenian laws, which would not be completed before the final restoration of the democracy in 403. At that point cases could be introduced to court only on the basis of written laws. In the 4th century all the laws of the city would be kept in a central location at the Metroon, so that each citizen could easily consult them whenever he wished.

In the 4th century laws were introduced or abolished by specialized boards of nomothetai.[5] Decrees of the assembly were no longer considered to be conceptually identical to laws. There were thought to be specific measures dealing with specific issues, usually concerns of short or medium term, but in reality, even in the 4th century, the distinction between laws and decrees was never rigid. The basic philosophy underlying the introduction of new laws at the heart of the Athenian legal system, even after the codification of the laws in the late 5th century, was need. Rather than introducing broad strokes of legislation the Athenians continued to introduce short, specific laws to respond to specific contemporary challenges. If the picture that we get from the texts of the Attic orators is accurate, it seems that the introduction of new laws slows down as the 4th century advances. One would think that the increased risk and more involved processes for the introduction of new laws started having an impact. Another factor may be reduced need for new legislation after the extensive legislative activity of the late 5th and early 4th century. The impression we get is that around 380 the Athenians reached a point where existing laws covered most of the needs of the state and the individual. The end of the independent Greek *polis* in the last decades of the 4th century was a game-changer. Although the Athenians continued to make new laws and decrees, and acted as if nothing had changed, in reality the politics, trajectory, and overall, the fate of their city would increasingly be in the hands of powerful despots and their favorites.

Modern scholars have often employed legal principles from Anglo-American Common Law, or continental European Civil Law, in order to understand and interpret Athenian law. Many a time Athenian law has been unfavorably compared with modern legal systems, under the assumption that they are more advanced. However, Athenian law, although it shares some features with Common Law (e.g. extensive use of juries and adversarial argumentation), and some with Civil Law (e.g. codified laws), it is neither, and in the words of D. M. MacDowell "The Athenians themselves . . . had no knowledge of Roman or modern jurisprudence."[6] This is why attempts to employ modern jurisprudence as a methodological approach for Athenian law usually has resulted in failure.[7] The Athenians were not the first to develop a legal system in the ancient world. The code of Hammurabi, the laws of Charondas, Zaleukos, and perhaps Lycurgus, and the well if only partially preserved law of Gortyn, are only a few examples of legal systems outside Attica. At its inception in the late 7th to the early 6th century the Athenian legal system in some ways resembled those early codes. But it started diverging and taking a life of its own from the moment when the Democratic Constitution was established. From that point onwards little by little the law of Athens became the voice of the Athenian Democracy and the expression of the will of the sovereign *demos*, at least in most aspects affecting public life. The private law of Athens remained more conservative and was guided by the dominant principle of the preservation and well-being of the *oikos*. Under these circumstances transplanting modern legal principles to the Athenian legal system is not only anachronistic; it is also ill-fitting and highly unsuitable as it cannot account for the nature, purpose, socio-political framework and developmental patterns of Athenian law. The answers that we seek about Athenian law, and its implementation in the court system of the first democracy are to be found not in principles of modern jurisprudence, but in the extant literature of the Athenians, their documents and decrees preserved in the form of inscriptions, and on occasion in the material evidence and art which they have left behind.

Sources of Athenian law

By far the most significant source of Athenian law is the extant corpus of over a hundred Attic law-court speeches, augmented by numerous fragments in the form of citations in the lexicographers and other later antiquity or Byzantine authors. These are thought to be transcripts of prosecution or defense speeches delivered in Athenian trials. Sometimes they have been revised for publication; on other occasions they may be crude copies of the speech composed by the litigant himself or a shadow writer on his behalf in preparation for delivery during the trial. It is impossible to tell for sure which speeches have been revised for publication, and to what extent, but in either form they often address legal issues, as litigants tried to persuade the jury that the law was on their side. Sometimes the extant speeches do even better: they quote verbatim the law itself, or at least the part of it which the litigant considered pertinent. Quotations of the law usually take one of these forms:

a) the text of the law itself, or at least an extract from it, is preserved verbatim in the form of an inserted document,
b) the orator quotes part of the law in his text, almost word for word, or
c) the orator paraphrases the law in his text.

As expected, the trustworthiness of the information decreases from a) to c). Authentic legal citations inserted in the texts of the Attic orators are a reliable source of Athenian law. Citations of the law by the speakers can be reliable, but they need to be treated with caution as they may be selective and designed to serve the best interests of the litigant's case. A paraphrase of the law can contain useful information, but needs to be treated with additional caution, as this information is offered to us through the prism of the litigant's interests.

The question on the reliability of legal documents inserted in the text of the Attic Orators is inextricably linked to a larger debate on the authenticity of all inserted documents, which has been going on for two centuries. In some instances, scholars have reached widespread agreement. All the documents found in D. 18 *On the Crown*, and Aesch. 1 *Against Timarchos*, are universally considered to be forgeries, probably composed in Roman times and inserted in some lines of the textual tradition, but not all, at a much later time.[8] On the other hand, most scholars (with the exception of Mirco Canevaro) have accepted the position of Engelbert Drerup that the documents in D. 23 *Against Aristocrates*, and D. 24 *Against Timocrates* are authentic.[9] Beyond reasonable doubt authentic are also the documents in D. 45 and 46, the two speeches *Against Stephanos*, and D. 43 *Against Makaratos*. The laws and decrees cited in And. 1 *On the Mysteries* are also authentic.[10] The authenticity of the documents cited in D. 21 *Against Meidias* and D. 59 *Against Neaira* is harder to ascertain. Canevaro and Harris believe that the documents of *Against Meidias* are forgeries, however I accept the position of D.M. MacDowell that the laws and public documents are authentic, while private testimonies are forgeries.[11] I have argued that the same applies to the documents of *Against Neaira*.[12]

It is clear that sometimes the orators themselves cited the law in their own manuscript and read it out in court themselves.[13] In this case, since the law was incorporated in the author's manuscript, it was copied along with the rest of his text, and ought to be considered authentic. The study of Friedrich Burger on the partial stichometry confirms that such citations by the orators were included in the very early edition, perhaps the first ever, of the speeches which contained stichometric marks.[14] By contrast all inserted documents were not included in the stichometric edition. Some scholars, on the basis of this consider all inserted documents to be forgeries.[15] However, we have solid proof to the contrary, because some inserted documents are certainly authentic, word for word citations of laws preserved in inscriptions. One such case is very telling: D. 43.57 (αἰδέσασθαι . . . ἐνεχέσθων) is a word for word citation of the homicide law of Drakon as transcribed in an inscription in 409 (*IG* i³ 104). However, what is more interesting is that the document in D. 43 is not a transcription of the entire law of Drakon, but only of select passages as needed for this case. This is very telling and supports the view of the overwhelming majority of scholars, who are prepared to accept that some of these documents are authentic, even if partial, citations of laws, decrees and other documents, and propose that the only way to decide is to consider each document on its merits.

An obvious question to ask is how authentic documents found their way back into the manuscripts of the orators if they had not been included there in the first place. The answer is simple: the rhetoricians of the Hellenistic period could find at least some of the authentic documents. Laws could be easily found in the Metroon, other documents which might have been inscribed on stone, like for example the decree awarding citizenship to the Plataians in 427, which was definitely inscribed on stone and placed on the Acro*polis*,[16] might be still around, and the archives of magistrates of the Athenian state would contain additional documents which a meticulous editor of a certain speech could recover. In most cases only some of the documents could be recovered. For example, testimonies of private citizens did not exist in official archives and could perhaps be recovered and inserted in the manuscripts of the orators only in those few cases where someone had gone into the trouble of keeping those documents together with the original manuscript containing the speech.[17]

At a later time, probably in the period of the second sophistic, rhetoricians and their students in the schools of later antiquity set out to compose some of the missing documents for a number of reasons. Sometimes it may have been the need to complete the picture, on other occasions such compositions may have been used for educational purposes, and sometimes we get the impression that they were playful compositions.[18] Perhaps the fact that documents, authentic or not, can only be found in a few speeches which seem to have been popular texts for the study of rhetoric in Roman times highlights the educational purpose of these documents. Second sophistic forgeries eventually made it into our manuscripts, maybe intentionally or simply because a scribe though that they had been accidentally omitted, and it is a challenging task for us to separate the authentic documents from the forgeries. This process is critically important, especially in the case of legal documents, because if they are authentic they are reliable and direct sources for Athenian law, and many of them seem to be, but if they are forgeries, they cannot be trusted, and all the information they provide must be discarded.

The *Athenaion Politeia* attributed to Aristotle, which has reached us through some lucky finds of papyri containing a large part of it, is another invaluable source of Athenian law. First, it provides a narrative on the evolution of Athenian law from Drakon to the time of Aristotle, and important information on all significant stops in the process. Second, it often proposes a rationale behind the introduction of legal provisions in the quarter of the millennium that had passed from Drakon's legislation to the 330s, when this work was composed. We do not always need to uncritically accept the author's reasoning, as he is sometimes speaking about events which had taken place centuries before his own time, and what he is saying may simply be his opinion and not some authoritative knowledge. However, we do need to take his opinions and propositions seriously into account, since he clearly had a first-hand understanding of Athenian law and Constitution, and undoubtedly a large number of sources, primary documents as well as historical narratives, not available to us. Third, the *Athenaion Politeia* provides first-hand, reliable accounts on the day-to-day operations of the machinery of the state in classical Athens, the method of appointment, duties and responsibilities of specific magistrates. Fourth, it is an invaluable source even for private Athenian law, because it explains in great detail how individual citizens could access the legal system in order to protect their private interests, their families and their property. Finally, the *Athenaion Politeia* often places in context isolated legal provisions scattered all over the place in Athenian authors.[19]

Classical Athenian inscriptions are a direct and unchallengeable source of Athenian law, even if fragmentary and narrowly focused upon specific issues. Sometimes, we are lucky to have an actual law or decree of the Athenian state, like for example a part of Drakon's homicide law, or a series of naturalization decrees which shed light on this legal procedure.[20] Attic inscriptions contain valuable information on the legal duties and responsibilities of the numerous magistrates of the state. Honorary decrees are a very important source for our understanding of what constituted lawful, honorable and praiseworthy conduct for state officials and private persons, Athenians and outsiders. A large number of Attic inscriptions are dealing with religious matters, especially festivals, and offer information for the intersection of secular and sacred law.[21] Inscriptions are also significant sources for our understanding of local government at the level of the deme, over which literary sources tend to be very sketchy. Finally, inscriptions offer substantial, even if not always easy to interpret, evidence for our understanding of traditional citizen bodies like the phratries and gene.[22]

Attic comedy, especially the plays of Aristophanes, have often been used as sources for Athenian law, not always with satisfactory results. The nature of comedy makes it both a valuable and a dangerous source. If jokes are taken at face value, they can be very misleading. For example, modern scholars have often projected modern homophobic views into jokes on anal intercourse, and as a result an entire literature on penetration as an important cultural, social and even political value in the Greek world has arisen, even though the Greeks did not even have a single word for penetration. One wonders what are the chances of a culture that loved words, and had no less than 105 words for male prostitute, not to have a single word for penetration (or homosexuality, as a matter of fact), if it were such a centrally important concept. It is much more likely that the whole matter is a misunderstanding largely owed to crude jokes in comedy.

On the other hand, comedy can be very valuable if correctly interpreted in context, as it provides a perspective that is often different from that of more elevated genres, like tragedy or philosophy, one which is probably closer to the common person and devoid of the pretensions of higher literature, and as such more realistic. Under such circumstances comedy can offer valuable insights into the background as well as the effects of laws in contemporary society. A good example of how comedy, correctly used, can be an indispensable guide in our attempts to understand such effects is the statute quoted in the speech *Against Neaira*, which prohibited marriage or the pretense of lawful marriage between a citizen and an alien.[23] The plays of New Comedy, and Latin adaptations by Plautus and Terence, allow us to see clearly the impact of this law upon 4th century Athenian society. The alien *hetairai* featuring in these plays can never marry their Athenian lovers, and this has significant consequences for the plots. Sometimes the marriage of a good-natured *hetaira* (χρηστὴ ἑταίρα) to her lover might be desired, and for this purpose comedy needs to resort to a recognition plot, where the woman is discovered to be an Athenian, and thus she can marry her beloved in a happy ending.[24] Comedy may also be offering some glimpses into the reasons which led to the introduction of this law: seductive alien *hetairai* with whom Athenian men had long-term love affairs, and sometimes deep emotional bonds, might have been one of the primary targets of the law, for the reasons that comedy suggests. As the number of *hetairai* in 4th century Athens was increasing along with economic recovery, a law drawing the line of how deeply they could be integrated into Athenian society may have been seen as necessary.

Beyond these major sources, information on Athenian law and the reasoning and impact of specific legal provisions can be found almost anywhere in Greek literature. Who can explain the rationale behind the Solonean legislation better Solon himself? The fragments from his poems that have reached us can shed light upon the guiding principles of his legislation, what he was trying to accomplish, and what he perceived to be the best course of action for a state with immense socioeconomic problems. Moreover, his poems, unaffected by the democratization of later centuries, offer a clear reminder that Solon after all functioned within the boundaries and parameters of the aristocratic state, and that only later his legacy was reinterpreted as the core piece of the democratic Constitution. Another striking example is the narrative of Xenophon on the unusual trial of the generals after Arginousai. Was it constitutional? One might argue the case both ways. It could be said that it was unconstitutional for a number of reasons, and not least because the generals should have been tried in court with the appropriate procedures. On the other hand, it can be argued that the sovereign Assembly had the authority to do so, because the assembly was the source of all authority. But perhaps it was for uncontrollable bursts like this, which several times led to the wrong decisions in the 5th century, that the Demos tightened the rules in the 4th century. In any case, the narrative of Xenophon raises important constitutional and legal questions.

Perhaps it is noteworthy that the most aspirational document on the Athenian Constitution, the supremely eloquent defense of Democracy in contrast to other constitutional forms, like that of oligarchic and authoritarian Sparta, is not found in the court documents of classical Athens, or in the *Athenaion Politeia*, the main purpose of which was to study the Athenian Constitution, but in the most influential work of classical historiography, the *History* of Thucydides, placed in the mouth of Pericles, the man often identified with the classical Democratic ideal.[25] The epideictic speeches of the Attic orators offer important insights on Athenian political propaganda, and help us flesh out the rationale behind some of the laws of Athens, especially those establishing the framework for the dealings of the Athenians with outsiders. The great tragic plays of the 5th century tell us a lot about Athenian society and the work of the legal system in it, even when the settings are placed in other cities in the mythical past. For example, the *Trachiniae* of Sophocles allows us to understand better the complex family dynamics in a society where the law only recognized monogamy and privileged the lawful wife, but a man was not expected to remain faithful to his lawful wife unless he so wished, while in the *Medea* of Euripides we might recognize the effects of the Periclean citizenship law upon the relationships of citizens with outsiders.

Later literature is far from unimportant. Authors like Plutarch, Athenaios, Libanios, Clement of Alexandria or Lucian had absorbed vast amounts of classical literature and often quote it in their works. They had at their disposal so much more than what we do, and they often preserved for us evidence which otherwise would have been lost.[26] But the dangers of using later sources are obvious, and we need to be cautious. While, let's say, something which we read in Plutarch's *Life of Solon* could be an accurate citation of something which he had read in a reliable source now lost to us, it could just as easily be a misunderstanding of a classical source, something which he remembered incorrectly, or perhaps a piece of information coming from an unreliable classical or Hellenistic source. This is why later antiquity authors need to be consulted, but their evidence needs to be assessed with extra care.

The lexicographers and grammarians of the Roman and Byzantine periods, from Harpocration to Suda, and even the works of the Paleologean period, can be important sources for Athenian law as they often explain obscure legal terms, which otherwise we would not know how to interpret. Harpocration's invaluable lexicographic activity has much enriched our understanding of Athenian legal procedures, because he had in his hands many more speeches from the Attic orators than we do, and he often quotes his source, along with any information he provides on a certain procedure. Although Suda is less focused, in some ways it is more comprehensive and takes into account many more sources than Harpocration. The same can be said about other major lexicographic works like those of Pollux,[27] Hesychios or Photios. On the other hand, the amount of reliable information about Athenian law that we can find in the Delcamation of later antiquity is surprisingly little. The declamation was not interested in real law per se, but rather in stretching the logic of real law to breaking point, in order to train rhetoric students how to argue the absurd and the impossible. Even if real laws were hidden in the declamations of Libanios or Chorikios, let's say, we would have no way of separating them from fictional statutes without independent corroboration, which defeats the object.

In sum, information about Athenian laws, their rationale and impact can be found in a broad array of sources. Not all of these sources are equal in terms of value, reliability or concentration, and we always need to exercise good judgment, even when a piece of evidence comes from a reliable source and appears to be of unassailable authority. While we may not always be able to prove the authority and reliability of our sources, exercising caution could help us avoid serious errors, and having some faith in the possibility that unlikely sources can contain reliable evidence may ultimately furnish us with an important piece of information which otherwise we would have missed. In this study I have tried to assess each piece of evidence according to its own merits, taking into account the sources, the nature of the sources, inter-textual support, and the internal logic of arguments and information. No methodology is foolproof, but, nonetheless, I am convinced that the key to our understanding of Athenian law it is still to be found in the rich body of literature which humanity has inherited from the Athenians.

Scholarship on Athenian law and society

Athenian law did not have a direct influence upon the development of modern legal systems, as it came under the heavy shadow of Roman law and was eventually forgotten. However, it would be a grave historical error to ignore its indirect influence through those democratic principles such as equality before the law, freedom of speech, religious tolerance, and the conviction that all citizens should responsibly participate in the running of the state, which have shaped political landscapes around the globe since the time of the Enlightenment. From the Renaissance onwards, Athenian Democracy has stood as an inspiring political model, run by aspirational principles such as these for the betterment of humanity. The law of Athens was the voice of the Democratic Constitution which put these principles into action and translated them into daily practice, and, in this respect, it has helped to shape those ideals which motivate our political direction as democratic societies.

Athenian law before the 20th century was mainly studied in the margins of historical or political studies on the Athenian Democracy. However, already from the later part of the 19th century scholars were developing an interest in the Athenian Constitution, to a large extent fueled by the exciting discovery of the papyrus with large sections of the *Athenaion Politeia* attributed to Aristotle, which was published by F.G. Kenyon in 1891. Occasionally other areas attracted scholarly interest, like for example finance and contract law, investigated by Ex. Caillemer in the 1860s and 70s. In 1897, L. Bauchet published the first major study on Athenian law, his four-volume *Histoire du droit privé de la république athénienne*. He employed principles and classifications of Roman law, and his work although a classic, stands as a perennial example why one should not the employ legal concepts, principles, methodology and classification from later legal systems for the study of the laws of Athens. A few years later the influential work of Justus Hermann Lipsius *Das attische Recht und Rechtsverfahren* (1905–15) studied extensively Athenian legal procedure for the first time. Around the same time Robert Bonner made his debut with a significant study entitled *Evidence in Athenian Courts* (1905). In subsequent years he produced numerous studies on Athenian law culminating in his two-volume collaboration with Gertrud Smith *The Administration of Justice from Homer to Aristotle* (1930–8), which focused on the evolutionary processes of Athenian law.

The immediate postwar era in European scholarship was dominated by the towering figure of Hans Julius Wolff. His prolific activity would continue until the 1980s, while some of his works, like his book on *paragraphe* (*Die attische* Paragraphe*: ein Beitrag zum Problem der Auflockerung archaischer Prozessformen*, 1966), the *graphe paranomon* (*Normenkontrolle und Gesetzesbegriff in der athenischen Demokratie. Untersuchungen zur* graphe *paranomon*, 1970), and several studies on Athenian family law remain important to the present day. Equally substantial was the contribution of Louis Gernet. His influential *Droit et société dans la Grèce ancienne* (1959) still remains useful for issues like the *diamartyria* and commercial law, while many of his conclusions have been adopted by later studies. The two-volume study of A.R.W. Harrison, *The Law of Athens* (1968–71), has been an important stop, especially in English-speaking scholarship, but it has been influenced by principles and classifications of Roman law. I have always found Harrison a stimulating background reading, always encouraging deeper thinking with probing questions, but I very rarely share his opinions.

A few years after the postmortem publication of Harrison's second volume, D.M. MacDowell published his book *The Law in Classical Athens* (1978). This undoubtedly has been the most influential study on Athenian law since its publication and remains an indispensable manual for students of Athenian law, from beginners to experts. The simple, carefully crafted language makes the book accessible even to beginners, but this simplicity is deceptive: behind every word and every sentence there is thorough scholarship and deep learning. McDowell's book has brought Athenian law even to non-specialists and has helped classicists and historians working in other fields to better understand it. MacDowell remained a dominant figure in the field for the last quarter of the 20th century, and his collected articles, which include a large number of studies on many aspects of Athenian law, were recently published under the title *Studies in Greek Law, Oratory and Comedy* (2017).

A few years later Michael Gagarin filled an important gap in the scholarship with his book on early Greek law (1986). In 1993, Stephen Todd sought to expand the field by introducing anthropological and comparative legal perspectives to the study of Athenian law, and "to change the way in which the subject is perceived and studied."[28] The overall product was a book, which although valuable for the study of Athenian law and full of insightful comments and perspectives, it did not have the impact which it deserved to have, because in design and style it is far less accessible than MacDowell's book. Near the end of the century Ilias Arnaoutoglou published the first major sourcebook on Greek laws, a very useful collection for students and specialists alike. In the new millennium the new sourcebook by David Phillips *The Law of Ancient Athens* (2013), focused on Athenian law, and exceeded the traditional limitations of sourcebooks by providing detailed information on the scholarship related to each topic and a brief but highly informative account of the sources in question. In this respect Phillips created a very usable book for students, but also a valuable resource for scholars.

These are some of the main stops in terms of large-scale, comprehensive studies dedicated to the study of Greek Law. However, beyond the accomplishments of these books much more attention has been lavished upon Athenian law, and outstanding works in the form of books, articles and book chapters, by prominent scholars like Michael Gagarin, Gerhard Thür, Alberto Maffi, Edward Harris, Eva Cantarella, Christopher Carey, M.H. Hansen, Ugo Enrico Paoli or Eberhard Ruschenbusch, have illustrated specific aspects of Athenian law with great wisdom and depth. The riches are such that it would be impossible to enlist here all scholars who have published exceptional work on Athenian law. I knew from the start that trying to incorporate every piece of worthy scholarship in this book would be a fool's errand. The printed volume alone with the bibliography of Athenian law published by M. Sundahl, Ilias Arnaoutoglou and David Mirhady (2011) is 657 pages long.[29] The best one could hope for is to include sufficient scholarship to produce an informed account and offer a clear idea of the main issues involved. For more detailed readings the immensely valuable, readily available and user-friendly online bibliography kept up to date by David Mirhady, Ilias Arnaoutoglou and Mark J. Sundahl is an indispensable resource, while the online bibliography of *Diotima* has been useful for works on women, gender, and the *oikos*.[30]

The social, political, and economic context of Athenian law has been studied by scholars interested in the subject since the 19th century, but with significant limitations until the 1960s. Most historical studies on classical Athens published before the 1960s were primarily concerned with "masculine" subjects like war and politics. There was a scarcity of reliable studies on private life, social history, and above all, the other half of the Athenian population which did not participate in war or politics. Aside from a pioneering article by A.W. Gomme, published in 1925,[31] the scholarship on Athenian women was very limited. A book by Paul Brandt, also published in 1925 under the pseudonym of Hans Licht, was the first attempt to study the sexual lives of the Greeks, and despite its limitations it still makes a great read.[32] In the immediate postwar years, the tireless activity of Robert Flacelière enriched our understanding of private life in classical Athens. Among his books the one on love in ancient Greece (*L'amour en Grèce*, 1960) and especially his influential work *La vie quotidienne en Grèce au siècle de Périclès* (1959), heralded a new era where the study of private lives was now a dignified subject of historical inquiry. Around the same time women classicists, like Jaqueline de Romilly and Claude Mossé set out to conquer new ground in French Academia with extraordinary scholarly accomplishments in the coming decades, including the book *La Femme dans la Grèce antique* (1983), and the influential work on citizenship (*Le Citoyen dans la Grèce antique*, 1993).

From the 1960s, as more women and openly gay professors populated the ranks of academia, the center of gravity shifted decisively towards the study of women, gender, sexualities, private life and the Athenian household. Moreover, a new generation of Classics undergraduate students brought up in the cultural and sexual revolution of the 1960s could no longer be motivated by the endless parsing of irregular verbs, and dictated a study of the subject from new angles, where gender, sexuality and private life, along with more traditional subjects like mythology, philosophy, drama and political history could be integrated into a learning experience which was relevant in the present, for the major battles of the 60s and 70s to achieve political, racial and gender equality. In the spirit of the times the pioneering collection *Goddesses, Whores, Wives and Slaves*, edited by Sarah Pomeroy in 1975, was the first of many such collections in the last quarter of the 20th century studying women in the ancient world. It was followed the collection edited by H.P. Foley *Reflections of Women in Antiquity* (1981) or the one edited by E. Fantham, et al., *Women in the Classical World* (1994), and several more. Even though the scholarship in the earlier collections was largely superseded by more refined studies in later years, their contribution was very significant, because they sparked a very lively debate which would lead to a much better understanding of these topics.

The first short monograph on the subject by Mary Lefkowitz entitled *Heroines and Hysterics* was published in 1981. Sarah Pomeroy remarked with amazement in her review of the book that "Lefkowitz's work demonstrates that the study of women has become a respectable subject in the field of classics during the past ten years."[33] More substantial monographs were to come in the last two decades of the 20th century: Eva Cantarella's *Pandora's Daughters: The Role and Status of Women in Greek and Roman Antiquity* (1987), followed by her *Bisexuality in the Ancient World* (1988, trans. 1992), marked a new era in the study of gender and sexuality. Even more substantial works were to follow in the 1990s, like Sue Blundell's *Women in Ancient Greece* (1995), and independently on the same year the German monograph by Christine Schnurr-Redford *Frauen im klassischen Athen: sozialer Raum und reale Bewegungsfreiheit* (1995). Around the same time, Elke Hartmann was cutting new ground in German-speaking classical scholarship with a series of studies which would culminate in her significant 2002 monograph *Heirat, Hetaerentum und Konkubinat im klassischen Athen.* The study of women in the ancient world, which hesitantly got moving in the mid-70s, has proliferated into a very large subject, and the debate is still going strong. These studies, with few exceptions, were not concerned with Athenian law but they have provided an important backdrop for a better understanding of many critical issues related to Athenian private and family law, inheritance law and to some extent finances and the law.

The 1980s saw the first specialized studies on women and law. One of the first authoritative works in the field was the monograph of David Schaps on the economic rights of women (1979), while a series of significant articles through the decade discussed a number of relevant topics. Near the end of the decade two dedicated monographs on Women and Athenian law were published, a comprehensive, rich and authoritative study by Roger Just (1989), was followed by a shorter book by Rafael Sealey (1990) more interested in comparisons between Athens and other Greek cities. In the final years of the 20th century several important studies on the Greek family were published, by Sarah Pomeroy, Cynthia Patterson and Cheryl Cox. The bleak image of women's oppression in the Greek *polis* which emerged in many studies of the 1980s, and rather had to do with modern struggles and sexual politics than clear evidence from classical sources, has been largely corrected in later studies. While Athenian women lacked important political rights compared to their modern counterparts, as all women anywhere in the world did before the 20th century, their lives were not spent in joyless isolation and oppression, devoid of opportunities for a positive contribution to society, as some 80s authors would have us believe.

Historical studies on sexuality, gender and masculinity proliferated since the 1970s starting with Kenneth Dover's high-impact work on Greek homosexuality (1978). At the time this study was a bold undertaking considering that relations between men were still a criminal activity in Scotland while he was working on the book at the University of St. Andrews, and undoubtedly that atmosphere of fear and disapproval surrounding same sex relations has left its permanent mark in the pages the book, as James Davidson has eloquently demonstrated.[34] The broad acceptance and inclusion of the book's findings in Michael Foucault's second volume of his *History of Sexuality* (1984) helped establish Dover's book as a standard work in the study of sexuality. In the end of the decade two more influential studies, David Halperin's *One Hundred Years of Homosexuality* and Jack Winkler's *The Constraints of Desire* added to the picture. A mighty orthodoxy was born, according to which Greek men took young boys as lovers in asymmetrical relations which ideally should be sexless, lest the boys' civic virtue would be compromised, and even if they became sexual, boys should only consent very reluctantly. The paradox of chasing young men with gifts and persistent petitions but not wanting sexual favors reminds us the joke of the comic poet Amphis (fr. 15) that it would be like someone chasing rich men but not wanting their money.

The entire edifice which Dover has created on very slender evidence, mostly from the rhetorical banalities of the speech *Against Timarchos*, and the misunderstanding of some vase paintings, was in line with 1970s hostile views of same sex relations, presenting them as deeply problematic, ideally sexless and remarkably joyless. Meanwhile, all the evidence in Greek authors about adults over 18 years of age engaging in same-sex relations was intentionally suppressed, because it did not fit into this model of a no-sex, no-fun educational relationship between the *erastes* and the *eromenos*. Challenges of this highly problematic model in the new millennium, especially the one led by James Davidson in his large 2007 study, were met with substantial resistance amid accusations of partisan views. However, slowly and bit by bit the dominance of this graceless 70s edifice designed to appease heterosexual sensibilities and present same-sex relations in the ancient Greek world as schematic, devoid of pleasure, and consequently non-threatening has been unraveling in the more culturally diverse climate of the new millennium.

The late 1990s also saw a rise in the study of Greek medical authors, as well as the social aspects of ancient medical science. The pioneering work of Lesley Dean-Jones *Women's bodies in classical Greek Science* (1993), followed by Helen King's *Hippocrates' Woman: Reading the Female Body in Ancient Greece* (1998) shed new light on the social aspects of female biology as perceived by Greek Medical Science. Three major studies on contraception and abortion around the new millennium, John Riddle's *Contraception and Abortion from the Ancient World to the Renaissance* (1993), Angus McLaren *History of Contraception: From Antiquity to the Present Day* (1992), and my study *Abortion in the Ancient World* (2003), added to the picture and allowed us to better understand ancient views on biology, contraception, fertility and the beginnings of life. Numerous other studies on Greek society and culture like Daniel Ogden's *Greek Bastardy in the Classical and Hellenistic periods*, two studies on prostitution by Edward Cohen (2016) and myself (2017), and many more works which would take too much space to enlist here have greatly advanced our understanding of the *oikos*, women, gender, masculinity, sexuality, the family, the economy and private lives of the 5th and 4th century Athenians. Armed with this new knowledge we can now understand much better the social, economic and cultural context of Greek law, we can provide more insightful and better documented explanations on the reasons which led the Athenians to introduce the laws which they did, and we can assess with greater accuracy the potential impact of specific legal provisions in the evolution of Athenian society from the years of empire-building in the aftermath of the Persian wars to the end of the Greek *polis*.

This is not a book about Athenian law, or about Athenian society, but rather a study which stands at the intersection between the two. As a concept this book arose out of the need to make sense of Athenian law, to explain why it evolved as it did and offer some insights into how the law influenced behavioral patterns. In general, I am not fond of sweeping anthropological or sociological modes of analysis, because I doubt that they serve well the study of history. Some abstraction is necessary if we are to discern patterns and come up with explanations of complex historical phenomena. But too much abstraction can create models which although neat and elegant they are unrealistic, they do not take into account the randomness of human behavior, they suppress inconvenient truths and facts, and they end up presenting an image of the past which although clear and digestible, it is a fake. The real picture is messier, with shadowy areas, and unpredictable, random departures from the rules, just as it happens in real life.

While in the sciences it is established practice to begin with a premise that needs to be proved or disproved by subsequent research, in the study of history this method is probably counterproductive; too often sources have been forced to fit into the mold of a preconceived thesis.[35] I am convinced that a historian should always start from the sources, and rather than push them where he/she wants to take them, follow their trail to its natural conclusion. Following the sources sometimes would lead us to crystal clear conclusions, but more often the picture will not be quite so clear and answers we get may be incomplete. Sometimes we may easily be able to fill in the gaps through logical extrapolation; occasionally a hint from the comparative study of another society might put us on the right track. But comparing different societies comes with its own set of problems.[36] Cultural comparisons are only useful if we are acutely aware of their limitations.[37] To quote D.M. MacDowell "They [i.e. suggestions about Athenian society] will not be proved true by evidence about villagers in Portugal or Morocco. Careful and accurate interpretation of the ancient Greek texts is required."[38] In this study I have been following the classical, and sometimes even postclassical sources as the trail has been meandering through a forest of possibilities. Sometimes the path has been clear and the process has inspired confident conclusions. On other occasions the final picture is far less clear. I am comfortable with uncertainty and open-ended solutions hoping that future research will offer more conclusive answers to some of these difficult questions.

Notes

1 Primarily the Funeral Speech of Pericles comes to mind at this point (Th. 2.36–46), but there are other narratives, especially in epideictic speeches (e.g. Lys. 2, D. 60) with similar themes.

2 See for example Isoc. 18.16, where Solon was the lawgiver setting the laws of the democracy, while Kleisthenes the person who established it after expelling the tyrants: ἣν ἐθελήσωμεν ἐκείνην τὴν δημοκρατίαν ἀναλαβεῖν, ἣν Σόλων μὲν ὁ δημοτικώτατος γενόμενος ἐνομοθέτησε, Κλεισθένης δ' ὁ τοὺς τυράννους ἐκβαλὼν καὶ τὸν δῆμον καταγαγὼν πάλιν ἐξ ἀρχῆς κατέστησεν. A similar concept is proposed by Aeschines when he says that Solon adorned the democracy with the best laws (3.257: Σόλωνα μὲν τὸν καλλίστοις νόμοις κοσμήσαντα τὴν δημοκρατίαν, ἄνδρα φιλόσοφον καὶ νομοθέτην ἀγαθόν). Later authors approved of this approach and repeat the term κοσμεῖν with reference to the laws of Solon (Plu. *Comp. Publ. Sol.* 2.1; Alex. *Fig.* 19 and 21.). The anachronisms in these elegant schemes matter little to their authors. For the author of the *Athenaion*

Politeia the issue is one of degrees: Solon established the democracy and Kleisthenes broadened its basis to make it more inclusive (*Ath.Pol.* 41.2: ἡ ἐπὶ Σόλωνος, ἀφ' ἧς ἀρχὴ δημοκρατίας ἐγένετο. . . . μετὰ <τὴν> τῶν τυράννων κατάλυσιν ἡ Κλεισθένους, δημοτικωτέρα τῆς Σόλωνος).

3 Gagarin 1981: 71–77.

4 Arist. *Ath. Pol.* 14.3 suggests that Peisistratos was ruling like a politician rather than a tyrant (πολιτικῶς μᾶλλον ἢ τυραννικῶς), probably meaning that he paid attention to formalities and the appearance of legitimate rule.

5 See the discussion in Chapter 1.

6 MacDowell 1978: 9.

7 For example, Harrison's otherwise highly respected book on Athenian law has unsuccessfully employed such methodologies, and more recently Adriaan Lanni has employed American Common Law principles, with equally dubious results. See the discussion in Chapter 1.

8 For the discussion see Droysen 1893: 95–266; Wankel 1976, ad loc.; Canevaro 2013: 237–318 with previous bibliography; Fisher 2001: 68; Drerup 1898: 305–308. The wild inaccuracies of these documents, like for example in D. 18.116, where Salamis supposedly had a river running through it, and it was in hostile territory for a group of Athenian soldiers, leave no room for doubt that these cannot be the documents read out in court.

9 Drerup 1898; Harris and Canevaro 2013.

10 See MacDowell 1962 ad loc.

11 MacDowell 1990 ad loc.; Harris and Canevaro 2013: 209–236.

12 Kapparis 1999: 56–59.

13 See for example 23.22 and the discussion in Kapparis 2015: 41–42.

14 Burger 1892. Early editions sometimes contained stichometric marks every one hundred lines (α′ = 100, β′= 200, etc), marking the length of the text, perhaps for commercial purposes. Some of these have been preserved in our medieval manuscripts and can be used to calculate whether the documents had been included in those early editions, by comparing the spaces in our editions from α to β to γ, etc. Burger proved that if the documents are included these spaces are uneven, while if they are left out they are roughly even. This means that inserted documents were not included in those early editions, with the exception of laws or other evidence which the orator had incorporated in the body of his speech. This should not surprise us, as documents were not read out by the orator, but by the clerk of the court. The orator only needed to remind himself to ask the clerk to read the testimony, and in order to do this he might write ΝΟΜΟΣ, ΜΑΡΤΥΡΕΣ, ΜΑΡΤΥΡΙΑ, ΟΡΚΟΣ, or something similar in his manuscript, and often this is what we find in speeches. The documents to be read out should have been handed over to the clerk of the court separately before the beginning of the trial. The experience should be similar to a modern paper with a powerpoint presentation, where the author instead of including the information of the slide in the paper, he/she only needs to include an instruction to remember to change the slide.

15 E.g. Westermann 1850; Harris and Canevaro 2013.

16 D. 59.104–106

17 This, for example, may have happened with the private testimonies of D. 43 and 45.

18 See the discussions in Martinez 2011 and Harris and Canevaro 2013: 1–36.

19 The monumental commentary of P.J. Rhodes (1981) remains an invaluable companion for this crucially important work.

20 E.g. *IG* i^{3} 104; ii2 1 and 10.

21 See Chapter 8.3.

22 See Lambert 1998, and especially his 2012 book on Athenian laws and decrees inscribed on stone, and also the discussion in Chapter 2.3.

23 D. 59.16; see also the discussion in Chapter 4.3.

24 See Kapparis 2017: 146–152, with previous bibliography, and the discussion in Chapters 4.3 and 6.4.
25 Th. 2.37 ff.
26 For example, our understanding of Greek comedy would be so much poorer without the countless citations of Athenaios.
27 For Pollux as a source of Athenian Law see Maffi 2007: 29–42.
28 Todd 1993: 29.
29 Sundahl, M., Mirhady, D., Arnaoutoglou, I. (Eds) *A New Working Bibliography of Ancient Greek* Law (7th – 4th Centuries BC). Academy of Athens Yearbook of the Research Centre for the History of Greek Law 42, Supplement 11. Athens: Academy of Athens, 2011.
30 URL: www.sfu.ca/nomoi/
31 A.W. Gomme "The Position of Women in Athens in the Fifth and Fourth Centuries " *CP* 20 (1925) 1–25.
32 The volume under the title *Sexual Life in Ancient Greece* was reprinted by Routledge in 2000.
33 *AHR* 87 (1982) 1367–8.
34 Davidson 2001: 3–51, and also more broadly in his 2007 book. Homosexual relations between men were decriminalized in Scotland in 1978, but after they were decriminalized in England in 1968, a moratorium on prosecutions had been extended to Scotland.
35 A good example of this might be the thesis of David Cohen that *moicheia* only applied to married women, while unequivocal evidence from the classical period which disproved this preconceived thesis was dismissed as unreliable. See Cohen in *RIDA* 31 (1984) 147–165; for the counter-argument see *CR* 42 (1992) 345–347; Carey CQ 45 (1995) 407–40417; Dover Gnomon 65 (1993) 657–660; Kapparis 1999: 295–301, with references to previous scholarship.
36 For example, scholars sometimes use the term "Mediterranean society" to describe the ancient Greek or Roman world, assuming that there are strong parallels with modern Mediterranean societies. However, such comparisons do not take into account the multiple cultural layers which have been added upon the Greek world over the centuries, Roman, Byzantine, Ottoman, Venetian, Western European and American, Christian, Islamic, Jewish, and so on. While modern Greece or Italy are geographically Mediterranean and undoubtedly have preserved some cultural elements unique to them through time, they are very different societies in many important ways from ancient Greece or Roman Italy.
37 For example, speaking about "oriental seclusion" when it comes to Greek women, even if metaphorically used, it is an unsafe parallel, because if nothing else it ignores the substantial influence of Islam on perceptions of feminine virtue in the modern orient. While some parallels may exist, we always need to be accurately aware of the differences too before citing them.
38 D.M. MacDowell, *CR* 42 (1992) 345–347.

1 The administration of justice in the *polis*

1.1 Sources

1 Only written laws are considered valid and constitute the basis for litigation (after 403):

> Νόμοι. Ἀγράφῳ δὲ νόμῳ τὰς ἀρχὰς μὴ χρῆσθαι μηδὲ περὶ ἑνός. Ψήφισμα δὲ μηδὲν μήτε βουλῆς μήτε δήμου νόμου κυριώτερον εἶναι. Μηδὲ ἐπ' ἀνδρὶ νόμον ἐξεῖναι θεῖναι, ἐὰν μὴ τὸν αὐτὸν ἐπὶ πᾶσιν Ἀθηναίοις, ἐὰν μὴ ἑξακισχιλίοις δόξῃ κρύβδην ψηφιζομένοις.
>
> Τί οὖν ἦν ἐπίλοιπον; οὑτοσὶ ὁ νόμος. Καί μοι ἀνάγνωθι τοῦτον.
>
> <Νόμος.> Τὰς δὲ δίκας καὶ τὰς διαίτας κυρίας εἶναι, ὁπόσαι ἐν δημοκρατουμένῃ τῇ πόλει ἐγένοντο. Τοῖς δὲ νόμοις χρῆσθαι ἀπ' Εὐκλείδου ἄρχοντος.
>
> (And. 1.87)
>
> Laws: In no circumstances shall magistrates enforce a law which has not been inscribed. No decree, whether of the Council or Assembly, shall override a law. No law shall be directed against an individual without applying to all citizens alike, unless an Assembly of six thousand so resolve by secret ballot.
>
> What was needed to complete the list? Only the following law, which I will ask the clerk to read to you.
>
> Laws: All decisions given in private suits and by arbitrators under the democracy shall be valid. But of the laws only those passed since the *archon*ship of Eucleides shall be enforced.[1]

2 The scrutiny of incoming magistrates:

> ἐπερωτῶσιν δ', ὅταν δοκιμάζωσιν, πρῶτον μὲν 'τίς σοι πατὴρ καὶ πόθεν τῶν δήμων, καὶ τίς πατρὸς πατήρ, καὶ τίς μήτηρ, καὶ τίς μητρὸς πατὴρ καὶ πόθεν τῶν δήμων'; μετὰ δὲ ταῦτα εἰ ἔστιν αὐτῷ Ἀπόλλων Πατρῷος καὶ Ζεὺς Ἑρκεῖος, καὶ ποῦ ταῦτα τὰ ἱερά ἐστιν, εἶτα ἠρία εἰ ἔστιν καὶ ποῦ ταῦτα, ἔπειτα γονέας εἰ εὖ ποιεῖ, [καὶ] τὰ τέλη <εἰ> τελεῖ, καὶ τὰς στρατείας εἰ ἐστράτευται. ταῦτα δ' ἀνερωτήσας,'κάλει' φησὶν 'τούτων τοὺς μάρτυρας'. ἐπειδὰν δὲ παρά-σχηται τοὺς μάρτυρας, ἐπερωτᾷ 'τούτου βούλεταί τις κατηγορεῖν'; κἂν μὲν ᾖ τις κατήγορος,

δοὺς κατηγορίαν καὶ ἀπολογίαν, οὕτω δίδωσιν ἐν μὲν τῇ βουλῇ τὴν ἐπιχειροτονίαν, ἐν δὲ τῷ δικαστηρίῳ τὴν ψῆφον· ἐὰν δὲ μηδεὶς βούληται κατηγορεῖν, εὐθὺς δίδωσι τὴν ψῆφον·.

(Arist. *Ath. Pol.* 55.3–4)

The questions put in examining qualifications are, first, "Who is your father and to what deme does he belong, and who is your father's father, and who your mother, and who her father and what his deme?" Then whether he has a Family Apollo and Homestead Zeus, and where these shrines are; then whether he has family tombs and where they are; then whether he treats his parents well, and whether he pays his taxes, and whether he has done his military service. And after putting these questions the officer says, "Call your witnesses to these statements." And when he has produced his witnesses, the officer further asks, "Does anybody wish to bring a charge against this man?" And if any accuser is forthcoming, he is given a hearing and the man on trial an opportunity of defence, and then the official puts the question to a show of hands in the Council or to a vote by ballot in the Jury-court; but if nobody wishes to bring a charge against him, he puts the vote at once.[2]

3 The law allowing a son to deny his old father sustenance, if the father had not educated him:

νόμον ἔγραψεν, υἱῷ τρέφειν πατέρα μὴ διδαξάμενον τέχνην ἐπάναγκες μὴ εἶναι.

(Plu. *Sol.* 22)

He introduced a law that a son is under no obligation to provide for his father who had not educated him.

Alexis, qui Athenienses ait oportere ideo laudari, quod omnium Graecorum leges cogunt parentes [ali] a liberis, Atheniensium non omnes nisi eos, qui liberos artibus erudissent.

(Vitr. 6. pr. 3)

Alexis said that the Athenians deserve special praise because, while all the laws of the Greeks compel the children to provide for their parents, those of the Athenians do not require everyone to provide for their parents but only those who had been educated by them in the liberal arts.

4 The law prohibiting bribery of public officials, and the offer of legal services for money:

Ἐάν τις συνιστῆται, ἢ συνδεκάζῃ τὴν ἡλιαίαν ἢ τῶν δικαστηρίων τι τῶν Ἀθήνησιν ἢ τὴν βουλὴν ἐπὶ δωροδοκίᾳ χρήματα διδοὺς ἢ δεχόμενος, ἢ ἑταιρείαν συνιστῇ ἐπὶ καταλύσει τοῦ δήμου, ἢ συνήγορος ὢν λαμβάνῃ χρήματα ἐπὶ ταῖς δίκαις ταῖς ἰδίαις ἢ δημοσίαις, τούτων εἶναι τὰς γραφὰς πρὸς τοὺς θεσμοθέτας.

(D. 46.26)

> If any man enter into a conspiracy, or join in seeking to bribe the Heliaea or any of the courts in Athens, or the Senate, by giving or receiving money for corrupt ends, or shall organize a clique for the overthrow of the democracy, or, while serving as an advocate, shall accept money in any suit, private or public, criminal suits shall be entered for these acts before the Thesmothetae.[3]

5 The law stating that a person who initiated a *graphe*, but failed to appear in court or received 1/5th of the votes is liable to a fine of 1000 drachmas:

> ὅσοι δ' ἂν γράφωνται γραφὰς ἰδίας κατὰ τὸν νόμον, ἐάν τις μὴ ἐπεξέλθῃ ἢ ἐπεξιὼν μὴ μεταλάβῃ τὸ πέμπτον μέρος τῶν ψήφων, ἀποτεισάτω χιλίας δραχμὰς τῷ δημοσίῳ.
>
> Those who on their own initiate a *graphe* according to the law: if someone does not appear to prosecute or appears but does not receive 1/5 of the votes, he is to pay a fine of 1000 drachmas to the public treasure.

1.2 The division of powers in the Athenian Democracy

The tripartite division of powers into executive, legislative and judicial, which has prevailed in constitutional forms since the time of the Enlightenment is typically attributed to Montesqieu (*L'Esprit de Lois*). It was conceived as a response to many centuries of authoritarian monarchies where one person held all powers concentrated in his (and occasionally her) hands, and all authority stemmed from his divine right to rule. And yet, this was not the first time in history when separation of powers with all the concomitant checks and balances was implemented. One could hardly think it possible to have a democratic constitution without separation of powers, checks and balances. The Athenian Democracy implemented even more rigorously separation of powers and had far more frequent and effective checks and balances than any modern democracy. This was the response to two centuries of tyrannical regimes, essentially dictatorships where one individual had seized power and held onto it, throughout the Greek world. In Athens itself half a century had gone by under the rule of the Peisistratids, which was preserved in the collective memory of the Athenian people for centuries as a situation that was to be avoided at all costs. Some of the extreme measures to which the Athenian state went from time to time, which to us may seem strange and perhaps outright unjust, like an ostracism, where a distinguished citizen was sent to exile for a decade for no other reason than the fear of his fellow citizens that he was getting too popular and too powerful, make sense only within this frame of mind, as reactions and precautions taken by the Athenian people to ensure that no person in future would ever be able to concentrate all powers of the state in his own hands.[4]

Kleisthenes introduced the democratic constitution in Athens only a few years after the fall of Hippias, the last tyrant of Athens. Its introduction could have been a gut reaction to the tyranny of the Peisistratids, and ironically the establishment of the first democratic constitution in history may owe its existence to a cruel dictator like Hippias. He was in exile at the time when democracy was established, plotting with the enemies of the city for his return to power, and in the Persian campaign against Athens, which culminated in the battle of Marathon in 490, he was following the Persian forces as an advisor, hoping to regain power once the city had been subdued. The Athenian victory at Marathon, and subsequent Greek victories in the Persian wars, not only dashed the hopes of the Peisistratids for a return to power, but also helped consolidate the Democratic Constitution. Kleisthenes insightfully determined that the new polity could only be successful if the old centers of power were diluted and integrated into the new Constitution under more egalitarian organizational structures designed in such a manner that no one group or individual could ever amass enough power in their hands to take over the state.

Kleisthenes did not abolish that bastion of old aristocratic power, the Areopagos Council, nor did he replace the old structural units of the citizen body, the four ancient Ionic tribes,[5] the genos or the phratry with its subgroups. He simply added elements like the Boule of the 500, the members of which were appointed by lot, or organizational structures, like the tribes and demes, in effect bypassing, but not abolishing the older structures which most Athenians held dear. The result was an organizational structure that is not dissimilar to modern democracies. There was a well-defined executive consisting of hundreds of magistrates, which oversaw the day to day running of the city, two councils, one conservative and august, which was stripped of most of its powers after the reforms of Ephialtes in 462, the other more representative of the people (δημοτικόν) with broader powers, and a popular assembly which in theory was the overall source of authority in the *polis* (κυριώτατος δῆμος). However, unlike modern representative republics, this was a direct democracy, where the only limitation to the powers of the people were the laws which the people had voted, as these were vetted (mostly in the 4th century) and applied by the popular law-courts (δικαστήρια).

The development of the popular law-courts seems to have been a gradual process. The laws of Solon gave citizens dissatisfied with the decisions of magistrates the right to appeal to the assembly (Heliaia).[6] However, it seems that as time went by the number of appeals was so large that the assembly could not hear them all, and it became necessary to spit into heliastic courts perhaps initially of 500 people, but then still smaller sections. Each one of them was a random selection of citizens chosen by lot, and, in this respect, it represented the entire citizen body. This is how the Athenians invented the jury system. D.M. MacDowell offers a very elegant answer to the critically important question of how these courts became the primary feature of the Athenian justice system. He suggests that Solon initially allowed appeals to the Assembly as a measure to limit the extensive authority of the magistrates of the aristocratic state and give ordinary citizens a last-resort measure against their power abuses. We can tell that much because in many Soloneal laws the hearing before the Heliaia is envisaged as an appeal process. Solon did not envisage the popular law courts system as we see it in the classical period, but this was the natural development from the system he created. As appeals cost nothing, dissatisfied litigants kept appealing more and more frequently. With the establishment of the democracy the dikasteria acquired new significance and came to be seen as a central, and indispensable feature of the new constitution.

1.3 The question on the rule of law in the Athenian Democracy

When Pindar subverted the phrase "νόμος ὁ πάντων βασιλεὺς θνατῶν τε καὶ ἀθανάτων"[7] he took a core concept of Greek political thought and gave it new meaning. However, the author of one of the Platonic letters quoting Pindar takes it literally as an assertion of the superiority of the law, when he explains that Lycurgus put the law above the power of the Spartan kings through the institution of the gerousia and the ephors. In the same spirit Herodotos has the dethroned Spartan king Demaratos tell Xerxes that the law is the true king of the Spartans:

> Ἐλεύθεροι γὰρ ἐόντες οὐ πάντα ἐλεύθεροί εἰσι· ἔπεστι γάρ σφι δεσπότης νόμος, τὸν ὑποδειμαίνουσι πολλῷ ἔτι μᾶλλον ἢ οἱ σοὶ σέ· ποιεῦσι γῶν τὰ ἂν ἐκεῖνος ἀνώγῃ· ἀνώγει δὲ τὠυτὸ αἰεί.[8]
>
> Although they are free, they are not free in everything. The law is their Lord, and they fear it much more than your men fear you. Thus, they obey everything it commands, and it always gives the same command.

In a similar spirit Athenian politicians in funeral speeches, philosophers in their works, and orators before the courts frequently repeat the topic of the superiority of the law in the Greek world, the civilizing benefits that come with this for the city and the individual, as well as the adverse consequences when the rule of law breaks down.[9] The Greeks invented the rule of law as a political concept and identified it with freedom from authoritarian rulers outside or inside the *polis*, with civilization, order, and a balancing force against the rule of nature where the strong vanquish the weak.

Adriaan Lanni sees a paradox in this core belief of the Greek city-states in the rule of law, because, she argues, the Greeks never achieved the rule of law.[10] Lanni is siding with a number of scholars, including David Cohen, Robin Osborne, Moshe Berent, Matthew Christ, Joshia Ober and Virginia Hunter, who have argued that Athenian courts did not reach their verdicts on the basis of the law, but rather made ad hoc decisions on the basis of much broader criteria, political, cultural, social or emotional.[11] This line of thought has been based upon the argument that Athenian legal procedure did not enforce rules of relevance, and as a consequence much attention was paid to matters beyond the law and the facts of the case such as the character of the litigants, their political beliefs, or other extra-judicial factors. Second, there was no consistency in the application of the law or the verdicts issued by Athenian courts. Third, there was no coercive force in the hands of the state and citizens had to take matters in their hands, prosecute opponents, and enforce the judgment of the courts themselves.

Some of the more extreme versions of this argument, mainly propagated by Cohen and Berent, have presented Athens as a leaderless, even if peaceful society, not a state but an assembly of individual Athenians feuding with each other. In this scenario the role of the courts was to release tensions rather than implement justice, and they often become the theater for long-term private feuds. Lanni, on the other hand, adopts a more moderate view which she calls the expressive effect of the law. She argues that Athens was a generally peaceful society despite the fact that the laws were not rigorously enforced through punitive measures because the laws had a preventative force and encouraged lawful behavior. As proof of this she cites the *hybris* law, which included slaves, even though no citizen would risk 1000 drachmas to go to court in order to defend a slave. The fact that the law prohibited this behavior had a normative effect in itself and resulted in milder treatment of slaves. The other example she cites is the *hetairesis* law. Athenian youths worried that if they engaged in homosexual affairs might be prosecuted for prostitution in later years, would be discouraged from engaging in such affairs. These examples, along with most of Lanni's arguments, have been effectively countered by Alberto Maffi in his thoughtful review of her 2016 book.[12]

Contrary to such views the great legal scholars of the 20th century, including Justus Hermann Lipsius, Robert Bonner and Gertrude Smith, A.R.W. Harrison and D.M. MacDowell, have assumed that the Athenians did not go through the trouble (and danger after 415, when the *graphe paranomon* was established) of introducing new laws just for the sake of it, but in order to apply them rigorously in their courts. In recent years, the arguments of the proponents of an "anarchist" Athens that never achieved the rule of law have been forcefully refuted by Edward Harris and Vasileios Adamidis. Harris, in several articles and a high-impact book, has convincingly and overwhelmingly defended the rule of law in Classical Athens, and argued that the Athenians made laws in order to follow them, and when they said that the rule of law equals civilization and progress they meant it. Vasileios Adamidis building on the position of Harris has argued that many of the elements which previous studies have considered to be extra-judicial were in fact an indispensable part of the legal process.[13]

I stand fully behind Harris and Adamidis on this issue and I would encourage the reader to turn to these studies for more detailed and thorough discussions. Here I will summarize why I stand behind Harris and Adamidis, by taking the principles for the rule of law as set by the *World Justice Project* (WJP hereafter) and measuring how classical Athens fares in comparison.[14] The WJP establishes four universal principles for the rule of law:

1 *Accountability*: The government as well as private actors are accountable under the law.
2 *Just laws*: The laws are clear, publicized, stable, and just; are applied evenly; and protect fundamental rights, including the security of persons and property and certain core human rights.
3 *Open government*: The processes by which the laws are enacted, administered, and enforced are accessible, fair, and efficient.
4 *Accessible and impartial dispute resolution*: Justice is delivered timely by competent, ethical, and independent representatives and neutrals who are

accessible, have adequate resources, and reflect the makeup of the communities they serve.

Before we proceed it is necessary to address in general terms some methodological parameters. First, perceptions on the rule of law in classical Athens have often been colored by the application and practices of Common Law in the USA (and on occasion the UK). However, any methodology based on the assumption that the modern US legal system represents the progress of humanity towards the rule of law, and that it should be used as a measure for what it means for a society to have achieved the rule of law ought to be considered as deeply flawed from the outset. The US legal system would probably fail all four WJP criteria, some of them abysmally.[15] Second, the view that Athens was a stateless society is based on wild oversimplifications of the way the numerous magistrates of the state operated and fails to take into account the evolution of the Athenian legal system from Drakon and Solon to 4th century radical democracy. It also demonstrates a distinct lack of appreciation for the socio-cultural context of Athenian law, as well as the layers of judicial processes meticulously engineered to implement justice according to the laws. Each one of these issues needs to be addressed, even if briefly, if we ever are to understand how Athenian law functioned.

1.4 Accountability of officials and individuals before the law

It may be fair to say that no society in history has held its public officials as accountable as the Athenian Democracy did. First, for most public officials a relatively short term in office guaranteed that they would not get too comfortable in the role and begin to look for ways to bypass safeguards against abuses of power. Most Athenian officials were appointed for a term of one year. Members of the Boule could be appointed twice in their lifetimes, but not in two successive years. One would think that simple arithmetic made this arrangement necessary, as the Boule had a large number of members to be filled from willing citizens. Members of the Areopagos served for a lifetime, but this was an exception to the rule and gave this ancient, august council it's unique place in the Athenian Constitution. Elected officials on the other hand, like the generals or the treasurer of the theoric fund, although they also served one-year terms, they could be reelected unlimited times. We can understand why in this case the Athenians allowed reelection: where ability, experience and honesty were crucially important it would not be wise for the state to intentionally refuse the services of the men who could serve it best. Besides, with elections every year the Assembly had complete control on how these important offices were manned.

In all cases, whether officials were elected or appointed by lot, whether they served for a year or for a lifetime, and whether their office was important or not, they were subject to constant scrutiny before they entered into office, during their tenure of office, and when they exited from office. Before entering into office all magistrates of the city, major or minor, including priests and ambassadors, had to undergo a scrutiny (*dokimasia*) before the court, at least in the 4th century.

Incoming members of the Boule were scrutinized by the outgoing Boule, but rejected candidates could appeal to the courts. The nine *archon*s with their assessors (πάρεδροι) were subject to a double scrutiny, first before the Boule and then before the Court, which symbolized the traditional prestige of their offices. In the 4th century the judgment of the court was the final one: even if someone had been rejected by the Boule, he could serve if the court accepted him.

The purpose of that scrutiny was to ascertain someone's basic suitability for public office, not his ability for the specific job. Candidates were asked questions inquiring whether they were of citizen birth, they had fulfilled their military obligations, they had been paying their taxes and dues and they were looking after their parents (S 2).[16] Essentially, the state wanted to know whether someone was a citizen with a basic sense of duty and responsibility before entrusting him with public office. Except for a few cases among the speeches of Lysias concentrated in the aftermath of the Peloponnesian war and the regime of the Thirty, and related to the traumatic experience of Athens in those years, we do not hear much about failed dokimasiai, which probably means that the vast majority of candidates went through their scrutiny without problems.[17]

Athenian officials could be terminated by the assembly even during their year of office, if they gave serious cause for concern. Each month in the main Assembly a question was asked whether state officials are properly performing their duties (ἐπιχειροτονία), and anyone who wished could call into question a magistrate's performance. If the Assembly voted against this magistrate (ἀποχειροτονία) his term in office came to an end, and he could be further prosecuted through the courts. Expectedly we only hear about important officials who were terminated by the assembly, most notably Pericles, who was removed from office as a general in 430, when during the plague the Athenians were very distressed and were looking for someone to blame for the war with Sparta, and their current misfortunes.[18] Another prominent case was the suspension and execution of the victorious generals at Arginousai for failing to pick up those at sea after the end of the battle.[19] However, it seems that such cases were rather exceptional and the vast majority of Athenian officials were able to complete their year without challenges.

In the end of their year in office all Athenian magistrates without exception had to undergo an auditing (εὔθυνα). Plutarch attributes the introduction of this procedure to Pericles and this may be correct, since the process is mentioned or alluded in 5th century authors, but not before.[20] How exactly an *euthyna* unfolded is not very clear, but seemingly it consisted of two parts, and it certainly was a serious affair. [21] The first stage was about finances and was performed by the *logistai*. If the magistrate was managing public money during his year in office he needed to provide full financial accounts. If he was not managing any public funds, he still could be in trouble if there was suspicion that he had accepted bribes or unlawfully profiteered from his office. When the logistai had completed their investigation, they brought the magistrate to a court in which they presided and asked whether anyone else had something to report. If the magistrate was found guilty of bribery (δώρων), embezzlement (κλοπῆς) or some other financial mismanagement (ἀδικίου) he needed to repay tenfold the sum he had taken.[22] If he was cleared of financial misconduct, he could proceed to the second part of his auditing which had to do with his overall conduct in office. This provided citizens who felt injured by the exiting magistrate a unique opportunity to hold him accountable for any grievances they had. We know that the officials in charge were the ten *euthynoi*, who sat in the agora and received complaints. But it is unlikely that they sent to court every minor grievance against each and every one of over a thousand magistrates, councilors, ambassadors and other state officials under audit, because in such a case the courts would be doing nothing else for the rest of the year. In all probability the *euthynoi* vetted the complaints and only if they felt that a charge was justified and sufficiently grievous they passed it to the appropriate magistrate for trial by jury. Otherwise, they pronounced the *euthyna* complete and this brought the magistrate's responsibility to a close. We have a number of cases in our sources which suggest that the *euthyna* was often seen as a place to settle scores, and someone's performance as a magistrate could provide an occasion for a full-scale assault on his character and conduct by a resentful enemy.[23]

With such formidable accountability safeguards in place for all state officials, major or minor, classical Athens undoubtedly met the requirement of accountable government under the rule of law. Athens would also comfortably meet the criteria of holding private citizens or groups accountable before the law. Proponents of the theory of a stateless Athens have often invoked the absence of a public prosecutor as evidence that justice in Athens rested upon private initiative. This view does not take into account the complexity or size of Athenian government, nor any evolutionary process from the aristocratic state to the radical democracy. Unlike Sparta, where a very small number of people[24] made all the decisions, important or trivial, Athens had a relatively large executive, consisting of hundreds of magistrates, and two Councils, the Boule with a fixed number of 500 members selected by lot and the Areopagos with probably a couple of hundred members at any time.[25] If to that one added 6000 citizens engaged in jury service throughout the year, a number of almost 10,000 citizens, or approximately one quarter of entire citizen body, were involved in the running of the state and its institutions at any given moment, that is, almost every Athenian who had the time and disposition to do so.

Far from lacking in enforcement powers, each magistrate, as well as the two Boulai, had the authority to impose on the spot a fine of 50 drachmas to violators of the law.[26] This sum was not a mere trifle for the ordinary citizen. One would need to serve as a juror for 100 days, with the standard compensation of three obols a day, in order to be able to pay off this fine. Fifty drachmas was also a large enough sum to be offered as a bribe by Meidias to the arbitrator to change his verdict.[27] Meanwhile an unpaid fine to the state instantly resulted in temporary atimia, with all its adverse consequences in public and private life, until the debtor paid it off. The poor jurors in the *Wasps* of Aristophanes would have found themselves in a conundrum. They could no longer serve in juries until they paid off the debt to the treasury, but since they did not have another source of reliable income, they could never hope to pay off such a fine. Moreover, considering that hundreds of magistrates could impose such fines with no possibility of appeal or cancellation, an unruly citizen could rapidly find himself in a lot of trouble and effectively disfranchised.

All relevant passages mentioning the right of a magistrate to impose a fine include an additional clause inviting the magistrate to refer the offender to court if he thought that the violation deserved a higher penalty. This should address one of the most contentious points made by those who believe in a stateless Athens, namely that the city never had a public prosecutor.[28] Athens never needed to have a single public prosecutor, or even a board of them, simply because every magistrate in the city could act as public prosecutor, and was explicitly invited to do so by the law, if it came to his attention that a serious violation had taken place under his watch, one that merited a harsher punishment than a hefty fine. Moreover, in those occasions when public prosecutors were needed, as for example in the case of magistrates undergoing their *euthyna*, special boards like the *euthynoi* were appointed to see it through the courts. Far from being toothless and helplessly reliant on private citizens to punish violators of the laws, all Athenian magistrates had substantial punitive powers of their own, and the state had vested with extensive prosecutorial discretion individual magistrates and purposefully appointed boards.

The proponents of the stateless model have also brushed aside a very inconvenient truth, namely the existence of a numerous and adequately equipped police force in Athens, with the authority to deal with ordinary crime. To offer one striking example, Virginia Hunter in her study *Policing Athens*, would rather put her faith on gossip and archaic structures as the means of social control, than in the actual police force of Athens, which she considers little more than comic fodder on the basis of some Aristophanic jokes.[29] However, laughing at the comic caricature of the stupid cop need not make a police force any less formidable or effective, especially in 5th century Athens where audiences routinely enjoyed the public ridicule of authority figures. A board of 11 magistrates plainly and ominously known as the Eleven, with the support of a thousand-strong body of public slaves, had the authority and resources to deal effectively with crime and perform the standard duties of a police force. We do not know why they were 11 in number and not the usual ten, but, given the challenging decisions that they might routinely need to make on the use of force and the permissible extent and nature of it, an odd number might be necessary as a tie breaker.

The Eleven were assisted by a substantial number of Scythian archers, who were public slaves. Suda gives their number as 1000. Andocides mentions the purchase of 300 Scythian archers, and Virginia Hunter on the basis of this, and because it is consonant with her objective to undermine this force, accepts the testimony of Andocides.[30] However, these two sources are not necessarily at odds because the purchase mentioned in Andocides, large as it was, might not amount to the total number of Scythian archers in the ownership of the Athenian state, and could simply be either the number of Scythian archers originally purchased, and then expanded to 1000, or a large purchase but not the entire force. Either way, the Eleven clearly had sufficient manpower at their disposal to perform the regular duties of a police force. Although the original Scythian archers might have actually come from Scythia, in later times it is quite likely that they also included slaves from other parts of the world. Regardless of their actual origin, they retained the characteristic Scythian dress with its distinct head-gear, dotted tunic and trousers, bow and unusual quiver,[31] no doubt because it had come to be identified as an easily recognizable uniform for the Athenian police force. This way anyone who needed their assistance might be able to identify them instantly, and the exotic uniform vested them with the authority of the state and the board of the Eleven, compelling citizens to obey their instructions, even though they were mere slaves. Elizabeth Baughman is probably right when she argues that they only used non-lethal force (typically a whip); this would be consonant with Greek concepts of supernatural pollution (*miasma*) from spilled blood, and the fact that we do not know of anyone who ever died in the hands of the Scythian archers, supports this conclusion.[32]

The attested duties of the Eleven, supported by the Scythian archers, were extensive. They were in charge of the prison (δεσμωτήριον) of Athens and had the authority to order the imprisonment of persons who had been led to them through *endeixis* or *apagoge* until their trial.[33] They also had the authority to pursue persons who had escaped from prison.[34] They kept in custody persons convicted to death until their execution, or persons convicted to slavery until their sale. The Eleven could order that someone is confined to the stocks for a period of five days, if that person had broken certain laws.[35] The Eleven had the authority to put instantly to death without trial criminals, like thieves, enslavers or robbers, who had been caught in the act and seized with *apagoge* and had confessed their crime. They also produced lists of the property items belonging to persons who had been convicted to death and confiscation of property. After their execution the Eleven enlisted the property (*apographe*) and if there were no claims to any part of it, it was handed over to the *poletai*, the state auctioneers, for sale. However, if anyone laid any claim, a *diadikasia* trial followed to determine the owner of the disputed property.[36] Finally, the Eleven could be asked to accompany magistrates during property seizures, and probably other activities for which in our times police presence would be necessary.[37] Very clearly the duties of the Eleven mirror similar duties in modern police forces. The large number of Scythian archers at their disposal makes clear that they were kept busy enforcing the laws and maintaining order and safety during public meetings and festivals, when large numbers of people converged in the city (and this is why their original residence was at the center of public activity, the Agora), secured dangerous criminals into custody until their trial, and with their assistants the Eleven kept the streets of the city safe.

Other state officials performed a number of additional duties which were necessary for the health and safety of the community, the protection of consumers and the smooth supply and operation of the markets. Among those we need to mention the *astynomoi*, who were in charge of health and safety issues around the streets, and performed duties in some ways similar to code enforcement officers in our times, such as making sure that people did not encroach on the streets nor build houses or parts of houses in the streets, that they did not extend overhead pipes or balconies over the streets, and that they did not dump waste or other health hazards in public areas.[38] One of their duties was to oversee the hiring of sex-entertainers around the city and make sure that fights did not erupt over them when masculine egos were competing.[39] The duty of the *astynomoi* was to make sure that clients were not overcharged above the two drachmas ceiling price, and if the demand exceeded availability they distributed the entertainers among customers by lot. The *agoranomoi* where the equivalent of public health officials making sure that the food sold in the marketplace was not spoiled or dirty. The importance of their office cannot be underestimated, if one considers how many deadly epidemics in history began with unhygienically prepared or handled food. The *metronomoi* made sure that merchants were using fair weights and standards, and the *sitophylakes* were making sure that the grain and bread supply in the city runs smoothly, and that there are no famines or unethical profiteering from the basic needs of the people.

Far from been a stateless society classical Athens had an admirable organizational structure of public officials ensuring that the laws are observed, order is maintained, health and safety are not compromised in a routinely crowded city, and businesses are regulated to ensure fairness and honesty in their transactions with clients. More to the point, Athenian officials had substantial punitive powers to assist them in their efforts to enforce laws, rules and regulations, and always the option to refer major offenders to court. This was more than what some modern states do to ensure the rule of law and the well-being of their citizens. Classical Athens was a peaceful, law-abiding society because it had good laws which were observed and properly enforced, and the state did not need to rely on willing individuals to make sure that offenders are punished and the law is applied. The fact that individual citizens also had the power to pursue through the courts their adversaries or persons who had broken the law adds an extra layer, another dimension to Athenian legal procedure, without necessarily detracting from the power of the state to enforce the laws. Individual citizens and city officials collaborated to ensure that no one was above the law, person or agency, and the statement of Aeschines that often personal animosities can be beneficial for public life sounds true in some respects.[40] The phrase βοηθεῖν τοῖς νόμοις (to assist the laws), which we often encounter in the Attic Orators and other texts was not a mere formality, but a genuine expectation from the citizens of the democracy.[41]

The reasons for all these different layers of law enforcement have as much to do with the gradual and not always linear or orderly development of the Athenian legal system from the aristocratic state of Drakon and Solon to the radical democracy of the 4th century, as with an inherent belief that the individual citizen of the democracy is not only entitled but also obligated to make sure that the laws are observed and prevail over individual or group interests or objectives. In the time of Solon magistrates like the *archon*s probably had broad punitive and prosecutorial powers. However, gradually after the establishment of the democratic constitution, as the individual citizen became more empowered the authority of the magistrates proportionally diminished. A clear example of this shift can be seen in the case of the laws for mistreatment of orphans and heiresses. The law of Solon as cited by Demosthenes clearly gave the *archon* the authority to punish abusers of orphans or heiresses, or to take them to court, if they deserved higher punishment. However, when the family of Demosthenes, while he was still under age, made a complaint to the *archon* that the orphans, Demosthenes and his sister, were mistreated by the guardians, he chose not to intervene with punitive actions. He lent a sympathetic ear, discussed matters with the wider family and all agreed that the best course of action was to wait for young Demosthenes to reach adulthood and go after the delinquent guardians himself. The *archon* here rather acted as legal counsel, than as a prosecuting magistrate.

The inevitable conclusion is that this extra layer in the Athenian justice system, where besides the magistrates of the state individual citizens too had the power to pursue offenders or adversaries for all kinds of cases, public or private and civil or criminal, was not there by design in the first place, but evolved along with the establishment of democracy and the empowerment of the individual citizen in it. The end result of this evolutionary process, as we encounter it in the texts of the 4th century, was an extraordinarily rigorous justice system, where the powers to bring offenders to justice were not limited to a handful of state prosecutors, but were the privilege and duty of every citizen. Every free person living in the Athenian Democracy had an open invitation to come to the aid of the laws and safeguard their rule, because society prospered under it.

1.5 Protections of core human rights in Athenian law

> Our constitution . . . favors the many instead of the few; this is why it is called a democracy. If we look to the laws, they afford equal justice to all in their private differences; if to social standing, advancement in public life falls to reputation for capacity, class considerations not being allowed to interfere with merit; nor again does poverty bar the way, if a man is able to serve the state, he is not hindered by the obscurity of his condition. [2] The freedom which we enjoy in our government extends also to our ordinary life. There, far from exercising a jealous surveillance over each other, we do not feel called upon to be angry with our neighbor for doing what he likes, or even to indulge in those injurious looks which cannot fail to be offensive, although they inflict no positive penalty. [3] But all this ease in our private relations does not make us lawless as citizens. Against this fear is our chief safeguard, teaching us to obey the magistrates and the laws, particularly such as regard the protection of the injured.[42]
>
> Th. 2.37

Thucydides places these words in the mouth of a man whom he believed to be the embodiment and chief agent of Golden Age Athens. Pericles in this most famous expression of Greek political thought, the defense of democracy, identifies among its major strengths the fundamental equality of all before the law regardless of birth, wealth or ability, the possibility of advancement in public life on the basis of someone's merits regardless of birth or social status, the freedom to find pleasure in private life as everyone wishes, without animosity or disapproval by his fellow citizens, and to believe in the rule of law and obey the magistrates, especially when the protection of the injured is concerned. One could comfortably read this as a declaration of fundamental human rights under equal for all and just laws.

From an evolutionary point of view the first law codes of Athens were not about equality for all or fairness; they were more concerned with helping the injured and alleviating some of the burden of the lower classes in the aristocratic state, and Solon actually said as much when he declared

> δήμωι μὲν γὰρ ἔδωκα τόσον γέρας ὅσσον ἐπαρκεῖν,
> τιμῆς οὔτ' ἀφελὼν οὔτ' ἐπορεξάμενος·
>
> For I gave the common folk such privilege as is sufficient for them, neither adding nor taking away[43]

In his poem Εὐνομίη he extolls the benefits which good laws bring in society,[44] but what *eunomie* meant to him was something very different from what it meant to 4th century Athenians. For Drakon, the first lawgiver of Athens, the objective was to provide some effective mechanisms which would pull the breaks to the most extreme abuses of the leading aristocracy. It seems that the limited, but successful scope of his legislative work, encouraged a more comprehensive body of laws in order to deal with the massive socio-economic problems which Athens was facing a quarter of a century later. Solon came in at a time when the misery of the lower classes must have been seen as a ticking time-bomb which one day could lead the city to tyranny, as it had already done in other parts of the Greek world. His role was to release tensions and establish a viable and comprehensive code of laws which was going to protect the interests of the upper classes but at the same time offer some relief to the lower classes.[45] With the pressure released Athens could be spared the fate of a tyranny. Although this scenario did not play out as envisaged and the tyranny of the Peisistratids followed, the laws of Solon became embedded in Athenian perception as the core legislation of the city, even when this was no longer true in the 4th century

The generally popular rule of Peisistratos broke down some barriers, reduced the power of the aristocracy and gave the people more confidence. When a few years after the fall of the Peisistratids Kleisthenes introduced the first form of democracy the Solonean *eunomie* (to be governed by good laws) was replaced by *isonomie* (equality before the law),[46] while the Solonean four-tier constitution was eventually replaced by *isopoliteia* (equality of citizen rights and status), and every citizen was given an equal right of speech (*isegoria*) and the ability to express his opinions without fear or restraint (*parrhesia*). All these principles defined the prized Greek concept of freedom (ἐλευθερία), and in Athens the predominant (but not universal) belief was that freedom and the principles which constituted it could only be guaranteed under the protective shield of the law in a democracy.

The fundamental right to life was guaranteed for all by Athenian law, and since it had religious aspects attached to it, the community had a number of compelling reasons to protect life and punish a killer severely.[47] Even if the victim was a lowly slave, a killing, intentional or not, invited supernatural pollution (*miasma*), and could infect anyone associating with the killer. This extra-legal dimension made it imperative for the community to avenge the spilled blood, and the law of Drakon sent after the killer the most inexorable prosecutors, the close relatives of the victim. They were the ones expected to prosecute and punish the killer, and we can imagine that they were motivated. In the times of Drakon this rule was probably necessary in order to bypass altogether partial and corrupt magistrates of the aristocratic state. As it was practiced in the classical period it ensured that someone's killing would almost never go unpunished, because under normal circumstances the victim's family would make sure that they vigorously pursued the killer through the homicide courts. State-sponsored killings, which go unpunished in offensive numbers around the world in our times, would never go unpunished in classical Athens, because the magistrates of the state did not have the authority to decline the prosecution of someone who killed under the authority of the state.[48] The family of the victim would ensure that no matter who the killer was or why he did it, he would be brought to justice, and his closer relatives were the only ones who had the authority to pardon someone who had killed accidentally and was sent into exile as a result. With blood relatives in charge of prosecution and redemption the right to life was perhaps better protected in Athens than in most places in history.

The dividing line between free persons and slaves was clearly marked by a decree passed in the archonship of Skamandrios,[49] which prohibited the torture or physical abuse of free persons by anyone, including the Eleven or other state officials, for any reason.[50] The right to own property also drew a line between free persons and slaves; free persons living in Attica could own property, but slaves were themselves property items. Citizens could own any kind of property but non-citizens could not own real estate, unless granted this right (*enktesis*) as a privilege. A free person's property was inalienable, and a set of strict laws penalizing theft and robbery with penalties, which could be as severe as death, guaranteed a person's right to his/her property.[51] Confiscation of property was only allowed as a punishment for certain offenses, while the state had no right of expropriation. Again, the protections of these fundamental rights afforded by Athenian law were in some ways more robust that they are in most countries in our times.

Education was an important preparation for all Athenian males as citizens of the democracy. Their families sent them to school between the ages of six and 14, where they were taught reading, writing, poetry, music and trained in sports.[52] A law mentioned by Plutarch and Vitruvius (citing Alexis) stated that a son who had not been educated by his father was not obligated to provide for him in his old age (S 3). Although this law is not attested in classical sources, we have no good reason to doubt its existence.[53] Such a law would be consonant with other measures which the Athenian state took in order to prevent parents from neglecting or abusing their children, like for example the Solonean law which permitted a man who had been procured by his father not to provide for him in his old age.[54] Considering that the latter law was centrally important for the protection of children of impoverished families in Solonean Athens, we might also consider the law requiring a father to offer his son some education to be also Solonean and motivated by the same spirit of child welfare.

Unlike the brutality of the Spartan educational system, the sole purpose of which was to turn Spartan children into formidable soldiers, the Athenian educational system took a well-rounded approach, as its primary objective was to educate the future citizens of the democracy, who could be effective in the battlefield, but also politically aware, successful in business and appreciative of their cultured city and all the opportunities it offered. Athens as the cultural center of the Greek world offered some unique opportunities of higher education. Throughout the classical period some of the most prominent minds from the entire the Greek world, like Gorgias of Leontini, Protagoras of Abdera or Aristotle from Stageira, came to Athens, accepted students, typically for very substantial fees, and offered them a higher education which was intended to stimulate the minds of students, challenge their assumptions and encourage them to question matters in the world around them, from politics, to cultural values and religion itself. In the 4th century higher education became more organized offering students a rich choice among several legendary institutions, like the Academy of Plato, the Peripatos of Aristotle, or the School of Rhetoric of Isocrates, and later on the Lycaeum under Theophrastos, the Gardens of Epicurus, and a whole host of other famous centers.[55] They stood as beacons of learning for a millennium, until Justinian closed in 529 the last remaining educational institution associated with Greek paganism, the Neoplatonic school of Athens.

Girls were not formally schooled like boys; they were taught at home by their parents and tutors how to read, write, and count, since these were essential skills for good housekeeping, how to cook, prepare and store foodstuff, spin wool and make cloth, and other such skills which would be relevant and important for their role as managers of a household when time came to get married.[56] Most higher education institutions only accepted men, but several schools like the Pythagoreans, the Epicureans, the Megarian school of Stilpon and the Cyrenaic school of Aristippos, accepted women too. A few open-minded women, some but not all of them *hetairai*, like Aspasia, Leontion, Theano, Periktyone or Themista (a married woman, core member of the Epicurean school), took advantage of the opportunities, and although their number was small, their contribution to history was enormous since they functioned as role-models of wisdom in the long, dark centuries that were about to follow the end of democratic Athens and its freedoms and ideals.[57]

The right to privacy is mentioned in the *Funeral Speech* of Pericles as a fundamental component of freedom within the democratic constitution, and implicitly contrasted with the Spartan way of life.[58] Athenian citizens and metics did not need to worry about the laws of the state or public disapproval for what happened behind the closed doors of the *oikos*. The state interfered only when the *oikos* was in danger from an intruder who had seduced one of its women and threatened to contaminate the citizen stock with improperly born offspring. The fierce set of adultery laws, which had evolved over the period of more than two centuries, set formidable protections to a citizen's right to family life and respect within the community.[59] While a blanket statement that the sexual morals and private habits of the Athenians were more relaxed than our own would be a serious oversimplification, the Athenians were more accepting of the private preferences, choices and tastes of their fellow citizens, like taking a concubine instead of the wife, having a lover, male or female, even though they were married, having love affairs or casual sex with prostitutes female or male, eating or drinking more than they should, following fashion trends in hairstyling and clothing, or engaging in unusual pursuits and novelties, like scientific experimentation or witchcraft.

For women some of these parameters were different, but not for all women in the same manner. Women who were part of the family structure, the *oikos*, fidelity to their husband, which ensured the legitimate birth of their children was of paramount importance, and affairs were not only socially unacceptable, but also had substantial legal consequences.[60] However, even the most respectable family women in Athens did not have their individuality stifled in a manner suggested in 20th century studies. They had a social life with other women, exits in style to the shops, the temples, festivals, or houses of friends and relatives, and were very much part of the life of the community.[61] On the other hand, an increasing number of women, citizen and metic, especially in the 4th century, chose to place themselves outside the traditional structures of the *oikos*. They took lovers, partied hard with the men, received a higher education, accumulated personal wealth which they spent for self-aggrandizement or expensive hobbies such as art collections and became iconic symbols of their gender for centuries to come. They were the ground-breaking women of classical Greece, some but not all, prominent *hetairai*, others simply unconventional figures who did not fit well into the respectable anonymity of family life. The mere fact that they could be themselves and had the freedom to push the boundaries in this manner is a testament to the fundamental freedoms which the rule of law guaranteed in the Athenian Democracy. The *polis* did not interfere in the private lives, interests and pursuits of its people unless it had specific reasons to protect an important aspect of public life.

Unlike modern legal systems, where someone needs years of professional training in the law, because the Corpus of laws is vast, complex and written in technical language, which is inaccessible to the ordinary person, the laws of the Athenian Democracy were brief, straightforward and using language that was technical but not forbidding for the average citizen. The laws of Drakon and Solon had been written in simple language, which anyone could understand in their time. In the 4th century they sounded archaic, and sometimes the language in them might need some interpretation,[62] but even so their meaning was crystal clear and easily understood by anyone. Subsequent legal provisions had the same level of brevity and clarity. Whether they had been introduced by specially appointed boards of legislators (*nomothetai*), or through decrees of the assembly, they were meant to be accessible to the ordinary citizen. The work of the Boule may have played a crucial part in this process: the Council of the 500 had the important task of preparing these proposals for the Assembly, and formulating them in the correct language. Although strict uniformity never was one of the goals of Athenian lawgivers, and the members of the Boule who oversaw the preparatory work and the formulation into the correct language changed too often to allow the crystallization of rigid terminology and phraseology, still the background work of the

Council must be credited to a substantial degree for the clarity and elegant simplicity of Athenian legal language.[63]

The laws of the state were not written for professionals, but for everyone, and they were displayed in public places so that anyone who wished could find them. The homicide laws of Drakon were copied for public display in the late 5th century on an inscription, part of which is still extant.[64] The laws of Solon were originally inscribed on *kyrbeis*, a term of uncertain meaning, and in the classical period they were inscribed on *axones*, namely revolving wooden tablets set on an axle, and placed in the Agora, so that anyone could easily consult them.[65] Such public displays of the laws are attested elsewhere in the Greek world, with the most famous example being the laws of Gortyn in Crete, inscribed in boustrophedon script on the walls of a circular public building.[66]

Between the years 410 and 403 extensive legislative work was done in order to tidy up the Athenian legal corpus, which by that stage had become a messy assemblage of ancient laws going back to the time of Drakon and Solon, and numerous laws and decrees introduced piecemeal in the past two centuries. It also seems that litigants in the 5th century could appeal to unwritten rules, like religious regulations or strong social conventions. All this had created a need to put some order into the Athenian body of laws, and this activity had started in the later years of the Peloponnesian war.

The reorganization of public life after the defeat and restoration of the democracy in 403 offered a unique opportunity for a fresh start. By that stage the legislative work of the past seven years had resulted in a tidier corpus of laws, which was written down, and in future it would form the basis of all legal action in the city. The relevant decree as quoted by Andocides (S 1) forbade the application of unwritten laws, declared valid laws of the state only the ones written down and approved during the *archon*ship of Eukleides (403), confirmed the validity of previous court or arbitration judgments passed under the democracy, and made it a requirement that no law could be introduced which did not apply to all Athenians, with the exception of personal decrees, like naturalization, which needed to be approved by a majority in a full assembly of 6000 citizens. In future copies of the written laws of the city would be kept at the *Metroon*, and any citizen could go there to find out what the law said on any particular matter.[67]

The stability of Athenian laws was not really in question: the core code of Solon and the even older laws of Drakon had remained valid, to some extent, for centuries. They enshrined the important rights to life, property, personal safety, inheritance and family life. A few other important laws, like the decree from the *archon*ship of Skamandrios, which prohibited the torture of free persons, were so old that no one could remember precisely when they had been introduced. The Periclean citizenship law, which in one brief, simple sentence (μὴ μετέχειν τῆς πόλεως, ὃς ἂν μὴ ἐξ ἀμφοῖν ἀστοῖν ᾖ γεγονώς)[68] set the boundaries between citizens and aliens for most of the classical period, remained in force, except for the years of the Peloponnesian war, when Athens had to adapt to the huge losses in an entire generation of young men. These are just a few significant examples. Despite the complaints of the orators about the instability and unnecessarily large number of laws in Athens,[69] in reality the Corpus of Athenian laws was relatively small and stable through the centuries.

The even application of the law is a difficult principle to assess in any society, as human justice is often dictated by human flaws, partiality, prejudice, politics, economics or other extra-legal factors. One of the core arguments of those who contend that Athens never reached the rule of law is the weight that extra-legal evidence seemingly had during a trial. Someone's previous record as a good or bad citizen, his character, liturgical service, or someone's involvement with the regime or the Thirty or democrats of Phyle,[70] are typically brought up by litigants trying to influence the verdict in their favor in the extant speeches. But, first and foremost, the Athenians were not unique in this respect; justice in every human society in history has been influenced by similar criteria.[71] Then, we should be careful not to confuse the rule of law with the rule of rhetoric. Such elements were not part of Athenian law but were part of the rhetorical strategy in an Athenian trial. The law was impartial and equal for all; people's perceptions were unequal and partial, and this is what the rhetorical strategies of the Attic Orators reflect. These strategies were aimed precisely at human weaknesses, fears, anxieties, prejudices, and day-to-day irritations, with the sole purpose to exploit them for the benefit of the litigant. On the other side of the coin, skilled litigators often exploited the positive sides of the human psyche, such as compassion, kindness, empathy and altruism.[72] As Vasileios Adamidis has correctly pointed out, such elements were part of the wholesome presentation of a litigant before the court.[73] More to the point, this material has always been a crucially important part of the rhetorical strategies of trials, from antiquity to the present day, and in all probability it will continue to be. The rule of law was established in classical Athens as in other societies through the centuries with these elements included, and not in their absence.

In conclusion, the Athenian Democracy comfortably meets the criteria for Just Laws. Its laws were clear, the body of laws relatively small and easily accessible to the layperson, and access to the justice system was free for all, at least as far as the state was concerned, with the exception of minor administrative fees. Behind the scenes a flourishing industry of legal services needed to keep a low profile, because the law explicitly prohibited profiteering from the justice system.[74] Equality before the law was an important political concept in the Athenian Democracy, and its laws were meant to be applied evenly, even though in reality the human factor and the power of rhetoric introduced inequalities. The laws of the Athenian state were firmly protecting fundamental rights, including life, property, security, privacy and family life, protection from torture, education, healthcare, and a safety net for those who needed extra help, like widows, orphans, the elderly, and persons with disabilities.[75]

1.6 Open government in the Athenian Democracy

The introduction of the laws of Drakon, and later Solon, was engineered by the aristocratic state for its own purposes, although the lower classes certainly benefitted from the establishment of coherent, stable, and in some aspects equitable laws. Those ancient laws remained at the core of the Athenian legal system, but many additional layers introduced in later centuries would modify them substantially, and on many occasions newer statutes or political and social developments would render them obsolete. After the establishment of the democracy the introduction of new laws was handled by the Assembly. A citizen who wished to introduce a new law would need to bring a proposal before the Boule (προβούλευμα). When the Boule had formulated the new decree and given its approval for presentation to the Assembly, the person could then bring the proposal before the people. If the Assembly approved it, it became a valid law of the Athenian state. This process probably worked well in the more restrained and better-controlled democracy under Kimon and Pericles. However, when the era of the demagogues and professional politicians arrived in the later part of the 5th century the entire process came under strain, as the relatively low levels of scrutiny for the introduction of new laws allowed some of the excesses of the demagogues in the years of the Peloponnesian war. The signs of dissatisfaction and disillusionment with the course of the city's politics under the demagogues are visible in the *Knights* of Aristophanes, and other plays from the later 420s.

Anxieties such as these were behind the introduction of a process which was intended to hit the brakes on the legislative processes of the Athenian Democracy. It allowed any citizen to bring an indictment for an illegal proposal (γραφὴ παρανόμων) against any decree of the Assembly which in the opinion of the prosecutor was contradicting an existing law.[76] Between the prosecution and trial the decree was suspended until resolution in court. If the prosecutor lost, the force of the decree was reinstated. If he won, the decree was annulled, and if less than a year had passed since its introduction, the proposer of the decree was also punished.[77] The trial was an *agon timetos*, which meant that the jury would assess the penalty. MacDowell writes: "whoever suggested it (i.e. the *graphe paranomon*) was no doubt a man who believed in the maintenance of law and the existing constitution".[78] This may be so, but in the 4th century the courts of the democracy used the *graphe paranomon* as an opportunity to rethink a decree in context, rather than stick to the technicalities of it.[79]

A famous example of this would be the *graphe paranomon* against Ktesiphon brought by Aeschines in 336. He indicted the decree of Ktesiphon, which was proposing to crown Demosthenes for his services, but when the case finally reached the courts in 330 Aeschines did not stand a chance of winning regardless of the merits of his case. The whole trial ended up being an epic *agon* on whether Demosthenes had been offering the right advice to the city all those years. By that stage the southern Greeks had been defeated at Chaironea, Philip and then Alexander had dominated the Greek World, Thebes had been razed to the ground, and the world of the independent Greek *polis* had changed beyond recognition. Squabbling about legal technicalities would seem pointless when history had proven with absolute certainty that the policies and warnings of Demosthenes were truthful and in the best interests of Athens, while the policies which Aeschines had advocated over the years had led to the submission of the entire Greek world to

Macedon, just as Demosthenes had been warning all along. Aeschines was decisively defeated in that trial and since he did not secure 1/5 of the votes and could not afford to pay the massive fine of 1000 drachmas, he was disfranchised and permanently left Athens.

The *graphe paranomon* was used extensively in the 4th century by politicians to settle scores, reverse measures or decisions which they did not like, attack opponents, or cancel naturalization decrees for political figures when they did not agree with their views. There are seven extant speeches on *paranomon* cases, and all amply demonstrate that this procedure dramatically changed the political landscape.[80] Prominent politicians became more cagey about what they put in writing before the assembly, and used minor political figures to do the dirty work by adding their name to proposals and taking upon themselves the risk, for monetary profit and career advancement in the ranks of a political party.

For example, the careful language of Demosthenes when speaking about diverting money from the theoric to the stratiotic fund in the later 340s, after his political friend and ally Apollodoros had been defeated in a *graphe paranomon* on this matter in 347–346 and was forced to pay the massive fine of 1 talent, shows the restraining impact which this law was having on the legislative work of the assembly.

The constitutional crises of the late 5th century, which twice in a decade had led to the replacement of the Democratic Constitution with unpopular oligarchic regimes, urged the Athenians to rethink the legislative process, so as to make it more difficult for antidemocratic forces to overturn the constitution. The solution was a conceptual separation between laws and decrees, and additional steps in the introduction of laws. The difference between laws and decrees in the 5th century was rather semantic. A decree (ψήφισμα) was a document which recorded the result of a vote, often inscribed on stone and placed in a public building related to its content.[81] A law was a more abstract concept indicating a permanent rule, like for example the laws of Solon. In reality the distinction was hazy. For example, the word *psephisma* would be used for one of the most fundamental laws of the Athenian state, the decree from the *archon*ship of Skamandrios which protected free persons from torture, and also for decisions of the Assembly pertaining to short-term, specific events, like for example the decision of the Assembly not to destroy Mytilene.[82] On the comic stage the Decree-seller (ψηφισματοπώλης) in the *Birds* of Aristophanes comes to Nephelokokkygia to sell laws (νόμους) to the new state.[83]

In the 4th century the Athenians tried to tidy up matters and differentiate between laws and decrees. A law could no longer be introduced with a simple vote of the assembly. The details of the procedure of *nomothesia*, namely the introduction of new laws and/or repeal of old laws, are contentious, but seemingly it was a three-stage process.[84] First someone needed to prepare a proposal with the Boule (*probouleuma*), second, the proposal needed to be approved by the majority of the Assembly, and finally it went to a board of legislators (*nomothetai*), for final approval, and only then it became a valid law the Athenian state.[85] By contrast, a decree was conceptualized as something less permanent, something pertinent to a specific issue, and did not require the same level of scrutiny. As before, one would need to secure a *probouleuma* and the approval of the Assembly before the decree took effect. For the most part the distinction of laws and decrees is observed in the 4th century, but it is not rigid, as a decree could still have lasting effect. Both laws and decrees could be challenged in court at any point after their successful introduction, the laws through a process called "to introduce an improper law" (νόμον μὴ ἐπιτήδειον θεῖναι),[86] and the decrees through a *graphe paranomon*. Some of the extant public forensic speeches in the Demosthenic Corpus (e.g. 20, 22, 23, 24, 25), as well as several titles of non-extant speeches, are related to such lawsuits and offer valuable insights in the legislative processes of classical Athens, how these were influenced by contemporary politics, and what was the role of the courts in such cases.

The power of the courts to cancel any law or decree approved by the Assembly is reminiscent of modern concerns about the interference of the courts in political matters and has led H. Hansen to form a theory that the courts and not the Assembly was the sovereign body of the Athenian Democracy.[87] The entire discussion is a moot point in the case of classical Athens. While the Athenian Democracy clearly separated the judicial from other powers and had incorporated a formidable set of checks and balances to make sure that no one person or group acquires so much power as to endanger the constitution, the people sitting in its courts were the same as the people sitting in the Assembly. The 6000 citizens manning the court system probably were, for the most part, the same people who had the time and disposition to join the main meeting of the Assembly (*kyria ekklesia*) each month. Each court section was a random selection by lot from this body, and it was large enough to be quite representative of the citizen body. This is why the courts were never viewed as an antagonist of the Assembly; they were viewed as a representative part of it with more time in their hands to look into the issues more carefully, and with stricter procedures so as to be harder to deceive with skillful rhetoric. Had the courts been viewed as antagonistic to the Assembly, we should be in no doubt that their powers would have been as effectively curtailed as those of the Areopagos in 462. But the courts were not viewed as antagonistic to the *demos*, because they were *demotic* (δημοτικόν).

The legislative processes of the Athenian *polis* and the openness of its government are remarkable. Without a doubt the direct democracy of Athens had the most open government than any human society before or since. Laws were not enacted by a small number of representatives, as it happens in our democracies, or as it happened in Sparta, where only an Ephor had the authority to propose a new law. Neither were laws enacted by government officials or judges. Any citizen could propose a new law. In the 5th century this process was risk-free and open to all, but as the process was abused and eventually turned against democracy itself in the final decade of the Peloponnesian war and its immediate aftermath, sensible safeguards were introduced in the 4th century. Additional scrutiny was required for the introduction of new laws, and the state expected of citizens who proposed laws and decrees to take responsibility by making sure that they introduced proposals that did not break existing laws, that they did not introduce laws harmful to the state and its institutions, and that they would make sure to repeal old ineffective laws before trying to introduce new ones. The *graphe paranomon* and *nomon me epitedeion thenai* procedures were the safeguards of the state that citizens did their due diligence before trying to change things, and ultimately took responsibility for their actions. These safeguards did not hinder the open government and the fair and efficient enactment of new laws. Ultimately, every citizen could still propose a new law, and the Assembly still retained the authority to accept or reject a proposal. What the safeguards did was to ensure that the introduction of new laws and important decisions on policy matters, domestic and foreign, were not a matter of whimsical decisions of the moment, but the result of thoroughly examined and carefully crafted planning.

1.7 Dispute resolution: processes and types of lawsuits

Those who believe that Athens never reached the rule of law often use as an argument the absence of rules of relevance and the excessive use of extrajudicial elements in the Athenian justice system. However, such views miss a large part of the picture. They only see the Heliastic courts, which had been envisaged as appeal courts, while at the same time they miss the rigorous scrutiny of the facts in the first stage of any private trial (except homicide), namely the public arbitration. They also fail to take into account the importance of dispute resolution, for public or private lawsuits, through private arbitration. This is why it is necessary to look at the entire picture of the Athenian legal system before we try to understand how facts were checked, evidence was presented, relevance rules were observed and decisions were made.

There was significant difference in the processes between public lawsuits, where anyone could bring a prosecution, and private lawsuits, where the injured party was seeking redress through the legal system. The vast majority of public lawsuits were *graphai*, indictments which, as the name suggests, began with a written complaint to the appropriate magistrate, usually the *thesmothetai*. *Graphai* related to religious matters were submitted to the *basileus*, those related to immigration violations were submitted to the polemarch, and *graphai* related to family law were submitted to the *archon*. A *graphe* always carried a risk of 1000 drachmas, a truly severe fine for a prosecutor who failed to appear in court on the day of the trial or did not secure 1/5 of the votes.[88]

Two more public procedures mentioned in our sources, the *probole* and the *eisangelia*, could also be initiated by anyone, but they did not carry the same risk. The *probole* was intended to prosecute violations during festivals, which had compromised the ceremonies, and also to prosecute sycophants.[89] The *eisangelia* was envisaged as an avenue to prosecute people whose activities put the safety of the state at risk, and in the private sphere to prosecute persons who had been abusing someone who could not defend him/herself, like an orphan or an heiress (*epikleros*). Since neither the *probole* nor the *eisangelia* carried a penalty risk, the state somehow needed to find a way to weed out frivolous prosecutions. The solution was a two-stage process. A *probole* first needed to be presented to the assembly, and if it won the approval of the assembly then it could proceed to the courts. The *eisangelia* was typically presented first to the Boule, but also on occasion to the assembly, and with their approval it could be brought to court. We do not know of any such case which was defeated either before the assembly or the Boule, and still proceeded to a court trial, and the silence may be significant; it could mean that a defeat in the assembly or the Boule was sufficient to kill off a prosecution initiated under one of these procedures. Relentless abuses of the *eisangelia* process in the 4th century resulted in a change of the law around 330, which brought the *eisangelia* in line with *graphe*. In future *eisangelia* cases would carry the same risk of 1000 drachmas.

Other public lawsuits, like the *apagoge* (arresting an alleged criminal and taking him to the Eleven), *endeixis* (indicting a criminal and maybe also arresting him) and *ephegesis* (leading a magistrate to an alleged crime-scene or criminal), were used for a variety of offences. For the most part these procedures could be used when someone had been caught red-handed, like a thief in someone's house, or an enslaver leading a free person to slavery. They could also be employed when someone was spotted in a place where he should not be. For example, a killer who for some reason had not been prosecuted by the family of the victim, or he had been prosecuted and chose to ignore the proclamations and mix with others in the Agora or a temple was subject to these procedures. Or a disfranchised man, who ignored the rules and still was mixing with citizens in the agora or the temples, was also subject to one of these procedures. Of the three, *endeixis* seems to be the broadest, and could be used to denounce a variety of alleged crimes, like for example the religious violation which Andocides had unwittingly committed when he placed a suppliant branch on the altar at Eleusis during the festival, unaware that this was forbidden by the sacred rules.[90]

Phasis and *apographe* were concerned with economic crime. *Phasis* was the primary procedure for most forms of economic crime, such as illegal sales of goods in the marketplace, improper possession of public property, violations of commerce laws, or crimes related to the estates of orphans.[91] The state had a vested interest in the fight against economic crime and wanted to encourage individuals to come forward with prosecutions of such offences. This is why the successful prosecutor in a *phasis* procedure was rewarded with half of the value of the assessed penalty. *Apographe* was the appropriate process for the confiscation of the property of persons convicted for certain crimes. The process began with a list of a person's property items.[92] If the list included items which belonged to someone else, that person could come forward and claim those items, and the court would determine the owner.[93] Once all possible claims had been settled the remainder of the property was handed over to the *poletai* for sale, and the successful prosecutor would receive one third of the value of the confiscated property.[94]

The trial in public cases was an entire day affair. Aeschines describes the process as following (with reference to a *graphe paranomon*):

> Εἰς τρία μέρη διαιρεῖται ἡ ἡμέρα, ὅταν εἰσίῃ γραφὴ παρανόμων εἰς τὸ δικαστήριον. Ἐγχεῖται γὰρ τὸ μὲν πρῶτον ὕδωρ τῷ κατηγόρῳ καὶ τοῖς νόμοις καὶ τῇ δημοκρατίᾳ, τὸ δὲ δεύτερον ὕδωρ τῷ τὴν γραφὴν φεύγοντι καὶ τοῖς εἰς

> αὐτὸ τὸ πρᾶγμα λέγουσιν· ἐπειδὰν δὲ τῇ πρώτῃ ψήφῳ μὴ λυθῇ τὸ παράνομον, ἤδη τὸ τρίτον ὕδωρ ἐγχεῖται τῇ τιμήσει καὶ τῷ μεγέθει τῆς ὀργῆς τῆς ὑμετέρας.
>
> The day is divided into three parts, when a *graphe paranomon* comes into court. The first lot of water is poured in for the prosecutor, the laws, and democracy: the second for the defendant in the *graphe* and those speaking on the actual case; and when the question of illegality is decided by the first vote, the third lot of water is poured in for the assessment of the penalty and the extent of your anger.[95]

Since the *graphe paranomon* was only one of several public lawsuits, it is fair to conclude that this procedure was followed in all public lawsuits. The process best described above would take a good part of the day. Equal time needed to be allocated for the speeches of the prosecution and the defense. Supporting speakers and advocates needed to speak within the time available to the litigant. The water-clock was only paused for the presentation of documents such as statements of witnesses, oaths, wills, etc.[96] We do not know the exact amount of time which each litigant had at his disposal. Peter Rhodes has calculated 2½ hours for each litigant, and this is probably not far off the truth.[97] If we add to that some time for the preliminaries before the prosecution began, perhaps a short, necessary break between prosecution and defense, the time taken for the assessment of the penalty if the defendant had been found guilty in a case where the court needed to assess the penalty, which should be another 2½ hours, this time for both sides, and also some time for bargaining and negotiation, which seems to have been happening between the successful prosecutor and the defendant with the objective to reach agreement and propose the same penalty,[98] then undoubtedly the trial would have taken the whole day.

Most cases in Athenian law were private lawsuits (δίκη ἰδία) initiated by the interested party. Private lawsuits did not carry large risks and penalties for the unsuccessful prosecutor, except the modest 30 drachmas fee (*prytaneia*) paid by the losing side. Private lawsuits, whether concerned with financial matters, like for example a suit for the return of a dowry (δίκη προικός), or with other forms of injury to the prosecutor, like for example the lawsuit for assault (δίκη αἰκείας), carried a financial reward for the successful prosecutor, the amount of which sometimes was defined by the law, as for example in cases of slander,[99] but more often was determined by the prosecutor at the time when he submitted the lawsuit.

The financial element made private lawsuits more attractive in those cases where the law allowed different avenues, as for example in cases of battery, where the victim of a physical assault could choose between a public lawsuit for deliberate wounding (γραφὴ τραύματος ἐκ προνοίας) or a private lawsuit for assault (δίκη αἰκείας). In the former case the prosecutor took significant risk, 1000 drachmas if he failed to secure 1/5 of the vote, and if successful he gained nothing other than some mighty revenge, since the convicted defendant was permanently exiled from Attica. However, if he chose a private lawsuit, he stood to gain financially, as his opponent could be forced to pay a very hefty compensation. In such cases the personalities of the litigants, the motives behind the lawsuit and the circumstances of the case would determine which path seemed preferable.[100]

Private lawsuits followed very different procedures from public lawsuits. First, they were submitted to different magistrates, the Forty in the time of the orators. Then, each case went to public arbitration. The arbitrator was appointed by the state through sortition and was answerable to an *euthyna* in the end of his year in office, which ensured full accountability. Unlike trials by jury an arbitration did not need to be completed on the spot; postponement and adjournment were permissible, while the arbitrator and the litigants could use the extra time to explore further the details of the case and the arbitrator could always try to forge a compromise. If he failed, or he felt that it was not appropriate to seek a compromise in that particular case, he ruled in favor of one side.[101]

Women could also give evidence in an arbitration since the witnesses were not subject to a prosecution for false testimony (*pseudomartyrion*), and on the whole the rules were far less rigid than they were in a trial by jury, for the simple reason that arbitrators did not operate under the same constrains of time and cost as the Heliastic courts. Thus, the Athenian arbitration in many ways resembles a modern trial, allowing each side to build their case without narrow constrains of time or the procedural restrictions of the courts over a number of days or weeks, if necessary. It also allowed for proper and thorough checks and objections to facts and figures. Speaking outside the subject, building elaborate rhetorical strategies, delivering high and mighty speeches and making arguments from character would probably be pointless before the arbitrator, as he could stop the litigant at any moment and ask as many questions on the facts and merits of the case, as he wanted, thus rendering those techniques familiar to us from jury trials meaningless.

If the arbitration failed to resolve the case, a final appeal was allowed before the courts. During the trial each litigant could speak twice. The prosecution went first, followed by the defense, and then the prosecution returned with a second, seemingly shorter speech (*deuterology*), followed by the defense with a second speech of equal duration. This format would be more appropriate especially when financial data and facts needed to be presented as it allowed each side to check the facts of the other side and respond with detailed figures. This format was also observed in homicide trials, where after the first set of speeches the defendant could choose to interrupt the trial and permanently leave Attica.[102] The prevailing principle in the procedures of an Athenian trial was that each litigant was legally entitled to an equal share of the court's time and an equal opportunity to voice his side of the story. The principle is echoed by the chorus in the *Heraklidai* of Euripides:

> XO: τίς ἂν δίκην κρίνειεν ἢ γνοίη λόγον,
> πρὶν ἂν παρ' ἀμφοῖν μῦθον ἐκμάθηι σαφῶς;[103]
>
> CHO: who would judge a trial or reach a decision,
> before properly hearing the story of each side?

Homicide cases were a special category of private lawsuits, partly because the laws which governed them were truly ancient, introduced by Drakon in 620, namely a quarter of a millennium before the time of the orators, and partly because they were closely associated with religion and fell within the competence of the chief magistrate of religious affairs in the state, the *basileus*. This strange mix of religious conservatism and antiquated legal procedure, which preceded the establishment of democracy by more than a century, gave homicide cases their peculiar character. They were private lawsuits because the law only allowed relatives up to second cousins, or the master of a slave, to prosecute the offender.[104] However, unlike most other private lawsuits, financial gain was decidedly not in the cards; the relative of the victim needed to bring this prosecution because the spilled blood of the victim needed to be avenged, and the killer was polluting anyone with whom he came into contact or shared a roof (*miasma*).[105] Homicide cases were not tried by regular courts, but by the Areopagos Council, or sections of it called ἐφέται, and this was surely a vestige from an early time when the Heliastic courts did not even exist as a concept.

Because of the religious aspects of homicide litigants took terrible oaths to bring destruction upon themselves and their families if they lied, and also to stick to the facts of the case. The general idea was that putting an innocent person to death would bring upon the community the same destructive force of the *miasma*, as it would have if a killer were allowed to walk free among them. This is why it was particularly important for homicide courts to reach the correct verdict. From the 5th century the law allowed any citizen to prosecute a killer with *apagoge*, but only if he had not been prosecuted by the family, or he was awaiting trial, and still entered public places and threatened with contamination anyone who came in touch with him. Such cases went to regular courts, because the offence under trial was not the homicide per se, but rather the reckless action of putting the entire community at risk by mingling with innocent persons.

The state also invited litigants to settle their differences outside the court system through private arbitration, by recognizing the rulings of private arbitrators as legal and final. At any point before the date of the trial, in public or private lawsuits, the litigants could elect to suspend the formal legal proceedings and entrust the case to private arbitration. The number of arbitrators was not set by law. It could be only one person who enjoyed the trust of both sides for his impartiality, or could be two, one representing each side, or three, so that a person trusted by both could be the tie-breaker, but at the same time each side had a person of their choosing on the panel to represent their interests. It appears that often private arbitration was about dispute resolution through compromise and mutual concessions. However, since there was no rule-book, and the arbitrators enjoyed the confidence and trust of the litigants, private arbitrators had so much more room for maneuvering in order to reach the desired resolution. Sometimes they used unorthodox methods and reached rulings which we might find weird, but they knew well the parties involved and the personalities that needed to be appeased, and, unlike the courts which had to go by the law, the arbitrators had the discretion to what was necessary to effect a fair and lasting resolution.[106]

Many of the criticisms of the Athenian legal system by those who believe that it never reached the rule of law only take into account the final stage of appeal before the court, for those cases which arbitration failed to resolve, and not the entire process. However, a closer look into the Athenian legal system demonstrates that it was much more involved than the short final performance before the jury. It was a long process which started with presentations before the responsible magistrate (ἀνάκρισις), followed by lengthy preparations, and in the vast majority of cases, namely all private lawsuits except homicide, by mandatory arbitration, which could extend over a number of days or weeks. During the arbitration evidence needed to be presented, facts and figures could be checked, and double checked, witnesses could be thoroughly cross-examined, surprises were not always effective, as the opposing side could ask for adjournment in order to respond, and the entire process was as thorough as any modern trial could be.

The great political trials in public lawsuits have more in common with modern appeal trials before higher or constitutional courts, discussing matters of greater significance for the community and the application of the law within these concerns, and as such they are conceptually broader and more encompassing, and this is what we see in the major public forensic speeches which have reached us. In those trials the political beliefs, good citizenship and standing of a litigant would be inextricably linked to the core of the case. For the Athenians it was important whether their politicians were men of good character, honest, trustworthy and consistently worthy citizens, as it would be for us. This is why these elements, which some scholars have deemed to be extra-judicial, were very much part of the equation in the major political trials for which the extant public-forensic speeches were delivered, as Vasileios Adamidis has demonstrated.[107]

The Athenian legal system easily meets the fourth universal principle of the WJP for fair and impartial resolution of disputes. The aim of the Athenian legal system was to produce a timely, competent, fair, ethical and impartial resolution, and this is why it had clear, established procedures in place. When time was of essence as in the case of commercial disputes (δίκαι ἐμπορικαί) or monthly lawsuits (ἔμμηνοι δίκαι), a rapid resolution process was built into the system, but for the majority of cases time limits were more flexible. The fair, ethical and impartial resolution of cases was assured by the equal time allocated to each side, the thorough steps leading up to the trial by jury, including public arbitration, the appointment of arbitrators by lot and the full accountability of arbitrators. But more importantly, the trial before large juries of one's peers, the members of which were selected randomly by lot, and, in this respect, they represented a cross-section of Athenian society, is the lasting legacy of the justice system of the first democracy. Ultimately, dispute resolution was not the domain of legal specialists or state magistrates, who could be partial, corrupt or selected on the basis of specific political views. The all-important duty of the implementation of the law was bestowed upon the communal sense of fairness and justice of a random, representative section of the litigants' peers, who after reviewing the evidence and listening to each side, would vote individually, in secret, for the side whom they believed to be in the right. This measure was important as a step designed to eliminate peer pressure and, in the words of a 4th century orator, allow each man to reach his own decision and cast his vote as if this was his own trial (ἀλλ' ὡς ὑπὲρ αὐτοῦ δικάζων οὕτως ἕκαστος ὑμῶν οἴσει τὴν ψῆφον).[108]

1.8 Blocking an improperly introduced lawsuit

Before the end of the 5th century illegally or incorrectly introduced cases (μὴ εἰσαγώγιμος), like for example bringing a case against a citizen before the polemarch under the assumption that he was an alien, or introducing a case on the basis of a non-existent contract, could be blocked by the opposing litigant with a rather antiquated procedure called διαμαρτυρία. The litigant could produce a witness before the magistrate who testified why the case was improperly introduced. If his opponent did not protest, this was the end of the proceedings. However, if the opponent objected (ἐπίσκηψις) the proceedings were temporarily halted giving the opponent the opportunity to bring a prosecution for false testimony (*dike pseudomartyrion*) against the witness. If the opponent won, this ended the proceedings; if he lost, the initial lawsuit resumed as before. Louis Gernet has proven that this was an ancient procedure relying on concepts such as the assertion of a single witness. Classical Athenian law typically required more involved and objective procedures, and probably this is the reason why *diamartyria* seemed inadequate to deal with a potential flood of blocked lawsuits in the wake of the general amnesty in 403, and was for the most part replaced by the *paragraphe*, except, it seems, in cases of *diadikasia* for property claims, where understandably the testimony of persons with precise knowledge of family affairs might still be particularly significant and necessary.[109]

The *paragraphe* was introduced shortly after 403 with a law proposed by Archinos, and Isocrates *Against Kallimachos* was delivered for the first ever *paragraphe* case.[110] A litigant who believed that for some reason his opponent had introduced the case incorrectly or illegally could block proceedings with a counter-suit (παραγραφή). Once a *paragraphe* was launched the initial legal proceedings came to a halt, until this case was decided. If the litigant lost, then the initial lawsuit could proceed as normal. If he won, his opponent had to drop the case or make a new prosecution adjusted for the points that had made his previous prosecution illegal. If, for example, someone had prosecuted his opponent before the polemarch assuming that he was an alien, as in the case *Against Pankleon*, and lost the *paragraphe* because his opponent had produced evidence that he was a citizen, the prosecutor could drop the case altogether,[111] or bring a new case before the appropriate magistrate for Athenian citizens. The loser in a *paragraphe* lawsuit had to pay a fine (*epobelia*) of 30 drachmas.[112] Several *paragraphe* speeches, all concerning commercial disputes, survive in a cluster among the speeches of Demosthenes (32–8). The *paragraphe* was sometimes used by litigants as a tactic to delay and disrupt proceedings (Dem. 21.84; 36.2), and to a large extent this is the reason why its use became widespread in the course of the 4th century.[113]

1.9 The "amateurism" of Athenian law?

Often, studies on Athenian law refer to the "amateurism" of the laws themselves and the processes by which they were enforced. I am convinced that "amateur" is the wrong word when speaking of Athenian jurors, legal processes, speakers and advocates. It is perfectly understandable why it has been extensively used, compared to modern times where the law and its application are limited to expert professionals. Ever since the Romans created an obfuscated legal system which required professional advocates, since it would have been impossible for the ordinary citizen to know the vast and complex body of law, the professional lawyer and judge became standard features in both Civil and Common Law systems. However, the fact that the legal system of the Athenian Democracy was based on different principles, which recognized the right and duty of the ordinary citizen to know the law and encouraged the citizen of the democracy to get personally involved in the implementation of the law on a day-to-day basis, does not make it a system of amateurs. This would be yet another oversimplification.

First, payment for legal services was very much present in the Athenian legal system. The dicasts could not be expected to devote so much of their time to the justice system for free. They were compensated at the rate of three obols per day, which was equal to the compensation of an unskilled worker. Although this surely was not the most attractive career option in town, it was a reliable minimum wage source, which for many poor Athenians could make the difference between food on the table and starvation.[114] This is why it is not difficult to believe Aristophanes, when he suggests in the *Wasps* that for some people, especially the elderly and those who lived near the city, jury service was a long-term occupation. Since there was no statutory limit to the number of times that someone could serve as juror, we can easily envisage the scenario where the majority of the men sitting in any specific jury had been doing this for years and some of them had heard thousands of cases. Even the new person could have behind him the experience of dozens of trials, by the end of his first year, and as a result he would be much more aware of the realities of jury trial and the slippery tricks of skilled litigants, and in time he would amass substantial legal expertise, by hearing the laws cited every day and participating in their application.

Even more formidable must have been the legal expertise of those judging in the homicide courts. The members of the Areopagos already had very significant administrative experience, since all of them had served as *archon*s. After they joined the Council they would remain members for life hearing only homicide or deliberate wounding cases, year after year. If it was true that they also served as *ephetai* in the rest of the homicide courts, we would be justified to conclude that their legal expertise in homicide law as well as their experience in trying homicide cases would be formidable. The Areopagus had an established reputation for fairness, and we can understand why this was the case.[115]

It is also a carefully cultivated myth that all litigants in Athenian courts were amateurs relying on their own elementary knowledge and understanding of the laws, and their own ability to plead their case before the jury. Often, litigants were supported by advocates, while for women litigants representation by an advocate was necessary. The advocate could be simply acting as a legal advisor in the background, suggesting strategies and offering help with the laws. As the body of laws grew larger in the course of the 4th century, legal experience was bound to become increasingly more important.[116] Experienced advocates like Lysias,

Isaios or Demosthenes certainly knew the laws well and could advise their clients accordingly. Often the advocate would do more than merely advise: he could act as a logographer, a shadow-writer who actually composed the speech that the litigant was going to deliver in the trial, or he could turn up in person and speak on behalf of the litigant.

We have more than a hundred speeches written for Athenian litigants by a small number of prominent orators, whose work later antiquity deemed to be sufficiently prestigious and worthy of preservation. Undoubtedly there were many more speechwriters and legal advisors whose works did not enjoy the same reputation in later times, but some of these works have survived because they were mistakenly attributed to the masters of Attic Oratory. The works of Apollodoros, the son of Pasion, are an excellent example of this: although he went to court countless times in his life and he was a very experienced litigator, expert in the laws, a formidable adversary and a very competent orator, we have seven of his speeches only because they were mistakenly attributed to Demosthenes. We know that paying dearly for the services of an experienced advocate was common practice for Athenian litigants, and some of the most illustrious orators and speechwriters of the time, like Lysias, Demosthenes or Hypereides, became very wealthy from this profession.

On many occasions we find experienced orators, like Demosthenes, speaking as advocates (*synegoros*) in support of litigants, either taking over the entire speech, as it happens in the case of Phormion (D. 36), supposedly on account of his imperfect Greek, or together with the litigant coming forward as a team and sharing the allocated time, as Theomnestos and Apollodoros do in the speech *Against Neaira*. This was perfectly permissible and common practice, so long as the advocate did not support the litigant for-profit. This was prohibited by the same law which penalized the bribery of public officials, and surely this fact is significant for our understanding of this law. It appears that being paid to serve as an advocate was similar in Athenian eyes to bribing a state official (S 4). In both cases profit could interfere with important public matters, such as the functions of the state and the implementation of justice, and have a detrimental effect on the principle of *isonomia*.

It is very much to the credit of the citizens of the first democracy that they understood the dangers of financial inequalities for the course of justice, and tried to prevent the agency of such factors with a clear, firm and determined law banning all profit for legal services. This is why sometimes we hear advocates stressing the bond of friendship or relationship with the litigant whom they support.[117] However, it would be naïve to take all these claims of unselfish motives literally. We should be in no doubt that Demosthenes was paid a very large amount of money to write the speech on behalf of Phormion, and that the orators and litigators of classical Athens, whose fame has far surpassed the geographical and chronological boundaries of classical Athens, like Lysias, Isocrates, Demosthenes, Hypereides or Isaios, were paid dearly for their services, even if no one would admit to this in court. The noble intentions of the law notwithstanding, human insecurity and the concomitant financial interference were not absent from the Athenian legal system, even if they were less pronounced than they are in modern, "professional" legal systems. For these reasons, we should not be buying into the "amateur" rhetoric of Athenian litigants, or their self-professed ignorance of the laws and inexperience in public affairs, as such claims often disguise fine-tuned tactics planned in the background by their expensive legal advisers.

The famous litigators, speech-writers and orators of classical Athens were not amateurs; they were as professional as they come. The judges were no amateurs either; many of them had probably clocked more hours in court than any modern judge would hope to clock in a lifetime of service. Even though they lacked the training of their modern counterparts, their long-term, day-to-day engagement with the legal system equipped them with substantial experience and expertise in legal matters. Ultimately, their lack of training in the law would not be much of a disadvantage in a society which intentionally kept its body of laws relatively brief and accessible to all.

1.10 Rules of evidence and the rule of law

One of the main points of those who argue that Athens never reached the rule of law is that Athenian courts lacked rules of evidence. According to this point of view extra-legal argumentation, such as character-evidence, or lists of someone's liturgies,[118] which would fail modern tests of relevance, were extensively used in Athenian courts, and had a detrimental effect upon the consistency of verdicts and the application of the law. Complex rules of evidence and detailed technicalities characteristic of Common Law systems, such as those in place in the US and UK in our times, have been set up, mostly by American and British researchers of Athenian law, as a golden standard which the Athenians have failed to reach. However, such comparisons of legal systems are unequal and fundamentally flawed as a number of studies has demonstrated. In the words of Stephen Todd "It is a wasted criticism, based on modernizing assumptions, to blame the Athenian dikasterion for failing to achieve that supposedly objective enactment of justice for which it was never designed."[119] Crude comparisons between legal systems based on different principles and modes of operation are bound to lead to misleading conclusions, especially when modern legal systems are idealized, despite thoroughly documented evidence of their serious failings,[120] and the Athenian system is perceived as primitive despite the fact that it was based on principles of democratic openness, fairness and accessibility which should be the envy of modern law.[121]

First and foremost, we should not jump to the conclusion that modern legal systems are producing fairer or more consistent verdicts, because they have complex rules of evidence, while Athenian courts produced ad hoc, inconsistent verdicts, because they failed to observe rules of relevance, and did not have sufficient records of precedent.[122] This is total guesswork; we do not know whether Athenian courts produced consistent or inconsistent verdicts because we have the verdicts in only a handful of cases, mostly major political trials, which would be a poor guide for any conclusions, in the first place. We rarely know the outcome on the overwhelming majority of lawsuits, and altogether we simply do not have enough data to reach any conclusion on the consistency of the verdicts in Athenian courts or the lack of it. Edward Harris has correctly asserted that the goal of Athenian courts was to achieve consistency – whether they were successful and to what extent we cannot tell.[123] We can only make the general observation that the Athenians trusted their legal system, perhaps more than we trust ours, and resorted to it frequently to resolve differences in public or private life. This is a very important factor in our discussion. In a direct democracy the justice system could only have functioned as it did if it enjoyed the trust of the citizens in its processes and the fairness of its verdicts; otherwise, the citizens of the democracy would have changed the system, radically, fundamentally, to its core concepts and foundations, because they could and had the power and the authority to do so. The justice system of the Athenian Democracy was as it was not because powerful elites had formed it to suit their interests, as it often happens in our times, but because this is how the citizens wanted it to be. The Athenians did not come up with a complex legal system, not because they could not devise one, but simply because they chose not to do so. The main strengths of the Athenian justice system lie in exactly the opposite traits: simple, easily accessible laws understood by every person concerned, open access and a strong communal sense of fairness and equality before the law, consistent principles of social justice, and affirmation of the democratic values of classical Athenian society.

Second, what is relevant and what is not in a legal case is very much a matter of interpretation; the difference between the Athenian and modern legal systems simply lies in the methods of interpretation, not in the essence of it. The carefully cultivated legal fiction in our times that increasingly complex and detailed sets of rules on evidence and relevance successfully remove the human factor from judicial process, minimize the impact of emotion on verdicts, and result in the employment of pure reason and impartiality in the entire process has been time and again discredited in the literature. It has been amply demonstrated that skilled litigators will always find a way of bypassing even the most technical and detailed rules, appeal to human emotion, and manipulate the anger, fear, empathy, resentments and insecurities of juries, as well as the political preferences, cultural crusades or religious sentiments of even the most rigidly professional judges. Ultimately, this is what has always been the strength of the professional lawyer, his or her ability to secure the desired verdict through the manipulation of human nature, within the procedural confines of each case. Just to give a couple of examples, modern legal literature has amply demonstrated that emotional victim statements can have a very profound impact upon the verdict and sentencing,[124] or that the unlimited use of gruesome photographs in modern trials, while in full compliance with the rules of evidence, clearly has a forceful emotional impact on juries, and this makes evidence such as this most compelling.[125] Such evidence is not designed to make an impartial, logical contribution to the case. It is designed to penetrate the rules of evidence and target the emotions of a jury, elicit anger, fear, empathy and a communal thirst for vengeance. Therefore, it succeeds in piercing right through the rules which are supposed to be there in order to prevent such influences, and strike its target with mathematical precision.

The Attic Orators were well aware of the potential impact of visual evidence on juries, as the excellent study by Peter O' Connell has amply demonstrated.[126] Emotional arguments and tactics intended to appeal to the emotions of the jury played a prominent role in both prosecution and defense speeches, as a number of thorough studies in recent years has discussed at length.[127] The orators understood the processes of persuasion, and the role of emotion and character, as much as their modern counterparts understand and employ them in their strategies. But while modern litigators need to take into account the rules of evidence and go through or around them, their ancient counterparts had somewhat different challenges to face.

While in a modern court-room, despite the rules of evidence, it is relatively easy to manipulate the emotions of a few people who have never sat in a jury before, and very likely will never sit again, for the ancient litigator the challenge was somewhat different and in some ways harder. He needed to appeal to the emotions of a large number of people, coming from all walks of life, with different ages and backgrounds. But more importantly, what made his task truly intimidating was the fact that many of the jurors had been sitting and listening to cases day after day for years, and even the least experienced among them could still have a couple of hundred trials under their belt. They had heard and seen it all and using old tricks to manipulate them could turn out to be in the best case unsuccessful, if not counterproductive, inciting anger instead of empathy and identification.

It is fair to say, that the rules of evidence in modern legal systems although well-intentioned have never been an effective screen against the manipulation of judges and juries by skilled litigators, while the absence of such rules did not automatically expose ancient juries to unfair manipulation, partly because the large number of jurors diluted strong emotional reactions by a few among them, and partly because the majority of jurors were very experienced, seasoned judges, and much less susceptible than modern jurors would be. Emotions always played a major part, as they do now, and so long as human beings and not machines sit in judgment emotions will always be a highly influential factor in deciding the outcome of trials. Aristotle in the *Rhetoric* acknowledges the actions and reactions of such factors and describes the inherent dangers and the efforts to minimize their impact:

> διαβολὴ γὰρ καὶ ἔλεος καὶ ὀργὴ καὶ τὰ τοιαῦτα πάθη τῆς ψυχῆς οὐ περὶ τοῦ πράγματός ἐστιν, ἀλλὰ πρὸς τὸν δικαστήν· . . . ἅπαντες γὰρ οἱ μὲν οἴονται δεῖν οὕτω τοὺς νόμους ἀγορεύειν, οἱ δὲ καὶ χρῶνται καὶ κωλύουσιν ἔξω τοῦ πράγματος λέγειν, καθάπερ καὶ ἐν Ἀρείῳ πάγῳ, ὀρθῶς τοῦτο νομίζοντες· οὐ γὰρ δεῖ τὸν δικαστὴν διαστρέφειν εἰς ὀργὴν προάγοντας ἢ φθόνον ἢ ἔλεον· ὅμοιον γὰρ κἂν εἴ τις ᾧ μέλλει χρῆσθαι κανόνι, τοῦτον ποιήσειε στρεβλόν. ἔτι δὲ φανερὸν ὅτι τοῦ μὲν ἀμφισβητοῦντος οὐδέν ἐστιν ἔξω τοῦ δεῖξαι τὸ πρᾶγμα ὅτι ἔστιν ἢ οὐκ ἔστιν, ἢ γέγονεν ἢ οὐ γέγονεν· εἰ δὲ μέγα ἢ μικρόν, ἢ δίκαιον ἢ ἄδικον, ὅσα μὴ ὁ νομοθέτης διώρικεν, αὐτὸν δή που τὸν δικαστὴν δεῖ γιγνώσκειν καὶ οὐ μανθάνειν παρὰ τῶν ἀμφισβητούντων.

> The arousing of prejudice, compassion, anger, and similar emotions has no connection with the matter in hand, but is directed only to the dicast . . . . For all men either think that all the laws ought so to prescribe, or in fact carry out the principle and forbid speaking outside the subject, as in the court of Areopagus, and in this they are right. For it is wrong to warp the dicast's feelings, to arouse him to anger, jealousy or compassion, which would be like making the rule crooked which one intended to use. Further, it is evident that the only business of the litigant is to prove that the fact in question is or is not so, that it has happened or not; whether it is important or unimportant, just or unjust, in all cases in which the legislator has not laid down a ruling, is a matter for the dicast himself to decide; it is not the business of the litigants to instruct him.[128]

Like Aristotle, Plato in the *Laws* suggests that the presiding magistrates need to instruct persons speaking outside the case to focus on the subject.[129] The speaker in Lysias 3 *To Simon* reiterates to the Areopagos that speaking outside the subject is not permitted in this court. However, this is nothing more than a rhetorical device, conveniently used in the epilogue. He has already made extensive use of character arguments, and much of what he has said is aimed at the emotions rather than the pure reason of the members of the Council, including some gruesome scenes of violence and blood, or some memorable scenes like the one where Theodotos, the young boy at the center of the quarrel was running through the streets naked.[130] It is clear that the stricter rules of evidence before the Areopagos Council proved as ineffective as the rules of evidence in modern courts can be. Euxitheos in the speech *Against Euboulides* tries the same rhetorical trick near his epilogue. He assures the jury that he has much more to say about the character and actions of his opponent, but he will refrain just in case they think that he is speaking outside the subject.[131]

The reactions of the orators to extra-judicial tactics tended to be more pragmatic: instead of trying to hide behind rules in order to block emotional or extra-judicial factors, they took more realistic approaches. If the opponent had spoken outside the subject, they could point it out and ask the jury not listen to him. If themselves planned to speak on a topic which might appear to be outside the subject, they could try to secure the approval of the dicasts by reassuring them that what they were saying was actually relevant. The speaker in a fragment of Isaios is promising the jury to willingly respond to accusations outside the subject.[132] Euxitheos in the speech *Against Euboulides* warns the jury that what he will say might appear to be ἔξω τοῦ πράγματος, and then he proceeds to accuse his opponent of *hierosylia*, namely stealing weapons dedicated to Athena. Undoubtedly this was intended to have a powerful effect on the jury, even though it has nothing to do with the *ephesis* on the citizenship of Euxitheos. Aeschines in *Against Timarchos* is pleading with the jurors not to accept a defense outside the subject, a curious plea considering that almost his entire speech has been outside the subject. Lykourgos in *Against Leokrates* makes a promise to the jury to speak only what is just, and not outside the subject. Then he proceeds to explain that not straying from the subject is good for the defendant because he can be judged without slander (διαβολή), and for the prosecutor too, because he can put forward his point without sycophantic intent.[133] Passages such as these indicate clear awareness of the impact of extra-judicial factors, and the need to diminish it though measured responses, reasoned explanations for the use of elements which might seem extra-judicial, and self-restraint. What complex rules try to accomplish in modern court rooms, Athenian litigants tried to accomplish with balanced approaches to extra-judicial factors, aware of the limitations as well as the dangerous power of such elements, for prosecutor and defendant alike.

Modern rules of evidence are designed to regulate character evidence, but obviously not with great success if one can judge by the number of people who are convicted every year not because there is strong evidence against them, but because of their criminal record, past misdeeds, and behavioral patterns, especially with regard to drug-related offences. So long as a defendant's criminal record, past conduct or pertinent character traits are admissible we should not be surprised if they play a disproportionate part in the outcome of the trial. In the United States Federal Rule of Evidence 404 permits the use of character evidence "for another purpose, such as proving motive, opportunity, intent, preparation, plan, knowledge, identity, absence of mistake, or lack of accident." Effectively this means that a prosecutor can base a large part of his strategy on the character of the accused, in order to provide a perhaps persuasive narrative on how the accused could and did commit the crime and why, on the basis of only circumstantial evidence which may seem to fit well with past conduct and character traits.

The Attic Orators often presented character evidence perfectly within these confines, as part of their narrative or proof, trying to explain why their opponent had acted the way he did. For example, when Euphiletos is explaining to the *ephetai* in the Delphinion court that Eratosthenes had seduced his wife, he creates the character of a serial seducer of women, whose actions with the wife of Euphiletos were just part of his customary pattern of behavior. The only concrete evidence presented is some highly suspect testimony from friends of Euphiletos. The entire case rests on the successful *ethopoeia* of the speech and has largely convinced modern audiences that Euphiletos acted within the law, even if coldly and unemotionally. In the speech *Against Timarchos* Aeschines created the portrait of a lecherous drunk dominated by his passions and won his case, while in the speech *Against Neaira* Apollodoros has successfully created a more nuanced portrait of the ageing *hetaira* as a woman who was not inherently bad, but many a time did bad things and broke the law motivated by necessity or the need to protect herself from the abusive men around her. As several scholars, and more recently Vasileios Adamidis, have convincingly argued this evidence was not perceived as extra-judicial by ancient juries, and with minor adjustments could easily pass the Federal US standard of evidence mentioned above.[134]

The alleged differences between the Athenian and modern legal systems with regard to the rules of evidence and relevance have been exaggerated. In one set of narratives the Athenian courts wildly allowed just about anything to be said, without any checks or restraint; in another set of narratives the Athenian courts believed that a broad range of proof was acceptable and relevant. None of these narratives is entirely accurate. The Athenians were aware of the dangers of extra-judicial factors and had the same desire to limit their impact and judge according to established laws, on the basis of rational arguments, within the broader frame of established social and civic values, such as empathy, compassion, justice, and democratic freedoms. However, trying to limit the impact of such factors with complicated legal rules would have privileged the professional lawyer, and this would be deemed undemocratic. The laws of the democracy were not meant to be the privilege of the few, but rather a common asset for the benefit of every citizen, publicized in buildings, temples, the Agora and the archive of the Metroon, accessible to everyone, but more importantly easily understood by everyone.

It was the right, privilege and duty of every citizen to know the laws himself, and to be able to appeal to them in order to punish offenders in court, or to seek redress from injustice done to him. Complicated procedural law would be unacceptable to this democratic sentiment. To balance the dangers of extra-judicial elements the Athenians took oaths to speak within the subject, at least in private lawsuits, and implemented some techniques within their speeches intended to alert juries.[135] The juries themselves perhaps were much less susceptible than commonly believed, considering the vast experience of Athenian discasts with trials, and the many long hours they spent hearing litigants trying to outwit each other, and the dicasts themselves.

1.11 Executive officers of the Athenian state

Legend has it that Kekrops, the first king of Athens, was born from the earth, and his bottom half was still shaped like a serpent.[136] He founded the Kekropid dynasty, which ruled Athens until the *archon*ship of Medon or Akastos (second half of the 11th century BC).[137] In the version of the *Athenaion Politeia* the king's rule was shared at some point with the new office of the polemarch, namely the "war-leader."[138] We are told that this change occurred because some kings had become soft in war affairs, and someone capable of taking care of the affairs of war became necessary. In this scheme of things, the king would be taking care of internal affairs and all things related to peace, while the polemarch would be taking care of war and external affairs. The concept of shared royal authority should not be strange to us as it had survived all the way to the classical period in the dual kingship of Sparta. Undoubtedly in the days when the kings had true power the dual kingship functioned as a guarantee that no one person could concentrate unlimited authority in his hands. According to legend Kodros was the last hereditary king of Athens. His son Medon was no longer going to be king, but rather a magistrate of the state serving for life and sharing power with the polemarch and a newly minted magistrate, the *archon*, who was going to be in charge of administrative duties which in a modern state we would mostly identify as the work of the civil service.

From the reign of Akastos, the heir of Medon, all three senior magistrates needed to take an oath to adhere to the agreements reached during the reign of Akastos, which seemingly outlined the privileges of the three magistrates in exchange for their service. Many years later, six additional magistrates were appointed, the *thesmothetai*, whose task was to write down and safeguard the rules and customs (*thesmoi*) of the city, for the purposes of dispute resolution.[139] By that stage the *archon*s had become annual, and their offices had been significantly diminished in both power and prestige. The nine *archon*s as we recognize them from the texts of the classical period were the main civil servants of the Athenian state. Although they no longer had the power to lead as they once did, their duties and responsibilities in the day-to-day running of the city's administration were so extensive and essential that we cannot even imagine the machinery of the state running without their dedicated, and yet unpaid, work.

In the classical period the office of each *archon* had retained many traditional features and duties from past times, including their role in religious rites and sacrifices. The *basileus* was in charge of the Mysteries and sacrifices around the city, the drinking completion of the Lenaia, and the introduction of religious offences to court. The polemarch was in charge of sacrifices for Artemis and Enyalios, the religious rites for Armodios and Aristogeiton and those killed at war, while the *archon* was in charge of most other festivals in the city.[140] Because of the extensive religious duties of the *archon*s, disabled persons were not permitted to occupy these offices on account of their physical condition.[141] Male prostitutes, parent abusers, draft-dodgers and tax-evaders were also disqualified, on account of their past conduct and unsuitable lifestyle.[142] Considering the importance of these offices for the religious life of the *polis* as well as the administration of the city and the justice system, the state was extra-careful in the scrutiny of the *archon*s and put them through a mandatory double scrutiny before the boule first, and then the courts. During their scrutiny in the Boule, after a few probing questions to verify their citizen status and suitability for office, people who might object to their appointment were invited to step up and speak. Then the Council voted. According to the *Athenaion Politeia*, in past times rejection by the Boule was final, but by the time of Aristotle it was advisory, unless the candidate chose to withdraw; the decision of the court was final.[143] Each of the three senior *archon*s appointed two assessors (*paredroi*) of his choosing. Their role was to assist the magistrates in their administrative duties, and they also needed to undergo a *dokimasia* before the court after their appointment and an *euthyna* in the end of their year in office. The office of the *paredros* was one of very few in the Athenian state made by appointment, and this is why it was coveted by politicians.[144]

The duties of the *basileus*, as described comprehensively in the *Athenaion Politeia*, include the oversight for the correct conduct of the Mysteries.[145] He was assisted in this task by four *epimeletai*, two selected by lot from the entire citizen body, one from the sacred genos of the Eumolpidai and one from the Kerykes. He also oversaw the procession and competition of the Lenaia with the assistance of the *epimeletai*. He oversaw all torch-races and sacrifices and settled disputes between gene and priests over jurisdiction. He accepted cases of *asebeia*, and other religious offenses, and also all homicide trials (which were perceived as religious offences). Upon acceptance of a homicide prosecution he issued proclamations to the alleged killer to refrain from the agora and other public places until the trial, so as not to contaminate other people if he truly was a killer. The proclamations were not just some antiquated religious formality: they had actual legal significance, and the person who violated them was subject to *apagoge*.[146] His wife also had religious duties to perform. Her title, *basilinna*, probably was a fossilized form from much earlier times, and her duties, with the assistance of several highly respectable women called the *gerairai* (reverent), quite possibly extended over the entire year. Apollodoros describes in considerable detail her role as the bride of the god Dionysos in the festival of Anthesteria, and informs us that because of these religious duties she needed to be a virgin at the time of her marriage with the *basileus*, and a citizen by birth.[147] In short, the *basileus* can be rightly considered to be the chief magistrate in charge of religious affairs in Athens, and in this capacity he oversaw many traditional rituals and introduced to court offences against the state religion and the gods. It seems that these responsibilities are a remnant from a time when the *basileus* was seen as the link between the gods and the city.

The office of the polemarch in the classical period is clearly a remnant of the role that this magistrate had in earlier times as the leader in war affairs and foreign relations. Even in the early years of the democracy we find the polemarch Kallimachos actually leading the ten generals at Marathon.[148] He doesn't seem to be the supreme commander of the army in the manner that the Spartan king would be, but rather the co-ordinator, the civilian authority overseeing the entire operation. Kallimachos was not commanding the generals on how they should conduct combat operations, however, his voice was important and his role in convincing each one of the generals to hand over his turn of command to Miltiades was critical for the success of the entire operation at Marathon. Such a role in the battlefield is not attested anywhere in later years, which probably means that as the democracy evolved the polemarch, as a senior civil servant, was limited to his religious, civil and judicial duties. Necessity undoubtedly contributed to this change because the polemarch could not be absent from Attica following the armies, when he had so many routine government duties to perform on a daily basis in the classical *polis*. Thus, eventually the responsibility of leading armies away from Attica, perhaps for months at a time he, fell squarely upon the shoulders of the ten generals.

The religious duties of the polemarch are those which belong to a war leader: he was in charge of sacrifices for Artemis and Enyalios, of funerary honors for the tyrannicides, Harmodios and Aristogeiton, and for those killed at war. The main core of his duties revolved around the legal affairs of metics, visitors and other foreigners in Athens. Anyone who wanted to bring a lawsuit against a non-Athenian, for whatever reason including citizenship and immigration violations, needed to initiate it through the polemarch. Strangely, the oldest and most significant among immigration violations, the *graphe xenias*, as well as the potential follow-up lawsuit the *graphe doroxenias* (if the prosecutor claimed that someone had been acquitted in a *graphe xenias* by offering bribes), needed to be brought before the *thesmothetai*. The reason behind this probably was that the accused had not yet been proven to be an alien, while in the rest of the immigration cases the law took it for granted that the accused was an alien. The polemarch was also the magistrate in charge of all property, inheritance or other disputes concerning the alien population of Attica, and it was his duty to look after orphans and *epikleroi* in metic families in the same manner that the *archon* was duty-bound to protect the interests of orphans and *epikleroi* in citizen families.[149]

The *archon* gave his name to the year, and upon entry to office ceremoniously proclaimed that no one would lose his property during this *archon*'s tenure. This guarantee of property rights undoubtedly was a relic from past times with little practical significance under the laws of the classical period, but nonetheless a ceremonial recognition of the inalienable right to own property in Attica.[150] A very important part of his office was the organization of the major public festivals and the appointment of *choregoi* for most of them.[151] If there were objections to the appointments on good legal grounds, such as that someone had very recently undertaken another liturgy, or proposals for property exchanges (*antidosis*), the *archon* he would introduce such cases to court, which would decide who should undertake the liturgy.[152] In family law he was the chief magistrate responsible for processing property disputes concerning orphans and heiresses (*epikleroi*), and for safeguarding the property and rights of these vulnerable groups against rapacious guardians and relatives. His authority in such matters remained extensive even in the 4th century. First, he had the authority to bypass the guardians, lease the property of an orphan under 14 years of age, and collect the income from the lease on behalf of the orphans. Second, he could punish offenders on his own authority (probably with a fine of up to 50 drachmas), or if he believed that they deserved higher punishment, he could always take them to court.[153] In short, the *archon* was the senior executive officer of the Athenian state managing some of the most important affairs in public life, like the numerous and sumptuous public festivals of the city. In private life he was expected to safeguard the well-being of those members in the family that could not protect themselves against abusers or thieves of their property by taking them to court.

The six Thesmothetai played a key role in the co-ordination of the Athenian justice system and carried much of the weight of processing and introducing to court public lawsuits. The *Athenaion Politeia* gives an extensive list of lawsuits introduced by the Thesmothetai. They included nearly all public lawsuits, *graphai, eisangeliai* and *probolai,* except for a few which traditionally came under the sphere of one of the other *archon*s, like for example the *graphe asebeias*, which as a religious offense came under the authority of the *basileus*, or immigration violations, like the *graphe aprostasiou*, which like other lawsuits concerning immigration came under the authority of the polemarch. The Thesmothetai also presided over all *dokimasiai*, but only over the *euthyna* of the generals. The *dokimasia* was probably a much faster process than the *euthyna*, since the presiding magistrate only needed to ask a few questions to verify that the person was eligible for office, and this is why they were able to process all of them fairly rapidly. However, the *euthyna* was a much more involved process even for minor magistrates, and this is why the Thesmothetai where in charge of the *euthyna* of the generals only, the most powerful people in Athenian administration and the ones most likely to face extensive scrutiny and challenges.

Among private lawsuits the *thesmothetai* only introduced one specific category to court, the monthly lawsuits (ἔμμηνοι δίκαι) for disputes related to commerce or mines. One would imagine that speed in the resolution of such cases was a very important factor. An economy like the one of classical Athens, which largely depended upon the enterprising spirit of its citizens, and the smooth trade with allied cities and outsiders, wanted to see any disputes rapidly resolved and business resuming, especially in the precious few summer months when calm seas and sunny weather made travel in the Mediterranean relatively easy and safe. It is not clear whether they introduced all monthly lawsuits or only the two mentioned in the *Athenaion Politeia*. The note in the *Athenaion Politeia* that the *thesmothetai* handled cases of *kakegoria* when a slave had spoken ill of a free person, has puzzled scholars, as there is no easy explanation why such cases needed special treatment compared to other *kakegoria* cases. It may have to do with some traditional reasoning which eludes us.

In the earlier days of the classical period the de facto leaders of the Athenian state, the people with most power, influence, and prestige came from the board of the ten generals. Theoretically the ten generals did not have any additional constitutional authority and powers except the leadership of the Athenian armies. However, unlike Sparta, where most of the power was yielded by the five ephors, the Democratic Athenian Constitution was set up to do the exact opposite, namely to avoid the concentration of substantial powers in the hands of any single magistrate. Not long after the establishment of the democracy some of the prominent generals of the Athenian state stepped in to fill the void of a constitutionally designated leadership role. This probably was the result of specific circumstances. These were years of great wars and empire building, and naturally the voices of the generals who carried the brunt of the city's efforts would be very influential in the assembly. Men like Miltiades, Themistokles, Kimon and Pericles were able to dominate the affairs of the assembly and prove themselves to be the effective leaders of Athens in their capacity as generals. War was not only an important part of foreign policy, which in its presence or absence defined the relationships of Athens with other states, but it pervaded important aspects of civilian life too, like public finances and how to best use the resources of the city, who should be appointed as ambassadors and be the face and voice of the city to outsiders, legal and commercial agreements with other Greek cities (σύμβολα), the policies defining the routes and supply of grain in a city with a very large population and not sufficient domestic resources, all these and many more were areas where the voice of the generals carried much weight. It is therefore not surprising to find some of them functioning as effective leaders of Athens for at least the first century of the democracy.

The death of Pericles in the turbulent years of the Peloponnesian war created a leadership vacuum which was filled by populist leaders. The era of the demagogues had arrived. During the war years the prominent generals who led the war effort undoubtedly carried much weight with the assembly, and a generalship was still the ultimate trophy on someone's path to power. All the prominent political figures of the time, who led the assembly and the city in the challenging years of the Peloponnesian war were generals. Kleon, an opponent of Pericles while the latter was alive, began as a political figure, but eventually he was elected general and for much of the 420s, at the height of his power, he led Athenian armies in various fields, most successfully in the effort to capture a Spartan force trapped on the island of Sphakteria, but unsuccessfully in his efforts to recover Amphi*polis*, where he was killed in 423. Two more prominent names from those years, Demosthenes and Nikias, played a major role in Athenian politics and the war effort. Both were prudent men who did not advise excesses, but the times they lived in belonged to bold, enterprising dreamers like Alcibiades. The unwillingness of the Athenian Democracy to make a decision whether the prudent politics of Nikias and Demosthenes, or the bold dreams of Alcibiades should define its course of action eventually led to the worst catastrophe that Athens and the Greek world as a whole was going to experience in that fateful summer of 415 in the great harbor of Syracuse, where the dreams of Athens at its finest hour were drowned with the loss of most of its fleet and thousands of men.

In the later years of the Peloponnesian war as the institutions of the democracy had begun to crumble under the weight of the losses and strains of the war a new brand of leader started to emerge, one whom we would more easily recognize as a political rather than a military leader, like Theramenes, the moderate oligarch, or Kritias, the hard-core member of the Thirty. Although many of them, like Theramenes, might serve for a period of time as generals, their legacy is primarily defined by their politics and statesmanship. In the course of the 4th century influential generals like Konon, Timotheos, Iphikrates, Chabrias or Chares, always had the ear of the assembly especially in matters related to war and foreign policy. However, increasingly the assembly came under the influence of professional politicians.

Although the word "professional" needs to be used with caution, as in theory these men were not paid for their services to the city, in reality politics became a desirable career which promised riches through indirect avenues, and this is why we see the power gradually shifting away from generals, like the famously honest Phokion, to career politicians like Euboulos. How clear the dividing line between politician and general had become by the second half of the 4th century becomes apparent by the closing lines of Aeschines' speech *On the False Embassy*, where he summons as advocates "Euboulos, one of the politicians and a prudent man, and Phokion, one of the generals most distinguished for his fairness".[154] Eventually in the course of the 4th century the word for "orator" (ῥήτωρ), would become a synonym for "politician" (πολιτικός), and it would be those *rhetores*, men like Demosthenes, Aeschines, Hypereides or Lykourgos, who would lead the assembly in the struggle with Philip during the final days of the independent Athenian *polis*. According to Plutarch, Phokion viewed this division of roles as a sign of decline in the public life of the city:

> He saw that the public men of his day had distributed among themselves as if by lot the work of the general and the orator. Some of them merely spoke before the people and introduced measures – men like Eubulus, Aristophon, Demosthenes, Lycurgus, and Hypereides; while such men as Diopeithes, Menestheus, Leosthenes, and Chabrias advanced themselves by holding the

> office of general and waging war. He therefore wished to resume and restore the public service rendered by Pericles, Aristides, and Solon, which was equally apportioned in both fields of action. For each of those men showed himself to be, in the words of Archilochus (Fr. 1 West),
>
> "As well a squire of Enyalius god of war,
> As versed in the lovely Muses' gifts."
>
> He also saw that the goddess Athena was a goddess of war as well as of statecraft, and was so addressed.[155]

Whether Phokion was right or wrong in his interpretation of the shift of power from the general to the politician as a sign of decline is open to interpretation. However, one thing is certain: as the Athenian Democracy evolved in the course of 200 years nothing ever remained static. Power kept shifting along with wealth and privilege, from the landed aristocracy and the old propertied families of the early 5th century to the merchants and traders in the years of Empire, and then to the bankers and entrepreneurs of the 4th century. Those incessant and not always easily detectable shifts were certainly influenced by the major political events and the frequent and often costly wars in which Athens was engaged throughout the course of the classical period. The Athenian Democracy along with its core political concepts, its laws, and procedures continued to change, sometimes driven by major shifts like the establishment of the Empire in the aftermath of the Persian wars, other times compelled by major trauma, as in the aftermath of the catastrophes in Sicily and Aigos Potamoi, and often by the need to respond to new challenges or improve visible flaws and weaknesses.

As time went by legal procedures evolved too, they became tighter, more consistent, more bureaucratic, more precise, more detailed. One wonders, if the Athenian Democracy had stayed in place, intact for a few more centuries, whether Athenian law would have come to resemble Roman law, as with time more and more detailed statutes would keep piling up creating eventually the need for legal scholarship, professional judges and lawyers, and ultimately for a comprehensive system of codified laws like the *Corpus Iuris Civilis*. While we can find some of the main ingredients in the Athenian legal system, like successive codifications of laws, professional legal advisors acting as "ghost" speech-writers, or sometimes openly as advocates, even if they were not supposed to be paid for the service, and dicasts who through their long-term day-to-day involvement with the legal system ended up with perhaps as much experience as a modern judge, there were some counter-forces in the Democratic constitution, some important safeguards, which not only discouraged, but altogether abhorred the establishment of a fully-fledged professional justice system.

Through the daily sortition of jurors, the stern prohibition of professional advocacy, the absence of professional judges and the free access to the legal system the Athenian Democracy sought to eliminate factors such as the undue influence of wealth, class, politics, ideology or power lobbies on its justice system. A simple, easily accessible and understood by the ordinary person body of laws ensured that the law was equal for all (*isonomia*), and that the ordinary person could protect his rights, his family and his property, as well as the property, safety, and healthy state of the *polis*, by directly accessing the system, and without the need for intermediaries. To the Athenians democracy meant direct access to public life, and their legal system accurately reflects this important principle.

Notes

1 Trsl. K.J. Maidment. All translations of Greek and Latin texts in this volume are mine, unless otherwise stated.

2 Trsl. H. Rackham.

3 Trsl. A.T. Murray. I have omitted the word "public" before "advocate" because it is not included in the original.

4 Athens was not unique among the Greek city-states in the stress it placed upon the importance of the separation of powers, checks and balances. Oligarchic Sparta was just as particular, and just as strict with these concepts. Its entire Constitution, which they attributed to the legendary lawgiver Lykourgos, was designed to prevent any particular individual or group from assuming too much power in their hands. First of all there were two kings, so that no single individual could be seen as the natural leader of Sparta, and they had little constitutional authority inside Sparta (but unchallengeable authority when leading the army outside Sparta). The Council of the Elders was a largely advisory body, while the five Ephors, who had most of the power of the state in their hands were only elected for one year, once in their lives. The brevity of the office in this case was the guarantee that the Ephors would not abuse their powers. Even men in Sparta's history who accomplished extraordinary things, like Pausanias the victorious leader of the Lacaedemonian armies in the battle of Plataia, or Lysander, the victorious general in the long war with Athens, where quickly reduced to size, when they appeared to be getting too big for their shoes. Pausanias met a cruel end in the hands of his fellow citizens, while Lysander, more honorably, was sent to fight in remote and unimportant parts of the Greek world, away from the big action arenas, until he was killed in battle.

5 Γελέοντες, Ὅπλητες, Ἀργαδεῖς, Αἰγικορεῖς named after the four sons of Ion, according to Herodotos (5.66); see also Plu. *Sol.* 23.5.

6 There is no firm evidence on the assembly of Solonean Athens, but "assembly" is the actual meaning of the word "Heliaia", not only in Athens but in many other Greek cities too (EM s.v. ἡλιαία, *IG* iv 479 ἁλιαίᾳ ἔδοξε [Nemea], 497 [Mycene], 557 [Argos], v 2 [Tegea]. One more indication that the word indicated the Assembly may be in the number of 6000 jurors routinely participating in the justice system of classical Athens. This was the number of citizens which the Pnyx could accommodate before its expansion in the 4th century, and was considered a "full house" in those cases when a quorum was required, such as νόμος ἐπ' ἀνδρί cases like ostracism or naturalization. Clearly 6000 was perceived to be the number of citizens who at any given time could enter the assembly area and vote, and the number seemingly stuck even when the Heliaia had been split into sections, the δικαστήρια, in the Classical period, in order to be able to deal with the large load of cases. See the discussion in MacDowell 1978: 29–34.

7 Pi. Fr. 169a Maehler: law, the king of all, mortal and immortal = Pl. *Grg.* 484 b. Using the myth of Herakles as justification of violence, Pindar's version gave precedence to natural law, where the one with greater prowess justly prevails. The purpose of the Pindaric version probably was to praise the natural physical prowess of exceptional athletes. Plato in *Gorgias* took it literally and employed it as a defense of the superiority of natural law, where the stronger have an inherent right to rule over the weaker.

8 Hdt. 7.104.
9 Hyp. *Epit*. 9 Jensen; Lys. 2.19; Th. 2.37; Hdt. 3.38; Pl. *Symp*. 196 c, *R*. 607 a, *Lg*. 691 a; Hip. *Aër*. 23 (where it is stated that the Europeans are braver than the Asiatics, precisely because they live by the law, and not under the commands of a king); D. 6.25 (where laws and freedom go hand in hand); Arist. Pol. 1313 a 4. For a more thorough discussion see Harris 2013, esp. pp. 3–18.
10 Lanni 2006 and 2016.
11 Cohen 1995; Osborne 1985: 40–58; Berent 2000: 2–34; Christ 1998; Ober 2009. Virginia Hunter (1994) also believed that the Athenians largely policed themselves, and Stephen Todd emphasized the political and extra-legal dimensions in Athenian trials, but neither of them could comfortably be grouped with the "anarchists" that perceive Athens to be a leaderless society, because both accept the application of the law by Athenian courts.
12 Maffi: *BMCR* 2017.10.22.
13 Harris 2013; Adamidis 2016.
14 The stated purpose of this important international project reads as following (data from their website): "The World Justice Project® (WJP) is an independent, multidisciplinary organization working to advance the rule of law worldwide. Effective rule of law reduces corruption, combats poverty and disease, and protects people from injustices large and small. It is the foundation for communities of equity, opportunity, and peace – underpinning development, accountable government, and respect for fundamental rights. Traditionally, the rule of law has been viewed as the domain of lawyers and judges. But everyday issues of safety, rights, justice, and governance affect us all; everyone is a stakeholder in the rule of law. Based on this, WJP's mutually-reinforcing lines of business employ a multi-disciplinary approach through original research and data, an active and global network, and practical, locally-led programs to advance the rule of law worldwide."
15 The unchecked abuses of police powers, the forced slave-labor and often brutal conditions in US prisons, the largely unchecked power of corporations, the influence of extra-legal factors such as race, ethnicity, religion, gender, sexual orientation, wealth and political connections in the law-making process as well as the verdicts, the routine employment of arcane and secretive processes, such as grand juries, especially when national security interests are invoked, all factors well documented in the literature, would raise strong doubts as to whether the US legal system meets the criteria for the rule of law (see for example, Bach 2010; Bandes 2000; Beckett and Sasson 2003; Colombatto 2007: 1163–80; Goldberg et al. 1999: 781–95; Hagan and Albonetti 1982: 329–55; Shiffrin 2000).
16 References to the sources cited in the opening section of each chapter are indicated by the letter S (for "source"), and the number of the source. Thus, here S 2 refers to source number 2 in section 1.1.
17 Some cases of rejection (ἀποδοκιμασία) are mentioned in D. 25.68; Lys. 13.10; see also the dokimasia speeches of Lysias (16, 25, 26, 31) and Weißenberger 1987; Wolpert and Kapparis 2011: 52–8. On the *dokimasia* see also Feyel 2009; Hashiba 1997: 1–10; Lepri Sorge 1987: 427–34; Adeleye 1983: 295–306; Todd 2010: 73–108, with response by Gagliardi. On the impact that the traumatic memories of the defeat in the Peloponnesian war and subsequent civil war had upon the Athenians see Wolpert 2001b.
18 Th. 2.65.3–4.
19 X. *HG* 1.7; Arist. *Ath. Pol*. 34; Hdt. 3.80; Ant. 6.43. Other examples include the generals Kephisodotos (D. 23.167) and Autokles (50.12), and all six Thesmothetai of the year 344/3 (D. 58.27–28).
20 Plu. *Per*. 32.5; Aesch. Prom. 324.
21 Athanasios Efstathiou (2007: 115) has sensibly suggested that the court hearing came at the end of the entire *euthyna* and not after the financial part. He thus understands

the *euthyna* as a three-tier process. He has argued that the financial scrutiny came first, followed by the more general part before the *euthynoi*, and the court hearing only came in the end of the process. This may well be right, but the main problem of his approach is that magistrates with open accusations of financial misconduct could still proceed to stage two before the *euthynoi* without clearance. This is not impossible but it could be a serious problem and capable of causing much confusion, if, let's say, charges of embezzlement were mixed together into a court case with a myriad of other accusations, drawing each other and allowing a dishonest magistrate to escape by creating diversions. Did the state care as much about the grievances of citizens against a former magistrate as it cared about recovering embezzled public money? And then, if both processes, the financial and the more general could be blended together in this manner, should we not expect a single body to handle both of them? With such objections in mind I find the process as described by MacDowell to be more logical, even if less smooth.

22 Arist. *Ath. Pol.* 54.2; Plu. *Per.* 32.5.

23 Demosthenes dramatically relates how Meidias maliciously succeeded in having an arbitrator disfranchised during his *euthyna*, because he found against him and then refused to accept a bride and change the verdict (D. 21.83–95). Even if Demosthenes has deliberately left out some misconduct which led to the disfranchisement of the arbitrator, still the case underlines the potential dangers for magistrates during their audit from angry adversaries who had the means and the occasion to seek vengeance. See also D. 25.37; Aesch. 1.1 (where Aeschines boasts that he never sought to put anyone into trouble during his *euthyna*), 2.178; Ant. 6.43; D. 19 and Aesch. 2 passim. We also have several titles of non-extant speeches delivered in cases arising from an *euthyna*: Din. Fr. 8: *Κατὰ Λυκούργου εὔθυναι*, Fr. 30: *Κατὰ Θεοδώρου εὐθυντικός*, Lyk. fr. 4. *Πρὸς Δημάδην ἀπολογία ὑπὲρ τῶν εὐθυνῶν*. See also Efstathiou 2007: 113–35 with previous literature; Oranges 2016: 81–97 (on the financial part of the euthyna); Piérat 1971: 526–73; Velissaropoulou-Karakosta 1993.

24 A total of 35, if we count the two kings, the Council of the Elders, and the five ephors.

25 Nine new members joined the Areopagos Council each year and remained in the Council for life. These were the retiring *archon*s of the previous year. If we assume an average tenure of 25 years as Areopagites, since some of the men could be in their thirties, while others in their sixties or seventies, this would yield a number of approximately 200 members. Both councils were called βουλή. (βουλὴ τῶν πεντακοσίων or βουλή ἡ ἀπὸ τοῦ κυάμου for the Council of the Five Hundred, or βουλὴ ἡ ἐν Ἀρείῳ Πάγῳ for the Areopagos Council).

26 For example, *IG* i3 82.24–28: hοι h]ιεροποιοὶ [νε]μόντον [α]ὐτοῖς ὀμὰ τὰ κρέα. τε̃ς δὲ πονπε̃ς hόπος [ἂν hος κάλλιστα] πενφθε̃ι hο[ι hι]εροπ[οι]οὶ ἐπιμελόσθον, καὶ ἂν τίς τι ἀκοσμε̃[ι, **κύριοι ὄντον αὐ] / τοὶ μὲν ζεμ[ιο̃ν μέχρι πε]ντέκοντα δραχμο̃ν καὶ ἐκγράφεν ἐ̣σ̣ [τὸς πράκτορας**· ἐὰ] / [ν] δέ τις ἄχς[ιος ε̃ι μέζον]ος ζε[μ]ίας, τὰς ἐπιβολὰς ποιό[ντ]ον [hοπόσας ἂν δοκε̃ι κ]/[α]ὶ ἐσαγό̣ν̣[τον ἐς τὸ δικας]τέ̣ρ̣ι[ο]ν τὸ το̃ ἄρχοντος. See also Aesch. 1.35 (forged document possibly using a classical source), D. 43.75; MacDowell 1978: 235–7. 50 drachmas is also a standard penalty in the Platonic *Laws* (e.g. 764 a 2; 844 e 3; 847 b 4; 953 b 4).

27 D. 21.85–96.

28 For example, Hunter 1994.

29 Hunter 1994.

30 Suda τ 771: Τοξόται· οἱ δημόσιοι ὑπηρέται, φύλακες τοῦ ἄστεος, τὸν ἀριθμὸν χίλιοι, οἵτινες πρότερον μὲν ᾤκουν τὴν ἀγορὰν μέσην σκηνοποιησάμενοι, ὕστερον δὲ μετέβησαν εἰς Ἄρειον Πάγον, ἐκαλοῦντο δὲ οὗτοι καὶ Σκύθαι καὶ Σπευσίνιοι; ἀπὸ Σπευσίνου τινὸς τῶν πάλαι πολιτευομένων συντάξαντος τὰ περὶ αὐτούς. "Archers: The public slaves, guards of the city, in number 1000, who formerly lived in the Agora, camping out in the middle, but later moved to the Areopagus. These were called 'Scythians' and 'Speusinioi,' from a certain Speusinos, one of the ancient

politicians, who organized their affairs" (Trsl. Elizabeth Baughman). On the dress and identity of the Scythian archers, and their representation in vase iconography see Gleba 2008: 3–13; Ivantchik 2006: 197–271; Braund 2006: 109–13. See also the brief informative article by Elizabeth Baughman published online (www.stoa.org/projects/*demos*/scythian_archers.pdf).

31 Instead of a cylindrical shape the Scythian quiver, as presented in vase iconography, was shaped like a lopsided funnel, to make access to the arrows easier.

32 However, we have several incidents of violence inflicted upon unruly citizens by the Scythian archers on the orders of Athenian magistrates trying to keep the peace (e.g. Ar. *Ec.* 143, *Eq.* 665, *Th.* 9.23, Lys. 445).

33 D. 24.63, 80, 105, 146; Din. 5.13; Hyp. Euxen. 22; Lys. 10.10.

34 D. 25.56; Ant. 5.14.

35 Lys. 10.16.

36 Arist. *Ath. Pol.* 52.1; D. 24.80, 162, 197; D. 35.47; Lys. 11.5; Isoc. 19.237.

37 D. 22.49; 24.197.

38 Arist. *Ath. Pol.* 50.

39 See the discussion in Kapparis 2017: 275–284.

40 Aesch. 1.2: Αἱ γὰρ ἴδιαι ἔχθραι πολλὰ πάνυ τῶν κοινῶν ἐπανορθοῦσι.

41 For example, Ar. *Plu.* 914; Lys. 10.32, 22,3; D. 21.225, 26.27; D. 42.15: χρὴ δ', ὦ ἄνδρες δικασταί, μὴ τοῖς ἰσχυροτέραν νομίζουσι τῶν νόμων τὴν αὑτῶν βδελυρίαν εἶναι, πλέον τούτοις τοῦ δικαίου νέμειν (εἰ δὲ μή, πολλοὺς ποιήσετε τοὺς καταγελῶντας τῶν ἐν τοῖς νόμοις δικαίων γεγραμμένων), ἀλλ' ἐκείνοις βοηθεῖν, οἵτινες ἂν τὴν τῶν νόμων φωνὴν ὑμετέραν εἶναι νομίζωσι "But, men of the jury, you should not grant more than their due to those who hold their own shamelessness to be stronger than the laws; if you do, you will multiply the numbers of those who mock at the just provisions of the laws. No; you should succor those who regard the voice of the laws as your voice" (Trsl. A.T. Murray); D. 43.84, 57.32; Lyc. 1.149.

42 Trsl. J.M. Dent.

43 Fr. 5 West; Trsl. J.M. Edmonds.

44 Fr. 4 West.

45 Part of Solon's solution was to divide Athenian society into four tiers according to their income (*pentakosiomedimnoi, triakosiomedimnoi, zeugitai, thetes*), rather than birth or privilege. This went a long way towards breaking down some barriers, because at least within each tier, concepts of equality of citizens started taking root. But the socioeconomic impact of the Solonean reforms is a much larger debate: see Ehrenberg 2010; Woodhouse 1938; Owens 2010; Blok and Lardinois 2006. For the laws of Solon see the recent collection with translation and brief commentary by Leão and Rhodes (2015), as well as the classic collection of Ruschenbush (1966).

46 Hdt. 3.80, which is the earliest reference to this principle, interestingly identifies it with the rule of the people (Πλῆθος δὲ ἄρχον πρῶτα μὲν οὔνομα πάντων κάλλιστον ἔχει, ἰσονομίην).

47 See the discussion in Chapter 8.5.

48 The only instances where a killing was considered justified was when someone had killed a person at war, by accident in an athletic contest or in bed with one of the women of his household. But even under these circumstances the killer was not immune from prosecution, as Lysias 1 *On the murder of Eratosthenes* proves. He still had to persuade a jury that the killing fell into one of these categories in order to be acquitted. If he failed, he was treated as a murderer. See the discussion in Chapter 8.5.

49 The exact date is unknown. The year 510/9, after the expulsion of the Peisistratids, would suggest itself, but there is no corroboration for this date.

50 With the exception of persons caught committing adultery, which could be abused by the *kyrios* of the woman, as a way to atone for his injured masculinity (see the discussion in Chapter 6.3).

51 See the discussion in Chapter 7.6.

52 See the detailed dissertation of Alexandrakis (1987) on this subject.

53 See the discussion in Schmitter 1975: 276–89.
54 Aesch. 1.13; see also Kapparis 2017: 156–8.
55 Further on the Athenian educational system see the valuable collection of essays edited by Yun Lee Too (2001), and also Poulakos and Depew 2004; Carcieri 2002 (with focus on the education of the citizens of the democracy); Morgan 1999: 46–61; Ober 2001: 175–207; Pritchard 2003: 293–349.
56 X. *Oec*. 7, with the corresponding commentary of Sarah Pomeroy provides an excellent resource for a better understanding of the schooling of a woman at home.
57 See Kapparis 2017: 125–38.
58 The Spartan state went to great lengths to make sure that a citizen was always under the watchful eye of the State. Boys were not brought up by their own families but grew up in barracks and stayed there until the age of thirty under constant surveillance. Even when they were allowed to go home and form families of their own, they still needed to be in the public eye for much of their day. Men, and uniquely in Sparta women too, trained daily in public areas naked, as was the Greek custom. The men had lunch and dinner in the messes, without exception, unless they were on campaign, or maybe short trips for a few days, and this included the two kings. In this manner the state could exercise absolute control on how much each person ate, what they ate, how fit they were for active duty in the army and what was in their minds, so that any subversive ideas could be caught and eliminated before they proliferated. In order to be able to exercise this level of control on a daily basis, the Spartan state required its citizens to live in five villages tightly clustered in an area of a few square kilometers, even though it had the largest territory of all Greek city-states. With this level of surveillance on a daily basis one would think that there were not many things in Sparta that stayed private, or secretive, and this undoubtedly was the objective of these arrangements. The primary sources for this are X. *Lac*. and Plu. *Lyc*.; See also MacDowell 1986 and Cartledge 2013.
59 See the discussion in Chapter 6.3.
60 See the discussion in Chapters 3.2 and 6.3.
61 See the discussion in Chapter 3.3.
62 See Lys. 10, with the substantial commentaries of Steven Todd and Michael Hillgruber on the speech.
63 See Rhodes 1972: 49–87; De Laix 1973.
64 *IG* i^3 104; see also Stroud 1968 and 1979.
65 See Ruschenbush 1966: 1–58; Leão and Rhodes 2016: 1–9.
66 *IC* 4.72; see also Willetts 1967; Gagarin 1982: 129–46.
67 Lyc. *Leoc*. 66; Harp. s.v.
68 Arist. *Ath*. 26.3; see also the discussion in Chapter 4.2.
69 See for example D. 24.139–40, where Demosthenes dramatically contrasts a tale about the way laws are introduced among the Locrians, with the volatility of Athenian laws. See also Isoc. 17.50; 18.40, D. 20.89, 93; 22.49.
70 On this topic see Wolpert 2002.
71 In modern courts someone's criminal record could be responsible for a much heavier sentence, compared to someone who committed the same offense without a criminal record, and often grave miscarriages of justice have been done because juries and judges were influenced by someone's previous record, appearance, perception or image. Character and previous conduct are important in modern court proceedings too, as are extra-legal factors like race. In 11 American states more than 50% of the prison population is black, while only 13% of the general population is black. (Data from www.sentencingproject.org/publications/color-of-justice-racial-and-ethnic-disparity-in-state-prisons/). In the words of two researchers on the issue "Intentional oppression is, sadly, not a prerequisite for injustice. Racial oppression has long thrived in this country, despite claimed good intentions and justified attitudes, policies, and practices." (Hanson and Hanson 2006: 480). Politics, religion, sexual orientation, education levels, mental illness, addiction to mood-altering substances, legal or illicit, cultural stereotypes, and economic factors can have a huge impact on verdicts, and

generate vastly uneven and inconsistent applications of the law. The modern legal literature on the subject is vast: for a first approach see Cole 1999; Hanson and Hanson 2006: 413–80 (a thorough discussion of narratives of racial injustice); Hagan and Albonetti 1982: 329–55; Coker 2002: 827–79.

72 Contrary to Matthew Christ (2012), I am convinced that altruism was an important quality in Athenian culture and life, public and private. Doing someone a good turn (εὐεργετεῖν or εὖ ποιεῖν) was the feature of a kind and good person long before Christianization, and certainly an Athenian cultural value glorified in the orators (e.g. Isoc. 12.1, Aesch. 19.330).

73 Adamidis 2016.

74 See Chapter 1.9.

75 See also Chapter 9.

76 Important studies on the *graphe paranomon* include Wolff 1970; Hansen 1974; Heftner 2012: 1–32; Sundahl 2000 (Diss.); Yunis 1988: 361–82.

77 On the statutory limit of one year and its rationale see Giannadaki 2014: 15–33.

78 MacDowell 1978: 50.

79 See the discussion in Schwartzberg 2012: 1049–62.

80 D. 18, 19, 20, 22, 23, 24; Aesch. 3. D. 25 and 26 are closely related, as they started from *paranomon* cases.

81 Although typically a *psephisma* refers to decrees of the Assembly, it can have a wider meaning. For example, on several occasions it refers to votes of the Boule (Is. 6.50; Lys. 13.20; D. 19.179).

82 Andoc. 1.43; Th. 3.49.4.

83 Ar. *Av.* 1038–1045 {ΨΗ.} Ψηφισματοπώλης εἰμὶ καὶ νόμους νέους

> ἥκω παρ' ὑμᾶς δεῦρο πωλήσων.
>
> . . .
>
> {ΠΙ.} Οὐκ ἀποίσεις τοὺς νόμους;
> Πικροὺς ἐγώ σοι τήμερον δείξω νόμους.

84 It appears that initially the proposal needed to be presented in several successive meetings of the Assembly to give people time to think about it carefully, and the *nomothetai* were chosen from the jurors of the year. But these arrangements did not last for long. Eventually the process was simplified to a single meeting of the Assembly, and the *nomothetai* were appointed as needed on each occasion from the entire citizen body.

85 On the *nomothetai* see the very informative introduction in Kremmydas 2012, and also Rhodes 1985: 55–60 and 2003: 124–9; Hansen 1985: 345–71.

86 On this procedure see the introduction of Kremmydas 2012, and also Calabi Limentani 1982: 357–68.

87 Hansen 1974.

88 It is broadly accepted that a prosecutor who initiated a public lawsuit but suspended proceedings was also liable to a fine of 1000 drachmas. However, it is proven beyond reasonable doubt by several passages that a *graphe* or other public lawsuit could be dropped without penalty before the trial, sometimes, but not invariably, in order to be entrusted to private arbitration (e.g. D. 45.4–5 suspending a *graphe hybreos*; D. 58.6 suspending a *phasis*; D. 58.36 a possible suspension of an *endeixis*; D. 59.45, and Aesch. 1.63, suspending an ἀφαίρεσις εἰς ἐλευθερίαν, D. 59.68 suspending a γραφὴ ἀδίκως ὡς μοιχὸν εἰρχθῆναι). The same applied to private lawsuits (e.g. Isoc. 2.10; D. 33.14). The phrase in the law ἐάν τις μὴ ἐπεξέλθῃ (S 5, and Lys. Fr. 19 Carey) must mean, "if the prosecutor does not turn up on the day of the trial"; this is the meaning of ἐπεξιέναι in the second part of the phrase ἢ ἐπεξιὼν μὴ μεταλάβῃ τὸ πέμπτον μέρος τῶν ψήφων. It was advantageous for the state to allow people to withdraw before the trial, as it cleared up the busy schedule of the courts. However, once the trial had been set up and

everyone else was present, except the prosecutor who failed to turn up, he was subject to a fine of $ 1000, and rightly so, since he had wasted an entire day of the court's time.

89 See the discussion in Chapter 8.4.

90 Andoc. 1; see also the introduction of MacDowell's commentary on the speech, and Hansen 1976.

91 For example, Isoc. 2.6–8, 4.2; D 38, 58.5–6; Arist. *Ath. Pol.* 51, and also MacDowell 1990: 187–198; Phillips 2013: 31; Bogaert 1962: 157–68.

92 For a detailed account of the process see Lys. 17.5–6, D. 53.1–3 and Wolpert and Kapparis 2011: 161–71.

93 Apollodoros in the speech *Against Nikostratos* is doing the opposite: he is claiming that some slaves who belonged to the confiscated property of Arethousios had been illegally appropriated by the brothers of Arethousios, and he is trying to recover them for the state.

94 Lys. 17.5–6, and D. 53.2 (τρίτα μέρη is an almost certain emendation of Lewis for τρία μέρη of the manuscripts at this point).

95 Aesch. 3.197; Trsl. D.M. MacDowell. See MacDowell 2000: 536–538; Worthington (2003: 364–371) has argued that some trials lasted for more than a day, but this is probably incorrect.

96 See, for example, the command to stop the water-clock for the recitation of documents in D. 20.96, 23.23, 45.8.

97 Rhodes 1981: 726–27.

98 For example, D. 53.18, 59.6–8; Lys. 1.29 (metaphorically; Euphiletos presents the pleas of Eratosthenes for his life as a request to come to an agreement, which the former found unacceptable and considered death as the proper punishment).

99 See Chapters 7.2 and 7.6.

100 See the discussion in Chapter 7.2.

101 For further discussion on arbitration as a democratic method of dispute resolution see Chapter 7.4.

102 See Chapter 8.5.

103 E. *Herakl.* 180–1.

104 D. 47.72: κελεύει γὰρ ὁ νόμος, ὦ ἄνδρες δικασταί, τοὺς προσήκοντας ἐπεξιέναι μέχρι ἀνεψιαδῶν (καὶ ἐν τῷ ὅρκῳ διορίζεται ὅ τι προσήκων ἐστίν), κἂν οἰκέτης ᾖ, τούτων τὰς ἐπισκήψεις εἶναι. The law permits, men of the jury, relatives up to second cousins to prosecute (and in the oath the prosecutor needs to state his relationship with the victim), and also the master of a slave, and these are the ones who need to initiate the prosecution. See also Is. 11.12; D. 43.62.

105 See the discussion on homicide cases in Chapter 8.5.

106 See the discussion in Chapter 7.4.

107 Adamidis 2016.

108 Isoc. 3.21.

109 The procedure of *diamartyria* is described in Lys. 13–14; see also Schönbauer 1964: 203–231; Gernet 1955: 83–102; MacDowell 1978: 212–14, and 216–19.

110 Isoc. 18.2; Harp. s.v. διαμαρτυρία.

111 The case against Pankleon (Lys. 23) was one of the first ever *paragraphe* cases to come to court. Pankleon maintained that his opponent had improperly sued him before the polemarch, because he was a Plataian, and therefore an Athenian citizen.

112 Isoc. 18.3.

113 See also Wolff 1966; Isager and Hansen 1975; MacDowell 1978: 214–19.

114 See the discussion in Chapter 9.5.

115 For example, Aesch. 1.92 (τῷ ἀκριβεστάτῳ συνεδρίῳ τῶν ἐν τῇ πόλει); D. 20.157; 23.65; And. 1.79; Lys. 6.14.

116 For example, D. 59.15, where an advocate is called to continue with the case, partly because of his experience with the laws; Ant. 5.14; D. 24.66, where the inexperience

(ἀπειρία) of a private citizen (ἰδιώτης) is contrasted with the legal expertise of professional politicians; 58.25; 59.72.

117 A very good example would be the narrative of Theomnestos (D. 59.1–15), where he explains at length his close relationship to his *synegoros*.

118 On the issue of the liturgies see the insightful and thorough response of Adamidis (2017: 85–96) to previous discussions.

119 Todd 1990: 19.

120 See for example Bach 2010; Beckett and Sasson 2003; Colombatto 2007: 1163–80; Godoy 2006 (with reference to Latin America); Goldberg et al. 1999: 781–95; Hagan and Albonetti 1982: 329–55; Cole 1999; Hanson and Hanson 2006: 413–80; Hagan 1982: 329–55; Coker 2002: 827–79.

121 See the difficulties pointed out by Todd 1990: 19–40.

122 Lanni 2006, 2016, and 2005: 112–28. Harris responds convincingly to the issue of precedent (2013: 246–273), but we always need to bear in mind that the Athenian legal system was not a Common Law system. Precedent might have an advisory role, but it was never binding. In this particular aspect the Athenian justice system resembles more Civil Law systems, where a set of laws introduced by the legislative branch of government is implemented by the courts. For Athenian juries the question was whether this particular defendant had broken one of the codified laws, typically ascribed to Solon, which the prosecutor alleged that he had broken.

123 Harris 2013: 246–73.

124 The recent trial of Larry Nassar, the former US gymnastics team doctor, who pleaded guilty to extensive sexual abuse of young athletes in his care is a good example of this. For weeks victim after victim took the stand with tales of horrific abuse, compiling sufficient emotional force to secure a sentence of 175 years. See also Goldberg 1999: 781–795; Erez and Rogers 1999: 216–239; Devine et al. 2001: 622–727.

125 See for example Bright and Goodman-Delahunty 2006: 183–202.

126 O' Connell 2017.

127 See Sanders and Johncock 2016; Griffith-Williams 2016: 41–55; Harris 2017: 223–42; Rubinstein 2016; 55–72.

128 Arist. *Rh.* 1354 a 16–31. Trsl. J. H. Freese.

129 Pl. *Lg.* 949 b.

130 Lys. 3.46.

131 D. 57.66.

132 Is. Fr. 3.1.2. Roussel.

133 Lyk. 1.11.

134 Adamidis 2017; De Brauw 2002: 161–76; Kremmydas 2013: 51–89 (on deception and characterization).

135 Whether the rule was different in public lawsuits, as Arist. *Ath. Pol.* 67 may imply, is difficult to tell, and our large public forensic speeches, like the speech *On the Crown*, or the two speeches *On the False Embassy*, are not a safe guide, as most of them seem to be published pamphlets of the original speeches, and extra-judicial elements, like poetry citations, could have been added at this stage. See the discussion in Rhodes 1981: 718–19.

136 On the myth of autochthony and its political and cultural implications see Chapter 2.2.

137 On the early kings of Athens see Flament 2011: 285–308. Robert Drews (1983) has argued that much of the material on the early kings is mythical or invented by classical authors.

138 Arist. *Ath. Pol.* 3; see also Rhodes 1981: 100 ff. On other versions of early Athens legends see Parker 1987: 187–214.

139 Gagarin (1981: 71–77) has argued that in early times the *thesmothetai* should be credited with making a significant contribution to the development of law in Athens.

140 See Lys. 6.4; D. 59.74; Aesch. 1.19; Arist. *Ath. Pol.* 5658.

141 See the discussion in Chapter 8.2.

142 See the discussion above.
143 Arist. *Ath. Pol.* 55.
144 Arist. *Ath. Pol.* 56.1, Kapparis 1998: 383–93.
145 Arist. *Ath. Pol.* 57.
146 See Chapter 8.5.
147 See D. 59.74–78; Kapparis 1998: 329–44 with previous scholarship.
148 Hdt. 6.109–110.
149 The main source is Arist. *Ath.Pol.* 58.
150 Arist. Ath. Pol. 56.1, and Rhodes 1981: 622.
151 In the time of the *choregoi* for the Lenaia were no longer appointed by the *archon*, as in the past, but were provided by the tribes. The same applied to the choruses for the *Thargelia* (Arist. *Ath.Pol.* 56.3).
152 See also the discussion in Chapters 8.3 and 9.5.
153 See the discussion in Chapter 9.2.
154 Aesch. 2.184: Παρακαλῶ δὲ Εὔβουλον μὲν ἐκ τῶν πολιτικῶν καὶ σωφρόνων ἀνδρῶν συνήγορον, Φοκίωνα δ᾽ ἐκ τῶν στρατηγῶν, ἅμα δὲ καὶ δικαιοσύνῃ διενηνοχότα πάντων.
155 Trsl. Bernadotte Perrin.

2 Citizens, metics and slaves in Athenian law and life

2.1 Sources

1 What is citizenship in the Greek *polis*?

ὥστε τίνα χρὴ καλεῖν πολίτην καὶ τίς ὁ πολίτης ἐστὶ σκεπτέον. καὶ γὰρ ὁ πολίτης ἀμφισβητεῖται πολλάκις· οὐ γὰρ τὸν αὐτὸν ὁμολογοῦσι πάντες εἶναι πολίτην· ἔστι γάρ τις ὃς ἐν δημοκρατίᾳ πολίτης ὢν ἐν ὀλιγαρχίᾳ πολλάκις οὐκ ἔστι πολίτης. τοὺς μὲν οὖν ἄλλως πως τυγχάνοντας ταύτης τῆς προσηγορίας, οἷον τοὺς ποιητοὺς πολίτας, ἀφετέον· ὁ δὲ πολίτης οὐ τῷ οἰκεῖν που πολίτης ἐστίν (καὶ γὰρ μέτοικοι καὶ δοῦλοι κοινωνοῦσι τῆς οἰκήσεως), οὐδ' οἱ τῶν δικαίων μετέχοντες οὕτως ὥστε καὶ δίκην ὑπέχειν καὶ δικάζεσθαι (τοῦτο γὰρ ὑπάρχει καὶ τοῖς ἀπὸ συμβόλων κοινωνοῦσιν [καὶ γὰρ ταῦτα τούτοις ὑπάρχει]· πολλαχοῦ μὲν οὖν οὐδὲ τούτων τελέως οἱ μέτοικοι μετέχουσιν, ἀλλὰ νέμειν ἀνάγκη προστάτην, ὥστε ἀτελῶς πως μετέχουσι τῆς τοιαύτης κοινωνίας), ἀλλὰ καθάπερ καὶ παῖδας τοὺς μήπω δι' ἡλικίαν ἐγγεγραμμένους καὶ τοὺς γέροντας τοὺς ἀφειμένους φατέον εἶναι μέν πως πολίτας, οὐχ ἁπλῶς δὲ λίαν ἀλλὰ προστιθέντας τοὺς μὲν ἀτελεῖς τοὺς δὲ παρηκμακότας ἤ τι τοιοῦτον ἕτερον (οὐδὲν γὰρ διαφέρει· δῆλον γὰρ τὸ λεγόμενον). ζητοῦμεν γὰρ τὸν ἁπλῶς πολίτην καὶ μηδὲν ἔχοντα τοιοῦτον ἔγκλημα διορθώσεως δεόμενον, ἐπεὶ καὶ περὶ τῶν ἀτίμων καὶ φυγάδων ἔστι τὰ τοιαῦτα καὶ διαπορεῖν καὶ λύειν. πολίτης δ' ἁπλῶς οὐδενὶ τῶν ἄλλων ὁρίζεται μᾶλλον ἢ τῷ μετέχειν κρίσεως καὶ ἀρχῆς.

(Arist. *Pol.* 1275 a 1–23)

So that we have to consider who is entitled to the name of citizen, and what the essential nature of a citizen is. For there is often a difference of opinion as to this: people do not all agree that the same person is a citizen; often somebody who would be a citizen in a democracy is not a citizen under an oligarchy. We need not here consider those who acquire the title of citizen in some exceptional manner, for example those who are citizens by adoption; and citizenship is not constituted by domicile in a certain place (for resident aliens and slaves share the domicile of citizens, nor are those citizens who participate in a common system of justice, conferring the right to defend an action and to bring one in the law-courts (for this right belongs also to the parties under a commercial treaty, as they too can sue and be sued at law – or rather, in many places even the right of legal action is not shared completely by resident aliens, but they are obliged to produce a patron, so that they only share in a common legal procedure to an incomplete degree, but these are only citizens in the manner in which children who are as yet too young to have been enrolled in the list and old men who have been discharged must be pronounced to be citizens in a sense, yet not quite absolutely, but with the added qualification of "under age" in the case of the former and "superannuated" or some other similar term (it makes no difference, the meaning being clear) in that of the latter. For we seek to define a citizen in the absolute sense, and one possessing no disqualification of this nature that requires a correcting term, since similar difficulties may also be raised, and solved, about citizens who have been disfranchised or exiled. A citizen pure and simple is defined by nothing else so much as by the right to participate in judicial functions and in office.[1]

2 Introduction to the deme and full citizen status

Ἔχει δ' <ἡ νῦν κατάστασις τῆς πολιτείας> τόνδε τὸν τρόπον. μετέχουσιν μὲν τῆς πολιτείας οἱ ἐξ ἀμφοτέρων γεγονότες ἀστῶν, ἐγγράφονται δ' εἰς τοὺς δημότας ὀκτωκαίδεκα ἔτη γεγονότες. ὅταν δ' ἐγγράφωνται, διαψηφίζονται περὶ αὐτῶν ὀμόσαντες οἱ δημόται, πρῶτον μὲν εἰ δοκοῦσι γεγονέναι τὴν ἡλικίαν τὴν ἐκ τοῦ νόμου, κἂν μὴ δόξωσι, ἀπέρχονται πάλιν εἰς παῖδας, δεύτερον δ' εἰ ἐλεύθερός ἐστι καὶ γέγονε κατὰ τοὺς νόμους. ἔπειτ' ἂν μὲν ἀποψηφίσωνται μὴ εἶναι ἐλεύθερον, ὁ μὲν ἐφίησιν εἰς τὸ δικαστήριον, οἱ δὲ δημόται κατηγόρους αἱροῦνται πέντε [ἄν]δρας ἐξ αὑτῶν, κἂν μὲν μὴ δόξῃ δικαίως ἐγγράφεσθαι, πωλεῖ τοῦτον ἡ πόλις· ἐὰν δὲ νικήσῃ, τοῖς [δ]ημόταις ἐπάναγκες ἐγγράφειν. μετὰ δὲ ταῦτα δ[οκ]ιμάζει τοὺς ἐγγραφέντας ἡ βουλή, κἄν τις δόξ[ῃ] νεώτερος ὀκτωκαίδεκ' ἐτῶν εἶναι, ζημιοῖ τ[ο]ὺς δημότας τοὺς ἐγγράψαντας.

(Arist. *Ath. Pol.* 42.1)

The present state of the constitution is as follows. The franchise is open to all who are of citizen birth by both parents. They are enrolled among the demesmen at the age of eighteen. On the occasion of their enrollment the demesmen give their votes on oath, first whether the candidates appear to be of the age prescribed by the law (if not, they are dismissed back into the ranks of the boys), and secondly whether the candidate is free born and of such parentage as the laws require. Then if they decide that he is not a free man, he appeals to the law-courts, and the demesmen appoint five of their own number to act as accusers; if the court decides that he has no right to be enrolled, he is sold by the state as a slave, but if he wins his case he has a right to be enrolled among the demesmen without further question. After this the Council examines those who have been enrolled, and if it comes to the conclusion that any of them is less than eighteen years of age, it fines the demesmen who enrolled him.[2]

3 Athenian military service for citizen men (*epheboi*)

ἐπὰν δὲ δοκιμασθῶσιν οἱ ἔφηβοι, συλλεγέντες οἱ πατέρες αὐτῶν [κ] ατὰ φυλάς, ὀμόσαντες αἱροῦνται τρεῖς ἐκ τῶν φυλετῶν τῶν ὑπὲρ τετταράκοντα ἔτη γεγονότων, οὓς ἂν ἡγῶνται βελτίστους εἶναι καὶ ἐπιτηδειοτάτους ἐπιμελεῖσθαι τῶν ἐφήβων, ἐκ δὲ τούτων ὁ δῆμος ἕνα τῆς φυλῆς ἑκάστης χειροτονεῖ σωφρονιστήν, καὶ κοσμητὴν ἐκ τῶν ἄλλων Ἀθηναίων ἐπὶ πάντας. συλλαβόντες δ’ οὗτοι τοὺς ἐφήβους, πρῶτον μὲν τὰ ἱερὰ περιῆλθον, εἶτ’ εἰς Πειραιέα πορεύονται, καὶ φρουροῦσιν οἱ μὲν τὴν Μουνιχίαν, οἱ δὲ τὴν Ἀκτήν. χειροτ[ο]νεῖ δὲ καὶ παιδοτρίβας αὐτοῖς δύο καὶ διδασκάλους, οἵτινες ὁπλομαχεῖν καὶ τοξεύειν καὶ ἀκοντίζειν καὶ καταπάλτην ἀφιέναι διδάσκουσιν. δίδωσι δὲ καὶ εἰς τροφ[ὴν] τοῖς μὲν σωφρονισταῖς δραχμὴν α′ ἑκάστῳ, τοῖς δ’ ἐφήβοις τέτταρας ὀβολοὺς ἑκάστῳ· τὰ δὲ τῶν φυλετῶν τῶν αὑτοῦ λαμβάνων ὁ σωφρονιστὴς ἕκαστος ἀγοράζει τὰ ἐπιτήδεια πᾶσιν εἰς τὸ κοινόν (συσσιτοῦσι γὰρ κατὰ φυλάς), καὶ τῶν ἄλλων ἐπιμελεῖται πάντων. καὶ τὸν μὲν πρῶτον ἐνιαυτὸν οὕτως διάγουσι· τὸν δ’ ὕστερον ἐκκλησίας ἐν τῷ θεάτρῳ γενομένης, ἀποδειξάμενοι τῷ δήμῳ τὰ περὶ τὰς τάξεις, καὶ λαβόντες ἀσπίδα καὶ δόρυ παρὰ τῆς πόλεως, περιπολοῦσι τὴν χώραν καὶ διατρίβουσιν ἐν τοῖς φυλακτηρίοις. φρουροῦσι δὲ τὰ δύο ἔτη χλαμύδας ἔχοντες, καὶ ἀτελεῖς εἰσι πάντων· καὶ δίκην οὔτε διδόασιν οὔτε λαμβάνουσιν, ἵνα μὴ πρό[φ]ασις ᾖ τ[ο]ῦ ἀπιέναι, πλὴν περὶ κλήρου καὶ ἐπικλή[ρου], κἄν τ[ι]νι κατὰ τὸ γένος ἱερωσύνη γένηται. διε[ξ]ελθόντων δὲ τῶν δυεῖν ἐτῶν, ἤδη μετὰ τῶν ἄλλων εἰσίν.

(Arist. *Ath. Pol.* 42. 2–5)

When the youths (Epheboi) have passed this examination, their fathers meet by their tribes, and appoint on oath three of their fellow tribesmen, over forty years of age, who, in their opinion, are the best and most suitable persons to have charge of the youths; and of these the Assembly elects one from each tribe as guardian, together with a director, chosen from the general body of Athenians, to control the while. Under the charge of these persons the youths first of all make the circuit of the temples; then they proceed to Piraeus, and some of them garrison Munichia and some the south shore. The Assembly also elects two trainers, with subordinate instructors, who teach them to fight in heavy armour, to use the bow and javelin, and to discharge a catapult. The guardians receive from the state a drachma apiece for their keep, and the youths four obols apiece. Each guardian receives the allowance for all the members of his tribe and buys the necessary provisions for the common stock (they mess together by tribes), and generally superintends everything. In this way they spend the first year. The next year, after giving a public display of their military evolutions, on the occasion when the Assembly meets in the theatre, they receive a shield and spear from the state; after which they patrol the country and spend their time in the forts. For these two years they are on garrison duty, and wear the military cloak, and during this time they are exempt from all taxes. They also can neither bring an action at law, nor have one brought against them, in order that they may have no excuse for requiring leave of absence; though exception is made in cases of actions concerning inheritances and wards of state, or of any sacrificial ceremony connected with the family. When the two years have elapsed they thereupon take their position among the other citizens. Such is the manner of the enrollment of the citizens and the training of the youths.[3]

4 The laws and procedures of naturalization in Athens

ὁ γὰρ δῆμος ὁ Ἀθηναίω ν κυριώτατος ὢν τῶν ἐν τῇ 88.5 πόλει ἁπάντων, καὶ ἐξὸν αὐτῷ ποιεῖν ὅ τι ἂν βούληται, οὕτω καλὸν καὶ σεμνὸν ἡγήσατ' εἶναι δῶρον τὸ Ἀθηναῖον γενέσθαι, ὥστε νόμους ἔθετο αὑτῷ καθ' οὓς ποιεῖσθαι δεῖ, ἐάν τινα βούλωνται, πολίτην, οἳ νῦν προπεπηλακισμένοι εἰσὶν ὑπὸ Στεφάνου τουτουὶ καὶ τῶν οὕτω γεγαμηκότων. ὅμως δ' ἀκούοντες αὐτῶν βέλτιον εἴσεσθε, καὶ τὰ κάλλιστα καὶ τὰ σεμνότατα δῶρα τοῖς εὐεργετοῦσι τὴν πόλιν διδόμενα γνώσεσθε ὡς λελυμασμένοι εἰσίν. πρῶτον μὲν γὰρ νόμος ἐστὶ τῷ δήμῳ κείμενος μὴ ἐξεῖναι ποιήσασθαι Ἀθηναῖον, ὃν ἂν μὴ δι' ἀνδραγαθίαν εἰς τὸν δῆμον τὸν Ἀθηναίων ἄξιον ᾖ γενέσθαι πολίτην. ἔπειτ' ἐπειδὰν πεισθῇ ὁ δῆμος καὶ δῷ τὴν δωρεάν, οὐκ ἐᾷ κυρίαν γενέσθαι τὴν ποίησιν, ἐὰν μὴ τῇ ψήφῳ εἰς τὴν ἐπιοῦσαν ἐκκλησίαν ὑπερεξακισχίλιοι Ἀθηναίων ψηφίσωνται κρύβδην ψηφιζόμενοι. τοὺς δὲ πρυτάνεις κελεύει τιθέναι τοὺς καδίσκους ὁ νόμος καὶ τὴν ψῆφον διδόναι προσιόντι τῷ δήμῳ πρὶν τοὺς ξένους εἰσιέναι, καὶ τὰ γέρρα ἀναιρεῖν, ἵνα κύριος ὢν αὐτὸς αὑτοῦ ἕκαστος σκοπῆται πρὸς αὑτὸν ὅντινα μέλλει πολίτην ποιήσεσθαι, εἰ ἄξιός ἐστι τῆς δωρεᾶς ὁ μέλλων λήψεσθαι. ἔπειτα μετὰ ταῦτα παρανόμων γραφὴν ἐποίησε κατ' αὐτοῦ τῷ βουλομένῳ Ἀθηναίων, καὶ ἔστιν εἰσελθόντα εἰς τὸ δικαστήριον ἐξελέγξαι ὡς οὐκ ἄξιός ἐστι τῆς δωρεᾶς, ἀλλὰ παρὰ τοὺς νόμους Ἀθηναῖος γέγονεν.

(D. 59.8889 –)

Although the Athenian people is the supreme authority over everything in the city and can do whatever it wishes, it considered becoming an Athenian citizen to be such a fine and solemn gift that it restricted itself with laws governing how they must make someone a citizen, if they wish to. These laws have now been besmirched by Stephanos here, and by those who have conducted marriages in this manner. However, after hearing these laws you will acquire a better knowledge and understand how these people have vilified the finest and most solemn gifts reserved for the benefactors of the city. First there is a law imposed on the people which lays down that it is not possible to make someone an Athenian unless he deserves to become a citizen because of good service to the Athenian people. Next, once the people is convinced and grants the award, it does not allow the act to become valid unless it is approved in the next assembly by secret ballot of at least six thousand Athenians. The law orders the presidents to place the urns and allow the vote as the people are coming in, before the foreigners enter and the fences are removed, so that each person may consider in his own mind who the man is that is going to be made a citizen and whether he is worthy of the award. After this it authorizes any Athenian who wishes to bring a prosecution for an illegal proposal, and there is the possibility of coming to court and proving that the man does not deserve the award but has become an Athenian against the laws.

5 The religious and judicial duties of the *polemarch*

δίκαι δὲ λαγχάνονται πρὸς αὐτὸν ἴδιαι μὲν αἵ τε τοῖς μετοίκοις καὶ τοῖς ἰσοτελέσι καὶ τοῖς προξένοις γιγνόμεναι. . . . αὐτὸς δ' εἰσάγει δίκας τάς τε τοῦ ἀπο[ς]τασίου καὶ ἀπροστας[ί]ου καὶ κλήρων καὶ ἐπικλήρων τοῖς μετοίκοις, καὶ τἆλλ' ὅσα τοῖς πολίταις ὁ ἄρχων, ταῦτα τοῖς μετοίκοις ὁ πολέμαρχος.

(Arist. *Ath. Pol.* 57)

Only private actions come before him, namely those in which resident aliens, both ordinary and privileged, and agents of foreign states are concerned. . . . The Polemarch, however, brings up in person cases in which an alien is charged with deserting his patron or neglecting to provide himself with one, and also of inheritances and wards of state where aliens are concerned; and in fact, generally, whatever the Archon does for citizens, the Polemarch does for aliens.

6 The law allowing enslavement as a penalty for someone who failed to pay back the ransom

ὅτι καὶ οἱ νόμοι κελεύουσιν τοῦ λυσαμένου ἐκ τῶν πολεμίων εἶναι τὸν λυθέντα, ἐὰν μὴ ἀποδιδῷ τὰ λύτρα.

(D. 53.12)

The laws order that the person who does not pay back the money to the one who ransomed him from the enemy, he is to become the slave of the ransomer.

7 Persons convicted in a *graphe xenias* but claiming that they were wrongly convicted because of false testimony must await for the *pseudomartyrion* trial imprisoned

οὐδὲ γὰρ οἱ τῆς ξενίας ἁλισκόμενοι ἀγανακτοῦσιν ἐν τῷ οἰκήματι τούτῳ ὄντες, ἕως ἂν τῶν ψευδομαρτυριῶν ἀγωνίσωνται, ἀλλὰ μένουσιν καὶ οὐκ οἴονται δεῖν ἐγγυητὰς καταστήσαντες περιιέναι. ἔδοξε γὰρ τῇ πόλει ἀπιστεῖν αὐτοῖς, καὶ οὐκ ᾤετο δεῖν διακρουσθῆναι τῆς τιμωρίας δι᾽ ἐγγυητῶν καταστάσεως, ἀλλ᾽ ἐνταῦθα μένειν αὐτοὺς οὗ καὶ ἄλλοι πολλοὶ τῶν πολιτῶν.

People convicted under the alien acts do not think themselves aggrieved when they are kept in yonder building[1] until the trial for false evidence is over; they simply stay there without expecting to get the freedom of the streets by putting in bail. The commonwealth, having decided to distrust them, did not choose to be cheated of retribution by the process of putting in bail, but preferred that they should stay in a place where many genuine Athenians have sojourned.[4]

2.2 Citizenship in the Greek *polis*

The term "citizen" in English, like its Greek equivalent "polites" indicates belonging to a city (Greek "*polis*"), rather than a kingdom, an empire, a province or any other political unit. It is an import from Greek political thought, which understood the individual as a person belonging to a specific city-state, with a civic identity profoundly defined by this bond. The citizens of the Greek city-state very proudly belonged to it and could not imagine themselves outside it. This is why they staunchly believed in the right of their city for self-determination and were prepared to defend this right with their lives, no matter how small or militarily and economically insignificant their city-state was. Greek city-states recognized common cultural and religious ties with other city-states and were happy to share in the common heritage of Hellenism, but at the same time they fiercely defended their political autonomy and understood themselves as sovereign and independent. Having their own laws, coinage and constitutional form was seen as proof of this independence.

For the individual in this political structure being a citizen of Athens, or Corinth, or Sparta, was a permanent identity. Although people sometimes migrated to other places in search of a better fortune or compelled by adverse circumstances, they never stopped being Athenian, Corinthian or Spartan. They retained their citizenship, along with the cultural identity coming with it and, as far as we can tell, only exceptionally would they assume a new citizen identity through naturalization.[5] Typically themselves and their descendants would retain their original citizenship for generations, and in the host city they would retain the status of a metic, a resident alien. For example, a person from Corinth who migrated to Athens would always remain Corinthian, him and his descendants, no matter how many generations they had lived in Athens, unless with a rare act of naturalization, granted only for great services to the city of Athens (*andragathia*), they were offered Athenian citizenship. Some cities, like for example Thespiae after the Persian wars, were more generous with citizenship grants,[6] while others, like Sparta, were much more stringent. But in the end each city valued its own separate identity, and its citizens were proud to belong to it.

The meaning of citizenship varied significantly from city to city, as Aristotle insightfully pointed out (S 1).[7] For example, being one of the *homoioi* of Sparta was quite different from being one of the citizens of the Athenian Democracy. The methods of introduction into the citizen body, the rights, duties and responsibilities, the level and methods of access to public life and the privileges of this limited group of adult male citizens differed, sometimes greatly, from city to city. A Spartan male infant once inspected and found to be sufficiently healthy for the rigors of the *agoge* was effectively accepted into the citizen body. He would not become a full citizen before the conclusion of his military training at his 30th year, but he would never need to face additional scrutiny to verify his citizen status. An Athenian male child, by contrast, would only be accepted into the citizen body after his 18th year of age, and only after successive scrutinies and the final vote of approval by the deme to which his family belonged.

A Spartan male would be for the most part a spectator in the political life of the city, while the decisions about all matters of importance were taken by a small group of 35 men, the five ephors, the two hereditary kings, and the 28 elders who together with the two kings formed the Spartan *Gerousia*. Although in theory a Spartan citizen was asked about the most important decisions in the city, in most cases he was simply expected to rubberstamp the decisions of the ephors by acclamation. By contrast the Athenian citizen viewed himself as the sovereign master of everything in the city. In the democratic assembly he expected politicians to advise, serve and flatter him, while he cast his vote in order to determine what the city needed to do on any and every matter.

The Greek city-states had their own mythologies on what it meant to be a citizen, regardless of the constitutional framework. These mythologies were often connected to history, tradition and religion, and they were more than simple, innocent tales. Such traditional concepts often served as the means of patriotic propaganda and were intended to justify territorial claims, identity politics, legal provisions and social norms. These tales often established rights and claims and provided justification for these. Several Greek city-states, including the Athenians, the Thebans and the Aeginetans, had cultivated myths of autochthony, claiming that they had sprung from the ground and had always lived in their area, as opposed to others who had encroached into territories that initially belonged to others. Marcel Detienne writes, with a hint of sarcasm,

> Nothing is commoner in Greece or elsewhere than to proclaim oneself an autochthon. Every village has its first man; some, like the Arcadians, know with certainty that the first living being made his appearance even before the moon appeared in a sky dominated by the sun alone.[8]

Athenian concepts of autochthony, and their employment by classical political thought, are well documented in our sources, and were initially explored in a large work by Pherekydes entitled *Αὐτόχθονες*. Suda informs us that this was a sizeable work on early Athens in 10 books.[9] Vincent Rosivach has argued that the myth of Athenian autochthony was a 5th century invention on the grounds that the earliest sources for it are mid-5th century authors like Herodotos.[10] More precisely, the reference to the work of Pherekydes, as well as the fact that the concept of autochthony was very traditional and widespread in the Greek world and beyond, confirm that the classical Athenians did not invent the concept altogether. What they did was to take a traditional myth and form it to serve the purposes of political discourse in the public fora of the classical period. Some obscure creation myths evolved to a concept of original inhabitants, who on account of priority had the best claim and strongest rights to the land which they inhabited.

For Herodotos and Thucydides, autochthony retained this meaning.[11] It is mostly used to explain territorial claims and rights.[12] However, later in the classical period the concept undergoes significant enrichment. Euripides repeatedly uses it to suggest that Athens is the greatest city on earth because its inhabitants are autochthonous, and therefore noble, and this concept of nobility (εὐγένεια) is central for the definition of autochthony in Aristotle's *Rhetoric*.[13] For Isocrates autochthony amounts to legitimacy (11.24: καλῶς καὶ γνησίως γεγόναμεν).[14] In Aristophanes autochthony generates military courage: the Athenians fought the Persians more bravely than anyone else because they were defending the land from which they were born.[15] Plato follows suite and explains that for the Athenians their land was a true mother, not a step-mother.[16] Later in the 4th century Apollodoros and Lykourgos would relate autochthony to citizenship.[17] Recently Josine Blok and Susan Lape have discussed this matter from different angles, and although their methodologies differ, both offer useful insights.[18] Several more studies have explored the autochthony theme in Athenian Drama and art, and the way such representations reflect Athenian civic ideology.[19]

By contrast, the Spartans never claimed autochthony in order to defend their right to inhabit Laconia. Instead the myth of the Heraclidae was employed to back the rightful claim of the Spartans on their city. According to it the descendants of Heracles and Dieaneira fled from the Peloponnese pursued by Eurystheus, only to return after his death and retake the cities that were rightfully theirs. The myth already appears in Tyrtaios, who asserts the divine right of the Spartans to Laconia. It was, he says, the gift of Zeus to the sons of Herakles. Both Spartan royal lines and the three traditional Doric tribes, Hylleis, Pamphyloi and Dymanes, referred their origins to the descendants of Heracles.[20] The memory of the Dorian invasion was still alive in archaic and classical Greece, and in order to counter the Athenian claim that they were migrants (ἐπήλυδες), and consequently had no legitimate claim to Laconia the Spartans adhered to the myth of the Heraclidae and claimed an ancestral and divine right upon Laconia.[21]

These few examples should be sufficient to illustrate that the perception and application of citizenship, and how it was conceptualized and legitimized in contemporary political discourse, varied greatly from one city to the next, and each one of the Greek city-states was proud of the fact that it could set its own laws and parameters in the way it defined what it meant to be a citizen of that particular city. For some, like for example classical Sparta, a citizen was born, never made; others, like Athens, had a more open-minded policy, and were willing under certain conditions to extend this ultimate privilege of citizenship to an outsider and his descendants. On occasion the city might have to resort to extreme measures in order to replenish an ailing population, like the Thespians did after the Persian wars. Seven hundred Thespian men, the entire fighting force of the city, had been killed with Leonidas in Thermopylae (480 BC). The only males left in the city were men too old or too young to take up arms. In these desperate times the Thespians were incentivized to welcome libertines and even slaves of good character from other cities and naturalize them as citizens. Even in post-classical Sparta the proposed reforms of Agis IV, as these were implemented by Cleomenes III, created many new citizens from respectable Perioikoi and alien mercenaries fighting for Sparta. The measure was desperately needed in order to replenish the depleted ranks of the full Spartan citizens (*homoioi*), only it was too little, too late.

The citizenship of women operated within very different parameters considering that in no Greek city-state women could vote or be voted to office or participate in the army and had limited access to the justice system compared to men. They could not be judges, and in Athens it was customary for their testimony to be related to the court through a male representative. However, they could directly give evidence during arbitration, and access the legal system through a male representative when their property or personal rights had been violated. Since Athenian law did not recognize collective responsibility for any crime, women were held personally responsible and could be prosecuted for crimes which they had committed, like homicide, theft, religious transgressions or violations of the immigration laws of the city.[22] They could also face property claims as heiresses. The participation of female citizens in public life was predominantly expressed in the religious sphere. The Periclean citizenship law introduced in 451 explicitly recognized the citizen status of Athenian women and made it an indispensable part of the life of the *polis* by requiring that both parents needed to be citizens before a person could be a citizen. In Sparta the law did not explicitly recognize the citizen status of women, probably because it did not need to do so. A marriage between a Spartan and an outsider or a *perioikos* would be unthinkable. A Spartan man could only marry the daughter of a Spartan family, and we are told that Spartan women had freedom and visibility in the public life of the city, they were far more assertive than their Athenian counterparts, and by the time of Aristotle they owned as much as 40 percent of the land of Laconia.

All three major powers in mainland Greece, Athens, Sparta and Thebes, were not really a single city but confederations of cities. Again, each one of them was very different from the other two. Attica was probably the oldest of these confederations. The quintessential epic hero of Athens, Theseus, was supposedly the one who unified the villages and cities of Attica into a single *polis*, which later also incorporated neighboring Eleusis. In reality Peisistratos did much of the work, and the unification of Attica had been complete before the classical period, and in time it created a well-integrated city-state with the largest population among all Greek poleis.[23] The component-cities, the demes of Attica, had retained their own institutions, political and religious, and after the foundation of the democracy by Kleisthenes, they became a key component for the Athenian *polis* as a whole.[24] The *polis* consisted of ten tribes, named after Athenian epic heroes,[25] and each tribe contained a number of demes from all three regions of Africa, city (ἄστυ), seaside (παράλιοι) and inland (μεσόγαια). The organization of everything in Athenian public life, from the number of men that were to serve in a military campaign, to contributions that needed to be levied, or of the number of children that were to take part in a choir, was based on this decimal system of tribes, and constituent demes.

Sparta was also a confederation, but unlike Athens she chose to remain stratified almost down to the end of her history as a city-state.[26] Although she had the most extensive territory of all Greek city-states, occupying the whole of the southern Peloponnese, thanks to relentless conquest in its early years, the Spartan citizens were only allowed to live in five villages huddled together in a small area, all within easy walking distance from each other.[27] The rest of their territory, including their farms (κλᾶρος) cultivated by the helots, they could visit for limited periods of time. This was the way of the state to always keep an eye on the conduct of each citizen. The rest of the free population of Laconia (περίοικοι) lived in villages all around. They were not citizens of Sparta, but they were Lacedaemonians, namely members of the greater confederation of which Sparta was the leading city. The helots, the enslaved populations of Messenia, were public slaves who belonged to the state of Sparta, and assigned to individual Spartans to work for them, in a climate of absolute obedience and fear. Thus Sparta always retained a strict horizontal stratification of its components, and only allowed movement upwards under exceptional circumstances, when a non-Spartan had excelled in valor, or near the end, when the city had become truly desperate for manpower.

The Boeotian League was a looser confederation of states and each one of the participating city-states was perceived as independent and voluntarily partaking in this union.[28] The Boeotian city-states had common cultural and religious ties, and most cities seem to be willingly participating in this Confederacy, but not all. The heavy shadow of Thebes, the most populous and powerful city in the Confederacy, dominated its affairs, especially in the 4th century, and those cities which openly resented Theban domination, like Plataia and Thespiae, were eventually attacked and destroyed. However, it would be a substantial historical error to reach the conclusion that it was only the forceful persistence of Thebes that held the Confederacy together. The Boeotian League operated on a model of representative government, which although it was not as democratic as that of Athens, it was certainly less oligarchic and authoritarian than that of Sparta. The eleven boeotarchs at the head of the league's government were elected representatives from all the cities of the Confederacy roughly according to their population, and each city had the right to veto centrally made decisions which concerned her. In their dealings with the outside world the Boeotians acted as one unit, and the insistence of Thebes to sign the peace treaty on behalf of all Boeotians in 371, just as Athens had signed on behalf of all the towns of Attica, and Sparta had done on behalf of all Lacedaemonians, infuriated king Agesilaos II, and led to the Spartan invasion of Boeotia and crushing defeat at Leuctra.

In later centuries these early confederacies provided models for unions of villages and cities into larger political units, like the Arcadian league, which came to its own in the late classical period, or the Achaean and Aetolian leagues in the latter years of independent Greece, before the Roman conquest.[29] While the stand-alone city-state, like for example Syracuse, the second most populous Greek city-state after Athens, or Corinth, at the doorstep of Attica, was the prevailing model, even in the classical period we can see that coalescence into larger units through forceful annexation, or voluntary participation into a confederate structure, came with concrete and serious advantages, which sometimes at least they seem to override concerns about independence and self-determination. It was certainly a harbinger of things to come. The end of the city-state as an independent political unit was accelerated by such historical forces, which favored the more populous, larger structures, like these confederations.

2.3 Introduction into the citizen body

A newborn child in a citizen or metic family needed to be officially recognized by his/her father as his own. Although the community was relatively certain about the mother, the father needed to confirm his acknowledgement of the newborn. This could legally happen at any point, even after the child had reached adulthood,[30] but to delay recognition of the child's legitimate birth could raise suspicions about the child's proper birth and possibly deprive this child of his/her right to citizenship with all ensuing privileges. This is why a public act of recognition before family and friends happened not long after the birth of a child. This took place in a private ceremony at home around the 10th day after birth. The details of the ceremony are not well understood since references to it in classical sources tend to be rather circumstantial, while dedicated entries in later lexicographers do not seem to be based on clear and reliable evidence. Richard Hamilton after studying the evidence concluded that there was a ritual which included running around the hearth (ἀμφιδρόμια), the purpose of which was probably symbolic, an act of acceptance of the infant into the *oikos*, of which the hearth was the focal point, and later in the evening there was a more public ceremony which included a sacrifice (δεκάτη) in the presence of family and friends.[31] This ritual signified to the community that there was a new member added to the family, and more importantly that the father acknowledged the child as his own, legitimately born, offspring.

Later on, as soon as they could attend the festival of the Apatouria, Athenian men who belonged to phratries and their subgroups, like the gene, would inform their phrateres and/or gennetai about the new addition to their family by means of a sacrifice and a feast during the third day of the festival, the *Koureotis*. The father needed to swear an oath that the child was legitimately born (ἐξ ἀστῆς γυναικὸς καὶ ἐγγυητῆς κατὰ τὸν νόμον),[32] and then the phrateres or gennetai accepted the child, and if they kept written registers, the child's name was inscribed in them. It appears that practice differed from phratry to phratry regarding the methods of admission as well as the record-keeping, as one would naturally expect of such ancient and traditional institutions.[33]

The phratry or genos could refuse admission if they had reasons to doubt the legitimate birth of a child. One such instance narrated in considerable detail by Apollodoros highlights the process in such cases. A man named Phrastor tried to introduce his son to the genos of the Brytidai, but there were some irregularities. Before the birth of the child, Phrastor had divorced his pregnant wife. Apollodoros alleges that he did so because he suspected that she was the daughter of an alien *hetaira*, and thus not a citizen, but then changed his mind and was willing to take back his son and present him to the phratry. This need not be the case. The divorce of a pregnant woman would be sufficiently irregular to raise questions about the status of the child, as it could easily imply that her husband suspected her of adultery. In any case, under these unusual circumstances the gennetai objected to the introduction of the child. Phrastor sued his genos, the case went to public arbitration, and he won, understandably so, since against the solemn affirmation given by the father, the gennetai could only present suspicions.[34]

Another case of irregular admission to a genos, this time the sacred genos of the Kerykes, presented by Andocides highlights the importance of the father's solemn affirmation for admission. Andocides in a memorable narrative relates the scandalous affair between Kallias and his mother-in-law Chrysilla. A son was born from this affair, certainly outside wedlock, whom Kallias was reluctant to recognize under the circumstances. The relatives of Chrysilla tried to shame him by turning up at the meeting of the genos and challenging him to recognize his son. Kallias refused at the time, but then, after his wife had divorced him he got back together with Chrysilla, now his former mother-in-law, and then he recognized his son, now grown up, and had him registered in the genos, despite the objections of some members. This incident makes clear that the father's word was what mattered most in cases of admission to these bodies.[35]

Other suspicious introductions attested in the Attic orators confirm this. We are told that Euktemon was able to introduce into the phratry the son of the libertine Alke, despite the fact that his mother was alien and a former prostitute. The introduction of the child was initially blocked by Philoktemon, the adult son of Euktemon, with the agreement of the phratry. However, Euktemon was able to arm-twist his son to agree to the introduction of the child, and once the family had resolved their differences the child was admitted solely on account of the word of Euktemon, who presented himself as the father.[36]

Even more remarkably, Mantitheos was able to introduce two boys whom he had refused to acknowledge until they were adults.[37] When reluctantly and under pressure he was compelled to acknowledge them as his own sons, they were admitted to the phratry and the deme without further problems. I think all these cases concur: if an Athenian man was willing to testify under oath that a child was his own and legitimately born, it would be very difficult for anyone to contravene the word of the father and cast doubt upon a child's legitimacy, at least in official settings. Gossip and rumor surely went around about the affairs of families, wives suspected of infidelity, children suspected of illegitimate birth, and citizen men believed to be cuckolded husbands, innocent victims of manipulation or masters of deceit.[38] However, rumor and innuendo could not be sufficient grounds to refuse a citizen the introduction of his child; solid proof would be needed to persuade a majority of his fellow-citizens to inflict upon him such a painful humiliation.

In the days before the reforms of Kleisthenes (504 BC), admission to the phratry would be sufficient proof of citizenship. However, Kleisthenes made the deme the basic citizen unit, and organized everything according to a decimal system corresponding to the ten new tribes which he created. Attica was divided into three geographical regions, the city (ἄστυ), the coastal areas (παραλία), and the inland areas (μεσόγαια). Each of these contained a number of demes (δῆμος), which roughly corresponded to geographical towns and villages that had preexisted the Kleisthenic reorganization. Kleisthenes then took some demes from each geographical region to form a tribe, so that no tribe was a localized entity, but all of them included towns and villages from all three geographical regions. Each of the tribes was cleverly named after an Athenian hero, to inspire patriotic pride. Thus, the reorganization of Attica under Kleisthenes, although artificial, was based on natural geographical units, and this is why it was easily accepted, and it endured.[39]

Undoubtedly part of the plan was to water down strong local allegiances that had supported the aristocratic state for centuries and create an organizational structure which was egalitarian, all-encompassing, and based on new ties and a sense of belonging to the demes, tribes and the great democratic city of Athens, rather than to old, localized, aristocratic institutions and structures.[40] We will never know the answer to the question why Kleisthenes decided at that stage to leave intact the old institutions and structures which he was in essence trying to replace, like the phratry and its subgroups. We may speculate that their traditional associations with religion could generate significant resistance to their replacement, which he did not consider a battle worth fighting at that stage.[41]

Athenian boys, when they reached the age of 18, were presented to the deme of their father for registration (ἐγγράφεσθαι εἰς ἄνδρας). The members of the deme had to decide first whether the person presented had reached the age of 18. This was not self-evident in a society which did not keep written records of births, and if the youth's appearance suggested that he was younger than 18, and/or the family failed to persuade the deme with witnesses that he was 18, then he was relegated back to the children (πάλιν εἰς παῖδας) until a later date. After that the members of the deme needed to be convinced that he was properly born (γέγονε κατὰ τοὺς νόμους). If they were satisfied that these conditions were met, then they voted to inscribe the new member on the deme's register, and this act conferred upon a man full Athenian citizenship.

The meaning of the phrase "properly born" was not a constant in time, but meant different things at different points of Athenian history. Before 451 it meant a free son born to an Athenian man, regardless of the status of his mother. After the introduction of the Periclean citizenship law, it meant the son of both an Athenian man and an Athenian woman (ἐξ ἀμφοῖν ἀστοῖν). In the early years of the Peloponnesian war this law was repealed, as Daniel Ogden and Edwin Carawan have argued, probably correctly, since Athenian families were trying to cope with the heavy losses of young men.[42] Undoubtedly it came to be perceived as heartless and serving no good purpose to leave many families without an heir, in such times. So, any free-born son in an Athenian family now had the right to full citizenship and succession rights.[43] After the end of the war, as the Athenians were trying to reorganize public life and restore the city to its prewar state, a decree of Aristophon in 403 reinstated the Periclean citizenship law. Thereafter citizen birth from both sides would be required for full citizenship. The author of the *Athenaion Politeia* has skillfully bypassed these uncertainties in the legal definition by simply using a vague expression (42.1: εἰ ἐλεύθερός ἐστι καὶ γέγονε κατὰ τοὺς νόμους).

Whether lawful marriage of one's parents was a condition for full citizenship, or citizen descent from both sides was sufficient, has been a highly contentious issue, which cannot be answered with certainty. D.M. MacDowell argued that citizen descent alone was sufficient, because a fair number of citizens mentioned in the Attic Orators were born outside wedlock. Peter Rhodes replied that these persons could have been born in the years of the Peloponnesian war, when more liberal policies on citizenship were adopted under compelling circumstances. Cynthia Patterson has summarized the long debate on the subject, which has led to no firm conclusions, simply because the available evidence can be interpreted both ways.[44]

After registration with the deme, the new citizens needed to pass an inspection (δοκιμασία) by the Boule, the purpose of which was to make sure that they are of the right age for military service, and if the Boule believed that a deme had registered an underage person, it had the authority to fine the magistrates responsible. As with other cases of *dokimasia*, very likely a rejected youth who did not want to go back to the boys and repeat the process of registration in the future could appeal the Council's decision to court and try to prove his age with the testimony of family and other persons who had known him for the whole of his life. One would imagine that such incidents were very rare. The young men who had passed the scrutiny before the Boule joined the *ephebes* for the customary two years of military service. Four trustworthy men for each tribe were elected to oversee the training of the *ephebes*, three from the tribe and one from outside. In addition, two instructors were chosen to teach the ephebes the arts of war.

Unlike the brutality of the Spartan *agoge*, the Athenian military service seemingly was more measured and purposeful. In the first year the ephebes were instructed in combat tactics and spend much of their time on guard duty in Piraeus and the fortresses of Attica. After the end of basic training they were offered a shield and a spear at public expense and spent their second year mostly on guard duty. In the two years of military service they were immune from prosecutions, and could not prosecute others, so as not to have distractions to their training. Exceptions were made for claiming an inheritance or an *epikleros*[45] since these issues were time-sensitive, or for accepting a hereditary priesthood, which could not have waited until the end of the military service.[46] After the two-year period the young men went home resuming their lives as full citizens and would remain under obligation to join military campaigns when the city needed them until their 59th year of age.

Failure to join the army, or cowardice during the campaign would result to disfranchisement. Athenian law recognized three distinct offences related to military service, ἀστρατείας (failure to join a campaign), λιποταξίου (abandoning one's rank), ῥιψασπίας (casting away one's shield and running).[47] The procedure for the prosecution of all three offenses was very similar. It required a *graphe* and a trial by a special jury consisting only of citizens who had served as soldiers in that campaign. Understandably this would be a tough jury to face, and on one occasion attested in the speech *Against Neaira* a man was convicted and disfranchised for failure to join a campaign even though he had a specific legal exemption as a tax collector.[48] Besides tax collectors, holders of public office, members of a chorus, or citizens who were ill or absent from Attica at the time of the campaign were also legally exempt. In all such cases, evidently, a person was either unable to join the campaign or the importance of his presence in the city superseded the needs of the campaign.

An Athenian man could marry once he reached adulthood, but typically he was not expected to commit before he had the means and maturity to look after a family, in his late 20s, 30s or even later. The daughters of relatives or family friends would often be potential wives, although there was no set pattern in such matters. A man might marry a woman from a family he trusted, or a complete, but attractive stranger, someone who came with substantial dowry, or someone who came with nothing, someone attractive or someone not so attractive but well-trained and suitable for the role of an Athenian wife, a young virgin in her mid-teens, or an older woman in her 20s or 30s, who had married before and even had children from another man, a modest and reserved person or a vivacious and capricious youth. All these options were open to an Athenian man, and his decision ultimately depended upon his character, expectations and personal circumstances.[49]

Unlike Sparta, where bachelors faced ridicule and sanctions by the ephors, an Athenian man was under no obligation to take a wife. He could choose to remain unattached for the whole of his life without adverse consequences for his public image or standing in society. Alternatively, he could choose to take a concubine instead of a wife. Since Athenian law recognized relationships with concubines and extended the protective umbrella of the adultery laws over concubines as well, such relationships were not informal; there were simply inferior to lawful marriage. This does not mean that concubines were necessarily low-class women, or any less respectable than Athenian wives. Greek women from other cities, even highborn ones, or individuals of extraordinary ability and talent, like the Milesian Aspasia, could only be concubines of Athenian men in the years when the Periclean citizenship law was in force. Retired alien *hetairai*, like Neaira, Phila or the anonymous concubine of Olympiodoros,[50] were typical concubines in Athenian households. Illegitimate daughters of citizens would also become concubines. A concubine it was a woman with whom a man chose to live his life, even though she could not offer him legitimate children, and in most cases she did not come with a dowry to contribute to the finances of the household, simply because he wanted to be with her and no one else.[51]

Sometimes citizen men who were emotionally attracted to other men might choose to marry in order to have children, or avoid marriage altogether and remain bachelors having casual affairs with youths and men for love or money, like the generally respectable Misgolas in the speech *Against Timarchos*, or the middle-aged speaker in Lysias 3. Alternatively, they might choose to form long-term relationships with other males which society would recognize as love affairs, acceptable and permissible, but not legally comparable to monogamous heterosexual relations like marriage or concubinage, since the men participating in such relations were not required to remain monogamous and were not covered by the adultery laws.[52] This was not based on prejudice against such relations, as it has happened for the most part of the Christian era until very recently when same sex relations have gained legal recognition, but upon the perception that fidelity in a relationship was a requirement placed upon women. No one ever expected a man to remain monogamous either in a heterosexual or a homosexual setting. Classical Athens did not frown upon same-sex relationships, casual or long-term, because they did not view them as different from heterosexual relationships. All forms of sexual expression were seen as part of a continuum of the human sexual experience.

Fatherhood came with a set of inescapable obligations. Boys needed to be educated and carefully instructed in the duties and responsibilities of citizenship, while girls needed to be instructed in domestic tasks so as to become capable managers of their future households. It was the responsibility of the family to make sure that husbands could be found for girls who reached marriageable age, usually around 14 or 15, and that a dowry would be provided to help them pay their way in life. The father, or other male relatives in his absence, were responsible for the introduction of boys to the phratry and the deme, and for their smooth integration into the citizen body. While a family's duty typically ended when a girl was given in marriage and a boy had reached his 20th year, and became legally independent, family obligations never really ended as Athenians expected their relatives to be there and support them in difficult moments, women who lost their husbands might want to find safe haven in the warm embrace of their family home, and from a legal perspective both boys and girls retained inheritance rights in their natal *oikos* for life.[53]

When male citizens reached their 59th year of age they served as public arbitrators in the transitional year between eligibility for active military service and retirement. The fee of one drachma paid to an arbitrator for each case in which he was involved offered some compensation for all the time and effort a citizen had to put into this important task, but it was too low to be seen as an attractive money opportunity, especially since cases before an arbitrator sometimes dragged on for some time. After the customary auditing (εὔθυνα) in the end of his year of service the citizen, now in his 60th year and no longer eligible for military service, could continue to play a very active role in public life for as long as he desired. Aristophanes in the *Wasps* tells us that retired older men, who had more time in their hands but at the same time a greater financial need for the meager compensation of three obols offered daily for dicastic service were the men that manned the courts of Athens in large numbers. However, the *Wasps* also offers valuable evidence for the other side of the coin, the affluent household of Bdelykleon where his retired father Philokleon has been well provided.[54]

An Athenian man could remain an active citizen of the democracy and *kyrios* of his household until the end of his life, if his health and disposition allowed it. His adult sons would be legally independent from his authority, but not from his financial control, since he remained the owner of the property of the family, unless he decided otherwise. Many a time, sons had to wait until the father died, before they could get their hands on his property. In the meantime, they could marry, create their own families, and if they could secure independent financing for their household through a rich marriage, some business enterprise, or some other avenue, they could truly become their own men. However, so long as they depended on the property belonging to their father for the financial needs of their family, as it often happened especially in farming communities, they were also subject to his whims, and this could go on for many years. Alternatively, an Athenian man could decide or be compelled by old age and infirmity to retire and hand over control of his household to his son, like Philokleon has done in the *Wasps*. In this case, the father, and his wife if still alive, would often stay with the son and his family in the same household. Households including three or four generations were common in classical Athens, and everywhere else until the 20th century. In this setting the son along with the property assumed the responsibility of providing for his parents, grandparents and even great-grandparents.[55]

When a man had more than one sons, he could choose to divide the property among them while he was still alive, and either stay with one of them, or keep a part of the property for himself and continue to live separately. There was no fixed pattern in such arrangements; elderly Athenian men settled their affairs according to their family dynamics, disposition, and financial circumstances. The family's obligation did not end with the death of a person. Funeral rites and rituals in remembrance of the dead were an important part of family life, as well as a legal obligation of someone's descendants. A citizen's life from the cradle to the grave was a continuous negotiation between his duties to the city and the community and his obligations to his family. The funerary monuments and inscriptions which have survived in the cemeteries of the city, like the one in Kerameikos, offer eloquent testimony to the strength of both, the importance of a man's standing in public life as well as the depth of family ties.

2.4 The rights, privileges and duties of Athenian citizen men

In the classical democracy any male citizen regardless of birth or wealth, could vote in the elections of magistrates, unless he was disfranchised (ἄτιμος). An enfranchised citizen was also eligible to stand for election, or participate in the sortation for those offices where the lot decided, unless his age or conduct had disqualified him, or did not meet some other criterion specific to a certain office.[56] Fifth century literature reveals some tensions between rich and poor, and sometimes between the old, landed classes and the traders and craftsmen of the agora, as these are manifested in the variety of texts from Old Comedy (especially the *Knights* of Aristophanes) and tragedy, to the Old Oligarch, and even Thucydides or Xenophon. These tensions twice led to the establishment of troublesome oligarchic regimes in the final years of the 5th century, which to some degree discredited the voices of inequality. In the 4th century, with the exception of a few authors from the Socratic circle, most notably Plato and Xenophon, we see a more egalitarian face of the Athenian Democracy. This does not mean that inequalities of wealth, or perceptions of class and privilege were gone; it only means that arguments based on these were not sanctioned by contemporary political thought or deemed acceptable in public discourse. The democracy of the 4th century, at least in theory, was for all citizens and open to all citizens.[57]

The right to own real estate in Attica was the exclusive privilege of Athenian citizens. Metics could own real estate only if given ἔγκτησις, namely the privilege to own land in Attica.[58] While many a time houses and farms were passed down from generation to generation, only Athenian citizens (and qualified metics) had the right to buy properties that came up for sale. This restriction created handsome opportunities for citizens in the housing market, since the thousands of metrics who had made Attica their home could only rent properties. Wealthier metics, like Kephalos, the father of Lysias, rented elegant houses, as the rich narrative of the speech *Against Eratosthenes* suggests. Working-class metic families rented in apartment complexes (συνοικία), owned by entrepreneurial citizens like Apollodoros or Euktemon.[59]

Only Athenian citizens were entitled to subsidies like money to buy seats in the theater (θεωρικά), or occasional cash or grain distributions, and certainly only citizens could seek compensation for services to the city like seating in a jury (δικαστικὸς μισθός), participating in the Assembly (ἐκκλησιαστικὸς μισθός) or serving as ambassadors.[60] Athenian citizens were exempt from certain taxes that burdened the metic population, such as the *metoikion*, or additional taxes for the privilege of trading in the Athenian agora.[61] However, the narrative of the speech *Against Timarchos* implies that Athenian prostitutes needed to pay tax (πορνικόν τέλος) like alien prostitutes. If my previous suggestion that in the classical period the prostitution tax was a πεντηκοστή, namely a 2% annual tax on the earnings from prostitution, is correct, this would explain why Athenian citizens were not exempt from it; pentekostai, such as the tax on imported wheat, were paid by citizens as well as non-citizens, one would think because they were an important source of income for the Athenian state in the 4th century.[62] Richer citizens and metics were also responsible for the numerous liturgies in the city, which included the equipment of war ships for a year (trierarchy), or the expenses and training of a chorus for a religious festival (choregy). In the 5th century this duty burdened only the richer citizens and metics, but as their number diminished after the Peloponnnesian war more people with lower incomes needed to pool together to meet these needs (symmories). [63]

Enfranchised male Athenian citizens had unfettered access to the legal system and were expected to represent the best interests of their family members, such as women, children, elderly parents or disabled family members who could not go to court themselves. As far as we know, there was no law explicitly barring women from the courtrooms, but a strong social convention, which had stood from time immemorial, demanded that the *kyrios* of the household was to represent his family members in court and speak on their behalf, as a plaintiff or to give evidence.

However, this was limited only to the final stage of a legal dispute, the trial before a Heliastic court. In all stages before women had direct access to the legal system. They could appeal to magistrates in order to ask for protection of their rights or to lay claims on property items, and they could appear before arbitrators as witnesses. For major property claims such as an inheritance, or more serious legal disputes which were likely to end up in court they would need to enlist the help of an adult male citizen, such as their *kyrios*, a legal guardian, a relative, or a paid advocate (who was not supposed to be paid).

Only enfranchised citizen men could sit as judges or serve in any of the numerous offices of the Athenian state. The *Wasps* of Aristophanes suggests that jury service was attractive to poor older men, because it provided a reliable modest income of three obols for every day of service, a sum equal to the wages of an unskilled worker. While we need to make allowances for the comic reality of the play, the concept that retired older men with more time in their hands and poor citizens with no reliable source of income would be attracted to the service sounds truthful. On the other hand, public office was a different reality. Most magistrates of the Athenian Democracy were selected by lot, while elected offices like those of the generals and the treasurers were highly competitive, as were the very few offices into which someone could be appointed, like the assessors of the three senior *archon*s.[64] Although the officers of the democracy were not supposed to be paid, but only occasionally compensated for living expenses, there were always plentiful opportunities for enrichment from corruption and misuse of public funds. This made some public offices attractive, especially in the 4th century, and it seems that at least for some Athenian citizens involvement in public life game with concrete, even if not always legal or transparent ways for enrichment.[65]

2.5 Metics

Unlike modern states, which impose formidable barriers before someone can immigrate into their territory, the Greek city-states operated an open entry policy. While their borders might be guarded with fortresses and other defensive structures and routinely patrolled, the purpose of such measures was to keep out invading armies not peaceful individuals. Any person who wished to peacefully enter their territory could do so without harassment. Beyond that, whether they could stay, how long they could stay, and how welcome they would be to settle down and become part of the local community, if they so wished, varied from one city to the next. While we are not well informed about the immigration policies of most Greek city-states, we have sufficient information about Athens and Sparta to safely conclude that their policies were diametrically opposite. With rare exceptions, a visitor to Sparta could only stay for a few days to conclude his business, and then he had to leave. The last thing the Spartan state ever wanted was aliens with foreign habits, lifestyles or viewpoints mingling with the citizens and corrupting the purity of the Spartan way of life. Notoriously xenophobic Sparta would go to great lengths to ensure that the interactions between her citizens and the outside world were as limited as possible, lest they would be infected with foreign customs. The dramatic structural changes in Spartan society during and after the Spartan hegemony in the end of the 5th century, proved that these concerns were both justified and a self-fulfilling prophecy: the Spartans were particularly prone to corruption by foreign lifestyles, simply because they had never been exposed to them before, and were totally unprepared to deal with the new, the strange, the different.

The Athenian immigration model was the exact opposite. Athens was open and welcoming to immigrants. Any person who wished to move into Attica to pursue opportunities in the large and diverse markets of the city was welcome to settle, work, and productively contribute to the life of the city. Especially in the years of the Athenian Empire, when opportunity in the imperial capital was abundant, many Greeks and non-Greeks settled in the city of Pericles, and some, like the Syracusan Kephalos, the father of the orator Lysias, not only prospered financially but were also rubbing shoulders with the city's elite intellectuals, politicians and powerbrokers.[66] Prominent philosophers and skilled craftsmen, like Gorgias of Leontini, Prodikos of Keos, Hippias of Elis, Aristotle of Stageira or Hippocrates of Kos, settled in the city for lengthy periods, attracted by the open intellectual atmosphere of Periclean Athens which created abundant employment opportunities. Their presence in the city spearheaded the cultural revolution of classical Athens which changed the trajectory of humanity forever.[67]

James Watson has plausibly argued that after the introduction of the Periclean citizenship law in 451, the status of non-citizens living in Athens was more sharply defined by contrast to citizens, and after that date non-citizens residing in Attica needed to register.[68] However, there is no positive evidence confirming this, and it is equally possible that metics were required to register even before 451. The first references to metics are found in Aischylos, in plays composed before 451. A long-standing debate on whether there were legal differences among the resident aliens of Attica, and whether all free non-citizens were metics, or metic-status was a privilege, has been decisively settled by David Whitehead. Recently Athina Dimopoulou-Piliouni re-opened the discussion, but Joshua Sosin in response re-iterated the now widely accepted view that as far as the law was concerned all non-citizen residents were metics.[69]

This by no means implies that all metics were the same. As there were substantial inequalities of wealth and social standing among the citizens, there were large inequalities of wealth and social status among metics too. Rich metics like Pasion or Phormion before their naturalization lived in very different conditions, and had very different opportunities from metics like the libertine Dion, who cohabited with a prostitute named Alke and her children from unnamed fathers in a small, wretched apartment in Piraeus that also served as a brothel.[70] There was also a vast difference in social status between Greek-born metics like Lysias, one of the most respected logographers and legal advisers in the city, or the great Aristotle, and the libertine Pittalakos, who owned a profitable but disreputable gambling establishment.[71]

Non-Athenians were welcome to go about their business without having to inform the Athenian authorities of their presence for a limited period of time, perhaps a month. However, if they wanted to stay longer they were required to register with the *polemarch*, the magistrate responsible for all the alien populations of Attica, place themselves under the protection of an Athenian sponsor, and start paying a special tax, called the *metoikion*. This was a fixed poll tax set at 12 drachmas a year for men and their families, and at six for single women. The registration, under the protection of an Athenian sponsor, had a symbolic meaning attached to it: through this act the alien person expressed his/her wish to take up residence in Attica, and the city welcomed the new resident by placing him/her under the protection of a citizen. After this day the new metic would be inscribed in a register and easily identified as such for all legal purposes.[72]

Beyond this symbolic act the sponsor does not seem to be playing any further role. Registration with the support of a citizen was important for Athenian legal procedure, because it established a very clear dividing line between citizens and all non-citizens living in the city. Registration and subsequent regular payment of the tax (*metoikion*) amounted to a de facto recognition of the status of metic in Attica, and this was not necessarily a bad thing. The life-long obligation to register and pay the metoikion had a positive side to it, especially for former slaves whose status might come into question. A registered metic who had paid his tax could not be wrongly haled back to slavery, because there was a solid and indisputable proof of his free status in the register of metics. This happened to a woman named Zobia. When an angry former lover attempted to sell her as a slave, her status as a free person was confirmed because her payment of the metoikion had been duly noted in the register of metics.[73]

There is no clear evidence that non-citizen concubines of citizens needed to register as metics and pay the metoikion. We know that men, either single or with families, and independent metic women needed to register. However, this raises an interesting question: would alien concubines of citizens be classed as independent metic women, when in fact they belonged to an Athenian household in a relationship which although inferior to lawful marriage, it was still recognized by Athenian law and custom?[74] There is absolutely no evidence that a citizen ever had to pay the *metoikion* on behalf of an alien member of his household. This is why there is a distinct possibility that non-citizen women who belonged to Athenian households as concubines, illegitimate daughters, bastard sisters, or other relatives were not expected to register as metics, and so long they accepted their status and did not transgress into the citizen body by pretending to be citizens they remained beyond the reach of the law. If they ever got married, their metic husband would continue to pay the metoikion of 12 drachmas for the whole of his family. Illegitimate non-citizen sons in Athenian household probably were in the same position until they reached adulthood. After that, once they became legally independent, they needed to register as metics. The silence of our sources on the issue is probably significant: this could genuinely have been a gray area, where custom and traditional family structures prevailed over the literal definitions of immigration law.

An alien who failed to register and take a *prostates* could be prosecuted with a *graphe aprostasiou*. The penalty was slavery.[75] The harshness of the penalty no doubt has to do with the fact that failure to register was perceived as a fraudulent act intended to blur the distinctiveness of the metic's subordinate status, as Stephen

Todd has observed.[76] Less clear is the purpose and scope of the *dike apostasiou* mentioned in the same breath with the *dike aprostasiou* in the *Athenaion Politeia*. Despite the assertion of Harpocration that such cases were found in plenty among the Attic Orators, we know very little about it from classical sources, and the lexicographers do not seem to know much more. It appears as if they are trying to guess what this process was about from the name of it. For example, when Photios attempts to explain what the γραφὴ ἀποστασίου was, he comes up with a convoluted answer that makes no sense: he says that it could be brought by slaves who claimed to be free against their alleged masters.[77] However, this was the procedure which we can identify as removal to freedom (ἀφαίρεσις εἰς ἐλευθερίαν, see below), it was initiated by a free person and required citizens to stand as sureties. Therefore, it cannot be the procedure which Photios mentions, and most likely he's making things up to compensate for his complete ignorance on what this procedure was.

Some of the other lexicographers may be better informed when they say that it was a process used against libertines who had walked away from their former masters. They seem to imply that the law barred liberated slaves from taking another *prostates*, instead of their former master, but this does not seem logical. It should make no difference for the Athenian state whether a libertine took his former master as his sponsor or chose someone else. Besides, many libertines living in Athens came from other places, and their former masters were not living in Attica. Again, the lexicographers are probably guessing. The most likely explanation is that the case applied to former slaves who had been set free by their masters under a *paramone* condition, namely a contract which specified a set of duties that a former slave would still have towards his former master, for a period of time which could be as long as the lifetime of the former master or even his children (see below). Such contracts which allowed former masters to extend control over their former slaves even after their liberation, were not uncommon, and one can understand that after some time they could be viewed by the former slave as a major nuisance and an unfair power game. This is why the desire to breach those terms and break free could be an understandable human reaction. It seems that the law, in order to protect such contracts allowed a *graphe apostasiou* (indictment for breaking away) against former slaves who had revolted against this extended control of their former masters and tried to break free, just as the lexicographers suggest. The penalty was to be sold back to slavery.

Both procedures, the *graphe aprostasiou* and the *graphe apostasiou*, needed to be brought before the *polemarch*, like all other public or private lawsuits where the defendant was a metic. The *Athenaion Politeia* (S 5) states that for the metic population the *polemarch* was in charge of all those duties which for citizens came under the authority of the *archon*, such as inheritance matters and disputes, appointment of guardians, *epidikasia*i for *epikleroi* and so on.[78] However, when the defendant was a citizen it is clear that the lawsuit needed to be brought before the appropriate authority for citizens, such as the *basileus*, the *thesmothetai* or the Forty, regardless of the citizen status of the plaintiff.[79]

The level of access which metics had to the Athenian legal system has been a contentious issue,[80] but probably it should not be. It would be unimaginable for anyone to live, work and feel safe in a society as litigious as classical Athens without access to the legal system. A free person, head of a free household, needed to be able to go to court and defend the best interests of his family, seek the punishment of persons who had wronged him or his family, or defend a family member who had been accused of running foul of the law. Most metics were businessmen, and any business enterprise at some point or other might require some litigation in order to defend its financial interests and respond to challenges by competitors or clients.[81] It would be imperative for anyone operating a business in classical Athens to be able to go to court if necessary. A rich banker like Pasion might be able to afford the legal services of a citizen,[82] but a tradesman, like the fuller Pankleon in Lys. 23, who ran a small workshop in the marketplace,[83] would not have the luxury of pricey legal teams. First it seems that he tried to avoid litigation at all costs, and when this turned out to be a serious mistake, as his enemies smelled blood and started circling around, he had to go in person to court. And what about some inheritance dispute between non-Athenians, or personal injury inflicted upon a metic in a violent assault, or the violation of his household by the seducer of one of the women in his family,[84] or a thief caught in his house red-handed? How could anyone ever safely live in Attica if he did not have the legal capacity and right to seek restitution through the justice system? This is why there can be no doubt that free resident aliens in Athens could go to court in person to take care of the affairs of their family or business.[85]

There is sufficient reliable evidence confirming that free non-citizens could give evidence in Athenian courts and also address the court either as prosecutors or as defendants. For example, Lysias was able to prosecute Eratosthenes in person and speak in court although he remained a metic for the whole of his life.[86] Euxitheos of Mytilene, accused for the murder of the Athenian Herodes, while tried in Athens spoke in person in his defense with a speech written by Antiphon.[87] In the speech *Against Neaira* Theomnestos suggests that Stephanos disguised some slaves (probably with African looks) as free men from Cyrene, so that they could give false testimony against his opponent Apollodoros in a homicide trial, but the plot failed.[88] But above all, the proposal to suspend the degree of Skamandrios and torture metics for information during the scandal of the Hermokopidai in 415, essentially treating free persons as slaves to be tortured for evidence, makes clear that free persons always had the right to give evidence in court without coercion, on an equal footing with Athenian citizens. Treating a free person with any less respect than that would be un-Greek, and a violation of those famous rules of civilized society on which all Greeks prided themselves.[89]

For a limited number of lawsuits, seemingly those concerning citizenship and immigration offenses, like the *graphe xenias*, or important matters concerning public life and the *polis*, which included the *graphe hybreos* or the introduction of new laws, the law explicitly specified that only an Athenian citizen could bring a lawsuit. While the standard expression for the introduction of a public lawsuit appears to be ὁ βουλόμενος οἷς ἔξεστιν (whoever wishes among those who have the right), for those cases which could be introduced only by an Athenian citizen the expression appears to be Ἀθηναίων ὁ βουλόμενος οἷς ἔξεστιν (whoever wishes among those Athenians who have the right).[90]

The contribution of metics to the Athenian economy was widely recognized, as several sources suggest. Metics owned profitable businesses like for example the Syracusan Kephalos, the father of Lysias, who probably owned the workshop which in 403 had passed to his sons,[91] the libertine Pitalakos in the speech *Against Timarchos* who owned and operated a profitable gambling establishment,[92] the Egyptian metic Athenogenes who owned a perfume factory and sold it to the naïve speaker in the speech of Hypereides *Against Athenogenes*, along with all its debts, Pasion and Phormion who made huge profits as bankers before their naturalization, and many more. Metics also flourished in the services industry. Lysias himself became wealthy as a logographer and legal advocate, metics like several of the Sophists and philosophers, most prominently Aristotle of Stageira, commanded large salaries in the higher education sector, while many practicing physicians in Athens were also metics, and some, like the skilled Demokedes, were appointed as public physicians at the service of the Athenian state with massive salaries.[93] Other artisans, craftsmen, and small businessmen and businesswomen lived and worked in Athens in large numbers.

While citizen women would take themselves out of the house to work under dire necessity and economic pressures, independent metic women needed to work, pay taxes, and provide for themselves. The recent monograph of Rebecca Kennedy on the metic women of Athens outlines their substantial contribution to the city's economy, as well as the ideology of immigrant women in Athenian society.[94] Employment opportunities for independent women existed in the health sector, where they could be working as midwives or nurses, in the fabric industry as weavers and cloth makers, in small businesses as sellers and shopkeepers, in the service industry as innkeepers, cooks, servers or bread sellers, and more prominently, in the large sex industry of classical Athens. The majority of high-end, free-born *hetairai* working in Athens, like for example Lais of Hykkara, Phryne of Thespiae, Sinope of Pontus, or Antikyra of Antikyra, were metics who were attracted to the large and diverse sex markets of Attica, and the same applied to many procurers and brothel keepers. Slave born *hetairai* also joined the metic class if an infatuated lover was willing to buy their freedom, as Neaira did, when Phrynion of Paiania bought her freedom from her Corinthian masters and brought her with him to Athens.[95]

As the Athenian state was willing to award honors to citizens, like *ateleia*, or *sitesis*,[96] it was also willing to award honors to non-citizens for exceptional services to the Athenian state. These honors could be awarded to metics, to persons who lived in other cities and had promoted the interests of Athens, and sometimes even to persons who had never set foot on Attica. The lowest ranking among them seems to have been ἰσοτέλεια, namely equality of taxation with citizens. In practical terms this meant that a metic did not have to pay the *metoikion* or any other contribution or tax that citizens did not have to pay.[97] *Isoteleia* often came as a package with the more generous and coveted right to own real estate in Attica (ἔγκτησις).[98] However, the most coveted prize at the top of the list was a naturalization grant (πολιτεία) through which the Athenian state welcomed an alien with all his existing descendants, into the citizen body.

Apollodoros, a naturalized citizen of Athens himself,[99] describes in great detail the complex and involved procedure required before someone could become an Athenian citizen.[100] First, the law set a single criterion for a citizenship award, that of ἀνδραγαθία, namely an extraordinary act which benefited the Athenian *demos*. While the way that the Athenian assembly and courts understood *andragathia* kept evolving, especially in the course of the 4th century, the requirement itself as the only criterion for naturalization remained unchanged. Inscriptions define *andragathia* as the willingness to do everything within one's power to benefit the Athenian people.[101] In practical terms it could mean anything which Athenian politicians, the Boule, or the Assembly wanted it to mean. In the 4th century naturalization grants often served shortsighted political expediency, and sometimes were offered to powerful men who did not always have the best interests of Athens in mind, while on other occasions, such grants were cynically motivated by money, and rich metics like Pasion and Phormion were able essentially to buy their citizenship through extravagant donations to the Athenian state.

References to naturalization of foreigners in Athens before the years of the Peloponnesian war are scarce and somewhat problematic.[102] The first well-attested naturalization was that of the Plataians in the early years of the war. This was motivated as much by necessity as by the wish to reward the staunch and faithful ally that had stood by the Athenians alone among Greek cities in the battlefield of Marathon in 490. When their city was destroyed after a long siege in 427 BC by the Peloponnesian alliance, the Athenians offered to the surviving Plataians citizenship and a permanent home in Athens. The decree which conferred citizenship upon the Plataians is partially quoted by Apollodoros.[103] Several more mass naturalizations followed in the years of the Peloponnesian war, like that of the Samians, or the heroes of Phyle.[104] There is little that someone would find objectionable in these cases. Those who were offered citizenship had a proven record of loyalty and good service to the city of Athens. However, in the course of the 4th century politicians started interpreting *andragathia* as convenient in the short term. Some of the new citizens, like the tyrant of Syracuse Dionysios I, were not always blindly loyal to the best interests of Athens, while others, like Charidemos, a high-profile leader of mercenary troops, sometimes fought against the Athenians in the service of their enemies. Some of those new "citizens" did not even live in Athens, and there lies the irony of the situation. Many hard-working metics, who had lived in Attica for generations, made strong contributions to the prosperity and well-being of the city, and some had suffered terrible losses side by side with citizen families in the hard years of the Peloponnesian war and the tyranny of the Thirty, like the orator Lysias, were never awarded Athenian citizenship, when men with a proven record of ill-will towards the city, and no plans of ever going anywhere near Attica, were offered citizenship as part of petty political maneuvering.

Naturalization remained an exceptional process which required a personal decree (νόμος ἐπ' ἀνδρί). Like other exceptional decrees which concerned a single individual, rather than the entire citizen body,[105] it needed to be approved by a "full-house" assembly of 6000 citizens.[106] In the 4th century, as naturalization degrees became much more frequent, the process became two-tier. A citizen who wanted to propose the naturalization of someone would follow the normal procedures of introducing a decree to the assembly, and if the decree was approved, confirmation was necessary by a "full-house" assembly of 6000. However, this second vote did not come with discussion; it took place before the start of the assembly, early in the morning, and expectedly it was a secret ballot, just like the ballot for ostracism was in the 5th century. The citizens cast their votes in urns just as they entered the assembly area to take their seats. If the majority of this "full-house" vote confirmed the positive vote of the previous assembly, the candidate was accepted as a new citizen, and was invited to register with a deme, and a phratry of his choosing.

This two-tier vote probably was a streamlining of the process. Since naturalization decrees required the approval of a "full-house" assembly in practical terms they could only be proposed in a busy *kyria ekklesia*, the main assembly of the month, since the other assemblies were less well attended and probably did not reach the quorum. As naturalization proposals became more and more frequent they probably took too much of the valuable time of the main assembly during the discussion stage. This is why a new, more efficient strategy was devised, whereby the decree and the discussion could take place in any assembly, while the quorum requirement could be met effortlessly, and without any additional demands upon the time of the main assembly, through a secret ballot in the morning before the formal opening of the day's agenda.

Like any other decree, a naturalization proposal was vulnerable to a *graphe paranomon*, which if successful in court, it would result in the cancellation of the naturalization award, and the punishment of the proposer if less than a year had lapsed between the passing of the decree and its indictment. Apollodoros mentions a couple of cases of revoked citizenship awards after a *graphe paranomon*.[107] The reversal of these awards in court undoubtedly had to do with the messy politics of the 340s. Although we do not have a speech delivered in such a case, we may get a good idea of how a naturalization decree could be attacked through the determined assault on the character and record of Charidemos, a naturalized citizen, in the speech *Against Aristokrates*.

Naturalized citizens were automatically offered all rights and privileges of citizens by birth, with the exception of some minor and unimportant restrictions undoubtedly motivated by religious observance.[108] They were not allowed to participate in the sortition for the nine *archon*s, or accept a hereditary priesthood. These offices had traditional religious duties and rituals, and the state was concerned about their correct performance. However, the offspring of naturalized citizens from citizen women were not subject to these restrictions. Their impact might be more long-lasting within city groups like the Plataians, where most men would choose wives from their own group, rather than Athenian women, thus perpetuating the restrictions.

Individually naturalized citizens where invited to register with a deme and phratry of their choosing, but it seems that in mass naturalizations of city groups like the Plataians or the Samians, the state performed the distribution to demes automatically. The decree on the Samians explicitly mentions that the distribution is to be done by the *archon*s (καὶ νε͂μαι [αὐτὸς αὐτίκα μάλα τὸς ἄρχοντας ἐς τὰ]ς φυλὰς δέκαχα). Perhaps in this practice we may detect a fear that the new citizens would live in large concentrations in certain areas of the city and as a result they would overwhelm the local demes. Through automatic distribution the city was hoping to scatter them throughout Attica, and thus facilitate their integration. By contrast, the metics who had joined the heroes of Phyle, although naturalized en mass, like the Samians or the Plataians, they were invited to choose their deme and phratry. These metics had been living in Attica for years, if not for generations, and had local connections with the area where they resided, so it made sense to allow them to choose their local deme and phratry.

There is no reference to the phratry in the decrees on the Plataians and the Samians. The decree on the Plataians mentions automatic distribution into demes and tribes (κατανεῖμαι δὲ τοὺς Πλαταιέας εἰς τοὺς δήμους καὶ τὰς φυλάς), while the decree on the Samians only mentions the ten tribes (καὶ νε͂μαι [αὐτὸς αὐτίκα μάλα τὸς ἄρχοντας ἐς τὰ]ς φυλὰς δέκαχα), which assumes distribution into demes, but not phratries. Some scholars have thought that this omission is not meaningful, but upon a more thorough consideration, it needs to be. City groups like the Plataians or the Samians were not invited to join Athenian phratries because of respect for their own traditional religious and civic institutions, rather than the intention to discriminate against them. The Samians as Ionians had their own phratries, festivals and religious rituals attached to them, and the stated intention of the naturalization decree was to allow them a substantial degree of autonomy (πολιτευομένος ὅπως ἂν αὐτοὶ βόλωνται . . . τοῖς δὲ νόμοις χρῆσθαι τοῖς σφετέροις αὐτῶν αὐτονόμος ὄντας). The decree on the Plataians is only partially quoted by Apollodoros, and for all we know it could have contained a similar clause. We know for sure that 30 or 40 years after the introduction of the decree the Plataians living in Athens were making a conscious effort to keep their separate city identity and gathered in a place called the "Fresh Cheese" on the first day of each month.[109] The Plataians shared with other Boeotians their own traditional religious associations and rituals, and these they undoubtedly wanted to keep in their new city. It is to the credit of the Athenian state that with tact and respect for religion and tradition it did not impose upon the new citizens at their hour of need its own sociocultural imprint, but allowed them to retain their own identity, while welcoming them into the citizen body. It seems that the founders of democracy understood that inclusiveness and diversity are essential features of this constitutional form.

2.6 Slaves

Athenian law for the most part treated slaves as objects belonging to a certain owner. The owner had the right to do as he/she pleased with them. A slave could be beaten with cruelty, raped, mistreated, or worked to exhaustion by his/her master with no consequences.[110] However, as with most things in the Athenian

Democracy, the picture is more complex once we look closer. The law afforded one basic protection to all slaves: if mistreated by their master they could sit as suppliants at the Theseion and request to be sold to another master. An ancient law prohibited the punishment of runaway slaves who had taken refuge at the Theseion, and a fragment from a play of Aristophanes suggests that they could stay there indefinitely, until a new buyer was found. [111] However, such cases were undoubtedly acts of extreme desperation: terrorized slaves would not often publicly rebel against cruel masters with the vague hope that a kinder person would be waiting to buy them at an inflated price, which surely the cruel master would demand before releasing the unruly slave.

A slave could not be killed with impunity, no doubt because, beyond financial implications, such an act endangered the community with supernatural pollution (*miasma*). Someone who had killed a slave could be prosecuted for homicide and tried at the Palladion court. [112] However, since the person legally entitled to initiate homicide proceedings was the slave's master, the killing of a slave by his own master would probably go unpunished.[113] Additional protection from abusive behavior was afforded to slaves through the law on *hybris*, at least in theory. In practice, since a *hybris* prosecution was a *graphe* carrying the substantial risk of 1000 drachmas for the prosecutor who had failed to secure 1/5th of the votes, it would require of a citizen to risk such a large fine in order to avenge a lowly slave. Moreover, the law on *hybris* had not been written with slaves in mind. Its purpose was to safeguard the rules of civilized society by asking all persons to treat with respect everyone else, regardless of who he or she was. Failure to do so was punishable not because the state cared about the honor and self-respect of slaves, but because it cared very much about the conduct of its citizens. It was the citizen's *hybris*tic behavior towards anyone *at all*, that concerned the lawgiver, not its impact on the slave. In any case, the argument is theoretical, since the possibility of a citizen bringing a *graphe hybreos* against another citizen on behalf of a slave seems remote at best, and never happened, as far as we can tell.

Beyond this, any other legal protection afforded to a slave would be the direct result of his/her monetary value. A vivid account of this theme is presented in the second mime of Herodas *The Pimp*. A brothel keeper is taking a client to court because the latter assaulted one of the girls in an incident fueled by alcohol. What the brothel keeper finds objectionable is not the assault, but the fact that it happened without his permission and that the client did not want to pay for the damage he caused on the girl. The entire logic of the argument is summed up by the pimp in the sentence "if something (sic!) inside the house inflames your passion, put the price in the hands of poor little Battaros, and then break your own things as it pleases you."[114] What afforded the sex-slaves of the ancient world some protection against beatings and physical punishment was rather the fact that cuts and bruises do not look attractive, and therefore reduce the value of a sex-slave, than any firm legal protections. The same applied in other walks of life. An abused, malnourished and sick slave would be unproductive, and this is why in the *Economics* of Xenophon Ischomachos is advising his wife that it is her duty to look after sick slaves, unpalatable as the task might be.[115] With such considerations in mind we can understand why the law did not allow anyone else to strike, punish or mistreat in any way someone else's slave without the master's explicit permission, and this included law enforcement.[116] In the event that someone's slave was tortured in order to give evidence for a court-case, with the master's permission, compensation needed to be paid for any harm coming to the slave as a result of this procedure.

The torture of slaves for evidence in a court case has been widely discussed, presumably because modern scholars seem shocked by this practice within the enlightened legal system of democratic Athens. However, the whole issue is a red herring: we are being deceived by treacherous rhetoric. An Athenian litigant who claimed that a slave belonging to his opponent had vital information for his case could request from his opponent to hand over the slave, to be tortured until his tormentor was convinced that the slave was telling the truth. Understandably the slave under torture would tell exactly what his tormentor wanted to hear, and the master of the slave was well aware of it. Therefore, it is not surprising that such requests were invariably refused. The real issue in this case is why such challenges were even made when everyone, including both litigants and the judges, knew that they will be refused because ultimately torture is an unreliable questioning tactic. What did the litigant stand to gain from such obviously futile methods? To this there can only be one short answer: these challenges were made out of desperation. When a litigant had absolutely no evidence in support of his claims, a diversionary tactic like this one might generate sufficient confusion to introduce at least an element of doubt and provide some explanation, however weak and insufficient, for the lack of evidence. At least in this manner a litigant could be claiming that there was substantial evidence, but his opponent was blocking access to it because he had something to hide. It is hard to imagine that Athenian juries put much faith into such tricks, but their frequency suggests that at least sometimes, in the right combination with other litigation tools, they could be helpful.[117]

Slavery in the ancient Greek world was not related to race or skin color, as in the colonial era. Although from time to time slave names like Xanthins (blondie), Pyrrhias (red-head) or Thratta (woman from Thrace) betray someone's complexion and ethnic origin, it was not these features that made them slaves. There were plenty of blonde and red-haired men and women among the citizen populations of Athens and the other Greek cities, while there was nothing inherently slavish in any geographic origin either. Despite some far-fetched attempts by philosophers like Aristotle or Plato to provide a rational, intellectually coherent explanation of slavery,[118] most people understood that it was circumstances that made someone a slave, and if these changed, someone could regain his/her freedom, and perhaps even his/her former position in society. Enslavement was a hazard of life in the ancient world, seen not as an inherent status, but as an unfortunate reversal of fate and circumstance.

Athenian audiences were moved by the fate of Hecuba, who had fallen from royalty to slavery in the course of a single day and accepted that such reversals of fortune could be part of the human existence. Many of the slaves who manned

Athenian businesses and households were the descendants of domestic slaves (οἰκογενής) who already belonged to the master, while others had been bought from slave traders or other owners (ἀργυρώνητος).[119] The more distant regions of the Mediterranean and the Black Sea, as well as the hinterlands of Scythia and Africa, were exposed to raids by slave traders, while in times when piracy was experiencing a surge people at sea were vulnerable to capture. War also fed the slave markets with captured enemy soldiers, but more importantly with the non-combatant populations of defeated cities, especially women and children. Classical literature abounds with stories, true or fictional, of the populations of entire cities being sold to slavery, or free persons, including some of the most famous personalities of the ancient world, captured by pirates and sold to slavery. Some were lucky enough to have a family with the financial capacity to buy back their freedom, but for many this dire reversal of fate became a permanent condition for themselves and their descendants.[120]

With such dangers lurking in every corner it is not surprising that Athenian law treated the attempt to enslave a free person with immediate and extraordinary severity. A slave merchant (ἀνδραποδιστής) caught trying to enslave a free person was subject to *apagoge*. He could be immediately arrested and taken to the Eleven and if he confessed he was immediately executed. If he did not confess but disputed the charges, the case would go to a trial, and the death penalty was invariably imposed upon convicted defendants.[121]

While Athenian law treated all slaves flatly, for the most part as property items belonging to a certain master, in real life there was substantial variation in the circumstances of slaves throughout Attica. First of all, some of the slaves were owned by the state itself (δημόσιοι). These included the Scythian archers, who assisted the Eleven in their duties as the police force of Athens. Not only did they mostly come from foreign lands but they also dressed in Scythian outfits throughout the classical period. We can see good reasons behind this practice: first, they often performed undignified duties such as arresting criminals or hailing convicted prisoners to their death. Second, they could be standing guard and keeping order in a city where all persons were at least in theory equal, and no one had an inherent right to give orders to the other. These tasks were well suited to a security force of outsiders, and the outlandish outfits of the Scythian archers functioned as an easily recognizable uniform of that un-Greek police force.[122]

Other public slaves performed the less glamorous tasks of the civil service, such as building and archive maintenance, and assisted the magistrates of the Athenian state in their daily duties.[123] Although these slaves were as vulnerable as privately owned ones to abuse and torture, the fact that they belonged to the state and could only be tortured with explicit permission of the magistrate in charge offered them some safety from the constant abuse to which privately owned slaves were subject at their owners' whims.[124] Another major difference was created by the fact that for the majority of public slaves who assisted Athenian magistrates when regular business hours ended, and the supervising officers went home, these slaves could live their lives with some privacy and peace. They lived independently, probably in accommodations near their workplace, and although their lives would be marked by poverty and reduced aspirations, their lot in life was much better than that of private slaves who never got a rest under the watchful eye of their master.

Other slaves living with relative independence included craftsmen who worked independently and offered part of their income to their master (χωρὶς οἰκοῦντες). There are several attested cases like this in the literature of the 4th century. Aechines mentions that the father of Timarchos owned a number of slaves who lived and worked independently. He enumerates nine or ten shoemakers, each of whom made a payment of two obols a day to his master (ἀποφορά), while the manager of the workshop paid three obols, a woman weaver, who took her fabrics to the market-place to sell them, and a painter. The speech of Hypereides *Against Athenogenes* offers important evidence on a family of slaves that managed and worked for their master a perfume factory, which they had run into serious debt. We hear of slave families that lived independently in farms which they worked for the master, and periodically had to pay him the *apophora*, while in Andocides a man named Diokles, the one responsible for mass denunciations during the scandal of 415, says that he set out early in the morning to go to Laureion in order to collect the *apophora* from one of his slaves there.[125] For all intents and purposes such slaves were similar to serfs or the Spartan helots, who also lived independently in the lands of their Spartan master, and worked under the obligation to bring him every year a fixed amount of produce.[126]

The plays of classical drama, the speeches of the Attic orators, as well as almost every source, literary, epigraphical, or artistic, offer ample testimony on the lives and contributions of the countless slaves that manned Athenian households, farms, workshops, brothels, or warehouses, as workers or servants tending to every need of their masters, including some intimate and unpleasant tasks like holding a pot for the master to urinate, or holding his head while vomiting.[127] Slaves typically performed most of the household's duties, like cooking, cleaning and maintenance of the household. They would also work in the fields for their master, and in busy times for agricultural tasks slaves were available for hire, in order to meet the need for extra hands.[128] Slaves also ran the industrial production of Athens. A very clear example of the extent to which slave labor ran those businesses is provided by Demosthenes, when he is enlisting the factories owned by his father Demosthenes senior, the number of slaves working in these factories, their monetary value, as well as the annual income which they yielded for their master.[129]

Some particularly dirty or undignified jobs, like being a wet-nurse or a fuller, were considered to be fit for slaves, and therefore unsuitable for free persons. The Plataian Pankleon found himself in the precarious position of having to defend his citizen status, because he was doing the humble job of a fuller, and Euxitheos had to defend his citizenship when it was questioned by Euboulides on the grounds that his mother had been a wet-nurse, which was not a job suitable for citizen women.[130] Working in a mill was seen as a particularly onerous task only fit for slaves. A man named Menon who had a free boy from Pellene working in his mill was sentenced to death, no doubt under accusations of *andrapodismos*. Being thrown into a mill to work was seen as a dire fate and masters threatened uncooperative slaves with labor in a mill.[131] One of the hardest and most dangerous tasks performed by slaves was the work in the mines. Especially when the hard labor was imposed as a punishment with no regard for the lives and well-being of the enslaved the conditions could be atrocious, and eventually lethal for most, as it was the case in the stone quarries of Syracuse for the defeated and captured Athenian armies.[132]

Slave labor was ubiquitous in classical Athens and a proper discussion of the economic, social and cultural implications of it far exceeds the purposes of this study.[133] The legal framework which allowed slavery to exist is not even mentioned in any source, because it was taken as a self-evident fact of life that did not need specific legislation to establish it. The relevant laws as we have them only regulate certain aspects of slavery, such as the prohibition of enslaving a free person under normal circumstances. This legislation obviously did not apply to enemy populations in war times, or to cases where slavery was imposed as a penalty for certain offenses. Athens did not allow the enslavement of free persons for debts since the time of Solon, but it allowed enslavement as a penalty for certain offences, mostly transgressions of the citizenship and immigration laws of the city.[134] The law also attempted to set a barrier to extreme abuses and killings of slaves, but it did not go far enough because of its reluctance to confront or limit the fundamental right of a master to do as he pleased with the slaves he owned. Thus, the countless slaves who run the capitalist economy of ancient Athens, spent their lives working very hard, with no rights or protections, at the complete mercy of a master who sometimes might be humane, but then again he could be fiercely cruel. Slaves could only escape this fate, if by a fortunate set of circumstances someone was willing to pay for their freedom, or if they succeeded in persuading a master to set them free or at least agree to a manumission contract, which could still come with harsh terms for the former slave (παραμονή), but at least gave him/her a chance to start again as a free man or woman.

2.7 Legal procedures for status disputes

The coveted privileges of citizenship were "a precious gift to be sought after with much trouble and expense" for those who were not born into it, in the words of Apollodoros.[135] This is why a law which was certainly in force in the 5th century and perhaps even before that, punished with enslavement a non-citizen who pretended to be a citizen. Someone suspected of being an alien but claiming to be a citizen could be prosecuted with a *graphe xenias*, and if convicted he would be sold into slavery. A convicted person who claimed that he lost the case because of someone's false testimony would need to stay in prison until the *dike pseudomartyrion* went to court. Exceptionally in this case the law did not allow the convicted person to provide sureties and remain free until the *pseudomartyrion* trial, because he was considered a flight risk (S 7). If he prevailed in the trial for false witnesses, the initial verdict was canceled. The *graphe xenias* primarily had in mind adult men who had already registered as citizens, and even though the law did not explicitly limit it to men, all attested *xenias* cases were brought against men.[136]

Among the fragments of Deinarchos we find an interesting case, which according to Dionysios Halicarnassus was an *eisangelia xenias* brought against a man named Agasikles. Harpocration agrees that the case was an *eisangelia*, but he does not mention *xenia* anywhere; instead, on several occasions he simply gives the title as "Against Agasikles." The combined testimony of Harpocration and Suda seems to suggest that the father of Agasikles was Scythian (perhaps a Scythian archer), and he worked in the marketplace making sure that the measures of grain sold were correct (προμετρητής), and that his son was assisting with the task when he was a boy.[137] Therefore, he should be a metic and not a citizen. The case is puzzling on several levels, as the meager evidence we have raises difficult questions. First, we have conflicting testimonies about the προμετρηταί. Harpocration, citing Deinarchos, mentions this case, and Suda adds that the *prometretai* were paid employees, which could mean that Skythes, the father of Agasikles, was a metic.[138] However, an entry in the *Lexica Segueriana* states that the *prometretai* were annual magistrates, and therefore citizens, and this sounds quite plausible, because the important task of ensuring that merchants in the market place were not cheating their customers in the sale of grain sounds like the job of state enforcers, rather than hired salespersons.[139] Although the testimony of the *Lexica Segueriana* seems more reliable, it is impossible to reconcile it with Harpocration's citation form the speech of Deinarchos. Was Skythes[140] a metic hired for the job, or a citizen performing his duty as a magistrate?

Then the legal procedure itself is equally puzzling, since there is no mention of an *eisangelia xenias* anywhere else. While it appears that Agasikles was accused of fraudulently usurping the rights of a citizen, if the case was indeed an *eisangelia*, the accusations of xenia probably were not the main thrust of the prosecution, but rather a circumstantial accusation in the margins, which Dionysios erroneously perceived to be the main accusation. This could explain why he thought that this was an *eisangelia xenias*, while the more careful Harpocration simply mentions that this was an *eisangelia* brought against Agasikles. If this explanation is correct, then the *eisangelia xenias* did not really exist, and this would be consonant with what we know about *xenias* cases. They always seem to be *graphai*, and the law explicitly stated that, like all other violations of citizenship and immigration status, they could only be introduced by an Athenian citizen (Ἀθηναίων ὁ βουλόμενος, rather than the standard ὁ βουλόμενος for regular public lawsuits). The evidence we have on this mysterious and intriguing case is too scanty and conflicting to reach any safe conclusions, but on balance it seems that cases of *xenia* could only be prosecuted through a *graphe*.

Unusually in Athenian legal procedure, cases involving *xenia* could be reopened if the prosecutor suspected that the defendant had been acquitted through bribery (like, for example, by buying off one or two crucial witnesses). This second trial could be initiated through a *graphe doroxenias*, and it seems that this is what happened to the *hetaira* Aristagora, who had been accused of failing to register as a metic (ἀπροστασίου). Although these cases were public and we should only have one speech against Aristagora, we have two, and some information about a *doroxenias* prosecution. It appears that the second speech *Against Aristagora* comes from the *doroxenias* trial, but later grammarians and rhetoricians were confused because of the similarity of subject between the two speeches and considered them to be two speeches delivered in the same trial, without thinking of the legal formalities.[141] A fragment from the speech cited by Harpocration renders strong support to this interpretation of the case:

> Ὑπερείδης ἐν τῷ κατ' Ἀρισταγόρας οὕτω γράφων· "ἐπεὶ καὶ ὁ τῆς δωροξενίας νόμος ἁρμόττων ἐστὶ τῷ νῦν ἀγῶνι παραχθῆναι· εἰ γὰρ καὶ τοὺς ἀποφυγόντας ξενίας εἴρηκεν ἐξεῖναι τῷ βουλομένῳ πάλιν γράψασθαι, ἐὰν μὴ δοκῶσι δικαίως τὸ πρῶτον ἀποπεφευγέναι, πῶς οὐ φανερόν ἐστι κατ' Ἀρισταγόρας τὸ δίκαιον?"[142]
>
> Hyperides in the speech *Against Aristagora* writes this: "because we can reach the conclusion that the law on *doroxenia* is appropriate for this case; if he says that is it permissible for anyone who wishes to bring a *graphe* against those who have been acquitted of *xenia*, if they appear to have been unjustly acquitted in the first trial, how is it not clear that justice is against Aristagora?"

Hypereides may have had to deal with a substantial procedural matter. The law which he is paraphrasing in the passage cited by Harpocration clearly mentioned that the *doroxenia* procedure applied to the *graphe xenias*, but did not mention any of the other procedures against illegal aliens, like the *graphe aprostasiou* or *apostasiou*. Hypereides quite possibly needed to convince the jury that all these procedures should also come under the *doroxenia* provisions, since they could be dealing with aliens who broke the law by misrepresenting their status and were improperly acquitted through bribery. His argument is that Aristagora certainly has done so, and this is why the *doroxenia* law should apply to her case. It appears that Aristagora was acquitted in the first trial. Hypereides renewed the attack with a *doroxenias* case, and most of the interesting and distasteful quotations to all things meretricious from the cases against Aristagora come from the second speech. If they are an indication, it appears that after the loss in the first trial, the determined prosecutor of Aristatora, possibly Hypereides himself, decided to drive her through the mud by speaking extensively about her career as a *hetaira*, even though this probably was of little relevance to the immigration case.[143]

In the early 4th century, probably in the 380s, another law was introduced, which seems to be primarily aimed at women. It prohibited the usurpation of citizenship rights for one's self and one's descendants either through marriage or pretense of marriage or any other device (τέχνῃ ἢ μηχανῇ ἡτινιοῦν) that the devious couple might try in order to legitimize their brood and pass them off as citizens. The law explicitly included alien men, too, but in practice it would be much more difficult for an alien man to fake marriage with a citizen woman, than an alien woman to fake marriage with a citizen man. This is why it seems that this law had alien woman rather than men in mind, and perhaps more specifically attractive alien *hetairai* capable of seducing Athenian men and inducing them to break the law for their sake. Violators could be prosecuted with a *graphe*, which followed the same guidelines as cases of *xenia*, and if convicted the alien partner would be sold into slavery and his/her property would be confiscated, while the citizen partner of the alien woman would be disfranchised.[144] An additional clause in the same law punished with disfranchisement any citizen who knowingly deceived another citizen and betrothed to him an alien woman under the pretense that she was a citizen and a relative of his, whom he had the legal right to betroth with *engye*.[145]

A strange incident in 346 sent ripples of anxiety through Athenian public life. A decree proposed by Demophilos required all demes of Attica to carry a scrutiny of all their members to ensure that they had been correctly inscribed in the registrers (διαψήφισις).[146] Those found to be fraudulently inscribed would be voted off (ἀποψήφισις) and could no longer be citizens. Persons rejected by the deme could accept the outcome and register as metics, which in reality meant that they would lose all real estate they owned and also the right to inherit their father. They would also need to dissolve their marriages to Athenian women, and their descendants, existing or future, would be downgraded to the status of metic too. Alternatively, they could appeal the decision of the deme to the courts. However, if they lost that appeal they would be sold into slavery. The stakes were high and the nervousness generated by this process is faithfully reflected in contemporary texts. Even persons who had been registered as citizens for many years had reasons to be worried, because as several texts suggest old animosities, local politics in the demes and even property bids by greedy relatives who were eyeing someone's inheritance could surface and play a major part in these proceedings.

Two extant speeches both delivered by citizens rejected during the *diapsepisis*, offer important testimony not only about the process but also the petty politics and unethical games behind these proceedings. Isaios 12 *In Defense of Euphiletos* has been delivered on behalf of a man who had been rejected during the process, it seems on account of personal animosities against his family and some rumors that he had been surreptitiously adopted as a child. A united family appears in court to quash such accusations, and the weighty testimony of the half-brother of Euphiletos in his defense should convince even the most skeptical juror, since the half-brother stood to gain the most if Euphiletos ceased to be a citizen, as he would inherit all the family property. This case shows that no one was really safe in this process, if even people who were members of large Athenian families willing to verify their citizenship status with many witnesses among close relatives could still be rejected.

Equally strong seems to be the claim to citizenship of a man called Euxitheos, who was rejected by the deme of Halimous, because allegedly his father Thoukritos was an alien, even though he was undoubtedly a citizen and had served in many offices, passing numerous *dokimasiai* and *euthynai* over the years. In this case it appears that the hostility of the demarch[147] of Halimous over local politics was the driving force behind his rejection. The rogue demarch ran the vote on Euxitheos late in the evening, when it was already dark and many of the demesmen had already left, while his supporters had stayed put to vote against Euxitheos. The evidence which Euxitheos presents in defense of his citizenship is very strong, and this suggests that he may be right when he cites local politics as the real reason behind his rejection.

Another case is mentioned by Aeschines in the speech *Against Timarchos*, which was delivered shortly after *the diapsephiseis*, and retains that raw feeling of anxiety in Athens about the process. A man named Philodades was rejected by his deme of Kydathenaion, after accusations brought by Timarchos, who at the time was an influential political figure. Timarchos maintained that Philotades was a libertine, who once belonged to him, and even appeared in court during the appeal of the case and gave evidence under oath to that effect. However, during the trial it was revealed that he had received a bribe of 20 minae from Leukonides, the brother in law of Philotades, through a third party, an actor named Philemon. If the plot succeeded and Philotades lost his citizenship and right to inherit, all the property of the family would be inherited by his sister, the wife of Leukonides, and this was the motive behind this treacherous plot. Both, Philemon and Leukonides were summoned as witnesses during the trial of Timarchos.[148]

The true motives behind the *diapsephisis* decree introduced by Demophilos are unclear. *Diapsephisis* as a vote to decide someone's claim to citizenship was the routine procedure in the demes when a new person was introduced at his 18th year of age and it was also standard practice in some phratries and gene.[149] However, a general *diapsephisis* in all the demes for the entire citizen body as it happened in 346 is unprecedented, and as far as we know, never repeated.[150] What makes the motives behind this process even more mysterious is the fact that it took place in a time of turmoil for the city, when the Athenians were divided over the right course of action towards Philip II, and in the final decade of true independence for the Athenian state. While one would think that in such critical times the citizens of Athens should be pulling together, it seems that they were doing the exact opposite: they were debilitating themselves through the spreading of fear, anxiety and discord. Perhaps this is the correct reading of this strange incident: it was a sign of the times in a deepening crisis when Athenian society was tearing itself apart through fear, suspicion, accusations and divisive politics, in the face the most serious threat to its independence in the city's history.[151]

When someone's freedom was disputed, and not simply his/her citizen status, two different and to some extent overlapping procedures could be followed. The first would be applicable to all metics in Athens, and simply required to check the register to verify whether someone had been properly registered with a *prostates*, and the payments of the metic tax (*metoikion*) were up-to-date. This apparently happened in the case of a metic woman, possibly a sex worker, named Zobia. When a former lover, whom she was pestering for money, seized and took her to the auction house for delinquent metics with the intent to have her sold as a slave, the fact that her payment of the metoikion was up to date secured her freedom. A check with a register verified that the woman was free and dutiful to her obligations as a metic.[152]

However, sometimes things could be more complicated, especially when the person alleged to be a slave had been seized and taken to the house of the alleged master, as a recaptured runaway slave would have been taken. Before the status of this person could be verified, first they would need to be rescued from the clutches of the alleged master. This is what happened to Neaira upon her return to Athens. Neaira had been set free when Phrynion, a former lover, was willing to buy her freedom from her masters. The act of her manumission had been witnessed by one Athenian man, a friend of Phrynion, and probably more witnesses on behalf of her Corinthian masters. Then she returned with him to Athens as his lover. Phrynion probably was an abusive man and mistreated her, so she ran away from him and stayed in Megara, working as a free *hetaira*, for a couple of years. Then she met Stephanos, the man who was going to become her life-long partner and followed him in Athens. Upon her arrival, Phrynion found out, went to the house of Stephanos with a gang of strong young men and seized her, claiming that she was a runaway slave of his. Before any decision could be made on her status as a free person, first she needed to be rescued from Phrynion. This procedure was called "extraction to freedom" (ἀφαίρεσις εἰς ἐλευθερίαν) and required the appointment of sureties, who would guarantee that she was not going to flee, and that she would appear in a trial that would determine her status. This particular case never went to trial because the two sides reached an agreement through private arbitration, which guaranteed Neaira's freedom.[153]

We can easily understand why a simple check with the register of the metics would not have been the right way to deal with a case like this. In order for this simpler avenue to be followed one would need to be a registered metic. However, if someone's status came into question before registration, because, for example, he/she had only been in Athens for a short period of time, as Neaira had been after her return, or because he/she was simply visiting and never intended to stay long enough to register as a metic, or in the case of women, because she was the concubine or blood relative of an Athenian citizen and a member of his *oikos*, and therefore not required to register as an independent metic (which also applied to Neaira's case), his/her name would not be inscribed on the register of metics proving his/her free status.

We do not know of any case of ἀφαίρεσις εἰς ἐλευθερίαν that ever reached the courts,[154] but we should not be surprised if lowly libertines could not afford the services of the expensive logographers whose works have reached us. However, there may be one additional dimension to the whole concept of *aphairesis* as it was actually practiced in Athenina litigation: in most cases it appears that the *aphairesis* was part of the legal maneuvering intended to force someone to the negotiating table. This seems to be the case with the *aphairesis* of Neaira or the libertine Pittalakos in Aeschines. Both cases ended up in arbitration and subsequent resolution away from the court system. A case mentioned by Isocrates also confirms this understanding of *aphairesis*: Pasion the banker removed to freedom a slave named Kittos who, according to his opponent, had knowledge of a large transaction which Pasion was denying. The reason was because he was unwilling to hand over the slave to be tortured by his opponent. Later, he changed his tactics and abandoned the *aphairesis* proceedings. Several other references in the speech *Against Pankleon* also confirm that *aphairesis* often was part of the legal maneuvering, and its true objective was to force the other side to the negotiating table, and ideally to a compromise deal.

Athenian law had established some rigorous processes in order to secure the rights of citizens, but also adequate legal protection among the large numbers of free non-citizens who lived in Attica. The metic population of the city was seen as a valuable resource of creative, hard-working, respectable families and individuals, who contributed to the welfare of the city, it's vigorous economy, it's defense and the life of the community. Especially in trying times like the years of the Peloponnesian war, Athenian and metic families suffered side-by-side, fought side-by-side, and in the end they joined forces on the Fortress of Phyle in a quest for freedom from Spartan-imposed tyranny. Two opposing forces seem to be at work in the Athenian state. On the one hand the strong sense of a separate identity of the Greek *polis* demanded a clear definition and privileged status for the citizen of the *polis*, but on the other hand the democratic sense of inclusivity in a diverse society opened up the city to outsiders willing to take advantage of opportunities and contributed to the well-being of the community, by inviting people from very different walks of life to come together, work for the common good and prosper. The legislation on citizenship and immigration in classical Athens seems to be a continuous balancing act between these two forces, enabling the citizens to be proud and privileged members of the city, but at the same time keeping the city open and welcoming to anyone who wanted to join it and contribute to its progress and well-being.

Notes

1 Trsl. H. Rackham.
2 Trsl. F.G. Kenyon.
3 Trls. F.G. Kenyon.
4 Trsl. A.T. Murray.
5 This is the case in Athens, about which we are better informed. It is quite possible that other Greek cities were more generous with naturalization awards and had more relaxed citizenship requirements, but we know almost nothing about the naturalization practices of most Greek city-states.
6 However, it must be noted that this generosity in Thespiai was tied to specific circumstances. 700 Thespians voluntarily stayed with the Spartans at Thermopylai and given the small size of the city, this loss was catastrophic.
7 The bibliography on the meaning and connotations of citizenship in the context of the ancient Greek *polis* is extensive. See the classic study of Claude Mossé (1993); Block 2017 (focusing on Athenian citizenship), and 2005: 7–40; Farenga 2006; Hansen 2006; Migeotte 2002: 13–26; Vatin 1984; Whitehead 1991: 135–54.
8 Detienne 2001: 53. See also Morales 2004: 273–9; Carnes 1990: 41–4.
9 Suda φ 216.
10 Hdt. 1.171–172 , 4.109, 4.197, 8.73.
11 See Hdt. 1.171–2, 4.109, 4.197, 8.73; Th. 6.2.2.
12 See also Pelling 2008: 471–83.
13 E. Ion 29–30, 589–590, 737, Fr. 360 Nauck 7–10; Arist. *Rh.* 1360 b 30–2.
14 See also Lys. 2. 43: γνησίαν δὲ καὶ αὐτόχθονα.
15 Ar. *V.* 1076, *Lys.* 1082.
16 Pl. *Mx.* 237 b, *Soph.* 247 c; see also Lys. 2. 43.
17 D. 59.74; Lyc. 1.41; See also Leão 2012: 135–52 for a discussion of autochthony and citizenship from a legal point of view in relation to the right of metics to own land in Attica (ἔγκτησις).

18 See Blok 2009: 251–75; Lape 2010.
19 See Calame 2011: 1–19; Nimis 2007: 397–420; Saxonhouse 1986: 252–73; Scodel 2006: 65–78; Shapiro 2006: 65–78; Westra 2006: 273–9.
20 Tyrtaeus Fr. 2 and 19; Ephorus *FGrH* 10 F 15; Herodian *De Prosodia* 241.26.
21 For the political implications of the myth in the classical period see Luraghi 2014: 133–51.
22 See the discussion in Chapter 3.3, and also Gagarin 1998: 31–51.
23 Diamant 1982: 38–47; Anderson 2000: 387–412; Frost 1990: 3–9.
24 The most important work on the demes is the classic study of D. Whitehead (1986); see also Traill 1986.
25 The names of the tribes were: Erechtheis (Ἐρεχθηΐς); Aigeis (Αἰγηΐς); Pandionis (Πανδιονίς); Leontis (Λεοντίς); Acamantis (Ἀκαμαντίς); Oineis (Οἰνηΐς); Kekropis (Κεκροπίς); Hippothontis (Ἱπποθοντίς); Aiantis (Αἰαντίς); Antiochis (Ἀντιοχίς).
26 Important books on Sparta include MacDowell 1986; Cartledge 2013 (on the various layers of Spartan society see pp. 52–170), and 1987; Hodkinson and Powell 2009 and 1997; Whitby 2013.
27 The five villages of Sparta were Limnai, Pitana, Mesoa, Kynosoura and Amyclae, which was 5 km away from the cluster of the other four.
28 On the Boeotian confederacy see Bruce 1968: 190–9; Buckler 2000: 431–46; Larsen 1955: 40–50; Pascual González 2006: 22–45.
29 See Pretzler 2009: 86–109; Roy 2000: 308–26; Arnaoutoglou 2009: 181–201; Hasegawa 1994: 79–89; Larsen 1971: 8186 – .
30 This happened for example with the two sons of Mantias from Plangon in D. 39 and 40, whose father recognized them as adults, and subsequently they were registered as citizens.
31 The relevant evidence is discussed by Richard Hamilton (1984: 243–51); see also Selfert 2011.
32 D. 59.60.
33 Is. 7.16, where the members of a phratry are following a procedure of διαψήφισις mirroring the admission processes to the deme, for the admission of new members, 3.76, 8.19; on phratries and their subgroups see Lambert 1998; Jones 1999; Cromey 2006: 41–69; Nilsson 1986; Flower 1985: 232–5; Ustinova 1996: 227–42; Hedrick 1991: 241–68. See also the discussion on the Apatouria in Chapter 8.3.
34 D. 49–63; see also Kapparis 266–95.
35 And. 1.124–9; see also MacDowell's com. ad loc.
36 Is. 6.19–24.
37 D. 39 and 40.
38 Is. 12 and D. 57 offer great examples of such gossip, and how destructive it could become, but in both cases the citizenship of Euphiletos and Euxitheos respectively was only questioned under the unusual circumstances of the *diapsephisis* generated by the decree of Demophilos in 346, which provided an opportunity to their enemies. Both men had been admitted to the phratry and the deme before the *diapsephisis*. We do not know the outcome of these cases, but both seem to be clear cases of citizen men unjustly attacked by their enemies, and both were confident that they could win, because they were risking enslavement as a penalty if they lost.
39 On the reforms of Kleisthenes see Hamilton 1993: 69–93; Thompson 1971: 72–9; Anderson 2003; Andrewes 1977: 241–8; Eliot 1963; Kienast 2005: 69–100; Martin 1974: 5–42; Stanton 1994: 161–207.
40 See Anderson 2003.
41 It appears that phratry membership was not extended to mass naturalizations, like those of the Plataians or the Samians in the years of the Peloponnesian war, and there was probably a good reason for that. These groups had their own religious associations, and the Samians as Ionians would have their own phratries. So, out of sensitivity and respect for the religious associations of these groups, and surely in order to

avoid imposing upon Athenian phratries to accept large numbers of new citizens, the provisions of the naturalization decrees that offered citizenship to those groups did not include the phratry. This position is not universally accepted; some scholars argue that the omission of the phratry in those decrees was not to be understood as exclusion from the phratry. However, when compared with individual naturalization decrees, where the phratry is explicitly mentioned, alongside of the deme and the tribe, the conclusion that membership of the phratry was not automatically extended to all new citizens in mass naturalizations, seems to be the most logical. See my previous discussion in Kapparis 1995: 361–74, and 1999: 397, with previous scholarship.

42 See Ogden 1996: 70–7; Carawan 2008: 383–406.

43 See the relevant discussion in Chapters 4.2. and 4.3.

44 See MacDowell 1976: 88–91 (reprinted in Arnaoutoglou et al. 2017: 261–4); Rhodes 1978: 89–92; Patterson 1990: 40–73.

45 Rhodes (1981: 509) understands that this provision concerned the son of an *epikleros*, who was supposed to take control of his maternal grandfather's property when he reached his eighteenth year, but the wording of the *Athenaion Politeia* at this point suggests the provision was broader and covered all affairs related to an *epikleros*, including laying claim to an *epikleros*. This provision would be essential in such cases, as the adjudication of an *epikleros* could have been completed by the time an ephebe finished his service, and it was legally imperative that he should be allowed to claim her, if he was the nearest relative.

46 Arist. *Ath. Pol.* 42.4–5; see also Rhodes 1981: 507–10. On the ideology of the ephebes see also Steinbock 2011: 279–317, and the study of Nigel Kennell (2006) for citizen training systems in the Hellenistic and Roman periods.

47 MacDowell 1978: 159–61.

48 D. 59.26–27.

49 See the discussion in Chapters 3.3 and 4.3.

50 D. 48.53–5; D. 59.

51 See the discussion in Chapter 4.4.

52 If, let's say, a man caught his male companion in bed with another man, he had no legal authority to punish the intruder or the unfaithful lover. Lysias 3 suggests that uncontrollable rage in such a case could land an aggressive lover in court with the very serious charge of deliberate wounding, which carried the penalty of permanent exile from Attica.

53 See the discussion in Chapter 3.

54 See also Purves 1997: 5–22.

55 See the discussion in Chapter 3.

56 See Chapters 6.4 and 1.4. Male prostitutes, parent abusers, persons who had wasted their patrimony, and persons convicted for military offenses, like desertion or cowardice were excluded from all offices. Members of the Boule needed to be at least 30 years old. Public arbitrators were all 59 years old. Naturalized citizens could not be appointed to hereditary priesthoods or participate in the sortation for the nine *archon*s. Disabled persons were also disqualified from the office of the nine *archon*s. Many offices had specific regulations for reasons related to the duties of these offices, and sometimes to tradition and religion. However, such regulations were never property-based. The objective was not to exclude poor, honest citizens from office, but to make sure that ineligible individuals could not stand for these offices. See also the discussion in Chapter 1. For Aristotle (S 1) voting and standing for office were the main qualifications of citizenship, but this is not universally applicable. The debate on what Athenian citizenship meant has been long: see Blok 2017; Boegehold and Scafuro 2002;

57 This is a much larger debate. The reader could benefit from a number of authoritative studies on the subject including but not limited to the following; Boegehold and Scafuro 2002; Cook 2012: 219–51; Develin 1973: 71–9; Farenga 2006; Scholz 2009:

171–92; Lape 2010; Whitehead 1991: 135–54; Lang 2004; Manuwald 2014: 225–43; Vester 2004; Ober 2009.

58 See the discussion in Chapter 2.5.

59 D. 53.13–14; Is. 6.20–1; Aesch. 1.43; D. 45.28 (where a *synoikia* is valued to 100 minae).

60 See the discussion in Chapter 9.5.

61 See che discussion in Chapter 2.5.

62 Kapparis 2017: 271–5.

63 See the discussion in Chapter 9.5.

64 See Kapparis 1998: 383–93.

65 See Chapter 9.5.

66 Kephalos is the host of the symposium in the backdrop of Plato's *Republic*. See also D. H. Lys. 1 Λυσίας ὁ Κεφάλου Συρακουσίων μὲν ἦν γονέων, ἐγεννήθη δὲ Ἀθήνησι μετοικοῦντι τῷ πατρὶ καὶ συνεπαιδεύθη τοῖς ἐπιφανεστάτοις Ἀθηναίων, and Plu. 835 C: Λυσίας υἱὸς ἦν Κεφάλου τοῦ Λυσανίου τοῦ Κεφάλου, Συρακουσίου μὲν γένος μεταναστάντος δ' εἰς Ἀθήνας ἐπιθυμίᾳ τε τῆς πόλεως καὶ Περικλέους τοῦ Ξανθίππου πείσαντος αὐτόν, φίλον ὄντα καὶ ξένον, πλούτῳ διαφέροντα·

67 The bibliography on the Athenian metic is extensive. The classic monograph of D. Whitehead (1977, with additions and refinements in 1986: 145–58) remains the most important study; see also Rubinstein 2018: 5–24; Kennedy 2014 for the metic woman; Akrigg 2015: 155–76; Bakewell 1999: 5–22; Meyer 2010; Nemeth 2001: 331–48.

68 For example, A. *Sept*. 546–548 (composed in 467): γοργὸν δ' ὄμμ' ἔχων, προσίσταται / Παρθενοπαῖος Ἀρκάς· ὁ δὲ τοιόσδ' ἀνὴρ / μέτοικος, Ἄργει δ' ἐκτίνων καλὰς τροφάς.

69 Sosin 2016: 2–13, in response to a Dimopoulou-Piliouni 2008: 27–50.

70 Is. 6.19–20.

71 Aesch. 1.64–78.

72 There is some evidence which seems to suggest that the demes kept registers of the metics living in their territory, but this evidence is not strong (see Rhodes 1981: 497 and MacDowell 1978: 77). This evidence consists of inscriptions which identify metics on the basis of the deme where they reside (e.g. *IG* I^3 476.fr XIII.col I.20: Τεῦκ/ρος ἐν Κυδαθεναίοι hοικο͂ν). However, this may simply be an easy way to identify someone, and by no means indicates a register kept by the deme. We can understand why demes kept registers of their citizen members, but there is no compelling reason why they should accept the responsibility of keeping registers for non-members. Since the registration of metics took place before the *polemarch* and not at the demes, it makes sense that he was the one keeping a central register and ensuring that all metics paid their taxes every year.

73 D. 25.57.

74 See Chapter 4.4.

75 D. 25.57, DL. 4.14; see also MacDowell 1978: 76–78; Rhodes 1981: 496–8; Todd 1993: 194–9.

76 Todd 1993: 194–9.

77 Phot. α 2640 <Ἀποστασίου> καὶ <ἀπροστασίου>· δικῶν εἰσιν ὀνόματα. ἀποστασίου μέν, ὅταν δοῦλος †ὑπ'† ἐλευθερίας ἐνίσταται, φάσκων μὴ προσήκειν τοῖς δουλοῦν αὐτὸν ἀντιποιουμένοις, οὗτος ἀποστασίου δίκην λαχεῖν λέγεται. ἀπροστασίου δέ, ὅτι τῶν μετοίκων ἕκαστος προστάτην †ἔχουσι† κατὰ νόμον ἕνα τῶν ἀστῶν, καὶ δι' αὐτοῦ τό τε μετοίκιον τίθεται κατὰ ἔτος καὶ τὰ ἄλλα διοικεῖται. ὅταν οὖν τις δοκῶν εἶναι μέτοικος προστάτην μὴ ἔχῃ ἢ μὴ δῷ τὸ μετοίκιον ἢ ἀστὸς εἶναι φάσκῃ παρεγγεγραμμένος εἰς τὴν πολιτείαν, ὁ βουλόμενος δίκην εἰσάγει πρὸς αὐτόν, ἥτις λέγεται ἀπροστασίου.

78 See also Chapter 5.

79 See for example D. 59: 64–7: Epainetos of Andros was not a citizen, or even a metic; it seems that he was a traveling merchant who frequently visited Athens for business

purposes, and it seems some pleasure too. When he was accused of adultery, falsely as he claimed, he submitted a countersuit intended to release him from his obligation to pay compensation to the *thesmothetai*, against a citizen man, the *kyrios* of the woman, with whom he allegedly had the affair.

80 See the discussion in Patterson 2000: 93–112; MacDowell 1978: 76–8; Rhodes 1981: 496–8; Todd 1993: 194–9.

81 Lysias takes pride in the fact that although his family had been living and running businesses in Athens for 30 years, they had never been involved in a lawsuit either as prosecutors or defendants. This he presents as extraordinary, and it probably was, if we contrast it, for example, with the astounding number of lawsuits in which Pasion and his successors in the bank routinely had to engage in order to defend their financial interests.

82 Isoc. 5.33: Πυθόδωρον γὰρ τὸν σκηνίτην καλούμενον, ὃς ὑπὲρ Πασίωνος ἅπαντα καὶ λέγει καὶ πράττει. Pythodoros the so called "tent-man," who does everything and speaks on everything on behalf of Pasion.

83 I am convinced that Pankleon was a Plataian, and therefore a citizen, but this does not alter the argument either way. Whether a citizen or a metic this poor man could not afford advocates acting or speaking on his behalf, and according to the narrative of Lys. 23, he had to take care of his legal affairs in person.

84 Metic families were explicitly covered by the adultery laws. See the discussion in Chapter 6.3.

85 It might be fair to say that metics in Athens were in a similar position as green card holders in the United States or the European Union in our times. While they have no right to vote or be voted into office and may have some additional restrictions and financial responsibilities according to immigration law, they have unfettered access to the justice system of the host country, without which residing there would have been perilous. The plight of undocumented immigrants in these communities, who are in a dangerously fragile position all the time, should underline for us the importance of open access to the legal system of the host country, without which living there should be a very unattractive option for any alien resident. Ancient Athens would not have been as attractive a destination as it was without necessary legal protections for its legal resident aliens.

86 Lys. 12. See the introduction and notes of Andrew Wolpert in Wolpert-Kapparis 2011: 29–51, and Wolpert's (2011) significant monograph on the memory of the Thirty in subsequent Athenian literature.

87 Antiphon 5, *On the Murder of Herodes*; on this unusual case see also Gagarin 1989; Erbse 1977: 209–27; Lattimore 1987: 502–4.

88 D. 59.9–10.

89 The Greek spirit as expressed through the mouth of Apollo in A. *Eum.* 182–97 abhorred mutilations, torment and castrations. Those who engaged in such inhumane acts were spat on by the gods (ἀπόπτυστοι θεοῖς).

90 See for example D. 24.23 or 43.10, as opposed to D. 59.16 Ἀθηναίων ὁ βουλόμενος οἷς ἔξεστιν, 21.47, 24.23 (revision of laws), or Lys. *In Defense of Pherenikos* (fr. 2 Carey), and Todd 1993: 196. The expression Ἀθηναίων ὁ βουλόμενος οἷς ἔξεστιν appears incorrectly several times in forged documents like for example D. 21.47, or Aesch. 1.32. Forgers repeatedly misunderstood the subtlety of the legal language.

91 See Lys. 12.8; Roismann and Worthington 2015: 121–2.

92 Aesch. 1.54–68. Aeschines calls him a public slave in an effort to present the man as even lower class than he actually was. However, there was no doubt that he was a free person, as Aeschines himself admits later on, when he mentions the removal of Pittalakos to freedom. Pittalakos was free, and probably sufficiently well off to set his eyes upon a citizen man with spectacular looks like Timarchos, if there is any truth in the account of Aeschines.

93 On Demokedes and other metics as public physicians see Chapter 9.6.
94 Kennedy 2014.
95 See the narrative of D. 59.18–40.
96 *Ateleia* meant exemption from taxes and liturgies; *sitesis* meant dining at the Prytaneion at the expense of the city (e.g. Ar. *Ra.* 764, And. 4.31, Pl. *Ap.* 37a). See Chapter 8.3. and 9.5. See also Rubinstein 2009.
97 For example, X. *HG* 2.4.25, *Vect.* 4.12; Harp. s.v. *IG* ii[2] 83, 109 fr. b. 20, 214.8. See also Maffi 1973: 939–64.
98 For example, *IG* ii[2] 83, 214.8; Arist. *Oec.* 1347 a 2. See also Pečirka 1966; Leão 2012: 135–52.
99 Apollodoros was a teenager when his father Pasion was granted Athenian citizenship for lavish contributions to the Athenian state, and was at that point naturalized along with his father. The precise date of this event is uncertain. See Deene 2011: 159–75, and also the excellent monograph of Jeremy Trevett (1991) for a wholesome image of Apollodoros as a family man, citizen, politician, businessman and author.
100 D. 59.88–93; see also Kapparis 1999: 360–70. The most authoritative study on naturalization in Athens is the four-volume account of Michael J. Osborne (1981–3).
101 For example, *IG* I[3] 102, 6–10: ἐπαινέσα]ι Θρασύβολον ὁς ὄντα ἄνδρα ἀγαθὸ[ν περὶ τὸν δε͂μ]ον τὸν Ἀθεναίον καὶ πρόθυμον π[οιε͂ν hó τι δύνα]ται ἀγαθόν· καὶ ἀντὶ ὁ͂ν εὖ πεπο[ίεκεν τέν τε πόλιν] καὶ τὸν δε͂μ[ο]ν τὸν Ἀθεναίο[ν.
102 See Osborne 1981, T1; Plu. *Sol.* 24; Arist. *Ath. Pol.* 13.5, *Pol.* 1275 b 36–7.
103 D. 59.104–106; see also my discussion of the decree in Kapparis 1995: 359–78. Mirco Canevaro (2010: 337–69) in a counter-argument maintains that the decree quoted by Apollodoros is a forgery. However, I have briefly voiced some objections to Canevaro's arguments in *Gnomon* 2015: 40–3, and siding with the majority of scholars I remain convinced that it is a partial quotation of the authentic decree.
104 *IG* II[2] 1 and 10.
105 One such decree would be an ostracism decree, where a citizen was sent to exile, not because he had done something wrong, but, on the contrary, because he was so distinguished that he posed a threat to democracy itself. Ostracisms were sometimes performed in the 5th century. The practice had lapsed in the 4th century.
106 6000 men was the maximum capacity of the Pnyx in the 5th century, so the quorum of 6000 meant that the Assembly area needed to be full. Clearly the purpose of this rule was to ensure that the enemies of a citizen could not just band together on a quiet day in the Assembly and pass a decree to harm him personally. This safety precaution made it very difficult to pass decrees on individuals without broad support.
107 D. 59.91; see also the discussion in Kapparis 1999: 370–1.
108 The nature and purpose of these restrictions is not dissimilar to the modern rule in the American Constitution that naturalized citizens cannot run for president of the United States, but their descendants can, since they will be citizens by birth. In practical terms this restriction is unimportant, since the possibility of a first-generation immigrant running for president would be totally negligible.
109 Lys. 23.6
110 Numerous references suggest that slaves had no way of fending off unwanted sexual advances by their masters (e.g. Lys. 1.12–13, where the sexual assault of the maid by the drunken Euphiletos is simply a matter of a joke, or Herodas 5, where the cruel treatment of the sex-slave Gastron by his mistress Bitynna is a disproportionate response to an alleged infidelity. See also Marshall 2013: 173–96.
111 Philochoros *FGrH* 328 F 177; Arist. Fr. 567; Sch. Aesch. 3.13; *EM* s.v. Θησεῖον.
112 See Chapter 8.5. for the discussion.
113 Plato's *Euthyphro* contains one such moral and legal dilemma, which provides the occasion for the dialogue. The father of Euthyphro was responsible for the death of a serf (πελάτης) attached to the farms of the family, but Euthyphro thinks that the

killing should not go unpunished and prosecutes his father for homicide. A discussion on what is holy and right will follow.

114 Herodas 2.81–3: εἴ σευ θ[ά]λπεταί τι τῶν ἔνδον,
ἔμβυσον εἰς τὴν χεῖρα Βατ̣ταρίωι τιμήν,
καὐτὸς τὰ σαυτοῦ θλῆ λαβὼν ὄκως χρήιζεις.

115 X. *Oec*. 7.37–8.

116 By contrast, in Sparta the helots assigned to a Spartan could be punished by other Spartan citizens, most notably the dreaded secret police of Sparta, the *krypteia*, which according to Aristotle (fr. 8.44.538 Rose = Plu. *Lyc*. 28) terrorized and killed helots at night with sole objective to strike fear. This interpretation of the krypteia has been questioned in recent years (see Handy 2005: 99–120; Link 2006: 34–43; Welwei 2004: 33–46), but it should not surprise us if authoritarian and cryptic Sparta resorted to such methods to keep the helot population permanently afraid.

117 I have explained my views on this issue in greater detail in Kapparis 1999: 424–36; see also Gagarin 1996: 1–18; Mirhady 1996: 119–31 and 2000: 53–74; Thür 1996: 132–134.

118 See Brunt 1993: 343–88; Millet 2007: 178–209; Garnsey 1996; Burns 2003: 16–36; Ross 2008: 53–67; Schlaifer 1936: 165–204; Bentley 1999: 100–13; Ambler 1987: 390–410; Cambiano 1987: 22–41; Smith 1983: 109–22. The theories of the philosophers have received attention in my opinion disproportionate to their actual reflection of contemporary realities and views on slavery. For most Athenians in the 4th century slavery simply was a convenient source of labour, and a long-established situation.

119 See, for example, Hekataios *FGrH* 264 F 25.1000: περὶ μὲν γὰρ τὴν θεραπείαν αὐτῶν οὐδεὶς ἦν οὔτ' ἀργυρώνητος οὔτ' οἰκογενὴς δοῦλος.

120 Several cities experienced catastrophic enslavement of their entire populations (ἐξανδραποδισμός), such as mighty Thebes (D. S. 17.1–16, Hyp. *Epit*. 7), Orchomenos and Koroneia (D. 19.112), Priene (Hdt. 1.161.3), Kedreia (X. *HG* 2.1.15), Krobyle and Tiristratis (D. 12.3) and countless other cities and towns in the course of ancient history. Famous people who were enslaved and then liberated by relatives or friends include Plato (D. L. 3.20) and Julius Caesar (Plu. *Caes*. 1–2). In the speech of Apollodoros *Against Nikostratos* (D. 53), Nikostratos is captured by slave-traders in a remote location, and then liberated by his family with a loan from Apollodoros. Capture by pirates and subsequent enslavement and liberation are crucial plot devices in the Hellenistic novel, including Chariton's *Chaireas and Kallirhoe*, Xenophon's *Ephesiaca*, or Longus *Daphnis and Chloe*. The list could increase exponentially.

121 Isoc. 19.90; D. 4.47; Hyp. *Athenog*. 5.23; Lyc. Fr. 10–11.1 Conomis; Lys. 10.10.

122 On the dress and identity of the Scythian archers, and their representation in vase iconography see Gleba 2008: 3–13; Ivanchik 2006: 197–271; Braund 2006: 109–13; see also the discussion in Chapter 1.4.

123 See for example *IG* ii^2 502 where a public slave named Antiphates has been sent to an expedition as a servant to the general; *IG* ii^2 583, where the public slave working at the Metroon is asked to fetch a decree of *isoteleia* and hand it over to the secretary to inscribe it; *IG* ii^2 839, where a public slave is employed as a scribe; *IG* ii^2 840, where a public slave is to be appointed as assistant to three members of the council overseeing a religious ritual, and so on. It appears that most jobs in the civil service of Athens were performed by public slaves under the authority of citizen magistrates.

124 See for example D. 53.24–5, where Apollodoros raises the prospect that public slaves ought to be tortured by the magistrates in charge or members of the council in order to give evidence, and states that himself as a private citizen would not have the authority to perform this task. In any case, the argument is entirely theoretical, because this never happened. As usual, such arguments were merely rhetorical, and the practical implications of this are that typically public slaves were safe from torture, and that unlike privately owned slaves they did not expect routine beatings or mistreatment.

125 Men. *Epit.* 380; And. 1.37.

126 In order to maintain full Spartan citizenship someone needed to be able to contribute to the mess every month 1 medimnos of barley (1 medimnos = approximately 30kg), 96 cups of wine (e.g. 3 cups a day), 5 minae (= 2.5kg) of cheese and 2 ½ minae (= 1.25kg) of figs. Surely at least an equal amount of these would be needed for the maintenance of the rest of the family, and this should give us some measure of the quantities which a helot had to pay to his Spartan master. On the institution of the Spartan helots see Luraghi 2009: 261–304; 2003: 109–41; Hodkinson 2008: 285–320; Cartledge 2003: 12–30.

127 For a small, random selection see Ar. *V.* 1–50; *Ra.* 1–37; E. *Med.* 49–95; Theocr. 2; Lys. 1.18; D. 59.120. For some unusual and intimate images of slaves with their masters see Getty Museum 86.AE.237 = Beazley online 10147; Berlin, Antikensammlung: F2309 = Beazley (2nd ed.) 373.46 = Beazley online 203944.

128 Apollodoros (D. 53.19–21) mentions two slaves owned by Arethousios who were hired out for agricultural tasks by their master. Arethousios arranged the hiring and received the payments on their behalf.

129 D. 27.9: "My father, men of the jury, left two factories, both doing a large business. One was a sword-manufactory, employing thirty-two or thirty-three slaves, most of them worth five or six minae each and none worth less than three minae. From these my father received a clear income of thirty minae each year. The other was a sofa-manufactory, employing twenty slaves, given to my father as security for a debt of forty minae. These brought him in a clear income of twelve minae." (Trsl. by A.T. Murray)

130 See Lys. 23, with my introduction and notes in Wolpert-Kapparis 2011: 59–64, and also D. 57.

131 See Aesop *Sententiae* 13; E. *Cyc.* 240; Lys. 1.18; D. 45.33.

132 Th. 7.87.

133 The reader could turn to Millett 2007; Osborne 1997; Finley 1980; Finley 1960.

134 See the discussion below in Chapter 2.7.

135 D. 59.13: δωρεάν, μετὰ πολλῶν ἀναλωμάτων καὶ πραγματείας πολίτης μέλλων ἔσεσθαι.

136 See Is. 3.37; Ar. *V.* 718 (fictional); Lys. 13.60, and fr. 350 Thalheim; D. *Ep.* 3.29; Hyp. Fr. 87–90 Jensen.

137 Din. Fr. 16 Conomis; see also Harp. s.v. προμετρητάς and Sud. π 2504.

138 Harp. s.v. προμετρητάς = Din. fr. 16.4 and 4a Conomis; Sud. π 2504: τούτου τοῦ ἔργου μισθὸν λαμβάνων.

139 <Προμετρηταί>: ἄρχοντές τινες ἐνιαύσιοι ἦσαν, οἱ τῷ δικαίῳ μέτρῳ διαμετροῦντες τὰ ὄσπρια καὶ τοὺς πυροὺς ἐν τῇ ἀγορᾷ.

140 The name Skythes need not mean that he was actually Scythian. It could be, as it turned out, an unfortunate name for a citizen, or even a nickname for a citizen man with red hair and Scythian features.

141 Like, for example D. 45 and 46, *Against Stephanos*, where the second speech is the *deuterology*. However, this was a *dike pseudomartyrion*, and as a private lawsuit required a set of two speeches, rather than a long one as in all public cases.

142 Harp. s.v. δωροξενία.

143 Hypereides may have been a former lover (Athen. 13.58), and possibly he had a child with Aristagora (the reference to *notheia* in Hyp. Fr. 17 Jensen could be an allusion to the presence of an illegitimate child). If such personal motives were involved, they could explain the viciousness of these repeated attacks.

144 In the unlikely event that the citizen partner was the woman, of course disfranchisement would be meaningless, and this is why the law only mentions disfranchisement as a penalty for a citizen man living in marriage (or pretending marriage) with an alien woman. For a more thorough discussion of this law see Chapter 4.2 and my discussion in Kapparis 1999: 198–206.

145 See the discussion in Kapparis 1999: 198–206.

146 See D. 57 passim; Is. 12 passim; Aesch. 1.86, 142, 2.182.

147 Robert Develin (1991: 75–79) has argued against David Whitehead that Euboulides was not the demarch of Halimous. Although Whitehead is probably correct, as this is the easiest reading of the text, it is not important for our understanding of the procedure.

148 Aesch. 1.114–16.

149 The verb διαψηφίζω (more often in the middle διαψηφίζομαι) literally means to choose by secret vote (Th. 4.88.1 κρύφα διαψηφισάμενοι, Andoc. 4.3 διαψηφισαμένων κρύβδην τὸν ὀστρακισθέντα) between one of two proposals. With reference to citizenship and immigration procedures see Is. 7.16 (introduction to phratry and genos); Arist. *Ath. Pol.* ἐγγράφονται δ' εἰς τοὺς δημότας ὀκτωκαίδεκα ἔτη γεγονότες. ὅταν δ' ἐγγράφωνται, διαψηφίζονται περὶ αὐτῶν ὀμόσαντες οἱ δημόται.

150 Two previous widespread *dokimasiai* of citizens are mentioned, but even if these are historical events (which is doubtful), they still bear little resemblance to the *diapsephiseis* of 346. The first even precedes the establishment of the democratic constitution and the organization of the citizen body into demes. Supposedly it took place at some point after the fall of the tyrants in the sixth century, and it may have been politically motivated (Arist. *Ath. Pol.* 13.5). Another set of widespread citizenship disputes seems to have taken place in 445–4, when the king of Egypt sent grain to be distributed among the citizens of Athens. However, Plutarch who mentions this does not speak of another general *diapsephisis* but rather of extensive litigation, with an impossible number of several thousands of suits and counter-suits around the city (Plu. *Per.* 37.4: ἐπεὶ δὲ τοῦ βασιλέως τῶν Αἰγυπτίων δωρεὰν τῷ δήμῳ πέμψαντος τετρακισμυρίους πυρῶν μεδίμνους ἔδει διανέμεσθαι τοὺς πολίτας, πολλαὶ μὲν ἀνεφύοντο δίκαι τοῖς νόθοις ἐκ τοῦ γράμματος ἐκείνου τέως διαλανθάνουσι καὶ παρορωμένοις, πολλοὶ δὲ καὶ συκοφαντήμασι περιέπιπτον. ἀπεκρίθησαν οὖν ἁλόντες ὀλίγῳ πεντακισχιλίων ἐλάττους, οἱ δὲ μείναντες ἐν τῇ πολιτείᾳ καὶ κριθέντες Ἀθηναῖοι μύριοι καὶ τετρακισχίλιοι καὶ τεσσαράκοντα τὸ πλῆθος ἐξητάσθησαν.) The historicity of this event is highly doubtful, at least in the way it is described by Plutarch. By the time it would take the courts to decide who was entitled to the grain and who was not, the grain would have turned to dust. Several attempts to link the narrative of Plutarch to the Periclean citizenship law have been unconvincing, because clearly it did not have retroactive validity. Kimon, for example, who was the son of a Thracian princess, and undoubtedly a *metroxenos*, continued to lead Athenian politics and armies until his death in Cyprus in 449. See the discussion in Rhodes 1981: 331–5.

151 For further discussion of the possibilities see the study by Carusi and Fantasia 2004: 187–216.

152 D. 23.56–8.

153 D. 59.38–43; see also Kapparis 1999: 248–53.

154 Another famous case of *aphaeresis* concerning the libertine Pittalakos in Aeschines (1.54–66) never reached the courts either. It went to arbitration, and it seems that the case was dropped altogether at some point later.

3 The Athenian *oikos*

3.1 Sources

1 The formation of an *oikos* is a natural process

ἀνάγκη δὴ πρῶτον συνδυάζεσθαι τοὺς ἄνευ ἀλλήλων μὴ δυναμένους εἶναι, οἷον θῆλυ μὲν καὶ ἄρρεν τῆς γεννήσεως ἕνεκεν, καὶ τοῦτο οὐκ ἐκ προαιρέσεως, ἀλλ' ὥσπερ καὶ ἐν τοῖς ἄλλοις ζῴοις καὶ φυτοῖς φυσικὸν τὸ ἐφίεσθαι.

(Aristotle, *Politics* 1252a 26–9[1])

It is necessary in the first place for those who cannot live without each other to come together, like the female and the male for the purpose of procreation, and to do so not because of choice, but as with other animals and plants the desire is instinctive.

2 Definition of *oikos*

ὀρθῶς Ἡσίοδος εἶπε ποιήσας "οἶκον μὲν πρώτιστα γυναῖκά τε βοῦν τ' ἀροτῆρα".

(Aristotle, *Politics* 1252b 10–12)

Correctly Hesiod said "at first an *oikos* is a woman, an ox, and a plough."

3 *Oikos* as the nucleus of the *polis*

ἡ δ' ἐκ πλειόνων οἰκιῶν κοινωνία πρώτη χρήσεως ἕνεκεν μὴ ἐφημέρου κώμη [. . .] ἡ δ' ἐκ πλειόνων κωμῶν κοινωνία τέλειος πόλις, ἤδη πάσης ἔχουσα πέρας τῆς αὐταρκείας ὡς ἔπος εἰπεῖν, γινομένη μὲν τοῦ ζῆν ἕνεκεν, οὖσα δὲ τοῦ εὖ ζῆν.

(Aristotle, *Politics* 1252b 15–16, 27–31)

The first society of several houses which was not a temporary settlement was called a *kome* [. . .] the purposeful society of several *komai* together is called a *polis*, and it is totally self-sufficient, initially formed for the purpose of living, but existing for the purpose of living well.

4 Purpose of the *oikos*

> βουλευόμενος δ' ἔγωγε ὑπὲρ ἐμοῦ καὶ οἱ σοὶ γονεῖς ὑπὲρ σοῦ τίν' ἂν κοινωνὸν βέλτιστον οἴκου τε καὶ τέκνων λάβοιμεν, ἐγώ τε σὲ ἐξελεξάμην καὶ οἱ σοὶ γονεῖς, ὡς ἐοίκασιν, ἐκ τῶν δυνατῶν ἐμέ. τέκνα μὲν οὖν ἂν θεός ποτε διδῷ ἡμῖν γενέσθαι, τότε βουλευσόμεθα περὶ αὐτῶν ὅπως ὅτι βέλτιστα παιδεύσομεν αὐτά· . . . · νῦν δὲ δὴ οἶκος ἡμῖν ὅδε κοινός ἐστιν. ἐγώ τε γὰρ ὅσα μοι ἔστιν ἅπαντα εἰς τὸ κοινὸν ἀποφαίνω, σύ τε ὅσα ἠνέγκω πάντα εἰς τὸ κοινὸν κατέθηκας. . . . ἀλλὰ σωφρόνων τοί ἐστι καὶ ἀνδρὸς καὶ γυναικὸς οὕτω ποιεῖν, ὅπως τά τε ὄντα ὡς βέλτιστα ἕξει καὶ ἄλλα ὅτι πλεῖστα ἐκ τοῦ καλοῦ τε καὶ δικαίου προσγενήσεται.
>
> (Xenophon, *Economics*, 7, 11–14)
>
> Making inquiries, I for myself and your parents on your behalf, who would be the best companion for household and children, I chose you, and your parents, as it seems, chose me among potential suitors. If god ever gives us any children, then we need to consider how best we educate them . . . but now this household is jointly ours, and I declare everything I have to be common, and you have contributed everything you brought in.[2] . . . However it is a characteristic of a wise man and woman to make sure that whatever they already have will remain in a healthy shape, and many more will be added in a fair and just manner.

5 The term "*oikos*" includes all property

> Οἶκος δὲ δὴ τί δοκεῖ ἡμῖν εἶναι; ἆρα ὅπερ οἰκία, ἢ καὶ ὅσα τις ἔξω τῆς οἰκίας κέκτηται, πάντα τοῦ οἴκου ταῦτά ἐστιν; Ἐμοὶ γοῦν, ἔφη ὁ Κριτόβουλος, δοκεῖ, καὶ εἰ μηδ' ἐν τῇ αὐτῇ πόλει εἴη τῷ κεκτημένῳ, πάντα τοῦ οἴκου εἶναι ὅσα τις κέκτηται.
>
> (Xenophon, *Economics*, 1.5)
>
> "What do we think an *oikos* is? Is it the same thing as an oikia? Or are the things which a person owns outside the oikia also all part of the *oikos*?" "In my opinion" said Kritoboulos, "even if they are not even in the same city as the owner, all the things that a person owns are part of the *oikos*."[3]

3.2 The *oikos* and the *polis*

The student of classical Athens might be greatly surprised by an apparent contrast between the pace of developments in public and private life. While legal, constitutional, and cultural developments in public life kept moving like an angry torrent, uprooting ancient strongholds of power and changing not only the shape of Athenian politics and society but also the entire path of human civilization, private life, by contrast, seems to be standing still. The 4th century Athenians were still following a definition of marriage so traditional that its institution was lost in the mists of time, and no one ever wondered when or why its basic rules had been set up, or why they were as they were. In matters related to adoption, inheritance, and the legal rights and responsibilities of the members of the household the ancient laws of Solon remained still valid two and a half centuries after their introduction, with only very minor modifications. Expectedly this did not happen without problems and difficulties. Some of the provisions of these laws were time and place-specific, created to address significant social and economic problems in the time of Solon. However, times had changed and 4th century Athens was no longer an impoverished state locked into a bitter class struggle; on the contrary, economically and politically she was the most successful city in the Greek world, and some of the Solonean laws no longer made sense, and were ignored or interpreted by the standards of the time, regardless of their original intent. Moreover, the constitutional frame itself had drastically changed from the time of Solon to the classical period, and some of the provisions of the Solonean legislation which were designed to address the balance of power between the old aristocracy and the common people were meaningless in the egalitarian democracy of the 4th century.

Despite such major changes it is remarkable that the Athenians never changed even legal provisions which were a dead letter long before the 4th century. Whether it was done out of reverence for the ancient code, or as a matter of deliberate policy, or simply because no one bothered to go through the trouble of a point by point overhaul of the Solonean legislation, the end result was the same. Family life in classical Athens was still regulated by a selection of ancient provisions and an entire set of unwritten traditions which appear to be immutable and unchangeable in time, and yet the Athenians, ever ready to question everything and change much in every other aspect of life, did not seem to be troubled by the perpetuity of family life and its institutions. S.C. Humphreys and J. Roy have interpreted this discrepancy as the result of a "striking restraint" on behalf of the *polis* to interfere into the affairs of private life within the *oikos*.[4] R. Wallace has also stressed the respect of private life by the *polis* citing the *Epitaphios* of Pericles.[5] By contrast Cynthia Patterson in a recent study has convincingly argued that the interaction between *oikos* and *polis* was one of the most significant factors in the historical development of the Athenian Democracy and the interests of the *polis*.[6]

In a sense, both of these approaches are correct and should be seen as different perspectives of the same historical reality. While introduction of new laws in private life is truly much slower than introduction of new laws regulating public life, this should not be interpreted as the result of a complete separation of spheres. A closer look suggests that this serene and timeless image of the unchanging Greek family is a mirage. The changes in family life are keeping pace with the dramatic evolution of public life, but they are less spectacular and more nuanced, and so are the shifts in the legal processes regulating family life. The most earth-shattering change in the evolution of family life was introduced in 451, when a law of Pericles established that someone can only be an Athenian citizen if he or she was born of two Athenian parents. This law changed significantly the structure of the Athenian family, because in future mixed marriages would be meaningless, since they could not produce legitimate offspring, and alien women living with Athenian men would thereafter be reduced to the status of a concubine. The effect of the Periclean law was intensified in the early 4th century with another law expressly forbidding the marriage or pretense of marriage between citizens and noncitizens. This law brought about further changes in the structures of the Greek *oikos*.[7]

Further changes in the family and family life tended to be subtler, the result of a slow evolutionary process, rather than a revolution. In the long run, from Solon to the 4th century, changing economics, demographics, morals, attitudes and cultural perspectives often rendered existing laws meaningless or obsolete and altered the administration of justice, even though the statutes themselves in theory remained unchanged. Two examples might be appropriate at this point. The law forbidding women to engage in financial transactions higher that one bushel of barley (Is. 10.10; this would be roughly the sum needed for the weekly expenses of the household), was still in the statute books in the 4th century, but changed economics and social attitudes had rendered it a dead letter, as women in the classical period often engaged in economic transactions higher than that without the supervision of a *kyrios*.[8] An even more striking example could be found in the law permitting the father of an unchaste unmarried woman to sell her into a brothel. While the law still remained in the statute books, changing morals had removed the option in practical terms, and such an action would not only be unacceptable in 4th century Athens, but the father might even face the very severe penalties of the laws of ἀνδραποδισμός for enslaving a free person. Slow-burning shifts and changes like this can be observed in many instances and will be discussed in the following chapters, along with the relevant laws which regulated the *oikos* and its affairs.

3.3 The *oikos* and its members

The core definition of the *oikos* is provided by Hesiod with the approval of Aristotle (S 2): in order to create a new *oikos* a man needed a wife, an ox and a plough (namely the means to support himself, the wife and any offspring to come). It goes without saying that most classical Athenian families would expect more of themselves or potential suitors of their daughters than the basic necessities of life, and property considerations would weigh significantly in the arranged marriages which started most Athenian *oikoi*. As D.M. MacDowell has convincingly demonstrated, followed by the majority of scholars, the Greek word οἶκος means house,[9] household, the property of the household and also family, all at once (S 5).[10] The *oikos* included the original couple that started it, their offspring, other relatives living with the family, like unmarried or widowed sisters, brothers, uncles, or aunts, and in one attested case an elderly libertine, former slave of the household, who returned to the *oikos* on her own free will, when she was widowed and had no one to provide for her.[11] It also included the slaves of the family, along with the rest of the assets and movables of the household.[12] Cheryl Cox, in her thorough study of the subject, has pointed out that the *oikos* is not a fixed entity, but rather an intricate network in a state of flux, temporarily or permanently including unmarried or widowed relatives, and an ever changing number of slaves.[13] One might add to this new acquisitions or liquidations of assets and movables, which render the property of the *oikos* mobile and ever changing too. Athens never had a similar rule to that of the large aristocratic estates in imperial Britain, where the eldest son and heir inherited the entire unit intact; the assets of the Athenian *oikos* would be split equally among legitimate male heirs, generating as many new oikoi as the number of legitimate sons, natural or adopted. On the whole, the Greek *oikos* should not be understood as a feudal, unchangeable structure, but rather as a flexible and encompassing unit, taking its shape at any given moment from the specific circumstances of the family at its nucleus.

The *oikos* was headed by the κύριος,[14] the senior adult male in the house. The *kyrios* of the house had certain duties and responsibilities towards its members and had to represent and defend the interests of the *oikos* in the public sphere and in the judicial system. Unlike the massive powers of life and death (*patria potestas*), which Roman law and custom bestowed upon the Roman *pater familias*, especially during the republic and early empire, the Greek *kyrios* had only modest legal authority. He had no legal control over other adult citizen males in his household, like unmarried sons, his elderly father or other relatives living with them. These men were legally independent and personally responsible for their own actions and life choices before the law, society and religion. The *kyrios* commanded authority and respect, but no true legal power. Numerous examples in our sources suggest that the wishes of the *kyrios* could not be ignored, but also that he had no special legal powers to impose them upon other adult males in his household, and quarrels between members of the *oikos* were not a rarity.[15] His power over other adult males in his household was primarily financial, which is not to be underestimated, as the holder of the purse can usually impose his will.[16] Other adult males of course had the choice to move out, if they resented the authority of the *kyrios* as, for example, young Clinia does in Terence's *Heautontimorumenos*.[17] When he is sternly reproached by his father he leaves to join the army causing great distress to the old man.

Other members of the *oikos* did not have this choice. The wife could leave her husband, assuming that her natal family had agreed to take her back, but this happened so rarely that in effect Athenian women were expected to make the marriage work no matter what.[18] Other free persons attached to the *oikos* by circumstances were theoretically capable of moving out, but the actual circumstances which had made them move into the *oikos* in the first place, like, let's say, widowhood, were probably compelling enough to keep them in the *oikos* and make them obey the wishes of the *kyrios*. Children and slaves did not have any option except to obey the *kyrios*. The authority of the *kyrios* over the members of the household was not so much a matter or specific legislation, as it was the result of tradition, circumstances and his direct control over the slaves and finances of the household.

The *kyrios* also had a bundle of responsibilities towards the members of his household, some of which were mandated by law, but most were traditional expectations. The most significant of these was to represent legally minor members of the household, namely persons who could not act independently in public life and the courts, like women, children and slaves. For example, if a man's daughter was prosecuted for impiety because she did something very inappropriate in a temple, the father was expectedly bound to represent and defend her in court. As far as we can tell, there was no law stating that he actually had to do so, but convention in this case was so strong that it practically had the same effect. On other occasions the law explicitly required the *kyrios* to act on behalf of the woman, such as in dowry disputes, and the arrangements of marital contracts (ἐγγύη).[19] Likewise the law sometimes explicitly required the *kyrios* to take action on behalf of a child, and it was generally understood that the father or guardian (who often, but not invariably was a close male relative, like the maternal grandfather in Lys. 32)[20] would need to represent an under-age person. The *kyrios* was also responsible for the actions of slaves from his household, his permission was necessary when slaves of his were requested to give evidence under torture, and as their legal owner he could sue for compensation if someone harmed them. He could also prosecute the killer of one of his slaves for homicide at the Palladion court.

The *kyrios* had the responsibility to provide for the household. He took his wife's dowry and merged it into the finances of the new *oikos*. Beyond that point he had a duty to provide for everyone in the *oikos*, and ideally to enlarge the property which he inherited.[21] Squandering one's inheritance not only brought shame but could also result in legal impediments for holding public office and speaking in the Assembly. The law on the scrutiny of the orators (δοκιμασία ῥητόρων), as quoted by Aeschines, explicitly disqualifies persons who have not looked after their parental inheritance from advising the city, on the grounds that they must be bad advisors; if they could not look after their own, how could they look after the city's property?

> "δοκιμασία," φησί, "ῥητόρων· ἐάν τις λέγῃ ἐν τῷ δήμῳ . . . ἢ τὰ πατρῷα", φησί, "κατεδηδοκώς, ἢ ὧν ἂν κληρονόμος γένηται"· τὸν γὰρ τὴν ἰδίαν οἰκίαν κακῶς οἰκήσαντα, καὶ τὰ κοινὰ τῆς πόλεως παραπλησίως ἡγήσατο διαθήσειν."
>
> (Aesch. 1.28)
>
> "Scrutiny" he says "of the speakers; if one speaks in the Assembly . . . and he has squandered his parental estate, or any other inheritance; because he believed that the person who has mismanaged his own household, will do the same to the common property of the city."

This is a 4th century law, but the principle, that persons who had mismanaged their inheritance should be barred from public office for fear that they would do the same to the affairs of the city, preceded the introduction of this law and was simply incorporated into it.[22] The orators mention several cases of men who squandered their parental inheritance. Aeschines for example devotes several sections of his speech *Against Timarchos* trying to prove that the latter had squandered his inheritance, and levels the same accusations against Demosthenes. In both cases the accusations cannot be taken seriously considering that both men were quite wealthy. More truth is probably to be found in the case of Kallias, the son of Hipponikos, who seems to have squandered one of the largest fortunes in the whole of the Greek world.[23] While on occasion it may be a matter of pride to tell the court that someone spent his inheritance to benefit the city through plentiful liturgies and trierarchies, typically accusations of squandering one's inheritance are meant to bring shame and damage to someone's image.[24] Isocrates with sadness and indignation remarks that the war which the politicians brought upon Athens turned many rich people into poor, and the politicians themselves from poor into rich.[25] While the ideal standard was to maintain and enhance the property of the *oikos*, circumstances like wars, civil strife, unforeseen factors such as weather phenomena in a city of mariners, and even dangerous litigation could have a large impact on the management of the family fortunes.

One of the main responsibilities of the *kyrios* was the welfare of his children. It was his duty to notify the community that a child had been added to the family by offering a sacrifice at the festival of the Apatouria, and to present the child for initial registration to the phratry and its subgroups, taking an oath that this was his child, and was legitimately born.[26] He also had the responsibility to support the child in all subsequent steps which led to adulthood and full recognition of the child as a citizen by the community. For a boy this meant presentation for the second time to the phratry and its subgroups in adolescence (κουρεῶτις), and presentation to the deme for full registration to the citizen body when he had reached his 18th year of age. In the event that any of these bodies disputed the right of the child to be registered it was the duty of the father to challenge their decision all the way to the courts.[27]

The *kyrios* needed to make sure that unmarried daughters or sisters under his protection would be given in marriage.[28] He was duty-bound to search for a suitable husband and when one had been found he had the legal obligation to seal the marital contract (ἐγγύη) on behalf of a woman. Even though it was not his legal duty to provide a dowry, and in theory he could conclude the transaction without one, in practice the woman's *kyrios* almost invariably would have to procure a dowry, as a contribution to the finances of her new *oikos*.[29] In the rare event of a divorce, the *kyrios* would need to take back the woman to his household, and make sure that her dowry was returned in its entirety. If the former husband refused or was unable to return the dowry, the *kyrios* had the legal duty to ensure that a high interest of 18 percent was paid on the capital of the dowry, and if the former husband failed in this obligation too, the *kyrios* would need to prosecute him, month after month, if necessary, for the interest (δίκη σίτου).[30]

The *kyrios* was expected and had the legal authority to keep order and discipline among the members of his household. The entertaining exchange between Strepsiades and his son in the *Clouds* of Aristophanes offers us some great insights into the disciplinary practices of the Greek household.[31] It would be normal for parents to hit their naughty children, but society considered it so heinous for someone to hit their parents, that it would disqualify them from holding office or speaking in the assembly.[32] The impeccable rationale of both father and son in this exchange sounds eerily familiar to readers through time:

1409 Φε: καὶ πρῶτ᾽ ἐρήσομαί σε τουτί· παῖδά μ᾽ ὄντ᾽ ἔτυπτες;
1410 Στ: ἔγωγέ σ᾽, εὐνοῶν τε καὶ κηδόμενος.
{Φε.} εἰπὲ δή μοι,
οὐ κἀμὲ σοὶ δίκαιόν ἐστιν εὐνοεῖν ὁμοίως

τύπτειν τ', ἐπειδήπερ γε τοῦτ' ἔστ' εὐνοεῖν, τὸ τύπτειν;
πῶς γὰρ τὸ μὲν σὸν σῶμα χρὴ πληγῶν ἀθῷον εἶναι,
τοὐμὸν δὲ μή; καὶ μὴν ἔφυν ἐλεύθερός γε κἀγώ.[33]

Ph.: First I will ask you this. Did you hit me when I was a child?
St.: Of course, because I love you and care for you
Ph.: So tell me now
Is it not fair for me to love you too
And hit you, because this is what "to love" means, "to hit"?
Why should your body be immune to beatings
And mine is not? Wasn't I born a free person too?

The punitive powers of the *kyrios* were limited. The Greek *kyrios* did not have rights of life and death or the power to abuse extensively or injure the members of his household. There were legal barriers to this and the state allowed for any neighbour or relative to bring a prosecution (εἰσαγγελία) against someone who abused certain members of his household, like orphans in his care or heiresses (ἐπίκληροι) under his authority.[34] A *kyrios* could not even kill his own slave, because even the killing of the slave could carry *miasma* and, at least in theory, result in a prosecution for homicide.[35] Any punishments which the *kyrios* could inflict had to be within reason and stemmed out of his authority as the head of the household and the necessity to maintain order within his own house, rather than any particular legislative arrangements. There is no known case of someone prosecuting a neighbor or family member for abusing members of his family. One would imagine that such interference into the affairs of someone else's *oikos* would be something that most citizens would be reluctant to do, but even the theoretical possibility that someone's enemy could take advantage and prosecute might in itself function as a deterrent for some of the most extreme domestic abuses. Moreover, since homicide and spilling blood were abominable in Greek religion one would think that most Athenian men would refrain from spilling kin blood in their own household for fear of dreadful vengeance by some of the darkest spirits in the Greek pantheon.

While the *kyrios* had the primary responsibility of providing for the household, other members of the *oikos* had to do their part in the maintenance and well-being of the unit. The women of the household, led by the wife of the *kyrios*, or the most senior woman, would be expected to manage the assets of the household and operate as the first line of production for its basic needs. The duties of the women inside the *oikos* are described in considerable detail in Chapter 7 of Xenophon's *Oeconomicus*, which provides valuable insights into the workings of an affluent Athenian *oikos*. The occasion for the narrative is the marriage of Ischomachos, a rich Athenian man to a teenage woman from a good family. Socrates enquires about the marital bliss in the house of Ischomachos and wants to know all the details about the workings of the household. Ischomachos obliges offering a full account on the training of his young wife for her duties as the mistress of the household as well as the conversations he had with her about the actual philosophy behind these arrangements.

Ischomachos begins by relating to Socrates a conversation with his wife about the reasons why they got married and their respective roles in the union. We are told that the gods built the bodies of men and women to suit their respective responsibilities. The male body they made bigger, stronger and better suited to outdoors tasks, and equipped it with courage so as to be able to face these tasks. Correspondingly they built the female body better suited to the indoors tasks, and equipped it with fear, because a more timid and sparing nature is better suited to taking care of infants and prudently managing the household. Aristotle also emphasizes this divinely ordained separation of spheres of influence between the male and the female, and sees it as a harmonious act of divine providence (τὸ θεῖον):

> Οὕτω προῳκονόμηται ὑπὸ τοῦ θείου ἑκατέρου ἡ φύσις, τοῦ τε ἀνδρὸς καὶ τῆς γυναικός, πρὸς τὴν κοινωνίαν· διείληπται γὰρ τῷ μὴ ἐπὶ ταὐτὰ πάντα χρήσιμον ἔχειν τὴν δύναμιν, ἀλλ᾽ ἔνια μὲν ἐπὶ τἀναντία, εἰς ταὐτὸν δὲ συντείνοντα· τὸ μὲν γὰρ ἰσχυρότερον, τὸ δ᾽ ἀσθενέστερον ἐποίησεν, ἵνα τὸ μὲν φυλακτικώτερον ᾖ διὰ τὸν φόβον, τὸ δ᾽ ἀμυντικώτερον διὰ τὴν ἀνδρείαν, καὶ τὸ μὲν πορίζῃ τὰ ἔξωθεν, τὸ δὲ σῴζῃ τὰ ἔνδον· καὶ πρὸς τὴν ἐργασίαν τὸ μὲν δυνάμενον ἑδραῖον εἶναι, πρὸς δὲ τὰς ἔξωθεν θυραυλίας ἀσθενές, τὸ δὲ πρὸς μὲν τὰς ἡσυχίας χεῖρον, πρὸς δὲ τὰς κινήσεις ὑγιεινόν· καὶ περὶ τέκνων τὴν μὲν γένεσιν κοινήν, τὴν δὲ ὠφέλειαν ἴδιον· τῶν μὲν γὰρ τὸ θρέψαι, τῶν δὲ τὸ παιδεῦσαί ἐστιν. Πρῶτον μὲν οὖν [νόμοι πρὸς γυναῖκα] [καὶ] τὸ μὴ ἀδικεῖν· οὕτως γὰρ ἂν οὐδ᾽ αὐτὸς ἀδικοῖτο. Τοῦθ᾽ ὑφηγεῖται δὲ [ὁ] καὶ ὁ κοινὸς νόμος· καθάπερ οἱ Πυθαγόρειοι λέγουσιν, ὥσπερ ἱκέτιν καὶ ἀφ᾽ ἑστίας ἠγμένην ὡς ἥκιστα δεῖν [δοκεῖν] ἀδικεῖν· ἀδικία δὲ ἀνδρὸς αἱ θύραζε συνουσίαι γιγνόμεναι.
>
> (Arist. *Oec*. 1343b 26–1344a 13)

> And so with this purpose in view Divine Providence has fashioned the nature of man and of woman for their partnership. For they are distinguished from each other by the possession of faculties not adapted in every case to the same tasks, but in some cases for opposite ones, though contributing to the same end. For Providence made man stronger and woman weaker, so that he in virtue of his manly prowess may be more ready to defend the home, and she, by reason of her timid nature, more ready to keep watch over it; and while he brings in fresh supplies from without, she may keep safe what lies within. In handicrafts again, woman was given a sedentary patience, though denied stamina for endurance of exposure; while man, though inferior to her in quiet employments, is endowed with vigor for every active occupation. In the production of children both share alike; but each makes a different contribution to their upbringing. It is the mother who nurtures, and the father who educates. We begin then with the rules that should govern a man's treatment of his wife. And the first of these forbids him to do her wrong; for if he observes this, he is not likely himself to suffer wrong at her hands. As the Pythagoreans declare, even the common rule or custom of mankind thus

> ordains, forbidding all wrong to a wife as stringently as though she were a suppliant whom one has raised from the hearthstone. And a man does wrong to his wife when he associates with other women.[36]

What follows in the account of Ischomachos about the education of his wife is the list of duties which she needed to perform in the household. Her first and most significant duty would be managerial. She should organize the tasks, delegate them to the servants and slaves of the household, supervise their proper execution, and make sure that throughout the year the household runs like a well-oiled machine. This may sound easier than it would be in reality, as much needed to be done in the ancient household on a daily basis, and the mistress of the house needed to stay on top of it. First, there were the routine daily tasks: one had to prepare dinner. Sometimes what was in storage would be sufficient, but the Athenians of the classical period were accustomed to more elaborate foods,[37] and could obtain the materials from the market place. So, a servant might need to be sent out to buy ingredients for the dinner.[38] Then, the dinner would need to be cooked. We are told that this was one of the basic skills which the young wife of Ischomachos already possessed when she came to him. Then, the mistress would need to delegate cleaning duties, and if she did not have enough servants to carry out the tasks she would probably need to get involved herself. If they had young children, the cleaning roster would certainly be more extensive, and water would need to be fetched, sometimes from a public fountain outside the house. Then, in certain times of the year, as crops and other goods were coming in from the farm, they would need to be processed. Firewood would need to be cut and stored in the autumn, ahead of the chilly Attic winter nights. The wool collected in the late spring would need to be cleaned, dyed, spun and woven into cloth over the summer months, to be ready for the winter. The grain collected in the summer would need to be stored safely for the year ahead.

The grape stomping in the late summer was an opportunity for some community entertainment, and the juice needed to be stored in jars to ferment until the late winter, when the jars would be reopened and families could taste the new wine in the Pithoigia, the first day of the Anthesteria. The collection and pressing of the olives in winter would bring in the famous Attic olive oil, which also needed to be stored in jars. Likewise, other crops, such as lentils, beans, figs and nuts would need to be dried, processed and stored away. The list is endless, as so many of the basic household necessities were actually produced in an affluent *oikos* and needed to be processed. Even in city households which did not have to process agricultural or animal produce, there would still be a significant amount of daily duties to be performed, as dictated by the more sophisticated needs of the city life-style. The busy Athenian calendar of religious festivals would add to the work of the women and servants of the *oikos*, as those often required the production of new outfits and festive garb, meals or baked goods, and came with parties, extra housework and additional clean up in the end. Running a busy household ideally aimed at self-sufficiency was a tall order, and Athenian women were anything but idle in the performance of their routine duties inside the *oikos*.

The other significant duty of the Athenian woman in the house was her role as a caretaker. Apollodoros is inviting the jury to recall how priceless a woman can be for a sick person,[39] and Ischomachos reminds his young wife how important this duty was, even if it was not the most pleasant.[40] As a mother the Athenian woman was expected to perform all those duties that mothers have performed through the ages. Ischomachos was convinced that this was part of the divine plan for the roles of the sexes, and this is why, he says, women love infants more than men.[41] Training the staff was also part of her duties; she needed to teach inexperienced slaves how to do things, and this Ischomachos finds very rewarding in the long run. The inevitable metaphor of the queen bee is brought in to suggest that a good wife will look after her household, rewarding the good and punishing the bad, in the same manner as the queen bee is looking after the hive.

Finally, one of the most significant duties of the wife was budgeting, handling the finances of the household and making sure that the resources available to her can make ends meet. Ischomachos advises that it is important to stick to the budget and not to spend in one month the entire year's resources.[42] In the *Ecclesiazousai* of Aristophanes one of the arguments in support of the proposal to hand over the city to the women is their ability to produce money out of nowhere (a key skill for a city hard-pressed for resources in the middle of the Corinthian war).[43] Euphiletos in Lysias' *On the murder of Eratosthenes* praises his wife for being a very capable and stringent manager of the resources of the household, which, he says, induced him to completely trust her in all affairs and give up his close oversight of everything.[44] This sentence of Euphiletos corroborates the narrative of Xenophon about the household of Ischomachos. In the speech *Against Spudias* we see the wife of Polyeuktos exercising this kind of control upon the household finances, budgeting, keeping accounts, and also a ledger noting the debt every time she lent money to one of her sons in law.

The image which a man wanted to project to his peers was that of a benevolent despot in his household. He should be the one in charge and only transfer responsibility to his wife when he was satisfied that she was sufficiently trained and up to the task. Beyond that point there was no shame in a man admitting that the affairs of the household were the domain of his wife. If anything, Ischomachos suggests that it would be shameful for a man to stay indoors and do a woman's work in the household, as it would be inappropriate for a woman to venture out into the world of men, in politics, the army, and the public life of the city. There are numerous examples of this powerful stereotype, where space transgressions of women into the public sphere of the *polis* and men into the domestic sphere of the *oikos* were seen as at least anomalous, if not problematic. One of the most striking examples of a male transgression is provided in the fascinating narrative of Ktesias about the Assyrian king Sardanapalus, who chose to spend his time with the women of the harem, wearing makeup and spinning wool with them.[45] Klytaimestra in the *Oresteia* is the female equivalent: a strong woman transgressing into the world of men and seeking power and authority in her own right.[46] However, a caveat is necessary at this point. Although literary figures like Sardanapallus or Klytaimestra are built on elements of reality, they need not be historically correct in their entirety, and great caution is necessary when using such stereotypes for the understanding of Athenian social history.[47]

The narrative of several Attic speeches, where strong women take care of the affairs of family and household with a firm hand, while men obediently follow their lead, may be partially refuting the carefully cultivated macho image of Euphiletos, the idealized image of the perfect Athenian male portrayed by Ischomachos, or the sharp division between *oikos* and *polis* suggested by high literature. These narratives imply that although the division of spheres and duties broadly operated as Xenophon and Lysias suggest, the image is much more nuanced and complex in its details. For example, women of the lower classes had to work outdoors, women who occupied high office as priestesses were required to function extensively in the sphere of the *polis*, while some men took a much more active and hands-on approach to the upbringing of their children and decisions within the *oikos*.[48] Consequently the gender imbalance which high literature suggests may have been exaggerated, while male dominance and female submission need to be interpreted in context, rather than to be accepted as a fixed historical certainty.[49]

It would be a grave historical error to view the *oikos* as a restrictive ring, a prison where the subordinates of the *kyrios* existed to serve him. Family relations were never like this in the Greek household, nor Greek women ever were the muted, meek figures portrayed in much of the scholarship in the 20th century. The narratives of Xenophon and Aristotle in their respective *Economics*, as well as numerous other sources suggest that the ideal relationship between the members of the *oikos*, as well as between the *oikos* and the *polis*, was one of cooperation and mutual support.[50] They view the *oikos* as a protective sphere which insulated its members from their enemies in the outside world, fended off attacks through the court-system, and ensured that its members had their day to day needs met, and were offered the conditions to prosper and increase their own fortunes as well as those of the household, may that be through successful business enterprise or a good marriage. Unmarried women had a safe place to stay until the day when they could start a new *oikos* with their own husband, and if that day never came at least they had a place where they could live their lives with dignity and respect, and have their basic needs met, while children had a place where they were protected, looked after, educated and prepared for adult life as the future citizens. Widows with children who found life too intimidating to manage on their own always had the choice to return to their natal *oikos* and raise their children within its protective shield.[51] Essentially the *oikos* was able to protect these members of the household who could not directly protect themselves through the legal system, and it was expected to create a financially stable, if not always affluent, environment, and a legally shielded unit, which the Athenian state felt that it had a duty to protect with a steady set of laws that changed very little through time. This is how the *oikos* formed the basis of the social structures of most Greek city-states, and the cell of which the entire body of the city-state was composed.

How significant this safety net was becomes clearer if one looks into the challenges which individuals faced when this network broke down. An impoverished widow in the *Thesmophoriazousai* of Aristophanes explains her options when she lost her husband:

> Ἐμοὶ γὰρ ἀνὴρ ἀπέθανεν μὲν ἐν Κύπρῳ
> παιδάρια πέντε καταλιπών, ἁγὼ μόλις
> στεφανηπλοκοῦσ' ἔβοσκον ἐν ταῖς μυρρίναις.
> Τέως μὲν οὖν ἀλλ' ἡμικάκως ἐβοσκόμην·
> [. . .]
> Ἀλλ' εἰς ἀγορὰν ἄπειμι· δεῖ γὰρ ἀνδράσιν
> πλέξαι στεφάνους ξυνθηματιαίους εἴκοσιν.[52]
>
> My husband was killed in Cyprus
> leaving me with five children, which
> I was barely able to feed by making myrtle-wreaths
> and in the past with difficulty I managed to feed them
> [. . .]
> But I must go to the market, because I have
> an order of twenty wreaths to make for the men.

A non-fictional example of this situation is attested in the speech *Against Euboulides*:

> μετὰ δὲ ταῦτα χρόνῳ ὕστερον παιδίων αὐτῇ δυοῖν ἤδη γεγενημένων, καὶ τοῦ μὲν πατρὸς στρατευομένου καὶ ἀποδημοῦντος μετὰ Θρασυβούλου, αὐτὴ δ' οὖσ' ἐν ἀπορίαις ἠναγκάσθη τὸν Κλεινίαν τὸν τοῦ Κλειδίκου τιτθεῦσαι, τῷ μὲν εἰς ἔμ' ἥκοντι κινδύνῳ νῦν μὰ τὸν Δι' οὐχὶ συμφέρον πρᾶγμα ποιήσασα (ἀπὸ γὰρ ταύτης τῆς τιτθείας ἅπασ' ἡ περὶ ἡμᾶς γέγονεν βλασφημία), τῇ μέντοι ὑπαρχούσῃ πενίᾳ ἴσως καὶ ἀναγκαῖα καὶ ἁρμόττοντα ποιοῦσα.[53]
>
> After some time she had two children, and when my father was on campaign out of town with Thrasyboulos, she was forced out of financial necessity to become the wet nurse of Kleinias the son of Kleidikos, always currently assisting me in this trial. By Zeus, what she did was not helpful, because that job was what gave rise to the current insult against us; however, she did what was necessary and appropriate for her circumstances.

The speaker implies that for a citizen woman like his mother falling so low as to do a job normally done by slaves, was an embarrassment, and ultimately put his own citizenship in jeopardy, because it generated rumors that the family was not really of citizen descent. However, at the same time he praises his mother for having the courage to do what was necessary in the dire circumstances in which she found herself, when the main breadwinner of the house was gone, and she had to become the defender and provider of the *oikos* on her own.

Aeschines speaks with disdain about Diophantos the orphan, a youth who did not have a family to look after him and had taken up prostitution to provide for himself while still under age.[54] Hypereides began the narrative in the speech *To*

Timandra by telling the jury how Timandra and her sister were left without a family and took up prostitution to survive.[55] New comedy has turned this into a standard theme. Typically the pseudo-*hetaira* character is removed from her family, and falls prey to unscrupulous procurers, but since she remains virtuous typically she is reunited with her family in the end, marries her beloved, and the *oikos* is safe again.[56] The cautionary tale of how a respectable citizen woman could be compelled to take up prostitution overwhelmed by adversity after the death of the breadwinner *kyrios* is brought to life in one of the mimes of Lucian: the mother Krobyle is instructing her naïve daughter Korinna on the benefits of taking up prostitution for both of them.[57] Surely such tales were not literary fantasy in a society where men were killed in droves in ceaseless warfare and families were left to wither in poverty and isolation. This is why the Athenian state had put in place rigorous rules, in order to make sure that in the event that the *kyrios* died, his dependents would be properly looked after, his under-age children would come under the protection of an adult male capable of looking after their interests, and they would not end up doing slave jobs or take up prostitution, while the state took it upon itself to ensure that his daughters would be given in marriage, and that their future husbands would not marry them in unconsummated unions only for their dowry.

Considering the importance of the *oikos* for society and the *polis* as a whole, it is no wonder that its continuation was perceived to be an important goal of the family, as well as the *polis* and the legal system. The natural and unproblematic continuation of the *oikos* was effected by legitimate sons, natural or adopted.[58] A man's son would inherit his property when he died and continue his *oikos*. If he had more than one son then the original *oikos* and its property would be split into two or three or as many parts as necessary, and several new *oikoi* would spring out of the original *oikos* of their father.[59] To keep things simple, if a man had legitimate sons, natural or adopted, the law mandated that his property should go to them and did not allow a man who already had one or more natural sons to adopt, or leave the whole or part of his property to anyone else. The Athenians never had a law like the *rhetra* of Epitadeus in Sparta, which allowed a man to make a will and leave his property to whomever he wished.[60] Athenian law firmly sided with the right of a man to inherit his father and wanted to make sure that this inheritance was not diminished through sharing with anyone else except his legitimately born brothers and sisters.[61]

Succession through legitimate daughters in the absence of a male heir could still continue the *oikos* but indirectly. If the daughter happened to be married and already have children when her father died, they were seen as the heirs of the grandfather and the property simply passed to her family without further complications. This was one of those grey areas in Athenian family law. While the sons of the deceased man's daughter, strictly speaking, were continuing the *oikos* of their father, in a sense they were also continuing the *oikos* of their maternal grandfather. In essence, this meant that direct descendants through a matrilineal line had precedence over lateral relatives. Sometimes, especially when a large fortune was at stake the family might actually adopt one of their sons into the *oikos* of his maternal grandfather. This effectively meant that the adopted son lost all inheritance rights in his own father's *oikos*, but probably this would not be a problem if the maternal grandfather's *oikos* had been affluent. By doing so the family not only found a way to directly continue the *oikos* of the deceased, but also ensured that there would be no claims to the estate by lateral relatives.

If a man died leaving behind unmarried daughters, or daughters married without children, they became heiresses to his fortune (ἐπίκληροι). From this point on the marriage of the *epicleros* and the fate of the fortune that went with her were no longer left up to the family to settle as they wished. A certain procedure was followed every step of which was clearly prescribed by law. The *epicleros* could be claimed in marriage by the nearest male relative of her father, and if he happened to be married and did not want to divorce his wife, or he was too old, or simply unwilling to marry the *epicleros* himself she could step aside in favor of his son or some other relative. How large the fortune coming with the *epicleros* was, and how attractive and young she was, surely would be important factors in this process. Even if the *epicleros* was poor, the nearest male relative of her father still had an obligation towards her. He still needed either to marry her or find her another husband, and even give a dowry out of his own property if necessary. It is very difficult to tell whether this convention was universally observed, or people found ways to get out of it, if they did not want to take care of the poor heiress, because in the few cases that we hear about relatives are boasting that they did their duty towards the poor *epicleros*.[62] This type of marriage was called ἐπιδικασία (adjudication), and came with some legal stipulations which may seem strange to the modern reader, like the condition that the husband was obligated to have sex with his wife three times a month with a view to the birth of children. Although this may seem like an unprecedented intrusion by the *polis* into the family's private life, the purpose of it was very clear and specific. The *polis* was aware that this was not an ordinary marriage, but an arrangement involving property, sometimes very substantial, and had a clear goal, which was the continuation of the *oikos*. The emotional disposition of the participants took secondary place to this important goal, and this is why the state wanted to make sure that the primary purpose of this union was achieved, and that someone did not marry an heiress only for her fortune. Beyond that it was hoped that, as with any other arranged marriage, eventually love and affection would develop between the couple. In the absence of natural heirs, an adoption was the best way to procure an heir for the *oikos*. The adoptee needed to be of citizen birth and would be usually male for obvious reasons. Sometimes men who had only daughters but no sons might adopt their son-in-law thus precluding the possibility of the daughter becoming an *epicleros* if they died before she had any children.

Leaving an heir was not only important for practical reasons but also essential for religious reasons, so that someone would look after the graves and perform the appropriate rituals for the dead. The dead members of the *oikos* in some way still belonged to it, they needed to be remembered, and they were buried in the family graves. When men were scrutinized for citizenship or for entry to office, one of the standard questions was where the family graves are, as they were seen as a focal point for the continuity of the family and its traditions.[63]

The legal protections of the *oikos* and family life were definitely extended to free non-Athenian families permanently residing in Attica. These families mostly from other parts of the Greek world, but also non-Greek in origin, could be a very mixed bag.[64] Some were very affluent and proud of their identity, others could be liberated slaves who had found freedom and a home in Attica. This is why it is reasonable to assume that individual traditions differed from family to family, and that metic households sometimes might adhere to their own traditions, rites and religious holidays. Athens was a tolerant place in this respect, and the *polis* did not interfere wih the private lives of its citizens so long as they obeyed the laws of Athens, paid their taxes, and fulfilled their obligations to the city like any other family. Although metic families were not allowed to intermarry with citizen families for the most part of the classical period, their right to a family life, within the safe space of their own *oikos* was respected and recognized by Athenian law in exactly the same terms as the rights of the citizen families. In this respect Athens was a welcoming place and always had large metic populations, perhaps more so in the years of prosperity under the Athenian Empire, or the middle of the 4th century, when the city experienced significant growth under the skilled economic policies of Euboulos.

The *oikos* was much more than a group of people bound by obligations and duties. It was first and foremost a κοινωνία,[65] a microcosm of a human society with its joys, anxieties and sorrows, celebrations, festivals, and occasions when the members came together, sometimes also joined by friends, relatives and neighbors to a happy feast, a problem-solving conference, or a mourning. The main life events like births, deaths and marriages would offer occasions for a gathering of the members of the *oikos* and their friends. A birth would be celebrated with the ἀμφιδρόμια and the δεκάτη, a marriage would be celebrated in a feast and a procession (πομπή) to the house of the groom, which would become the *oikos* of the new couple, while a funeral dinner (περίδειπνον) would bring together relatives and friends. The men of the *oikos* might invite their friends to join them for a symposion, a party which could be ranging between polite conversation and a wild brawl under the influence of alcohol and the sounds of the exuberant flute, with prostitutes and entertainers in the mix. Expectedly such events were not attended by the women of the house, and some references suggest that the more wild of the attested feasts took place in the houses of bachelors, where there were no respectable women to be offended by the presence of prostitutes and overt sexuality.[66] The members of the *oikos* also participated in social occasions, events, public celebrations and festivals around the city throughout the year, with the only exception of disfranchised men or women caught committing adultery, who were excluded from public temples and celebrations.[67]

Each citizen was responsible to the same degree for the smooth operation of the democratic constitution and the legal system in the direct democracy of Athens, and having friends, political allies, and family members behind him was a safeguard that he would have loyal supporters in public life. Tensions within families had to be set aside when they ventured out into the public life, because solidarity out there mattered a lot, and we actually see both of these aspects of the Athenian family evidenced in the classical texts. We find references to tensions within families, but we also find references to brotherhood and mutual support among family members. One's family were his natural allies because they were always there, and in this respect the men of an *oikos* brothers, sons, and fathers, needed to stick together and defend the interests of the family in the outside world.[68] They did not always do it, and family relations were not unproblematic, but perhaps more than in any other place in history family solidarity would be essential for the citizens of the democracy, especially when they had to face opponents in court or in the political arena, and needed the backing of their friends and relatives.

Notes

1 The same arguments are repeated in the first book of the *Economics* of Aristotle, and elsewhere in his work.
2 Meaning her dowry, which was joined with his property to form the family property of the new *oikos*. Assuming that the couple did not divorce, one day their children would inherit the combined family property.
3 Translation by D.M. MacDowell.
4 Humphreys 1977: 97–107; Roy 1999: 1–17. Further on the relationship between *oikos* and *polis* and the involvement of the law into the affairs of the *oikos* see Patterson 2009; Crane 1997: 198–229; Fartzoff 1984: 171–184 and his subsequent 1991 book; Adam-Magnissali and Cudjoe 2010: 67–93; Ferrucci 2006: 183–210 and 2013: 263–84; Lacey 1968; Lape 2002: 117–139; Leão 2005: 5–31; MacDowell 1989: 10–21; McGowan 1997: 63–84.
5 Wallace 1997: 151–66, citing Th. 2.37.
6 Patterson 2009.
7 See Chapters 4.2 and 4.3 for the discussion.
8 See for example D. 41.9, where a widow is engaging in transactions much higher than one bushel of barley without the supervision of a *kyrios*, and also Schaps 1979: 52–6; Hunter 1994: 20–9; Foxhall 1989; Harris 1992; Cohen 1998, and the discussion in Chapters 3.3, and 5.3.
9 About *oikos* as housing see Mértaux 1999: 392–405 and Napolitano 2014.
10 MacDowell 1989: 10–21 = Arnaoutoglou et al. 2017: 171–184; Cheryl Cox (1998: 130–67) discusses in considerable detail the definition of the *oikos*, and also concludes that it should be understood as a unit broader than the nuclear family. See also Irigoyen Troconis 2004: 141–51. Gherchanoc (2012: 15) succinctly defines the *oikos* as following: "Précisément, oikos signifie, en grec, la demeure, la maison, le lieu où l'on habite, chez soi; il désigne également le patrimoine; enfin, c'est la communauté humaine du mari et de la femme destinée à se reproduire, du père et des enfants, du maître et de l'esclave, constituée par le fait qu'ils partagent la même nourriture et les mêmes cultes sous l'autorité d'un même kurios (le chef de l'oikos, à la fois mari, père et maître). Cette communauté (koinônia) ou famille, plus petite unité de la cité d'après Aristote, serait unie par des liens avant tout naturels, si l'on excepte les relations entre maître et esclaves. [Specifically, *oikos* means, in Greek, the residence, the house, the place where one lives, their place; it also refers to the patrimony; finally, it is the human community of the husband and the wife destined to reproduce, father and child, master and slave, constituted by the fact that they share the same food and the same worship under the authority of the same *kyrios* (the head of the *oikos*, simultaneously husband, father and teacher). This community (κοινωνία), or family, smallest unit of the city after Aristote (see S 1 and 3) would be united by bonds primarily natural, except for the relationship between master and slave]."

11 D. 47.55–6: τιτθή τις ἐμὴ γενομένη πρεσβυτέρα, ἄνθρωπος εὔνους καὶ πιστὴ καὶ ἀφειμένη ἐλευθέρα ὑπὸ τοῦ πατρὸς τοῦ ἐμοῦ. συνῴκησεν δὲ ἀνδρί, ἐπειδὴ ἀφείθη ἐλευθέρα· ὡς δὲ οὗτος ἀπέθανεν καὶ αὐτὴ γραῦς ἦν καὶ οὐκ ἦν αὐτὴν ὁ θρέψων, ἐπανῆκεν ὡς ἐμέ. . . . καὶ τῇ γυναικὶ βουλομένῃ ἦν τοιαύτην οἰκουρὸν μετ' αὐτῆς με καταλιπεῖν. [There was an old woman, who had been my nurse, a loyal and trusted servant, who had been set free by my father. When she was set free she took a husband. When he died and she was old and there was no one to provide for her she came back to me. . . . With the agreement of my wife, I left her as her domestic assistant].

12 For the slaves in the household see the informative collection Pettinato-Moggi, et al. (eds) 1997; Ferrucci 2002: 29–50. Mark Griffith (2011: 175–208) and Cheryl Cox (1998: 168–208) offer useful accounts of the peripheral members of the *oikos*.

13 Cox 1998: 130–208.

14 Literally κύριος means lord or leader.

15 See Humphreys 1989: 34–45; Strauss 2002; Cox 1998: 68–104; MacDowell 1989: 10–21. The *Wasps* of Aristophanes provides excellent insights into such relations at a first, literal level, as well as in the inversion of roles between two adult males of the household, where Bdelykleon, the son, is actually becoming the "baby-sitter" of his naughty old father, and acting in a way in which the father would act towards his son in a regular household. Philokleon is retired from the leadership of the household, and now his son Bdelykleon is the *kyrios* of their *oikos*. Both men are legally independent, and equal before the law. In this respect, Bdelykleon has no legal right to impose his will on his father, but he does so, as he tries to prevent him from giving in to his addiction for jury duty. Bdelykleon is able to do so because he is now the one whom the slaves of the household obey. These same slaves once obeyed Philokleon when he was leader of the household, but after his retirement the center of gravity has shifted to his son, who can order the slaves to lock Philokleon in the house for his own good. In this case the authority of Bdelykleon stems out of his position as head of the household, and is the result of an unwritten perception of the center of power in it.

Another enlightening example of such relations we find in the narrative of Isaios about Euktemon. There are two adult males in the same household, Euktemon and his son Philoktemon, who clash over the older man's infatuation with a libertine, a former prostitute named Alke. Euktemon falls in love with her, moves out of the house causing great distress to his existing family, and is manipulated into introducing Alke's illegitimate son as his own into the phratry. Philoktemon takes the side of his mother and blocks his father's attempts, and what follows is a back-and-forth between father and son until eventually Philoktemon is persuaded to allow his father to introduce the boy into the family. The narrative of Isaios undoubtedly suggests that neither of the two men has the authority to impose his will upon the other, and that any resolution to the quarrel has to come through compromise. Many more examples of such squabbles between fathers and sons can be found in new comedy, where sons try to fool or cajole their fathers into giving them the money to liberate a *hetaira* with whom they have fallen in love (see e.g. Plautus *Bacchides, Mostellaria*, al; with a twist in *Aulularia*, where the hen-pecked father is assisting his son to extract the money from his wife, the scary Artemona). See also Strauss 2002.

16 See for example Luc. *DMeretr*. 10, where the young Kleinias is forced by his father to quit the *hetaira* with whom he was going out and join a philosopher's school, or Ael. *Ep*. 19, where the father is threatening that he will force his son to divorce his wife (a former prostitute flute-player), and as a punishment to make him work hard in the fields. The only way fathers could force their sons in this manner was through economic sanctions.

17 The play is based on a Menandrian comedy with the same title. A point as basic for the plot as the initial quarrel between father and son probably comes from the original play.

18 For further discussion see Chapter 6.2 on divorce.

19 See for example the paraphrase of the law on the δίκη σίτου (see also Chapter 6.2) in D. 59.52: κατὰ τὸν νόμον ὃς κελεύει, ἐὰν ἀποπέμπῃ τὴν γυναῖκα, ἀποδιδόναι τὴν προῖκα, ἐὰν δὲ μή, ἐπ' ἐννέ' ὀβολοῖς τοκοφορεῖν, καὶ σίτου εἰς Ὠιδεῖον εἶναι δικάσασθαι ὑπὲρ

τῆς γυναικὸς τῷ κυρίῳ. [According to the law which orders that if someone divorces the woman, he is to return the dowry, and if he does not return it, he is to pay interest at the rate of nine obols to the drachma (18%), and the *kyrios* is to bring the lawsuit for the interest to the Odeon.] See also Is. 3.30 where the husband initiated proceedings on behalf of his wife so that she could claim her inheritance after the passing of her father, D. 43.9, where someone goes to court to fight for his wife's inheritance. See also Chapter 4.3 on marriage.

20 See Chapter 9.2.

21 On the financial interests of the *oikos* see Cox 1998; Gardner 1989: 51–62; Herz 2009: 177–94; Humphreys 1977: 97–104; Jorquera Nieto 1994: 213–18; Mirón Pérez 2004: 61–79; Pesando 1987; Richarz 1991: 141–51; Wolpert 2001a: 415–24.

22 See Chapter 6.4, and the discussion in Kapparis 2017: 161–171.

23 For example, Protag. Fr. 11 DK; Isoc. 4.31; Andoc. 1.130–131; Lys. 19.48. The passage of Lysias suggests that the actual property of Hipponikos may have been overestimated during his lifetime, but nonetheless it appears that Kallias lost much of the property which his father had left him.

24 For example, in Aesch. 3.19 spending one's inheritance on trierarchies is mentioned with praise, however in most cases it is meant to damage a litigant's image: e.g. Aesch. 1.94–106, 170; Din. Dem. 71.

25 Isoc. 17.124: ὁρῶντες διὰ τὸν πόλεμον καὶ τὰς ταραχὰς, ἃς οὗτοι πεποιήκασιν, τῶν μὲν ἄλλων πολιτῶν πολλοὺς ἐκ τῶν πατρῴων ἐκπεπτωκότας, τούτους δ' ἐκ πενήτων πλουσίους γεγενημένους. [We see that because of the war and the other upheavals that they (the politicians) have created, many of the other citizens lost their parental inheritance, while themselves have become a rich even though before there were poor.]

26 See Lambert 1998, and the discussion in Chapter 8.3.

27 See the discussion in Chapter 2.3.

28 On occasion one might arrange a marriage for his mother too, or even his wife, if he expected that he might die soon, or he needed to divorce her in order to marry an *epikleros* (heiress). In this case, the husband by arranging the marriage of his current wife to another man indicated to the community that he loved and respected her, and that the arrangement was motivated purely by financial considerations, and not character disagreement or infidelity. See the discussion in Chapter 5.4.

29 See Chapter 5.3.

30 The δίκη σίτου was an ἔμμηνος δίκη, namely a monthly lawsuit. The interest had to be paid monthly, and if the former husband failed to pay, he could be taken to the court at Odeon, where with an expedited process he would be ordered to pay. See Chapters 5.3 and 7.6.

31 Ar. *Nu.*1320–461.

32 See Chapter 1.11.

33 Ar. *Nu.* 1409–14.

34 See Chapter 9.2

35 The possibility for such prosecutions in real life were minimal, because the person who was supposed to prosecute for the mother of a slave was the *kyrios* himself. In an interesting twist, in the opening scenes of Plato's *Euthyphro*, Socrates is informed that Euthyphro is on his way to prosecute his own father for the killing of one of their slaves.

36 Translation by G.C. Armstrong, *Aristotle. Aristotle in 23 Volumes*, Vol. 18, Cambridge, MA, Harvard University Press; London, William Heinemann Ltd. 1935.

37 See for example, Davidson et al. 1995; Alcock 2006; Davidson 1995: 204–213; a thorough discussion of the expensive eating habits of some Athenians can be found in his 1997 book *Courtesans and Fishcakes*.

38 See for example Lys. 1.8.

39 D. 59.56: ψυχαγωγούμενος ἐν τῇ ἀσθενείᾳ τῇ θεραπείᾳ <τῇ> ὑπό τε τῆς Νεαίρας καὶ τῆς θυγατρὸς αὐτῆς (ἐβάδιζον γὰρ πρὸς αὐτόν, ὡς ἠσ θένει καὶ ἔρημος ἦν τοῦ

θεραπεύσοντος τὸ νόσημα, τὰ πρόσφορα τῇ νόσῳ φέρουσαι καὶ ἐπισκοπούμεναι· ἴστε ἤπου καὶ αὐτοὶ ὅσου ἀξία ἐστὶν γυνὴ ἐν ταῖς νόσοις, παροῦσα κάμνοντι ἀνθρώπῳ). [He was made comfortable in his illness by Neaira and her daughter (they went to his house, when he was ill and had no one to treat him, offering beneficial medicine and looking after him. You know yourselves how valuable a woman can be in sickness, at the side of a sick person.]

40 7.37–8: ἐπιμελημάτων ἴσως ἀχαριστότερον δόξει εἶναι, ὅτι, ὃς ἂν κάμνῃ τῶν οἰκετῶν, τούτων σοι ἐπιμελητέον πάντων ὅπως θεραπεύηται. Νὴ Δί', ἔφη ἡ γυνή, ἐπιχαριτώτατον μὲν οὖν, ἂν μέλλωσί γε οἱ καλῶς θεραπευθέντες χάριν εἴσεσθαι καὶ εὐνούστεροι ἢ πρόσθεν ἔσεσθαι. ["You may find that this one of your least pleasant duties: When one of the servants is sick, you need to look after them so that they can recover". "But of course" my wife said "this would be a very pleasant duty, if the ones who are cured are going to be grateful and even more dedicated than before."]

41 X. Oec. 7.24: τοῦ στέργειν τὰ νεογνὰ βρέφη πλέον αὐτῇ ἐδάσατο ἢ τῷ ἀνδρί. [He (sc. The divine providence) gave her a larger portion of the ability to love newborn infants.]

42 X. Oec. 7.36:

43 Ar. Ec. 236 χρήματα πορίζειν εὐπορώτατον γυνή. [A woman is very capable of finding money.]

44 ἐν μὲν οὖν τῷ πρώτῳ χρόνῳ, ὦ Ἀθηναῖοι, πασῶν ἦν βελτίστη· καὶ γὰρ οἰκονόμος δεινὴ καὶ φειδωλὸς {ἀγαθὴ} καὶ ἀκριβῶς πάντα διοικοῦσα. [In the beginning, men of Athens, she was the best of all women; she was a very capable manager, and very careful, and administered everything with precision.]

45 Ctesias *FGrH* 688 f 1b 23.

46 Maria Fialho (2010: 113–121) explains the anomaly as a result of the long absence of the *kyrios*, which created the circumstances for his wife to take over his role. See also MacEwen 1990: 16–34, as well the entire volume edited by MacEwen (1990) on the image of Klytaimestra in the ancient and modern tradition. Michael Shaw (1975: 255–66) sees a polarization between *oikos* and *polis*: when women act outside their traditional roles as mothers, wives or legal minors, they transgress into the world of men. Helene Foley (1982: 1–21) accepts the concept of transgression from one sphere to the other but sees it as a dialectic between the two spheres rather than a contrast. Judith Fletcher (1999: 108–25) has argued that the women in Lysistrata are so far removed from their traditional role as child-bearers that once they take the oath they start acting like men. Froma Zeitlin (1981: 301–27) has discussed female characters on stage within the context of gender and genre transgressions. The discussion on gender transgressions in Drama, as well as a possible dialectic between *oikos* and *polis* are far more extensive and exceed our purposes at this point.

47 In a previous paper I have suggested that the images of women coming from high literature are probably distorted to fit into this stereotype, while real women probably had more in common with the less limited, more irreverent, livelier and freer female characters of Attic Comedy.

("Aristophanes, Hippocrates and Sex Crazed Women", in *Ageless Arts, the Journal of the Southern Association for the History of Medicine and Science*, vol. 1: 47–57. Available at www.sahms.net/uploads/3/4/7/5/34752561/kapparis_final.pdf).

48 The speech of Lysias *On the property of Aristophanes* (19), and several plays of New Comedy, like for example the *Adelphoe* of Terence, based on plays of Menander and Diphilos, provide ample evidence of fathers actively involved in the upbringing of their children and their role within the *oikos*. See also Cox 2012: 278–87.

49 For example, in the speech *Against Spudias* the formidable wife of Polyeuctos and her daughters seem to be managing the affairs of the broader family, while the husbands are content to follow their lead. In the speech *Against Neaira* the former *hetaira* clearly runs everything in the household and gives it a distinct aura which breaks with traditional family conventions. In the speech against Diogeiton, the widow stands up to the *kyrios* of the household, her own father, in order to protect the best interests of

her children, and the narrative makes clear that she put up a determined and prolonged fight to protect the interests of the household against the rapacity of her father. For images of the *oikos* in Greek Drama see Cox 2012: 278–87; Crane 1997: 198–229; Fartzoff 1984: 171–184, and 1991; Fiahlo 2010: 113–121; Foley 1982: 1–21; Gambón 2009; Gardner 1989: 51–62; Luschnig 1990: 9–39; Morenilla Taléns 2009: 195–206; Pomeroy 1998; Proffitt 2011: 152–174; Salmenkivi 1997: 183–194; Syropoulos 2001: 5–18; Traill 2008. Wallace 1997: 151–66.

50 For a short introductory article on the topic see Tsouyopoulou-Saveriadou 1994: 41–9. Indispensable commentary and context on the *Economics* of Xenophon and Aristotle is provided by Pomeroy (1994 and also 1998) and Hunter (1994).

51 See, for example, Lys. 3.6 where the widowed sister and nieces of the speaker are living in his *oikos*, or D. 47.55 where an old servant, who had been set free and taken a husband, returns to live with the family after his death, and finds safety in her original *oikos*, this time as a free employee of the household. By contrast, the mother of Demosthenes chooses to stay in her husband's *oikos* as an independent widow.

52 Ar. *Th.* 445–458. Father discussion on the challenges of widowhood can be found in Chapter 5.

53 D. 57.42; the speaker was facing a challenge of his citizen status. His accusers were saying that he could not be an Athenian citizen because, among others, his mother had worked as a wet nurse, which was a job typically not done by citizen women. His response is that citizens sometimes were forced to do undignified jobs in order to survive and be able to feed their families.

54 Aesch. 1.158. The fact that Diophantos has to prosecute a client who had not paid for services provided through the *archon*, whose task was to look after orphans around the city, indicates that he was still under age. If he had been registered with a deme, he could have prosecuted the client himself. See Chapter 6.4.

55 Hyp. Fr. 164–5 Jensen.

56 As for example Palaestra in Plautus *Rudens*, who is fleeing from her captors.

57 Luc. *DMeretr.* 6; See also Gilhully 2006: 274–91, and the discussion in Kapparis 2017: 56–9.

58 About succession along agnatic lines see Cox 1998: 68–104; Hunter 1993: 100–21.

59 In this respect the Athenians were pragmatic, compared, let's say, to archaic and early classical Sparta, where the family property could not be divided, but had to be transferred as a whole to the eldest son, while other sons would need to acquire property through marriage into families without sons, at the risk of losing their full citizen status and become "inferiors" (ὑπομείονες) if they failed to do so. This discouraged healthy birth rates, and the anemic efforts of the state to stimulate birth rates proved totally ineffective. By the middle of the 4th century Sparta had less than 1000 full citizens, and this was her undoing as a great power in the Greek world. Athens on the other hand had no difficulty maintaining its status as the most populous city in the Greek world throughout the classical period, despite almost ceaseless warfare and astronomical losses of men.

60 For the *rhetra* of Epitadeus and the significant social changes in which it resulted, some of them certainly unintended and undesirable, see Christien 1974: 197–221; MacDowell 1986, and the discussion in Chapter 5.6.

61 See the discussion in Chapter 5.2–5.3.

62 For example, And. 1.117–122; for the *epicleros* and inheritance law in general see Chapter 5.4.

63 See the discussion in Chapter 1.4

64 See Chapter 2.5.

65 X. *Oec.* 7.19

66 About the symposion see Chapter 6.4.

67 The law is cited verbatim by Apollodoros in D. 59.87. More information about these celebrations is offered in the coming chapters. The very informative dissertation of Florence Gherchanoc (2012) is very useful for a better understanding of the celebratory occasions within the *oikos*. Martina Seifert in an indispensable study (2011) focuses upon the children within the *oikos*, and the various ceremonious occasions in their development. See also Simon 2002; Parke 1977; Burkert 1985; Oakley and Sinos 1993; Rehm 1994; Dillon 2003; Sutton 2004: 327–50.

68 Among numerous examples one might mention a positive and a negative one. The family of Euphiletos in Is. 12 is a positive example of how effective strong ties among its members could be in public life. The citizenship of Euphiletos had been questioned, but his brother, the person who stood to lose most if Euphiletos won, as he would see his inheritance cut in half if the citizenship of his brother was restored by the court, strenuously defends him. The father, mother, and even husbands of the sisters of Euphiletos all appear in court to support him with their testimony, too. It is difficult to imagine that the opponents of Euphiletos could succeed against such a united and determined family with strong ties of blood and loyalty. A negative example might be the family of Nikostratos in D. 53. While the same strong bonds of blood and loyalty undoubtedly seem to bind them too, their actions and motives are much darker, and the reader of the speech would rather think of them as a gang of criminals than a strong Athenian family.

4 The formation and purposes of marriage

Wives and concubines

4.1 Sources

1 The primary law on marriage (594 BC)

ΝΟΜΟΣ: Ἣν ἂν ἐγγυήσῃ ἐπὶ δικαίοις δάμαρτα εἶναι ἢ πατὴρ ἢ ἀδελφὸς ὁμοπάτωρ ἢ πάππος ὁ πρὸς πατρός, ἐκ ταύτης εἶναι παῖδας γνησίους. ἐὰν δὲ μηδεὶς ᾖ τούτων, ἐὰν μὲν μὴ ἐπίκληρός τις ᾖ, τὸν κύριον ἔχειν, ἐὰν δὲ ᾖ, ὅτῳ ἂν ἐπιτρέψῃ, τοῦτον κύριον εἶναι.[1]

(D. 46.18)

LAW: The woman given into lawful marriage by either her father, or brother from the same father, or her paternal grandfather, one can have legitimate children from her. If none of them is alive, if she is not an *epikleros* (heiress), let her husband keep her, but if she is, her husband is to be the man who has been appointed.

2 The *engye* formula

[{Σω}].λοιπόν ἐστιν ἡμῖν ἐγγυᾶν.
{(Κα)} ἀλλ' ἐγγυῶ παίδων ἐπ' ἀρότωι γνησίων
τὴν θυγατέρ' ἤδη μειράκιόν σοι προῖκά τε
δίδωμ' ἐπ' αὐτῆι τρία τάλαντα.

(Menander, *Dyskolos*, 841–44[2])

All that is left for us is to proceed with the agreement.
I offer my daughter to you, young man, as your wife
for the birth of legitimate children, and with her
I offer a dowry of three talents.

3 The law on the *epidikasia* of poor heiresses (594 BC)

ΝΟΜΟΣ: Τῶν ἐπικλήρων ὅσαι θητικὸν τελοῦσιν, ἐὰν μὴ βούληται ἔχειν ὁ ἐγγύτατα γένους, ἐκδιδότω ἐπιδοὺς ὁ μὲν πεντακοσιομέδιμνος πεντακοσίας δραχμάς, ὁ δ' ἱππεὺς τριακοσίας, ὁ δὲ ζευγίτης ἑκατὸν πεντήκοντα, πρὸς οἷς αὐτῆς. ἐὰν δὲ πλείους ὦσιν ἐν τῷ αὐτῷ γένει, τῇ ἐπικλήρῳ πρὸς μέρος ἐπιδιδόναι ἕκαστον. ἐὰν δ' αἱ γυναῖκες πλείους ὦσι, μὴ ἐπάναγκες εἶναι πλέον ἢ μίαν ἐκδοῦναι τῷ γ' ἑνί, ἀλλὰ τὸν ἐγγύτατα ἀεὶ ἐκδιδόναι ἢ αὐτὸν ἔχειν. ἐὰν δὲ μὴ ἔχῃ ὁ ἐγγυτάτω γένους ἢ μὴ ἐκδῷ, ὁ ἄρχων ἐπαναγκαζέτω ἢ αὐτὸν ἔχειν ἢ ἐκδοῦναι. ἐὰν δὲ μὴ ἐπαναγκάσῃ ὁ ἄρχων, ὀφειλέτω χιλίας δραχμὰς ἱερὰς τῇ Ἥρᾳ. ἀπογραφέτω δὲ τὸν μὴ ποιοῦντα ταῦτα ὁ βουλόμενος πρὸς τὸν ἄρχοντα.

(D. 43.54)

LAW: In regard to all heiresses who are classified as Thetes, if the nearest of kin does not wish to marry one, let him give her in marriage with a portion of five hundred drachmae, if he be of the class of Pentacosiomedimni, if of the class of Knights, with a portion of three hundred, and if of the class of Zeugitae, with one hundred and fifty, in addition to what is her own. If there are several kinsmen in the same degree of relationship, each one of them shall contribute to the portion of the heiress according to his due share. And if there be several heiresses, it shall not be necessary for a single kinsman to give in marriage more than one, but the next of kin shall in each case give her in marriage or marry her himself. And if the nearest of kin does not marry her or give her in marriage, the *archon* shall compel him either to marry her himself or give her in marriage. And if the *archon* shall not compel him, let him be fined a thousand drachmae, which are to be consecrated to Hera. And let any person who chooses denounce to the *archon* any person who disobeys this law.[3]

4 The Periclean citizenship law (451 BC)

ἐπὶ Ἀντιδότου (451–50 BC) διὰ τὸ πλῆθος τῶν πολιτῶν Περικλέους εἰπόντος ἔγνωσαν μὴ μετέχειν τῆς πόλεως, ὃς ἂν μὴ ἐξ ἀμφοῖν ἀστοῖν ᾖ γεγονώς.

(Arist. *Ath.* 26.3)

In the archonship of Antidotos after a proposal by Pericles they decided, because of the multitude of the citizens, to exclude from the city those who were not born from two citizen parents.

5 The reversal of the Periclean citizenship law (429 BC)

στρατηγὸς αἱρεθείς, ᾐτήσατο λυθῆναι τὸν περὶ τῶν νόθων νόμον, ὃν αὐτὸς εἰσενηνόχει πρότερον, ὡς μὴ παντάπασιν ἐρημίᾳ διαδοχῆς [τὸν οἶκον] ἐκλίποι τοὔνομα καὶ τὸ γένος.

(Plu. *Per.* 37)

When he was elected general, he requested the abolition of the law on illegitimate children, which he had introduced himself, so that his name and family would not be entirely eclipsed in the absence of an heir.

6 The Periclean law reinstated (403 BC)

ΝΟΜΟΣ: νόθῳ δὲ μηδὲ νόθῃ μὴ εἶναι ἀγχιστείαν μήθ' ἱερῶν μήθ' ὁσίων ἀπ' Εὐκλείδου ἄρχοντος (cf. also Is. 6.47, with almost identical wording).

(D. 43.51)

LAW: an illegitimate son or daughter is not to participate in the anchisteia (e.g. retain inheritance rights), and the holy and sacred rites, if born after the archonship of Eucleides.

7 The law prohibiting mixed marriages altogether, as well as any pretence (c. 380 BC)

ΝΟΜΟΣ: Ἐὰν δὲ ξένος ἀστῇ συνοικῇ τέχνῃ ἢ μηχανῇ ἡτινιοῦν, γραφέσθω πρὸς τοὺς θεσμοθέτας Ἀθηναίων ὁ βουλόμενος οἷς ἔξεστιν. ἐὰν δὲ ἁλῷ, πεπράσθω καὶ αὐτὸς καὶ ἡ οὐσία αὐτοῦ, καὶ τὸ τρίτον μέρος ἔστω τοῦ ἑλόντος. ἔστω δὲ καὶ ἐὰν ἡ ξένη τῷ ἀστῷ συνοικῇ κατὰ ταὐτά, καὶ ὁ συνοικῶν τῇ ξένῃ τῇ ἁλούσῃ ὀφειλέτω χιλίας δραχμάς.

(D. 59.16)

LAW: If an alien man lives in marriage with a citizen woman through some trickery or device, he is to be indicted to the *thesmothetai* by any Athenian who wishes and has the right to do so. If he is convicted, he is to be sold, himself and his property, and the successful prosecutor is to receive the one third. Likewise, if an alien woman lives in marriage with a citizen man, the same penalties apply, and the man living in marriage with the foreign woman is to be fined one thousand drachmas.

8 The law prohibiting the fraudulent betrothal of a foreign woman to an Athenian citizen (c. 380 BC)

ΝΟΜΟΣ: Ἐὰν δέ τις ἐκδῷ ξένην γυναῖκα ἀνδρὶ Ἀθηναίῳ ὡς ἑαυτῷ προσήκουσαν, ἄτιμος ἔστω, καὶ ἡ οὐσία αὐτοῦ δημοσία ἔστω, καὶ τοῦ ἑλόντος τὸ τρίτον μέρος. γραφέσθων δὲ πρὸς τοὺς θεσμοθέτας οἷς ἔξεστιν, καθάπερ τῆς ξενίας.

(D. 59.52)

LAW: If someone betroths an alien woman to an Athenian man under the pretence that she is his relative, he is to be disfranchised, and his property is to be confiscated, and the successful prosecutor is to receive the one third. An indictment is to be brought to the *thesmothetai* by anyone who is legally entitled, as in cases of *xenia*.[4]

4.2 The ever-shifting definition of marriage

In early times the Athenians could marry other Greeks without restriction, and the children of one Athenian parent would be citizens themselves. In fact, some of the most prominent men in the city had been the offspring of mixed marriages especially among the upper classes, as often aristocrats married wealthy, aristocratic foreigners. For example, Kleisthenes, the founder of democracy was the offspring of Megakles of the Almaeonidae, and Agariste, the daughter of the tyrant of Sikyon, while Kimon was the son of Miltiades, the glorious victor at Marathon, and the Thracian princess Hypsipyle. It is understandable why mixed marriages were not uncommon among the lower classes too in a trading city with large numbers of foreign visitors and open immigration policies. If the figure given by Plutarch comes from a reliable source, in the middle of the 5th century 10 percent of the entire citizen body were offspring of mixed unions (μητρόξενοι).[5]

This policy came to an end at the height of the Athenian Empire in 451 when a law introduced by Pericles made Athenian parentage from both sides a mandatory requirement for citizenship (S 4).[6] The law, as it has been preserved in several sources, was a very simple piece of legislation only stating the requirement of Athenian parentage from both sides. However, its consequences were far-reaching and affected many areas of public and private life. According to Plutarch, approximately 5000 people lost their citizenship as a result of this law, approximately 10 percent of the citizen body, and this did not happen easily or smoothly.[7] It happened, he says, over a period of time and was the result of vicious and prolonged litigation all over the city. MacDowell correctly disputes this, and it is true that there is not much evidence of extensive litigation resulting from the law of Pericles shortly after the middle of the 5th century. First and foremost, the Periclean citizenship law was not retroactive. Persons of mixed origin already registered as citizens were not disqualified. However, our sources from that period are limited and Plutarch's information may be supported by a passage from the *Wasps* of Aristophanes.[8] There is a distinct possibility that the law strengthened xenophobic views and encouraged prosecutions for *xenia*, even if this may not have been the intention of the creator of this law.[9] While the numbers of Plutarch must be exaggerated, we should not be too quick to dismiss the possibility that there were quite a few *xenia* lawsuits initiated by men emboldened by the Periclean citizenship law against their enemies.

The law did not expressly forbid mixed unions, nor required that Athenians in mixed unions needed to divorce. However, given that the Solonean law on marriage expressly stated that the purpose of the union was to produce legitimate children (S 1), it would make no sense in future to conduct a marriage between an Athenian and an alien, when the offspring would automatically be excluded from citizenship. The long-term impact of this law was very significant and changed the way the Athenians understood marriage.[10] First, it terminated the practice of alliances through marriage with rich and powerful families in other Greek cities, and this affected mostly the upper classes and conceivably strengthened the Democratic Constitution by depriving the aristocrats of the ability to count on the muscle of foreign alliances. It also closed quite decisively a possible avenue for outsiders to become part of Athenian society. Immigration was high during the Athenian Empire, as many outsiders came to the wealthy capital in search of a better life and more opportunity. Until 451, these outsiders, especially women, had a path of greater integration into Athenian society through marriage with an Athenian citizen. Although themselves would not become Athenian, their children would be. The Periclean citizenship law drew a very clear line between Athenians and outsiders. Thereafter, anyone wishing to become an Athenian would need to take his chances through an impossibly difficult naturalization process. Considering that this process only allowed the naturalization of a foreigner on grounds of great service to the city of Athens,[11] through a personal naturalization decree approved in a "full house" vote of at least 6000 citizens, it effectively meant that the path of metics towards greater integration into Athenian society was now effectively and permanently blocked. Those who were not born Athenian would forever remain alien, themselves and their descendants, with rare exceptions.

One of the most profound consequences of this law was the attention which the Athenian woman was about to receive. Until then, as far as the *polis* was concerned, outside the sphere of religion the Athenian woman was invisible, unless she committed a serious crime, or she was involved in some property claim, and she was readily replaceable with a richer or prettier alien woman. This changed overnight with the Periclean citizenship law. From then on, the Athenian woman was going to become the necessary vessel for the continuation of the citizen stock, and as such an instrument for one of the most important goals of the *polis* and the *oikos*, and an inalienable and integral part of the *polis*. This renewed attention to the Athenian female caught the eye of the lawgiver. With a law, which seems to have been enacted not long after 451, she could no longer avoid punishment if caught committing adultery. Now the stakes were higher for the *polis*, and a mandatory divorce was required in order to make sure that the offspring of adulterous relationships would not be surreptitiously passed off as citizens. Moreover, the woman herself was going to face harsh penalties which amounted to *atimia*, her effective expulsion from the public life of the community.[12] Other laws seemingly were adapted to this new social reality, like, for example, the rule which required that the wife of the *archon basileus* needed to be of citizen birth. This rule, along with the other, more traditional requirements of her role, was inscribed on a stone stele and placed outside in the sanctuary of Dionysus at the Marshes (ἐν Λίμναις) and was still legible about 100 years later even though it had faded by that stage.[13]

We should be in no doubt that the law had a serious impact upon the position of the Athenian woman even within the *oikos*. The citizen woman must have felt empowered certain in the knowledge that only her own children could be the future citizens, while any illegitimate brood of her husband from concubines, prostitutes or slaves could no longer qualify for citizenship or have any claim on the family property; the marginalization of illegitimate children was complete. Nonetheless, an Athenian man could always make arrangements for his illegitimate children *inter vivos*. While they had no automatic claim to the family property, there was nothing stopping a man from offering a sum of money to an illegitimate son, let's say to start a business, and he would probably be expected to offer a dowry, even if smaller, to an illegitimate daughter given in marriage to a non-Athenian man or in concubinage to an Athenian man. A law mentioned by Harpocration limited the sum which could be offered to an illegitimate child to 1000 drachmas (νοθεῖα).[14] A passage of Aristophanes implies that this limit might have applied only to arrangements made in a will, and this may well have been the case, but the existing evidence is not sufficient to corroborate this conclusion.[15] This amount was substantial enough to give an illegitimate son a head-start in life, or to provide a modest dowry for a daughter, but not too large to be seen as a threat to the interests of the *oikos* and its legitimately born heirs.

The reasons behind the introduction of the citizenship law in 451 have been the subject of extensive speculation. Aristotle says that it was done because Athens had too many citizens. In a significant passage in the *Politics* he writes the following:

> οὐ μὴν ἀλλ' ἐπεὶ δι' ἔνδειαν τῶν γνησίων πολιτῶν ποιοῦνται πολίτας τοὺς τοιούτους (διὰ γὰρ ὀλιγανθρωπίαν οὕτω χρῶνται τοῖς νόμοις), εὐποροῦντες δὴ ὄχλου κατὰ μικρὸν παραιροῦνται τοὺς ἐκ δούλου πρῶτον ἢ δούλης, εἶτα τοὺς ἀπὸ γυναικῶν, τέλος δὲ μόνον τοὺς ἐξ ἀμφοῖν ἀστῶν πολίτας ποιοῦσιν.[16]
>
> But they make these men citizens when there is shortage of legitimate citizens (they introduce these laws because of the lack of manpower). However when the population increases, they incrementally leave out first those born from male or female slaves, then those born from the free women [concubines], and finally they only make citizens those born of two citizens.

MacDowell advises caution on modern interpretations of the Periclean citizenship law, such as the preservation of the racial purity of the Athenians or their fear that their own daughters might not be able to find husbands, saying "these suggestions seem to spring from the interests and moral beliefs of those who make them."[17] He argues that the only interpretation offered by an ancient source is that of Aristotle, that the citizen body had become too large. Stephen Todd, on the other hand, places less faith in Aristotle, on the grounds that this might be his own personal view of the law.[18]

The statement of Aristotle is based upon his observation of the reasons why the Athenians reinstated the Periclean citizenship law in 403, and at least in the latter case he diagnoses the motives of the Athenians correctly. During the Peloponnesian war, when Athens was low in manpower, and many families were in danger of being left without an heir, the Periclean citizenship law was invalidated and children from concubines or even slaves were accepted as citizens. When after the war the fortunes of the city started to recover then all others were excluded except those born of Athenian women. His interpretation of the Periclean law itself as the result of a policy intended to reduce the number of citizens may have merit, if we consider that the direct democracy of the Greek *polis* was conceptualized with a limited number of citizens in mind. The Pnyx, the assembly area, could not accommodate more than 6000 people, which at the time when the Periclean citizenship law was introduced, would be not much more than 10 percent of the citizen body. The concept of a constitutional form where every citizen had an equal right to vote and participate in the running of the state in person, while representation in public life was considered to be the most recognizable feature of oligarchy, could only function if the number of citizens was limited. At the height of the Athenian Empire the population of Athens was growing, not least because the prosperity and prestige of the city had attracted metics from every corner of the Greek world and beyond, and metics marrying citizens would be increasing the number of Athenian citizens at a faster pace. Athens was already about ten times larger than the magic number of 5000 citizens, which some considered to be the ideal number for a *polis*, and seems to have been roughly the number of citizens in rival, and much admired Sparta at that time.[19] The pressure to put the brakes to Attica's population explosion and keep the Athenian democratic institutions functional might truly be the reason why the man who has come to embody the Athenian Democracy at its finest hour proposed this law, even though by doing so he was also excluding from citizenship his youngest son who had his name. The sincere motive of Pericles might have been to safeguard the Athenian Democracy, and as Cynthia Patterson has argued, to make its administration more effective.[20]

The Periclean citizenship law was repealed in 429 with the proposal of Pericles himself, as Daniel Ogden and Edwin Carawan have convincingly demonstrated (S 5).[21] Plutarch describes how the great general, crushed with grief after the death of both his legitimate sons, his sister, and other relatives from the plague, begged the assembly to reverse his own law. The historical irony was not missed. The assembly approved his proposal, no doubt because many hard-pressed families around the city were in a very similar situation and could no longer afford to exclude illegitimate children from citizenship and succession. This more inclusive view of the *nothoi* has left some traces in the drama of the period. Euripides keeps returning to the subject: several times he stresses in his plays the physical equality and common nature (φύσις) of the *nothoi* with the *gnesioi*, making the point that the *nothoi* are only disadvantaged when it comes to the law.[22] In a fragment from his lost *Andromeda* he says that the *nothoi*, even though they are equal to the *gnesioi* in every respect, they are suffering from the "disease" of the law (τῶν γνησίων γὰρ οὐδὲν ὄντες ἐνδεεῖς/νόμῳ νοσοῦσιν).[23] In *Andromache* we read that many *nothoi* are morally superior to the *gnesioi* (νόθοι τε πολλοὶ γνησίων ἀμείνονες).[24] Such sentiments would be echoed from time to time even in 4th century authors, when the Periclean citizenship law had been reinstated. The idealized king Nikocles prides himself in not making any distinction between his illegitimate and his legitimate children, because all are worthy of their privileged bloodline, and Hekataios in his praise of the Egyptians stresses that no child is ever considered illegitimate, even those born of slave mothers.[25]

The law of Pericles was reinstated with a decree of Aristophon and Nikomenes in 403 (S 6),[26] along with the general re-organization of the city. The timing of it may seem strange when considering how many lives had been lost in Athens after a 30-year war, and how many families pinned up their hopes on their illegitimate offspring. This is why the law did not apply retroactively; devastated families who relied upon illegitimate children for the succession and continuation of the *oikos* could continue to do so. The law only applied to those born after 403, thus recognizing the grim practicalities of a painful past, but also expressing the optimism that a better future lies ahead, where the Athenians would not need to resort to such measures in order to preserve their families, and the democracy could function better, strong as in the golden years of Pericles.

Not long after the last μητρόξενοι had been registered with the demes, probably around 380,[27] a new law was introduced intended to tie up loose ends, remove all uncertainty about mixed unions, and ensure that no pretext could be used in future to introduce into the citizen body anyone who was not Athenian on both sides. After the Periclean citizenship law mixed marriages had not been prohibited, as such; they were simply made pointless. The new law went one step further and actively prohibited mixed marriages with very severe penalties. The alien partner was to be sold into slavery and any property he/she might have was to be confiscated, while the citizen partner of an alien woman was liable to a huge fine of 1000 drachmas (S 7). In an additional clause anyone who had deceived an Athenian and betrothed to him an alien woman under the pretense that she was his own relative and an Athenian citizen was liable to even harsher penalties, such as disfranchisement and confiscation of his property. The determination of this law to put an end to all mixed unions and any subterfuge possibly used to sneak an alien into the citizen body is unmistakable.

The reasons which might have prompted this legislation are not clear, but we can make some educated guess. It would be reasonable to assume that for a few years after 385, when the last μητρόξενοι had been registered with the demes, quite a few people were claiming that they had actually been born before the archonship of Eukleides, especially women whose age was more difficult to verify, and perhaps there was some concern that 20 years after the reinstatement of the Periclean citizenship law, the citizen body was still rife with non-Athenians or half-Athenians. The slow, incremental implementation of the decree of Aristophon and Nikomenes over a period of almost 20 years could easily have created the impression that after all this time nothing had actually changed or was about to change without decisive action.

One other factor, which may have created some urgency for additional legislation banning mixed marriages once and for all, could be the rise of the *hetaira* as a cultural icon. After the turn of the century the profitable business of high-end prostitution started spilling out of Corinth to its neighboring cities, the prosperous Megara, and of course Athens. As the finances of the city were recovering through renewed capitalist enterprise and commerce, and its central position in the Greek world was reasserted, Athens became an attractive destination for top of the range *hetairai* from the whole of the Greek world. Some of the women were liberated slaves, like Neaira or the famous Bacchis, who provided the character for several plays, others were free-born Greek women, like Sinope from Pontus or Lais from Hykkara, and some, like Lais the younger or Mania, were local Athenian girls. Foreign women vastly outnumbered the local ones in this business, and quite possibly a few of them ended up married to citizens under subterfuge that they were properly born Athenians. This kind of deception should not be too hard to orchestrate in the case of women, since the state kept no records on their births, deaths or marriages.[28] The anxiety that an ever-increasing number of seductive alien women, adept at manipulating infatuated men, could be sneakily marrying bachelors destined for Athenian women and introducing their illegitimate brood into the citizen body, might have triggered strict legislation intended to stop them.

It was never the intention of the lawgiver to stop citizens from cohabiting with aliens, have affairs with alien *hetairai*, or interfere in any way with the lovelives of the Athenians. This kind of interference would be undemocratic, and the Athenians prided themselves in their freedom to live their private lives as they pleased. The law was only concerned with the composition of the citizen body, and it only prohibited mixed marriages, or the pretense of a lawful marriage between a citizen and an alien. The law certainly did not prohibit other unions, not tried to stop citizens from taking alien concubines, and spending their lives with them if they so wished, and in fact such unions were protected by the rigorous adultery laws of Athens.[29] Ultimately this law had nothing to do with the living arrangements of citizens and non-citizens alike; it only had to do with the proper birth of the citizens of Attica, and was only invoked when someone had tried to introduce an improperly born person into the citizen body. We should be in no doubt that this is the case, not only because Apollodoros explicitly says so (see below), but also because the status of Phano is crucial for his strategy when he invokes this law in the prosecution of Neaira. Without a doubt this was the one thing that he needed to focus upon if he wanted to prove that Stefanos and Neaira had breached this law.

The law changed forever the relations of Athenians with foreigners. In 4th century sources we find that the separating lines between Athenians and foreigners were sharp. Apollodoros would try to place an admittedly alien 60-year-old woman into slavery, because, he alleged, she had the temerity to have children with an Athenian man and seek to legitimize them. Her partner, however, denied that she was the mother of his children. In Isaios 3 the relatives of a young woman are trying to steal her sizeable inheritance alleging that she was illegitimate because her mother was an alien *hetaira*. In comedy this divide between citizens and non-citizens is very clearly visible, as it creates an insurmountable barrier for lovers of unequal status. The barrier is sometimes crossed through a classic recognition plot, when it turns out that the woman who was thought to be an alien turns out to be a citizen. This plot twist allows the two lovers to get legally married in the end and offers the audience the awaited happy ending. For example, the kind and likable Glykera in Menander's *Perikeiromene* turns to be a citizen woman who had been exposed at birth and is a recognized by the baby clothes which she was wearing when she was exposed. This plot twist allows her to marry her lover, the short-tempered Demeas. In *Misoumenos*, we have another such example, where the virtuous Krateia is recognized as a citizen in the end and marries the soldier Thrasonides. The character of the "pseudo-*hetaira*", who turns out to be a citizen woman of good character and can therefore legally marry her beloved, as the audience wishes, is rather standard in the plays of New Comedy, and underlines the fact that the law under discussion had a very dominant effect in shaping the relations of Athenians with non-Athenians in the 4th century.

The possibility that the law was actually targeting the group which seems most affected in the plays of New Comedy, remains distinct. The lengthy argument of Apollodoros in the closing sections of the speech *Against Neaira*, where he states that if this law were to be invalidated prostitutes would take the place of Athenian wives and property born Athenian women would have no option but to turn to prostitution, seems to actively support the association between this law and the attempt of the Athenian state to keep the offspring of alien *hetairai* outside the citizen body. For Geoffrey Bakewell this anxiety, where the *kyrioi* of eligible Athenian women feared that nubile metic women would snatch potential bridegrooms, lies at the core of this law.[30] It certainly prevented the numerous alien sex workers of Attica from transitioning into wives of Athenian citizens when they moved past their prime and would be looking for a more settled and secure lifestyle at the side of an infatuated lover.[31] At best, they would have to be content in the role of a concubine, and accept the fact that their position would always be vulnerable, since they could not give birth to legitimate offspring.

4.3 Lawful marriage: types and purpose

In the legal documents of the classical period the word used for marriage is not a noun, but a verbal form, an infinitive with article, meaning "the act of living together" (τὸ συνοικεῖν), because, at least from a legal perspective, marriage was not understood as an abstract concept or an institution,[32] but rather as a composite process, in effect for as long as the participants continued to live together. In order for the process to be valid in the eyes of the law, it needed to be initiated through a legal act, a contract (ἐγγύη) or an adjudication (ἐπιδικασία).[33] However, the contract was not enough for the marriage to come into effect (unlike modern marriage papers, which once signed make the marriage legal and binding regardless of the living conditions of the couple). The process came to full effect when the couple moved in together. Usually the bride moved into the house of the bridegroom after a wedding feast and a ceremonial procession from her parental house to that of her husband.[34] In most cases the wedding ceremony followed shortly after the legal arrangements, but this was not always the case. Years could go by between the contract or the adjudication and the actual wedding, especially when the bride was too young for the consummation of the marriage.[35] The marriage continued to stay in effect for as long as the couple lived together. If one of them moved out, this was divorce, simple and easy.[36]

The dominant view of the Athenians on the purpose of marriage is summarized by a 4th century orator as following:

> τὸ γὰρ συνοικεῖν τοῦτ' ἔστιν, ὃς ἂν παιδοποιῆται καὶ εἰσάγῃ εἴς τε τοὺς φράτερας καὶ δημότας τοὺς υἱεῖς, καὶ τὰς θυγατέρας ἐκδιδῷ ὡς αὑτοῦ οὔσας τοῖς ἀνδράσιν. τὰς μὲν γὰρ ἑταίρας ἡδονῆς ἕνεκ' ἔχομεν, τὰς δὲ παλλακὰς τῆς καθ' ἡμέραν θεραπείας τοῦ σώματος, τὰς δὲ γυναῖκας τοῦ παιδοποιεῖσθαι γνησίως καὶ τῶν ἔνδον φύλακα πιστὴν ἔχειν.
>
> (D. 59.122)

> For this is what to be married means, to have children and to introduce the sons to the phratry and the deme, and to give the daughters in marriage to their husbands as one's own [legitimate] offspring. We keep *hetairai* for pleasure, concubines for the daily care of our bodies, and wives in order to have legitimate children and a faithful guardian of our household.

The primary purposes of marriage, according to Apollodoros, are the birth of legitimate children and good household management, and other contemporary sources support this statement.[37] These purposes of marriage were not incompatible with a good sex life or love and emotional attachment.[38] Although marriage by love was possible, if the plots of new comedy and a few indirect references in the Attic Orators are to be taken at face value, arranged marriages were the rule in Attica.[39] The participants did not expect to be in love before they entered the union, but rather to allow such feelings to develop in time.

As Xenophon states,[40] the choice of a suitable mate was a very important part in the process. Numerous cases suggest that Athenian men, when looking for a wife, often considered brides among their relatives and friends.[41] The only blood relationship which Athenian law considered inappropriate for marriage was that of a brother and sister from the same mother. Brothers and sisters from the same father could in theory marry, but such unions where extremely rare.[42] More distant relatives, on the other hand, such as cousins, nephews or nieces frequently made suitable mates.[43] We should be in no doubt that in real life too, as it often happens in fiction, attractive women were prizes to be won by potential mates. In choosing a wife the possibilities were endless, depending on a man's temperament and expectations, and there is no reason to assume uniformity of practice.

Young women did not choose their husbands; this was done by their parents, especially the father. Expectedly, a father might be looking for very different qualities in a potential husband for his daughter than what the woman herself would be looking for. A man's good financial and social standing, and his family's good reputation would strongly recommend him, while his looks or age would be far less important.[44] This should not be taken as an indication that the woman had no say; a determined young woman always has her way of prevailing over her father. Older women, especially widows, understandably had more of a say. In one such case in the speech of Isaios *On the Estate of Menekles* the brothers of the woman leave the decision whether she should remarry entirely up to her.[45] Widows with children could even choose to stay in their deceased husband's house, or return to their natal *oikos*, and we have examples of both types of arrangements.[46] However, ultimately the decision, negotiations and legal formalities of a marriage were a man's job, and the marriage contract was not between the woman and her husband, but between the men, the woman's *kyrios* and her husband.

Given the vulnerability of the woman in this situation and the importance of these arrangements for her future, the law only allowed her closest male relatives, father, brother or paternal grandfather, to arrange a marriage contract (*engye*) on her behalf (S 1). This law is in line with other provisions related to marriage and inheritance, which always favored the agnatic side. Its language betrays that it was Solonean,[47] and it stands to reason that Solon simply incorporated into law what had been widespread social practice in his time. In subsequent centuries the Athenians saw no good reason why they should tamper with this time-honored process, and it appears that this Solonean law continued to be the primary text which regulated the legal provisions of marriage for centuries. Although the law does not seem to mention the current husband of a married woman, several passages suggest that as her *kyrios* he also had the legal right to give her in marriage to another man. This could happen, for example, if he wanted to free himself in order to claim an *epikleros*, or he expected to die and wanted to make sure that his wife will be well looked after in future.[48]

The actual procedure of the *engye* seems to be straightforward: the two men, the woman's *kyrios* and her future husband, came together in the presence of witnesses to negotiate and seal the contract. Although the dowry was not a legal requirement, rarely a woman would be given in marriage without any dowry (ἄπροικος).[49] The negotiations on the dowry, which might be the most difficult part in the process, were not only concentrated on the sum of the dowry, but also on the forms which it took. A dowry could be cash, real estate, like a house or a field, movables like furniture or clothing, and valuables like jewelry or cups made of precious metals. Non-monetary items needed to be assessed, so that in case of divorce there would be no disagreement on the value of the dowry which needed to be returned.[50]

Once the form and value of the dowry had been agreed, all that remained was to seal the deal with a traditional formula. Several examples in New Comedy allow us to understand what the formula was like. With minor variations all suggest that the father of the bride said to the bridegroom, "I give you my daughter for the birth of legitimate children, and with her I offer a dowry of this amount". The bridegroom responded "I accept and I will cherish her" (S 2 and note). The standard phrase ἐπ᾽ἀρότω γνησίων παίδων (for the birth of legitimate children), which has an archaic and poetic coloring, suggests that the formula was probably a very traditional text, most likely in meter.[51] A handshake in the presence of the witnesses completed the process. In future, if there was any question about the legality of that contract, the witnesses would be called to testify and confirm its validity. Since the Athenians mistrusted written contracts not verifiable by witnesses, *engye* in its traditional form remained an oral process, and written marriage contracts did not make their appearance until later in the classical period and did not become widespread before the Hellenistic period.[52]

The alternate form of marriage, the ἐπιδικασία (adjudication), was reserved for these cases where there was no father, brother or paternal grandfather alive to give a woman in marriage (S 1). In that case a woman became an ἐπίκληρος (heiress), which meant that in the absence of a male heir she inherited the property of her father.[53] Strictly speaking, she did not own the property, and neither did her future husband. The law explicitly stated that the owner of the estate would be her son, once he reached his 20th year of age (ἅμα ἡβήσῃ ἐπὶ δίετες, see Chapter 5.4 for the discussion). When he took control of the estate, he was obliged to pay for the maintenance of his mother, instead of her husband, who would normally be expected to provide for her. The process of *epidikasia* had two objectives: the first was to take care of the woman and make sure that she would be well-looked after; the second was to make sure that the property remained in the family and was inherited by a direct descendant of the deceased, who would thus be seen as the heir to his grandfather's *oikos*. Both objectives seemed to be best achieved if the woman were to be given in marriage to the closest male relative of her father.

As an uncle or cousin, he should be well-disposed towards her, and the property would stay within the family. In order to make sure that heirs, preferably male, were born, who would inherit their grandfather, the law required the husband of the *epikleros* to have intercourse with her at least three times a month.[54] Plutarch approves of the wisdom of Solon in this instance, even though he admits that at first sight the law appeared to be ridiculous and pointless (ἄτοπος δὲ δοκεῖ καὶ γελοῖος). The objective, he says, was to make sure that the husband did not take an *epikleros* only for her money.

A marriage through *epidikasia* began with a claim of the woman and her property submitted to the *archon* by her father's closest male relative. If he was too old, or unwilling to divorce his wife, as one would imagine that it often happened, he could step aside in favor of the second closest male relative, like, for example his son, or a younger brother, and so on.[55] Many a time it was not obvious who was the eldest, closest male relative of the woman's father, and in a case like this, more distant relatives could be entering competing claims, especially if the property was large, or the woman exceptionally attractive. In a society which did not keep exact records of births or deaths, and relied on witnesses to clarify familial relations, deciding who had the better claim was not always straight-forward. One such complicated case is illustrated in two extant speeches delivered in the same trial.[56] They reveal an incredibly complex network of relatives, and trying to sort out the genealogy and correctness of each claim appears to be a daunting task even for a scholar who has the time to patiently navigate through both texts. One can hardly imagine how an Athenian jury could reach a fair decision just by hearing the claimants speak on the fly.

It is not clear what happened when only one claimant had submitted a request to the *archon*, and the actual wording of the law ὅτῳ ἂν ἐπιτρέψῃ is not helping, because it is not obvious who the subject of ἐπιτρέψῃ was. One would imagine that in an uncontested case the *archon* would validate the claim and complete the *epidikasia* without further ado. However, if more than one claimants appeared, the case went before a jury (διαδικασία), which decided who had the strongest claim. The winner would then proceed to marry the woman and take her property along with her.

If the *epikleros* happened to be poor and there was no property going with her, a Solonean law made specific arrangements, ordering the closest male relative of her father to marry her himself, or give her in marriage with a dowry out of his own property. The sum of the dowry was fixed and specified in the law and varied according to the financial muscle of the donor (S 3). It is doubtful whether these sums, in accordance with the four Solonean classes, would be observed in the classical period, but the principle that no citizen woman should be left outside the protective sphere of the *oikos* for lack of property and an immediate family to take care of her, is abundantly evident in this provision. When those who were expected to make sure that this woman is given in marriage and becomes part of a family were not around, the state ordered more distant relatives to step into their shoes and perform their duty, whether they liked it or not, adding a moral imperative "to do the right thing" to the economic compulsion.[57] Once the legal formalities of the *epidikasia* were finalized, if the woman was over 14 years old, she moved in with her husband and the marriage process was complete. If she was under age, she would stay with her natal family, under the protection of a guardian (ἐπίτροπος) until she reached the age of 14.

Richard Cudjoe in a significant article has questioned whether the *epidikasia* was an alternate form of marriage.[58] He argues that the *epidikasia* was primarily concerned with property and its main purpose was to determine the relationship of the claimants with the *epikleros*, and ultimately who was her *kyrios*. He also maintains that "any decision about the married life of the *epikleros* was a later discretionary one taken by her successful claimant after the *epidikasia*, and quite independent of the *archon*'s executive fiat."[59] Cudjoe also argues that once the *epidikasia* had been completed the *kyrios* of the woman could marry her himself or give her in marriage to someone else with a dowry, thus expanding the provisions of the law on the poor *epikleros* (S 3) to all *epikleroi*.

Cudjoe is aware of the main difficulty of his thesis, namely that there is not a single case of a rich *epikleros* attested in the sources who did not become the wife of the successful claimant.[60] This undermines both his thesis that the marriage arrangements were discretionary, and his argument that the *epidikasia* was not an alternate marriage procedure. The reason why there is not a single such case attested, but in all cases the *epikleros* had to become the wife of the person who won her, was that the process of the *epidikasia* was the first, obligatory and necessary step to a marriage. Moreover, unless the *epidikasia* was an alternate marriage path, the entire set of arrangements about the *epikleros* does not make sense. If, for example, the person who won the right to the *epikleros* could just as easily marry her off to a stranger and keep for himself the property of her father, then that property would be permanently lost to the woman and her children; this would run against everything we know about an *epikleros* and her fortune. As mentioned above, the whole purpose of a marriage to her father's nearest relative was for the property to stay within the family along with the woman, not without her. For these reasons it is necessary to adhere to the traditional view advocated by MacDowell, Wolff, Todd and others that the *epidikasia* was an alternate form of marriage.[61] The corrected text of the primary law on marriage (S 1) clearly indicates that the *engye* was the first legal step for a valid marriage by contract, and the *epidikasia* was its replacement, as the first legal step for a valid marriage in these instances when an *engye* could not be performed.

The Athenians had a comparable concept to the modern "age of consent."[62] Young children were carefully protected and never left unattended. In their early years they were often looked after by a nurse (τίτθη or τροφός). Boys who were sent to school where accompanied by a *paidagogos*, typically a slave in charge of their safety and well-being, and young girls were never away from the watchful eye of the family. However, a time came when Athenian parents needed to acknowledge the sexual autonomy of the children. For girls this typically meant to be given away to their first marriage, and for boys it meant to have more freedom to engage in consensual love affairs with women or men. Marriage was not even a possibility for boys before registration with the deme, and typically came much later, when they had the means to provide for a family.[63]

The passage into sexual maturity happened around the age of 14 or 15. The practice of the Athenians is in line with the average age of consent throughout the world today.[64] By this stage a woman would be mature enough for sexual relations,[65] but not sufficiently self-assured to defy a husband's authority and control. According to Xenophon,[66] it was an important part of the careful upbringing of a young woman to be shielded from the world and go to her husband with very little life experience, which would render her more susceptible to his instruction and ready to be molded to his needs and wants.[67] An additional reason for an early marriage undoubtedly was the fact that the natal family did not have to battle with teenage hormones and the ever-increasing possibility of premarital sexual relations. Once the woman was married she became the responsibility of the husband in more than one ways, and the marriage would provide a safe outlet for her physical needs. Greek medical theory endorsed these arrangements, as ancient physicians were convinced that sexual abstinence was harmful for the woman, while regular intercourse by broadening the mouth of the womb allowed the menstrual blood to flow freely and was therefore beneficial.[68]

4.4 Alternative unions and concubines

From early times some Athenian men chose to keep concubines, instead of taking a lawful wife, and from time to time they could keep a concubine in addition to a lawful wife.[69] The concubine typically was not a paramour, "the other woman"; she was a woman with whom a man lived without prior lawful marriage through *engye* or *epidikasia*, either because of legal impediments, like for example inequality of status, or because of personal choices and reasons. In the years when the Periclean citizenship law was not valid (before 451, and between 429 and 403) the dividing line between wives and concubines was rather blurry. Even though legal marriage might not have taken place, in the end of the day the children of the concubine could also be citizens, like the children from a lawful wife. Therefore, a concubine, even though she might be treated as inferior in some aspects of public life, like for example certain roles in religious festivals reserved for married women, and she could be facing some disadvantages in the community, still she could be the mother of citizens and a respectable mistress in her own household. During these periods it is difficult to define the difference between the wife and the concubine in legal terms. Perhaps one prominent example would suffice: Aspasia, the intelligent and deeply cultivated woman from Miletos, who lived with Pericles as his concubine, was as much of a "first lady" as Athens could have ever had, and the numerous jokes about her in Attic comedy confirm that in the eyes of the Athenian public she held her own special place at the side of the leading man of the city.[70]

For the periods when the Periclean citizenship law was in force the difference between the wife and the concubine was unmistakably clear. The children from the concubine could not be citizens or heirs to their father's property, and in the 4th century they faced serious penalties if they attempted to enter into a marriage with a citizen. Therefore, the lawful wife (γυνὴ ἀστὴ καὶ ἐγγυητὴ κατὰ τὸν νόμον) was the only vessel for legitimate succession. Given this clear delineation of roles, one pressing question remains: why would an Athenian man take a concubine when he could have taken a wife, and a sizeable dowry coming with her?[71] There is only one clear answer to this question, and I think it ought to be "because he wanted to." Let us consider a few examples of Athenian men who shared their lives with concubines rather than lawful wives. Perhaps the best attested example was that of Stephanos of Eroiadai, who spent more than 30 years of his life with the former *hetaira* Neaira.[72] They met at a time when she was coming out of her prime and looking for a way to settle into respectable anonymity. He was captivated by her considerable charms and it was love at first sight. It appears that by this stage Stephanos was a widower with four young children, three of which were boys, so he no longer had a pressing need to take a wife and produce an heir and could allow himself the luxury of a relationship based on physical attraction and love.

The case of Olympiodoros appears to be similar in some important aspects.[73] We are told that he never married nor had any children, but instead he liberated a former *hetaira* and made her his lifelong companion and mistress of his household. The speaker also informs us that the female relatives of Olympiodoros were envious of her status and affluence, when she was going about wearing beautiful clothes and expensive golden jewelry.

The case of the concubine of Philoneos in the speech of Antiphon *On the Stepmother* appears to be broadly similar with the previous two, but with an unhappy ending.[74] While Stephanos and Olympiodoros continued to live with their concubines in committed relationships, Philoneos simply got tired of his and wanted to get rid of her by establishing her in a brothel. The narrative implies that the woman was still a slave, and certainly vulnerable. Unlike Neaira, who chose to run away from the abusive Phrynion,[75] the concubine of Philoneos tried to influence his feelings and make him fall in love with her again through a love-potion. The plans of Philoneos, which understandably made his mistress feel insecure, cost him his life. In a series of events reminiscent of the tragic end of Herakles and Dieaneira, that love-potion turned out to be lethal: Philoneos and a friend of his both died from it, while the woman herself was tortured and executed for his murder. Even in this sad tale of insecure, deadly love, we can see the same pattern: a citizen man kept a concubine for as long as he was in love with her. However, this story also underlines the vulnerability of the concubine; without the legal protections, support from social norms, and empowerment through a dowry which a lawful wife enjoyed, the concubine was much more susceptible to the whims and mood changes of a volatile partner and knew that she always had to keep trying to earn his love, because without it she had nowhere to stand.

Another famous couple, Pericles and Aspasia, may be conforming with the general pattern if we believe the tradition that Aspasia was a former *hetaira*.[76] However, their relationship appears to be much more than a love-affair based on physical attraction. This extraordinary woman, who made an impression upon some of the greatest minds of her time as an intellectual, scholar and teacher, was able to attract the leading man of Athens at the height of his power exactly because she stood out, and she was not like an anonymous, respectable wife.

The final example in this subjective list adds some important information. Alke the concubine of Euktemon, does not seem to be an exclusive life partner, like the women mentioned above.[77] She is a lover, former prostitute and currently a procuress, setup in a separate residence. For some time Euktemon only visited her and spent part of his time there, while the rest of the time he spent in his house with his wife and family. It appears however, that Euktemon was eventually seduced by the concubine and induced to abandon his family, move in with her, and introduce her eldest son into the phratry as his own. This was perceived as *casus belli* by his adult son Philoktemon, who stepped forward to defend the interests of his mother and younger brother(s). What the existing sons of Euktemon stood to lose was a significant part of their inheritance, which would go to their newly minted "brother," the son of Alke. A protracted and very public quarrel eventually came to an end with an uneasy compromise between father and son. The case suggests, just as Athenaios confirms,[78] that Greek wives would not tolerate the presence of a concubine, and that if a man wanted to keep a concubine in addition to his lawful wife, not only he needed a separate residence for her, but he should also be prepared to face jealousy and ever-lasting arguments.[79] However, at the same time, as far as the law was concerned, it was a man's prerogative to keep a concubine in a separate residence, if he wished and could afford it, or to keep a female or male lover, or have a string of encounters with prostitutes of either sex, or use his slaves to satisfy his passions.

The pattern which emerges from these show-cases is that, many a time, Athenian men fell in love with alien *hetairai*, and chose to spend at least part of their lives with them. These unions were not casual. The law recognized them, since concubines were covered by the adultery laws in the same way as wives. The Drakonian law which defined adultery explicitly included not only free concubines, but even slaves whom a man might keep for the birth of free children.[80] It was forbidden to seduce someone else's woman, regardless of her status, simply because the crime in the eyes of the law was the violation of another man's private sphere. The procedure and penalties in a case like this would be exactly the same as those for the seduction of a wife.[81]

Illegitimate children from concubines were the responsibility of their father, who was expected to send the boys to school and supervise their good upbringing, and to find husbands for the daughters. A sensible plan for an illegitimate son might be to send him to learn some craft or trade like masonry, carpentry, medicine, music or similar, which would help him secure a living. Since, non-citizens could not own real estate and illegitimate children had no inheritance rights, a caring father might offer some cash which could help his son start a business and could make arrangements *inter vivos* which would be impossible after his death. He could also give a dowry to an illegitimate daughter, and it was his duty and legal right to look for a husband for her among respectable metic families or other non-citizen men making a successful living in an open and diverse city like Athens. Even though the law excluded a concubine's children from citizenship and inheritance, this does not necessarily mean that they were abandoned to their fate by their families.

4.5 Conclusions

The legal and social structure of the Athenian marriage is in some ways similar to our marriage, but also in some important ways very dissimilar. Affection, love, and sexual compatibility were part of the Athenian marriage too, but the pathways to reach this state of affairs were very different. While the rhetoric of modern marriage, at least in the western world, assumes that the two participants met before marriage and fell in love, and more often than not lived together for some time and had sexual relations before marriage, in the ancient world none of this was required, and in fact it was positively discouraged for young women to have eyes for potential husbands. The marriage was usually arranged and the choice of husband mostly reflected the wishes of the woman's father, and it is a fair bet that a father would not admire good looks or dashing youth in a potential husband for his daughter. He would be searching for a man of some means to keep a family, respectable in the community, and reliable. The potential husband did not expect love at first sight either; he would be satisfied with a respectable woman and a good dowry. Love, affection and sexual compatibility came later, and sometimes never really came, but this probably did not matter as much to an Athenian couple as it would matter to a modern couple.

While half of marriages end up in divorce in some parts of the western world in our times, only eight cases of divorce are attested in classical Athens.[82] The reason for such a low divorce rate has much to do with expectations. While in a modern marriage emotional connectivity is considered paramount, and when it is gone, the whole marriage starts to fail, Athenian marriages had no anxieties over this. The purpose of marriage was to have children, to bring them up properly, and to create a safe and productive household. So long as these expectations were met, the marriage would seem successful, and the participants felt no need to question it. The asymmetrical power distribution in the couple, as well as the fact that men could have other outlets to emotional or sexual needs not met at home meant that men did not feel an urgent need to dissolve a marriage not based on emotional connectivity, and women would need to accept that a man who was a good provider, a good father to his children and a respectable member of the community, was as good a husband as they come. With such objectives Athenian marriages were much less volatile, less troublesome, and lasted for a lifetime.

Notes

1 The text as it appears here includes a transposition of μὴ from its place in the manuscripts (ἐὰν δὲ {μὴ} ᾖ), to the position before ἐπίκληρός τις ᾖ. I proposed this transposition in the study "The Demosthenic edition of Mervin Dilts, and the textual transmission of Apollodoros". In Grusková, Jana and Bannert, Herbert (eds) *Demosthenica libris manu scriptis tradita*, Wiener Studien, Beiheft 36, Vienna 2014, 107–28.

The reason for the transposition is that the law in the transmitted text says the exact opposite of what it should be saying, while the transposition corrects the error.

2 The same formula with minor variations is also attested in several other instances, e.g. Men. *Mis.* 444–6; *Per.* 1013–6; Fr. Dubium 35 Sandbach; Sam. 726–8. The version in the *Samia* seems to be the most complete because the father also mentions that the event is taking place before witnesses, and the future husband replies with three presents with future force: ἔχω, λαμβάνω, στέργω (I have her, I take her, I love her). It would be tempting to think that this was the standard reply of the bridegroom which sealed the deal, but since this is the only one of the attested instances which includes this sentence, it might simply be specific to this play. Still it is a distinct possibility that this was part of the standard formula, on the grounds that the pledge of the woman to her husband has a ritualistic character, and if the *kyrios* of the woman had to deliver some formulaic sentence, it would be reasonable to assume that the bridegroom needed to respond with a formulaic sentence too, promising to take the woman and cherish her.

3 Translation by A.T. Murray.

4 Very likely this reference to *xenia* has to do with the persons entitled to bring this prosecution. *Xenia*, a prosecution intended to disqualify someone from citizenship by proving that he/she was actually an alien, could only be brought by Athenian citizens. Most public lawsuits could be introduced by any free adult male (ὁ βουλόμενος), but immigration offences understandably could only be introduced by an Athenian citizen (Ἀθηναίων ὁ βουλόμενος). *Xenia* was probably the oldest immigration process in the statute books which had this limitation, and this is why the author of this law refers to it when he wants to introduce a similar restriction.

5 Plu. *Per.* 37. The term μητρόξενος refers to a person born of an Athenian father and a foreign mother. Typically this would be the pattern in Athens, as an Athenian woman given in marriage to a foreign man would probably be living in her husband's city (e.g. D. 24.202–3, where the sister of Timocrates was given in marriage to a man from Kerkyra, and at the time of the trial she was living in the island with her husband). However, on the rare occasion where an Athenian woman had married a non-Athenian man and the child was born and brought up in Athens, as far as we know, there was no impediment for this child to be considered Athenian before 451.

6 Arist. *Ath.* 26,4, *Pol.* 1275 b 31, 1278 a 34; Plu. *Per.* 37. Despite a large body of literature on this law, its true intention and the reasons behind its introduction are still vigorously debated. See Rhodes 1981: 331–5; Patterson 1981, passim; Walters 1983: 314–36; Raaflaub 2004: 15–16, 217; Ober 1989: 81; Ogden 1996: passim; Kapparis 2005: 72–6; Blok 2017: 141–70.

7 Plu. Per. 37. A gift of corn from the king of Egypt which needed to be distributed among the citizens was the motivator for the aggressive disfranchisement of the offspring of mixed unions.

8 Ar. *V.* 716–8, and Sch. Ar. V. 718. See also Chapter 3.3.

9 For the laws and procedures on *xenia* see Chapter 2.7.

10 Mark Griffith (2011: 175–208) has reached the opposite conclusions on the basis of evidence from drama, mostly tragedy. He notices that after 451 the patterns of mixed marriages among the elites do not appear to be significantly different from what they were in previous years. This is an interesting vector of approach; however, the plots of Greek Drama have their origins in very traditional themes and can only be used sparingly and with extreme caution as a historical source for classical Athens. Let's say Phaedra, the Cretan wife of Theseus, need not all of a sudden become Athenian just because a new law was introduced in Athens discouraging mixed marriages. At the same time, it is noteworthy that the theme of the wife versus the alien concubine/mistress features heavily in some plays, like the *Medea* of Euripides or the *Trachiniai* of Sophocles, and very much so in the plays of New Comedy and their Latin adaptations a century later. Particularly interesting is the reference to the fact that Herakles

as a *nothos* cannot inherit Zeus, in the *Birds* of Aristophanes (1648–1651), because the play was produced in 414, when the Periclean citizenship law was in disuse and *nothoi* could inherit their fathers. This case demonstrates that drama suited its own purposes and did not always follow the laws of real life. For the use of plays as evidence for marriage rituals and customs see also Pilitsis 1981.

11 ἀνδραγαθία περὶ τὸν δῆμον τὸν Ἀθηναίων: see Chapter 2.3.

12 D. 59.87; see the discussion in Chapter 6.3.

13 D. 59.76; See Kapparis 1999: 335–6.

14 Harp. s.v. Νοθεῖα: τὰ τοῖς νόθοις ἐκ τῶν πατρῴων διδόμενα οὕτω καλεῖται, ἦν δὲ μέχρι χιλίων δραχμῶν· [Notheia: this is how the sum offered out of the parental estate to illegitimate children is called.]

15 See Ar. *Av.* 214.

16 Arist. *Pol.* 1278 a 29–33.

17 MacDowell 1978: 67–70.

18 Todd 1993: 177–81.

19 See, for example, Pl. *Lg.* 740 d 4 ff.; Arist. *Pol.* 1265a; X. *Hel.* 5.3.16.

20 Patterson 1981: 97–104.

21 Plutarch (*Per.* 37), our main source on the events surrounding the dismantling of this legislation in the assembly, actually says that the request Pericles was personal; he simply asked the assembly to allow him to legitimize his own son from Aspasia. I have expressed my disagreement with the view that the younger Pericles, the son of the general from Aspasia, was offered citizenship through a personal naturalization decree, because he did not meet the all-important condition of *andragathia* (Kapparis 1999: 200–1). The anecdote in Plutarch (*Per.* 37) introduces a personal touch in order to underline the irony of Pericles suffering the dire consequences of his own law. The rule obviously applied to all Athenians, as it is certain that all μητρόξενοι in those years where citizens. See Ogden 1996: 70–7; Carawan 2008: 383–406.

22 Euripides Fr. 141, 168 and 337 Nauck. In the contrast between *physis* and *nomos,* the latter need not be taken narrowly to mean only "law"; it can also be taken in a broader sense to mean "custom," or "perception." Here I have translated it as "law" out of convenience as I could not think of a word with an equally broad semantic field.

23 E. Fr. 141 Nauck.

24 E. *Andr.* 638.

25 Isoc. 14.42; Hecat. *FGrH* 264 F 25.1262–3.

26 The historian Karystios (Fr. 11), who attests that the proposers of the decree reinstating the Periclean law were Aristophon and Nikomenes, has a similar tale to tell about Aristophon, as that of Pericles. He says that Aristophon by proposing this decree declared his own son from the *hetaira* Choregis illegitimate. This could not be the case, because the decree of Aristophon only applied to those born after 403. If we were to believe the story, we would need to understand that the son of Aristophon was not already born but came later.

27 In a previous study I have argued that a date around 380 is likely for the introduction of this law, as it seems to be taken for granted in 4th century comedy, and it seems that it was a well-established law by the 340s, when the case against Neaira went to court (see Kapparis 1999: 97–205).

28 See, for example, the accusations of Apollodoros about Phano, who was supposedly an illegitimate daughter of Neaira, but her family gave her a new name and new identity and presented her as a citizen woman. In all probability, Apollodoros is misrepresenting her status, but the fact that he could plausibly make a case like this before an Athenian court suggests that such behaviors did not sound outlandish to his audience. Likewise, when the speaker in Isaios 3 alleges that Pyrrhos had been living with an alien concubine who claimed to be his wife, he is probably lying, but the possibility of something like this happening was real. Another case can be found in one of the letters

of Aelian (*Ep.* 16), where the son of a farmer takes a flute-player to his father under the pretense that she is a properly born woman whom he wishes to marry.

29 Olympiodoros, for example (D. 48.53), never married but spent his entire life with his concubine, a former *hetaira* whom he liberated. Stephanos, on the other hand, seems to have been married in his younger days, but spent much of his adult life with his concubine Neaira, again a former *hetaira* (see D. 59, and the discussion below).

30 Bakewell 2008: 97–109.

31 Two examples of Athenian-born *hetairai* who transitioned into wives spring to mind. One must be the naughty wife of Pyrrhos, who clearly was Athenian and was legally betrothed to him, but at the same time it looks as if she had been a *hetaira*, and like her husband, she continued to love a spirited party, even as a married woman. By the sound of it, their union was legal, even though her behavior may have been unusual for most Athenian couples; but then again this was not just an ordinary couple. The other example probably is Plangon in D. 39 and 40. Even though the speaker does not explicitly say that she was a *hetaira*, he implies it many times, and calls her by her first name, which he should not have done unless she had been a *hetaira*.

32 The Greek word for "marriage" is γάμος, the same word used for "wedding". It appears that the original meaning of γάμος was "wedding" (e.g. Hom. *Il.* 18.491), and this is the meaning consistently encountered in the Attic Orators. However, from early times it's semantic field was expanded to include "marriage" (e.g. Hom. *Od.* 1.249) and has retained this all-encompassing meaning throughout the millennia and all the way to the modern language. Perhaps the reason why legal documents avoid the noun "γάμος" may be that in the classical period it meant "marriage" mostly in a metaphorical, sometimes euphemistic sense (already attested in Hom *Il.* 5.429).

33 See S 1–3 and the discussion below.

34 The procession is well described in Hyperides *Against Lykophron* 3–7 and depicted in several Attic vases (e.g Bonn, Akademisches Kunstmuseum: 994; Athens, National Museum: 1453 = Beazley 1127.18). The standard works on the wedding rituals are Rehm 1994 and Oakley and Sinos 1993. See also Smith 2005; Kavoulaki 1997: 351–71; Sutton 1997: 27–48.

35 In one extreme case, the bride was only five years old. The father of the orator Demosthenes in his deathbed betrothed his young daughter to Demophon, with a massive dowry of two talents (D. 27.4–5). Demosthenes senior was motivated by the desire to settle his family affairs before his death when he entered into this unusual arrangement. In effect, this meant that the husband of his daughter could take control of her dowry right away, while the marriage would not come into full effect for another ten years or so, when the sister of Demosthenes would be old enough to move in with her husband. This case underlines the dangers of such arrangements, since the marriage was never consummated, and Demosthenes had to sue for the recovery of the dowry when he became an adult.

36 The following studies on marriage remain important: MacDowell 1978: 84–89, and 1989: 10–21; Harrison 1968: 296–303; Todd 1993: 204–16; Pomeroy 1975: 62–8; Foxhall 1989: 22–44; Just 1989: 40–75; Patterson 1998: 107–14; Hunter 1994, esp. Chapter 1. For a collection of sources on marriage see Phillips 2013: 137–53.

37 See, for example, the opening sections in the *Economics* of Aristotle, and Xenophon's similarly worded statement in his *Economics* (7): βουλευόμενος δ' ἔγωγε ὑπὲρ ἐμοῦ καὶ οἱ σοὶ γονεῖς ὑπὲρ σοῦ τίν' ἂν κοινωνὸν βέλτιστον οἴκου τε καὶ τέκνων λάβοιμεν, ἐγώ τε σὲ ἐξελεξάμην καὶ οἱ σοὶ γονεῖς, ὡς ἐοίκασιν, ἐκ τῶν δυνατῶν ἐμέ. [I deciding for myself, and your parents on your behalf who would be the best partner for the household and for the birth of children, I chose you, and your parents, as it seems, among potential suitors chose me.] See also Cox 1998: 38–67.

38 In Athenian drama love and affection within marriage are often celebrated, and two striking examples spring to mind, the profound love of Dieaneira for her husband in the

Trachiniai of Sophocles, and the biting love of Medea for Jason in Euripides *Medea*. On the other hand, comedy celebrated the overt and pronounced sexuality of the married Athenian woman especially in the three extant women's plays, The *Thesmophoriazousai*, the *Ekklesiazousai* and *Lysistrata*. New Comedy built most of its plots upon the assumption that young love is an important, even if not indispensable, part of marriage. Attic Oratory on the other hand, places more emphasis on the practical aspects of marriage, such as the legitimacy of the children and the management of the *oikos*, perhaps with good reason, as these two aspects of marriage were the ones more often giving rise to legal disputes.

39 See for example Lys. 19. 14–7, where the speaker's mother and sisters were all married without a dowry to "good" (βελτίω, κοσμίοις, σώφροσι) men, no doubt because they were supremely attractive.

40 *Economics* 7.10–12.

41 See for example the language of friendship used in Is. 2.4–5, in order to explain the choice of a husband: Ἐπώνυμος γὰρ ὁ Ἀχαρνεύς, ὁ πατὴρ ὁ ἡμέτερος, ὦ ἄνδρες, φίλος ἦν καὶ ἐπιτήδειος Μενεκλεῖ καὶ ἐχρῆτο οἰκείως· ἦμεν δὲ αὐτῷ παῖδες τέτταρες ἡμεῖς, δύο μὲν ὑεῖς, δύο δὲ θυγατέρες. Τελευτήσαντος δὲ τοῦ πατρός, ἐκδίδομεν ἡμεῖς τὴν πρεσβυτέραν ἀδελφήν, ἐπειδὴ εἶχεν ὥραν, Λευκολόφῳ, προῖκα ἐπιδόντες εἴκοσι μνᾶς. Καὶ ἀπ' ἐκείνου τοῦ χρόνου τετάρτῳ ἔτει ἢ πέμπτῳ ὕστερονἥ τε ἀδελφὴ ἡμῖν ἡ νεωτέρα σχεδὸν ἡλικίαν εἶχεν ἀνδρὶ συνοικεῖν, καὶ τῷ Μενεκλεῖ ἡ γυνὴ τελευτᾷ ἣν εἶχε πρότερον. Ἐπειδὴ οὖν ἐκείνῃ τὰ νομιζόμενα ἐποίησεν ὁ Μενεκλῆς, ᾔτει τὴν ἀδελφὴν ἡμᾶς, ὑπομιμνῄσκων τήν τε φιλίαν τὴν τοῦ πατρὸς καὶ ἑαυτοῦ, καὶ ὡς πρὸς ἡμᾶς αὐτοὺς ἦν διακείμενος· καὶ ἡμεῖς εἰδότες ὅτι καὶ ὁ πατὴρ οὐδενὶ ἂν ἔδωκεν ἥδιον ἢ ἐκείνῳ, δίδομεν αὐτῷ, οὐκ ἄπροικον, ὡς οὗτος λέγει ἑκάστοτε, ἀλλὰ τὴν ἴσην προῖκα ἐπιδόντες ἥνπερ καὶ τῇ πρεσβυτέρᾳ ἀδελφῇ ἐπέδομεν· καὶ ἐκ τοῦ τρόπου τούτου, πρότερον ὄντες αὐτοῦ φίλοι, κατέστημεν οἰκεῖοι. [My father, gentlemen, Eponymus of Acharnae, was a friend and close acquaintance of Menecles and lived on terms of intimacy with him; there were four of us children, two sons and two daughters. After my father's death we married our elder sister, when she reached a suitable age, to Leucolophus, giving her a dowry of twenty minae. Four or five years later, when our younger sister was almost of marriageable age, Menecles lost his first wife. When he had carried out the customary rites over her, he asked for our sister in marriage, reminding us of the friendship which had existed between our father and himself and of his friendly disposition towards ourselves. Knowing that our father would have given her to no one with greater pleasure, we gave her to him in marriage – not dowerless, as my opponent asserts on every possible occasion, but with the same portion as we gave to our elder sister. In this manner, having been formerly his friends, we became his kinsmen.] (Translation by Edward Seymour Forster)

42 See Sch. Ar. Nu. 1371; D. 57. 20–21.

43 For example, Apollodoros, the son of Pasion, betrothed his daughter to his wife's brother Theomnestos (D. 59.2–3), and comments that this union strengthened the family bonds between himself and his in-laws. In Lys. 32, Diodotos married his niece, the daughter of his brother Diogeiton, and we are left to understand that the wealth of Diodotos had something to do with this arrangement (ἐργασαμένου δὲ Διοδότου κατ' ἐμπορίαν πολλὰ χρήματα πείθει αὐτὸν Διογείτων λαβεῖν τὴν ἑαυτοῦ θυγατέρα, ἥπερ ἦν αὐτῷ μόνη· [*Diodotos made a lot of money in commerce, and Diogeiton persuaded him to marry his only daughter*]).

44 A good example of this can be found in the first marriage of Phano in the narrative of *Against Neaira* (D. 59.52–4). The young Phano was unenthusiastic about her father's choice of a husband for her. Her father had chosen a man with good financial standing, thrifty, stern, and from the sound of it considerably older, while she had in mind someone more urbane and elegant; the result of their epic fighting was an acrimonious divorce while she was pregnant with his son.

45 Is. 2.8: ὅ τι γὰρ <ἂν> ἐκείνη πεισθῇ, τοῦτ' ἔφαμεν ποιήσειν. [Whatever she was persuaded to do, we agreed that we would go along with it.]

46 For example, Kleoboule, the mother of Demosthenes chose to remain in her husband's *oikos* (D. 27), while in Lys. 3 the sister of the speaker with her daughters are living with her middle-aged, unmarried brother (Lys. 3.7).

47 See, for example, the archaic form δάμαρτα for "woman," never used in legal documents of the classical period, but standard in the time of Solon.

48 In D. 57.40–1, the husband arranged the next marriage for his wife, with whom he had a daughter, so as to be free to marry a rich *epikleros*, but the woman was given away to her new husband by her brother. In D. 27.5 Demosthenes senior on his death-bead gave away his wife to Aphobos with a massive dowry. The size of the dowry indicates his wish to ensure the well-being of his widow. Likewise, Diodotos in Lys. 32.6 on his way to a military campaign, where he was actually killed, made arrangements for the next marriage of his wife, in the event that he would not return, leaving her a very large dowry. Finally, Pasion gave in marriage his wife Archippe to Phormion on his death-bead. His son Apollodoros later disputed the legality of these arrangements (D. 45 and 46), but the matter of fact was that Archippe's marriage to Phormion was valid and produced legitimate offspring. It must be noted that Archippe's status was more complicated: see Carey 1991: 84–9.

49 See, for example, 19.14–7; Is. 3.8, 28–9 (where it appears that Pyrrhos married an Athenian *hetaira* through ἐγγύη, without a dowry, because he was infatuated with the woman), D. 40.20 and 25. On the dowry see the discussion in Chapter 5.3.

50 In the case of divorce, the former husband needed to return the entire sum of the dowry. If, as the manager of the property, he had liquidated assets which were part of the dowry, he could instead return their value in money, and this is why it was important in the case of non-monetary assets to agree on their value during the *engye*.

51 For the marriage formulas in the Greek and Jewish traditions see Katzoff 1996: 223–34.

52 On marriage contracts in later times see Hanafi 2001.

53 Not all women in families without a male heir became *epikleroi*. It was all a matter of timing and circumstances. A man who had only daughters could give them in marriage while he was alive. If they already had children at the time of his death, his remaining property would go to them, and would be integrated into the *oikos* of their husbands and inherited by their children. One such case is the family situation in D. 41, where the two daughters of Polyeuktos were not *epikleroi*. They had been given in marriage by their father while he was alive, and presumably they had children. After their father's death, the remaining property was managed by their mother, the remarkable widow of Polyeuktos. When she died too, the two daughters and their husbands divided the remaining property, equally, but then disputes arose, which were argued in court by the two husbands. On the other hand, if a man died before he had the chance to give his daughters in marriage, they became *epikleroi*, and could only be given in marriage through *epidikasia*. The same applied if at the time of his death his married daughter did not have any children. She still became an *epikleros*, and the closest male relative of her father could take her away from her husband, along with the property coming with her. A woman could also become an *epikleros* to other relatives like her grandfather, or brother in the absence of a male heir, and the same rules applied. Every time a childless woman stood to inherit a relative she became an *epikleros*. If she already had children, then she simply inherited, and the property theoretically belonged to her children. For further discussion on the *epikleros* see Chapter 5.4.

54 Plu. *Sol*. 20. 2–5.

55 In one such case, Kallias persuades Leagros, who had the highest claim towards a poor but seemingly very attractive *epikleros*, to step aside with a promise of money, and let him claim her. Then Kallias himself steps aside and allows his son to claim the woman (And. 1.117–22). If Andocides is telling the truth here, it looks as if the woman was the object of a capricious desire. The rich son of Kallias wanted her so badly that he was prepared to eliminate all suitors with a higher claim through bribery or blackmail.

56 Is. 11, *On the Estate of Hagnias*, and D. 43 *To Makaratos*.
57 In the words of Andocides (1.119), διὰ τὴν ἡμετέραν ἀρετὴν τάδε ἔσται.
58 Cudjoe 2005: 55–88.
59 Cudjoe 2005: 57.
60 Cudjoe 2005: 86: "It seems apparent also that the situation whereby a rich *epikleros* had been claimed without the successful claimant marrying her is non-existent in the sources."
61 See MacDowell 1978: 95–98; Wolff 1946: 70; Karabelias 1979: 201–23.
62 An interesting but inconclusive discussion on the issue is provided by David Cohen (1993: 5–16). Cohen is asking the right questions but is looking into the *graphe hybreos* for answers, for which there is no evidence that it was ever used for such cases. Thus, the article remains largely speculative. See also my discussion in Kapparis 2017: 194–6.
63 See Isager 1981: 81–96 and the discussion in Chapter 8.
64 See the online data for the age of consent around the world today in www.avert.org/age-of-consent.htm. The world-wide average is typically around 16, while in Europe it tends to be around 15, and in China it is 14. In some countries it is as early as 12. Greek sources which set an age of consent around 14 or 15 include X. *Oec*. 3.13 and 7.5; Arist. *Ath*. 56.7 (cf. MacDowell 1978: 98; here it is stated that the *archon* should lease out the property of the *epikleros* until she is 14 years old; presumably after that she moves in with the husband selected through the *epidikasia*); Philo *De Josepho* 43 and X. *Lac*. 3.1, where it is stated that in the whole of Greece, except Sparta, when children reach adolescence, they are no longer accompanied by paidagogoi, and are given autonomy to do as they please (αὐτόνομοι). See also Cudjoe 2005: 71 and 78.
65 A significant passage from the *Republic* of Plato (460 e 4–5) suggests that the ancient world was well aware of the potential complications of an early pregnancy, and that the age between 20 and 40 was perceived to be the optimal childbearing age of a woman.
66 X. Oec. 7.5: Καὶ τί ἄν, ἔφη, ὦ Σώκρατες, ἐπισταμένην αὐτὴν παρέλαβον, ἣ ἔτη μὲν οὔπω πεντεκαίδεκα γεγονυῖα ἦλθε πρὸς ἐμέ, τὸν δ' ἔμπροσθεν χρόνον ἔζη ὑπὸ πολλῆς ἐπιμελείας ὅπως ὡς ἐλάχιστα μὲν ὄψοιτο, ἐλάχιστα δ' ἀκούσοιτο, ἐλάχιστα δ' ἔροιτο. [And what could she, Socrates, know, when I took her? She came to me when she was not even fifteen, and before that time she had lived under the most careful supervision, so that she could see as little as possible, and hear as little as possible, and ask as little as possible.]
67 It is probably a historical irony that Chrysilla, the ideal wife of Ischomachos, went on to have an affair and a child outside wedlock with the husband of her daughter, and ultimately steal her daughter's husband (And. 1.124–128 and Harvey 1984: 68–70).
68 See Kapparis, K. 2014. "Hippocrates, Aristophanes and Sex-Crazed Women" in *Ageless Arts, The Journal of the Southern Association for the History of Medicine and Science*, 47–57.
69 Concubinage is well attested in myth and the epic tradition; some famous examples include Chryseis and Briseis, captured noble women who became the concubines of their captors, and the many concubines of Priam. From Attic Drama Medea and Iole are two easy examples. On concubinage the studies of Maffi (1985: 177–214), and Sealey (1984: 111–33) remain important.
70 On Aspasia see Cratin. Fr. 259; Ar. *Ach*. 523–9; X. *Mem*. 2.6.36, *Oec*. 3.14; Pl. *Mx*. 235 e ff.; Aeschines Socraticus *Fragments*; Athen. 5.61 ff. and also Henry 1995.
71 However, illegitimate daughters would be offered a modest dowry when given away as concubines by their fathers or other relatives (Is. 3.39: καὶ οἱ ἐπὶ παλλακίᾳ διδόντες τὰς ἑαυτῶν πάντες πρότερον διομολογοῦνται περὶ τῶν δοθησομένων ταῖς παλλακαῖς· [Even those who give their own relatives as concubines agree on what is going to be given to the concubines.]).
72 See D. 59 passim.
73 D. 48.53–5.
74 Ant. 1.14–20.

75 D. 59.35.

76 This vexed and inconclusive discussion is thoroughly presented in Madeleine Henry's excellent monograph on Aspasia (Henry 1995).

77 Is. 6.19–21.

78 Athen. 13.3

79 In the Hellenistic period the kings and potentates in the kingdoms of the Diadochoi took prominent *hetairai* as their concubines and kept them in their palaces along with the lawful wives, who had no choice but to put up with them, but these un-Greek customs did not come to pass before the demise of the classical *polis*. One infamous example would be Demetrios Poliorketes, who kept his favorite concubines, the flute player Lamia and the *hetaira* Leaina, in the same residence, for a time the Parthenon, while his queen Phila, accustomed to the polygamy of Macedonian royalty, was simply expected to tolerate his notorious indiscretions.

80 This probably had a different meaning in the time of Drakon than it did in the classical period. In the 5th and 4th century the Drakonian law would be interpreted to mean that someone's concubine whether free or slave, was his and no one else's, and this is why no other man had the right to seduce her with impunity. See also Chapter 6.3.

81 In a widespread medical anecdote which we find in Aristainetos, the deleterious desire of a young man for his father's concubine would have been tantamount to *moicheia*, had the doctor on call not convinced the father that allowing his heartbroken son to sleep with his concubine is simply therapy (Aristaenet. 1.13: ἀναγκαίαν τινὰ σωτηρίαν οὐ μοιχείαν τὸ πρᾶγμα καλῶν). The same story is involving the great Alexandrian physician Erasistratos in the version of Suda (ε 402).

82 See Chapter 6.2.

5 The continuation of the *oikos*

Inheritance and succession

5.1 Sources

1 The main law regulating succession and inheritance (594 BC)

> ΝΟΜΟΣ: Ὅσοι μὴ ἐπεποίηντο, ὥστε μήτε ἀπειπεῖν μήτ' ἐπιδικάσασθαι, ὅτε Σόλων εἰσῄει τὴν ἀρχήν, τὰ ἑαυτοῦ διαθέσθαι εἶναι ὅπως ἂν ἐθέλῃ, ἂν μὴ παῖδες ὦσι γνήσιοι ἄρρενες, ἂν μὴ μανιῶν ἢ γήρως ἢ φαρμάκων ἢ νόσου ἕνεκα, ἢ γυναικὶ πειθόμενος, ὑπὸ τούτων του παρανοῶν, ἢ ὑπ' ἀνάγκης ἢ ὑπὸ δεσμοῦ καταληφθείς.[1]
>
> (D. 46.14)
>
> LAW: Any citizen, except those who have been adopted, and have not renounced the adoption or succeeded to an estate under an *epidikasia*, shall have the right to dispose of his property as he wishes, if there is no legitimate male issue, unless he has been overcome by mental impairment, old age, drugs or illness, or influenced by a woman or pressured by necessity or imprisonment.

2 An addendum to the law of succession for cases when legitimate male heirs do not reach adulthood (594 BC)

> ΝΟΜΟΣ: Ὅ τι ἂν γνησίων ὄντων υἱέων ὁ πατὴρ διαθῆται ἐὰν ἀποθάνωσιν οἱ υἱεῖς πρὶν ἐπὶ δίετες ἡβᾶν, τὴν τοῦ πατρὸς διαθήκην κυρίαν εἶναι.
>
> (D. 46.24)
>
> LAW: If the father of legitimate sons makes a will, and the sons die before reaching their 20th year, the will of the father is to be valid.

3 Law on succession by legitimate daughters (594 BC)

> Καὶ τῷ μὲν πατρὶ αὐτῆς, εἰ παῖδες ἄρρενες μὴ ἐγένοντο, οὐκ ἂν ἐξῆν ἄνευ ταύτης διαθέσθαι· κελεύει γὰρ ὁ νόμος σὺν ταύταις κύριον εἶναι δοῦναι, ἐάν τῳ βούληται, τὰ ἑαυτοῦ·
>
> (Is. 10.13)
>
> Her father, if he had no sons, he would not have been able to make a will excluding her; for the law states that he has the right to leave his property

to whoever he wishes, so long as he includes her [sc. a legitimate daughter] in the arrangement.

4 The law on the *epikleros* (594 BC)

ΝΟΜΟΣ. Ἣν ἂν ἐγγυήσῃ . . . ἢ πατὴρ ἢ ἀδελφὸς ὁμοπάτωρ ἢ πάππος ὁ πρὸς πατρός. . . . ἐὰν δὲ μηδεὶς ᾖ τούτων, ἐὰν μὲν μὴ ἐπίκληρός τις ᾖ, τὸν κύριον ἔχειν, ἐὰν δὲ ᾖ, ὅτῳ ἂν ἐπιτρέψῃ, τοῦτον κύριον εἶναι.[2]

(D. 46.18)

LAW: The woman given into lawful marriage by either her father, or brother from the same father, or her paternal grandfather . . . . If none of them is alive, if she is not an *epikleros* (heiress), let her husband keep her, but if she is, her husband is to be the man who has been appointed.

5 Who owns the property of the *epikleros* (594 BC)

ΝΟΜΟΣ: Καὶ ἐὰν ἐξ ἐπικλήρου τις γένηται καὶ ἅμα ἡβήσῃ ἐπὶ δίετες, κρατεῖν τῶν χρημάτων, τὸν δὲ σῖτον μετρεῖν τῇ μητρί.

(D. 46.20)

LAW: And if someone is the son of an *epikleros*, two years after he reaches manhood [i.e. 20 years old], he shall assume control of the estate and pay for his mother's living expenses.[3]

6 The law on the welfare of widows, heiresses and orphans (594 BC)

ΝΟΜΟΣ. Ὁ ἄρχων ἐπιμελείσθω τῶν ὀρφανῶν καὶ τῶν ἐπικλήρων καὶ τῶν οἴκων τῶν ἐξερημουμένων καὶ τῶν γυναικῶν, ὅσαι μένουσιν ἐν τοῖς οἴκοις τῶν ἀνδρῶν τῶν τεθνηκότων φάσκουσαι κυεῖν. τούτων ἐπιμελείσθω καὶ μὴ ἐάτω ὑβρίζειν μηδένα περὶ τούτους. ἐὰν δέ τις ὑβρίζῃ ἢ ποιῇ τι παράνομον, κύριος ἔστω ἐπιβάλλειν κατὰ τὸ τέλος. ἐὰν δὲ μείζονος ζημίας δοκῇ ἄξιος εἶναι, προσκαλεσάμενος πρόπεμπτα καὶ τίμημα ἐπιγραψάμενος, ὅ τι ἂν δοκῇ αὐτῷ, εἰσαγέτω εἰς τὴν ἡλιαίαν. ἐὰν δ' ἁλῷ, τιμάτω ἡ ἡλιαία περὶ τοῦ ἁλόντος, ὅ τι χρὴ αὐτὸν παθεῖν ἢ ἀποτεῖσαι.

(D. 43.75)

LAW: The *archon* is to look after the orphans and the heiresses and the deserted oikoi and the women who remain in the *oikos* of their dead husband claiming that they are pregnant. He is to look after them and not to allow anyone to treat them abusively. If someone abuses them or does something illegal, he has the authority to impose a fine to the extent of his powers.[4] If he appears to deserve a more severe penalty, the *archon* is to serve him with a five days notice, and writing on the indictment the penalty which he thinks is fair, he is to introduce the case to the heliaia. If he is convicted, the heliaia is to decide what punishment or fine is appropriate for the convicted man.[5]

7 The law on the *anchisteia* and the order of priority for inheritance. (594 BC)

ΝΟΜΟΣ. Ὅστις ἂν μὴ διαθέμενος ἀποθάνῃ, ἐὰν μὲν παῖδας καταλίπῃ θηλείας, σὺν ταύτῃσιν, ἐὰν δὲ μή, τούσδε κυρίους εἶναι τῶν χρημάτων. ἐὰν μὲν ἀδελφοὶ ὦσιν ὁμοπάτορες· καὶ ἐὰν παῖδες ἐξ ἀδελφῶν γνήσιοι, τὴν τοῦ πατρὸς μοῖραν λαγχάνειν· ἐὰν δὲ μὴ ἀδελφοὶ ὦσιν ἢ ἀδελφῶν παῖδες, [. . .] ἐξ αὐτῶν κατὰ ταὐτὰ λαγχάνειν· κρατεῖν δὲ τοὺς ἄρρενας καὶ τοὺς ἐκ τῶν ἀρρένων, ἐὰν ἐκ τῶν αὐτῶν ὦσι, καὶ ἐὰν γένει ἀπωτέρω. ἐὰν δὲ μὴ ὦσι πρὸς πατρὸς μέχρι ἀνεψιῶν παίδων, τοὺς πρὸς μητρὸς τοῦ ἀνδρὸς κατὰ ταὐτὰ κυρίους εἶναι. ἐὰν δὲ μηδετέρωθεν ᾖ ἐντὸς τούτων, τὸν πρὸς πατρὸς ἐγγυτάτω κύριον εἶναι. νόθῳ δὲ μηδὲ νόθῃ μὴ εἶναι ἀγχιστείαν μήθ᾽ ἱερῶν μήθ᾽ ὁσίων ἀπ᾽ Εὐκλείδου ἄρχοντος.

(D. 43.51)

LAW: Whenever a man dies without making a will, if he leaves female children his estate shall go with them, but if not, the persons herein mentioned shall be entitled to his property: if there be brothers by the same father, and if there be lawfully born sons of brothers, they shall take the share of the father. But if there are no brothers or sons of brothers, their descendants shall inherit it in like manner; but males and the sons of males shall take precedence, if they are of the same ancestors, even though they be more remote of kin. If there are no relatives on the father's side within the degree of children of cousins, those on the mother's side shall inherit in like manner. But if there shall be no relatives on either side within the degree mentioned, the nearest of kin on the father's side shall inherit. But no illegitimate child of either sex shall have the right of succession either to religious rites or civic privileges, from the time of the archonship of Eucleides.[6]

8 The law on the statutory time-limit for inheritance disputes with guardians (5th–4th century)

βούλομαι καὶ τοῦτον ὑμῖν τὸν νόμον εἰπεῖν, ὅστις διαρρήδην λέγει,[7] ἐὰν πέντ᾽ ἔτη παρέλθῃ καὶ μὴ δικάσωνται, μηκέτ᾽ εἶναι τοῖς ὀρφανοῖς δίκην περὶ τῶν ἐκ τῆς ἐπιτροπῆς ἐγκλημάτων. καὶ ὑμῖν ἀναγνώσεται τὸν νόμον. ΝΟΜΟΣ.

(D. 38.17)

I also want to read to you this law, which expressly states, if five years go by and they do not bring a case to court, it will no longer be permitted for orphans to make claims against their guardians. He will read you the law. LAW.

9 The law on the poor *epikleros*

ΝΟΜΟΣ. Τῶν ἐπικλήρων ὅσαι θητικὸν τελοῦσιν, ἐὰν μὴ βούληται ἔχειν ὁ ἐγγύτατα γένους, ἐκδιδότω ἐπιδοὺς ὁ μὲν πεντακοσιομέδιμνος πεντακοσίας δραχμάς, ὁ δ᾽ ἱππεὺς τριακοσίας, ὁ δὲ ζευγίτης ἑκατὸν πεντήκοντα, πρὸς οἷς αὐτῆς. ἐὰν δὲ πλείους ὦσιν ἐν τῷ αὐτῷ γένει, τῇ ἐπικλήρῳ πρὸς μέρος ἐπιδιδόναι ἕκαστον. ἐὰν δ᾽ αἱ γυναῖκες πλείους ὦσι, μὴ ἐπάναγκες εἶναι πλέον ἢ μίαν ἐκδοῦναι τῷ γ' ἑνί, ἀλλὰ τὸν ἐγγύτατα ἀεὶ ἐκδιδόναι ἢ αὐτὸν ἔχειν. ἐὰν δὲ μὴ ἔχῃ ὁ ἐγγυτάτω γένους ἢ μὴ ἐκδῷ, ὁ ἄρχων ἐπαναγκαζέτω ἢ αὐτὸν ἔχειν ἢ ἐκδοῦναι. ἐὰν δὲ μὴ ἐπαναγκάσῃ ὁ ἄρχων, ὀφειλέτω χιλίας δραχμὰς ἱερὰς τῇ Ἥρᾳ. ἀπογραφέτω δὲ τὸν μὴ ποιοῦντα ταῦτα ὁ βουλόμενος πρὸς τὸν ἄρχοντα.[8]

(D. 43:54)

LAW: In regard to all heiresses who are classified as Thetes, if the nearest of kin does not wish to marry one, let him give her in marriage with a portion of five hundred drachmae, if he be of the class of Pentacosiomedimni, if of the class of Knights, with a portion of three hundred, and if of the class of Zeugitae, with one hundred and fifty, in addition to what is her own. If there are several kinsmen in the same degree of relationship, each one of them shall contribute to the portion of the heiress according to his due share. And if there be several heiresses, it shall not be necessary for a single kinsman to give in marriage more than one, but the next of kin shall in each case give her in marriage or marry her himself. And if the nearest of kin does not marry her or give her in marriage, the *archon* shall compel him either to marry her himself or give her in marriage. And if the *archon* shall not compel him, let him be fined a thousand drachmae, which are to be consecrate to Hera. And let any person who chooses denounce to the *archon* any person who disobeys this law.

5.2 Succession by natural legitimate sons

The laws of Athens governing inheritance and succession had not changed since the time of Solon, with the exception of a few minor modifications.[9] There is something perennial about these laws alongside an unmistakably archaic character. While it appears that families came together and dissolved, and properties were passed on from the one generation to the next in unchanging, predictable patterns, some of the arrangements on inheritance and interstate succession have surprised modern scholars and appear to be strange when viewed from an outsider's perspective. In order to understand Athenian inheritance laws and practices, we need to place them in context and comprehend the purposes which they served.

Direct succession could only take place through legitimate sons, natural or adopted. If the *kyrios* of the *oikos* had one legitimate son, he directly inherited his father after his death. The *kyrios* also had the option to retire and hand over control of the *oikos* to his son when he was too advanced in years to effectively exercise his duties.[10] If there were more than one son they were entitled to an equal share of the father's property after his death. Alternatively, a father could go ahead and divide the property equally among his sons while he was still alive.[11] In such cases the father might keep for himself and his wife some of the property, which would be divided among the sons after the death of their parents.[12] While the inheritance speeches in the corpus of Isaios, as well as some in Demosthenes, Lysias and Isocrates, and fragments in other orators, suggest a variety of patterns and practices in the actual distribution of estates, the basic premise, that legitimate sons were entitled to equal parts of their father's property, was never in question and any attempt to circumvent it resulted in litigation.

5.3 Legitimate daughters and dowry

Legitimate daughters did not directly continue the *oikos* of their father, as at some point they were expected to leave their natal family and start a new *oikos* with their husband. However, unlike the Roman *cum manu* marriage, an Athenian woman never lost inheritance rights in her natal *oikos*, and never acquired any inheritance rights in her husband's *oikos*. In a sense it is as if she was given on loan to her husband's *oikos*, she could be reclaimed at any time (and she readily was if she became an *epikleros*), and every last obol of her dowry needed to be returned in case of divorce. On the other hand, an Athenian marriage was different from the Roman *sine manu* marriage in two important aspects: the Athenian wife came under the legal authority of her husband, and her children retained some inheritance rights to her natal family's *oikos*, albeit secondary to those of the agnatic line. A legitimate daughter could only continue her father's *oikos* through her children, and even then, this was a secondary option to be taken only in the absence of direct male heirs.

In families with male and female offspring legitimate daughters could be given in marriage before or after the death of their father, as a brother also had the legal right to arrange a marriage with *engye*. On the other hand, in families with only female offspring one would imagine that there was a certain urgency in arranging marriages as soon as possible, because if by the time of the death of her father a woman already had children then the succession was secure and the woman could not be claimed as *epikleros*; she could stay with her husband and her children, and her father's property simply joined that of the family to be inherited by the children along with the property of their father.[13] However, if at the time of her father's death the woman was either unmarried, or married without children, then she became an *epikleros*, and might be pursued primarily for her property. It is reasonable to assume that most fathers would prefer the stability of an arranged marriage with a husband of their choice for their daughter instead of the vicissitudes of an *epidikasia* (see the discussion below).

Almost invariably a woman married with *engye* would be given part of the family property in the form of a dowry agreed during the *engye*,[14] although this was not a legal requirement for a lawful marriage.[15] Poorer Athenians might have to borrow or collect funds through an *eranos* among relatives and friends, in order to be able to provide for the future of a daughter.[16] The dowry would stay with her until her death, as it was meant to be what provided for her sustenance, and after her death it would be inherited by her children. The question is why, if the dowry was not legally required, families almost never gave a daughter in marriage without one, and the answer to it can be found in several legal arrangements regulating aspects of the institution.

The primary law on succession by legitimate daughters (S 3) made it illegal to exclude them from any arrangement on the family property. A legitimate daughter had an inalienable right to a share of the family property, and under normal circumstances, when she was given away in marriage through *engye*, the dowry was the standard way for her to obtain her share of the property. This share typically was smaller than the one going to male heirs,[17] expectedly so, since they would have the primary financial responsibility for their households, while her share was only meant to be a contribution to her husband's *oikos*. The provision which in case of divorce allowed the former husband to keep the dowry for some time, if he made monthly payments at the high interest rate of 18 percent for the maintenance of the woman (σῖτος),[18] suggests that the dowry was also seen as the means for the citizen woman to pay for her way in life. The same underlying principle can be recognized in the provision that the son of an *epikleros* is to pay for his mother's maintenance (τὸν δὲ σῖτον μετρεῖν τῇ μητρί) once he reaches his 20th year of age and takes control of the property that came with her (S 5). These principles are also visible in the fact that the dowry was not limited to citizen women. Sometimes women given as concubines, like illegitimate daughters of citizens or respectable metic women, also received a dowry which was meant to pay for their sustenance and offer them a more secure position in their new household by making it unappealing for their partner to repudiate them and lose the dowry.[19]

Plutarch attests a Solonean law which restricted the dowry a woman could carry to three garments and low value household utensils.[20] This law probably made sense in the tense, economically depressed climate of Solonean Athens, but clearly it was ignored in later times, when the finances of the city recovered. In the classical period there is no doubt that the law was obsolete as even women from the lowest income families would get significantly larger dowries than what this law allowed.[21] Two important studies, the classic work of Augustus Boeckh, and the excellent monograph of David Schaps on the economic rights of Athenian women agree that a dowry could start at 10 minae for families at the lower end and go as high as 2 talents, with an average of 20–30 minae for most families.[22] The dowry could consist of cash, real estate, jewelry, clothing, other valuables such as golden or silver cups, furniture or whatever else the families had agreed upon, while its value was formally assessed during the *engye*.[23] In case of divorce the former husband ought to return a sum equal to the agreed one, but not necessarily the same items. For some prominent families a large dowry may have been a question of status. For example, the dowry given by Hipponikos, perhaps the richest man in Greece at the time, to his daughter Hipparete when she married Alcibiades was legendary and it appears that the family was making a statement of its wealth and power (Ἱππονίκῳ δὲ τῷ Καλλίου πατρί, δόξαν ἔχοντι μεγάλην καὶ δύναμιν ἀπὸ πλούτου καὶ γένους).[24] On several occasions in our sources exceptionally large dowries are given by dying men to their daughters,[25] and this surely reflects their anxiety for the future of their loved ones, and their desire to make sure that they would be well looked after.

On the basis of a few passages like the famous remark of Poseidippos "everyone raises a son, even if he is poor, and exposes a daughter, even if he is rich"[26] several scholars, most notably Sarah Pomeroy and Mark Golden, have argued that there was widespread exposure of female infants in classical Athens, and the dowry has taken much of the blame for this.[27] The argument has been that since families would be hard-pressed to secure dowries for daughters, they would be more likely to expose them as infants. However, the evidence in support of this suggestion is rather anecdotal and not very reliable, and this is why the majority of scholars, including A.W. Gomme, Averil Cameron and D. Engels, have firmly rejected the view that the exposure of female infants was common in Athens.[28] More recently Wayne Ingalls has mounted a targeted challenge to the view that the dowry was a cause for selective infanticide.[29]

Lin Foxhall approaching the subject from a different angle has argued that the dowry was actually a source of strength for the woman in the household, as it gave her a voice and discouraged the husband from divorcing her and losing the dowry.[30] While one should not overstate the point, as an Athenian man always had a choice of another marriage and a new dowry, especially when no children were involved, there is ample evidence suggesting that the dowry gave the woman power and a stronger voice in the household (παρρησία, in the words of Menander[31]), while the comedians exploited the theme of the domineering female with the large dowry. Antiphanes joked that there is no load heavier than a woman with a large dowry, and Alexis said that men are enslaved by women when they put a dowry in the place of honor.[32] The formidable Artemona in Plautus *Asinaria* is a classic embodiment of this theme: she has everyone in the household under her thumb and never lets anyone forget that it is her dowry that provides for the entire household.

5.4 *Epikleros*

If a man died leaving behind only legitimate daughters, but no son to inherit him, then these daughters became the vessels for the continuation of the *oikos* of their father. The English term "heiress" is only an approximate translation for the Greek ἐπίκληρος.[33] The Athenian *epikleros* did not actually inherit the property of her father; it would be more accurate to say that the property went with her and was to be inherited by her sons, who would be seen as the actual successors to their grandfather. This is why it was very important to secure a husband for the *epikleros* and to have legitimate children from the union. As explained in the previous chapter, the Athenians were concerned about the welfare of women accompanied by large properties, and had instituted a series of rigorous procedures to make sure that the *oikos* would continue, the women would be properly looked after, the property would stay within the family, and eventually a male heir in a direct line of succession would come in possession of the property and assets of the *oikos*.

How seriously the Athenian state took this process can be demonstrated by the fact that the wider family did not have a choice when it came to securing a suitable husband for the heiress, nor could they simply give her in marriage. By default, when the situation occurred the woman could only be given in marriage with the approval of the *archon*, whose responsibility was to ensure that she would be married to a person legally entitled to take her and the property that came along with her. The law actually took the extraordinary step of defining who this person ought to be. He had to be the closest male relative of her father, and if more than one man fitted this description (e.g. two first cousins), then the older of the two had priority. If he happened to be married and did not wish to divorce his wife in order to marry the *epikleros*, he could always step aside in favor of his son, and if he simply did not wish to pursue the claim, he could always step aside and allow the next person in line to claim the woman and her property.

Much depended on the particular circumstances of the case, such as who the woman was, how attractive she was, whether she would be of childbearing age, and most important how large was the fortune accompanying her. One would imagine that a rich, and maybe even a poor but attractive *epikleros* would not be short of suitors. However, a poor *epikleros* with modest appearance might not have any suitors, and this is why the law intervened and forced the nearest male relative of her father either to marry her himself or to give her a dowry out of his own property and find her husband (S 9).

This legal provision is important for our overall understanding of the institution of the *epikleros*. If the state were simply concerned with interstate succession, and the fate of the *oikos* and the property, then this provision would not have been introduced at all. Since there was no significant property left, there would be no need for the state and its institutions to be concerned. However, the fact that the law compelled the relatives to secure a husband for the woman at their own cost suggests that this legal provision should be interpreted as part of the wider social security network of the Athenian Democracy.[34] A woman outside the structures of the *oikos* was legally, economically and personally vulnerable, and this is why the Athenian state wanted to make sure that no citizen woman would find herself in that position.[35]

If more than one person was claiming an *epikleros* in marriage, the *archon* needed to refer the case to court under a process of διαδικασία. The difference with any other form of lawsuit was that in a *diadikasia* there were no accusers or accused, but two or more contestants. It was up to the jury to decide who had the better claim, and if several of the surviving cases are any indication, this was no mean feat in a state which did not keep written records of births or deaths, and no family registers enlisting all members.[36] What made the process even more difficult was that several women could simultaneously become *epikleroi* to the same estate, and by the time their descendants started claiming parts of the property, it would be a herculean task to tell who had the better claim in the order set by the law defining the *anchisteia*, the family lines (S 7).

All violations of provisions related to an *epikleros* needed to be referred to the *archon*. The law encouraged citizens to report abuses against an *epikleros* and violations of the pertinent laws with *eisangelia*, a public procedure which unlike other public cases (e.g. *graphai*), did not carry any kind of risk for the unsuccessful prosecutor (S 6).[37] Any citizen could initiate the *eisangelia* and even if he failed to obtain one 5th of the votes there was no liability, because the state wanted to encourage prosecutions of such abuses. Matters related to metic women who became *epikleroi* to their father or brother had to be brought before the *polemarch*, not the *archon*, as expected, since the *polemarch* was the magistrate in charge of the non-citizen populations of Attica. While the Attic Orators typically portray the *epikleros* as vulnerable, a potential victim at the mercy of determined suitors hungry for her wealth, comedy, on the other hand, sometimes portrays her as the domineering mistress, bossing around everyone else in a household funded by her wealth. A fragment from the *Plokion* of Menander compares the rich *epikleros* with the mythological monster Lamia terrorizing everyone in the house.[38] Another fragment of Menander presents the *epikleros* as punishment disguised as a blessing:

> ὅστις γυναῖκ' ἐπίκληρον ἐπιθυμεῖ λαβεῖν
> πλουτοῦσαν, ἤτοι μῆνιν ἐκτίνει θεῶν,
> ἢ βούλετ' ἀτυχεῖν μακάριος καλούμενος.[39]
>
> Anyone who wishes to marry a rich *epikleros*
> He is punished by angry gods
> Or he wishes to be called fortunate, even though he is miserable

5.5 Illegitimate children

After 403, when the decree of Aristophon and Nikomenes excluded illegitimate children from the *anchisteia* and reinstated the Periclean citizenship law, a man who had only illegitimate children would be exactly in the same position as someone who did not have any children at all, as far as inheritance law was concerned. Illegitimate children could certainly care for a parent in life, or after death by performing the necessary funeral rites, and could offer much love and support, but under no circumstances could inherit their father or be seen as his successors. His property would go to lateral relatives with an order of eligibility clearly defined by law (S 7). Whether illegitimate children were excluded from succession since the time of Solon, or the decree of Aristophon created a new restriction is not certain. MacDowell, with good reason, doubts the reliability of the evidence from the *Birds* of Aristophanes, which states that a Solonean law excluded illegitimate children from the line of succession.[40] The Aristophanic text as it is worded is ambiguous and confusing.[41] On the other hand, it would be difficult to ignore the Aristophanic passage altogether, as it was written in 414, namely several years before the decree of Aristophon, and during a time when the *nothoi* had full inheritance rights, so the joke would not make any sense unless some form of exclusion of the *nothoi* from inheritance had pre-existed 403. This is why, the exclusion which it suggests, garbled as the wording may be, could be Sononean, and was only suspended during the years of the Peloponnesian war. If so, the decree of Aristophon simply revived a traditional legal concept. On the whole, since such a law is not mentioned anywhere else, and 4th century orators by default refer to the decree of Aristophon and Nikomenes, we cannot be certain what was the situation before, but we have some grounds to suspect that *nothoi* had limited inheritance rights, if any at all, since the time of Solon.

If this conclusion is correct, then we must also understand that the Periclean citizenship law in 451 redefined the meaning of *nothos*. Before 451 a *nothos* would be a child born outside wedlock through *engye* or *epidikasia*. For example, Pericles junior, the general's son from the concubine Aspasia would be a *nothos* even before 451, because his parents were never married. However, children born of mixed marriages between Athenians with non-Athenians would be *gnesioi*, as they had been legitimately born in wedlock. For example, Kimon, the son of Miltiades with the Thracian princess Hypsipyle, would be considered legitimate, and he certainly was heir to his rich and illustrious father, since he was born in proper marriage. After 451 legitimate children of mixed unions (μητρόξενοι) effectively found themselves in the same position as the *nothoi*, and eventually came to be considered *nothoi* themselves.[42] The legal disadvantages of the *nothoi* were suspended during the Peloponnesian war, but the decree of Aristophon enshrined them firmly into law in 403, excluding the *nothoi* from citizenship and inheritance (except perhaps a modest bequest up to 10 minae).[43] In the 4th century, all children of a citizen with a non-citizen would be considered *nothoi*, and the occasional call for more respect and equal rights for the *nothoi* (see Chapters 4.2 and 4.4) simply confirms the rule that illegitimate children routinely faced legal inequality, discrimination and prejudice, and were treated as inferiors in most aspects of public and private life.

5.6 Wills and succession by adopted children

Persons with no legitimate sons were allowed to adopt an heir even before the time of Solon.[44] In our times, adoption of an adult while possible is rather rare, but in the ancient world it was common, as an adoption was not only about "creating a life-long family bond and legal connection,"[45] but first and foremost about securing an heir. Every student of the ancient world will be familiar with the issues related to the succession of Augustus, an adopted son of Julius Caesar himself, eventually settled through the adoption of Tiberius into the Julian family, or the good fortune of the empire when four of its best rulers in a row had to settle succession through the adoption of an accomplished adult, thus creating a chain of five good emperors in Rome's finest hour. The Greeks, like the Romans viewed adoption primarily as a means of securing an heir, and this is why they often, but not invariably, adopted adult citizens, whom they could trust with their property and the continuation of their *oikos*. This aspect of adoption has been emphasized by Claudine Leduc in a significant article on the subject, where adoption is linked with the institution of the *epikleros* as two pathways leading to the same objective, namely the continuation of the *oikos*.[46] This did not necessarily exclude emotional factors, such as the development of strong family bonds between adopter and adoptee, or the very human behaviors of caring for a child or an ageing parent. Lene Rubinstein in her authoritative monograph on adoption in 4th century Athens correctly stresses the emotional aspects of adoption, especially *inter vivos*.[47]

Adoption was not an option for a person who already had living legitimate sons (S 1–2). The law expressly prohibited it, and the reasons are obvious: an adoption would cut a slice from the share of legitimate natural sons and there was no reason for it, since the succession of the *oikos* had already been secured. In the event that the natural son(s), died before the father, then he had the right to adopt from the moment that he was left without an heir (S 2). An adoption could be arranged *inter vivos*, through a will, which means that it took effect after the death of the adopter, or even posthumously by the members of the family. In the years when the Periclean citizenship law was in effect, the adoptee would need to be a citizen-born child or adult, as adoption could not be used as a means of brining non-citizens into the citizen body. As far as we can tell, the law did not prohibit adoption of non-citizens, but since these adoptees could not be heirs to their adopted father, one would imagine that such adoptions were done for emotional reasons and had no legal purpose.

Adoption could be an appealing option for men with only legitimate daughters, as this meant that a trusted person, often a close relative would be brought into the household to take the place of a brother for them, and as such not only take care of them in legal matters but also look after their interests in life and offer emotional support as a brother would. Alternatively, an adopted son could also become the husband of a legitimate daughter. Such arrangements meant that a legitimate daughter would not become *epikleros* after her father's death, and as such a soft target for ruthless relatives going after her property. Among numerous examples one could mention the will of Aristotle, as it is a textbook case for some important aspects of adoption.[48] The philosopher had two children, a legitimate daughter from his wife Pythias, and an illegitimate son named Nikomachos from his concubine Herpyllis, probably a former *hetaira*. Since neither could be his legal heir, Aristotle adopted in his will his nephew Nikanor, with the provision that he will marry the daughter of the philosopher, when she reaches maturity. As a failsafe, if something were to happen to Nikanor before the girl reached adulthood, Aristotle named Theophrastos as his alternate adopted son and possible husband to his daughter. Nikanor as the *kyrios* of the household was also going to take care of young Nikomachos and Herpyllis, and make sure that they are well looked after. Aristotle went one step further and specified which property items belonged to Herpyllis, including a house for her to reside in and furniture to her liking, thus making sure that she would not be short-changed by his heir. Through these provisions Aristotle was trying to ensure that his *oikos* would continue and the members of his household would not be mistreated or neglected.

Another interesting case study would be the adoption of Leokrates into the family of his uncle Polyeuktos. The adopted son married the younger daughter of Polyeuktos with a significant dowry (40 minae) at the time of the marriage, and with the understanding that after the death of Polyeuktos he would inherit the remaining property and continue his *oikos*. This adoption was done *inter vivos* and certainly came with an emotional baggage, which eventually created animosities and the arrangement fell through. Perhaps the apparent inequality of the arrangement, treating the one daughter in a more privileged way over the other had something to do with it. It is clear that the adoption of Leokrates went beyond financial calculations, and Polyeuktos saw in his nephew a future son and heir, until for reasons that are left unexplained the two men fell out. Leokrates walked away from the adoption and Polyeuktos took back his daughter with the dowry, and remarried her to Spudias, but this time without an adoption. Consequently, after the death of Polyeuktos, and since both women seemingly had children by that time, they were to divide his property into two equal parts. The case reveals that there was nothing permanent in an Athenian adoption, unless the two parties wanted it to be permanent, and either the adopter or the adoptee could at any point walk away from the arrangement if it no longer seemed suitable. However, this rarely happened, as many a time significant financial interest overrode emotional outbursts within families.

Although adoption was often accompanied by marriage to one of the legitimate daughters of the family, this was not a requirement. The law simply required that legitimate daughters could not be left out of the arrangements (S 3), if the adoption was made through a man's will, that is, when he would no longer be around to protect his daughters' interests. Consequently, unless the will of her father specified that the adopted son needed to marry the woman himself, her adopted brother once he was formally a member of the family had the legal right to give her in marriage with *engye* to another man, and offer her a dowry, like a natural brother would have done. The law on wills and adoptions had two objectives: the first was to secure an heir for the *oikos*, and the second was to make sure that in the process the property rights of legitimately born women would not be ignored.

An adoption became official when the adopter presented the adoptee to his phratry and his deme. Once the adoptee had been accepted into the deme of his adopter, then the process was complete and all legal ties with his natal *oikos* were severed. The adopted son no longer retained any inheritance rights in his father's *oikos*. One would imagine that such an arrangement was not only convenient for the adoptee, who stood to inherit everything in his new *oikos*, but also for his natural brothers, who could keep his share of the property in his natal *oikos*. In this respect, an adoption to another *oikos* could be a "win-win" scenario for a family with several legitimate sons, and not enough property to be split among them, and this is why it seems that it was quite extensively practiced without significant family antagonisms in most cases. Sometimes the adoptee was female, and the law placed no impediment to it.[49] However, since the ultimate objective of succession could only be indirectly accomplished through a female line, the inevitable conclusion is that such arrangements were infrequent and dictated by emotional considerations. If the adoptee was a woman, very likely the adopter would offer a sacrifice on her behalf in the phratry, thus letting the community know about the adoption. However, since practices in phratries seem to vary in relation to women, it is difficult to tell whether any additional steps were necessary before the adoption was considered legally complete.

An adoption through a will was different from an adoption *inter vivos* in one significant aspect. In the latter case the adoptee could take residence in his new *oikos*, and if a marriage had been included in the package, he could move in with his wife, as Leocrates does in the above-mentioned case, and be integrated into the adopter's immediate family with all the positive and negative emotional implications that this might entail. However, an adoption through a will did not take effect until the death of the adopter. This more cautious approach meant that the adoptee did not need to build a close emotional relationship with his new *oikos* before it was necessary, and the adopter remained in firm control of his family, property and entire *oikos* until the end, without having to explain his actions to another adult citizen man.

A will was an expression of a man's desire to control the fortunes of his *oikos* even after his demise, and this is why sometimes even men with legitimate sons could make a will arranging the affairs of the family after their death. So long as the basic premise, that the property was to be equally split between legitimate sons, was observed, additional clauses settling other affairs of the family could be included. There are several examples of this. In the speech of Lysias *Against Diogeiton*, Diodotos on his way to a military campaign, in which he was killed, deposited a will with his brother, and father-in-law Diogeiton, making clear his wishes about the affairs of his family in the event that he did not return.[50] Diodotos had three legitimate children, two sons and one daughter, and he left a property of approximately 13 talents. In his will he stated that his wife was to be given in marriage again with a dowry of 1 talent, and his daughter was to receive another talent for her dowry. The two sons were to split the remaining 11 talents. These arrangements did not really break the law which forbade a man with legitimate sons to make a will, because they did not violate the property rights of the sons, and for this reason they could not be contested in court, as there was nothing to contest. Beyond that, the terms in the will of Diodotos were non-binding family arrangements, which could be ignored without legal consequences. For example, when his brother and father-in-law decided to give his daughter, the widow of Diodotos, in marriage, he did not honor the terms of the will and gave her a dowry of 50 minae, instead of a talent. Another instructive example of a will of this kind is that of the father of Demosthenes, who again had an under-age legitimate son, when he made his will. Like the case of Diodotos, the wishes of Demosthenes senior for the members of his family as stated in his will were largely ignored.

The will of the banker Pasion, a naturalized citizen of Athens, who also had two legitimate sons at the time of his death, one of them an adult, was more effective in settling the affairs of his household, but this happened only because his adult son Apollodoros initially cooperated.[51] When Pasion was terminally ill he was worried about the extravagance of his elder son, and probably felt weary of entrusting the management of the entire property to him. In order to shield the portion of the property belonging to his younger son Pasicles, who was still under-age, he made a will, where he split the property in two, Apollodoros got his inheritance immediately to do as he pleased, while his trusted bank manager Phormion was placed as a guardian to Pasikles and was to manage his portion until the boy came of age. Moreover, Phormion was to take the widow of Pasion as his wife. There should be no doubt that Apollodoros initially went ahead with this arrangement. He was 24 years old and accustomed to a lifestyle reserved for the sons of the upper strata of Athenian society. Caring for his younger brother in addition to a demanding family business was a task that he was happy to entrust to other people. This conclusion is inevitable because if Apollodoros had objected to the will of Pasion as vehemently as he appears to be objecting to it 25 years later in the two speeches *Against Stephanos*, all he would need to do is ignore the will after the death of his father and assume direct control of the *oikos* as its *kyrios* according to the law on succession by legitimate sons, until his brother reached adulthood.

After the death of Pasion, Apollodoros as the only adult male in the household would be *kyrios* of his younger brother and his mother, and he could simply put a stop to all arrangements made by his father. He was under no legal obligation to allow the marriage of his mother, and by right he was the legal guardian of his brother and *kyrios* to the *oikos* of Pasion. However, it seems that at first Apollodoros accepted these arrangements until it was too late to reverse them. By 365, namely six years after the death of Pasion when the speech *Against Nikostratos* was delivered, Apollodoros was engaged in litigation with his brother's guardian, and eventually his brother, claiming that they had defrauded him.[52] The legal battles would go on for about a quarter of a century, and the former slave Phormion would become rich enough to buy his way into Athenian citizenship through very generous contributions to the Athenian state, just as Pasion had done before him. Meanwhile, Apollodoros although still quite rich, had seen a reduction of his massive property to the value of three talents by 348, if we believe that he is telling the truth about his alleged "poverty."[53] When Apollodoros finally challenged the legality of the will of Pasion 24 years after his death, even though from a legal point of view he appeared to be right, his arguments must have sounded pointless after the passage of so much time.

The profound impact of the laws on testamentary succession upon family and social structures are nowhere seen more clearly than in the contrast between Athenian and Spartan inheritance law. In Sparta before the *rhetra* of Epitadeus (5th century), adoption into the *oikos* of a man who did not have a son to inherit him was the only way for second or third sons of Spartan citizens to gain a lot of land (κλᾶρος), and full Spartan citizenship (*homoios*) along with it, since the lot of their father had to pass to the eldest son intact. The system worked, because strict regulation along these lines guaranteed that the ancestral lots remained of a standard size, sufficient to provide for the Spartan citizen and his family, as well as the helots who worked the land for him. The number of spare sons and families without a male heir naturally balanced each other, and the number of full citizens in Sparta remained steady, close to the ideal number of 5000 full citizens for a Greek *polis*.

The *rhetra* of Epitadeus was a simple piece of legislation deregulating succession and allowing a man to leave his property to whomever he wished *inter vivos* or through a will.[54] The phrase ᾧ τις ἐθέλοι (to whomever he wished) included women, and not only Spartan men, which Aristotle considered the root of the insurmountable demographic problems which Sparta was facing in his time. This deregulation destroyed the fundamental "one lot for every Spartan" principle of the Spartan system, which guaranteed the prized equality of the Spartan *homoioi*. From that moment forward lots could be essentially bought and sold, which facilitated the accumulation of resources in fewer and fewer hands, and to the disfranchisement of an ever-increasing number of citizens. In the time of Aristotle, it seems that 40 percent of the land was owned by women, which in Athens would be inconsequential as citizenship was not tied to land ownership, not since the archaic period, but in Sparta it was devastating because it meant that large numbers of its male citizens would become disfranchised Inferiors (ὑπομείονες) because they did not own land. Thus, a simple deregulation of the inheritance law, which was fundamentally incompatible with Sparta's rigid structures proved to be the most devastating blow to the system of Lycurgus, and rapidly accelerated the demise of Spartan power by eroding the numbers at the core of its armies, the elite Spartan citizen battalions.

In Athens, property concentration or large ownership did not interfere with the political system in the same way, as free-market forces were built into it, and citizenship was conferred on the basis of birth, not income. Therefore, one would expect the Athenian system to be more deregulated, but paradoxically it was not. The Athenians never reached the point of complete freedom to dispose of one's property as one wished; on the contrary, a set of firm rules established in the archaic period mostly by Solon provided for every eventuality and regulated with precision how property could be transmitted from one generation to the next with the very clear objective to preserve the *oikoi* and keep the property within the family. While a man always had the right to buy or sell property, he could not deprive his sons of their livelihood after his death, even if he so wished. Unless he took the extreme measure of renouncing a son (ἀποκήρυξις)[55] he had no choice but to leave his property to him, and when daughters came into the picture the intricate network of rules regulating succession was an inescapable net which might allow some room for maneuvers but it would never allow actions outside its scope.

While the laconically phrased *rhetra* of Epitadeus essentially unraveled Spartan society, the more complicated and thoughtful laws of Solon were intended to maintain the constellation of *oikoi* which constituted the *polis*, and proved very successful in preventing large accumulations of wealth in a few hands, along with all the socio-economic problems which this would entail, and Solonean Athens had experienced first-hand. While in a basically capitalist economy like that of classical Athens there were substantial inequalities of wealth, the principle of the preservation of the *oikoi* at which the state was aiming allowed a large number of citizens to remain financially comfortable and able to exercise their rights and duties in the first democracy. It seems that Solon instinctively operated on the economic principle that regulation of market forces favors a healthy middle class, which in turn favors political stability and social cohesion, while lack of regulation favors the accumulation of wealth in fewer hands, which in turn fosters extreme political forces, instability and an endless host of social problems. The society which he was trying to regulate was an imbalanced and unstable one, and it is to his credit that with the system of laws regulating succession and inheritance which he devised he contributed to a large degree to the economic and social stability which was necessary for the first democracy to come to life and flourish a century later.

Notes

1 See also other partial and slightly modified citations of the same law in D. 44.68: 'ὅσοι μὴ ἐπεποίηντο' φησίν 'ὅτε Σόλων εἰσῄει εἰς τὴν ἀρχήν, ἐξεῖναι αὐτοῖς διαθέσθαι ὅπως ἂν ἐθέλωσιν,' ὡς τοῖς γε ποιηθεῖσιν οὐκ ἐξὸν διαθέσθαι. ["Whoever has not been adopted" he says "when Solon entered into office, shall have the right to dispose of his property as he wishes," because those who have been adopted do not have the right to dispose their property through a will]. See also Is. 6.28 τοῖς φύσει υἱέσιν αὐτοῦ οὐδεὶς οὐδενὶ ἐν διαθήκῃ γράφει δόσιν οὐδεμίαν, διότι ὁ νόμος αὐτὸς ἀποδίδωσι τῷ υἱεῖ τὰ τοῦ πατρὸς καὶ οὐδὲ διαθέσθαι ἐᾷ ὅτῳ ἂν ὦσι παῖδες γνήσιοι. [no one includes in a will any kind of inheritance to natural sons, because the law itself bestows the father's property to the son and does not allow a man to make a will if he has legitimate sons.]

2 The text as it appears here includes a transposition of μὴ from its place in the manuscripts (ἐὰν δὲ {μὴ} ᾖ), to the position before ἐπίκληρός τις ᾖ. I proposed this transposition in the study "The Demosthenic edition of Mervin Dilts, and the textual transmission of Apollodoros". In Grusková, Jana and Bannert, Herbert, (eds) *Demosthenica libris manu scriptis tradita*, Wiener Studien, Beiheft 36, Vienna 2014, 107–28. The reason for the transposition is that the law in the transmitted text says the exact opposite of what it should be saying, while the transposition corrects the error.

3 See also Hyp. Fr. 192, for an actual case where this law was applied: ΠΡΟΣ ΧΑΡΗΤΑ ΕΠΙΤΡΟΠΙΚΟΣ. ἐπεὶ δὲ ἐνεγράφην ἐγὼ καὶ ὁ νόμος ἀπέδωκε τὴν κομιδὴν τῶν καταλειφθέντων τῇ μητρί, ὃς κελεύει κυρίους εἶναι τῆς ἐπικλήρου καὶ τῆς οὐσίας ἁπάσης τοὺς παῖδας, ἐπειδὰν ἐπιδιετὲς ἡβήσωσιν. [TO CHARES ON GUARDIANSHIP. When I was registered [with the deme] and the law put me in charge of the property left to my mother, which states that the children are to be the *kyrioi* of the *epikleros* and the entire property, when they reach 20 years of age.]

4 Typically the limit for such fines was 50 drachmas for individual magistrates and 500 for the Council of the Five Hundred (MacDowell 1978: 235–37).

5 See also D. 35.48; Is. 6.36.

6 Translation by A.T. Murray.

7 After λέγει the orator switches from indirect to direct discourse without warning, because from ἐὰν πέντ' ἔτη he is quoting the wording of the law, which is going to be read in full by the clerk immediately after ΝΟΜΟΣ.

8 The text of the law as transmitted here must have undergone significant revisions in the classical period to include sums in drachmas, which could not have been included in the original Solonean law, and a hefty fine of 1000 drachmas for the *archon* who failed in his duty to compel the relatives of a poor *epikleros* to give her in marriage. It appears that, as it often happened, that the original Solonean core has undergone revisions and additions. The alternative would be that the document was forged, which although not beyond the realm of possibility in this instance, it seems less likely, since the document adds a significant amount of information on monetary figures according to the Solonean classes, which seems credible.

9 For an overview of inheritance laws and practices see MacDowell 1978: 92–108 and 1989: 10–21; Todd 1993: 216–31; Gagliardi 2002: 5–59; Ruschenbush 1962: 307–11; Asheri 1963: 1–21; Schaps 1979; Boeckh 1842; Cox 1989: 34–46; Foxhall 1989: 22–44; Hodkinson 1989: 79–121; Just 1989: 83–104; Humphreys 2002: 340–7; Hunter 1994, as well as the ever-useful commentary of Wyse on the speeches of Isaios (1904).

10 A detailed example of this setting can be found in the *Wasps* of Aristophanes, where Philokleon has retired and handed over control to his son Bdelykleon. After the transition of power from father to son, the property and slaves of the household passed under the authority of Bdelykleon, while Phikokleon was meant to enjoy a comfortable retirement.

11 One good example would be the *oikos* of Bouselos. The author of the speech *Against Makaratos* describes the succession to the house of Bouselos as following:

Βούσελος γὰρ ἦν ἐξ Οἴου, ὦ ἄνδρες δικασταί, καὶ τούτῳ ἐγένοντο πέντε υἱεῖς, Ἁγνίας καὶ Εὐβουλίδης καὶ Στρατίος καὶ Ἅβρων καὶ Κλεόκριτος. καὶ οὗτοι ἅπαντες οἱ τοῦ Βουσέλου υἱεῖς ἄνδρες ἐγένοντο, καὶ διένειμεν αὐτοῖς τὴν οὐσίαν ὁ πατὴρ Βούσελος ἅπασιν καλῶς καὶ δικαίως, ὥσπερ προσῆκεν. νειμάμενοι δὲ τὴν οὐσίαν, γυναῖκα αὐτῶν ἕκαστος ἔγημεν κατὰ τοὺς νόμους τοὺς ὑμετέρους, καὶ παῖδες ἐγένοντο αὐτοῖς ἅπασιν καὶ παίδων παῖδες, καὶ ἐγένοντο πέντε οἶκοι ἐκ τοῦ Βουσέλου οἴκου ἑνὸς ὄντος, καὶ χωρὶς ἕκαστος ᾤκει τὸν ἑαυτοῦ ἔχων καὶ ἐγγόνους ἑαυτοῦ ποιούμενος. [Bouselos was from Oeum, men of the jury, and he had five sons, Hagnias, Euboulides, Stratios, Habron, and Kleokritos. All these sons of Bouselos reached adulthood, and their father Bouselos distributed his property among them in a good and fair manner, as appropriate. Whey had distributed the property, each one of them took a wife according to your laws, and they all had children and grandchildren, and five oikoi were created out of the one *oikos* of Bouselos, and each one of his sons was living separately in his own house with his own descendants.] The passage implies that in other cases the sons might stay in the father's house and bring up their children in crammed quarters, waiting for the time to receive their inheritance. One would imagine that the arrangement of splitting the property while the *kyrios* was still alive would be more desirable if there were several sons in the family, as in the case of Bouselos. In the speech *Against Nikostratos* (D. 53.27–8), several brothers (at least three) had divided the property.

12 In several cases the widow remains in control of a portion of the estate, which would go to her children after her death. The widow of Polyeuktos in the speech *Against Spudias* was in control of the larger part of the family property. The two daughters of the family had received their dowry, and their parents were in charge of the rest of the property. When their father died, the mother continued to be in charge, and upon her death the two daughters, who by that stage had children and could not be claimed as *epikleroi*, divided the remaining property between themselves. In the speech *Against Nikostratos* (D. 53.27–8) it seems that several brothers (at least three), had divided the property among themselves, while a part had been retained by their mother, surely to be equally divided among them after her death.

13 See, for example, the detailed account of such a case in D. 41.

14 Biscardi 1988: 225–35. For further discussion on the dowry see Wolff 1944: 43–95; Schaps 1979: 74–88; Hunter 20–9; Foxhall 1989: 22–44; Blundell 1995: 115–16; Ingalls 2002: 246–54; Wagner-Hasel 2009: 143–81.

15 See Lys. 19,14, Is. 3,29, 35–6; Arist. Fr. 1.14.93.4–5 Rose; Men. *Dysc*. 308.

16 See Philo *De Fuga et Inventione* 29; Millett *Lending* 62–3. An *eranos* was a loan collected through contributions of a fairly large group of people, and had to be repaid in small installments, sometimes without interest, and sometimes with interest, but probably lower than the interest paid to banks and other lenders.

17 But not so in Men. *Dysc*. 536–40, where the father splits the property in two and gives half to his daughter as a dowry, and half to his son, who is still expected to provide for himself and his parents. Of course, the evidence from comedy is not always to be taken as historical, but it is possible that this happened from time to time in real life too.

18 D. 29.17; 59.52.

19 See Is. 3.39 and Grzybek 1989: 206–12.

20 Plu. Sol. 20.6: τῶν δ' ἄλλων γάμων ἀφεῖλε τὰς φερνάς, ἱμάτια τρία καὶ σκεύη μικροῦ τιμήματος ἄξια κελεύσας, ἕτερον δὲ μηδέν, ἐπιφέρεσθαι τὴν γαμουμένην. οὐ γὰρ ἐβούλετο μισθοφόρον οὐδ' ὤνιον εἶναι τὸν γάμον, ἀλλ' ἐπὶ τεκνώσει καὶ χάριτι καὶ φιλότητι γίνεσθαι τὸν ἀνδρὸς καὶ γυναικὸς συνοικισμόν. [From all other marriages [except the *epidikasia*] he took away the dowries, allowing the bride to carry only three garments and utensils of small value, and nothing else. For he did not want the marriage to be a financial transaction but the joining of man and woman for child-bearing, caring and love.]

21 Beate Wagner-Hasel (2009: 143–81) has argued that the three garments were only the gifts-in-return (Gegengaben) which the bride brought for the bridegroom, and could be

of very high value, but this is not what Plutarch says. He clearly indicates that Solon limited the dowries, one would imagine in order to alleviate the burden on the poorer citizens, and to address biting social concerns such as envy and antagonism, and, indeed, to set marriages on a foundation of true love and affection. The most reasonable explanation is that this law was meant to address situations specific to Solonean Athens, and this is why it was ignored in later centuries.

22 See, for example, Is. 8.8; 2.5; Lys. 16.10; 32.6; D. 27.5 (the two-talent sum here may be inflated); 59.52; Boeckh 1828: 2.283; Schaps 1975: 99. Sums of five or ten talents mentioned in comedy are probably exaggerations (e.g. Men. *Dysc.* 843–4, three talents; Ep. 10.134 Sandbach, four talents; *Per.* 1015 three talents). The 20 talents given as a dowry to Hipparete, the wife of Alcibiades (And. 4.13), which was supposed to be the largest dowry ever given, may also be an exaggerated figure, as it only appears in later sources, like the speech *Against Alcibiades* (And. 4.13), which is probably a later antiquity rhetorical exercise, and Plutarch (*Alc.* 8.3). Classical sources mention the legendary dowry, but do not attach a figure to it (e.g. Isoc. 4.31). Both the scribe of *Against Alcibiades* and Plutarch (who appear to be somehow connected, but it is not possible to tell who came first), mention that the dowry was given in two installments, ten talents at the time of the marriage, and ten after the birth of a child. Since this practice is not attested anywhere else, the lack of parallels adds to our suspicions about this account.

23 For example, in D. 41.5–6 a house is included in the dowry, while in D. 41.27 the dowry includes expensive jewelry and clothes. In Is. 5.26 an apartment complex (συνοικία), assessed at 40 minae, is given as a dowry. In Men. *Dysc.* 737–8 it is a farm, half of it, while the other half is going to go to the brother of the bride.

24 Plu. *Alc.* 8.3.

25 For example, the dying Demosthenes the elder offers his five-year-old daughter a two talents dowry (D. 27.5), and Diodotos before leaving for a military campaign, from which he did not return, left his daughter one talent (Lys. 32.6).

26 Poseidippos *Ἑρμαφρόδιτος* Fr. 11: υἱὸν τρέφει πᾶς κἂν πένης τις ὢν τύχῃ, θυγατέρα δ' ἐκτίθησι κἂν ᾖ πλούσιος.

27 See Pomeroy 1983: 207–22, and 1997: 116–21; Golden 1981: 316–31; Patterson 1985: 103–23.

28 Bolkestein 1922: 222–39; Gomme 1933; Cameron 1932: 105–14; Eyben 1980: 5–82; Engels 1980: 112–20, Kapparis 2002: esp. Chapter 5.

29 Ingalls 2002: 246–54.

30 Foxhall 1989: 22–44; for a similar approach to the dowry see also Grzybek 1989: 6–12.

31 Men. *Sententiae* 13.21.

32 Antiphanes Fr. 329 (or Alexis 341: the paternity of this fragment is disputable); Alexis Fr. 146.

33 ἐπίκληρος literally means "someone who comes with the inheritance" (the force of ἐπὶ here is "with"). Important studies on the *epikleros* are MacDowell 1978: 92–108; Todd 1993: 216–31; Maffi 1990: 21–36; Karnezis 1979: 145–71; Balogh 1953: 683–719; Cudjoe 2005: 55–88 (discussed in some detail in Chapter 4.3); Katz 1992: 692–708; Ledl 1907; Gernet 1921: 337–79.

34 See Chapter 3.3.

35 A fictional account of Lucian pictures one such scenario. When the breadwinner of the family, a blacksmith, died leaving behind a widow and an underage daughter, the two women tried to make ends meet, first by selling his equipment, and then through menial jobs. The mother kept going hoping that one day her daughter would be able to provide for the household, and when she reached an appropriate age the mother was happy to instruct her on how to become a skilled *hetaira* and generate wealth for herself and her mother. Thus, in this perhaps not so fictional account an Athenian woman took to prostitution because of poverty.

36 Two speeches composed for the same inheritance, Is. 11 *On the Estate of Hagnias* and D. 43 *To Makaratos* underline the potentially immense complexity of extended family relations, and the difficulties of deciding who has the strongest claim.

37 See also the discussion in Chapter 9.2.

38 Men. Fr. 402–3.

39 Men. Fr. 585.

40 Ar. Av. 1660–6: Ἐρῶ δὲ δὴ καὶ τὸν Σόλωνός σοι νόμον· "Νόθῳ δὲ μὴ εἶναι ἀγχιστείαν παίδων ὄντων γνησίων· ἐὰν δὲ παῖδες μὴ ὦσι γνήσιοι, τοῖς ἐγγυτάτω γένους μετεῖναι τῶν χρημάτων." [I will recite for you the law of Solon: "An illegitimate child is not to partake in the *anchisteia*, if there are legitimate children; if there are no legitimate children, the nearest relatives are to inherit."] See also MacDowell 1978: 99.

41 We may read in it that illegitimate children were excluded, along with lateral relatives, only when their father also had legitimate children, but we may also read that illegitimate children were always excluded and lateral relatives inherited a man with no legitimate children.

42 Already in Herodotos (5.94) Hegesistratos, the son of Peisistratos with an Argive woman is considered *nothos*, and in the *Birds* of Aristophanes (1652) it is clearly stated that Herakles is *nothos* on account of the fact that his mother is a non-Athenian (ὤν γε ξένης γυναικός). However, there is not enough clarity on this issue as it is entangled with the unanswerable question whether the Periclean citizenship law stopped mixed marriages or simply discouraged them.

43 See Harp. s.v. νοθεῖα, and the discussion in Chapter 9.

44 See the wording in D. 46.14: ΝΟΜΟΣ: Ὅσοι μὴ ἐπεποίηντο, ὥστε μήτε ἀπειπεῖν μήτ' ἐπιδικάσασθαι, ὅτε Σόλων εἰσῄει τὴν ἀρχήν (S 1), which indicates that there were adopted people even before Solon.

45 I borrow the phrase from the booklet of the state of Florida on adult adoptions – www.floridaschildrenfirst.org/wp-content/uploads/2011/06/Adult-Adoption-Booklet-with-forms.pdf

46 Leduc 1998: 175–202.

47 See Rubinstein 1993, for a list of known cases of adoption and useful discussions.

48 See D. L 5.11–16.

49 See for example Is. 11.8 and 44.

50 Lys. 32.4–7.

51 About the affairs of Pasion and his family see D. 36, 45 and 46.

52 D. 53.9.

53 D. 59.3–8.

54 Plu. *Agis* 5.3; Arist. *Pol.* 1270 a 15–34. Some scholars have doubted the existence of the *rhetra* of Epitadeus (e.g. Hodkinson 1986: 378–406; Schütrumpf 1987: 441–57), but the majority have accepted the reliability of the testimony of Plutarch and Aristotle (MacDowell: 1986, 99–110; Asheri 1963: 1–21; Marasco 1980: 131–45; Christien 1974: 197–221; Avramovic 2005: 175–86).

55 An *apokeryxis* meant that the son was excluded from the *oikos* and disinherited, but this did not affect his standing with the city or his citizenship rights (e.g. Pl. *Lg.* 928 e 7–8 παῖς ἀποκεκηρυγμένος οὐκ ἂν ἐξ ἀνάγκης ἄπολις εἴη). Such incidents were rare, and the *apokeryxis* often was rather a method of blackmail and control of an unruly son, than a complete breakdown in family relations. See, for example, D. 39.39; Ptol. Ascal. *Diff.* 390, 9: <ἀποκήρυκτος> μέν ἐστιν ὁ ἐπὶ ἀδικήματι ὑπὸ τοῦ πατρὸς ἐκβληθεὶς τῆς οἰκίας [*apokeryktos* is the one who has been expelled from the house of his father because of some wrongdoing]; Antiphon, Fr. 66, Thalheim; Cobetto Ghiggia 2008: 627–40; Albertoni 1923; Photiades 1925.

6 The *oikos* in peril

Divorce, adultery, prostitution

6.1 Sources

1 The primary law on divorce and the return of the dowry (c. 355 BC, in its current form)

> κατὰ τὸν νόμον ὃς κελεύει, ἐὰν ἀποπέμπῃ τὴν γυναῖκα, ἀποδιδόναι τὴν προῖκα, ἐὰν δὲ μή, ἐπ' ἐννέ' ὀβολοῖς τοκοφορεῖν, καὶ σίτου εἰς Ὠιδεῖον εἶναι δικάσασθαι ὑπὲρ τῆς γυναικὸς τῷ κυρίῳ.
>
> (D. 59.52)

> According to the law which states, if he divorces the woman, he is to return the dowry, and if he does not, he is to pay an interest of nine obols to the drachma (18 percent), and a *kyrios* of the woman can bring a lawsuit at the Odeon on behalf of a woman for her maintenance.

2 The Law of Drakon on Homicide as the primary text defining adultery

> Ἐάν τις ἀποκτείνῃ ἐν ἄθλοις ἄκων, ἢ ἐν ὁδῷ καθελὼν ἢ ἐν πολέμῳ ἀγνοήσας, ἢ ἐπὶ δάμαρτι ἢ ἐπὶ μητρὶ ἢ ἐπ' ἀδελφῇ ἢ ἐπὶ θυγατρί, ἢ ἐπὶ παλλακῇ ἣν ἂν ἐπ' ἐλευθέροις παισὶν ἔχῃ, τούτων ἕνεκα μὴ φεύγειν κτείναντα.[1]
>
> (D. 23.53)

> If someone kills in an athletic contest without intent, or by taking someone down in the street, or accidentally at war, or after catching him with his wife, mother, sister, daughter or concubine kept for the birth of free children, the killer is not to be punished under these circumstances.

3 The law permitting bodily humiliations of an adulterer

> οἳ κελεύουσι μέν [sc. οἱ νόμοι], ἐάν τις μοιχὸν λάβῃ, ὅ τι ἂν οὖν βούληται χρῆσθαι.[2]
>
> (Lys. 1.49)

> The laws state that if someone catches an adulterer he can do to him whatever he wishes.

4 The law addressing false accusations of adultery

κατὰ τὸν νόμον ὃς κελεύει, ἐάν τις ἀδίκως εἵρξῃ ὡς μοιχόν, γράψασθαι πρὸς τοὺς θεσμοθέτας ἀδίκως εἰρχθῆναι, καὶ ἐὰν μὲν ἕλῃ τὸν εἵρξαντα καὶ δόξῃ ἀδίκως ἐπιβεβουλεῦσθαι, ἀθῷον εἶναι αὐτὸν καὶ τοὺς ἐγγυητὰς ἀπηλλάχθαι τῆς ἐγγύης· ἐὰν δὲ δόξῃ μοιχὸς εἶναι, παραδοῦναι αὐτὸν κελεύει τοὺς ἐγγυητὰς τῷ ἑλόντι, ἐπὶ δὲ τοῦ δικαστηρίου ἄνευ ἐγχειριδίου χρῆσθαι ὅ τι ἂν βουληθῇ, ὡς μοιχῷ ὄντι.

(D. 59.66)

In accordance with the provisions of the law, which lays down the following: if anyone wrongly imprisons a man as a seducer, the victim may bring an indictment before the *thesmothetai* on the grounds that he was wrongly imprisoned, and if he secures the conviction of the man who imprisoned him and it is judged that he was the victim of an unjust plot, he is to be innocent and the sureties are to be free from liability; but if he is judged to be a seducer, it is laid down that the sureties must hand him over to the successful litigant, and he is to inflict upon him in the courtroom any punishment he wishes, without using a knife, as one would with a seducer.

5 The law excluding prostitutes from the force of the adultery statutes

τόν τε νόμον ἐπὶ τούτοις παρεχόμενος, ὃς οὐκ ἐᾷ ἐπὶ ταύτῃσι μοιχὸν λαβεῖν ὁπόσαι ἂν ἐπ' ἐργαστηρίου καθῶνται ἢ πωλῶνται ἀποπεφασμένως.[3]

(D. 59.67)

He produced the law on the subject, which forbids accusations of adultery with one of those women established in brothels or visibly practicing any form of prostitution.

6 The law ordering mandatory divorce after adultery (after 451 BC)

ΝΟΜΟΣ ΜΟΙΧΕΙΑΣ. Ἐπειδὰν δὲ ἕλῃ τὸν μοιχόν, μὴ ἐξέστω τῷ ἑλόντι συνοικεῖν τῇ γυναικί· ἐὰν δὲ συνοικῇ, ἄτιμος ἔστω. μηδὲ τῇ γυναικὶ ἐξέστω εἰσιέναι εἰς τὰ ἱερὰ τὰ δημοτελῆ, ἐφ' ᾗ ἂν μοιχὸς ἁλῷ· ἐὰν δ' εἰσίῃ, νηποινεὶ πασχέτω ὅ τι ἂν πάσχῃ, πλὴν θανάτου.[4]

(D. 59.87)

After he catches the seducer, the man who caught him shall not be permitted to continue living with the woman in marriage. If he continues living with her in marriage he is to be disfranchised. And whoever is caught with a seducer shall not be permitted to enter the public temples. If she enters, she is to suffer whatever humiliation she suffers, except death, with impunity.

7 The law allowing a public prosecution for adultery

εἰσὶ δὲ καὶ γραφαὶ πρὸς αὐτοὺς (sc. τοὺς θεσμοθέτας) . . . καὶ μοιχείας.[5]

(Arist. *Ath.* 59.3)

Public prosecutions are introduced to them (namely, the *thesmothetai*) . . . and for adultery.

8 The law imposing sanctions upon family members for procuring their children

Διαρρήδην γοῦν λέγει ὁ νόμος, ἐάν τινα ἐκμισθώσῃ ἑταιρεῖν πατὴρ ἢ ἀδελφὸς ἢ θεῖος ἢ ἐπίτροπος ἢ ὅλως τῶν κυρίων τις, κατ' αὐτοῦ μὲν τοῦ παιδὸς οὐκ ἐᾷ γραφὴν εἶναι, κατὰ δὲ τοῦ μισθώσαντος καὶ τοῦ μισθωσαμένου, τοῦ μὲν ὅτι ἐξεμίσθωσε, τοῦ δὲ ὅτι, φησίν, ἐμισθώσατο. Καὶ ἴσα τὰ ἐπιτίμια ἑκατέρῳ πεποίηκε, καὶ μὴ ἐπάναγκες εἶναι τῷ παιδὶ ἡβήσαντι τρέφειν τὸν πατέρα μηδὲ οἴκησιν παρέχειν, ὃς ἂν ἐκμισθωθῇ ἑταιρεῖν· ἀποθανόντα δὲ θαπτέτω καὶ τἆλλα ποιείτω τὰ νομιζόμενα.

(Aesch. 1.13[6])

The law explicitly says that, if a father, or brother, or uncle, or guardian, or any other person with legal authority, procures a boy, there will be no prosecution against the boy himself, but against the person who hired him and the one who hired him out, against the former, because he hired him, against the latter, he says, because he hired him out. The penalty he made equal for both, and it is not obligatory for the boy who had been hired out as a prostitute to maintain his father or provide a dwelling for him once he reaches adulthood; however when the father dies, he must bury him and perform the rest of the traditional rites.

9 The law on *hetairesis*, banning male prostitutes from certain public offices, and from speaking in the Assembly

ἄν τις Ἀθηναίων, φησίν, ἑταιρήσῃ, μὴ ἐξέστω αὐτῷ τῶν ἐννέα ἀρχόντων γενέσθαι, ὅτι οἶμαι στεφανηφόρος ἡ ἀρχή, μηδ' ἱερωσύνην ἱεράσασθαι, ὡςοὐδὲ καθαρῷ τῷ σώματι, μηδὲ συνδικησάτω, φησί, τῷ δημοσίῳ, μηδὲ ἀρξάτω ἀρχὴν μηδεμίαν μηδέποτε, μήτ' ἔνδημον μήτε ὑπερόριον, μήτε κληρωτὴν μήτε χειροτονητήν· μηδὲ κηρυκευσάτω, μηδὲ πρεσβευσάτω, μηδὲ τοὺς πρεσβεύσαντας κρινέτω, μηδὲ συκοφαντείτω μισθωθείς, μηδὲ γνώμην εἰπάτω μηδέποτε μήτε ἐν τῇ βουλῇ μήτε ἐν τῷ δήμῳ, μηδ' ἂν δεινότατος ᾖ λέγειν. Ἐὰν δέ τις παρὰ ταῦτα πράττῃ, γραφὰς ἑταιρήσεως πεποίηκε καὶ τὰ μέγιστα ἐπιτίμια ἐπέθηκεν.

Aesch. 1.19–20 (c. 400)[7]

If any Athenian, he says, works as a prostitute, he cannot be appointed as one of the nine *archon*s (I believe because this is a crowned office), nor assume any priesthood (because his body is not clean), nor become a public advocate, nor serve as a magistrate either at home or abroad, appointed by lot or elected; he is not to serve as a herald or an ambassador (and he is not to judge those who have served as ambassadors, or engage in sycophantic activities for money), nor can he voice his opinion either in the Council or in the Assembly, not even if he is a highly accomplished speaker. If someone disobeys these laws, the lawgiver has established a graphe for prostitution and the most severe penalties.

10 The law on the scrutiny (*dokimasia*) of the speakers in the Assembly

"δοκιμασία," φησί, "ῥητόρων· ἐάν τις λέγῃ ἐν τῷ δήμῳ τὸν πατέρα τύπτων ἢ τὴν μητέρα, ἢ μὴ τρέφων, ἢ μὴ παρέχων οἴκησιν·" τοῦτον οὐκ ἐᾷ λέγειν. Νὴ Δία καλῶς γε, ὡς ἔγωγέ φημι. Διὰ τί; ὅτι εἴ τις, οὓς ἐξ ἴσου δεῖ τιμᾶν τοῖς θεοῖς, εἰς τούτους ἐστὶ φαῦλος, τί ποτε, φησίν, ὑπ' αὐτοῦ πείσονται οἱ ἀλλότριοι καὶ ἡ πόλις ὅλη; Καὶ τίσι δεύτερον ἀπεῖπε μὴ λέγειν; "ἢ τὰς στρατείας," φησί, "μὴ ἐστρατευμένος, ὅσαι ἂν αὐτῷ προσταχθῶσιν, ἢ τὴν ἀσπίδα ἀποβεβληκώς," δίκαια λέγων. Τί δή ποτε; ἄνθρωπε, τῇ πόλει ὑπὲρ ἧς τὰ ὅπλα μὴ τίθεσαι ἢ διὰ δειλίαν μὴ δυνατὸς εἶ ἐπαμῦναι, μηδὲ συμβουλεύειν ἀξίου. Τρίτον τίσι διαλέγεται; "ἢ πεπορνευμένος," φησίν, "ἢ ἡταιρηκώς"· τὸν γὰρ τὸ σῶμα τὸ ἑαυτοῦ ἐφ' ὕβρει πεπρακότα, καὶ τὰ κοινὰ τῆς πόλεως ῥᾳδίως ἡγήσατο ἀποδώσεσθαι. Τέταρτον τίσι διαλέγεται; "ἢ τὰ πατρῷα," φησί, "κατεδηδοκώς, ἢ ὧν ἂν κληρονόμος γένηται"· τὸν γὰρ τὴν ἰδίαν οἰκίαν κακῶς οἰκήσαντα, καὶ τὰ κοινὰ τῆς πόλεως παραπλησίως ἡγήσατο διαθήσειν, καὶ οὐκ ἐδόκει οἷόν τ' εἶναι τῷ νομοθέτῃ τὸν αὐτὸν ἄνθρωπον ἰδίᾳ μὲν εἶναι πονηρόν, δημοσίᾳ δὲ χρηστόν, οὐδ' ᾤετο δεῖν τὸν ῥήτορα ἥκειν ἐπὶ τὸ βῆμα τῶν λόγων ἐπιμεληθέντα πρότερον, ἀλλ' οὐ τοῦ βίου.

(Aesch. 1.28–30 (4th century))[8]

Who did he consider unsuitable for speaking? Those who have lived inappropriately; he does not allow these men to address the assembly. Where does he say so? "Scrutiny," he says, "of the Speakers: If someone is addressing the Assembly, while he is beating his father or mother, or he does not provide for them or offer them accommodation," he does not allow this man to speak, by Zeus, rightly so in my opinion. . . . After this whom did he bar from speaking? "The man," he says, "who has not taken part in the military campaigns assigned to him, or has dropped his shield," correctly so. . . . Then, whom does he address after that? "A man who has been a male prostitute," he says, "or has sold his body," because he believed that a man who has sold his own body to be abused, he would easily sell the common affairs of the city. Then whom does he mention? "If he has squandered his parental estate," he says, "or his inheritance," because he believed that a man who has mismanaged his own estate, would dispose of the goods of the state in a similar fashion. The lawgiver did not believe that it was possible for the same man to be bad in his private life, but good in public. Moreover, the lawgiver did not think that a man should step on the roster, having taken care of his speech, but not his own life.

6.2 Divorce

There is unanimous agreement in the literature that divorce in classical Athens was easy.[9] Since marriage was not so much perceived as an institution, but rather as an on-going arrangement with very practical objectives, not surprisingly it could be terminated at any moment. Divorce was just as easy as the husband asking or forcing his wife to return to her natal family, or the wife simply walking out on the husband and going back to her own family. Unquestionably it was easier for a man to dismiss his wife than for a woman to walk away from her marriage. In practical terms, the husband did not stand to lose anything else except his wife's dowry, which always needed to be returned to the full, regardless of the circumstances for the divorce. This dowry might be substantial and its loss a powerful deterrent for divorce,[10] but a man could always replace it by taking in a new wife and another dowry. On account of this, Stephen Todd has suggested that divorce was frequent, but the findings of subsequent studies, especially the core study by Louis Cohn-Haft, do not support this and argue that the divorce rate in classical Athens was actually very low.[11] The reasons for this will be discussed below.

Previous studies have sidestepped the most powerful deterrent for divorce, namely the presence of children.[12] In none of the known cases of divorce there were any children in the marriage at the time when it was dissolved. In one case the woman was pregnant, but there is no clear indication of how advanced the pregnancy was, and for all we know it is quite possible that the father-to-be was unaware of his wife's pregnancy at the time when he made the decision to send her back to her father.[13] If so, we must conclude that, as far as the evidence allows us to see, divorce was a realistic possibility only for as long as the marriage was childless, and that the birth of a child, especially a son, exponentially strengthened and cemented the position of the mother in the household. There is no evidence to suggest that the law prohibited divorce after the birth of a child. However, as it has happened in many societies throughout history, a strong social convention made the dissolution of a marriage with children much harder.

Securing legitimate heirs was the main purpose of an Athenian marriage, while emotional fulfillment, although an important part of it, took second place. It would only be reasonable to assume that since this primary purpose had been achieved a divorce would be pointless, unless of course adultery was involved, in which case the divorce was mandated by law (S 6, and the discussion below). A strong social convention along these lines would also help explain the very small number of instances of divorce known to us. If a woman with children could not really be divorced, then the dissolution of a marriage was reserved for those rare occasions when a childless couple had strong practical reasons (like, for example, claiming an *epikleros* or securing an heir) for breaking the arrangement (τὸ συνοικεῖν), and this seems to be the case in at least six out of the eighth cases of divorce known to us.[14]

A divorce initiated by the woman was more complicated, as she first needed the consent of her natal family, to whom she was going to return. Their agreement was essential, because they would be expected to provide for her after the divorce and her father or brother needed to make sure that her dowry was fully recovered, which in itself might be a challenging task against an aggrieved former husband.[15] Then, the woman needed to appear in person before the *archon* and declare that she had left her husband.[16] The reason for this practice remains a matter of speculation. MacDowell suggested that the woman needed to register the intent to leave her husband so that he would have the option to intervene, if he disagreed with the divorce, but since he had no legal power to stop his wife from leaving, or her family from taking her back, this reason seems insufficient. Carlos Noreña interprets this requirement within the context of the different roles of wife and husband in the *oikos*, and other scholars have offered a variety of explanations.[17]

Since no ancient source explains to us why this procedure was followed, we can never be sure about the reasons why the wife needed to register the divorce she initiated, while the husband did not, but given that the *archon* was the magistrate in charge of the property and marriage arrangements in the case of an *epikleros* (see previous chapter), it is reasonable to assign to him a similar regulatory role in the case of a wife wishing a divorce from her husband. This role was to make sure that property transfers were done smoothly and legally, and that women were not defrauded of their property and rights by rapacious male relatives. His function in the case of divorce should have been to make sure that the dowry was to be returned by the former husband, or at least proper interest payments were to be made on a monthly basis. Registering the divorce with the *archon* would signify the official date from which a husband who had failed to return the dowry would need to start paying the hefty 18 percent interest on the capital (*sitos*). The woman's physical presence before the *archon* made sure that the date of the *apoleipsis* would be properly and officially registered, excluding future speculation or fraudulent claims (like for example the one reported in D. 30). This is why the burden fell upon the woman to appear before the *archon*: it was her dowry that was at stake, and it was her initiative that dissolved the marriage.

Some sources suggest that it was possible to tear away a woman from her marriage (ἀφαίρεσις). A long-standing debate has tried to determine under which circumstances this could happen and whether the woman had a say on this.[18] Joseph Modrzejewski has probably correctly suggested that a woman could be removed from her existing marriage only when she had no children. This was certainly the case when she became an *epikleros*;[19] she needed to leave her existing husband and marry the man who had prevailed during the *epidikasia*. However, in other instances where a divorce seems to have been initiated by the woman's natal family, it is possible that her consent was essential. The virtuous wife of Menekles initially refused to give her consent to a divorce agreed between her old husband and her brothers. Menekles apparently was acting with her best interests in mind and felt that it was not right for his wife to grow old and childless at his side. The orator does not explain why Menekles was so sure that he was responsible for their childlessness, but one might suspect some underlying medical condition exacerbated by his age. Eventually she was persuaded to agree to an amicable divorce, and her ex-husband adopted one of her brothers as his heir.

In the one attested instance where a divorce was initiated by the woman's father, that of the younger daughter of Polyeuktos, who was removed from her husband Leokrates, it is not clear whether her consent was asked.[20] In terms of an overall impression it appears that the women in the house of Polyeuktos were no pushovers, and if the dynamics of the family offer any indication, it does not seem likely that the woman who demanded, and had, jewelry worth the value of a house (10 minae) was removed from her marriage against her wishes.

A marriage ended automatically and regardless of the wishes of the pair when the woman had been caught committing adultery (S 6). A law, which was probably introduced some time after the Periclean citizenship law of 451, removed from the husband the option to forgive his wife and continue living with her. The reason for this uncustomary intervention of the *polis* into the affairs of the *oikos* is clear: the *polis* was concerned about a very public matter, the legitimacy of the children and the true Athenian descent of the citizen stock. An adulterous relationship cast suspicion upon the paternity of the offspring born in the marriage, and this was an uncertainty that the city was not prepared to tolerate after the introduction of the Periclean citizenship law. For this reason, the state took the extraordinary step of breaking up the marriage.

The initial demand that the dowry is to be returned in full, in the event of divorce, regardless of the circumstances, probably was established practice even before the time of Solon, and the lawgiver merely adopted it. A refusal or delay to return the dowry could trigger a δίκη προικός, the objective of which was to force the delinquent ex-husband to return the entire sum at once. However, such proceedings could take time, and for as long as the former husband was withholding the dowry, the family of the woman could not arrange for her another marriage, unless they were really wealthy, and moreover had to pay for her maintenance and expenses while someone else was profiting from her dowry. This is why another legal process was enacted around the middle of the 4th century in line with other monthly lawsuits,[21] the purpose of which was to ensure that legal proceedings would be concluded rapidly, within the space of a month.[22] According to the new law for every month that the ex-husband was withholding the capital of the dowry he needed to pay interest at a rate of nine obols to the mina.[23] The interest was payable on the first of every month, and if the former husband failed to make the payment the *kyrios* of the woman could submit a lawsuit, which needed to be brought to trial and decided within the month. This lawsuit was called "trial for the maintenance" (δίκη σίτου), and the court which accepted such cases was based in the Odeon of Pericles.[24] Through the constant payments of interest at a high rate the law put pressure on the former husband to return the dowry.

After the introduction of this procedure the *kyrios* of the woman had a choice to make, when pursuing the ex-husband through the courts. If he wanted the immediate return of the entire capital of the dowry, for whatever reason, the δίκη προικός was the appropriate procedure. If on the other hand, he was content to allow the ex-husband to keep the dowry and make payments of interest he stood to make good profit, and might choose the δίκη σίτου, for missed payments. Considering that for an average dowry of 30 minae the annual interest would be 540 drachmas, a sum comparable to the annual pay of a skilled laborer, it might be in the interests of the *kyrios* of the woman to allow the ex-husband to keep the dowry and draw an income from it, for as long as the latter also found some advantage in this arrangement.

The ease with which an Athenian marriage could be legally terminated is a reflection of the concept of marriage as a practical arrangement with specific objectives. It was a contract between two families which could be readily disentangled in its initial stages, before the birth of children. Once this major objective of a marriage had been achieved, and the continuation of the *oikos* was guaranteed, either directly through legitimate sons, or indirectly through legitimate daughters, then the contract was solidified, and a disentanglement was neither practicable nor desired any more. A divorce would create the unnecessary situation where the woman's natal family would need to provide for her all over again, maybe strive to recover her dowry, and seek to arrange another marriage for her. This is why, unless extraordinary circumstances occurred, such as the possibility to claim a wealthy *epikleros*, or the destruction of the marital bond through adultery, divorce was not in the cards.

About half of the marriages enacted in the US end up in divorce, and the percentage stands even higher at 60 percent for second marriages. Among the most common reasons which divorcing couples enlist is marrying too young, changing or unmet expectations, getting into the marriage for the wrong reasons, not having a shared vision of the future, loss of intimacy, financial worries, different priorities and interests, or inability to resolve conflict. Most of these situations do not seem to apply to Athenian marriages, at least not to the extent that they could result in a divorce. Women typically entered their first marriage at a very young age, but men were not expected to marry until they had the means and maturity to sustain a family. This in itself suggests that for a man the decision to marry was not taken lightly, and, in most cases, it was not the byproduct of hormonal enthusiasm. Then, the expectations were different: while there was hope that love and affection would eventually develop in a couple, they were neither deemed indispensable, nor their absence was perceived to be a good reason for divorce. Husbands and wives did not expect to socialize together, except perhaps on religious occasions, pursue common interests or maintain excitement in their marriage. Men were expected to spend much of their time outdoors, while women would look after the household, and routinely socialize with female friends, relatives and neighbors.

The roles and expectations of each side were largely prescribed by traditional social norms. A husband was not even expected to be faithful to his wife, so long as he respected her space and kept his affairs away from the family home. However, he was expected to provide for his family, and beware of profligate spending of the family property for his pleasures. He was also expected to take care of his family members, provide for their education, represent them in the institutions of the *polis*, and keep order and discipline in his household. A wife was expected to remain faithful to her husband, look after the household and its interests, bring up her children and make a home for the entire *oikos*. So long as these traditional expectations were met, the marriage was considered successful, and intimacy beyond what was required for childbirth was certainly desirable, but not indispensable.[25] Couples with children would not divorce simply because the "spark" had gone out of the relationship. A careful consideration of these factors can explain with abundant clarity why, although from a legal point of view the dissolution of the marital bond was very easy, in practice Athenian marriages rarely ended in divorce.

6.3 Adultery (μοιχεία)[26]

The first body of laws introduced by Drakon in 621/620 recognized the seduction of a respectable woman as a very serious offense, an affront to her *kyrios*, and an injury grave enough to break up a family. In the case of a married woman (or someone's concubine), it was viewed as an insult to her husband's masculinity. The law considered equally harmful the seduction of an unmarried woman as it would limit her chances of a successful marriage, and it interfered with another man's household so disrespectfully. Moreover, adultery was seen as a crime of power and abuse from one man towards another, rather than an offence against abstract institutions. On account of such considerations, Drakon was prepared to bypass the probably partial justice system of the aristocratic state and place the power to avenge the injury directly into the hands of the *kyrios* of the woman, by allowing him to kill a man caught in bed with his wife, sister, daughter, mother or concubine.[27] The law did not question the status, wealth, social standing or citizenship of the man or the woman, but offered equal protection to all free men by giving them the power to punish the offender on the spot.

The Drakonian law should not be viewed as a license to kill, but rather as an immediate and powerful deterrent. The fact that we know only one such case, where the husband killed a man allegedly caught in bed with his wife, unequivocally suggests that most Greek men would not risk bringing upon themselves and their family the deadly curse of the gods (*miasma*)[28] in order to punish the lover of an unfaithful wife. Even this one case, the killing of Eratosthenes by Euphiletos (Lysias 1), raises red flags. Euphiletos only summons some of his friends as witnesses, who could be very easily lying. Beyond this, there is not a shred of independent evidence that Eratosthenes had an affair with his wife. It is quite likely that Euphiletos fabricated an adulterous affair as a way to extricate himself out of any culpability for what may have been the cold and calculated murder of young Eratosthenes for reasons unknown to us.

In addition to any religious horrors that the *miasma* raised for the Greeks, killing was a very risky option. The victim's family most likely would prosecute for homicide, and the killer needed to be able to convince the judges at the Delphinion court (ἐφέται)[29] that adultery had taken place. If he failed, he would be treated as a killer and executed. The risk was too great for any fair-minded person to take, and this is precisely the point. This law was not addressing even-tempered individuals; it was willing to offer something similar to a temporary insanity defense to the *kyrios* who acted in justified rage, but not to sanction killing. This is where, in my opinion, the otherwise tight-knit defense of Euphiletos fails: his meticulous and elaborate preparation of the killing of Eratosthenes is not the work of a furious cuckolded husband striking before he had the time to think, but that of a cold-blooded murderer, wrapped in a mantle of calculated righteousness and haughty morals.[30]

The first systematic attempt to build a legal framework for adultery cases was made by Solon a quarter of a century later. The Drakonian law enlisted the categories of women with whom *moicheia* could be committed, and although it only meant to define non-culpable homicide, in subsequent centuries the Athenians would continue to use this text as a point of reference for defining adultery. Solon certainly accepted this definition of adultery and set out to circumscribe and clarify it. The law of Drakon was open to abuse in the hands of unscrupulous procurers, who could invoke it and blackmail clients for much more money than the agreed fee. Since financial compensation was always a realistic, perhaps less honorable, but also less odious alternative to manslaughter, trapped men would happily pay to escape with their lives. This is why a Solonean law cited by Apollodoros prohibited accusations of adultery with women who were practicing some form of prostitution, whether organized in a brothel or free-lance (S 5).[31] By doing so, Solon formally recognized prostitution as an activity that was taking place in a variety of forms around the city and set the boundaries between women who were to be treated as prostitutes and women who were respectable members of the *oikos*. In later centuries he would be remembered as the founder of brothels in Athens.[32]

Another law enacted for the same purpose addressed the situation where someone had been fraudulently accused of adultery, trapped and forced to agree to pay compensation. This law offered a way out of this arrangement, if the accused was able to prove that he had not committed adultery.[33] The accused needed to submit a countersuit to the *thesmothetai* for unlawful entrapment with accusations of adultery. If he succeeded in court he was released of the agreed compensation, and those who had acted as sureties that he would pay were also released of any obligation. However, the procedure was not without risks for if he failed he could be treated as an adulterer and face public humiliation before the court. The clause permitting the humiliation of an adulterer seems to be another piece of legislation enacted by Solon as a more humane alternative to the killing of an adulterer permitted by the law of Drakon (S 3). Since this law permitted only the physical abuse of an adulterer, but prohibited bloodshed, it was seen as a way for the humiliated *kyrios* to get his own back without the need to become a killer or offend the gods. We are told that the preferred forms of humiliation were the depilation of the adulterer's pubic hair and penetration with a large vegetable like a radish.[34] Both of these humiliations were meant to avenge the injured masculinity of the *kyrios* by feminizing the adulterer.[35]

The dissolution of a marriage after adultery was not optional in the classical period, at least after the introduction of a law which threatened the cuckolded husband with disfranchisement, if he refrained from divorcing his unfaithful wife (S 6). I have previously argued that the law was probably introduced in the 5th century, after the Periclean citizenship law, and its main objective was to safeguard the purity of the citizen stock.[36] A woman who had committed adultery could not be trusted and her offspring, which might not be the children of her husband, should not be allowed to be introduced into the citizen body as his children. This is why the law in this case took the unusual step of directly interfering with the affairs of the *oikos* and ordering the dissolution of the marriage. This predominant concern about the legitimacy and proper birth of the children who would become the citizens of Athens in the future is the underlying reason behind the strict requirement of fidelity of an Athenian wife to her husband; his fidelity was not necessary since any children born of his affairs with prostitutes or slaves were instantly recognized as illegitimate.

This law for the first time also penalized the woman. Until then the *polis* had ignored the adulteress and considered her seducer to be the culprit. We should not doubt that even before the introduction of this law the woman would suffer indignities at home, and in Solon's time an unmarried woman caught in bed with a man could be legally procured by her father,[37] but the *polis* was not concerned with her fate. This changed when the Periclean citizenship law made the citizen woman a joined contributor of citizenship. From this point forward, the *polis* turned its attention upon the woman too and imposed upon her the most severe sanctions. A permanent ban from all public temples amounted to a ban from public life. The woman could no longer go to the temples to pray, attend festivities, participate in rituals and public celebrations, and play a role in the life of the community. Aeschines uses the term ἀτιμία, the same word used for a man's disfranchisement, and describes as following the penalties which she was about to face if she decided to ignore the ban:

> Τὴν γὰρ γυναῖκα ἐφ' ᾗ ἂν ἁλῷ μοιχὸς οὐκ ἐᾷ κοσμεῖσθαι, οὐδὲ εἰς τὰ δημοτελῆ ἱερὰ εἰσιέναι, ἵνα μὴ τὰς ἀναμαρτήτους τῶν γυναικῶν ἀναμειγνυμένη διαφθείρῃ· ἐὰν δ' εἰσίῃ ἢ κοσμῆται, τὸν ἐντυχόντα κελεύει καταρρηγνύναι τὰ ἱμάτια καὶ τὸν κόσμον ἀφαιρεῖσθαι καὶ τύπτειν, εἰργόμενον θανάτου καὶ τοῦ ἀνάπηρον ποιῆσαι, ἀτιμῶν τὴν τοιαύτην γυναῖκα καὶ τὸν βίον ἀβίωτον αὐτῇ παρασκευάζων.
>
> (Aesch. 1.183)

> He [sc. Solon] does not allow the woman with whom an adulterer has been caught to wear jewelry, or to enter into the public temples, so as not to corrupt respectable women by mixing with them. If she enters or wears jewelry, he orders any person to rip off her clothes and remove the jewelry and hit her, but not to kill her or cause permanent injury, disfranchising this woman and making her life unlivable.

All previous statutes assumed that the adulterer was caught *flagrante delicto* and did not address the possibility that someone who had not been caught in the act could still have committed adultery. There is some evidence suggesting that another law permitted a public prosecution for adultery (γραφὴ μοιχείας), and one would think that it could be applicable to those cases where there was strong suspicion of illicit sexual acts, but the naughty couple had not been caught in the act. This evidence comes from a passing reference in the *Athenaion Politeia*, and the assertion that the law permitted a *graphe* for adultery in the speech of Hypereides in defense of Lykophron.[38] The fact that Ariston, the prosecutor of Lykophron, did not choose this process, but brought a rather far-fetched and ill-fitting *eisangelia* against him may be an indication of the unappealing nature of this procedure.[39] A *graphe* was always a dangerous process, because if the prosecutor failed to secure at least 20 percent of the votes he was liable to a huge fine of 1000 drachmas. On top of that having to prove an illicit affair without hard evidence, such as an arrest *flagrante delicto*, would be challenging, and for a cuckolded husband or the maligned *kyrios* of a naughty unmarried woman having to risk a huge fine and becoming a laughing stock, in addition to the injury inflicted by the seduction might be too much to bear. This is why in all known cases of adultery the *kyrios* has gone to great lengths to entrap the seducer and catch him in the act. These considerations may suggest that the *graphe moicheias* remained largely a theoretical possibility, rarely if ever employed in actual practice, and this is why we do not hear more about it.

Adultery was a grave offence from one man against another man and his household, and threatened his marriage, his family, the legitimacy and status of his children, and his overall standing as a proud citizen in the community and the *polis*. The laws penalizing it were introduced in different periods of Athenian history, and each one of them was intended to deal with a different aspect of it. The self-help law of Drakon was an effective way even for men of the lower socio-economic classes to protect their families, and an insightful piece of legislation intended to reduce the impact of potentially biased magistrates in the aristocratic state. The more humane Solonean alternatives were designed to allow the husband to avenge his injured honor without having to resort to murder, and to discourage fraudulent entrapment under the power of the adultery laws by offering to victims a legal way out of contractual obligations agreed under duress. The final piece was a law which ordered the mandatory divorce of the adulteress, one would think in order to bar illegitimate offspring from citizenship, and for the first time severely penalized the woman too through permanent exclusion from the temples and public life. The severity of the Athenian adultery laws, which remained consistent through the centuries, should be read as a sing of the firm determination of the *polis* to protect family life and safeguard the proper birth and legitimacy of the future citizens of Athens.

6.4 Prostitution

The Greek city-states never tried to penalize or ban prostitution because their religion did not generate a moral imperative against it, and secular morality accepted it with raw pragmatism.[40] The Greeks accepted it as a fact of life with greater or lesser degrees of tolerance, considered it an occupation and taxed its earnings, and in some cases allowed it to become an important cultural feature in public and private life. The aforementioned law of Solon recognized organized and free-lance prostitution in Athens and defined it by separating sex workers from family women. Solon also introduced laws penalizing the procurement of free persons, which made sense in an economically depressed society like Solonean Athens, but were forgotten in later centuries (S 8).[41] Aeschines also mentions a law nowhere else attested, but conceivably still valid in the classical period which threated a slave with 50 lashes, if he pursued a free boy with erotic intent.[42] Another law intended to protect children from the actions of adult traffickers, family members or outsiders, was the one which did not permit any action or legal consequence against a juvenile forced into prostitution.[43] Persons only became liable for prosecution under the laws regulating male prostitution (see below) when they reached adulthood, and "came to know the laws of the city," in the words of Aeschines.[44] Another Solonean law, which allowed the father to sell an unchaste daughter has correctly been interpreted by Allison Glazebrook as a regulatory law on prostitution.[45] In Solon's time a father did not normally have the right to prostitute his daughter. However, this law appears to be an exception clause, which allowed him to do so as a punishment for her unruly behavior. A woman who did not protect her chastity before marriage, and chose to have an adulterous affair, by default placed herself outside the protective sphere of the *oikos* and the force of the adultery laws and could be treated as a prostitute.

The Solonean laws regulating prostitutional activities are consistently aimed at the protection of free persons from exploitation, especially minors incapable of giving consent. The lawgiver clearly mistrusted family members as much as he mistrusted outsiders. In a society where poor citizens had been offering their own freedom as collateral for loans, and many had ended up slaves before Solon freed them and forbade enslavement for debts, it is not surprising to find that the wise lawgiver was gravely concerned about the trafficking and exploitation of children, and decisively tried to stop it.

Considering Solon's thoughtful measures intended to protect children from sex-slavery and exploitation by family members and strangers alike, it may seem paradoxical that in later centuries he was considered to be the founder of prostitution, and widely praised for his insight to use brothels as a safety valve for the urges of young men, and as an effective mechanism to protect the *oikos* and its womenfolk.[46] There has been some debate as to whether there is any truth in this, and some scholars have even given credit to a tale from later antiquity that Solon established and managed brothels, and used their earnings to fund the building of the temple of Aphrodite Pan*demos*.[47] Two studies by Frank Frost and Vincent Rosivach agree that it is highly unlikely for Solon to be the founder of brothels.[48] I have argued that Solon's contribution to the establishment of prostitution in Athens was made through his legislative work. He recognized that prostitution was practiced in Athens in his time in a variety of forms, organized in brothels and freelance in the streets, and while attempting to exclude sex workers from the force of the adultery laws at the same time he defined prostitution as legal activity in all its forms. Moreover, his laws intended to protect children from trafficking and exploitation ended up regulating the markets of prostitution in his time, and some of them would have a lasting impact in the regulation of the proliferating sex-markets of the coming centuries.

The Solonean laws on procuring were for the most part ignored in later centuries. As Edward Cohen has amply demonstrated, prostitution could be very much a family business in classical Athens, and the procurement of free persons and slaves in a variety of organized or freelance settings was widespread.[49] These laws had been introduced at a time of economic distress as a measure intended to shield children and young adults from desperate family members and ruthless procurers.

However, as the economic realities of Athens changed so did the scruples which had dictated these laws. In the vigorous markets of the empire sexuality was a desirable commodity and the agents who provided it no longer had to fear antiquated laws. Although Solon's laws on procuring in theory remained in effect, along with his other laws regulating the markets of sex, in reality they were a dead letter and had no impact in the development of the cultural and economic climate which in the time of Athenaios would be remembered with nostalgia as the golden era of the Athenian *hetaira*.

Little information is preserved about prostitution at the height of the Athenian empire, not least because its chief historian had no appetite for salacious tales. The plays of Old Comedy suggest that prostitution was thriving in Athens, but they only offer sketchy details. This changed in the 4th century, when the interests of comedians shifted from political to character humor and eventually situational comedy. The *hetaira* took center stage, and had entire plays named after her in Middle Comedy, while in the plots of New Comedy and their Latin adaptations by Plautus and Terence the *hetaira* is often a key, even if stereotypical character. To this evidence, orators, historians and philosophers add a massive amount of material, all suggesting that under the Athenian Democracy the protections for privacy and freedom in a citizen's personal life allowed the sex markets to flourish. In a city with open borders policies and large numbers of transient people, typically male traders and merchants on long voyages from home, as well as a large number of prosperous local individuals willing to spend on their pleasures the demand was high, and the markets strived to meet it. The area around Kerameikos and the neighborhoods of Piraeus near the harbor were the main activity areas.[50] From cheap brothels, where even a male slave could occasionally afford a fleeting encounter with a low-end, probably slave prostitute, to very exclusive *hetairai* charging as much as 6000 times more for a longer term affair,[51] the sex markets of Athens could accommodate all tastes, sexual preferences, and financial capacities, and the law had nothing much to say about it, other than a few regulatory rules intended to make the markets run smoothly rather than to restrict or penalize sexual activities.

One such rule intended to minimize quarrels over sex-entertainers and to prevent customer gauging is attested by the *Athenaion Politeia*.[52] The law set the ceiling price of two drachmas for the hiring of entertainers, such as flute players, dancers or acrobatic performers, and if more than one person wanted to hire the same entertainer the magistrates in charge, the *astynomoi*, were required to draw lots in order to decide the winner. These entertainers routinely offered sexual services in addition to the entertainment, for which they would need to be compensated extra. It was only fair that the host of the party paid the two drachmas for the entertainment alone, while the person or persons who enjoyed sexual favors would pay for those. Some evidence suggests that entertainers could be auctioned in the end of the party for sexual services, and on other occasions it may simply have been matter of negotiation between their procurer and interested clients.[53] This law was intended to protect, the host of the party by making sure that he did not feel compelled to pay for anything else except the entertainment, and made sure that the host could not find himself in a position where he could be blackmailed and exploited by unscrupulous procurers. Moreover, the law enabled the smooth operation of the entertainment business and prevented quarrels between customers over an attractive entertainer.

Harpocration cites a passage of Hypereides quoting a law according to which women misbehaving in the streets were punished with the huge fine of 1000 drachmas.[54] It is only reasonable to assume that the law had in mind prostitutes, since a few independently wealthy *hetairai* were the only women capable of paying such a fine. Besides, one wonders what kind of misbehavior would warrant such a fine other than lewd acts in back alleys, or indiscreet and provocative soliciting of clients in the streets and public places. Very likely this is the kind of behavior which the lawgiver was so sternly trying to discourage.

Another law quoted by Apollodoros invalidated a man's will if it had been made, among others, under the influence of a woman.[55] Kallistratos, the speaker of *Against Olympiodoros* interprets this law as a reference to prostitutes (γυναικὶ πειθόμενος πόρνῃ), and explains its intent as an attempt to safeguard the property of the *oikos* from the rapacious appetites of prostitutes, while at the same time he goes to great lengths to explain the adverse impact upon the *oikos* and its members when a prostitute has a decisive influence.[56] The wording of this law did not exactly specify prostitutes. Like comparable modern laws, it simply wanted to ensure that the person was of sound mind and free from undue influence or compulsion when making a will. Nonetheless, this law was probably the strongest safeguard ensuring that the property of the *oikos* would stay within the family and could not go to some ruthless and seductive *hetaira*, who had offered friendship and companionship to a childless and lonely man in his deathbed with a view to inheriting his property.

According to Athenaios, Polemon in the study on the dedications of the Acr*opolis* mentioned a decree that prohibited giving the names of Four-Year festivals to prostitutes.[57] It is difficult to imagine how such a decree could be enforced, not least because when the parents named a child, let's say, Pythias, how could they know whether she will become a *hetaira* when she grew up? Or, should a Corinthian *hetaira* named Pythias change her name, and risk losing her clientele in the process, every time she made a longer visit to Athens? Such a law, dictated by religious scruple, would only make sense if it applied to pseudonyms given to prostitutes later in life, and even then it would be almost impossible to enforce. In fact, we know of several *hetairai* named after four-year festivals, like Olympias, the mother of Bion Borysthenites, or the illustrious Pythionike, the lover of Harpalos.

The famous judgment of Bochoris represents an intriguing, although legally challenging concept in the policing of ancient prostitution. It seemingly represented an unofficial precedent for the legal principle that payment was only due for services rendered. The story is related by Plutarch as following:

> ἀπομνημονεύεται δὲ τῆς Λαμίας καὶ πρὸς τὴν λεγομένην Βοκχώρεως κρίσιν ἀντίρρησις. ἐπεὶ γάρ τις ἐρῶν ἐν Αἰγύπτῳ τῆς ἑταίρας Θώνιδος ᾐτεῖτο συχνὸν χρυσίον, εἶτα κατὰ τοὺς ὕπνους δόξας αὐτῇ συγγενέσθαι τῆς ἐπιθυμίας

> ἐπαύσατο, δίκην ἔλαχεν ἡ Θῶνις αὐτῷ τοῦ μισθώματος. ἀκούσας δὲ τὸν λόγον ὁ Βόκχωρις ἐκέλευσε τὸν ἄνθρωπον ὅσον ἠτήθη χρυσίον ἠριθμημένον ἐν τῷ ἀγγείῳ διαφέρειν δεῦρο κἀκεῖσε τῇ χειρί, τὴν δ' ἑταίραν ἔχεσθαι τῆς σκιᾶς, ὡς τὴν δόξαν τῆς ἀληθείας σκιὰν οὖσαν. οὐκ ᾤετο ταύτην εἶναι τὴν κρίσιν ἡ Λάμια δικαίαν· οὐ γὰρ ἀπέλυσεν ἡ σκιὰ τῆς ἐπιθυμίας τοῦ ἀργυρίου τὴν ἑταίραν, τὸ δ' ὄναρ ἔπαυσεν ἐρῶντα τὸν νεανίσκον.
>
> (Plu. Demetr. 27.11)
>
> Lamia is also mentioned in the so-called response to the judgment of Bocchoris. While someone in love with the *hetaira* Thonis in Egypt was frequently harassed for money, he had a dream that he slept with her and his desire ceased. Thonis sued him for her fee. Bocchoris, when he heard the case, ruled that the man ought to bring the sum which she was claiming in a vessel and move the vessel here and there with his hand, while the *hetaira* was going to take hold of the shadow, because a dream is the shadow of reality. Lamia did not believe that this judgment was fair, because it was the dream that released the young man from his desire, not the shadow of the desire for money.

The fact that the judgment of Bocchoris seriously annoyed Lamia, the haughty and powerful mistress of Demetrios Poliorcetes, perhaps should be taken as an indication that this almost certainly mythical incident still had some bite, and could be used as an unwritten rule, a legal argument to defend clients against unreasonable demands by capricious mistresses, as it firmly suggested that one could not seek compensation for anything else except sexual services rendered, or agreed upon in advance, sometimes even with a written contract.

The use of contracts in prostitution has been studied in some detail by Edward Cohen. Although he probably places too much trust in the evidence from comedy, where absurd requirements are included in the contracts for comic effect, his conclusion that they were binding, legally enforceable agreements is broadly correct.[58] The evidence for contracts outside comedy is rather slim,[59] yet the possibility certainly was there, and one can reasonably understand that before an infatuated lover was prepared to splash a sum of money equal to the value of a house on a fickle man or woman, he might want some safeguards that this person was going to stay with him for a considerable, and explicitly agreed, period of time, and that certain expectations would be met without the need for quarrels. Many centuries later the 14th Novella of Justinian, in a frontal assault on prostitution throughout the Empire, invalidated all contracts between clients and prostitutes or their agents, and coming full circle, reiterated the ancient, forgotten Solonean ban on procuring.

Two more regulatory laws cited by Aeschines (S 9 and 10) have been perceived as centerpieces of Athenian culture and history in the 4th century, and generated a long, intense debate since the 1970s, despite the fact that they only addressed a tiny demographic, and only one case ever went to court on the basis of these laws. The first of these was a law intended to stop male prostitutes who were also active in politics from speaking in the assembly, accepting public office, and serving as priests or ambassadors. Violators of this law could be prosecuted with a *graphe* for *hetairesis* (γραφὴ ἑταιρήσεως), and the penalty, to be decided by the jury, could be quite severe (τὰ μέγιστα ἐπιτίμια). Some scholars believe that this law was introduced by Kleon before 426, but the evidence for this is very weak.[60] Another possible *terminus post quem* is a reference in the speech of Andocides *On the Mysteries*,[61] but again this interpretation of the passage of Andocides is very doubtful. The earliest date for which we can be certain that this law was in effect is c. 355, when the speech of Demosthenes *Against Androtion* was delivered.[62] Demosthenes thoroughly discusses the content and objectives of this law in this passage.

The other law mentioned by both Aeschines and Demosthenes, which sought to regulate the activities of politicians who had also being prostitutes, is in some ways narrower than the hetairesis law, as it only deals with speakers in the assembly, but in some other ways it is wider in scope as prostitution is one of several activities that would disqualify a citizen from speaking in the assembly. This is probably a 4th century law which had also been in effect before 355, since it is discussed in the speech *Against Androtion*. It may seem superfluous that the Athenians had two different laws to deal with the same violation, but it is evident that the law on the scrutiny (δοκιμασία) of the speakers in the Assembly did not introduce any new legal provisions; this law simply brought under a single umbrella existing laws which were thought to be relevant to the integrity and suitability of persons who advised the assembly.

While in the 4th century even minor magistrates of the Athenian state were scrutinized before their entry to office,[63] it might have seemed odd at some point that the speakers in the assembly, namely the individuals who directed public policy in the most important matters, were completely unaccountable. From a practical point of view, it would be impossible to introduce for the speakers in the assembly a type of scrutiny similar to that of other magistrates considering that any citizen could at any meeting stand up and address the assembly. This is why they introduced some basic rules intended to discourage persons who were obviously unsuitable for the task from advising the assembly. So long as individuals voluntarily observed this disqualification, they could still remain part of the *polis*, vote, go to the temples, participate in public festivals, retain full access to the justice system, and continue to enjoy all the other privileges of Athenian citizenship. Violators of this law could be prosecuted with a process called *epangelia* (ἐπαγγελία), a denunciation to the *thesmothetai*, in every other respect similar to a *graphe*, and carrying the same risk of 1000 drachmas for the prosecutor who failed to secure 20 percent of the votes. The penalty was total disfranchisement (ἀτιμία).

Demosthenes and Aeschines offer very different interpretations about the motives of the lawgiver and the objectives of these laws. Aeschines opts for a barrage of moralizing platitudes and argues that these laws were part of a master plan by Solon to police the morals of the citizens from the cradle to the grave, very similar to the constant oversight to which authoritarian Sparta subjected its citizens. As part of the "master plan," Aeschines pulls under the same umbrella a series of scattered laws and regulations from all over the place: school-safety rules, obsolete Solonean laws about procurement or the order of the speakers in the assembly that had not been observed for centuries,[64] as well as some regulations about the conduct of meetings in the assembly in his day. Some scholars have accepted the Aeschinean "master plan" as an adequate explanation of the motivation behind these laws.[65] However, accepting the Aeschinean narrative as historically valid would be deeply problematic, for a number of reasons. First, half of these laws were not valid in the time of Aeschines, and the rest were disparate pieces introduced centuries apart for very different purposes. Second, and most important, this kind of authoritarian oversight of the citizens' sex-lives would be un-Athenian; it would run counter to the core belief that in the democracy people trust each other to live as they please in their private lives, as glorified in the *Epitaphios* of Pericles.[66]

There is overwhelming evidence to support the Periclean tenet, and to suggest that the Athenians were not overridden by anxieties about homoerotic behavior, and in fact, they accepted it as an alternative, effortlessly interchangeable with heterosexual love, and certainly as a part of a person's normal erotic experience. Their most celebrated heroes, the tyrannicides Harmodios and Aristogeiton, were widely thought to be lovers, as were Achilles and Patroclus, and even Zeus himself had plenty of male lovers.[67] Moreover, the fact that the prosecution of Timarchos was unprecedented, and remains unique in the Athenian political life, rather suggests that it was a political stunt which benefited from the climate of the time to score an unexpected victory. As the negotiations for the peace of Philokrates, of which Aeschines was a great proponent, were under way, the defense of Timarchos, a staunch anti-Macedonian, was running against the political currents, and this is why it was drowned in the unstoppable torrent of Aeschinean rhetoric.

The rationale behind these laws is summarized very differently by Demosthenes in an account that precedes that of Aeschines by a decade. He argues that the prohibition from speaking in the Assembly is not particularly punitive because most Athenians entitled to speak do not exercise this right, anyway (τοῖς πολλοῖς ὑμῶν ἐξὸν λέγειν οὐ λέγετε). The lawgiver introduced this measure because he did not consider it safe for the democratic constitution to allow male prostitutes to advise the Assembly. In a democracy everyone can speak their mind, and unworthy men have the capacity to destroy democracy and offer such advice to the citizens that could make everyone else like them. Thus, as a precaution intended to prevent the *demos* from making mistakes, the lawgiver did not allow prostitutes to address the Assembly. It is interesting that, unlike the moral banalities of Aeschines, Demosthenes chooses an interpretation for these laws which is very "masculine," pragmatic and rooted in public life.

While scholars have often interpreted these laws on the basis of modern sensibilities and even as part of a broader debate on human sexuality, gender and LGBTI rights, the main fact remains that these were not mainstream statutes seeking to regulate the lives of all citizens.[68] The demographic which they affected would be tiny, if any at all. In fact, once we discard the insults which Athenian politicians traded with each other, when they called an opponent "a whore," it would be impossible to find any reliable evidence about a single individual who was a politician and a prostitute. This includes Timarchos, who although maligned by Aeschines and ultimately disfranchised, does not fit the profile of a male prostitute. The citizen male prostitutes that we know about with some certainty were invariably men of low birth and income, like Theodotos, a Plataian youth probably from a poor family, Diophantos an orphaned teenager, Aristion, the son of a Plataian pharmacist, and a few others, all from the lowest socio-economic strata of Athenian society. Timarchos was born in an affluent, respectable Athenian family, and was well-connected in the upper echelons of Athenian society, and so he did not have the motive to take up prostitution. Aeschines makes wild allegations which he is unable to substantiate, and fails to provide even a scrap of evidence proving that Timarchos ever took money for sexual services. Almost certainly the charges of prostitution leveled against Timarchos were false, made up from rumor and innuendo about an exquisitely good looking young man who liked to live big, and enjoyed parties, *hetairai*, gambling and the good life. If Timarchos is taken out of the equation too, we do not know of a single Athenian politician who can credibly be considered a prostitute. Citizen prostitutes, male or female, were typically persons of low birth from poor families, not powerful and influential political figures.

This is why, given what we know about male prostitution in Athens, it is difficult to imagine a demographic targeted by these laws. So, whom were they targeting and why? The answer may be lying hidden in the actual wording of Aeschines when he explains the purpose of the *hetairesis* law and says that male prostitutes were disqualified from the archonships and priesthoods, because the office had religious duties (μὴ ἐξέστω αὐτῷ τῶν ἐννέα ἀρχόντων γενέσθαι, ὅτι οἶμαι στεφανηφόρος ἡ ἀρχή, μηδ' ἱερωσύνην ἱεράσασθαι, ὡς οὐδὲ καθαρῷ τῷ σώματι). Disabled persons were also disqualified from these offices, even when they had led an exemplary life, as were the first-generation new citizens of Athens, the naturalized Plataians (but not their sons born from Athenian wives), even though the city had nothing but the highest praise for their bravery and unwavering loyalty and dedication to her interests.[69] The question is what male prostitutes had in common with these groups, and the answer ought to be, religious observance. Like disabled persons or first-generation Plataians, male prostitutes were deemed to be unsuitable for the extensive religious duties which offices like the nine *archons* or the various priesthoods around the city entailed.

A rule like this, dictated by religious scruple could come into effect regardless of any actual demographic in real life. When laws are passed to deal with real life problems, the targeted demographic is of the utmost significance; however, when a law is passed for the purposes of religious observance, it does not matter whether one or one million people are affected by it, as it would take only one transgressor to offend the gods and unleash their wrath. Far from expressing the moral milieu of mid-4th century Athens, the *hetairesis* law was not even concerned with the number of affected individuals, which would be very small at best, but with the correct performance of duties with a heavy religious component to it. The law on the *dokimasia* of the orators did not even remotely contend to be concerned with moral issues; its main objective was to make sure that persons unsuitable for leadership, either because of their physical condition or actions which did not inspire trust in their ability to manage the affairs of the city would not be sitting on the driving seat of the *polis*. The original interpretation of this law by Demosthenes as a safety measure for the well-being of the *polis* is probably more accurate than the exaggerated, conflicted, inaccurate and highly rhetorical banalities of Aeschines on the morals of his contemporaries.

Prostitution was not perceived as a threat to the family and society in a moral sense before the 2nd century AD, when increasingly intolerant attitudes, imported probably from eastern cults and cultures, began to permeate the body of Graeco-Roman thought and started changing the cultural and ideological landscape, and inadvertently preparing the ground for Christian ideology. In the classical period prostitution might be seen as a threat to the property of the *oikos*, and this concern was justified considering that a man could pay sums in the range of 20–30 minae to free a *hetaira*, and this was only the beginning for he would need to provide for her extravagant ways for the rest of his life, if he remained true to his promise to keep her as his concubine.[70] The entire prostitution industry was set up to profit from men's desires, to fleece them like sheep, as Plautus comically suggests in the *Bacchides*.[71] The laws regulating prostitution certainly reflect this anxiety: while they do not infringe upon private life, people's morals or financial decisions, they are certainly set up to prevent the property of the *oikos* from ending up in the hands of prostitutes by invalidating the will of a man made under the undue influence of a woman.

The laws also reflect the other major anxiety, vividly portrayed by Apollodoros in his closing remarks during the trial of Neaira, namely the blurring of the distinctions between prostitutes and citizen women.[72] He imagines a scenario where prostitutes emboldened by the acquittal of Neaira will take the place of the wives of Athenian men, while citizen women won't be able to find husbands, and will take up prostitution. It appears that the law prohibiting the marriage of a citizen with a foreigner under any circumstances was introduced to target attractive alien women like the numerous *hetairai* living and working in Athens. The law wanted to make sure that the boundary between the alien *hetaira* and the Athenian wife remained impermeable, and that any offspring of Athenian men from prostitutes remained firmly excluded from the *anchisteia*, and, more importantly, that Athenian men did not feel obligated to accept and legitimize such children. By drawing such boundaries, the law allowed the men of Athens to have their pleasures, but at the same time made sure that these pleasures did not interfere with the traditional institutions and structures of the *oikos*, family life, and the upbringing of the future citizens of Athens. The law also made sure that those male citizens who had chosen to prostitute their bodies, while not outright excluded or penalized, had a diminished influence in the running of the city and the direction of the political life and institutions.

Notes

1 See also Lys. 1.29–31; 13.66; X. *Hier*. 3,3; Aristaenet. 1.13; 2.17.

2 See also X. *Mem*. 2.2.5; Ar. *Nu*. 1083; Sch. Ar. Nu. 1083; Sch. Triclin. Nu. 1083; Sch. Tzetz. Ar. Plu.168; Luc. Peregr. 8; Catullus 15.17–19.

3 See also Lys. 10.15–19; Plu. *Sol*. 23; Argentarius *AP* 403, 7–8; Arist. *EE*. 1121 b 23–25.

4 See also Aesch. 1.183.

5 Cf. Hyp. Lyc. 10: αὐ̣[τὸς] δ̣’ ὑπερπηδήσ[ας ἅπ]αντας τοὺς ν̣[όμο]υς εἰσαγγελία[ν δέδ]ωκας ὑπὲρ ὧ̣ν [γρα]φαὶ πρὸς τοὺςθεσ[μοθ]έτας ἐκ τῶν νό[μων] εἰσίν, ἵνα π[ρῶ̣τον μ]ὲν ἀκίνδ[υνος εἰσ]ίῃς εἰς τὸ[ν̣ ἀγῶνα,] ἔπε[ι̣τ]α ἐξ[ῆι σοι τραγ]ῳ̣δίας γρ[άψαι εἰς τὴ]ν εἰσαγγελ[ίαν οἵας]π̣ερ νῦν γέγρ[αφας [You bypassed all the laws and introduced an *eisangelia* for matters for which the law permits regular indictments (graphai) to the *thesmothetai*, first in order to introduce this case without danger to yourself, and second in order to be able to include in the *eisangelia* all these tragedies which you have now written].

6 Aeschines (1.184) mentions one more law on procuring which threatened all procurers with the death penalty. It is far from certain that this law ever existed, since it contradicts the one mentioned in 1.13, which seems to be the real Solonean law on procuring, and moreover prostitution was continuously present in Athens with a visibility which would have been impossible had such a law been in operation. Most likely Aeschines is misrepresenting the law at this point, but even if such a statute had ever existed, it had fallen in disuse well before the classical period.

7 A significant clue for the dating of this law to the turn of the 4th century is provided by the usage of ἑταιρεῖν to indicate male prostitution. The term is not attested in this sense in the 5th century. In addition, the usage of συνδικισάτω in the technical sense to act as one's advocate, or partner in legal proceedings" is only attested once in the 5th century (A. *Eu*. 579), but frequently after the turn of the century (e.g. And. 1.150; Is. 4.3; D. 45.84).

8 The procedure of the *dokimasia* of public officials is not attested in the 5th century and in all probability such *dokimasiai*, including the one of the speakers in the assembly, were not instituted before the reorganization of public life after 403, if not several decades later. See Chapter 1.4.

9 See, for example, Todd 1993: 214; MacDowell 1988: 88; Cohn-Haft 1995: 1–14; Noreña 2008; Rosivach 1984: 193–230.

10 MacDowell 1978: 88; Foxhall 1989: 22–44; Cohn-Haft 1995:1–14.

11 There are eight known cases of divorce in classical Athens: And. 4.14; Lys. 14.28; Is. 2.7–12; 3.78; 30.4 ff; D. 41.4; 57.41; 59.51 and another divorce of the same woman in 82–83.

12 With the possible exception of Joseph Mélèze-Modrzejewski (1981: 258–60), who has argued that the presence of children terminated the right of the woman's father to break the marriage and take her back (aphaeresis). However, the suggestion of Mélèze-Modrzejewski although a possibility lacks support in the sources.

13 D. 59.51–63. The orator seems to imply that Phrastor, the husband, dismissed Phano, his pregnant wife, because he believed that she was an alien, and consequently had no interest in the child, since it could not become his heir. However, the actions of Phrastor suggest otherwise: first, he recognized his son after he was born, then when some members of his *genos* expressed doubts about the citizen status of this son, Phrastor sued them and forced them to accept him. The actions of Phrastor on their own cannot conclusively prove that he did not know about the pregnancy when he decided to divorce his wife, but they surely cast serious doubt upon the account of Apollodoros, and leave open the possibility that the divorce happened in early pregnancy before Phrastor knew that his wife was carrying his son and heir.

14 The two divorces of Phano (D. 59.51 and 82–83) seem to be the exception, but it is quite likely that these two cases are seriously misrepresented by Apollodoros.

15 See for example the difficulty which Stephanos had with the recovery of the dowry after his daughter's first divorce (D. 59.51–60).

16 See D. 30.15, 17, 26; Is. 3.78; Andoc. 4.14; Plu. Alc. 8.5; Rosivach 1984: 193–230; MacDowell 1988: 88; Cohn-Haft 1995: 1–14; Noreña 2008.

17 Noreña 2008, and especially n. 32.

18 Rosivach 1984: 193–230; Karnezis 1978: 145–71; Paoli 1946: 363–76; MacDowell 1988: 88; Cohn-Haft 1995: 1–14; Noreña 2008.

19 Méléze-Modrzejewski 1981: 258–60. If she had children, they were seen as the heirs to their maternal grandfather, and their mother could remain married to their father (see Chapter 5.3–4).
20 D. 41.3–6.
21 The earliest attested reference to this procedure is in Isaios 3.9 and 78. The date of the speech is uncertain (Wyse 1904: 276–77), but if Blass is correct that this is one of the later speeches of Isaios (1874: vol. 2, p. 537), a date after 355 would accommodate the introduction of the monthly lawsuits, including this one. See also D. 59.50–52.
22 It is not clear what the term " monthly lawsuit" (ἔμμηνος δίκη) actually meant. Some have understood it as meaning that lawsuits where accepted once a month, while others believe that such cases needed to be concluded within the space of a month. I side with the latter point of view. I do not see how it would speed up legal proceedings if such lawsuits were merely accepted on a monthly basis. The speedy resolution of such cases would only make sense if by the end of the month all lawsuits submitted in that month had been brought to trial and completed. Since these lawsuits were instituted to address time-critical claims, like maritime disputes in the summer months, which needed to be resolved while the good weather was holding, it would only make sense if they were resolved within a month from the moment of submission. See MacDowell 1978: 146 and 231–34.
23 Namely 1.5 percent per month = 18 percent per annum.
24 See Kapparis 1999: 272–74.
25 For these traditional roles within the *oikos* see Chapter 3.3.
26 The precise meaning of the Greek word μοιχεία has caused significant controversy. It indicated any extra-marital consensual affair with a free woman who belonged to another man's *oikos*. David Cohen (1984: 147–65 and 1990: 147–65) has tried unsuccessfully to limit it to marital relations. This view is flatly contradicted by the law of Drakon and the detailed narrative of *Against Neaira* (64–70), and has been rejected in subsequent studies (e.g Carey 1995: 407–17; Ogden 1997: 25–41). I use the word "adultery" with a degree of approximation to convey the term "*moicheia*" in English, and I prefer it to "seduction" because "adultery" would be the *terminus technicus* found in the statute books for similar offenses in our times.
27 The meaning of the phrase ἐπὶ παλλακῇ ἣν ἂν ἐπ' ἐλευθέροις παισὶν ἔχῃ [concubine kept for the birth of free children] is not clear. It probably had a different meaning in the time of Drakon, than it did after the Periclean citizenship law came into effect. Nonetheless, in the classical period it was interpreted as a reference to all concubines in relationships with citizen or non-citizen free men, and covered all long-term relationships with free or slave-women, and not only the marital bond. In this respect the law was very broad. One should never mess with another man's woman, whoever she was.
28 See the discussion in Chapter 8.5.
29 See the discussion in Chapter 8.5.
30 For a discussion of the case see Todd 2007: 43–60; Wolpert-Kapparis 2011: 17–20; Avezzù 1985.
31 See also the discussion in Kapparis 1999: 295–300 and 309–12.
32 See also Philemon, *PCG* Fr. 3; Plu. *Sol.* 23; Athen. 13,25; Eust. *Com. Il.* 4.331; Frost 2002: 34–46; Rosivach 1995: 2–3; Kapparis 2017: 33–45.
33 See D. 59.65–66, and Kapparis 2017: 307–9.
34 See for example Ar. Nu. 1076–83:

> ἥμαρτες, ἠράσθης, ἐμοίχευσάς τι, κᾆτ' ἐλήφθης . . .
> {Κρ.} τί δ' ἢν ῥαφανιδωθῇ πιθόμενός σοι τέφρᾳ τε τιλθῇ;
>
> [You did something wrong, fell in love, committed adultery and then you were caught . . .
> What if he is penetrated with a radish, listening to you, and depilated with ash?]

35 See Kapparis 1996: 63–77.

36 Kapparis 1999: 354–359, and 1995: 197–22.

37 See Glazebrook 2006: 33–53.

38 Arist. *Ath. Pol.* 59.4: εἰσὶ δὲ καὶ γραφαὶ πρὸς αὐτοὺς . . . καὶ μοιχείας. [One can bring a graphe to them (the *thesmothetai*) for . . . and adultery.] Hyp. *Lyc.* 10 responding to a charge that Lykophron had seduced the wife of Charippos: αὐ[τὸς] δ' ὑπερπηδήσ[ας ἅπ]αντας τοὺς ν[όμο]υς εἰσαγγελία[ν δέδ]ωκας ὑπὲρ ὧν [γρα]φαὶ πρὸς τοὺςθεσ[μοθ] έτας ἐκ τῶν νό[μων] εἰσίν, ἵνα π[ρῶτον μ]ὲν ἀκίνδ[υνος εἰσ]ίῃς εἰς τὸ[ν ἀγῶνα,] ἔπε[ιτ]α ἐξ[ῇι σοι τραγ]ῳδίας γρ[άψαι εἰς τὴ]ν εἰσαγγελ[ίαν οἵας]περ νῦν γέγρ[αφας. [You bypassed all the laws and introduced an *eisangelia* for matters for which the law permits regular indictments (*graphai*) to the *thesmothetai*, first in order to introduce this case without danger to yourself, and second in order to be able to include in the *eisangelia* all these tragedies which you have now written.] In a forthcoming article I argue that the trial of Mithridates for adultery, even though he had never had engaged in intimate acts with Kallirhoe, in the novel of Chariton (5.6), explores the dynamics of this topic where someone is accused of adultery on the basis of circumstantial evidence, but without proof of illicit sexual acts.

39 Ariston chose an *eisangelia* for the prosecution of Lykophron because at the time it was a risk-free process (Hyp. *Lyc.* 10 ἵνα π[ρῶτον μ]ὲν ἀκίνδ[υνος εἰσ]ίῃς εἰς τὸ[ν ἀγῶνα [in order to introduce this case without danger to yourself]). Although this procedure seems to be quite ill-fitting for the particular case, at least it was risk-free at the time when this persecution was brought to court. It is difficult to tell whether the adultery was the main charge or a secondary charge in the margins of this prosecution. Abuses of the *eisangelia* brought about a change to the law in 330 BC, and after that the *eisangelia* carried the same liability of 1000 drachmas, like the *graphe* (18.250; Hansen 1975: 29–31; Carawan 1985: 115–40, and the discussion in Chapter 9.2.).

40 For a more thorough discussion of prostitution in classical Athens see Kapparis 2017 (especially pp. 153–264 on the laws regulating prostitution and trials involving prostitutes in Athenian courts) and Cohen 2016.

41 It is possible that the provision which allowed a son not to provide for his old father, if he had been procured (Aesch. 1.14), was perceived as a valid law by 4th century Athenians, but we know of no such case, not surprisingly; citizen men and women who took up prostitution typically were fatherless children from broken homes.

42 Aesch. 1.139: Πάλιν ὁ αὐτὸς εἶπε νομοθέτης· "δοῦλον ἐλευθέρου παιδὸς μήτ' ἐρᾶν μήτ' ἐπακολουθεῖν, ἢ τύπτεσθαι τῇ δημοσίᾳ μάστιγι πεντήκοντα πληγάς." [Again the same lawgiver [Solon] said "a slave is not to fall in love or pursue a free boy, or he is to receive fifty lashes with the public whip".]

43 Aesch. 1.13, 18, 39.

44 Aesch. 1.18: Κἀκεῖνο δέ μοι συνδιαμνημονεύσατε, ὦ ἄνδρες Ἀθηναῖοι, ὅτι ἐνταῦθ' ὁ νομοθέτης οὔπω διαλέγεται αὐτῷ τῷ σώματι τοῦ παιδός, ἀλλὰ τοῖς περὶ τὸν παῖδα, πατρί, ἀδελφῷ, ἐπιτρόπῳ, διδασκάλοις καὶ ὅλως τοῖς κυρίοις· ἐπειδὰν δ' ἐγγραφῇ εἰς τὸ ληξιαρχικὸν γραμματεῖον, καὶ τοὺς νόμους εἰδῇ τοὺς τῆς πόλεως, καὶ ἤδη δύνηται διαλογίζεσθαι τὰ καλὰ καὶ τὰ μή, οὐκέτι ἑτέρῳ διαλέγεται, ἀλλ' ἤδη αὐτῷ ὦ Τίμαρχε. [Remember also, men of Athens, that until that point the law-giver does not even address the boy directly but those around him – the father, the brother, the guardian, the teachers, and those responsible for him. However, once he is inscribed into the register of the citizens, comes to know the laws of the city, and is in the position to know the difference between what is good and what is not, the lawgiver is no longer addressing others but Timarchus himself.]

45 Plu. Sol. 23: ἔτι δ' οὔτε θυγατέρας πωλεῖν οὔτ' ἀδελφὰς δίδωσι, πλὴν ἂν μὴ λάβῃ παρθένον ἀνδρὶ συγγεγενημένην. [He does not allow men to sell their daughters or sisters, unless he finds out that his unmarried daughter has been with a man.] For the discussion and previous bibliography see Glazebrook 2005: 33–34; Just 1989: 70, and MacDowell 1978: 80 and 125.

46 Philemon Fr. 3, 1–9: σὺ δ' εἰς ἅπαντας εὗρες ἀνθρώπους, Σόλων·

σὲ γὰρ λέγουσι τοῦτ' ἰδεῖν πρῶτον νόμον,
δημοτικόν, ὦ Ζεῦ, πρᾶγμα καὶ σωτήριον,
(καί μοι λέγειν τοῦτ' ἐστὶν ἁρμοστόν, Σόλων)
μεστὴν ὁρῶντα τὴν πόλιν νεωτέρων,
τούτους τ' ἔχοντας τὴν ἀναγκαίαν φύσιν
ἁμαρτάνοντάς τ' εἰς ὃ μὴ προσῆκον ἦν,
στῆσαι πριάμενόν τοι γυναῖκας κατὰ τόπους
κοινὰς ἅπασι καὶ κατεσκευασμένας.

[But you Solon found it for all humans,
They say that you first saw that particular law
A popular, by Zeus, and terrific thing
(And it is fitting for me to say so, Solon)
Seeing that the city is full of young men,
Satisfying their physical needs
By committing crimes against those whom they shouldn't touch
You bought and established women in certain locations,
Common for everyone and available.]

47 Athen. 13,25; Eust. *Com. Il.* 4.331.
48 Frost 2002: 34–46; Rosivach 1995: 2–3; see also Glazebrook 2006: 33–53 and Henry 2011: 14–33; Kapparis 2017: 33–45.
49 Cohen 2015: 131–53.
50 Kerameikos, near the Agora captured the clientele coming into the city from all over Attica, while the brothels near the harbor were aimed at visitors and sailors. Both areas apparently prospered from these activities (see for example Is. 6, where Euktemon seemingly had a συνοικία [condominium] which served as a brothel in Piraeus and a tavern run by a libertine retired prostitute and surely serving more than wine in Kerameikos).
51 For the lower end see Antiphanes 293; Epicrates Fr. 3; Loomis 1988: 173 and n. 29; D. L. 4.16; for the 30 minae figure see Aesch. Ep. 7.3; Plautus *Rudens* 45, *Curculio* 344. Sums higher than this attested in New Comedy are generally considered dramatic exaggerations, not realistic prices. See the discussion in Kapparis 2017: 302–312.
52 Arist. *Ath. Pol.* 50.2 and Rhodes 1981: 574.
53 For example, X. *Symp.* 2.1–2; Persaios Fr. 451 von Arnim = Athen. 13.86.
54 Hypereides Fr. 14 Jensen (= Harp. s.v. ὅτι χιλίας).
55 D. 46.14: Ὅσοι μὴ ἐπεποίηντο, ὥστε μήτε ἀπειπεῖν μήτ' ἐπιδικάσασθαι, ὅτε Σόλων εἰσῄει τὴν ἀρχήν, τὰ ἑαυτοῦ διαθέσθαι εἶναι ὅπως ἂν ἐθέλῃ, ἂν μὴ παῖδες ὦσι γνήσιοι ἄρρενες, ἂν μὴ μανιῶν ἢ γήρως ἢ φαρμάκων ἢ νόσου ἕνεκα, ἢ γυναικὶ πειθόμενος, ὑπὸ τούτων του παρανοῶν, ἢ ὑπ' ἀνάγκης ἢ ὑπὸ δεσμοῦ καταληφθείς. [Any citizen, with the exception of those who had been adopted when Solon entered upon his office, and had thereby become unable either to renounce or to claim an inheritance, shall have the right to dispose of his own property by will as he shall see fit, if he have no male children lawfully born, unless his mind be impaired by one of these things, lunacy or old age or drugs or disease, or unless he be under the influence of a woman, or under constraint or deprived of his liberty.] (Loeb translation by A.T. Murray). The same law is quoted with minor variations by Hypereides (5.8) and Plutarch (265e; *Sol.* 21.4).
56 D. 48.56.
57 Athen. 13.51 (= Polemon Fr. 3a); cf. Herm. *Inv.* 1.2.47–8 Rabe; Syrianus *Sch. ad Hermog.* 4.188 Walz.

58 See Cohen, E.E. 2000: 113–48; Cohen, Edward E. 2000: 109–22; Cohen 2007: 201–24; 2015: 97–114.
59 See Lys. 3.
60 Kenneth Dover has argued that the earliest evidence about the existence of a law penalizing prostitutes involved in politics is found in a passage from the *Knights* of Aristophanes (Ar. *Eq*. 876–880; Dover 1978: 34), where Paphlagon boasts that he stopped those who enjoy passive sex (κινουμένους) from becoming politicians by disfranchising (ἐξαλείψας) Gryttos. See also Lanni 2010: 56: Lanni's argument rests upon Dover. However, there is no parallel where ἐξαλείφω means to disfranchise, or any other detail establishing a clear link between this passage and the *hetairesis* law. MacDowell, with his impressive credentials in both Aristophanes and Athenian law does not mention such a connection between this law and the passage of the *Knights* in his thorough discussion of Athenian laws related to homosexuality (MacDowell 2000: 13–27). See the discussion in Kapparis 2017: 161–71.
61 And. 1.95, 100.
62 D. 22.21–32.
63 For further discussion see also Chapter 1.4.
64 Kapparis 1998: 255–9.
65 For example, Cohen 1987: 9–10; Lanni 2010: 79–119.
66 Th. 2.37: οὐ δι' ὀργῆς τὸν πέλας, εἰ καθ' ἡδονήν τι δρᾷ, ἔχοντες, οὐδὲ ἀζημίους μέν, λυπηρὰς δὲ τῇ ὄψει ἀχθηδόνας προστιθέμενοι. ἀνεπαχθῶς δὲ τὰ ἴδια προσομιλοῦντες τὰ δημόσια διὰ δέος μάλιστα οὐ παρανομοῦμεν. [We are not angry with our neighbor if he does something for pleasure, nor we look annoyed, which is not injurious per se, but it is unpleasant. While in our private lives we conduct ourselves without anger, in public life we do not break the laws out of reverence.]
67 On the subject I find the accounts of Davidson (2007) and Cantarella (2002) more trustworthy than the influential study of Dover (1978). However, this lengthy debate is outside the purposes of this volume. For a most useful collection of sources on the subject see Hubbard 2003.
68 Adriaan Lanni (2010: 45–67) maintains that these laws had a widespread normative effect but there is no evidence to support this suggestion.
69 See D. 59.92–106 and Kapparis com. ad loc.
70 See the discussions in Kapparis 1999: 394–7.
71 Plautus *Bacch*. 1121–1122: Bacch. quis hás huc ovís adegit?/ Nic. Ovís nos vocánt pessumaé. [Bacch. Who brought these sheep here?/ Nic. The bitches are calling us "sheep."]
72 D. 59.110–115.

7 Criminal justice

Violence and property crimes

7.1 Sources

1 Athenian laws intended to curb violence among citizens

> οἱ μὲν γὰρ νόμοι πολὺ τἀναντία καὶ τὰς ἀναγκαίας προφάσεις, ὅπως μὴ μείζους γίγνωνται, προείδοντο, οἷον (ἀνάγκη γάρ μοι ταῦτα καὶ ζητεῖν καὶ πυνθάνεσθαι διὰ τοῦτον γέγονεν) εἰσὶ κακηγορίας δίκαι· φασὶ τοίνυν ταύτας διὰ τοῦτο γίγνεσθαι, ἵνα μὴ λοιδορούμενοι τύπτειν ἀλλήλους προάγωνται. πάλιν αἰκείας εἰσί· καὶ ταύτας ἀκούω διὰ τοῦτ' εἶναι τὰς δίκας, ἵνα μηδείς, ὅταν ἥττων ᾖ, λίθῳ μηδὲ τῶν τοιούτων ἀμύνηται μηδενί, ἀλλὰ τὴν ἐκ τοῦ νόμου δίκην ἀναμένῃ. τραύματος πάλιν εἰσὶν γραφαὶ τοῦ μὴ τιτρωσκομένων τινῶν φόνους γίγνεσθαι. τὸ φαυλότατον, οἶμαι, τὸ τῆς λοιδορίας, πρὸ τοῦ τελευταίου καὶ δεινοτάτου προεώραται, τοῦ μὴ φόνον γίγνεσθαι, μηδὲ κατὰ μικρὸν ὑπάγεσθαι ἐκ μὲν λοιδορίας εἰς πληγάς, ἐκ δὲ πληγῶν εἰς τραύματα, ἐκ δὲ τραυμάτων εἰς θάνατον, ἀλλ' ἐν τοῖς νόμοις εἶναι τούτων ἑκάστου τὴν δίκην, μὴ τῇ τοῦ προστυχόντος ὀργῇ μηδὲ βουλήσει ταῦτα κρίνεσθαι. εἶτ' ἐν μὲν τοῖς νόμοις οὕτως·
>
> (D. 54–17–9[1])

The laws take entirely the opposite view, and they have planned in advance with regard to excuses based on necessity so that they not lead to even more serious offenses. For example, (I was forced to investigate and learn about this thanks to Conon) there are suits for slander. [18] It is said that they exist for the following reason, in order that men not be induced to strike each other when they are being insulted. There are also suits for battery, and I am told that they exist so that, if someone is losing a fight, he does not defend himself with a stone or some other weapon, but waits for legal compensation. There are also public suits for wounding in order that murders not occur when people are inflicting wounds. [19] Precautions have been made for the least serious offense, I believe, slander, to prevent the last and most serious one, murder, and that men not be spurred on little by little from slander to blows, blows to wounds, and wounds to murder, but the law has penalties for each of these offenses so that the judgment is not based on the anger or whim of the individual.

2 The law on violence (including sexual violence and rape)

Βιαίων: ὄνομα δίκης κατὰ τῶν βίᾳ πραττόντων ὁτιοῦν· ὁ δὲ ἁλοὺς ἀποτίνει εἰς τὸ δημόσιον ἴσον ὅσον τῷ ἑλόντι. Δημοσθένης κατὰ Μειδίου. εἰσὶ δὲ καὶ ἐν τοῖς Λυσιακοῖς φερόμενοι λόγοι βιαίων. καὶ δῆλον ὅτι οὐκ ἐπὶ φθορᾷ παρθένων μόνον οὔτε τὸ ὄνομα οὔτε ἡ δίκη ἐλέγετο, ἀλλὰ καὶ ἐπ' ἄλλων.

(Harp. s.v. *biaion*)

Biaion: the name of a lawsuit brought against those who did anything at all by force; the convicted man pays to the public treasury an equal amount as he does to the successful prosecutor. Demosthenes *Against Meidias*. There are also some speeches for *biaion* among those attributed to Lysias. It is clear that this particular lawsuit, and its name, applied not only to the corruption of virgins, but also to other offenses.

3 Solon's law on rape and sexual assault

ΝΟΜΟΣ: Ἀκούετε, ὦ ἄνδρες, ὅτι κελεύει, ἐάν τις ἄνθρωπον ἐλεύθερον ἢ παῖδα αἰσχύνῃ βίᾳ, διπλῆν τὴν βλάβην ὀφείλειν· ἀν δὲ γυναῖκα, ἐφ' αἷσπερ ἀποκτείνειν ἔξεστιν, ἐν τοῖς αὐτοῖς ἐνέχεσθαι· οὕτως, ὦ ἄνδρες, τοὺς βιαζομένους ἐλάττονος ζημίας ἀξίους ἡγήσατο εἶναι ἢ τοὺς πείθοντας· τῶν μὲν γὰρ θάνατον κατέγνω, τοῖς δὲ διπλῆν ἐποίησε τὴν βλάβην, ἡγούμενος τοὺς μὲν διαπραττομένους βίᾳ ὑπὸ τῶν βιασθέντων μισεῖσθαι, τοὺς δὲ πείσαντας οὕτως αὐτῶν τὰς ψυχὰς διαφθείρειν, ὥστ' οἰκειοτέρας αὑτοῖς ποιεῖν τὰς ἀλλοτρίας γυναῖκας ἢ τοῖς ἀνδράσι, καὶ πᾶσαν ἐπ' ἐκείνοις τὴν οἰκίαν γεγονέναι, καὶ τοὺς παῖδας ἀδήλους εἶναι ὁποτέρων τυγχάνουσιν ὄντες, τῶν ἀνδρῶν ἢ τῶν μοιχῶν.

(Lys. 1. 32–3)

LAW: You hear, men, how the law orders if a person rapes a free man or boy to pay double damages, and if he rapes a woman, from that group in which it is permitted to kill [the seducer], to apply the same penalty. Hence, men, the lawgiver believed that those who use force deserve a lesser penalty than those who persuade. He assigned death as a punishment for the latter and double damages for the former because he recognized that those that accomplish their ends with force are hated by those who are violated. Those who use persuasion so corrupt the women's minds that they make other men's wives closer to themselves than their husbands and all of the household becomes under their control, and it becomes uncertain who are the children's fathers, the husbands or the seducers. The lawgiver, therefore, established the death penalty for them.[2]

4 Definition of assault (*aikeia*)

ἡ δὲ αἴκεια τοῦτ' ἔστιν, ὃς ἂν ἄρξῃ χειρῶν ἀδίκων πρότερος.

(D. 47.40)

This is what assault means, whoever raises his hand first to strike.

5 The law stating the penalty for deliberate wounding and providing a definition of the injury

ἐὰν μέν τις ἀνδρὸς σῶμα τρώσῃ, κεφαλὴν ἢ πρόσωπον ἢ χεῖρας ἢ πόδας, οὗτος μὲν κατὰ τοὺς νόμους τοὺς ἐξ Ἀρείου <πάγου> φεύξεται τὴν τοῦ ἀδικηθέντος πόλιν, καὶ ἐὰν κατίῃ, ἐνδειχθεὶς θανάτῳ ζημιωθήσεται·

(Lys. 6.15)

If someone injures a man's head or face or hands or feet, he is to be exiled from the city of the injured man according to the laws of the Areopagos; and if he returns he is to be denounced and punished by death.[3]

6 A possible definition of intent in Athenian law

ἔπειτα δὲ καὶ οὐδεμίαν ἡγούμην πρόνοιαν εἶναι τραύματος ὅστις μὴ ἀποκτεῖναι βουλόμενος ἔτρωσε. τίς γὰρ οὕτως ἐστὶν εὐήθης, ὅστις ἐκ πολλοῦ προνοεῖται ὅπως ἕλκος τις αὐτοῦ τῶν ἐχθρῶν λήψεται; ἀλλὰ δῆλον ὅτι καὶ οἱ τοὺς νόμους ἐνθάδε θέντες, οὐκ εἴ τινες μαχεσάμενοι ἔτυχον ἀλλήλων κατάξαντες τὰς κεφαλάς, ἐπὶ τούτοις ἠξίωσαν τῆς πατρίδος φυγὴν ποιήσασθαι· ἢ πολλούς γ' ἂν ἐξήλασαν· ἀλλ' ὅσοι ἐπιβουλεύσαντες ἀποκτεῖναί τινας ἔτρωσαν, ἀποκτεῖναι δὲ οὐκ ἐδυνήθησαν, περὶ τῶν τοιούτων τὰς τιμωρίας οὕτω μεγάλας κατεστήσαντο, ἡγούμενοι, ὑπὲρ ὧν ἐβούλευσαν καὶ προὐνοήθησαν, ὑπὲρ τούτων προσήκειν αὐτοῖς δίκην δοῦναι·

(Lys. 3.41–3)

Besides, I did not see that there was any premeditation of wounding in the case of a man who gave a wound without meaning to kill. For who is so simple as to premeditate a long time ahead how some enemy of his shall come by a wound? Why, it is clear that even the makers of our laws did not think well, when people happened in a fight to break each other's heads, to make it a case for banishment from their country; else they would have exiled a goodly number. But in the case of any persons who, designing to kill, wounded others without being able to kill them, they appointed the punishment in that degree of severity, judging it meet that where they had shown design and premeditation they should pay the penalty: though if they might not have succeeded, none the less their best efforts had been exerted.[4]

7 The law of *hybris*

ΝΟΜΟΣ: Ἐάν τις ὑβρίζῃ εἴς τινα, ἢ παῖδα ἢ γυναῖκα ἢ ἄνδρα, τῶν ἐλευθέρων ἢ τῶν δούλων, ἢ παράνομόν τι ποιήσῃ εἰς τούτων τινά, γραφέσθω πρὸς τοὺς θεσμοθέτας ὁ βουλόμενος Ἀθηναίων οἷς ἔξεστιν, οἱ δὲ θεσμοθέται εἰσαγόντων εἰς τὴν ἡλιαίαν τριάκοντα ἡμερῶν ἀφ' ἧς ἂν γραφῇ, ἐὰν μή τι δημόσιον κωλύῃ, εἰ δὲ μή, ὅταν ᾖ πρῶτον οἷόν τε. ὅτου δ' ἂν καταγνῷ ἡ ἡλιαία, τιμάτω περὶ αὐτοῦ παραχρῆμα, ὅτου ἂν δοκῇ ἄξιος εἶναι παθεῖν ἢ ἀποτεῖσαι. ὅσοι δ᾽ ἂν γράφωνται γραφὰς ἰδίας κατὰ τὸν νόμον, ἐάν τις μὴ ἐπεξέλθῃ ἢ ἐπεξιὼν μὴ μεταλάβῃ τὸ πέμπτον μέρος τῶν ψήφων, ἀποτεισάτω χιλίας δραχμὰς τῷ δημοσίῳ. ἐὰν δὲ ἀργυρίου τιμηθῇ τῆς ὕβρεως, δεδέσθω, ἐὰν ἐλεύθερον ὑβρίσῃ, μέχρι ἂν ἐκτείσῃ.

(D. 21.47)

LAW: If some one commits outrage against another, whether it be a child or woman or man, whether free or slave, or commits some other offense against another, let him, whoever wishes of those Athenians who are permitted, lodge a public suit before the *thesmothetai*, and let the *thesmothetai* bring it to the Heliastic court within thirty days from the indictment if public business does not prevent it, but if it does, as soon as first possible. Whomever the Heliastic court condemns, let it immediately impose a penalty on him whichever it thinks he deserves to suffer or pay. If any of those who lodge public suits in accordance with this law does not go to court or going to court fails to receive one 5th of the votes, let him pay a fine of 1,000 drachmas to the city. If he is fined for outrage, let him be imprisoned, if he committed outrage against a free individual, until he pays it.[5]

8 Solon's law on slander

Ἐπαινεῖται δὲ τοῦ Σόλωνος καὶ ὁ κωλύων νόμος τὸν τεθνηκότα κακῶς ἀγορεύειν. καὶ γὰρ ὅσιον τοὺς μεθεστῶτας ἱεροὺς νομίζειν, καὶ δίκαιον ἀπέχεσθαι τῶν οὐχ ὑπαρχόντων, καὶ πολιτικὸν ἀφαιρεῖν τῆς ἔχθρας τὸ ἀίδιον. ζῶντα δὲ κακῶς λέγειν ἐκώλυσε πρὸς ἱεροῖς καὶ δικαστηρίοις καὶ ἀρχείοις καὶ θεωρίας οὔσης ἀγώνων, ἢ τρεῖς δραχμὰς τῷ ἰδιώτῃ, δύο δ᾽ ἄλλας ἀποτίνειν εἰς τὸ δημόσιον ἔταξε. τὸ γὰρ μηδαμοῦ κρατεῖν ὀργῆς ἀπαίδευτον καὶ ἀκόλαστον, τὸ δὲ πανταχοῦ χαλεπόν, ἐνίοις δ᾽ ἀδύνατον· δεῖ δὲ πρὸς τὸ δυνατὸν γράφεσθαι τὸν νόμον, εἰ βούλεται χρησίμως ὀλίγους, ἀλλὰ μὴ πολλοὺς ἀχρήστως κολάζειν.

(Plu. *Sol.* 21)

Praise is given also to that law of Solon which forbids speaking ill of the dead. For it is piety to regard the deceased as sacred, justice to spare the absent, and good policy to rob hatred of its perpetuity. He also forbade speaking ill of the living in temples, court-of-law, public offices, and at festivals; the transgressor must pay three drachmas to the person injured, and two more into the public treasury. For never to master one's anger is a mark of intemperance and lack of training; but always to do so is difficult, and for some, impossible. 90And a law must regard the possibilities in the case, if its maker wishes to punish a few to some purpose, and not many to no purpose.[6]

9 The primary law on slander

ὁ νομοθέτης οὐδεμίαν ὀργῇ συγγνώμην δίδωσιν, ἀλλὰ ζημιοῖ τὸ ν λέγοντα, ἐὰν μὴ ἀποφαίνῃ ὡς ἔστιν ἀληθῆ τὰ εἰρημένα.

(Lys.10.30)

The lawgiver makes no allowance for wrath, but punishes the person who said it, if he cannot prove that what he said was truthful.[7]

10 The penalty for slander

Οὕτω δ' ἡγήσαντο δεινὸν εἶναι τὸ τύπτειν ἀλλήλους ὥστε καὶ περὶ τῆς κακηγορίας νόμον ἔθεσαν ὃς κελεύει τοὺς λέγοντάς τι τῶν ἀπορρήτων πεντακοσίας δραχμὰς ὀφείλειν.

(Isoc. 20.3)

They considered it so terrible to strike one other that they even set up a law about defamation, which states that those using one of the forbidden words are liable to a fine of 500 drachmas.

11 The law forbidding the use of certain words, unless they are truthful

'ἄν τις κακῶς ἀγορεύῃ,' 'τὰ ψευδῆ' προσέθηκεν, ὡς, εἴ γε τἀληθῆ, προσῆκον.

(D. 23.50)

"If someone is speaking ill," then he added "telling lies," for if it is the truth, they it is appropriate to say it.

12 The law on private arbitration

Ἐὰν δέ τινες περὶ συμβολαίων ἰδίων πρὸς ἀλλήλους ἀμφισβητῶσι καὶ βούλωνται διαιτητὴν ἑλέσθαι ὁντινοῦν, ἐξέστω αὐτοῖς αἱρεῖσθαι ὃν ἂν βούλωνται [διαιτητὴν ἑλέσθαι]. ἐπειδὰν δ' ἕλωνται κατὰ κοινόν, μενέτωσαν ἐν τοῖς ὑπὸ τούτου διαγνωσθεῖσι, καὶ μηκέτι μεταφερέτωσαν ἀπὸ τούτου ἐφ' ἕτερον δικαστήριον ταὐτὰ ἐγκλήματα, ἀλλ' ἔστω τὰ κριθέντα ὑπὸ τοῦ διαιτητοῦ κύρια.[8]

(D. 21: 93–4)

If some parties are in disagreement with each other over private contracts and they want to choose anyone to be an arbitrator, let them be allowed to choose whomever they want. And when they have agreed on their choice, let them adhere to the decisions of that man, and afterwards let them not transfer the same charges from him to another court, but let the decisions of the arbitrator be enforced.[9]

13 A thorough description of private arbitration

Κληροῦσι δὲ καὶ <τοὺς> <τετταράκοντα>, τέτταρας ἐκ τῆς φυλῆς ἑκάστης, πρὸς οὓς τὰς ἄλλας δίκας λαγχάνουσιν . . . . καὶ τὰ μὲν μέχρι δέκα δραχμῶν αὐτοτελεῖς εἰσι δ[ικά]ζε[ι]ν, τὰ δ' ὑπὲρ τοῦτο τὸ τίμημα τοῖς διαιτηταῖς παραδιδόασιν· οἱ δὲ παραλαβόντες, [ἐ]ὰν μὴ δύνωνται διαλῦσαι, γιγνώσκουσι, κἂν μὲν ἀμφοτέροις ἀρέσκῃ τὰ γνωσθέντα καὶ ἐμμένωσιν, ἔχει τέλος ἡ δίκη. ἂν δ' ὁ ἕτερος ἐφῇ τῶν ἀντιδίκων εἰς τὸ δικαστήριον, ἐμβαλόντες τὰς μαρτυρίας καὶ τὰς προκλήσεις καὶ τοὺς νόμους εἰς ἐχίνους, χωρὶς μὲν τὰς τοῦ διώκοντος, χωρὶς δὲ τὰς τοῦ φεύγοντος, καὶ τούτους κατασημηνάμενοι, καὶ τὴν γνῶσιν τοῦ διαιτητοῦ γεγραμμένην ἐν γραμματείῳ προσαρτήσαντες, παραδιδόασι το[ῖ]ς δ' τοῖς τὴν φυλὴν τοῦ φεύγοντος δικάζουσιν . . . . οὐκ ἔξεστι δ' οὔτε νόμοις οὔτε προκλήσεσι οὔτε μαρτυρίαις ἀλλ'ἢ ταῖς παρὰ τοῦ διαιτητοῦ χρῆσθαι ταῖς εἰς τοὺς ἐχίνους ἐμβεβλημέναις. διαιτηταὶ δ' εἰσὶν οἷς ἂν ἑξηκοστὸν ἔτος ᾖ . . . . τὸν δὲ τελευταῖον τῶν ἐπωνύμων λαβόντες οἱ τετταράκοντα διανέμουσιν αὐτοῖς τὰς διαίτας καὶ ἐπικληροῦσιν ἃς ἕκαστος διαιτήσει· καὶ ἀναγκαῖον ἃς ἂν ἕκαστος λάχῃ διαίτας ἐκδιαιτᾶν. ὁ γὰρ νόμος, ἄν τις μὴ γένηται διαιτητὴς τῆς ἡλικίας αὐτῷ καθηκούσης, ἄτιμον εἶναι κελεύει, πλὴν ἐὰν τύχῃ ἀρχὴν ἄρχων τι[ν]ὰ ἐν ἐκείνῳ τῷ ἐνιαυτῷ ἢ ἀποδημῶν· οὗτοι δ' ἀτελεῖς εἰσὶ μόνοι. ἔστιν δὲ καὶ εἰσαγγέλλειν εἰς τοὺς διαιτητάς, ἐάν τις ἀδικηθῇ ὑπὸ τοῦ διαιτητοῦ, κἄν τινος καταγνῶσιν, ἀτιμοῦσθαι κελεύουσιν οἱ νόμοι. ἔφεσις δ' ἔστι καὶ τούτοις.

(Ath. Pol. 53.1–6)

They also elect by lot forty persons, four from each tribe, who are the court before which the other suits are brought. . . . They have summary jurisdiction in claims not exceeding ten drachmas, but suits above that value they pass on to the Arbitrators. These take over the cases, and are unable to effect a compromise, they give judgment, and if both parties are satisfied with their judgment and abide by it, that ends the suit. But if one of the two parties appeals to the Jury-court, they put the witnesses' evidence and the challenges and the laws concerned into deed-boxes, those of the prosecutor and those of the defendant separately, and seal them up, and attach to them a copy of the Arbitrator's verdict written on a tablet, and hand them over to the four judges taking the cases of the defendant's tribe. . . . The litigants are not permitted to put in laws or challenges or evidence other than those passed on by the Arbitrator, that have been put into the deed-boxes. Persons fifty-nine years of age may serve as Arbitrators. . . . The Forty take the last one of the Name-heroes and distribute the arbitration-cases among those of his year and assign by lot the cases that each is to arbitrate upon; and it is compulsory for each of them to complete the arbitration of the cases allotted to him, for the law enacts the disfranchisement of anybody who does not become Arbitrator when of the proper age, unless he happens to hold some office in that year or to be abroad, these being the only grounds of exemption. Anybody unjustly dealt with by the Arbitrator may indict him before the Arbitrators and the laws prescribe the penalty of disfranchisement for an Arbitrator found guilty; but the Arbitrators also have an appeal.[10]

14 The law on theft

Ὅ τι ἄν τις ἀπολέσῃ, ἐὰν μὲν αὐτὸ λάβῃ, τὴν διπλασίαν καταδικάζειν, ἐὰν δὲ μή, τὴν διπλασίαν πρὸς τοῖς ἐπαιτίοις. δεδέσθαι δ' ἐν τῇ ποδοκάκκῃ τὸν πόδα πένθ' ἡμέρας καὶ νύκτας ἴσας, ἐὰν προστιμήσῃ ἡ ἡλιαία. προστιμᾶσθαι δὲ τὸν βουλόμενον, ὅταν περὶ τοῦ τιμήματος ᾖ.

(D. 24.105)

If someone loses something and recovers it, then the penalty is twice the value of the object; if he does not recover it, then the penalty ought to be twice the value of the object plus additional penalties. He (the thief) is to be bound by the foot in the stocks for five days and five nights, if the court imposes this punishment. Moreover, anyone can propose an additional penalty during sentencing.

15 The law permitting *apagoge* for theft

καίτοι γ' ὁ Σόλων, ὦ ἄνδρες δικασταί, . . . οὐχ ὅπως ἀσφαλῶς κακουργήσουσι φαίνεται παρασκευάζων τοῖς τοιούτοις, ἀλλ' ὅπως ἢ μὴ ἀδικήσουσιν ἢ δώσουσι δίκην ἀξίαν, καὶ νόμον εἰσήνεγκεν, εἰ μέν τις μεθ' ἡμέραν ὑπὲρ πεντήκοντα δραχμὰς κλέπτοι, ἀπαγωγὴν πρὸς τοὺς ἕνδεκ' εἶναι, εἰ δέ τις νύκτωρ ὁτιοῦν κλέπτοι, τοῦτον ἐξεῖναι καὶ ἀποκτεῖναι καὶ τρῶσαι διώκοντα καὶ ἀπαγαγεῖν τοῖς ἕνδεκα, εἰ βούλοιτο. τῷ δ' ἁλόντι ὧν αἱ ἀπαγωγαί εἰσιν, οὐκ ἐγγυητὰς καταστήσαντι ἔκτισιν εἶναι τῶν κλεμμάτων, ἀλλὰ θάνατον τὴν ζημίαν. καὶ εἴ τίς γ' ἐκ Λυκείου ἢ ἐξ Ἀκαδημείας ἢ ἐκ Κυνοσάργους ἱμάτιον ἢ ληκύθιον ἢ ἄλλο τι φαυλότατον, ἢ εἰ τῶν σκευῶν τι τῶν ἐκ τῶν γυμνασίων ὑφέλοιτο ἢ ἐκ τῶν λιμένων, ὑπὲρ δέκα δραχμάς, καὶ τούτοις θάνατον ἐνομοθέτησεν εἶναι τὴν ζημίαν.

(D. 24.113–14)

And yet Solon, gentlemen of the jury, and even Timocrates cannot pretend to be a legislator of the same calibre as Solon, so far from providing such defaulters with the means of swindling in security, actually introduced a law to ensure that they should either refrain from crime or be adequately punished. For a theft in day-time of more than fifty drachmas a man might be arrested summarily and put into custody of the Eleven. If he stole anything, however small, by night, the person aggrieved might lawfully pursue and kill or wound him, or else put him into the hands of the Eleven, at his own option. A man found guilty of an offence for which arrest is lawful was not allowed to put in bail and refund the stolen money; no, the penalty was death. Or suppose that he stole a cloak, or an oil-flask, or any such trifle, from the Lyceum, or the Academy, or Cynosarges, or any utensil from the gymnasia or the harbors, above the value of ten drachmas, for such thefts also Solon enacted the capital penalty.[11]

16 Monthly cases

κληροῦσι δὲ καὶ <εἰσαγωγέας> ε' ἄνδρας, οἳ τὰς ἐμμήνους εἰσάγουσι δίκας, δυοῖν φυλαῖν ἕκαστος. εἰσὶ δ' ἔμμηνοι προικός, ἐάν τις ὀφείλων μὴ ἀποδῷ, κἄν τις ἐπὶ δραχμῇ δανεισάμενος ἀποστερῇ, κἄν τις ἐν ἀγορᾷ βουλόμενος ἐγράζεσθαι δανείσηται παρά τινος ἀφορμήν· ἔτι δ' αἰκείας καὶ ἐρανικὰς καὶ κοινωνικὰς καὶ ἀνδραπόδων καὶ ὑποζυγίων καὶ τριηραρχικὰς καὶ τραπεζιτικάς. οὗτοι μὲν οὖν ταύτας δικάζουσιν ἐμμήνους εἰσάγ[ον]τες, οἱ δ' ἀποδέκται τοῖς τελώναις καὶ κατὰ τῶν τελωνῶν, τὰ μὲν μέχρι δέκα δραχμῶν ὄντες κύρι[οι], τὰ δ' ἄλλ' εἰς τὸ δικαστήριον εἰσάγοντες ἔμμηνα.

(Arist. *Ath. Pol.* 52.2–3)

They also elect by lot five men as Introducers, who introduce the cases to be tried within a month, each official those of two tribes. These cases include prosecutions for non-payment of dowry due, actions for the recovery of loans borrowed at a drachma interest,[1] and of capital borrowed from one party by another wishing to do business in the market; and also actions about outrage, friendly-society business, partnerships, slaves, draft animals, naval command,[2] and bank cases. These officials, therefore, bring into court and decide these suits within a month; but the Receivers[1] decide suits brought by tax-farmers or against them, having power to deal summarily with suits up to ten francs but bringing the others into the Jury-court within a month.[12]

7.2 Assault and slander: violence in Athenian law and life

In recent years much discussion has arisen from two diametrically opposite points of view, one presented by David Cohen, the other by Gabriel Herman, regarding attitudes to violence in classical Athens.[13] Cohen has argued that, in line with other Mediterranean societies,[14] classical Athens was a relatively violent and antagonistic society, while the feuds between individuals and families were often fueled by social constructs such as masculine honor and pride. Gabriel Herman on the other hand, in a significant behavioral study of classical Athens takes exactly the opposite point of view, that this was a very peaceful, law-abiding society and that no form of violence was ever tolerated. The subsequent discussions on who was right go far beyond the purposes of this inquiry, and on balance I am inclined to side with Werner Riess (but with less emphasis on the ritualistic aspects of violence), and Nick Fisher, both of whom argue that Athens was relatively free of physical violence and crime because conflict was channeled away from violent confrontations towards the courts, the gymnasium, religious expressions or other, usually safer forms of antagonism in public and private life.[15]

The Athenian Democracy had powerful mechanisms to counter machismo and violent confrontations, and re-channel negative emotions, allowing them to be expressed in a more controlled, even if not necessarily less aggressive or dangerous manner. It was exactly this ability of the Athenian male to control his emotions through the use of reason that placed him at the top of the Aristotelian *scala naturae*. These mechanisms were complex, and it would be a herculean task to attempt a discussion here. From the competition in the gymnasium, and in athletic events, to rhetorical contests (*agon*) and adversarial litigation in its court system the First Democracy had devised a whole range of measures intended to channel the energies, competitive instincts and masculine egos of its citizens away from violent conflict and criminal behavior, and into more noble and less detrimental forms of antagonism.

There is no doubt that Athenian law set harsh penalties for violent behavior among the citizens, and quite possibly perceived violence as an escalation, which if diffused early in the process could be contained with minimal consequences, assuming that we believe Isocrates (S 8), the speaker in Lysias 10, and the speech *Against Konon* (S 1).[16] Ariston, the speaker in *Against Konon*, sees a clear pattern in the laws intended to prevent the escalation of violence from verbal exchanges all the way to murder. He argues that the law forbade citizens even to use certain words, because the belief was that first come words, words can lead to blows, blows can lead to more serious injuries, and more serious injuries can lead to death. In this pattern the speaker reads the clear intention on behalf of the law-giver to stump out violence by tackling it at its initial stages and before it escalates. Generally, we should be very skeptical of "master plans" suggested by the Attic Orators, which pull together distinctly different pieces of legislation under a single objective. However, in this particular case there is a natural order to the escalation of violence from an angry verbal exchange all the way down to a lethal assault, and for this reason it may be prudent to give some credence to the suggestion that Athenian law intended to stop violent confrontations among citizens by forbidding even angry, slanderous exchanges, before things got worse.

The law recognized that it would be impossible to eliminate angry exchanges between citizens at all times and set the more realistic goal of regulating the circumstances under which more control than usual would be required (S 6). Plutarch praises the insight of Solon to compose a reasonable and practically enforceable law (πρὸς τὸ δυνατὸν γράφεσθαι τὸν νόμον), rather than one which would be very difficult for most people to follow, and impossible for some (τὸ δὲ πανταχοῦ [sc. κρατεῖν ὀργῆς] χαλεπόν, ἐνίοις δ' ἀδύνατον). In his paraphrase of the Solonean law, Plutarch mentions certain places where using bad language would be forbidden such as temples, law-courts or archives, and certain occasions like public competitions. The narrative of Lysias 9 adds the time when a magistrate was performing his official duties to the list.[17] He also mentions a prohibition to speak ill of the dead, which is confirmed as a valid law of the Athenian state in the 4th century by the narrative of *Against Leptines* and of the speech *Against Boiotos, on the Dowry*.[18] The penalty seems to have been 1000 drachmas, double the penalty for the defamation of a living person.[19] A law mentioned by Hypereides forbade the defamation of the tyrannicides, Harmodios and Aristogeiton, the iconic heroes of the Athenian state.[20]

Several sources also mention that there were certain forbidden words (ἀπόρρητα) which citizens could not use to insult one another under the threat of a 500 drachma fine (S 8), unless they were speaking truthfully.[21] The speech of Lysias *Against Theomnestos* is giving us an idea of the kind of words included in this list.[22] He mentions ἀνδροφόνος (murderer), πατραλοίας (father-beater), μητραλοίας (mother-beater), ῥίψασπις (shield thrower), λωποδύτης (thief), and ἀνδραποδιστής (enslaver). It is clear from the context of *Against Theomnestos* that these words were forbidden not out of sensitivity, but because each one of them was a grave offense with serious criminal and civil penalties, ranging between exclusion from public office (as in the case of persons who mistreated their parents) to the death penalty (as in the case of a murderer or an enslaver). The law forbade the use of words which were associated with serious crimes, unless the accusations were truthful. So, if someone called another person a "murderer," he would need to be able to stand by his word, and if sued, he would need to be able to prove that his opponent was truthfully a murderer, or else he was liable to a fine of 500 drachmas. To put it in perspective, this fine would be roughly equivalent of two and a half years of wages for an unskilled worker, or a year and a half of wages for a skilled worker. The penalty was not negligible and in it we should discern the firm determination of the law to keep the lid on slanderous exchanges which implicated citizens in illegal activities and prevent angry reactions by those unjustly accused of such crimes.

A prosecution for slander was a private lawsuit (*dike kakegorias*), and a later source states that 200 drachmas from the penalty paid by the unsuccessful defendant went to the state, while 300 went to the prosecutor.[23] Isocrates in the speech *Against Lochites* also mentions a fixed penalty of 500 drachmas, however, Demosthenes, seems to have won double that amount from Meidias. The penalty for the initial lawsuit for *kakegoria*, which Meidias lost in absentia, when he failed to appear at the arbitration, was 1000 drachmas.[24] The most likely explanation is that at some point in the 4th century, the penalty for κακηγορία was doubled. If correct, this information suggests that the law gave a financial incentive to insulted men to take their case to court. However, the speaker in *Against Theomnestos* reveals that defamation lawsuits were thought to be petty and the sign of an unpolished and litigious man (ἀνελευθέρων γὰρ καὶ λίαν φιλοδίκων εἶναι νομίζω κακηγορίας δικάζεσθαι), and he would rather have avoided this one if he could.[25] Perhaps we can understand his point of view: few people in our times would be willing to engage in litigation over defamation or bad language, unless it threatened directly an important aspect of their professional or personal lives, and Athenian practice seemingly was moving along the same lines. While most people might ultimately brush aside an insult, sometimes the consequences could be too severe if this defamation came to be believed as truthful, as in the case of the forbidden words, and, in these instances, they might feel compelled to challenge their detractor in court.

Regardless of the frequency of *kakegoria* lawsuits, the Athenian legal system intended to firmly discourage citizens from hurling insults at each other, because it made the assumption that angry words, even when they were inconsequential on their own, still had the potential to escalate a conflict and lead to a violent assault. Such an escalation is attested in several court cases. Perhaps the most famous among these is the escalation of the quarrel between Demosthenes and Meidias, which indeed started with a sharp verbal exchange and resulted in physical assault and bitter lawsuits. According to Demosthenes, the quarrel began when Meidias challenged him to an exchange of properties (*antidosis*).[26] The real objective seemingly was to stop the lawsuit which Demosthenes had initiated against his guardians. During the process Meidias and his men turned up in the house of Demosthenes and used very inappropriate language in the presence of his mother and young sister. Demosthenes felt the need to defend the honor of his household and responded with a lawsuit for defamation (*dike kakegorias*). The case went to public arbitration, as all private lawsuits would in the 4th century,[27] and Meidias lost in absentia.

Meidias subsequently tried to bribe the arbitrator to change his verdict, and when the latter refused Meidias went after him during his *euthyna* and succeeded in disfranchising him. Demosthenes pursued Meidias with a lawsuit for ejectment (*exoules*), the process typically used when fines from previous litigation had not been paid before the deadline. What followed was a dramatic escalation of the case, and Meidias ended up punching Demosthenes in the face while the latter was performing as a chorus leader during the festival of Dionysia. A denunciation to the assembly followed (*probole*), which voted against Meidias and referred the case to court. Meidias was convicted and had to pay a substantial fine of 30 minae. As Andrew Wolpert puts it,

> Thirty minas might not have been a hefty fine for Meidias, but for most Athenians it was a substantial sum of money. He was probably spared an even greater fine only because the skirmish between the two men was fairly minor.[28]

Another well-known case of violence among citizens is the beating of a man named Ariston by Konon and his sons (D. 54). Ariston describes with memorable images not only the aggression of Konon and his sons, but also their bragging and posturing, as well as his own long and slow recovery from the wounds. Given the aggravated circumstances and the presence of many witnesses, Ariston could reasonably expect to win a sizeable compensation. If the compensation was 500 drachmas for defamation, one would imagine that it would be significantly higher for a violent assault. Ariston also had the option to pursue Konon through a *graphe hybreos* and seek the death penalty in the event of conviction. In this case he would not be suing for the assault, but for the arrogant attitude of his opponent, his contempt for him and the laws of the city. However, such a case would have been much riskier, as proving *hybris* was always going to be tricky,[29] and a bad loss would incur a fine of 1000 drachmas. There was nothing to be gained from this option, other than revenge, and much to be lost if something went badly wrong.

In an *aikeia* prosecution, one had to prove first that he did not initiate the violence, and second that he was physically assaulted. The rule that the person who started the violence was the one liable for punishment was inscribed in the law (S 5) and was an important factor in all violence disputes. It would matter little if the perpetrator was the one who had suffered the most injuries. Whoever started it, was the one responsible before the law, and this is clear from a number of sources.[30] The question who started it first is very significant in the speech

Against Euergos and Mnesiboulos,[31] where two men, the speaker and his opponent Theophemos, have both sued each other for *aikeia* over the same incident.[32] These lawsuits were part of a whole series of legal engagements between the two men, and besides what they may tell us about the *dike aikeias*, they also suggest two seemingly contradictory conclusions. First that, as Riess, Herman and Fisher have argued, the Athenians channeled their quarrels through their justice system, because this was the lawful and democratic thing to do, but then again, that litigation was not the panacea for all violent tendencies, especially when seething anger was festering for a long period of time.[33]

The two men, the speaker and Theophemos, had been engaged in litigation for some time, and, at some point, they ended up assaulting each other. Then, they sued each other with a *dike aikeias*. The lawsuit of Theophemos went to court first and he won. Then, instead of a de-escalation of the quarrel the whole fight turned so ugly that during an incident an old servant of the speaker was injured while she was trying to protect a cheap, ordinary cup, which the men of Theophemos were trying to snatch from her bosom, where she had hidden it. About a month later, the old woman died from her injuries. The speaker for reasons of religious observance, if we believe him at this point, decided not to prosecute Theophemos for homicide, and one might think that after such a tragedy he would back down and put this whole matter to rest; apparently, he did not. Instead, he is using the death of the old woman as a powerful weapon in his quest for vengeance.[34] At the time when the present trial took place he was planning to pursue Theophemos for assault over the initial incident, and he was preparing for it by taking Euergos and Mnesiboulos, the key witnesses of Theophemos, to court for false testimony (*pseudomartyrion*). If he won, he would have stripped his opponent of his witnesses, and his chances of winning his *dike aikeias* too would be much better. Perhaps it may be worth remembering that this prolonged, ugly and ultimately lethal quarrel started over some pieces of naval equipment.

The doctor who examined the old woman quite possibly was one of the witnesses invited to testify on her condition after the assault.[35] The physician who tended to the wounds of Ariston was also invited to testify separately as an expert witness in *Against Konon*.[36] The expert independent testimony of a physician appears to be critical in cases of assault. Moreover, during the entire debate on violence scholars have neglected to discuss the role of the physician in cases like that of the old woman who died as a result of the assault. However, this may be an important part of the debate considering the limited abilities of ancient medicine in cases of serious traumatic injury, and the possibility of murder charges, if the victim succumbed to his/her injuries. The law did not hold doctors responsible for the death of the patient in their care, and automatically absolved them of all liability, even if their treatment was to blame for the death of their patient.[37] Given the limitations of ancient physicians, one would imagine that without such a law no one in the ancient world would have been able to practice medicine without constant fear of prosecution. The law clearly considered responsible for the death of the victim the perpetrator of the violence, namely the person who had started the deadly incident.

The theme is explored in the third tetralogy of Antiphon. In this hypothetical scenario an old man attacked a younger man, while both were drunk. The younger man hit back and injured him. The injuries were not critical, but an incompetent doctor was put in charge, who against the advice of other physicians followed a course of treatment that proved fatal. The young man was prosecuted for the death of the old man, and the question is who was responsible, the person who injured him, the doctor, or the victim himself who started the fight. Naturally the prosecution tries to put all the blame upon the younger man who injured the victim, arguing that if he had not hit the old man, there would have been no need to call upon the incompetent doctor. The defense tries to shift the blame by arguing that the injuries of the victim were not critical, and that ultimately it was the doctor who killed the man, not the defendant. However, in the end it is clear that the aggressor who started the fight ought to be responsible. The defense argues that the old man himself was responsible for his own demise, because he first attacked the younger man, who was forced to defend himself, and thus the aggressor brought upon himself his own death.

The narrative of the speech *Against Konon* on the role of the physician in the treatment of the injured Ariston throws new light on the reasons why Athenian law so firmly discouraged violent confrontations, even minor ones:

> Τότε μὲν τοίνυν παραχρῆμ' ὑπὸ τῶν πληγῶν ἃς ἔλαβον καὶ τῆς ὕβρεως οὕτω διετέθην, ὡς ἀκούτε καὶ μεμαρτύρηται παρὰ πάντων ὑμῖν τῶν εὐθὺς ἰδόντων. μετὰ δὲ ταῦτα τῶν μὲν οἰδημάτων τῶν ἐν τῷ προσώπῳ καὶ τῶν ἑλκῶν οὐδὲν ἔφη φοβεῖσθαι λίαν ὁ ἰατρός, πυρετοὶ δὲ παρηκολούθουν μοι συνεχεῖς καὶ ἀλγήματα, ὅλου μὲν τοῦ σώματος πάνυ σφοδρὰ καὶ δεινά, μάλιστα δὲ τῶν πλευρῶν καὶ τοῦ ἤτρου, καὶ τῶν σιτίων ἀπεκεκλείμην. καὶ ὡς μὲν ὁ ἰατρὸς ἔφη, εἰ μὴ κάθαρσις αἵματος αὐτομάτη μοι πάνυ πολλὴ συνέβη περιωδύνῳ ὄντι καὶ ἀπορουμένῳ ἤδη, κἂν ἔμπυος γενόμενος διεφθάρην· νῦν δὲ τοῦτ' ἔσῳσεν τὸ αἷμ' ἀποχωρῆσαν. ὡς οὖν καὶ ταῦτ' ἀληθῆ λέγω, καὶ παρηκολούθησέ μοι τοιαύτη νόσος ἐξ ἧς εἰς τοὔσχατον ἦλθον, ἐξ ὧν ὑπὸ τούτων ἔλαβον πληγῶν, λέγε τὴν τοῦ ἰατροῦ μαρτυρίαν καὶ τὴν τῶν ἐπισκοπούντων.
>
> ΜΑΡΤΥΡΙΑΙ
>
> At that time, then, as the immediate result of the blows and the maltreatment I received, I was brought into this condition, as you hear from my own lips, and as all the witnesses who saw me at the time have testified. Afterwards, although the swellings on my face and the bruises, my physician said, did not give him great concern, continuous attacks of fever ensued and violent and acute pains throughout all my body, but especially in my sides and the pit of my stomach, and I was unable to take my food. Indeed, the surgeon said that, if a copious hemorrhage had not spontaneously occurred, while my agony was extreme and my attendants were at their wits' end, I should have died from internal suppuration; but as it was, this loss of blood saved me. To prove now that these statements of mine are true, and that from the blows which these men dealt me there resulted an illness so severe that it brought

> me to the point of death. Read the depositions of the surgeon and of those who came to see me.[38]
>
> TESTIMONY

The doctor is actually called twice on the stand. The first time he is asked to testify what he first saw when he was called in shortly after the beating, namely, that the litigant had suffered substantial bruising and injuries as a result of the assault. Then, after describing the course of the treatment, and how close to death he came as a result of his injuries, the litigant asks the doctor to take the stand again, this time to testify on the progression of the treatment and confirm that in the coming days his patient came close to death as a result of his injuries.

What is remarkable in the narrative of Ariston is that, although he acknowledges that his doctor had very little to do with the improvement of his condition, he nowhere appears to be critical of his doctor's conduct or ability. On the contrary he demonstrates complete confidence in his doctor's skill and ability and is prepared to summon him as an expert witness. Ariston accepts as a fact of life the possibility that the doctor could have been mistaken in his earlier diagnosis, and that if things had gone wrong and he had died, it would not have been the fault of the doctor but of his assailant.

The uncertainties of ancient medical treatment in cases of assault have been left out of the debate on violence in classical Athens, but they should not be, because an injury which in our times might be considered minor, like a small cut which had the potential to get infected, could prove fatal in a society without antibiotics.[39] The limitations of medical science could much sooner result in the death of an injured man from causes inside the body that were beyond a physician's reach. In that case the law was clear. The responsibility never rested with the physician, no matter how incompetent, but always with the person who initiated the fight, and after the death of the victim the case would be treated as homicide.[40] Thus a minor quarrel in the heat of the moment, sometimes under the influence of alcohol, could result in homicide charges, as in Tetralogy 3 of Antiphon. The law firmly discouraged violence because its consequences could be unanticipated and very severe.

The most serious form of physical assault was the γραφὴ τραύματος ἐκ προνοίας (a *graphe* for deliberate wounding). The fact that it was tried by the Areopagos Council probably has to do with historic reasons,[41] but nonetheless suggests that Athenian law viewed this offence as one step below homicide, and the prescribed penalties of permanent exile and confiscation of property were more severe than the penalty imposed in some forms of homicide. Remarkably this particular lawsuit appears to be a *graphe*, when all other violent assault cases, including homicide, were *dikai*, and it would be the only public type of lawsuit to be brought before the Areopagos. Moreover, it appears that a similar process with homicide was followed during the trial, with a strong religious component and the customary exchange of oaths and curses (*diomosiai*).[42] These peculiarities have generated considerable discussion, and three possibilities have been proposed.

Chiara Pecorella Longo has maintained that *trauma ek pronoias* was prosecuted through a *dike*, like homicide and all other cases of violent conduct brought before the Areopagos, and that the four sources which speak of a *graphe traumatos ek pronoias* are merely using loose phraseology, as Pollux does.[43] Hansen proposed a more diplomatic solution arguing for the existence of both a *dike* and a *graphe traumatos*, which is unlikely, because, although sometimes there is duplication in Athenian legal procedure, there is no parallel where a *dike* and a *graphe* were in existence for exactly the same offence, and having the same penalties.[44] Moreover, as Longo has pointed out, such a possibility would not make sense, as a *dike* was relatively safe for the unsuccessful prosecutor, while a *graphe* which he lost with less than 1/5 of the votes, would result in an enormous fine of 1000 drachmas. The obvious question is why anyone would risk a huge fine in a public lawsuit, when he could safely reach the same outcome through a much safer private lawsuit.

On balance, I find more appealing the third option advocated by several scholars including MacDowell, and more recently David Phillips in an article dedicated to this procedure, that the *trauma ek pronoias* was a *graphe*, just as Demosthenes and Aeschines suggest.[45] The similarities with the *dike phonou* notwithstanding, Phillips does not accept that the *trauma ek pronoias* is simply a lawsuit for attempted murder, as it has been argued,[46] although sometimes it could be very similar to it. Phillips suggests that trauma was a *graphe* for two reasons: first, because an injured person might not always be able to pursue his assailant with a *dike*, if his physical condition did not permit it; and, second, because violent confrontations many a time happened in groups or gangs.[47] In such situations the flexibility afforded by a public lawsuit would ensure that the perpetrators could not avoid punishment by disabling or intimidating a victim into silence. Although the procedure for trauma to some extent imitated the proceedings and penalties for homicide, and on some occasions could be used for attempted murder, at the same time it was a different process, introduced at a later date to deal with a significantly broader range of violent offences than an unsuccessful murder attempt, and quite possibly to deal with endemic violence in a place with as many economic and social problems as Solonean Athens.

It may seem strange that in the 4th century the law was asking of a person who might have been beaten within an inch of his life to risk a huge fine of 1000 drachmas in order to bring his attackers to justice. However, the objection is not insurmountable if we take into account that Athenian law already provided a much safer and more profitable alternative in the *dike aikeias*, while a substantial risk might seem just right when the main objective was to vengefully inflict a permanent and devastating punishment upon the opponent, and there was no profit to be made from it either. It seems only fair that the law would not want such prosecutions to be taken lightly and to this end a *graphe* was the appropriate avenue, and also a deterrent from frivolous lawsuits.

The two extant speeches on trauma cases fit the profile of a determined quest for vengeance. Lysias 3 was delivered in defense of a middle-aged man who had a long-standing quarrel with a younger man named Simon over a Plataian rent-boy named Theodotos. Both men seemingly were in love with the youth, and neither would back down until the quarrel escalated into a brawl and Simon was injured. He then prosecuted the speaker for *trauma ek pronoias*. Simon was not after compensation in this case; he wanted revenge, and if he succeeded in having the speaker permanently exiled and his property confiscated, he would have decisively won the contest over Theodotos too. The other case, Lysias 4, is also a quarrel over a love-affair, this time a woman, who was originally a slave-prostitute, and the two men were sharing her favors until one of them fell in love with her and tried to lock the other out of the relationship. Again revenge, the desire to see a rival exiled from Attica, and subsequent victory in the erotic contest might make the risk of a *graphe* worthwhile.[48]

The third attested case, a bitter quarrel between two half-brothers, also fits the profile. A man called Mantitheos was fighting with his half-brothers over family and property matters, and, at some point, one of them, Boiotos, asked the physician Euthydikos to deliberately inflict cuts and bruises upon him. The doctor expectedly refused, but then Boiotos inflicted cuts and bruises upon his own head. He subsequently claimed that the injuries were caused by his half-brother and prosecuted Mantitheos for deliberate wounding. However, during the trial Euthydikos, the doctor, took the stand and revealed that he had been asked to injure Boiotos deliberately. The jury believed the doctor and Mantitheos was acquitted. Vengeance and a desire to have Mantitheos permanently exiled, which would leave Boiotos and his brother Pamphilos as the unopposed heirs to the prosperous *oikos* of Mantias, were the true motives behind this determined attempt. With so much at stake, the risks of a *graphe* might seem less intimidating. We do not know much about a 4th case against a man named Lysitheos, preserved in the form of scant fragments among the speeches of Lysias, but as in the previously mentioned cases it seems that there was a home invasion at some point, which led to the prosecution.[49]

Whether the use of a weapon marked the dividing line between *aikeia* and *trauma ek pronoias*, has been discussed by several scholars.[50] In my opinion there can be no certainty over this issue because the two key passages are problematic.[51] It is quite possible that, while the use of a weapon might be a clearer indication of intent, it was not indispensable, if intent could be sufficiently demonstrated by other means, such as a long-standing quarrel which provided the motive for the assault, as for example in the case of Mantitheos and his half-brother Boiotos, where a weapon is not explicitly mentioned.[52] Deliberate wounding focused on someone's purposeful attempt to injure an opponent, rather than his unsuccessful attempt to kill him.[53] Intent (πρόνοια) was the key component in this particular case, which should exclude fights erupting in the heat of the moment without pre-existing animosity. In all cases of deliberate wounding that we know about there seems to be long-standing animosity, which is fueling a desire for revenge, and perhaps this slow-burning anger is what motivated the alleged victims to risk 1000 drachmas in order to chase a hated opponent out of the borders of Attica, once and for all.

7.3 *Hybris*

Hybris is difficult to define within the Athenian legal system, not least because poets used the word to castigate a broad array of human behaviors, and our most important source for Athenian law, the Attic Orators, also used the term with "many facets," to use the words of G. Rowe, who has investigated its multiple shades of meaning and usage as a rhetorical tool in *Against Meidias*.[54] It was not a specific offence as such but rather an attitude, a behavioral pattern incongruous with the concept of *isonomia* and the principles of freedom and respect for other citizens in the Athenian Democracy. This is why a Solonean law (S 7) established a public lawsuit (*graphe hybreos*) intended to punish this kind of behavior, allowing a prosecutor broad discretion for defining how this particular case constituted *hybris*.

D.M. MacDowell understood the concept of *hybris* as having power and misusing it self-indulgently to harm others for pleasure. He pointed out that there is considerable overlap between *hybris* and other offenses such as assault, battery or slander, and concluded that the difference between these and *hybris* "lay in the motive and state of mind of the offender." On account of this, MacDowell rightly concluded that *hybris* was very difficult to prove in a court setting. He explains his conclusion as following:

> In a court it is difficult to establish a state of mind. It may be fairly easy to prove that someone hit you, but much harder to prove that what made him hit you was self-indulgent egotism and not some other motive or accident.

Nick Fisher agreed that it was an offence too difficult to prove, and in the case of rape or sexual offences, a *hybris* prosecution could be counter-indicated, as it would bring more shame to the family, and still might be unsuccessful.[55] Edward Harris has objected to this on basis of evidence of the *Old Oligarch*, which enlists *hybris* prosecutions as one of the reasons why the Athenian court system was clogged with a multitude of lawsuits and has suggested that the *graphe hybreos* was used for a broad variety of offenses, including sexual violence.[56]

At first glance the evidence paradoxically seems to support both positions at the same time. Several *hybris* cases are attested in the sources. Most of them are only titles preserved in the lexicographers, and in this respect offer no significant evidence on the subject.[57] We do not even know whether these cases were actual *graphai hybreos*, or just lawsuits introduced through a different procedure, but heavily employing *hybris* as a rhetorical argument, like the speech *Against Meidias*, which was introduced to court through a *probole*.[58] There are three securely attested cases of *graphe hybreos*. One was the *graphe* brought by Apollodoros against Phormion not long after the death of his father (371 BC). Apollodoros tells us that he was outraged by the illegal will of his father, through which Pasion betrothed his wife Archippe to Phormion with a significant dowry, and also handed over the guardianship of Pasikles, his younger son, to his trusted bank manager.[59] Upon his return he launched a *graphe hybreos* against Phormion, but it seems that this was nothing more than a ploy to force a better financial settlement upon Phormion. The fact that the will of Pasion was only advisory from a legal point of view, since he already had legitimate sons, makes clear that Apollodoros was prepared to accept the arrangement if his terms were met, and that the whole maneuvering, including the *graphe hybreos*, was part of the bargaining process. When they reached an agreement Apollodoros withdrew the *graphe*, and the case never went to court.

The second case never went to court either. Isaios mentions it as part of a complex web of property disputes surrounding the estate of Kirron, and was brought against a man named Diokles, who seemingly was responsible for the disfranchisement of the husband of a woman whose estate he had improperly seized. In this instance it appears as if the *graphe hybreos* was used as part of the property dispute, and we are told that the perpetrator has yet to be punished (οὐδέπω τούτων δίκην δέδωκε).[60] The phrase is ambiguous and can mean either that the case was eventually abandoned, or that it is still pending and has not yet come to trial. Either way, it does not help us answer any question about the *graphe hybreos* as a viable process in a real court setting.

The third case mentioned in a fragment from the speech *Against Dorotheos*, attributed to Hypereides, does not help much either.[61] We are told that Hipponikos, the son of Kallias prosecuted the comic poet Autokles with a *graphe hybreos*, when during a quarrel over a field the latter punched him in the jaw. While this case confirms that the *graphe hybreos* could be used for violent attacks, we do not know whether it ever reached the courts, or anything else about it. It is noteworthy that Hipponikos was the richest man in Athens, so a procedure like *dike aikeias* would be pointless, since he did not need any compensation, and on the other hand he could so easily afford a fine of 1000 drachmas, if he badly lost the case. Still, since we are only told that Hipponikos prosecuted Autokles we may take it an indication that this is all that happened, and that this case too never went to trial. Conceivably, when the wrath of Hipponikos over the punch subsided, he found an honorable way to settle that did not involve a vengeful trial.

Apollodoros mentions one more possibility in the speech *Against Nikostratos*, which underlines the wide range of cases which this procedure could theoretically cover.[62] He says that during his dispute with Nikostratos, his opponent sent a citizen-born boy from the neighborhood to damage the flowering rose beds. They were hoping that Apollodoros would catch the boy and restrain him thinking that he was a slave. This would provide the excuse for a *hybris* prosecution against him. In any case this never happened. The entire body of the Attic Orators is littered with possible cases of *hybris* which never happened.[63] The question is why, when it came to the crunch, the litigants always chose a different avenue, in all the cases we know about, and the answer surely has to do with the viability of a *hybris* lawsuit, as well as the fact that there was a high risk involved in it and nothing to be gained from a successful prosecution other than vengeance. While it is possible that some of these cases went to court, we cannot verify this, and, as far as we can tell, it is equally possible that all these cases were part of legal maneuvering and were dropped before they went to trial, like the two cases above, on which we are better informed.

As a matter of fact, we cannot pinpoint a single case of a *graphe hybreos* that ever went to trial. This certainly corroborates the skepticism of MacDowell about the viability of a lawsuit where a prosecutor taking considerable risk had to dispute not the actions of his opponent, but his thoughts, attitudes and values, and trust the subjective judgment of the jurors to interpret these as he did. As for the risk, perhaps it may be useful to remember at this point that it only took a single heavy loss in a *graphe* prosecution for Aeschines to be disfranchised and compelled to leave Athens. When he did not secure the one 5th of the votes in the case *Against Ktesiphon*, he was unable to pay the fine of 1000 drachmas, became ἄτιμος and left the city, through the treacherous politics of which he had been skillfully navigating for most of his life. The risk was always substantial, and unless one was too rich to care and too thirsty for revenge to be hindered by rational considerations, a more profitable and less perilous procedure like the *dike aikeias* or the *dike biaion* would seem like much safer choice.

7.4 Non-violent conflict resolution: arbitration

The citizens of the democracy were expected to settle their differences without resort to violence, because this is what separated enlightened, civilized Athens form lawless barbarians. Democracy celebrated the rule of law over the right of might, while its citizens considered it to be their duty to help the weak prevail over the strong, when justice was on their side.[64] As Derek Roebuck has suggested, settling disputes through negotiation dialogue and compromise, before litigation or violence was central in the Athenian Democracy. Perhaps nothing demonstrates with greater clarity the firm intention of the first Democracy to resolve disputes through dialogue and compromise than its extensive use of arbitration.[65] By law, all private disputes were referred to an arbitrator appointed by the state (κληρωτὸς διαιτητής). All Athenian men served as public arbitrators during the 59th year of their life, the last one before they retired from active military service. One would imagine that by this stage of their lives they would have not only the necessary life experience but also the right temperament for the challenges of the job.

In many ways, a modern trial has more in common with an Athenian arbitration than with heliastic court trials. First, the proceedings did not need to be completed in one day. Parties could ask for postponement, or recess to present new evidence, women could give evidence too, and the process allowed for a more rigorous scrutiny of the facts through dialogue, questioning, requests for relevant evidence and further documentation, oaths or challenges, and as much back and forth as it was deemed necessary. Conceivably in such a setting one's rhetorical prowess would be far less decisive than it could be in the staged speeches of a court-trial.

The arbitrator could simply rule for one side, or he might try to strike a compromise. If he succeeded in working out a solution acceptable by both sides, it was more likely that the litigants would adhere to his ruling. However, if one side was still unhappy, they could appeal to the courts, and only then the case could come to trial. The decision of the court was final, but a determined litigant could always find a way to continue the fight through the courts, by bringing a different lawsuit (like for example a prosecution for false testimony against a key witness of his opponent). While arbitration was risk-free for litigants and witnesses alike (a prosecutor had to pay the arbitrator a *parastasis* fee of only one drachma[66]), once the case went to the courts, much more was at stake. The losing party would need to pay compensation, sometimes a hefty one, and also the πρυτανεῖα (a fee of up to 30 drachmas), while the witnesses for each side were responsible for their testimony and could be prosecuted for false witnesses by the litigant against whom they testified (ὑπεύθυνοι). Surely a reasonable compromise during the arbitration might seem appealing, if all these risks could be avoided, but the point need not be overstated, because angry people often do not behave reasonably.

The aforementioned risks of a court trial grew exponentially in public cases, where the prosecutor was risking a huge fine of 1000 drachmas, and the penalties were typically severe (e.g. a massive fine, disfranchisement, exile, confiscation of property or death). This is why it should not surprise us to see that the Athenians quite often behaved reasonably and chose a far less risky alternative. The quarreling parties had the option of bypassing the state system altogether and appointing their own arbitrators. The law (S 13) only required one arbitrator, but in practice people routinely appointed two or three (one from each side, and sometimes a tie-breaker, a third arbitrator trusted by both).[67] This guaranteed that each side was well represented and its interests would not be ignored. The ruling of the private arbitrators could not be appealed, since they had been selected by the quarreling parties themselves and enjoyed their trust for an impartial judgment. This rule probably would not stop a determined litigant from finding another avenue to pursue his case through the courts, but still it empowered private arbitration with the authority of the state and recognized its rulings as binding and final. In a private arbitration a compromise would be high on the agenda, and we have a few cases where seemingly absurd rulings were pronounced in order to effect this compromise.

Perhaps the clearest example of such a ruling is the one on the status of Neaira.[68] Two determined lovers were fighting over the splendid *hetaira*, and her personal freedom was at stake was. One of these men, Phrynion, was a former lover, who had paid dearly for her freedom but subsequently proved to be abusive and this is why she left him; the other, Stephanos, was her current lover, who had sworn to love and protect her for the rest of their lives. The judgment of the arbitrators was a compromise with each side gaining something important to them, but no one prevailing outright. Phrynion and Stephanos were to share the company of Neaira. She was going to stay for half a month with each man, while she had her personal freedom formally recognized, which meant that she did not need to face a trial to prove that she was a free person (ἀφαίρεσις εἰς ἐλευθερίαν).[69] But the most insightful part in the arbitrators' ruling was a provisional authorization to alter the arrangements by common agreement. The arbitrators understood that such an arrangement could not be long-lasting, and allowed it to be altered without further ado, if both sides were willing to accept the new terms. Their ruling was designed to mollify the bruised male egos and allow time and persuasion to procure a final resolution. Not long after Phrynion drops out of the picture. One would imagine that Neaira persuaded him to let her be with Stephanos, and eventually he accepted the situation.

Arbitration was a civilized and democratic alternative for the resolution of disputes, which did not entail the dangers of court trials, or the perilous consequences of a violent confrontation. It was safe and effective, assuming that the quarreling parties were willing to listen to the voice of reason and make concessions in order to resolve the case. In some important ways arbitration was the embodiment of democratic discourse as it allowed a resolution through negotiation, concession and the search for common ground, and served as a model of how a citizen in a democracy should aspire to deal with confrontations and violations of his own space and rights. Evidence, debate, fact-checking, the willingness to make concessions for the common good, and ultimately the rule of law over personal animosity and aggression, were the features of arbitration which made it a favorable option for the citizens of the First Democracy.

7.5 Sexual violence

A precise legal definition of the boundaries between sexual violence and consensual activities is one of the most elusive issues of our times, and perhaps it has been so throughout history. What the Greeks understood as rape, how they responded to it, and whether they considered it a more serious crime than consensual seduction (μοιχεία) have been vigorously debated since the 1990s when an article by Edward Harris challenged the orthodoxy that adultery was considered to be a more serious crime than rape. Harris argued that a man caught in the act with someone's wife would not be treated more leniently if he was a rapist; he could still be killed with impunity, or alternatively a rapist could still be prosecuted with a *graphe hybreos* and receive the death penalty.[70] In a more recent article Harris refined his views and questioned whether the modern concept of rape can be applied to the Athenian legal system altogether and argued that the Greeks did not have a precise equivalent.[71] Harris acknowledges that classical Athens was not free of sexual violence in real life and in art, but he tries to draw attention to the differences, the most substantial of which would be that rape in a male-dominated world was defined by the consequences which it had upon the *oikos*, rather than the victim.

Harris is undoubtedly right in his assertion that sexual violence does not exist in a cultural vacuum, and that it is defined within the context of the values and beliefs of a certain society. It is therefore imperative to try and understand sexual violence in context. The terminology of rape has much to tell us about Greek attitudes to it. In the legal documents of archaic and classical Athens we encounter expressions describing rape, like βίᾳ διαπράττεσθαι, βίᾳ αἰσχύνειν, βίᾳ πράττειν,[72] or adjectives describing violent acts (βιαίων).[73] The noun βιασμός, which is the primary term for rape all the way to the modern language, is first attested in Menander,[74] which suggests that the Greeks probably did not use a noun for rape until the time of Menander, because they understood it as an action, or a series of actions, and not as a legal concept. In all its expressions, either as a verbal process, as an adjective, or, from the later classical period, as a noun the one constant feature of rape in Greek is violence (βία), which suggests that rape was viewed and treated as a crime of violence.[75]

The view of Harris that rape was not treated as an offense less serious than adultery was effectively challenged by Christopher Carey and Roseanna Omitowoju.[76] Both reasserted the traditional view, also supported by MacDowell, that rape was a less serious offense than adultery.[77] The narrative of Lysias 1 *On the Murder of Eratosthenes* seems to support this position, although Stephen Todd has advised caution when taking the arguments made in the speech at face value.[78]

The evidence drawn from the actual laws on rape and adultery strongly supports the traditional view. Adultery was covered by an entire array of laws introduced over a period of 200 years,[79] and ranging from death with impunity for the killer, to the very severe penalties of bodily humiliations and unlimited confinement, which normally were only allowed for slaves.[80] Moreover, two different types of *graphai* were directly associated with it, one which allowed anyone who wished to prosecute someone for adultery (γραφὴ μοιχείας), and one which in some ways went in the opposite direction and was meant to protect citizens from fraudulent accusations of adultery (γραφὴ ἀδίκως ὡς μοιχὸν εἱρχθῆναι). By contrast rape was only covered by a private lawsuit for violence (δίκη βιαίων), which penalized the force exerted upon the victim, and the convicted defendant had to pay a sum assessed by the court in compensation to the victim, and an equal amount of it to the state. In the worst-case scenario, the convicted rapist would not be able to pay his fine to the state and suffer disfranchisement. Even in this extreme scenario, the penalty is much lighter, and the limited legal options, compared with the broad array of laws on adultery, confirm beyond reasonable doubt that adultery was seen as a much more serious offence, probably because, just as Lysias suggests, it required the consent and complicity of the woman, and her full cooperation in deceiving her *kyrios*, and as such it represented a constant threat from within for his *oikos* and the legitimacy of his children.[81]

The suggestion that rape amounted to *hybris*, and could therefore be punished through a *graphe hybreos*, first suggested by Harris, and accepted in some later studies, has been effectively answered by Carey.[82] While *hybris* remained a theoretical possibility for the victim of a sexual assault, the crime which such a lawsuit would seek to punish was not the sexual assault but the attitude of the aggressor, his contempt for the victim and the rules of civilized society. This is why, as explained above, a *graphe hybreos* remained a largely theoretical possibility, and there is not a single attested instance where the *graphe hybreos* was used to prosecute a sex offender, in any setting or scenario. Scholars sometimes have used the possibility of the *graphe hybreos* as a convenient solution for the inconvenient truth that the Greeks did not consider rape as serious an offense as adultery. Unlike adultery, which they clearly perceived to be a sexual crime, they viewed rape as a crime of violence in par with theft and physical assault, and the actual law on rape, which also penalizes property crimes and other violent incursions, confirms that they grouped it with violent crime, rather than with sexual offences.

7.6 Property crimes and disputes

Ever since the time of Solon Athens had been moving towards a free economy based increasingly on enterprise, business, trade and certain types of large scale manufacturing, like pottery, metalwork and cloth. This type of economic activity, when compared with the more traditional land ownership, was often translated in the texts of the classical period as a contrast between city and country, old aristocracy versus "the mob", or oligarchy versus democracy.[83] In the years of the Athenian empire the city had become a complex economy combining the old and the new, and this activity continued and occasionally intensified in the 4th century, when the city had to rely on its own ingenuity and enterprising spirit. This level of economic activity could not have continued without a transparent and workable system for settling financial disputes. Our sources attest several different types of lawsuits for economic disputes such as a trial for damages (δίκη βλάβης), a trial for money (δίκη ἀργυρίου), a trial for the produce (δίκη καρποῦ), or a trial for rent (δίκη ἐνοικίου).[84] Essentially these are all different manifestations of the same procedure, a private lawsuit to settle a financial dispute. If the sum which the prosecutor was claiming was greater than 100 drachmas but less than 1000 he had to pay an administrative fee of three drachmas (πρυτανεῖα). If the disputed sum was greater than 1000 drachmas, then the prosecutor had to pay a fee of 30 drachmas. If he prevailed, his opponent had to compensate him for the *prytaneia*, in addition to any other sum which he needed to pay.[85]

When two or more persons entered a competing claim to an estate, an inheritance, or some other right or privilege, the process of *diadikasia* was followed, where there were no prosecutors or defendants, and the claimants from an equal footing had to make their case, while the court was to decide who had the better claim. Women are often listed as claimants in *diadikasia* cases, as are magistrates in pursuit of official interests and even larger bodies like gene and demes.[86] Women would typically be represented by an advocate or some other representative in the ensuing trial. Since there were no prosecutors or defendants in *diadikasia* cases the process was risk-free for all parties.

Theft, arguably the most common and widespread among property crimes, was categorized in Athens, as in modern legal systems, according to the amount stolen and the circumstances under which the offence occurred. Non-violent theft of low-value items was a relatively light offence, while aggravated robbery could be punished by death with a summary arrest and subsequent execution. Someone had the right to search the house of a person he suspected of theft for the stolen goods. A passage of Aristophanes suggests that he needed to do so naked (γυμνούς), and the Scholiast of Aristophanes confirms that persons in search of public money or stolen objects had to enter naked, so as not to be able to implant anything into the house of their opponent.[87] A person who had evidence suggesting that someone had stolen from him could bring a prosecution for theft (δίκη κλοπῆς). If he prevailed, his opponent had to return the stolen property and pay in addition a sum equal to twice its value. If the court deemed it necessary, the thief could also be confined in the stocks for five days and nights and pay additional penalties (S 15).

Demosthenes attributes this law to Solon and the language of the document confirms that this is correct.[88] Demosthenes at this point mentions an entire array of Solonean laws on theft and praises the insight of the lawgiver to impose double penalties on convicted thieves, and publicly shame them for the rest of their lives.[89] The goal was, he says, to make sure that thieves had a lot to lose if they were caught, and the heightened risk should discourage such behavior. This is certainly the case with the Solonean laws on theft allowing for self-help. Killing a thief found in one's house, injuring him while fleeing from the crime-scene, or seizing him and haling him to the Eleven (*apagoge*), were all permitted by the Solonean law. Self-help is a predominant characteristic of the Draconian homicide law, allowed under specific circumstances,[90] and it is possible that Solon retained this feature from the Drakonian legislation on theft. The reasons why the law in this case would allow self-help are obvious. A home invasion, either during the day or at night, could lead the frightened members of the household to defensive action and result in injury or the death of the intruder. In this case the law was prepared to exonerate the killer of the invader, whether this happened in the house itself, or while the intruder was trying to escape.

The alternative of *apagoge* to the Eleven is an equally strong measure which the law applied, because if the offender confessed he was immediately put to death, and if he did not, but was convicted in the ensuing trial, he would still be put to death. The only difference compared with direct self-help was that the owner of the house, instead of spilling blood himself, with the intimidating religious consequences which bloodshed carried, he turned the offender to the magistrates of the state either for summary execution, or a trial resulting in the death penalty. *Apagoge* was permitted if someone was caught stealing anything at all during the night, or anything above the value of 50 drachmas during the day. The sum was reduced to ten drachmas if the person was caught stealing clothing, jars or other such ordinary items from gymnasia or harbors (λωποδύτης), one would imagine because such places were more vulnerable to thieves, and the law firmly wanted to discourage it with the most severe penalties. Stealing from a temple or stealing items of religious significance was punished with a fine amounting to ten times the value of the stolen goods.

There is no doubt that theft was considered to be a very serious offence in Athenian law and punished with rather extraordinary severity. The reasons for this may be historical. While our sources from the classical period preserve the image of a prosperous, law-abiding, democratic society, we can only guess what crime in Solonean Athens was like. In a society where most of the wealth was concentrated in a few hands, while the vast majority of the population was struggling to survive from year to year, to the point of having to borrow on their freedom in order to stay alive, one would imagine that property crime was high and home robberies not infrequent. In this social setting laws empowering individuals to defend their lives and homes at any cost would be deemed necessary, because they offered potential victims some reassurance and the means to respond to intruders, and also because they might function as a stronger deterrent for potential thieves and robbers than more standard law enforcement tactics.

In a city with a large trading economy largely based on seafaring mercantile and maritime laws were necessary and specifically designed to resolve commercial disputes as expediently as possible.[91] Such legislation came into effect in the early years of the Athenian empire, and with adjustments and modifications stayed in place for the remainder of the life of the *polis*. Its main characteristic was the push to resolve potential disputes rapidly before the sailing season. During the sailing season, namely the summer months from May to August, no such cases could be introduced to court, so as not to inhibit trade through potential disputes. The most common type of dispute seems to be over a loan to buy cargo, which used the cargo itself as security. The speech *Against Zenothemis* vividly describes one such dispute with all the tricks and twists employed by dishonest merchants trying to seize the cargo for themselves.[92]

An important part of the 5th century legislation intended to facilitate trade and commerce was the establishment of treaties with other cities (σύμβολα), which tried to reconcile differences in local laws, and provided for the speedier resolution of a case in the local courts where the dispute had erupted. This may have been less complicated than it sounds in the years of the Athenian empire, when the leading city had the means to make sure that the cities of the empire were run under a democratic constitution and with laws which although by no means identical were not too dissimilar to Athenian mercantile law. Such legislation was good for business and substantially contributed to the prosperity of the cities of the empire through the course of the 5th century.[93]

The polemarch, the magistrate in charge of aliens in Athens, the *nautodikai* and the *xenodikai* were the magistrates in charge of dealing with such cases, although we do not know for sure whether they simply introduced the cases to court, or actually resolved them. If the absence of commercial cases before the middle of the 4th century from the extant corpus of the Attic Orators is significant, then such cases were actually decided by these special magistrates through a process which was different from the adversarial speeches of a heliastic trial, and the aforementioned passage of Xenophon seems to be clearly hinting at that.[94]

Around the middle of the 4th century sweeping reforms did away with these arrangements and seemingly all distinctions along the lines of citizenship or nationhood. All mercantile and trade disputes were referred to ordinary courts, regardless of who the litigants were. In future citizens and aliens alike were to introduce such cases to the *thesmothetai*. MacDowell discussing the reasons for this change rightly concludes that

> Greek merchants in the 4th century were becoming a cosmopolitan community, in which the old distinctions of citizenship and nationality were unimportant. The new mercantile laws recognized this fact, and where an important step towards the unity of the Greek World.[95]

One additional reason maybe the fact that around the middle of the 4th century the Athenian economy relied much more heavily for its prosperity upon trade and commerce, now that the dreams of Empire had disintegrated along with the second Athenian League (355 BC).

An important part of the new legislation, which arose from the need to resolve quickly some types of financial disputes, in order to facilitate commerce and allow mariners to make the most of the sailing season, was the establishment of monthly lawsuits (ἔμμηνοι δίκαι). The *Athenaion Politeia* contains a list of such cases (S 17). The lawsuits on this list had to do with commerce, debts, disputes of property items, including slaves or domestic animals, or monthly interest on a capital. This is why it is surprising to find in the list cases of physical assault (αἰκείας). Since there is no good explanation why such cases belong to that list, it is possible that the author of the *Athenaion Politeia* included them by mistake, or that there is a textual error at this point.

MacDowell has accepted the view of Edward Cohen that monthly lawsuits could be submitted to the five *eisagogeis*, the magistrates in charge, every month, but the resolution of each case might take much longer than a month.[96] However, this does not make sense. What useful purpose would such legislation serve, and why would it matter when the lawsuit had been submitted, if the actual resolution could take years? And then, why would anyone need to go to court every month to claim the interest on a loan if he was not going to get his money any time soon? This legislation only makes sense if cases which demanded quick resolution, like the cases included in the list of the *Athenaion Politeia* (S 17), were actually resolved within a month. Let's say, if a person who owed interest for the month did not meet his obligations on the first day of the month, when such debts became due, he could be sued for the interest of this month, and the case needed to be resolved before next month's interest payment was due. This is why monthly lawsuits were particularly useful for mercantile disputes: the speedy resolution within a month guaranteed that visiting merchants would not be delayed in Athens for months and years at a time. The agony of Strepsiades in the beginning of the *Clouds*, as he is dreading the first day of the month when he needs to make payments to his debtors, or else be brought to court for the interest is what pushes him to enroll in the school of Socrates. His hope is to become so competent in oratory that he would defeat his debtors in court and evade payment. Even though the monthly lawsuits as we know them from the forensic documents of the middle 4th century had not been introduced in the time of Aristophanes, the anxiety of Strepsiades underlines the spirit which led to the introduction of the ἔμμηνοι δίκαι in the next century.

A well-known type of a monthly lawsuit is the one for the interest of a dowry (δίκη σίτου). If the former husband failed to return the dowry after a divorce he was liable to pay interest at a fixed rate of 18 percent.[97] The high interest rate was meant to discourage the former husband from keeping the dowry for too long, but if, let's say, he had tied the dowry into a business investment and was unable to return it for some time, the law made sure that the family of his former wife was adequately compensated and that the maintenance of the woman would be paid from the interest of her dowry, as the actual name of the lawsuit (*sitou*) suggested. If the family insisted in having the entire sum of the dowry returned, so as to be able to arrange another marriage for the woman, then a lawsuit for the return of the dowry (δίκη προικός) was the best option. However, if they were happy to receive the monthly interest payments for some time, then the dowry effectively functioned as a high interest loan.

The withheld dowry started accruing interest as soon as the husband sent his former wife back to her natal family or the wife left her husband and registered the divorce (ἀπόλειψις) with the *archon*, so as to make sure that her former husband could not dispute the date of the divorce and try to cheat his former wife out of the interest. If the monthly interest had not been paid for whatever reason, the woman's *kyrios* could sue for the interest. This was an *emmenos dike*, which could be repeated every month until the former husband paid his debts to the family and returned the dowry. We know that the venue for this kind of lawsuit was fixed. Every month the *eisagogeis* accepted *dikai sitou* at the Odeon of Pericles, which was also used as a court. It is likely that the *eisagogeis* accepted all monthly lawsuits at the Odeon, and not only those for the interest on the dowry. Given the scarcity of divorce in classical Athens, there would be no need for specific arrangements for the interest on the dowry and on account of this we can safely conclude that every month all *emmenoi dikai* were introduced and processed at the Odeon.

Observing the legislation of Athens related to property disputes we can discern two distinct tracks, one pertinent to the *oikos*, the other dictated by policies at the level of the *polis*. The laws related to the protection of the property of the *oikos* from thieves and robbers, as well as the related issues of the safety of its members, where ancient. Some went even as far back as the time of Drakon, while most have been introduced by Solon and stood for centuries with only minor modifications and additions through time. On the other hand, legislation related to the broader economic policies of the city was more susceptible to change and was aligned with the political and economic circumstances of the Athenian *polis*. In the 5th century, when the leading city was aiming at the creation of wealth throughout the empire, which in turn would enrich the coffers of the imperial capital in the form of tribute, Athens introduced extensive legislation intended to facilitate commerce and trade, and through international treaties established a legal framework for a speedier and fairer resolution of disputes between its citizens and her allies and trading partners. When all ambition for empire had disintegrated in the 4th century, the city needed to rely even more than before on the commercial genius of its citizens, while at the same time adopting a less imperious, more egalitarian, outward looking, inclusive and cosmopolitan attitude towards her trading partners in a rapidly changing world.

Notes

1 Translation: Andrew Wolpert (2011).
2 Translation Andrew Wolpert (2011).

3 See also Lys. 3.38, which adds confiscation of property as a penalty, on top of the exile. This was standard practice for offences punished with exile.

4 Translation by W.R.M. Lamb. While this interpretation of intent is undoubtedly customized to suit the best interests of the speaker, it seems to be corroborated by a passage of Plato (*Lg* 876e–877a): ἡ δὴ γραφὴ περὶ τραύματος ὧδε ἡμῖν κείσθω· Ἐάν τις διανοηθεὶς τῇ βουλήσει κτεῖναί τινα φίλιον, πλὴν ὧν ὁ νόμος ἐφίησιν, τρώσῃ μέν, ἀποκτεῖναι δὲ ἀδυνατήσῃ, τὸν διανοηθέντα τε καὶ τρώσαντα οὕτως οὐκ ἄξιον ἐλεεῖν, οὐδὲ αἰδούμενον ἄλλως ἢ καθάπερ ἀποκτείναντα ὑπέχειν τὴν δίκην φόνου ἀναγκάζειν· [Let the prosecution for wounding be as following: if someone deliberately attempts to kill a friend, except those permitted by the law, and injures him, but fails to kill him, the person who did the planning and inflicted the injury is not worthy of pity, or any kind of leniency, but is to be punished for murder, as if he had killed.]

5 Translation by Andrew Wolpert (2011).

6 Translation by Bernadotte Perrin. See also D. 20.104; 40.49.

7 See also D. 23.50 'ἄν τις κακῶς ἀγορεύῃ,' 'τὰ ψευδῆ' προσέθηκεν ["If someone is speaks ill of someone", "telling lies" he added.]

8 E.M. Harris (in Canevaro and Harris 2013: 231–233) has argued that this document is probably not authentic because some items which should have been included in the authentic document are not present. The document speaks about one arbitrator when often more than one were appointed, and it contains some grammatical forms and expressions which belong to a later time, but not to the language of a classical law. However, problems of missing content can be easily overcome, if we assume that the present piece is only a partial quotation of the law. Moreover, one arbitrator was legally sufficient, and one only has been appointed on several occasions (e.g. Isoc. 2.14; D. 40.16, 44; 52.14). The fact that litigants often appointed more than one (e.g. D. 33.14; 59.45) perhaps supports the authenticity of the document, as a forger might be tempted to use the plural; however, the lawgiver did not need to mention more than the legally required one arbitrator. The linguistic problems cited by Harris are not decisive either. (The forms μενέτωσαν and μεταφερέτωσαν are not attested before the second quarter of the 4th century but are in existence at the time when the speech was delivered; see MacDowell 1990: 228, Threatte *Grammar* 2, 462–466. The form τὰ κριθέντα is uncommon, but, again, not impossible as it is also attested in D. 23.66). Thus, the language of the document suggests a date not earlier than the second quarter of the 4th century, which may be taken to imply that this law was introduced to streamline arrangements on private arbitration which had been in existence long before. This law was wrongly inserted by a later editor in the place where the law on public arbitration was needed, and this may also speak for its authenticity; forgers tend to keep closely to the context, as they understand it. A forger would not compose the wrong law, but probably one that sounded like the right one. In terms of content, I agree with the comment of Kaja Harter-Uibopuu (2002: 54): "This law contains the main elements of arbitration in a very precise and short manner: the arbitrator is chosen by the two parties. According to the mutual agreement – which used to contain an implementary clause – the decision should be final and there is no way of transferring the dispute to a court."

9 Translation by Andrew Wolpert.

10 Translation by Harter-Uibopuu (2002: 47–69).

11 Translation by A.T. Murray.

12 Translation by H. Rackham.

13 Cohen 1995; Herman 2006.

14 See also Gilmore 1990. The suggestion that classical Athens conforms to the Mediterranean anthropological model is perilous. What we understand as the Mediterranean anthropological model is not a perennial and immutable standard but the result of thousands of years of cultural evolution with layers from many civilizations added upon the

Greek world over the centuries, Roman, Byzantine, Ottoman, Venetian, Western European and American, Christian, Islamic, Jewish, and so on. While modern Greece or Italy are geographically Mediterranean and undoubtedly have preserved some cultural elements defined by tradition and climate, in essence they are very different societies in many important ways from ancient Greece or Roman Italy, expectedly so, since they have been at the crossroads of diverse cultural influences for millennia.

15 A central tenet for Riess is that the lower classes did not resort to the courts as often, and instead they used religious avenues, such as curse tablets, to get back at their enemies. While there is some truth in this, the thesis is, in my opinion, exaggerated. The fact that most of the forensic speeches which have reached us were prepared by pricy logographers for affluent litigants is not necessarily significant. These 100 or so speeches, which have survived, must be a mere drop in the ocean, once we consider how many courts were operating every day in the city, and also that Athenian trials were concluded in a single day. The reason why these speeches have been preserved was that later antiquity rhetoricians were interested in their authors (except perhaps a few fortunate accidents of transmission, like for example the seven speeches of Apollodoros which were mistaken for Demosthenic texts). If anything, we sometimes hear the opposite, namely that it was rich people who avoided the courts and would rather pay off their prosecutors, because they had much more to lose (e.g. D. 58.65; Isoc. 3.15; Lys. 24.17).

16 Isoc. 20.3; Lys. 6.9. There are some similarities between this policy of the Athenian state and modern concepts of "zero tolerance" towards crime. Both accept, rightly or wrongly, that an early intervention can be effective in preventing escalation. See, for example, Greene 1999: 171–87.

17 Lys. 9.5–16.

18 D. 40.49 τῶν νόμων ἀπαγορευόντων μηδὲ τοὺς τῶν ἄλλων πατέρας κακῶς λέγειν τεθνεῶτας, οὗτος, οὗ φησιν υἱὸς εἶναι, τοῦτον λοιδορήσει, ᾧ προσῆκεν καὶ εἴ τις ἄλλος ἐβλασφήμει περὶ αὐτοῦ ἀγανακτεῖν. [When the laws forbid to speak ill even of the fathers of other people once they are deceased, he is going to mock the man whose son he claims to be, when it would have been appropriate to be indignant, if someone else had tried to mock him.] See also D. 20. 104.

19 *Lex.Rhet.Cant.* s.v. κακηγορίας = Hyp. Fr. 100 Jensen.

20 Hyp. *In Philippidem*, Fr. "Ar." 15b.2.

21 See also Lysias 10 passim; D. 18.123; 21–79–89; 58.40. For truth as a defense see D. 23.50.

22 Lys. 10. 6–15.

23 *Lex. Rhet. Cant.* s.v. κακηγορίας.

24 Isoc. 3.3; D. 21.88–89. See also the study of Serena Bianchetti (1981: 65–87).

25 The speaker assures the jury that under normal circumstances he would not have prosecuted Theomnestos, but in this case he did because Theomnestos had accused him of killing his father. Theomnestos had not actually used the forbidden word ἀνδροφόνος, but the speaker argues that this is an unimportant technicality, since the meaning of what he said amounted to the false use of the forbidden word.

26 D. 21.77 ff.

27 On public arbitration see Chapter 1.7.

28 Wolpert and Kapparis: 2011: 81. For a concise but informative account see the introduction of A. Wolpert (2011: 79–83).

29 See the discussion in Chapter 7.3.

30 Michael Gagarin (2005: 365–376) has pointed out that the opponents in disputes about violence go to great lengths to emphasize that their opponent started it all.

31 See for example D. 47.7, 9, 36, 39, 47.

32 The gripping narrative of Apollodoros, who undoubtedly has composed the speech *Against Euergos and Mnesiboulos* (D. 47), devotes almost a third of the speech to the

initial quarrel over some naval equipment, because it makes Theophemos look really bad and an irresponsible citizen, although, strictly speaking, it is of little relevance to the *pseudomartyrion* case.

33 On enmity in the Attic Orators see the excellent monograph of Andrew Alwine (2015).

34 This may also explain why he did not pursue his opponent for homicide. Since the old woman was only a libertine, a fine would be the typical penalty that his opponent could suffer for unintentional homicide. Instead, the speaker is capitalizing on the death of the woman and using it as a powerful weapon in this trial, and probably he would also use it in the subsequent *aikeias* trial, essentially putting his opponents on trial for her murder too, and subliminally imply to the jury that they could not possibly allow these killers to get away with it, because, if nothing else, they could risk the anger of the gods.

35 Several witnesses are invited to testify on the poor condition of the woman after the assault in section 67, one of whom may have been the attending physician.

36 D. 54.10.

37 Antiphon 3.5: Εἰ δέ τοι καὶ ὑπὸ τοῦ ἰατροῦ ἀπέθανεν . . . ὁ μὲν ἰατρὸς οὐ φονεὺς αὐτοῦ ἐστιν, ὁ γὰρ νόμος ἀπολύει αὐτόν [If he died because of the doctor . . . the doctor cannot be prosecuted as the killer, because the law absolves him]. Even the most skilled physician in the ancient world could not guarantee a cure, and even if he was quite confident that he could produce one for a certain condition, he could not guarantee that there would be no serious side effects. The Greeks understood the limitations of their medicine but were nevertheless prepared to trust it without asking too many questions. They did not *expect* to be cured by their physicians; they only hoped that they might be.

38 D. 54.11–12.

39 It might be worth remembering at this point that two warrior kings, Kambyses of Persia, and Emperor John II Komnenos, of Byzantium, both escaped the perils of years of warfare and court intrigue only to die from small accidental cuts during relaxation time. Herodotos (3.64) says that Kambyses died by a scratch from his sword on the thigh, while Ktesias (*FGrH* 3c 688 F13) gives a slightly different version saying that Kambyses died from a scratch on the thigh, as he was practicing his hobby of woodwork. Likewise, the narrative of Kinnamos (24–25) dramatically describes how an accidental scratch from an arrow in John's quiver got infected and resulted in the death of one of the most pious and beloved monarchs of Byzantium, and arguably of the empire along with him.

40 This possibility weighs heavily in the mind of Theophemos in the speech *Against Euergos and Mnesiboulos*, when he explains to the jury that he did his opponents the courtesy of inviting them to bring in their own physician to treat the old woman after the assault and make the best they could to avoid homicide charges; they did not do as he suggested, and then he invited his own physician who told him that the woman was on the verge of death (D. 47.62).

41 D. 23.22–24; Lys. 3.1 ὦ βουλή. Traditionally the Areopagos tried cases of deliberate homicide, deliberate wounding, deliberate poisoning and arson (Arist. Ath. 57.3 εἰσὶ δὲ φόν[ου] δίκαι καὶ τραύματος, ἂν μὲν ἐκ προνοίας ἀποκτείνῃ ἢ τρώσῃ, ἐν Ἀρείῳ πάγῳ, καὶ φαρμάκων, ἐὰν ἀποκτείνῃ δούς, καὶ πυρκαϊᾶς· ταῦτα γὰρ ἡ βουλὴ μόνα δικάζει.).

42 See Todd 1993: 268–76; Phillips 2007: 84; Hansen 315–16; MacDowell 1963: 92.

43 Dem. 54.18 τραύματος πάλιν εἰσὶν γραφαὶ; Aeschin. 2.93; 3.51, 212. Longo 1981: 246–61, supported by Pollux 8. 40 (where among others he speaks of *graphai phonou*, when homicide cases were certainly *dikai*, and *graphai traumatos*), and Arist. Ath. εἰσὶ δὲ φόν[ου] δίκαι καὶ τραύματος, ἂν μὲν ἐκ προνοίας ἀποκτείνῃ ἢ τρώσῃ, ἐν Ἀρείῳ πάγῳ, καὶ φαρμάκων, ἐὰν ἀποκτείνῃ δούς, καὶ πυρκαϊᾶς· ταῦτα γὰρ ἡ βουλὴ μόνα δικάζει. [The Areopagos Council tries prosecutions for murder and wounding, if someone intentionally kills or injures, and poisoning, if someone kills by giving a poison, and arson, and these are the only cases which the Council tries.]

44 Hansen 1983: 307–20.
45 MacDowell 1978: 124; Phillips 2007: 74–105.
46 For example, Todd 1993: 268–76
47 It is noteworthy that in both extant trauma speeches (Lys.3.18–19; 4.6–8.), and also in the rowdy Symposion of Lucian (17 ff.), when a bowl breaks out, which results in significant injuries, many more than two people are involved.
48 For a thorough and thoughtful discussion of this case see Spatharas 2006: 87–106, and the discussion by Stephen Todd (2013) on both speeches.
49 Lys. Fr. Carey.
50 For example, MacDowell 1978: 123–4; Phillips 2007: 74–105, Spatharas 2006: 105. On the other hand, Stephen Todd (1993: 268–76) is skeptical.
51 D. 54.18 is not really speaking about any weapon used by the assailant. This passage is actually speaking about the victim of the assault who when cornered might grab a stone or some other defensive weapon in self-defense. In this respect, its testimony in support of the view that a weapon marked the line between *aikeia* and *trauma* is problematic. The other passage (Lys. 4.6) is equally problematic. The speaker makes a remark that if he was planning to kill his opponent, he might have brought a knife, and the fact that he didn't should be taken as evidence that he did not intend to kill him. This does not necessarily mean that without the knife the case could not be *trauma*.
52 D. 40.32–3.
53 For a more thorough definition of intent see Loomis 1972: 86–95.
54 Rowe 1993: 397–406. For an understanding of *hybris* as a cultural construct, as well as a rhetorical instrument see: Fisher 1992; 1997: 44–84; 2005: 67–89; Cairns 1996: 1–32; Gagarin 1979: 229–36; MacDowell 1976: 14–31; 1978: 129–32; Spatharas 2009: 30–52; Todd 1993: 270–1; Harris 2004: 41–83 (especially in connection to sexual violence).
55 Fisher 2005: 69–89; see also Fisher 1992, and 1998: 68–97.
56 X. *Ath.* 3.5; MacDowell 1976: 28–9; contrary Harris 2004: 63, n. 44. The key phrase διὰ χρόνου in the *Old Oligarch* means "throughout the year" and indicates that prosecutions for some offences like *hybris* or impiety were not fixed to a specific time in the calendar year and could be introduced to court at any time. However, it does not indicate *how often* such prosecutions were submitted. Harris has overstated the significance of this passage to boost his argument.
57 These cases are: Deinarchos *Against Proxenos*, *Apology of hybris for Epichares*; Lysias *Against Callias*, *To Sostratos*; Ps-Lysias *Against Diocles*.
58 Edward Harris (2008: 81) understood that the *probole* was only an advisory process, and that the case went to court through a *graphe hybreos*. However, the critical passage from the speech itself does not seem to support this interpretation: D. 21.28: μὴ δὴ τοῦτο λέγειν αὐτὸν ἐᾶτε, ὅτι καὶ δίκας ἰδίας δίδωσ' ὁ νόμος μοι καὶ γραφὴν ὕβρεως· δίδωσι γάρ· ἀλλ' ὡς οὐ πεποίηκεν ἃ κατηγόρηκα, ἢ πεποιηκὼς οὐ περὶ τὴν ἑορτὴν ἀδικεῖ, τοῦτο δεικνύτω· τοῦτο γὰρ αὐτὸν ἐγὼ προὐβαλόμην, καὶ περὶ τούτου τὴν ψῆφον οἴσετε νῦν ὑμεῖς. [Do not allow him to tell you that the law also permits private *dikai* and a *graphe hybreos*. Yes it does. However, he should prove that either he did not do what I am accusing him of doing, or although he did these things he has not violated the sanctity of the festival. This is what I am accusing him of through this probole, on which you will be casting your vote.] Demosthenes says that although the law allowed him several possibilities, such as a private lawsuit, or a *graphe hybreos*, he did not choose any of these, but instead chose the *probole*, because the assault happened during the festival, and this was the most appropriate procedure. He also explicitly confirms that the case on which the jury was about to vote was the *probole*. MacDowell is convinced that the current case was a *probole*, which Meidias lost, and was fined 30 *minae* (Aesch. 3.52). Andrew Wolpert in his 2011 study of the speech agreed with the conclusions of MacDowell (Wolpert and Kapparis 2011: 79–83). Aeschines thinks

that Demosthenes sold out in this case, and that he could have exacted a much more severe punishment, but, to be fair, 30 minae was a truly hefty fine for a mere punch, and Demosthenes was able to exact such a hefty punishment only because it happened during the festival. This penalty also suggests that the case was not a *graphe hybreos*. One would imagine that the successful prosecutor in a *graphe hybreos* would request the death penalty, just as D. 54,1 suggests. See also the discussion in Chapter 8.4.

59 D. 45.4–5. Pasion while in his deathbed left a will in which he betrothed his wife and mother of his two sons to Phormion, with a significant dowry. He also made Phormion the guardian of his younger, still-underage son Pasikles, probably because he was worried that his extravagant elder son would squander much of the property before Pasikles came of age. His elder son Apollodoros was 24 years old, and at the time he was absent on a trierarchy. Strictly speaking, the will of Pasion was not legally binding, since a Solonean law did not allow a man who had living legitimate sons to make a will (see Chapters 5.2. and 5.6.). At best it should be considered to be an advisory document of his wishes to his family and could not be enforced in a court of law. If Apollodoros, the sole adult male left in the *oikos* of Pasion, had chosen at that point to act as the *kyrios* and take control of the estate and the guardianship of his brother, and take back his mother, no one would have a legal right to stop him. However, we are told that children were already born to this mother from Phormion, and he alludes to a premarital relationship between his mother and Phormion on which he refuses to give details out of respect for her. Thus, Apollodoros found himself before a fait accompli and was forced to accept the marriage of his mother and try to settle the property affairs. At least this is what he says. In reality, probably the arrangement suited this young, rich play-boy, as I have argued in Chapter 5.6. He did not have to shoulder the responsibility of looking after his mother and younger brother, and Phormion would be doing most of the work in the bank, while himself could be enjoying the benefits of the arrangement. This is probably the real reason why he went along with it, and only later, when these arrangements did not work as he had anticipated, he engaged in prolonged litigation with his step-father and brother.

60 Is. 8.40–1.

61 Hyp. Fr. 97 Jensen.

62 D. 53.16.

63 There are 444 references to *hybris* and *hybris*tic behavior in the Attic orators, according to the TLG. Some famous cases include the *probole* against Meidias, the case *Against Lochites* (on the process, and why *hybris* was not chosen to prosecute Lochites see Spatharas 2009: 30–52), and homicide trial on the killing of Eratosthenes, where the defendant Eupiletos actually tells the *ephetai* at the Delphinion court that Eratosthenes committed *hybris* against him personally, when he decided to enter his house and seduce his wife (ἐμὲ αὐτὸν ὕβρισεν εἰς τὴν οἰκίαν τὴν ἐμὴν εἰσιών).

64 See for example Hyp. *Lyc*. Ar. 9: ἤ ἔστιν τι τῶν ἐν τῆι πόλει τούτου δημοτικώτερον, τοῦ τοὺς δυναμένους εἰπεῖν τοῖς ἀδυνάτοις τῶν πολιτῶν κινδυνεύουσι βοηθεῖν. [Is there anything more democratic in the city than those who are capable speakers helping those citizens who are not good with speaking, when they are in court?]. Th. 6.38; Isoc.18.20; 21.178; Sch. Dem. 22.91.

65 For a glimpse into the role and importance of arbitration in democracy see Reuben 2004: 279–320; Roebuck 2001.

66 Harp. s.v. παράστασις

67 See also n. 8.

68 D. 59.45–8.

69 See Chapter 2.7.

70 See Harris 1990: 370–77.

71 Harris 2004: 41–83.

72 See Lys. 32–3; Harp. s.v. βιαίων

73 D. 37.33; Lys. Fr. 140 Carey *Κατὰ Φιλωνίδου βιαίων*; Harp. s.v. βιαίων.

74 Men. *Ep*. 435; *Sam*. 278. The assertion of the *Anonymus Seguerianus* (s.v. βιασμός) that Eupolis (Fr. 64) used this word is not helpful in any way, as there is no context, and for all we know this usage might have nothing to do with sexual assault.

75 In Latin on the other hand the emphasis in the noun *raptus* (from which the English "rape" is derived) is in the act of seizing something which does not belong to the person who took it, from the stem of *rapio* "to seize and carry off." The Greek equivalent ἁρπαγή, although it often refers to rape, especially in mythology, has a softer tone to it, as it typically is an act motivated by infatuation or eros, and at least in poetry it can be seen as a privilege and an honor for the victim, like the ἁρπαγὴ of Ganymede by Zeus in the form of an eagle, or that of Europa by Zeus in the form of a bull.

76 Carey 1995: 407–17; Omitowoju 2002.

77 MacDowell 1978: 124–6

78 Todd 1993: 276–7.

79 On the adultery laws see the discussion in Chapter 6.3.

80 It must be noted that impunity for bodily humiliations was also considered a very severe penalty, as a decree introduced in the *archon*ship of Skamandrios strictly prohibited the torture or physical abuse of free persons and marked the dividing line between free men and slaves. The adultery law of Solon allowed the cuckolded *kyrios* of an adulteress to treat her lover like his slave.

81 Lys. 1.32–3: τῶν μὲν γὰρ θάνατον κατέγνω, τοῖς δὲ διπλῆν ἐποίησε τὴν βλάβην, ἡγούμενος τοὺς μὲν διαπραττομένους βίᾳ ὑπὸ τῶν βιασθέντων μισεῖσθαι, τοὺς δὲ πείσαντας οὕτως αὐτῶν τὰς ψυχὰς διαφθείρειν, ὥστ' οἰκειοτέρας αὑτοῖς ποιεῖν τὰς ἀλλοτρίας γυναῖκας ἢ τοῖς ἀνδράσι, καὶ πᾶσαν ἐπ' ἐκείνοις τὴν οἰκίαν γεγονέναι, καὶ τοὺς παῖδας ἀδήλους εἶναι ὁποτέρων τυγχάνουσιν ὄντες, τῶν ἀνδρῶν ἢ τῶν μοιχῶν. [He assigned death as a punishment for the latter and double damages for the former because he recognized that those that accomplish their ends with force are hated by those who are violated. Those who use persuasion so corrupt the women's minds that they make other men's wives closer to themselves than their husbands and all of the household becomes under their control, and it becomes uncertain who are the children's fathers, the husbands or the seducers. The lawgiver, therefore, established the death penalty for them.] See also Ogden 1997: 25–241.

82 Harris 1990; Threatt 2009: 87–8.

83 Important texts highlighting these tensions are the pseudo-Xenophontean The *Old Oligarch* (or *Athenian Constitution*), and the opening part of the *Clouds* of Aristophanes,

84 For example, D. 29.16; 49.20; 52.16; 48.45; Harp. s.v. καρποῦ δίκη;

85 D. 47.64; Pol. 8.38; Ar. *Nu* 1131–200.

86 See, for example, D. 28.17; 43.7; 44.40; Lyk. Fr. 7, and Fr. 20 Conomis; Carawan 2010: 381–400; Fabbri 2014: 35–44.

87 Ar. *Nu*. 499 and Sch. Ar. *Nu*. 499.

88 D. 24.114.

89 D. 24. 114–15: ᾤετο γὰρ δεῖν τόν γε τὰ αἴσχρ' ἔργ' ἐργαζόμενον μὴ ἃ ὑφείλετο μόνον ἀποδόντ' ἀπηλλάχθαι (πολλοὶ γὰρ [ἂν] αὐτῷ ἐδόκουν οὕτω γ' οἱ κλέπται ἔσεσθαι, εἰ μέλλοιεν λαθόντες μὲν ἕξειν, μὴ λαθόντες δ' αὐτὰ μόνον καταθήσειν), ἀλλὰ ταῦτα μὲν διπλάσια καταθεῖναι, δεθέντα δὲ πρὸς τούτῳ τῷ τιμήματι ἐν αἰσχύνῃ ζῆν ἤδη τὸν ἄλλον βίον. [He thought that the person who committed shameful acts, should not be absolved after returning only what he took, because this way would become thieves thinking that if they avoided detection, they could keep their booty, if they got caught, they would only have to return what they took. For this reason he ordered that the penalty was to be double the value of the stolen object, and that in addition to this penalty he was to be bound, and live in shame the rest of his life.]

90 See the discussion in Chapter 8.5.

91 It is possible that certain months of the year were allocated to the trial of specific lawsuits, so that those living outside Athens knew when their presence in the city would be required, when they had a part to play in such cases (MacDowell 1978: 224–34).

However, the evidence for this is not clear. What is more certain is that the Athenians tried to have mercantile cases resolved during the sailing season, with varying degrees of success as a passage of Xenophon (Vect. 3.3) indicates, which expresses dissatisfaction at the pace of such proceedings and bemoans the damage they are doing to trade: εἰ δὲ καὶ τῇ τοῦ ἐμπορίου ἀρχῇ ἆθλα προτιθείη τις ὅστις δικαιότατα καὶ τάχιστα διαιροίη τὰ ἀμφίλογα, ὡς μὴ [ἀπο]κωλύεσθαι ἀποπλεῖν τὸν βουλόμενον, πολὺ ἂν καὶ διὰ ταῦτα πλείους τε καὶ ἥδιον ἐμπορεύοιντο. [If someone were to offer prizes for the mercantile magistrates who processed disputes as fairly and rapidly as possible, so that someone willing to sail was not prevented, for these reasons many more people would take up commerce with greater eagerness.]

92 On the speech Against Zenothemis see the introduction and notes by Andrew Wolpert (Wolpert and Kapparis 2011: 13–149). On trade and maritime law see Cohen 1973; 1963; 1997; 1990: 57–79; 2015: 393–424; Millett 1983: 36–52; de Ste Croix 1984: 41–59; Garnsey et al. 1983; Morley 2007; Reed 2003; Von Reden 1995: 24–37; Casson 1990: 195–206.

93 The standard study for the *symbola* is Gauthier 1972; see also his later study for such treaties in the Hellenistic period (1999: 157–174). Among primary sources important are *IG* ii^2 46, a treaty between Athens and Troizen, and 144, which although badly mutilated provides hints for the large variety of legal matters covered by such treaties; Th. 1.77.1; Antiphon 5.78.

94 X. *Vect.* 3.3.

95 MacDowell 1978: 234.

96 MacDowell 1978: 231–4; Cohen 1973: 23–59.

97 D. 59.52 ἐπ’ ἐννέ’ ὀβολοῖς τοκοφορεῖν. 9 obols to the mina for the month, would amount to 18 drachmas per mina (100 drachmas) per annum.

8 Religion, the state and the law

8.1 Sources

1 The religious and judicial duties of the *basileus*

ὁ] δὲ <βασιλεὺς> πρῶτον μὲν μυστηρίων ἐπιμελεῖ[ται μετὰ τῶν ἐπι μελητῶν ὧ]ν ὁ δῆμ[ος χ]ειροτονεῖ, δύο μὲν ἐξ Ἀθηναίων ἁπάντων, ἕνα δ' [ἐξ Εὐμολπιδῶν, ἕνα] δ' ἐκ Κηρ[ύκω]ν. ἔπειτα Διονυσίων τῶν ἐπὶ Ληναίῳ· ταῦτα δέ ἐστι [πομπή τε καὶ ἀγών. τ]ὴν μὲν οὖν πομπὴν κοινῇ πέμ‖πουσιν ὅ τε βασιλεὺς καὶ οἱ ἐπιμεληταί, τὸν δὲ ἀγῶνα διατίθησιν ὁ βασιλεύς. τίθησι δὲ καὶ τοὺς τῶν λαμπάδων ἀγῶνας ἅπαντας· ὡς δ' ἔπος εἰπεῖν καὶ τὰς πατρίους θυσίας διοικεῖ οὗτος πάσας. γραφαὶ δὲ λαγχάνονται πρὸς αὐτὸν ἀσεβείας, κἄν τις ἱερωσύνης ἀμφισβητῇ πρός τινα. διαδικάζει δὲ καὶ τοῖς γένεσι καὶ τοῖς ἱερεῦσι τὰς ἀμφισβητήσεις τὰς ὑπὲρ τῶν ἱερῶν ἁπάσας οὗτος. λαγχάνονται δὲ καὶ αἱ τοῦ φόνου δίκαι πᾶσαι πρὸς τοῦτον, καὶ ὁ προαγορεύων εἴργεσθαι τῶν νομίμων οὗτός ἐστιν. εἰσὶ δὲ φόν[ου] δίκαι καὶ τραύματος, ἂν μὲν ἐκ προνοίας ἀποκτείνῃ ἢ τρώσῃ, ἐν Ἀρείῳ πάγῳ, καὶ φαρμάκων, ἐὰν ἀποκτείνῃ δούς, καὶ πυρκαϊᾶς· ταῦτα γὰρ ἡ βουλὴ μόνα δικάζει. τῶν δ' ἀκουσίων καὶ βουλεύσεως, κἂν οἰκέτην ἀποκτείνῃ τις ἢ μέτοικον ἢ ξένον, οἱ ἐπὶ Παλλαδίῳ. ἐὰν δ' ἀποκτεῖναι μέν τις ὁμολογῇ, φῇ δὲ κατὰ τοὺς νόμους, οἷον μοιχὸν λαβών, ἢ ἐν πολέμῳ ἀγνοήσας, ἢ ἐν ἄθλῳ ἀγωνιζόμενος, τούτ[ῳ] ἐπὶ Δελφινίῳ δικάζουσιν· ἐὰν δὲ φεύγων φυγὴν ὧν αἴδεσίς ἐστιν, αἰτίαν ἔχῃ ἀποκτεῖναι ἢ τρῶσαί τινα, τούτῳ δ' ἐν Φρεάτου δικάζουσιν, ὁ δ' ἀπολογεῖται προσορμισάμενος ἐν πλοίῳ. δικάζουσι δ' οἱ λαχόντες τα, πλὴν τῶν ἐν Ἀρείῳ πάγῳ γιγνομένων, εἰσάγει δ' ὁ βασιλεύς, καὶ δικάζο[υ]σιν ἐν ἱερ[ῷ] καὶ ὑπαίθριοι, καὶ ὁ βασιλεὺς ὅταν δικάζῃ περιαιρεῖται τὸν στέφανον. ὁ δὲ τὴν αἰτίαν ἔχων τὸν μὲν ἄλλον χρόνον εἴργεται τῶν ἱερῶν, καὶ οὐδ' εἰς τὴν ἀγορὰν ν[όμος] ἐμβαλεῖν αὐτῷ. τότε δ' εἰς τὸ ἱερὸν εἰσελθὼν ἀπολογεῖται. ὅταν δὲ μὴ εἰδῇ τὸν ποιήσαντα, τῷ δράσαντι λαγχάνει, δικάζει δ' ὁ βασιλεὺς καὶ οἱ φυλοβασιλεῖς, καὶ τὰς τῶν ἀψύχων καὶ τῶν ἄλλων ζῴων.

(Arist. *Ath. Pol.* 57)

The Basileus in the first place superintends the mysteries, in conjunction with the Superintendents of Mysteries. The latter are elected in the

Assembly by open vote, two from the general body of Athenians, one from the Eumolpidae, and one from the Ceryces. Next, he superintends the Lenaean Dionysia, which consists of a procession and a contest. The procession is ordered by the Basileus and the Superintendents in conjunction; but the contest is managed by the Basileus alone. He also manages all the contests of the torch-race; and to speak broadly, he administers all the ancestral sacrifices. Indictments for impiety come before him, or any disputes between parties concerning priestly rites; and he also determines all controversies concerning sacred rites for the ancient families and the priests. All actions for homicide come before him, and it is he that makes the proclamation requiring polluted persons to keep away from sacred ceremonies. Actions for homicide and wounding are heard, if the homicide or wounding be willful, in the Areopagus; so also in cases of killing by poison, and of arson. These are the only cases heard by that Council. Cases of unintentional homicide, or of intent to kill, or of killing a slave or a resident alien or a foreigner, are heard by the court of Palladium. When the homicide is acknowledged, but legal justification is pleaded, as when a man takes an adulterer in the act, or kills another by mistake in battle, or in an athletic contest, the prisoner is tried in the court of Delphinium. If a man who is in banishment for a homicide which admits of reconciliation incurs a further charge of killing or wounding, he is tried in Phreatto, and he makes his defense from a boat moored near the shore. All these cases, except those which are heard in the Areopagus, are tried by the Ephetae on whom the lot falls. The Basileus introduces them, and the hearing is held within sacred precincts and in the open air. Whenever the Basileus hears a case he takes off his crown. The person who is charged with homicide is at all other times excluded from the temples, nor is it even lawful for him to enter the marketplace; but on the occasion of his trial he enters the temple and makes his defense. If the actual offender is unknown, the writ runs against "the doer of the deed." The Basileus and the tribe-*basileus* also hear the cases in which the guilt rests on inanimate objects and the lower animal.[1]

2 The duties of the *basileus* concerning the management of sacred properties

εἰσφέρει δὲ καὶ ὁ βασιλεὺς τὰς μισθώσεις τῶν <τε>μενῶν, ἀναγράψας ἐν γραμματεί[οις λελ]ε[υ]κωμένοις. ἔστι δὲ καὶ τούτων ἡ μὲν μίσθωσις εἰς ἔτη δέκα, καταβάλλεται δ' ἐπὶ τῆς [θ′] πρυτανείας. διὸ καὶ πλεῖστα χρήματα ἐπὶ ταύτης συλλέγεται τῆς πρυτανείας. εἰσφέρεται μὲν οὖν εἰς τὴν βουλὴν τὰ γραμματεῖα κατὰ τὰς καταβολὰς ἀναγεγραμμένα, τηρεῖ δ' ὁ δημόσιος·

(Arist. *Ath. Pol.* 47)

Further, the *basileus* brings before the Council the leases of the sacred enclosures, written on whitened tablets. These too are leased for ten years, and the instalments are paid in the *prytany*; consequently it is in this *prytany* that the greatest amount of money is collected. The tablets containing the lists of the instalments are carried into the Council, and the public clerk takes charge of them.

3 All priests and priestesses are responsible under the law

Οἷον τοὺς ἱερέας καὶ τὰς ἱερείας ὑπευθύνους εἶναι κελεύει ὁ νόμος, καὶ συλλήβδην ἅπαντας καὶ χωρὶς ἑκάστους κατὰ σῶμα, τοὺς τὰ ἱερὰ μόνον λαμβάνοντας καὶ τὰς εὐχὰς ὑπὲρ ὑμῶν πρὸς τοὺς θεοὺς εὐχομένους, καὶ οὐ μόνον ἰδίᾳ, ἀλλὰ καὶ κοινῇ τὰ γένη, Εὐμολπίδας καὶ Κήρυκας καὶ τοὺς ἄλλους ἅπαντας.

(Aesch. 3.18)

For example, the law directs that priests and priestesses be subject to audit, all collectively, and each severally and individually – persons who receive perquisites only, and whose occupation is to pray to heaven for you; and they are made accountable not only separately, but whole priestly, families together, the Eumolpidae, the Ceryces, and all the rest.[2]

4 The law on the *probole*

ἀναγνώσεται δὲ πρῶτον μὲν ὑμῖν τὸν νόμον καθ' ὃν εἰσὶν αἱ προβολαί· μετὰ δὲ ταῦτα καὶ περὶ τῶν ἄλλων πειράσομαι διδάσκειν. Λέγε τὸν νόμον.

> ΝΟΜΟΣ: Τοὺς πρυτάνεις ποιεῖν ἐκκλησίαν ἐν Διονύσου τῇ ὑστεραίᾳ τῶν Πανδίων. ἐν δὲ ταύτῃ χρηματίζειν πρῶτον μὲν περὶ ἱερῶν, ἔπειτα τὰς προβολὰς παραδιδότωσαν τὰς γεγενημένας ἕνεκα τῆς πομπῆς ἢ τῶν ἀγώνων τῶν ἐν τοῖς Διονυσίοις, ὅσαι ἂν μὴ ἐκτετισμέναι ὦσιν.

Ὁ μὲν νόμος οὗτός ἐστιν, ὦ ἄνδρες Ἀθηναῖοι, καθ' ὃν αἱ προβολαὶ γίγνονται, λέγων, ὥσπερ ἠκούσατε, ποιεῖν τὴν ἐκκλησίαν ἐν Διονύσου μετὰ τὰ Πάνδια, ἐν δὲ ταύτῃ ἐπειδὰν χρηματίσωσιν οἱ πρόεδροι περὶ ὧν διῴκηκεν ὁ ἄρχων, χρηματίζειν καὶ περὶ ὧν ἄν τις ἠδικηκὼς ᾖ περὶ τὴν ἑορτὴν ἢ παρανενομηκώς, καλῶς, ὦ ἄνδρες Ἀθηναῖοι, καὶ συμφερόντως ἔχων ὁ νόμος, ὡς τὸ πρᾶγμ' αὐτὸ μαρτυρεῖ.

(D. 21.8–9)

He will first read to you the law that establishes *probolai.* Next I will attempt to explain the other matters. Read the law.

> LAW: The *prytaneis* convene the Assembly in the precinct of Dionysus on the day after the Pandia. At this meeting, they conduct business first on sacred matters, then let them bring forth the *probolai* that there are for the procession or the contests at the Dionysia and whichever have not been paid for.

This is the law, men of Athens, for which there are *probolai*, and it states, as you have heard, to convene the Assembly in the precinct of Dionysus after the Pandia, and here, after the presiding officers (*proedroi*) bring to a consideration matters that the *archon* oversees, to deliberate also about the offenses or violations anyone has committed concerning the festival. This law is good, men of Athens, and useful, as the dispute itself shows.[3]

5 *Probole* against *sykophants*

> ἐπὶ δὲ τῆς ἕκτης πρυτανείας πρὸς τοῖς εἰρημένοις καὶ περὶ τῆς ὀστρακοφορίας ἐπιχειροτονίαν διδόασιν, εἰ δοκεῖ ποιεῖν ἢ μή, καὶ συκοφαντῶν προβολὰς τῶν Ἀθηναίων καὶ τῶν μετοίκων μέχρι τριῶν ἑκατέρων, κἄν τ[ι]ς ὑποσχόμενός τι μὴ ποιήσῃ τῷ δήμῳ
>
> (Arist. *Ath. Pol.* 43.5)

In the sixth presidency in addition to the business specified they take a vote on the desirability of holding an ostracism, and on preliminary informations against persons charged as malicious informers, citizens and resident aliens, up to the number of not more than three cases of either class, and charges of failure to perform a service promised to the People.[4]

6 Late 5th century copy of Drakon's homicide law[5]

Διόγν[ε]τος Φρεάρριος ἐγραμμάτε[υε]·
Διοκλε̄ς ἐ̄ρχε·
ἔ̣δοχσεν τε̄ι βουλε̄ι καὶ το̄ι δέμοι· Ἀκα[μ]αντ̣ὶς ἐπ[ρ]υτάνευε, [Δ]ιό[γ]-
νετος ἐγραμμάτευε, Εὐθύδικος [ἐ]πεστάτε, ..Ε.3ΑΝΕΣ εἶπε· τὸ[ν]
Δράκοντος νόμον τὸμ περὶ το̄ φό[ν]ο ἀναγρα[φ]σά[ν]τον οἱ ἀναγραφε̄-
ς το̄ν νόμον παραλαβόντες παρὰ το̄ β[α]σ̣[ι]λ̣έ[ος με]τ[ὰ το̄ γραμμ]ατέο-
ς τε̄ς βουλε̄ς ἐστέλει λιθίνει καὶ κα[τ]α[θ]έντ[ον πρός]θε[ν] τε̄ς στο-
ᾶς τε̄ς βασιλείας· οἱ δὲ πολεταὶ ἀ̣πομι[σθο]ς[άντον κατὰ τὸν ν]όμο-
ν, οἱ δὲ ἑλλενοταμίαι δόντον τὸ ἀρ[γ]ύ[ρ]ι[ον].
προ̄τος ἄχσον.
καὶ ἐὰμ μὲ 'κ ἐκ [π]ρονοί[α]<ς> [κ]<τ>[ένει τίς τινα, φεύγ]ε[ν· δ]ι-
κάζεν δὲ τὸς βασιλέας αἴτ̣ιο[ν] φό̣ν̣[ο] [β]ολ-
εύσαντα· τὸς δὲ ἐφέτας διαγν[ο̄]ν̣[α]ι. [αἰδέσασθαι δ' ἐὰμ μὲν πατὲ]ρ ε̄-
ι ε̄ ἀδελφὸ[ς] ε̄ hυε̄ς, hάπαντ[α]ς, ε̄ τὸν κ̣ο[λύοντα κρατε̄ν· ἐὰν δὲ μὲ] ḥο̄-
τοι ο̄σ̣ι, μέχρ' ἀνεφ[σι]ότετος κ̣αὶ [ἀνεφσιο̄, ἐὰν hάπαντες αἰδές]α̣ς-
θαι ἐθέλοσι, τὸν κο[λύ]ον̣τα [κ]ρα[τε̄ν· ἐὰν δὲ τούτον μεδὲ hε̄ς ε̄ι, κτ]έ-
νει δὲ ἄκο[ν], γνο̄σι δὲ ḥοι [πε]ντ[έκοντα καὶ hε̄ς hοι ἐφέται ἄκοντ]α̣
κτε̄ναι, ἐσέ<ς>θ[ο]ν δὲ ḥ[οι φ]ρ[άτορες ἐὰν ἐθέλοσι δέκα· τούτος δ]ὲ ḥο̣-
ι πεντέκο[ν]τ[α καὶ] hε̄ς ἀ<ρ>[ι]στ̣[ίνδεν hαιρέσθον. καὶ hοι δὲ πρ] ότε[ρ]-
ον κτέ[ν]α[ντ]ε[ς ἐν] το̄[ιδε το̄ι θεσμο̄ι ἐνεχέσθον. προειπε̄ν δ]ὲ το̄ι κ-
τέν̣α̣ν̣[τι ἐν ἀ]γορ[ᾶι μέχρ' ἀνεφσιότετος καὶ ἀνεφσιο̄· συνδιόκ]εν
δὲ [κ]ἀνεφς[ιὸς καὶ ἀνεφσιο̄ν παῖδας καὶ γαμβρὸς καὶ πενθερὸ]ς κ-
αὶ φρ[ά]τ[ο]<ρ>[ας .] αἴτι-
ος [ε̄ι] φό[νο .1226.12 τὸς πεντέκοντ]α κ̣αὶ
hένα . φόνο
hέ̣λ̣ος[ι .1635.17 ἐὰν δ]έ [τ]ις τ-
ὸ[ν ἀν]δ̣ρ[οφόνον κτένει ε̄ αἴτιος ε̄ι φόνο, ἀπεχόμενον ἀγορᾶ]ς ἐφο-

ρί[α]ς κ[α]ὶ [ἄθλον καὶ hιερο͂ν Ἀμφικτυονικο͂ν, hόσπερ τὸν Ἀθεν]αῖον κ-
[τένα]ν[τα, ἐν τοῖς αὐτοῖς ἐνέχεσθαι· διαγιγνόσκεν δὲ τὸς] ἐ[φ]έτα[ς]
.3Ε.1839.19τει ἐμεδ-
[απεῖ .1941.20]ΟΝΑΤ.
.2145.22ΑΝΑ..
Ν[.1839.19 ἄρχον]τα χερ-
ο͂ν ἀ[δίκον .1430.14 χερ]ο͂ν ἀδίκον κ-
τέ[νει .37.3]Σ[.819.9 διαγιγνόσκ]εν δὲ τὸς ἐ-
[φέτ]ας .1736.17ΕΙΣΕ ἐλεύθ-
ε[ρ]ος ἐ͂ι. κα[ὶ ἐὰν φέροντα ἒ ἄγοντα βίαι ἀδίκος εὐθὺς] ἀμυνόμενο-
ς κτέ[ν]ει, ν[εποινὲ τεθνάναι .819.9]

(*IG* i³ 104)

Diognetos of Phrearrhioi was secretary.

Decree of 409/8 Diokles was *archon* (409/8). The Council and the People decided. AkamantisV was in *prytany*. Diognetos was secretary. Euthydikos was chairman. – phanes proposed: 5 the inscribers or writers-up of the laws shall inscribe Draco's law on homicide, taking it over from the king, with the secretary of the Council, on a stone stele and set it down in front of the royal stoa. The official sellers shall make the contract in accordance with the law, and the Greek treasurers shall provide the money.

"Draco's law" First axon. And or Even if anybody kills anybody not from forethought, he shall be exiled. The kings shall pronounce responsible for homicide [the one who himself killed or the one?] who planned it; the appeal judges shall decide it. There shall be reconciliation, if there are a father or brother or sons, to be granted by all, or the objector shall prevail. If these do not exist, then as far as cousinhood and cousin, if they are all willing to grant reconciliation, or the objector shall prevail. If none of these exists but he killed unwillingly and the fifty-one appeal judges decide that he killed unwillingly, let ten members of the phratry allow him to enter if they are willing: let these be chosen by the fifty-one on the basis of their excellence. And those who killed previously shall be liable to this ordinance. There shall be a proclamation against the killer in the agora by those as far as cousinhood and cousin; there shall join in the prosecution cousins and cousins' sons and brothers-in-law and fathers-in-law and phratry members . . . is responsible for homicide . . . the fiftyone . . . convict of homicide . . . If anybody kills a killer, or is responsible for his being killed, when he is keeping away from a frontier market and Amphictyonic contests and rites, he shall be liable to the same things as for killing an Athenian; the appeal judges shall decide . . . 36 . . . he is a free man. And if he kills a man by defending immediately when the man is forcibly and unjustly taking and removing, that man shall have been killed without penalty.

7 The competence of the Areopagos Council in homicide cases

ΝΟΜΟΣ ΕΚ ΤΩΝ ΦΟΝΙΚΩΝ ΝΟΜΩΝ ΤΩΝ ΕΞ ΑΡΕΙΟΥ ΠΑΓΟΥ. Δικάζειν δὲ τὴν βουλὴν τὴν ἐν Ἀρείῳ πάγῳ φόνου καὶ τραύματος ἐκ προνοίας καὶ πυρκαϊᾶς καὶ φαρμάκων, ἐάν τις ἀποκτείνῃ δούς.[6]

(D. 14.23)

LAW FROM THE HOMICIDE LAW PLACED IN THE AREOPAGOS. The Areopagos Council is to try cases of homicide and deliberate wounding and arson and poison, if someone kills by administering it.

8 The killer of a murderer is liable to a murder prosecution

ΝΟΜΟΣ: Ἐὰν δέ τις τὸν ἀνδροφόνον κτείνῃ ἢ αἴτιος ᾖ φόνου, ἀπεχόμενον ἀγορᾶς ἐφορίας καὶ ἄθλων καὶ ἱερῶν Ἀμφικτυονικῶν, ὥσπερ τὸν Ἀθηναῖον κτείναντα, ἐν τοῖς αὐτοῖς ἐνέχεσθαι, διαγιγνώσκειν δὲ τοὺς ἐφέτας.

(D. 23.37)

LAW: If any man shall kill a murderer, or shall cause him to be killed, so long as the murderer absents himself from the frontier-market, the games, and the Amphictyonic sacrifices, he shall be liable to the same penalty as if he killed an Athenian citizen; and the Criminal Court shall adjudicate.

9 The law forbidding the punishment for murder of someone who has left Attica to go into exile

ΝΟΜΟΣ: Ἐάν τίς τινα τῶν ἀνδροφόνων τῶν ἐξεληλυθότων, ὧν τὰ χρήματα ἐπίτιμα, πέρα ὅρου ἐλαύνῃ ἢ φέρῃ ἢ ἄγῃ, τὰ ἴσα ὀφείλειν ὅσα περ ἂν ἐν τῇ ἡμεδαπῇ δράσῃ.

(D. 23.44)

LAW: If any man outside the frontier pursue or violently seize the person of any homicide who has quitted the country, and whose goods are not confiscate, he shall incur the same penalty as if he so acted within our own territory.

10 The law on killers who violated the terms of their exile

ΝΟΜΟΣ: Φόνου δὲ δίκας μὴ εἶναι μηδαμοῦ κατὰ τῶν τοὺς φεύγοντας ἐνδεικνύντων, ἐάν τις κατίῃ ὅποι μὴ ἔξεστιν.

(D. 23.51)

LAW: No man shall be liable to proceedings for murder because he lays information against exiles, if any such exile return to a prohibited place.

11 The law exonerating a killer under certain circumstances

ΝΟΜΟΣ: Ἐάν τις ἀποκτείνῃ ἐν ἄθλοις ἄκων, ἢ ἐν ὁδῷ καθελὼν ἢ ἐν πολέμῳ ἀγνοήσας, ἢ ἐπὶ δάμαρτι ἢ ἐπὶ μητρὶ ἢ ἐπ᾽ ἀδελφῇ ἢ ἐπὶ θυγατρί, ἢ ἐπὶ παλλακῇ ἣν ἂν ἐπ᾽ ἐλευθέροις παισὶν ἔχῃ, τούτων ἕνεκα μὴ φεύγειν κτείναντα.

(D. 23.53)

LAW: If a man kill another unintentionally in an athletic contest, or overcoming him in a fight on the highway, or unwittingly in battle, or in intercourse with his wife, or mother, or sister, or daughter, or concubine kept for procreation of legitimate children, he shall not go into exile as a manslayer on that account.

12 The law allowing someone to kill in self-defense a person who has illegally seized him

ΝΟΜΟΣ: Καὶ ἐὰν φέροντα ἢ ἄγοντα βίᾳ ἀδίκως εὐθὺς ἀμυνόμενος κτείνῃ, νηποινεὶ τεθνάναι.

(D. 23.60)

LAW: If any man while violently and illegally seizing another shall be slain straightway in self-defence, there shall be no penalty for his death.

13 The law punishing with disfranchisement anyone who improperly alters the homicide law of Drakon

ΝΟΜΟΣ. Ὃς ἂν ἄρχων ἢ ἰδιώτης αἴτιος ᾖ τὸν θεσμὸν συγχυθῆναι τόνδε, ἢ μεταποιήσῃ αὐτόν, ἄτιμον εἶναι καὶ παῖδας [ἀτίμους] καὶ τὰ ἐκείνου.

(D. 23.62)

Whosoever, whether magistrate or private citizen, shall cause this ordinance to be frustrated, or shall alter the same, shall be disfranchised with his children and his property.

14 The laws on the proclamations for murder in the Agora

ΝΟΜΟΙ: Προειπεῖν τῷ κτείναντι ἐν ἀγορᾷ ἐντὸς ἀνεψιότητος καὶ ἀνεψιοῦ, συνδιώκειν δὲ καὶ ἀνεψιοὺς καὶ ἀνεψιῶν παῖδας καὶ γαμβροὺς καὶ πενθεροὺς καὶ φράτερας. αἰδέσασθαι δέ, ἐὰν μὲν πατὴρ ᾖ ἢ ἀδελφὸς ἢ υἱεῖς, ἅπαντας, ἢ τὸν κωλύοντα κρατεῖν. ἐὰν δὲ τούτων μηδεὶς ᾖ, κτείνῃ δὲ ἄκων, γνῶσι δὲ οἱ πεντήκοντα καὶ εἷς, οἱ ἐφέται, ἄκοντα κτεῖναι, ἐσέσθων οἱ φράτερες, ἐὰν ἐθέλωσι, δέκα· τούτους δὲ οἱ πεντήκοντα καὶ εἷς ἀριστίνδην αἱρείσθων. καὶ οἱ πρότερον κτείναντες ἐν τῷδε τῷ θεσμῷ ἐνεχέσθων.

(D. 43.57)

LAW: Proclamation shall be made in the market-place to the shedder of blood by a kinsman within the degree of cousin and cousinship, and cousins and sons of cousins and sons-in-law and fathers-in-law and clansmen shall join in the pursuit. To secure condonation, if there be father or brother or sons, all must concur, or whoever opposes shall prevail. And if there be none of these and the slaying was involuntary, and the Fifty-one, the Ephetae, shall agree that the slaying was involuntary, let the clansmen, ten in number, grant the right of entrance to the shedder of blood, if they see fit; and let these be chosen by the Fifty-one according to rank. And those who had shed blood before the enactment of this statute shall be bound by its provisions.

15 The opening procedures and oaths of a homicide trial

> ἴστε δήπου τοῦθ' ἅπαντες, ὅτι ἐν Ἀρείῳ πάγῳ, οὗ δίδωσ' ὁ νόμος καὶ κελεύει τοῦ φόνου δικάζεσθαι, πρῶτον μὲν διομεῖται κατ' ἐξωλείας αὑτοῦ καὶ γένους καὶ οἰκίας ὅ τιν' αἰτιώμενος εἰργάσθαι τι τοιοῦτον, εἶτ' οὐδὲ τὸν τυχόντα τιν' ὅρκον [τοῦτο ποιήσει] ἀλλ' ὃν οὐδεὶς ὄμνυσ' ὑπὲρ οὐδενὸς ἄλλου, στὰς ἐπὶ τῶν τομίων κάπρου καὶ κριοῦ καὶ ταύρου, καὶ τούτων ἐσφαγμένων ὑφ' ὧν δεῖ καὶ ἐν αἷς ἡμέραις καθήκει, ὥστε καὶ ἐκ τοῦ χρόνου καὶ ἐκ τῶν μεταχειριζο- μένων ἅπαν, ὅσον ἔσθ' ὅσιον, πεπρᾶχθαι. καὶ μετὰ ταῦθ' ὁ τὸν τοιοῦτον ὅρκον ὀμωμοκὼς οὔπω πεπίστευται, ἀλλ' ἐὰν ἐξελεγχθῇ μὴ λέγων ἀληθῆ, τὴν ἐπιορκίαν ἀπενεγκάμενος 69.1 τοῖς αὑτοῦ παισὶν καὶ τῷ γένει πλέον οὐδ' ὁτιοῦν ἕξει. ἂν δὲ δόξῃ τὰ δίκαι' ἐγκαλεῖν καὶ ἕλῃ τὸν δεδρακότα τοῦ φόνου, οὐδ' οὕτω κύριος γίγνεται τοῦ ἁλόντος, ἀλλ' ἐκείνου μὲν οἱ νόμοι κύριοι κολάσαι καὶ οἷς προστέτακται, τῷ δ' ἐπιδεῖν 69.5 διδόντα δίκην ἔξεστιν, ἣν ἔταξ' ὁ νόμος, τὸν ἁλόντα, πέρα δ' οὐδὲν τούτου. καὶ τῷ μὲν διώκοντι ὑπάρχει ταῦτα, τῷ δὲ φεύγοντι τὰ μὲν τῆς διωμοσίας ταὐτά.
>
> (D. 23.67–9)

You are all of course aware that in the Areopagus, where the law both permits and enjoins the trial of homicide, first, every man who brings accusation of such a crime must make oath by invoking destruction upon himself, his kindred, and his household; secondly, that he must not treat this oath as an ordinary oath, but as one which no man swears for any other purpose; for he stands over the entrails of a boar, a ram, and a bull, and they must have been slaughtered by the necessary officers and on the days appointed, so that in respect both of the time and of the functionaries every requirement of solemnity has been satisfied. Even then the person who has sworn this tremendous oath does not gain immediate credence; and if any falsehood is brought home to him, he will carry away with him to his children and his kindred the stain of perjury – but gain nothing. If, on the other hand, he is believed to be laying a just charge, and if he proves the accused guilty of murder, even then he has no power over the convicted criminal; only the laws and the appointed officers have power over the man for punishment. The prosecutor is permitted to see him suffering the penalty awarded by law, and that is all. Such are the prosecutor's rights. As for the defendant, the rules for his oath are the same.

8.2 The intersection of religion and the law

The intersection between religion and the law has been centrally important for the development of nearly every legal system in the western world from antiquity to the present day. For most of the Christian era the traditions, beliefs and customs of the Church have cast a heavy shadow upon legal systems, while the Enlightenment and Humanist movements in the past couple of centuries have only diminished their influence to a limited extent. This is why sometimes looking into ancient Greek culture as an example of a society with advanced political, social, ideological and cultural institutions, and free from the domineering influence of monotheism can be very informative. Immediately we will notice some significant differences in the way religion influenced the creation of law, and law was incorporated religion, but at the same time we will notice that Greek religion was just as integrated into the legal system and many a time influenced the introduction and interpretation of laws or decrees and used the legal system to demand restitution for wrongs against the gods, their sanctuaries, their rituals and their festivals.[7]

While in the Christian era the law often aims at establishing moral imperatives consonant with the teachings of the Church, the intersection between Greek religion and the law had much to do with ritual correctness, but very little to do with moral imperatives. One striking example should suffice: When Alcibiades was accused of imitating the secret rituals of the Eleusinean Mysteries in 415, the city was not concerned with his morals or those of his companions, since they did not seem to have a high opinion of these in the first place. What scared and upset the city was the incoming wrath of the two goddesses, whose rituals had been violated, in the middle of a precarious situation as the fleet was sailing for Sicily. It was the violation of the rituals, and not the immorality of those concerned, which led the city to take some extraordinary measures.[8] In every single instance where someone in Athens was prosecuted on the basis of religious considerations, the prevailing concerns had to do with ritual correctness, and the violation of very specific and concrete rules about religious observance, while moral or spiritual concerns would only be symptomatic expressions of a person's impiety in the periphery of the matter.

The second most significant difference between ancient religions and Christianity in their interactions with the law is the absence of a holy book of unchallengeable authority in Greek religion, while Christianity after the 4th century accepted a Canon of books, and attributed to it divine authority, that cannot be argued or reasoned with, with far-reaching consequences.[9] A good example of the implications of drawing authority from a holy book may be the recent acrimonious debate on the constitutional rights of same-sex couples to form families with equal legal rights as opposite sex couples. The primary objection of some Christian groups is based on a few probably misunderstood passages from the Leviticus and the Pauline letters, and this has been deemed as sufficient reason to deprive a significant number of the population of basic human rights, such as a right to form a family, inheritance rights or tax equality. The difference could not be greater in ancient Greek religion. The absence of a dogmatic authority allowed and fostered debate on all matters related to the individual and his/her standing in society. All matters could be argued, debated, sometimes *ad naueseam*, and occasionally a broad consensus was reached (as for example in the case of *hybris* as a cultural construct),[10] while on many matters plurality of thought and diversity of opinions were the rule. In the ancient Greek world humans did not need the gods to tell them how they should think.

Another major difference can be found in the organization of religious life. While Christianity after the 3rd century adopted a rigorous, exclusively male hierarchy, with sole purpose the administration of the Church, Greek religions never adopted a hierarchical administration, never limited access to priesthood along gender lines, and for the most part their priesthood was composed of ordinary persons, who took turns into office. Typically, male deities had male priests and female deities had priestesses, however the distinction was not absolute. For example, Apollo had priestesses who prophesized in Delphi, Zeus had priestesses for the same purpose in Dodona, Philochoros mentions some priestesses of Dionysos, while an inscription of the late 4th century mentions a priestess of Pluto related to the rituals of the Thesmophoria (which might explain why she needed to be a woman, in an all-female festival).[11] Some of the priesthoods were hereditary among the members of certain ancient families. The priestess of Athena, for example, always came from the *genos* of the Eteoboutadai, while the two sacred *gene* in Eleusis, the Kerykes and the Eumolpidai, always provided the *dadouchos* and the hierophant.

Many priesthoods were filled through sortition, like most other offices in the city.[12] Moreover, the nine *archon*s, and other magistrates, who were also appointed by lot, had extensive religious duties. In particular the *basileus* can be rightly considered to be the chief religious magistrate in the city, in charge of sanctuaries and religious properties and all major festivals. He also introduced to court offenses related to religion, like impiety or homicide (S 1–2). The religious dimensions of the offices of the nine *archon*s dictated certain precautions and restrictions, lest the gods be offended. Persons with physical imperfections, or persons whose ill-behavior, or lifestyle choices might be offensive to the gods, like those who had mistreated their parents or squandered their patrimony, or male prostitutes, were disqualified from these offices.[13]

If seen from a different angle these provisions are significant because they mean that the vast majority of citizens were just as qualified as any other person to fill these offices. One did not need to be a religious zealot, did not need to possess any divinely inspired insights or wisdom and did not need to have any particular skills in order to become the priest or priestess of one of the major gods in the Greek pantheon. While the Greek priests and priestesses enjoyed respect in the community as servants of the gods, they did not presume to tell anyone how they should live, what they should believe in, or whom they should vote into office. They could routinely be consulted on matters of ritual and correct performance of religious duties for the god or goddess they served, but after all, they were ordinary citizens dedicating some of their time to the service of the gods and the city, and were subject to an *euthyna*, like other magistrates of the state (S 3) for their conduct in office, because no one expected priests and priestesses to be beyond corruption or flawed human behaviors.

This left a significant vacuum. Who was going to decide on moral behaviors, social issues, or what was good or bad? It appears that in the classical period this role fell upon the individual as a citizen, and as a participant in social groups. Moral philosophy in the form of the sophistic movement in the 5th century, and prominent moral philosophers such as Plato, Aristotle, Zenon and Xenokrates, or several philosophical schools like Platonism, the Peripatetics, the Cynics, the Stoics, the Epicureans and others in the 4th and 3rd century, explored every conceivable question related to the human condition, and each came up with answers which although many a time did not have widespread appeal, they kept the discussion going for centuries, inviting humans to use their logical faculties in order to decide what was good and what was bad, what was appropriate, moral, expedient or correct. This relativism dominated the Greco-Roman viewpoint of the world for nearly a millennium, and only came to an end when a new religion, which had spread like fire, demanded and promoted single-minded certainty within the strict hierarchy of the Church and its teachings.

This is broadly the cultural context of Greek Law. It was not born out of a necessity to safeguard the morals or immortal souls of the citizenry, nor was it guided by principles which could not be debated, revised, or ultimately rejected because they came from a superior and eternal moral authority. The gods of the Greeks did not dictate irrefutable principles, but this had not resulted in a world in chaos. The Greek word for the world was *cosmos*, which meant "order." Everything in the cosmos had been arranged in order, and human societies also needed order, and it was up to them to figure out through reasoning what was the best way to do that. Greek law was born out of this profound belief in order, in a meaningful, even if not equitable, division of rights and responsibilities, and this was the underlying principle of the legislation which Solon outlined in his poem *Εὐνομίη*. The core concept of the word νόμος is about a workable distribution (νέμεσθαι) of duties and responsibilities in the best possible way to serve justice (δίκη).[14]

The laws of the Greek city-states were created over the centuries as responses to specific problems, conditions, needs or demands. They were practical measures for practical purposes, and this functionality is easily visible in most provisions once they are placed in context. Religion does not have an impact upon those underlying principles, not in most cases, but this does not mean that religion does not intersect with these laws. Religion sometimes provides a theoretical framework behind certain legal provisions. It certainly does so in the case of homicide law; homicide was offensive to the gods as well as to men, and this is why in addition to secular provisions about the persecution of offenders, trial and punishment, a thick layer of religious elements was added, like curses, oaths, proclamations and strange-looking regulations intended to deal with the religious aspects of homicide, and to avoid angering the gods.

On other occasions religion set some requirements which could not be violated if the community desired the favor of the gods. All legal provisions related to festivals, cults or religious matters were established with this principle in mind. The city and its citizens should not offend the gods with improper conduct or incorrect ritual, because this would have consequences for all, and this is why it was the duty of the law to ensure that rituals were properly performed and that deliberate violations or other offenses against the gods would not remain unpunished. Finally, religion could be used as an enhancement of the principles of justice, as we often read in the Attic Orators. What is just and fair is favored by the gods, and since they can see everything, even what humans cannot see, like what each judge has voted, they are more likely to show favor to those who have acted according to their wishes and the commands of justice.

In the following sections I shall discuss briefly the intersection of religion and the law with regard to homicide, impiety, festivals, and the rhetorical arguments of the Attic Orators based on religion. These subjects are vast, and a comprehensive discussion far exceeds the purposes of this study. My objective here is to outline these associations in order to demonstrate how religion as a communal motivator has influenced the creation of Athenian law, and how the law enhanced, but also sometimes limited with a firm hand, the standing and influence of religion in everyday Athenian life and society.

8.3 State religion, festivals and the law

In no area is the integration of religious rite into the functions of the state more visible than in the numerous festivals celebrated with grandeur and partly funded from the public purse. We should be in no doubt that the practice is truly ancient. From the early times when human communities formed permanent settlements, religious rites and festivals were employed to boost the community spirit, create an identity and differentiate from "others", secure good harvests or hunting, and vanquish their enemies through the favor of the gods.[15] Ever since the colossal study of James George Frazer *The Golden Bough* familiarized western audiences with the universal practices and principles of world religions in the 1890s, anthropology and historical sciences have studied thoroughly the links between religion and social structures. This vast discussion is beyond our purposes; readers interested in the functions and expressions of religion in the ancient Greek society have an abundance of high quality works to choose from. My purpose here is to briefly discuss the legal framework surrounding the major festivals of Attica, and how it interacted with social values.

The Panathenaia was in some ways the most "Athenian" of all festivals. Dedicated to the patron goddess of the city, it embodied musical and athletic competitions, spectacles and processions, large sacrifices and a communal collaboration for the weaving of the *peplos* of Athena at the Great Panathenaia every four years. The spectacular festival was a showcase of Athenian power and greatness to the large numbers of visitors from allied cities and the rest of the world, who arrived to celebrate and to be entertained.[16]

In the speech *Against Neaira*, an entourage of Corinthian *hetairai* arrives in the city during the Panathenaia to attend the festival and entertain the guests in a private party staged around the festival.[17] Surely such parties around the festival were routine in Athens, with so many guests and visitors in the city. A large amount of archaeological evidence, inscriptions, vase paintings and sculptures, including the frieze of the Parthenon, confirms the central importance of the festival in Athenian public life. Numerous inscriptions which touch upon every aspect of the festival offer clear testimony to its political and cultural significance, and the great care which the *polis* took of the festivities. For example, one such inscription includes a decree of the Assembly (c. 335/334 BC), which settles all kinds of details of the festival, from the portions of the sacrificial meats set aside for the *archon*s and the treasurers of the goddess, to costs of the sacrificial animals and the *pannychis*.[18] D.M. Lewis considered this to be the law for the Lesser Panathenaia.[19] Numerous other inscriptions include decrees dealing with various aspects of the celebrations, some record decrees for persons to be honored during the festival, and some are decrees honoring the officials of the festival for the successful performance of the festivities.[20]

The Great Dionysia offered another occasion for the Athenian *polis* to showcase her power, foster diplomatic relations and keep the ties between Athens and her allies strong.[21] Representatives from the entire Delian League (later the *arche* "empire") were sent to Athens in official embassies. They were entertained in the theater during the Dionysia attending the tragic contests, and surely fed with a fair amount of Athenian propaganda. This was the greatest opportunity available to the city to win hearts and minds among the representatives of the allies, and yet it seems that sometimes it was tactlessly missed. A passage of Isocrates describes one such occasion where the city officials acted with arrogance and imprudence during the festival, and as a result they weakened the prestige of the city and offended the allies.

> Οὕτω γὰρ ἀκριβῶς εὕρισκον ἐξ ὧν ἄνθρωποι μάλιστ' ἂν μισηθεῖεν, ὥστ' ἐψηφίσαντο τὸ περιγιγνόμενον τῶν πόρων ἀργύριον διελόντες κατὰ τάλαντον εἰς τὴν ὀρχήστραν τοῖς Διονυσίοις εἰσφέρειν ἐπειδὰν πλῆρες ᾖ τὸ θέατρον· καὶ ταῦτ' ἐποίουν καὶ παρεισῆγον τοὺς παῖδας τῶν ἐν τῷ πολέμῳ τετελευτηκότων, ἀμφοτέροις ἐπιδεικνύοντες, τοῖς μὲν συμμάχοις τὰς τιμὰς τῆς οὐσίας αὐτῶν ὑπὸ μισθωτῶν εἰσφερομένας, τοῖς δ' ἄλλοις Ἕλλησι τὸ πλῆθος τῶν ὀρφανῶν καὶ τὰς συμφορὰς τὰς διὰ τὴν πλεονεξίαν ταύτην γιγνομένας.
>
> For so exactly did they gauge the actions by which human beings incur the worst odium that they passed a decree to divide the surplus of the funds derived from the tributes of the allies into talents and to bring it on the stage, when the theatre was full, at the festival of Dionysus; and not only was this done but at the same time they led in upon the stage the sons of those who had lost their lives in the war, seeking thus to display to our allies, on the one hand, the value of their own property which was brought in by hirelings, and to the rest of the Hellenes, on the other, the multitude of the fatherless and the misfortunes which result from this policy of aggression.[22]

Augustus Boeckh, who is very critical of the extravagance of the Athenian state for the celebration of public festivals (δημοτελῆ ἱερά), on account of the fact that this generosity was funded from the oppression of the Allies, sees this magnificence, which was unprecedented in the Greek world, as a folly, albeit a nobler and more elegant one, since it embraced the entire citizen body.[23] A passage of Demosthenes backs Boeckh's criticisms. The orator covertly criticizes his fellow citizens for spending too much money, time, effort and manpower in the preparation of the Panathenaia and the Dionysia, while the preparations for the fleet are anemic, and as a result Athenian fleets always arrive late and underpowered for the task. Of course, Demosthenes had already set his sights on the moneys of the theoric fund, which he was hoping that he would be able to divert to military purposes, but he would not succeed in this objective before Philip had already interfered with the grain routes, and by then it was too late to halt his inevitable march to final victory.[24]

Demosthenes singled out these two festivals, because they were the most important in the life of the *polis*, but also the most costly and ostentatious, since they were both attended by large numbers of foreigners who probably were judging the city by what they experienced during their visits for the festival. Perhaps equally popular with foreigners was the other major festival of the Athenian state, the Eleusinian Mysteries, but unlike the previous two which were celebrated in the center of the city with splendor, the Mysteries were celebrated in Eleusis, 20km to the west of the *asty*, and the core of the festival consisted of secret rituals limited to the initiates and was celebrated within the confines of the Telesterion, away from public view.[25] As such the Mysteries did not offer a conspicuous platform for state-sponsored propaganda to the same extent as the Panathenaia or the Dionysia. Nonetheless, how important this cult was in the communal conscience of the Athenians can be seen with absolute clarity in the decisive and unprecedented actions of the city in 415, when reports reached the Assembly that a group of men, one of whom was the general Alcibiades, then at the height of his powers, had staged a mockery of the Mysteries in a private house.

The ensuing scandal, which led to executions, threats of torture of free persons for information[26] and mass imprisonment of hundreds of citizens shook Athenian public life to its foundations. Politically motivated scaremongering, that actions so offensive to the two goddesses might doom the Sicilian expedition, which was under way, led to the recall of Alcibiades, the visionary force behind this expedition, which ironically after his defection to Sparta resulted in the catastrophe that the city was trying to avert.[27] This whole affair illustrates the inextricably entangled relationship between religion and the state in some important ways. While no one would ever consider classical Athens to be a theocratic society, sacred law which settled religious affairs, such as the correct performance of rituals, or the punishment of violators who might have offended the gods with their actions, was always an important concern for the state, because an offended God was not an enemy that the Athenian state would like to have. In this respect, religious violations acquired a secular dimension and needed to be addressed on the basis of secular laws in the courts of the democracy.

Crime and punishment seem to be entangled even more closely in the expiation ritual of the Thargelia, where there is some evidence that a criminal (or two) every year, we are told the ugliest one, was to be treated like a scapegoat, and expelled from the city, according to Harpocration, or executed, according to Suda, in order to purify the city. Even if such a ritual took place in pre-classical times (and the evidence is too weak to safely reach this conclusion even for the archaic period), it certainly did not happen in the classical period. It is most unlikely that such a spectacular method of execution was in operation and we do not hear anything at all about it from the classical authors. It is equally unlikely that someone was sent into exile as part of the purification of the city, and again we do not hear anything at all about it anywhere in classical literature. Besides, this kind of guilt transfer, which allows one person to be punished for the crimes of another, would not be consonant with the core philosophy of democratic Athenian law that only recognized personal responsibility for one's crimes.

The state was equally meticulous in the preparation of the five women – only festivals celebrated each year.[28] The most prominent among them, the Thesmophoria, in honor of Demeter, Persephone and Pluto, was funded and prepared by the state with meticulous care, before male workers for the festival withdrew and left the Thesmophorion to the women for a traditional ritual of fertility, and regeneration of the vital forces of nature. Several inscriptions attest the great care which the Athenian state took during the preparations of the festival.[29] One of them makes detailed arrangements for the sacrificial items needed by the priestesses, another clarifies details of the ritual, and another proposes improvement in the physical space of the festivities.[30]

The other major women's festival, the Haloa, was celebrated in late December at the Telesterion in Eleusis in honor of Demeter, Persephone and Dionysos. As I have suggested in a previous publication, the Haloa probably was a winter solstice festival, since this is the only event of note related to fertility in late December.[31] At the point when the sun's rays were at their weakest, a festival to stimulate them would seem appropriate, and the rituals of the festival, which seemingly included bonfires (a standard solstice custom in the Greek folk tradition), support this suggestion. Women from all over Attica gathered to Eleusis for the festival. The city provided wood for the bonfires and the *archon*s prepared a buffet with delicacies in the court-yard of the Telesterion on behalf of the city. However, only the women were allowed in the Telesterion, where they sat around fires in the cold December night chatting, joking and enjoying themselves. The scholiast of Lucian considered the obscene talk about male anatomical parts to be ritualistic, but Brumfield, probably correctly, points out that obscene conversations and jokes in a single-sex environment need not be part of a ritual, but simply merriment and lighthearted conversation.

Unlike the Thesmophoria, which was attended by respectable married women, the Haloa seems to have been a more open festival welcoming all women, and this is why the numerous prostitutes of Attica had made it their own, joining other women for the festivities, and threw private parties all over Attica during the festival, undoubtedly with a view to meeting new clients, and celebrating with the current ones. In a festival like the Haloa we get the impression that we are observing the openness and diversity of the Athenian Democracy at work. The city was prepared to throw a party, provide the food, the firewood and one of the most sacred places in the city as the venue, under the auspices of its most senior civil servants, the nine *archon*s, in an all-inclusive festival where no woman was turned away, no matter who she was, where was she from, or what she did for a living.

The oldest festival of Dionysos in Athens, the Anthesteria, was steeped in traditional ritual involving the magistrates of the state in ways which might seem alien in the democracy of the classical period, but were reminiscent of times past when the *basileus* (king-*archon*) had the authority and prestige to represent the city in its dealings with the god.[32] The festival was celebrated for three days in February, when all the trees blossom in the Greek countryside and there is the promise in the air that nature is coming back to life after the slumber of the winter months. The Anthesteria were celebrated in other cities around the Greek world, seemingly with different customs, but the one thing they have in common was the welcoming of Dionysos returning from the underworld (ἄνοδος). The opening of the jars with the new wine, which had been fermenting since the late summer, took place in the first day of the festival (Pythoigia) and we can see the symbolism of the return of Dionysos in this.

The actual ritual celebrating the return of the God from the underworld formed the main event of the festival in the second day. This was celebrated centrally in the sanctuary At the Marshes (ἐν Λίμναις) with the ritual of the sacred marriage between the wife of the *basileus* (*basilinna*), and the God. Then, a wedding procession took the newlyweds to the Boukoleion, the ancient residence of the *basileus*, for the consummation of the marriage. I have argued in a previous publication that the "bridegroom" was a herm of the god, whom the *basilinna* addressed in highly stylized erotic language in a secret ritual at the Boukoleion.[33] The key role of the wife of the *basileus* in this ritual imposed certain restrictions on his choice of a wife. See needed to be in her first marriage and also of citizen stock. I have argued elsewhere that the first of these restrictions was very ancient, while the second came into effect after the Periclean citizenship law in 451, and then an inscription outlining both restrictions was placed in the open air in the sanctuary At the Marshes. About a century later Apollodoros could still see the inscription written in the old Attic Alphabet, but the letters had somewhat faded. The third day of the festival was celebrated locally with broth and low-key activities, as most people were nursing massive hangovers from the previous two days of serious drinking.

The Apatouria was another Athenian festival, which was inextricably linked with the city and its institutions, perhaps in a more important way than any other. This was the festival of the ancient Ionian tribes, phratries, and gene, and served the important purpose of the first introduction of children born to Athenian families into the community.[34] The actual practices for the presentation of new children, as well as new marriages, or adoptions, probably differed from phratry to phratry, but the purpose was the same. Such events played the role which registries of births, marriages, or adoptions play in modern societies, and it is possible that at least some of those bodies kept written registers of their members. When Kleisthenes introduced the deme as the basic unit of the citizen body, he did not abolish those traditional associations and their role as the guardians of Athenian identity. He simply added another layer only for adult male citizens, the registration with the deme when a man reached his 18th year of age. In the classical period all demes kept a written register of their members, but the phratry still remained the first access point, the place where citizens would first record the addition of children, male or female, natural or adopted, to their family, and also their new marriages, and since it was more encompassing, and not limited only to adult male citizens, these presentations to the phratry during the Apatouria retained significant legal weight in cases of dispute of someone's citizen status, adoption, or marriage. Unlike the deme, which was organized on democratic and egalitarian principles, phratries and gene remained traditional bodies sometimes run on the basis of elitist, non-democratic rules and principles, and the reasons why they were able to retain this traditional character under the classical democracy, were their associations with religion and the fact that by the 4th century membership to these bodies, although widespread, was not required for citizenship.

This list of festivals is by no means exhaustive; many more were celebrated under the auspices of the *polis*. The ones mentioned above were the most important and perhaps for this reason, they assumed a high degree of integration between state and religion. The state generously funded these festivals and was prepared to ensure their correct and spectacular performance, with laws and regulations, and also especially appointed magistrates. In return, the state used these festivals for its own ends, from the record-keeping for marriages, births and adoptions to political propaganda aimed at citizens and foreigners alike and intended to raise the profile of the city of Athens and present her as a worthy leader of the Greek world.

8.4 Prosecutions on religious grounds

The numerous festivals and religious rites of Attica were regulated with a complex and extensive body of sacred laws, most of which had been handed down from generation to generation, and were specific to the festival, temple, sanctuary, or rite concerned. Sacred law was usually interpreted and enforced by the priest, priestess or other sacred officials in charge. Much of this body remained largely apocryphal to the general public, and, when necessary, specific inquiries could be made to religious officials. Oracles could be consulted, especially the two ancient and revered sanctuaries of Apollo at Delphi, and Zeus at Dodona, and their responses could become the subject of public debate in the Assembly, or in the law-courts.[35] The ἐξηγηταί is another source of wisdom on religious matters, especially matters of purification. This mysterious group of religious savants is mentioned a few times, but we do not know who they were, how they were appointed or what were their qualifications. The term was familiar to Herodotos,[36] while Plato in the *Laws* mentions several times such officials in charge of traditional religious rites.[37] More significant are two references where the *exegetai* are consulted for matters of homicide, and their opinion is considered sufficiently important to influence legal proceedings.[38]

While it seems that the advice of oracles or *exegetai* was sought under extraordinary circumstances, the priests and priestesses of the gods would often voice opinions on matters of religious correctness and ritual. In sanctuaries it was not unusual to have specific rules, and fortunately quite a few inscriptions with such rules have been preserved for us. They could be concerned with dress code, correct preparation for the ritual, rules about purification after sexual intercourse, childbirth or a miscarriage, specific qualifications about persons who were expected to perform certain rites, and so on.[39] The list is long, and it is outside our purposes to explore these rules in detail. However, one important question about the relationship between sacred law and the secular laws of the Athenian Democracy needs to be addressed, especially since the boundary between the two is sometimes hazy.

Atonement for violations of sacred law typically included religious duties, such as sacrifices, offerings to a temple or purifications, and it was up to the believers, either as individuals or as a group all the way to city level, to heed the wishes of the gods and their representatives.[40] If they did not, they should fear the anger of the gods but not the laws of the city. The boundary was crossed, and the secular laws of the city were involved when violations were more serious or extensive and could be seen as an affront to the gods, sufficiently grave to put the entire community at risk from their wrath. When, for example, Alcibiades and his friends supposedly had mocked the Mysteries of Demeter, the affair crossed the boundary and from a violation of sacred law it actually became a crime in secular law, because the impious actions of this group were putting in peril the entire expedition on its way to Sicily. It appears that for the boundary to be crossed and a religious violation to become a matter of secular law two conditions needed to be met, first the action needed to be intentionally offensive, and not simply the result of negligence or omission, and second the violation needed to be serious enough to be putting the entire community at risk from the fury of an offended deity. While, of course, there is a certain amount of subjectivity in judging what is serious and what is not, or whether an offensive behavior was deliberate or not, the basic principle remains: the state got involved, and the secular courts meted out severe punishments for an intentional and grave affront to the gods. How exactly such principles were translated into real court cases is a more complicated matter, as piety was only one, and probably not the most important, among the factors which led to the introduction of such cases to court.

Subjective as these perceptions were, still things were not in a state of flux. For a case to be introduced in court one needed to present a written, secular law, which had been violated (at least after 403), and the secular laws which dealt with religious offenses were limited in number and somewhat specific. The two primary laws for the prosecution of offences related to religion in the courts of the city were the *probole*, which allowed prosecutions for specific violations during a festival, and *asebeia*, where the prosecutor needed to prove that someone had violated a religious rule or rite with blatant disrespect for the gods and the religious traditions of the city. Atonement for accidental violations of sacred rules typically was done with religious measures, such as sacrifices, donations to a temple or purifications. On a few instances where the secular courts were used to attack opponents for accidental violations of sacred rules, these prosecutions led to acquittals.[41] It is clear that in prosecutions for religious offences before the secular courts one needed to prove that any religious violations were willful and motivated by human arrogance and intentional disrespect for the gods and the traditional rites.

Plutarch mentions a decree introduced by Diopeithes, which allowed the prosecution with *eisangelia* of persons who denied the existence of the gods (τὰ θεῖα μὴ νομίζοντας) or spread teachings about celestial bodies (λόγους περὶ τῶν μεταρσίων διδάσκοντας).[42] However, these provisions suspiciously echo the *Clouds* of Aristophanes, and there is no evidence from the classical period that such a decree ever existed. Even Socrates, whose prosecution in real life was tailored on the persona which Aristophanes had created in the play, was not prosecuted with *eisangelia*, but with *graphe*,[43] and half a century later the *hetaira* Phryne was also prosecuted with a *graphe asebeias*, when she faced similar charges.[44] MacDowell, with considerable reservations, has suggested that Anaxagoras and Protagoras had been prosecuted in accordance with the decree of Diopeithes, but after 403 its provisions lapsed, and this is why the *graphe asebeias* needed to be used in subsequent years.[45] However, besides the hypothetical nature of this argument, since the persecutions of Anaxagoras and Protagoras are not confirmed historical facts, the primary objection against this interpretation would be the fact that natural philosophy and scientific inquiry into all things celestial, flourished in 5th century Athens, which could not have happened under the fear of an *eisangelia* from religious conservatives.[46] Jakub Filonik after a thorough discussion of these cases concludes that the evidence for the decree of Diopeithes and atheism trials in 5th century Athens is unreliable, and incongruent with the large variety of opinions and the intensity of discussions on the nature of the divine in classical Athens, as well as the intellectual climate which made such a discussion possible.[47] It is much easier to believe that the information of Plutarch is inaccurate, and that charges of atheism, attempts to abolish the traditional pantheon, improper introduction of new cults, or unholy rituals of magic, always came under the umbrella of *asebeia*, because they could be interpreted as a calculated affront to the gods.[48]

Peter Rhodes believes that the *probole* was unusual as a legal procedure because it began with a non-binding vote in the Assembly, which might or might not end up in court, with no consequences for the prosecutor who decided to abandon the procedure after that first stage. However, the *probole* was not unique in this respect: many other legal procedures had two stages, the first of which could be final if the parties involved decided to accept the verdict and abide by it,[49] but it would only be advisory and could be overturned if an appeal was launched to the courts. The most important question about the two-stage process in a *probole* must be why was the first vote needed at all. An answer cannot be given with absolute certainty, but it seems that it has to do with the nature of this procedure. As with an *eisangelia*, the other public prosecution which began with a denunciation, in a *probole* someone declared before the Assembly his intention to prosecute another citizen for a violation which concerned the entire community and sought public support for this undertaking. If the vote in the Assembly indicated that the proposal did not have sufficient support to go ahead, it could be pointless for the prosecutor to proceed to a trial.

There is no reference to a risk factor of 1000 drachmas for the prosecutor who failed to secure 1/5th of the votes in a *probole* trial, and if this is not an accident of transmission, then like the *eisangelia* a *probole* was risk free. This would make sense since the state wanted volunteer prosecutors to denounce and pursue violations of religious rite, especially during the sumptuous festivals on which the city was spending lavishly. If this is the case, then we may have a convincing explanation why procedurally the first vote in the assembly was necessary. Like the *eisangelia*, a *probole* was a risk-free procedure, and this is why the law required a two-tier process, in order to prevent abuses. Since there was no risk, the first vote in the boule for the *eisangelia*, and in the Assembly for the *probole*, had a vetting purpose to discourage frivolous prosecutions. There is no evidence of an *eisangelia* or *probole* which was voted down in the boule or the assembly, but still proceeded to a trial by jury. This may indicate that although an appeal to the courts may still have been theoretically possible, in reality a discouraging first vote would have stopped such a process in its tracks. Thus, the first vote was the safeguard of the state that these procedures would not be abused. When this safeguard proved insufficient to stop the abuses of the *eisangelia* in the 4th century the state changed the law and brought the *eisangelia* in line with the *graphe*, which had always carried a high risk. A *graphe* did not need a primary vote either by the Assembly or the Boule, because it carried the risk of 1000 drachmas for a prosecutor who failed to secure 1/5th of the votes. This is why I am convinced that the first vote was initially conceived as a measure of vetting frivolous prosecutions in the two procedures which did not carry a risk factor, but was never deemed necessary for a *graphe*, because the high-risk factor was deemed sufficient to deter frivolous prosecutions.

The two-tier system for risk-free public prosecutions clearly did not work as envisaged in the case of the *eisangelia*. Fourth century politicians took advantage of it, and with one excuse or another were able to push through the boule *eisangelia* cases which when viewed with the distance of time may seem to us preposterous.[50] However, it seems that the *probole* was never misused in a similar manner. There is only one probole case in the surviving corpus of Attic oratory (Demosthenes *Against Meidias*),[51] and sparse references to the procedure in other places, which suggests that it was probably used much more sparsely than the *eisangelia*, and there may be good reasons why the *probole* was not hijacked in the same way by 4th century politicians.

While it is clear that the *probole* was not limited to religious offenses, it was still a restricted procedure because the law clearly specified not only the circumstances under which a *probole* could be brought, but also specific times of the year when such cases could be introduced to the Assembly. *Probolai* for religious violations in relation to the festivals could only be introduced to the Assembly immediately after the Pandia (early April).[52] In the time of Demosthenes this particular assembly took place in the theater of Dionysos. We are not told why a change of venue was deemed necessary, but we can hypothesize that this special setting added a ceremonial aspect to the meeting and invited the citizens to take more seriously violations against the festivals and religious rites of the city. The only other attested instance where *probolai* were allowed to be brought before the assembly is that against sycophants. This one too could be brought only once a year, on the sixth *prytany*, and the law took it one step farther in order to prevent an overwhelming number of cases brought against political figures in the city: it capped the number to three citizens and three metics (S 5). These measures were undoubtedly designed to ensure that frivolous prosecutions using the risk-free option of the *probole*, either under the pretense of religious violations or sycophantic activities, would not be abused by politicians, and as far as we can tell these measures were successful.

Eisangelia could be brought for religious offenses, as the denunciations during the scandal of the Hermocopidae, and the alleged decree of Diopeithes suggest. However, it was not the correct procedure for such offenses, because the emphasis of the law on *eisangelia*, as partially quoted in the speech of Hypereides *For Euxenippos*, was on offenses that we would identify as treason which threatened the entire structure of the state, and we obtain some measure of how an *eisangelia* case could be argued to this effect in the scant fragments of the speech of Hypereides *For Lykophron*. It appears that the prosecutor in an *eisangelia* case did not only need to prove that an offense against the gods had been committed, but also that this offense posed an imminent threat for the entire state and the Democratic Constitution. This might have been easier in 415, when the Athenians were jumpy over the Sicilian expedition, but not quite so easy in normal times. Trying to argue an *eisangelia* case for religious offenses would have been like trying to argue an off-focus, two-tier case, and inviting the jury to make the equation that someone guilty of some religious transgression was a traitor to the city, and a threat to its very existence. Athenian juries may have been excitable, but perhaps not this naïve. Given these challenges we should not be surprised that *eisangelia* was rarely used to prosecute religious offenses.

The public procedure most often used to prosecute religious offenses was the γραφὴ ἀσεβείας. Although it carried a substantial risk, it was tailored to the needs of such a case. One needed only to prove that the person had intentionally violated religious rules, and with their conduct they had offended the gods.[53] It goes without saying that piety alone would probably be an insufficient motive for a prosecutor to take such a risk. As Jakub Filonik has amply demonstrated, the *graphe asebeias* was often motivated by politics, or ideology and culture in a broader sense. His conclusion offers an insightful explanation of the purpose and employment of the *graphe asebeias* in classical Athens:

> There was no systematic religious repression in Athens. Rather, the historical record cites a handful of individual trials for impiety out of nearly two centuries of Athenian Democracy, more often than not placed in a very particular political context. Those individual trials or sometimes groups of trials reflect important turning points in the life of the community, more often than not being linked to various periods of instability, crisis, anxiety, sometimes even coups d'état, war, and, last but not least, either a threat of falling under foreign domination or frustration at the defeat.[54]

It is indeed at those turning points in Athenian history that we observe the few well-attested *graphai asebeias*. Perhaps the most iconic among them, the trial of Socrates, took place exactly at one of those pivotal moments in Athenian history. The Athenian Empire had just been defeated and the city was trying to recover from the wounds of a long and bloody war, and civil strife. As part of this recovery process a reorganization of public life in 403 was followed by some soul-searching, an effort to find out what had gone wrong, and why the great Athenian dream had crashed and burned. Someone must have been responsible for this catastrophe. While the majority of scholars agree that Socrates became the scapegoat, the finer points which led the Athenians to execute perhaps the greatest and most revolutionary mind in their entire history, whose heavy influence was to change the course not only of Athens but of the entire human history, still remain a matter of contention, and do not concern us at this point.[55]

The prosecution of Socrates was a three-prong attack, as citations from the prosecution in the *Apology* of Plato reveal:

> Σωκράτης ἀδικεῖ καὶ περιεργάζεται ζητῶν τά τε ὑπὸ γῆς καὶ οὐράνια καὶ τὸν ἥττω λόγον κρείττω ποιῶν καὶ ἄλλους ταὐτὰ ταῦτα διδάσκων.
>
> (Pl. *Apol.* 18 b – c)
>
> Socrates is committing a crime and inquiring what is under the earth and in the heavens and is turning a lesser argument into a better one and is teaching others how to do so.
>
> Σωκράτη φησὶν ἀδικεῖν τούς τε νέους διαφθείροντα καὶ θεοὺς οὓς ἡ πόλις νομίζει οὐ νομίζοντα, ἕτερα δὲ δαιμόνια καινά.
>
> (Pl. *Apol.* 24 b – c)
>
> He says that Socrates is committing a crime corrupting young men and refusing to believe in the gods in whom the city believes, but instead believes in some new deities.

The most serious among these charges, under which the case came to court as a *graphe asebeias*, was that Socrates wanted to do away with the state religion, and replace the traditional pantheon with deities of his own invention. The charge here was not that he was attempting to introduce new deities, but that he completely intended to abolish traditional religion and replace it with a new one of his own making. Such an impious act could only invite the wrath of the traditional gods, in whom the city and most members of the jury certainly believed. Of course, anyone who has read the *Clouds* of Aristophanes would recognize this charge from the comic image of Socrates replacing Zeus with the new deities, the Clouds, and Plato in the *Apology* recognizes that the comic caricature of Socrates in the play provided the inspiration for these charges:

> ταῦτα γὰρ ἑωρᾶτε καὶ αὐτοὶ ἐν τῇ Ἀριστοφάνους κωμῳδίᾳ, Σωκράτη τινὰ ἐκεῖ περιφερόμενον, φάσκοντά τε ἀεροβατεῖν καὶ ἄλλην πολλὴν φλυαρίαν φλυαροῦντα, ὧν ἐγὼ οὐδὲν οὔτε μέγα οὔτε μικρὸν πέρι ἐπαΐω.
>
> (Pl. *Apol.* 19 b – c)

> You have seen all this in yourselves in the comedy of Aristophanes, some Socrates going about, claiming to be walking in the air, and talking a lot of nonsense about which I know nothing great or small.

Undoubtedly related to this comic image of Socrates is the other charge that he was engaging in improper inquiries, which endangered the traditional ethical code of conduct for a citizen. Surely anyone who had seen the play would remember the famous competition between the Just (κρείττων λόγος) and the Unjust Argument (ἥσσων λόγος), which results in a sound defeat for the Just Argument. It appears that the accusers of Socrates had even adopted the terminology of Aristophanes in order to suggest to the jury that Socrates was a dangerous man because he had the skill to present flawed reasoning as superior. Although the details are not clear, it seems that exactly this moral reversal was what upset audiences during the original performance of the *Clouds*, and the play flopped. In the revised version, the one we have, the victory of the Inferior Argument comes with severe consequences, and the burning of the school of Socrates provides a very different resolution to the play than the customary party. Undoubtedly the prosecutors of Socrates were hoping to tap into the same feeling of outrage which led to the flop of the original play and necessitated a revised version that ended with the burning of the school of Socrates as the appropriate remedy.[56]

The third charge brought against Socrates, that he was corrupting the young men of Athens with his teachings, is a direct consequence of the previous two charges. A teacher who doesn't believe in the traditional religion and intents to upset the moral order of things by presenting unacceptable behaviors, like the maltreatment of one's parents, as the morally superior choice must be exerting a deleterious influence upon his students. According to the weighty testimony of Xenophon, the prosecutors of Socrates used men like Alcibiades and Kritias as examples of the bad influence he was having upon his students, and the detrimental consequences which such an influence had for the entire city, under oligarchy or democracy.[57]

Ultimately Socrates was not convicted for impiety because anyone seriously believed that he threatened traditional Athenian religion. It was his associations with men like Kritias and Alcibiades, which surely proved weighty in the minds of the jurors, as well as the general perception that the ideology which created and fostered such men was responsible for the woes of the city. In Socrates they had a convenient scapegoat, a caricature popularized on the comic stage, who could easily be blamed for everything that went wrong for the Athenians in the last quarter of the 5th century.

One might argue that the elevation of the birds to a higher status than that of the Olympian gods in the *Birds*, was equally subversive and irreverent as the elevation of the Clouds to deities. Perhaps the ludicrous figure of Dionysos in the *Frogs*, or the supremely irreverent presentation of the *Thesmophoria* as a female conspiracy, should be considered equally offensive to traditional religious standards as the views presented by the Socratic Thinkery in the *Clouds*. And yet, the *Frogs* won first prize, and none of these plays upset Athenian audiences or led to prosecutions for impiety. What was different in the case of Socrates was that his mesmerizing personality and teachings were seen as a threat to the established order and upset many people. It is no wonder that when they had the opportunity they voted to remove permanently from the city this bad influence on its young people and its morals. Piety had very little to do with his prosecution; fear, anger, and a thirst to exact vengeance from someone, for all the ills that had befallen the city in the past 30 years under the direction of some of his students were the true motives behind the conviction and death of the philosopher.

Similar fears seem to be larking behind another notorious prosecution, which took place about half a century later, but it unmistakably echoes the charges brought against Socrates. At another critical turning point in Athenian history, when the city-state as an independent political unit was about to dissipate, and along with it the way of life which it had represented for a long time, the *hetaira* Phryne was prosecuted with a *graphe asebeias* for being a bad influence on the young men of Athens, for introducing a new deity, and for offending traditional religious rights. A quote from the prosecution speech summarizes the charges as following:

> ἀσεβείας κρινομένη ἡ Φρύνη· καὶ γὰρ ἐκώμασεν ἐν Λυκείῳ καὶ καινὸν εἰσήγαγε θεὸν καὶ θιάσους ἀνδρῶν καὶ γυναικῶν συνήγαγεν· ‘ἐπέδειξα τοίνυν ὑμῖν ἀσεβῆ Φρύνην, κωμάσασαν ἀναιδῶς, καινοῦ θεοῦ εἰσηγήτριαν, θιάσους ἀνδρῶν ἐκθέσμους καὶ γυναικῶν συναγαγοῦσαν’. ψιλὰ γὰρ νῦν τὰ πράγματα διηγεῖται.
>
> (Anon. Seg. *Ars Rhet.* 215 Hammer)
>
> Phryne is on trial for impiety, because she was carousing in the Lycaeum and introduced a new god, and put together groups (θίασοι) of men and women. “I have demonstrated to you that Phryne is impious, and that she was shamelessly carousing, and introduced a new deity, and gathered together illicit groups of men and women.” At this point he is only providing the mere facts of the case.

We should be in no doubt that, as in the case of Socrates, it was not piety or concern for religious matters behind the prosecution of Phryne. In fact, the religious accusations are so thin that later antiquity felt the need to invent an entire mythology surrounding this trial. It is as if Phryne *should* have done something much more offensive, in order to be prosecuted for impiety. In later antiquity mythology, indeed, she has done something spectacularly offensive, and also tantalizingly erotic: she stripped naked during a festival at Eleusis in full view of a large crowd of worshipers.[58] During the trial, Hypereides sensed danger, and in a bold move revealed her breasts to the jury with the plea not to kill the servant of Aphrodite. The jury was moved and Phryne was acquitted.

Craig Cooper, in a thorough study of the available evidence, concluded that most of the stories about Phryne’s trial found in later antiquity authors are inventions.[59] Perhaps Cooper did too good a job discrediting the late antiquity traditions, so much so that Christine Havelock came to the conclusion that Phryne is a largely fictional figure, and Jakub Filonik has questioned whether the trial ever took place at all.[60] This level of skepticism is unnecessary when we have extracts from the prosecution speech of Euthias and the defense speech of Hypereides preserved in ancient grammarians and rhetoricians. Especially the defense speech of Hypereides was so famous as a supremely urbane sample of classical Attic oratory that it was translated into Latin by Messala. The first three words of this translation preserved by Quintilian (*bene fecit Euthia*) very much remind us of the opening lines of Lyias 24 (ὀλίγου δέω χάριν ἔχειν, ὦ βουλή, τῷ κατηγόρῳ).

More recently scholars have been considering the possibility that the disrobing of Phryne in court may not to be total fiction either; such a bold visual stunt would be unparalleled, as far as we can tell, but not inconceivable, as litigators in Athenian courts often included into their tactics the element of surprise. Visual stunts such as inviting a blind man to give evidence against his nephew in the speech *Against Timarchos*, or coming to court with (self-inflicted) cuts and bruises in order to accuse the opponent of a brutal attack in the second speech *To Boiotos*, are attested in the Attic Orators, and have been the subject of an excellent monograph by Peter O'Connell.[61] On balance, the stories about the disrobing of Phryne during the festival and later in court seem to be anecdotal, but we should not discount with absolute certainty the possibility that there is some truth in them. Perhaps not all legends need to be discredited as pure fiction.

Regardless of the actual details of the case, the trial of Phryne is part of a greater pattern, a whole string of persecutions against women around the middle of the 4th century, mostly alien and several of them *hetairai*. Some were prosecuted for immigration offenses, while others seem to be prosecuted for impiety. In both cases the charges appear to be superficial, disguising hidden agenda. The priestess Theoris of Lemnos was prosecuted for impiety and executed. It seems that she was accused of being a *pharmakis* (poisoner). The narrative of Demosthenes *Against Aristogeiton*, our most important primary source of the incident, allows us to understand that Theoris was using drugs, filters, incantations, and other magical rituals pretending to offer help and treatment for illnesses, including mental illness and brain damage from a stroke.[62] If so, what the Athenian jury understood as impiety was some kind of parareligious healing, which included drugs, incantations and probably magical rites. Why within the plurality of ancient healing techniques and self-professed healers this particular one was seen as a danger to the public is unclear due to insufficient evidence.

Even less clear is the motivation behind the prosecution and conviction of the priestess Ninos. Demosthenes and Dinarchos only mention that she was prosecuted by Menekles and convicted. The Scholiast of Demosthenes provides more details. He actually tells us that she was convicted to death because (like Phryne and Socrates) she was a bad influence on young people, since she supplied them with love filters. Moreover, it seems that she was running some kind of cult which required initiation, and her initiation rituals were viewed as a mockery and an insult of the true Mysteries (γέλωτα εἶναι καὶ ὕβριν κατὰ τῶν ὄντως μυστηρίων).[63] Assuming that the information of the Scholiast of Demosthenes is reliable, we can recognize in this case a familiar pattern. Just as with the notorious scandal of 415, Ninos was convicted because she was performing initiation rituals which were perceived as a mockery of the Eleusinean Mysteries. A similar story about Aeschylos, who was accused of mocking the mysteries, and only escaped punishment when he claimed that he had not been initiated, and therefore he could not have known that he was unwittingly imitating the mysteries,[64] underlines the same theme, namely that the Athenian state was prepared to jump the gun and mete out severe, and maybe unjust, punishments upon anyone who even seemed to be parodying the Mysteries. Whether in any of these cases someone had purposefully imitated these ancient and revered rituals, for religious purposes or merely as a mockery, is irrelevant. So long as someone's actions could be presented as a mockery of the Mysteries, a credible case of impiety with the gravest consequences could be built against this person.

The cynical modern historian might wonder whether Alcibiades and his friends were actually mocking the Mysteries in 415, or simply some party game was purposefully misinterpreted to such effect, in order to bring down the most haughty and powerful man in the city. Likewise, one might wonder whether an initiation ritual into a cult performed by Ninos could be purposefully misinterpreted as a mockery of the Mysteries. But while in the case of Alcibiades we can see a clear motive to bring him down, in the case of the priestess Ninos it is much more difficult to see why someone would seek her death. Esther Eidinow in an intriguing monograph has explored the reasons behind the prosecutions of several women for impiety in classical Athens. She insightfully avoids firm certainty in her answers, but ultimately suggests that these prosecutions were the result of several factors among which fear and envy held central place. We have insufficient knowledge of the cases against Ninos, Theoris, and the sister of Lakedaimonios,[65] but we should be able to confirm that envy and fear played a major role in the prosecution of Phryne. The prominent *hetaira* was a self-marketing machine who attracted much attention upon herself with lavish gifts to her native Thespiae and to Delphi, the commissioning of statues of herself with famous sculptors like Praxiteles, and her ostentatious lifestyle. It would be easy for someone like her to inspire envy among her contemporaries, but also fear that their cultural values are threatened by the excesses of the famous *hetaira*.

These cases do not have in common some overwhelming sense of piety; if anything, there is a distinct lack of piety in all of them. Religion is nothing more than a veneer, an excuse to settle in the courtroom old scores, attack opponents or put away persons whom they considered dangerous for unrelated reasons. Undoubtedly the motives behind the denunciations of 415 where political; in sacrilege the enemies of Alcibiades found a convenient weapon against a man who had dominated the Athenian political landscape in the past few years. They feared and mistrusted his charisma but had not been able to curb his rise to power. The alleged offenses against the gods were a gift for the enemies of Alcibiades, because at this stage the panic and hysteria which they generated was just about the only thing which could reduce the great man.

Much has been said about the motivations behind the trial of Socrates but as far as I know no one has suggested that his accusers were motivated by genuine piety. Most researchers see Socrates as the scapegoat for all the wrongs of

Athenian society, which led to the catastrophic defeat in the Peloponnesian war. Someone needed to be held responsible, someone larger than the politicians of the time, someone whose influence was seen as so far reaching and detrimental that it eroded the very foundations of the Athenian Democracy. We can be certain that Athenian public opinion was not concerned with scientific inquiries, investigations into celestial bodies, or even the nature of religion and the gods themselves. That was what philosophical investigation was about in a democratic, culturally open society. They would not even be upset or offended by jokes about the gods in comedy, and we do know for sure that Athenian comedians could be irreverent. Surely no one was offended when Aristophanes replaced the Olympian gods with birds, presented the gods like a selfish bunch of morons, and ultimately made them subject to the will of the Birds.

There were additional motives why when Aristophanes replaced the gods with the Clouds, the audience was outraged, the play flopped, and a quarter of a century later the real Socrates was punished for the sins of the fictional Socrates of the *Clouds*. While the *Birds* was a colorful fantasy, the *Clouds* in its original form seemed to carry a dangerous message, which rewarded immoral behavior and dishonesty, and threatened to use the enormous power of the newly discovered rhetoric and reasoning to tear apart the very fabric of society. The crushing defeat in the Peloponnesian war with all the suffering it brought, the defection of Alcibiades, and the tyranny of Kritias, seemed to confirm the dangers which men like Socrates and his pupils posed for Athenian society. Religion had little to do with it, but politics, social factors, and emotions like fear and anxiety had much to do with the conviction of Socrates.

Perhaps similar anxieties are to be found behind the prosecution of several women in the middle of the 4th century. It speaks volumes that even in a case like the one against Neaira, which had a political background and used the citizenship and immigration laws of the city as a means of an unmistakably political attack directed against her partner Stefanos, 1/6th of the speech is devoted to religion. It is perhaps not difficult to understand how Ninos, a priestess who was performing initiation rituals, could become the target given the hysteria which gripped the city over similar allegations in 415. However, the case of Theoris is less straightforward. Eidinow correctly has avoided the temptation of seeing the case against Theoris as a witch-hunt, as we understand it in the Christian era, but has sought to understand how magic, filters, incantations, potions, and alternative healing practices could be seen as dangerous in pagan pluralism. There is no easy answer to this, and we probably need to try and understand it in the wider context of anxieties caused by a major political, economic and cultural shifts in the final days of the Greek city-state.

Such anxieties surely were behind the prosecution and trial of Phryne, the ostentatious *hetaira* who had acquired so much wealth and prestige that her statue in Delphi, sculpted by no other than the great Praxiteles, stood in the neighborhood of the statues of gods, heroes and kings.[66] In some ways Phryne seems to be the embodiment of the fears expressed by Apollodoros that if prostitutes take center stage in Athenian society, they will displace respectable women, and present an invitation to citizen women to take up prostitution.[67] Exaggerated and rhetorical as this statement may have been, it could still carry a powerful message to the members of the jury. We know of several citizen women who took up prostitution in the 4th century, such as Mania, Gnathaina, Lais the Younger or Thais, just to mention a few. Surely what motivated them was hope for a better life inspired by a woman like Phryne. She was wealthy, fiercely independent, provocative, ostentatious, and generous in a very public way. Phryne was an aspirational woman at a time when feminine virtue was identified with anonymous respectability. In some ways she had a similar catalytic effect upon traditional Athenian culture and ideology as Socrates had in the previous century, a mesmerizing aura, and this is why like Socrates she was perceived as a threat by some. Fortunately for her an Athenian jury could not see a *hetaira* as equally dangerous as a subversive philosopher, and if there is any truth in the tale of her disrobement in court, all it would take was showing off one's breasts to convey very clearly the message that she was merely a pretty woman, and not some menace to society, or a threat to the traditional religious rites of the city.

8.5 Homicide

It may seem curious to the modern scholar that homicide was classed among religious offenses in Athens, both in terms of legal procedure and conceptual associations.[68] Like other religious offenses, homicide cases were introduced by the *basileus*.[69] The trial itself contained some unusual features not encountered in any other procedure, such as oaths and curses, as well as a requirement to stick to the facts of the case, and not to speak outside the subject. Unlike any other procedure, homicide cases were not tried by the heliastic courts, but from the archaic period to the end of the Athenian Democracy and beyond, they were tried by the Areopagos, or subsections of it consisting of 51 men, called the *ephetai*. The processes and concepts related to homicide seem to be static in time, stuck in the archaic period, unaffected by the earth-shattering changes which led from the aristocratic state to the radical democracy.

This legal conservatism was the direct result of the fact that the laws on homicide never changed; the Athenians continued to use the laws of Drakon without additions or alterations. To put this into perspective, most Solonean laws although still valid in the classical period, at least in theory, were adapted along the way to the processes and concepts of the Democratic Constitution as these continued to evolve from Kleisthenes to the end of the Greek *polis*. By contrast, the homicide laws of Drakon were neither adapted to function harmoniously with the legal procedures of the democracy, nor were susceptible to shifting cultural concepts and ideologies. In the 4th century they seem like a fossilized oddity preserved in a time capsule from a remote past. What shielded Athenian homicide laws from the changes around them was precisely their inextricable association with religion. They remained as static and unchanging as sacred law, one would imagine because humans were not supposed to tamper with the eternal order of the gods on matters of life or death.[70]

The origins and core concepts of Athenian homicide law can be traced back to the blood feuds of the aristocratic state. Unusually, unlike classical law, which had in mind individuals, homicide law had in mind entire families. While it did not go as far as attributing collective responsibility to families, only a relative of the deceased could prosecute his/her killer,[71] and only family members (*anchisteia*) could pardon the killer of someone, provided that the killing was accidental and the family unanimously agreed to forgive him and allow him to return from exile.[72] The relative of the victim could bring a homicide case before the *basileus* in the first ten months of the year. No new homicide cases were accepted in the last two months, as there was insufficient time for the completion of the preliminaries by the outgoing *basileus*. These included three preliminary hearings (προδικασίαι) accompanied by proclamations (προαγορεύειν), one in each month, barring the potential killer from the agora, public temples and all public gatherings (εἴργεσθαι τῶν νομίμων).[73] While it is not clear why three proclamations, instead of one, were deemed to be necessary, we can understand the underlying reason behind such a ritualistic approach. The ultimate objective was to prevent the spread of deadly *miasma*, which a killer carried and could transmit to anyone who shared the same roof.

Μίασμα was a form of "supernatural infection", in the words of D.M. MacDowell, which could spread from person-to-person with disastrous consequences, from shipwrecks to failing oracles and sacrifices.[74] The opening scene of the masterpiece of Sophocles *Oedipus Tyrannus* is based precisely upon this concept. Oedipus has unclean hands because he has killed his father, albeit in self-defense, but the *miasma* which he carries has infected the entire community, and the deadly contagion is not limited to humans, but it has already spread to animals and even the crops, and the entire land is suffering from the sins of a single man.[75] In Aeschylus *Eumenides* the priestess of Apollo supernaturally sees *miasma* as an image of blood dripping from the hands of Orestes (αἵματι στάζοντα χεῖρας).[76] This concept of *miasma* as a deadly contagion dominates Greek homicide laws and perceptions and is certainly not limited to Athens. When, for example, we are told that the Spartans exposed disabled babies, rather than actively engage in a mercy killing, the underlying concept was that killing would have exposed the families and the entire community to the dangers of *miasma*, while exposure amounted to passing the responsibility over to the gods.[77]

In Athenian legal practice most of the peculiarities of homicide procedure, as well as the persistent conservatism of Athenian homicide law, can be definitely attributed to the attempts to prevent contagion and protect the community from the pollution, which stained the hands of a killer. First and foremost, the perception of homicide as a religious offense is directly related to the doctrine of pollution. The killer had not only injured the family of the victim, but also offended the gods. This perception of crime is limited to homicide and other religious offenses and does not extend to secular violations of the law. Most of the Athenian criminal justice was perceived as a secular affair.

Second, the initiation of a homicide prosecution was highly unusual exactly because of its connection to religion. Proclamations, the set number of three preliminary hearings, but most importantly, for all intents and purposes, the imposition of temporary disfranchisement (ἀτιμία) upon a citizen who had not yet been found guilty of any crime are unique to homicide and certainly related to the doctrine of *miasma* (S 14). In particular, the imposition of temporary disfranchisement upon someone simply accused of homicide is what made such prosecutions attractive as weapons in public life and the political arena. We know of several cases where a homicide prosecution was used as a political weapon to temporarily remove someone from public life.[78] The danger of contagion was ever present even during the trial, and this is why homicide trials were always held in the open air. Moreover, several passages suggest that a proclamation for homicide could change the behavior of society towards the suspected killer. People might avoid close contact with him/her, they might be unwilling to share a roof, or participate in the same religious rites.[79] As a result, the person simply accused of homicide could become a social pariah in the months leading to the trial, excluded from public life, social interaction, and even the solace provided by religion in difficult times.

The opening scenes of a homicide trial must have appeared to 4th century Athenians like an awesome, archaic ritual (S 15). Unlike any other trial, here the litigants took terrible oaths, invoking disaster upon themselves and their families if they lied. There was also a rule that the litigants in their speeches should stick to the facts of the case. Of course, this had relative significance because the interpretation of what constituted relevant evidence was left up to the litigant. And yet, in the few extant speeches from homicide cases we can actually see that diversions and digressions common in other cases are not found in abundance. For the most part the litigants seem to be adhering to the facts of the case.

However, despite all the emphasis on the religious aspects of homicide, and the ensuing theatrics, an Athenian homicide trial was not an exercise in superstition and supernatural fears. Rational arguments were needed to win a case, arguments made persuasively and with sufficient clarity to win the votes of a very experienced body of judges. The members of the Areopagos had significant administrative experience before they even entered into this august, ancient Council. Every year those who had finished their term in office as one of the nine *archon*s joined the Areopagus Council for life. Some of these men would spend decades of their lives hearing homicide cases. It should come to us as no surprise that the Areopagos had a formidable reputation for fairness. Unlike heliastic courts which sometimes could be swayed by skillful orators or react emotionally to cases, the austere and experienced members of the Areopagos would probably need something more than cheap rhetoric or commonplace emotional manipulation to be persuaded. This was seen as an important safeguard because, as a passage of Antiphon states, condemning an innocent person to death would be as offensive to the gods as allowing a killer to walk free in their midst.[80] We have sufficient evidence to be sure that the Areopagos tried cases of intentional homicide of Athenian citizens, and if the defendant was found guilty, the penalty was always death. Given the non-negotiable outcome of a "guilty" verdict, a defendant was allowed to interrupt the trial after the first set of speeches and voluntarily go into permanent exile, where his life was safeguarded by the law of Drakon. If an angry relative of the victim pursued and killed him while in exile, his killer was himself guilty of homicide (S 7–10).

We are far less sure about the composition of the juries in the other three homicide courts.[81] The Palladion tried cases of unintentional manslaughter of citizens, or killings of foreigners or slaves, and could impose the penalties of exile or fine, quite possibly exile for the killing of a free person, and the fine for the killing of a slave. The Delphinion tried cases of justified homicide. The defendant did not contest the accusation that he had killed someone; he only claimed that the law exonerated him. This law was an old Draconian statute which clearly defined a limited set of circumstances where someone was not to be punished for killing another person. These cases were an accident during an athletic competition, at war or in the street (probably in self-defense, arguably like Oedipus, when he killed the hubristic Laius), or catching someone in bed with his wife, concubine, mother, sister or daughter (S 11).[82] A man was also exonerated if he killed in self-defense someone who was illegally attempting to take him away (S 12). Finally, the court of Phreatto tried persons who had fled Attica after accusations of homicide but wished to return. Since they were suspected of killing they were not allowed to step on land and spread pollution. Instead they stood in a boat, while the judges were sitting on land across. If the defendant was acquitted then he was allowed to step off the boat to dry land.[83]

The judges in the Palladion and Delphinion were called *ephetai*. We know that they were 51 in number, over 50 years of age and in the early days they were selected on merit (ἀριστίνδην). The majority of scholars believe that in the classical period they were a subcommittee of the Areopagos, probably chosen by lot, but we have no positive confirmation of this in our sources.

Finally, nothing illustrates more vividly the fear of supernatural contagion among the Athenians, than the trial of animals, inanimate objects and unknown killers, in the Prytaneion. This was more than a mere formality, as it required the attention of the *basileus* as the presiding magistrate, along with the *phylobasileis*, the kings of the four ancient Ionian tribes. Animals or objects found guilty were cast out of the borders of Attica. It is astonishing that even non-humans could carry and spread the contagion of *miasma*, and this is why even non-humans were liable to the penalties of homicide law.

In the 5th century, new legislation allowed for *apagoge*, *endeixis* or *ephegesis* for homicide cases. They could be initiated when a citizen spotted a suspected killer in the Agora or a sacred place polluting with his presence those around him. The citizen could then seize the alleged killer and take him to the Eleven (*apagoge*), denounce him (*endeixeis*) or take the magistrate to him (*ephegesis*). That person could have been someone against whom a proclamation had been issued and he chose to ignore it, someone against whom a proclamation had not yet been issued because it was near the end of the year, or someone who, for whatever reason, had not been prosecuted even though he had killed someone. One such case was that of Agoratos, who during the Thirty caused the death of a man named Dionysios by denouncing him. After the restoration of the democracy Dionysiodoros, the brother of Dionysios had been unable to prosecute the man who deliberated his brother's death because of the amnesty. But then, he denounced Agoratos (*endeixis*) on the grounds that as a killer he was spreading contagion to those with whom he came into contact.[84]

In these procedures, if the defendant confessed he was instantly executed, but if he did not, like most people in the face of imminent peril, the case went for trial to a regular court. It is remarkable that through the employment of these procedures normal homicide processes were bypassed. However, in this case it was not the homicide that was a primary offense, but the grossly negligent, callous and potentially lethal behavior of the defendant, who did not care if he put an entire community at grave risk by mixing with others and spreading his contagion. The homicide charges were relevant only at the base level, because if they were true, then the grossly irresponsible citizen was putting everyone at risk. However, it was the serious threat from the behavior of the defendant to the community, rather than the actual killing, that was at the center of this prosecution, and this is why it was referred to regular courts, like all other cases of *apagoge*, *endeixis*, or *ephegesis*.[85]

The four extant speeches from homicide trials (Ant. 1, 5, 6, Lys. 1), as well as the three sets of model speeches in the tetralogies of Antiphon,[86] illustrate that two seemingly opposing elements were inextricably linked together. Reason and superstition were harmoniously collaborating in order to secure the vote. It is not an accident that Antiphon and Lysias, the two most prominent litigators for homicide trials, were also the two larger than life names responsible for the firm establishment of rhetoric in the Athenian legal system. Especially in those cases where the verdict was very literally a matter of life or death, rhetorical prowess mattered even more, and all four speeches, each in their own different way, are remarkable samples of Attic Oratory. While all of them take for granted the doctrine of *miasma* and the powerful religious extensions of homicide cases, each utilizes arguments from the sphere of the divine and the supernatural in different ways. Antiphon 5 *On the Chorister*, and 6 *On the Murder of Herodes* contain most of the references to the religious aspects of homicide, but not without good reason: in both cases religious and supernatural arguments serve well the objectives of the litigants, and this is why they have a prominent place in the development of the case. More subtle is the employment of the supernatural in Antiphon 1 *On the Stepmother*, where the speaker is deliberately presenting himself as another Orestes intent on punishing his stepmother, whom he calls a Klytaimestra, for the killing of his father.[87] The deployment of the argument evokes undertones similar to the dramatic quest for vengeance in the awe-inspiring opening scenes of Aeschylus *Eumenides*. By contrast, the religious element is entirely absent in Lysias *On the Murder of Eratosthenes*, and this is deliberate. Emphasis on the *miasma* in the hands of a killer would not serve well Euphiletos, who was admitting that he had killed Eratosthenes, but claimed that he had done so in mitigating circumstances, which rendered the killing permissible. The defense of Euphiletos is squarely based on an outstanding narrative and sound logical arguments, while with masterful ethopoeia Lysias has created the portrait of a law-abiding avenger.

We should be in no doubt that rational 5th and 4th century Athenians needed coherent arguments and convincing rhetoric in order to be persuaded. Religion was an important part of this rhetoric and could be manipulated and folded into the argument to enhance and enrich logical considerations. The awe-inspiring rituals of a homicide trial, their archaic character, and their supernatural undertones gave homicide cases a unique character and separated them from ordinary cases. Homicide trials were not trivial affairs and were not meant to be, as they stood in a hazy dividing line between religious crimes, which primarily offended the gods, and secular crime, which threatened the fabric of society.

Notes

1 Trsl. F.G. Kenyon, with minor modifications.
2 Trsl. Charles Darwin Adams.
3 Trsl. Andrew Wolpert.
4 Trsl. H. Rackham.
5 The text is the one of *IG*i[3], while the translation is the one provided by S. Lambert and P.J. Rhodes on the site *Attic Inscriptions Online* (www.atticinscriptions.com/inscription/StroudDrakon/42-7-l-12).
6 All translations of laws from Demosthenes in this section come from the translation of A.T. Murray.
7 The most recent and thorough discussion of the topic can be found in Evans 2010; see also Rhodes 2009: 1–13.
8 For the scandal and the events surrounding it, the classic commentary of MacDowell on Andocides 1 (1962) is still the best source of information. See also Marr 1971: 326–38; McGlew 1999: 1–22; Prandi 1996: 65–70; Will 1977: 92–6.
9 The precise number of canonical books varies from one Christian tradition to another, from 66 in Protestantism to 81 in Ethiopian Orthodoxy.
10 See the recent discussion in Phillips 2014: 75–97.
11 Philochoros, *FGrH* 328 F 206; Pl. *Phdr*. 244 b; DS 14.13.4; Thgn. 1.807, *Suppl. Epigr. Gr*. 23.80, col. 1, fr. b, 4. See also *Suppl. Epigr. Gr*. 36.206, which outlines the rituals and sacrifices to Pluto, along with those to the two goddesses, during the Thesmophoria. The plural in line 11 ἱέρειαι should be referring to the priestess of Demeter and Kore, and the priestess of Pluto working together.
12 For example, D. 57.47 εἰ μὲν ἔλαχον ἱερεύς; *IG* ii[2] 1 1334.13–14: τῶν λαγχανουσῶν ἱερειῶν εἰς τὴν θεόν.
13 See the discussion in Chapter 1.4.
14 See Solon's own explanation of these principles in Fr. 36 West.
15 For the role of religion in the early Greek *polis* see Hägg 1996;
16 For this aspect of the festival, as a showcase of Athenian power, see Shapiro 1996: 215–25 and Shear 2001 (Ph.D. Diss).
17 D. 59.24.
18 On the *pannychis* of the Panathenaia see Pritchett 1986: 179–88.
19 *IG* ii[2] 334; see also Lewis 1959: 239–47.
20 For example, *IG* ii[2] 212, 351 (330/329 BC, honoring the Plataian citizen Eudemos with ἔγκτησις), 456, 457, 492, 784 (an honorary decree for the ἀθλοθέται). Other important works on the Panathenaia include Spetsieri-Choremi and Palagia 2004; Boegehold 1996; 95–105; Neils 1996; Sourvinou-Inwood 2011 (on the myths related to the festival), and certainly the accounts in the general books on Greek religion and festivals mentioned above (n. 9).

21 On the Dionysia and its intersection with the life of the *polis* see also Goldhill 1990: 97–129; Rhodes 2011: 71–4; Wilson 2009: 8–29; Connor 1990: 7–32; Finkelberg 2006: 17–26.

22 Trsl. by George Norlin.

23 See Boeckh 1857: 290–8.

24 A decree of Demosthenes reversed the policy of the years of Euboulos and legalized the transfer of moneys from the theoric to the stratiotic fund, but not before 339/8, when Phillip attacked Byzantium and threatened the vital grain supplies destined for Athens. A direct confrontation between the city and Phillip was under way, which would be resolved in the battlefield of Chaironea with the crushing defeat of the southern Greek states.

25 The classic study on the Eleusinian Mysteries is Mylonas 1961; see also Sourvinou-Inwood 2003: 25–49; Skov 1975: 136–47; Evans 2002: 227–54; Clinton 1974 (with emphasis on the priests and officials of the Mysteries).

26 Andoc. 1.43. A decree which had been introduced in the *archon*ship of Skamandrios prohibited the torture of free persons, and the Athenian state took this prohibition very seriously. The precise year of its introduction is unknown, but it is generally believed to be around 510, after the fall of the Peisistratids. The unprecedented proposal to suspend the decree, made by Peisandros in the middle of the scandal of 415, clearly did not materialize. The fact that this decree needed to be suspended before anyone could be tortured for information reveals how seriously the Athenian authorities took this decree; no exception was ever allowed, not even in a time of crisis.

27 See Andoc. 1.11.

28 On women and religion see Parca and Tzanetou 2007; Blundell and Williamson 1998; Brumfield 1981; Prytz 1975: 78–87; Skov 1975: 136–47.

29 On the Thesmophoria see also Stehle 2007: Chlup 2007: 69–95; 165–85; Trümpy 2004: 13–42; Stallsmith 2008: 28–45; Lowe 1998: 149–73; Clinton 1996: 111–25.

30 *IG* ii^2 1117, 1184; *SEG* 36.206; see also Broneer 1942: 250–74.

31 See the discussion in Kapparis 1999: 413–18. The most important sources for the festival are the narrative of Apollodoros in *Against Neaira* (116), and the learned scholiast of Lucian (279.24 Rabe). The most reliable study on the subject is that by A.C. Brumfield (1981); see also the relevant sections in Sfameni-Gasparo 1986; Foxhall 1995: 97–110; Lowe 1998: 149–73; Parker 1979: 256–7; Skov 1975: 136–47.

32 The most significant source on the Anthesteria and the ritual of the sacred marriage is Apollodoros *Against Neaira* (74–84); see also my commentary on these sections (1999: 324–44). Important studies on the Anthesteria and the sacred marriage include Hamilton 1992 (with emphasis on the iconography of the festival); Avagianou 1991; Nissinen 2008; Craik 1987: 21–34.

33 Maurizio Lisa has argued that the Anthesteria were an assembly of disorderly, aimless processions which performed identities that could not be expressed in the city center. This argument, in my opinion, totally misses the point and character of the festival, and is based on misinterpretations of the evidence.

34 The most important book on the phratries and their role in Athenian public life is Lambert 1993, while the discussion of Nicholas Jones (1999, esp. Chapters 5 and 6) was an important addition to the debate. See also Cromey 2006: 41–69; Nilsson 1986; Flower 1985: 232–5; Ustinova 1996: 227–42; Hedrick 1991: 241–68; Seifert 2011; Evans 2004: 1–25.

35 For example, D. 19.297–9; 21.51–4; 43.66–7; Epistulae 1.16; 4.3; Aesch. 3.107–12. The close connection of the Oracle at Delphi with Sparta induced the Athenian state to seek answers from the oracle of Dodona, perhaps more often than expected, given than Delphi was so close, and Dodona so far from Athens.

36 Hdt. 3.31: ἐξηγηταὶ τῶν πατρίων θεσμῶν, for the Persian judges.

37 Pl. *Lg*. 759 c 7, d 5, e 2; 828 b 4.

38 Pl. *Euthyphro* 9 a; D. 47.68; see the discussion in Chapter 8.5.

39 For example, an inscription from Attica (*IG* ii^2 333) is concerned with cultic objects for various festivals and seems to be imposing punishment with lashes on negligent public slaves, in charge of them. An inscription from the temple of Despoina at Lykosoura prohibits gold, purple, flowery or black dresses, shoes or rings. Any of these items brought into to the temple will need to be dedicated to the goddess (*IG* v^2 514. 3–9). An inscription from Delos prohibits entry to a drunk person or someone wearing a flowery dress (*IG* xi 4.1300). An inscription from Kos ordains that the priest of Zeus is not to enter a house where someone has died before five days have passed, a house where a woman has given birth before three days have passed, and a house where a woman has had an abortion for five days after the event (see R. Herzog 'Gesetze von Kos' in *Abhandlungen der preussischen Akademie der Wissenschaften, Jahrgang 1928, philosophisch-historische Klasse*, p. 15). One such remarkable document from Philadelphia (*LSA* 20) has been heavily influenced by the ethics of the Hippocratic Oath, and forbids unmarried women who are not virgins to enter the sanctuary (see my discussion of the document in Kapparis 2002: 214–18). For the body of Greek sacred laws and relevant discussion and analysis see Sokolowski 1969 (the classic collection); Lupu 2005 (additional documents); Lambert 2005: 125–59 (Athenian laws and decrees with religious regulations preserved in inscriptions); Lewis 1959: 239–47 (law on the Lesser Panathenaia); Parker 2004: 57–70 (what are sacred laws); Rhodes 2009: 1–13; Robertson 2013: 195–244.

40 See for example the recommendations of the oracles in D. 21.53–4, and 43.66–7. The sacred laws of the Greek cities are full of such instructions of atonement.

41 For example, the prosecution of Andocides by Kallias, for accidentally placing a suppliant branch on the altar in Eleusis during the Mysteries, seems to be based on an unintentional violation. Andocides claims that he did not know that it was not permitted to do so during the festival. Of course, the entire prosecution was not motivated by piety, but in the end Andocides was acquitted (See And. 1 for this narrative). Likewise, Aeschylos was accused of accidentally revealing parts of the secret ritual of the Mysteries in one of his plays but was acquitted when it was clear that he had not been initiated in the Mysteries, and therefore any similarities were coincidental (ClemAl. *Str.* 2.14.60.3). The details of the story, as given by Clement are inaccurate, since impiety was not introduced to the Areopagos, but while the story may be true, it is possible that Clement used the Areopagos in his narrative to add gravitas to the proceedings. The case of the hierophant in the speech *Against Neaira* (59.116), who was punished for improperly sacrificing during the Haloa is different, because he was a religious figure who willfully violated sacred law, and therefore in his case a plea of ignorance did not apply.

42 Plu. *Per.* 32.

43 See for example Pl. *Apol.* 19 b 1–2, 26 b 4.

44 David Phillips (2013: 485) has argued that the prosecution of Phryne actually was an *eisangelia*, but there is absolutely no evidence for this, while all available evidence speaks about a *graphe asebeias* (e.g. Alciphron 4.3; Anon. Seg. *Ars Rhetorica* 215; Chorikios 29.2.45 and 76; Eustathios *Com. Il.* 4.579).

45 MacDowell 1978: 200–2.

46 Tim Whitmarsh (2015: 71–137) is willing to accept that the trials for atheism are true and that science was inhibited, but the evidence for the trials is much later (found in authors like Plutarch or Clement of Alexandria) and anecdotal in nature (see for example the criticisms of Dover 1975: 24–54), while, on the other hand, works like Aristotle's *Meteorologica* or *About the Sky*, some of the Platonic Dialogues, or the works of Eudoxus could not have been produced in a city which only a few years before was willing to execute scientists. Although a narrative of religious persecutions, and a reaction to the birth of reason and science may sound alluring, it is a false one, and probably

a product of the second sophistic. The Athenian Democracy happily accommodated cultural diversity, and this openness is what allowed reason, science, medicine, rhetoric and philosophy to be born and thrive in that particular time and place.

47 Filonik 2013: 11–96; Wallace 1994: 127–55 and 1996: 226–40.

48 On atheism as a cultural phenomenon in the Greek world see Whitmarsh 2015 and O'Sullivan 2011: 167–85.

49 For example, an *eisangelia* to the Boule could be a two-stage process, with one vote before the Boule and the final, decisive vote before the court, or a *dokimasia* before the Boule, could also be a two-stage process, with a final appeal to the courts. In fact, every single *dike* was a two-stage process, starting with public arbitration and only ending up in court, if one of the parties was still dissatisfied with the solution produced during the arbitration.

50 For example, the modern reader might react with disbelief to the charges of *eisangelia* against Lykophron brought by Ariston and Lykourgos, on the grounds that Lykophron was a danger to the Athenian *polis*, even though he had been living in Lemnos for more than three years and had no involvement in Athenian politics, or that he had corrupted many unnamed women and he was a dangerous, serial seducer, when Lykophron was in his fifties and living away from Athens. It certainly looks as if feeble excuses were used to bring this *eisangelia* to court. The true motives behind it seemingly included old animosities and a property grab. For the case against Lykophron see Phillips 2006: 375–394.

51 The quarrel between Demosthenes and Meidias preceded the events which resulted in the *probole* against Meidias. If we believe the narrative of Demosthenes, when he was appointed *choregos* Meidias did his best to sabotage him and publicly embarrass him, and then punched him in the face during the festival. Undoubtedly there were multiple witnesses to this and the initial vote in the assembly went against Meidias. What happened beyond this point is a matter of interpretation of an ambiguous phrase of Aeschines (3.52: καὶ ταῦτ' ἤδη τὰ περὶ Μειδίαν καὶ τοὺς κονδύλους οὓς ἔλαβεν ἐν τῇ ὀρχήστρᾳ χορηγὸς ὤν, καὶ ὡς ἀπέδοτο τριάκοντα μνῶν ἅμα τήν τε εἰς αὑτὸν ὕβριν καὶ τὴν τοῦ δήμου καταχειροτονίαν ἣν ἐν Διονύσου κατεχειροτόνησε Μειδίου. [Let me remind you the affair with Meidias, and the punches which he received in the orchestra while he was a charges, and how he sold-out for a mere 30 minae the *hybris* and the vote of the assembly, when the people voted against Meidias in the theater of Dionysos.] MacDowell, with the majority of scholars, initially believed that Demosthenes dropped the case and did not take Meidias to court after winning the vote of the assembly, and that the speech as we have it was never delivered. Later he revised his views, and in his monumental commentary of the speech Against Meidias reached the conclusion that the case went to court, Demosthenes won, and then proposed a penalty of 30 minae, which for a rich man like Meidias, would be rather light. We may be able to see a respectable compromise in this outcome. Demosthenes agreed to the lesser penalty proposed by his opponent (συγχωρεῖν), probably in exchange for a final settlement of their differences and an end to the hostilities between Meidias and himself. If seen in this light, this outcome may not have been quite as dishonorable as Aeschines suggests.

52 According to Suda (s.v.) the Pandia was celebrated on the 14th of Elaphebolion (March/April).

53 David Cohen (1988: 695–701) correctly points out the difficulties of defining *asebeia* as a legal concept. It simply seems to be the case that the Athenians used a very broad definition of what constituted *asebeia*: anything that might offend the gods could be considered to be *asebeia*, as Plato suggests in the *Euthyprho*.

54 Filonik 2013: 83.

55 For more detailed readings of the trial of Socrates, and its socio-political background see Brickhouse and Smith 1989; Connor 1991: 49–56; Samaras 2007: 1–11.

56 It would appear that the original play ended soon after line 1302. Pheidippides had learned well the skill of rhetoric and with his help Strepsiades was able to vanquish his tormentors and lenders. After that it was time for a celebratory party. This version seemed to condone immoral behaviors, benefiting from the extraordinary powers of the new tool of rhetoric. The final scenes of the play, which include the beating of Strepsiades by his son, his defeat in the subsequent argument with his son, where against all custom and reason he is compelled to accept that his son was right to hit him, and the burning of the school of Socrates as the necessary way to purge this evil from the city, where added later as remedies to the offending ending of the original *Clouds*.

57 X. Mem. 1.2.12: Ἀλλ' ἔφη γε ὁ κατήγορος, Σωκράτει ὁμιλητὰ γενομένω Κριτίας τε καὶ Ἀλκιβιάδης πλεῖστα κακὰ τὴν πόλιν ἐποιησάτην. Κριτίας μὲν γὰρ τῶν ἐν τῇ ὀλιγαρχίᾳ πάντων πλεονεκτίστατός τε καὶ βιαιότατος ἐγένετο, Ἀλκιβιάδης δὲ αὖ τῶν ἐν τῇ δημοκρατίᾳ πάντων ἀκρατέστατός τε καὶ ὑβριστότατος. [But his accuser argued thus: Among the associates of Socrates were Critias and Alcibiades; and none wrought so many evils to the state. For Critias in the days of the oligarchy bore the palm for greed and violence: Alcibiades, for his part, exceeded all in licentiousness and insolence under the democracy.] (Trsl. E.C. Marchant).

58 Athen. 13.59. The tales of Phryne's unveiling have provided inspiration for more than a dozen art works in the modern era.

59 The various versions of the story range from no nudity in Poseidippos (apud Athen. 13.60), to complete nudity in Quintilian (*Inst.* 2.15.9), while most Greek authors who mention the incident speak of partial nudity (only the breasts: Hyp. Fr. 178; Anon. Sch. in Hermog. 7.335 Walz). A. Casanova (1962), and more recently Jakub Filonik (2013: 65–6), are prepared to put some faith in the account of Poseidippos because of its chronological proximity and the fact that there is no nudity, but the process as described there is not consonant with what we would expect of an Athenian trial. We need to conclude that his account is no more reliable that those of later antiquity authors.

60 Havelock 1995: 3–4 and 42–7; Filonik 2013: 66.

61 Aesch. 1. 104; D. 40.33; see also O'Connell 2017.

62 D. 23.79–80.

63 See D. 39.2, 40.9; Din. Fr. 33.1 Conomis (= D. H. *Din.* 11); Sch. Dem. 19. 495a-b.

64 ClemAl. *Str.* 2.14.60.3.

65 The speech *Against Euboulides* (D. 57.8) mentions a *graphe asebeias* brought by Euboulides against a citizen woman, the sister of Lakedaimonios. No further details are given, except that she was comfortably acquitted, while her accuser did not even secure the 1/5 of the votes.

66 See Kapparis 2017: 321–5.

67 D. 59.113.

68 Homicide procedures have been thoroughly explored in a number of important studies. The classic work of D. M. MacDowell (1963) remains a central point of reference, while many of the finer points have been thoroughly discussed by Carawan (1998, and also 1991: 1–16 and 1993: 235–70), Gagarin (1981, and also 1978: 111–20; 1979: 301–23; 1990: 81–99; 2000: 569–79), Phillips (2008); Wallace 1984; Stroud: 1979; Tulin (1996); Riess 2008: 49–94; Evjen (1962); Hansen (1978) and others. Engaging closely with this rich literature would require a volume in itself. I have benefited greatly from these studies as background material for this short account.

69 On the role of the *basileus* in homicide cases see Gagarin 2000: 569–79.

70 The static and ritualistic aspects of Draconian laws are thoroughly explored by Carawan (1998). Although the reader may feel that some of the ritualistic aspects of oaths and other paraphernalia in homicide trials have been overemphasized, Carawan's work remains a standard for our understanding of these aspects of Athenian homicide law.

71 The most significant text confirming that only relatives were allowed to bring a homicide case is D. 47.73. The passage is at the core of Tulin's discussion (1996); see also Oliver (1950) for the role of the *exegetai* in the affirmation of this rule.

72 The relevant portion of the law has been preserved in an inscription dated in 409/408, which recorded Drakon's homicide law (S 6), and is confirmed by literary sources. See Stroud 1979.

73 See for example Ant. 5.4; 6.34–40; D. 23.42, 47.69; Arist. *Ath. Pol.* 57.2; Isoc. 11.157;

74 MacDowell 1978: 110; see also Ant. 5.82–3. The literature on *miasma* is too large to engage in detail here. The study of Robert Parker *Miasma* (1976) occupies central position; see also Arnaoutoglou 1993: 109–37; Robertson 2013: 195–244; Giordano 2014: 291–310; Visser 1984: 193–206; Todd 2017: 325–64; McPherran 2002: 105–30; Blickman 1986: 193–208; Harris 2015: 11–35.

75 S. *O.T.* 1–462; see also Harris 2010: 122–46 for a discussion of the finer points pertaining to the possible guilt of Oedipus according to Athenian homicide law.

76 A. *Eu.* 41–2; see also Kennedy 2009: 19–46; Carrara 2007: 3–16; Sommerstein 2010: 25–38.

77 Important studies on *miasma* include the classic work of Robert Parker (1976).

78 For example, in Antiphon's speech *On the Chorister* (34–40), the speaker argues that his opponents prosecuted him for the homicide of the choir boy Diodotos, only because he was the prosecutor in a major public trial for bribery and corruption. The relatives of Diodotos in collusion with the men he was prosecuting accused him of homicide in order to stop him from going to the trial. If they had succeeded in this plot and he were not able to appear in court on the day of the trial, the bribery case would have collapsed. As it happened, because these events took place in the last two months of the year, when no homicide prosecutions were accepted, the ploy failed, the bribery case went to court, and the defendants lost and were punished. Another striking example is the prosecution of Apollodoros by Stephanos for homicide in 346 BC (D. 59.9–10; see also my previous discussion in Kapparis 1999: 182–90). This was clearly a political move. Apollodoros had been a staunch supporter of the anti-Macedonian party, and a couple of years ago he had attempted to divert public funds into military purposes. Clearly he was seen as an outspoken opponent of any peace deal with Phillip, and the supporters of the peace tried to temporarily remove him from public life while the peace negotiations were taking place through a homicide prosecution. In the worst-case scenario for his opponents Apollodoros would be absent from public life for a period of four months, from the moment of the initial proclamation until his trial, and if they succeeded in this ploy, he could be permanently exiled from Attica for the murder of an alien woman. As it happened, the entire plot collapsed in court and Apollodoros was acquitted, but even so, his opponents had succeeded in their objective to remove him from public life during the critical stages of the negotiations over the peace of Philocrates.

79 See, for example, Ant. 5.82–3 and 6.45–6, where the defendants are citing their full participation in public life, smooth interaction with other people, and unhindered participation in religious rights in the months leading to the trial as evidence that they were not guilty. The argument is that if they had been killers, infected with *miasma*, they would transmit it to those around them spreading disaster, disease, and the displeasure of the gods.

80 On the Areopagos see Wallace 1984; Sealey 1983: 275–96; Carrara 2007: 3–16; Pedersen 1990: 73–8; Sommerstein 2010: 25–38; De Bruyn 1995 (more on the political aspects of the competence of the Areopagos).

81 On the other Athenian homicide courts see Boegehold 2009; Sealey 1983: 275–96; Carawan 1991: 1–16; Lanni 2012: 119–35; Travlos 1974: 500–11 (on the *Palladion*); Miles 1950: 219–24 (*Phreatto*); Carawan 1990: 47–67 (*Phreatto*).

82 The entire case of Lysias 1 rests precisely upon this law. Euphiletos has argued that he caught his wife in bed with Eratosthenes and killed him (for the particulars of the case see Todd 2007: 43–60). Lysias has built a tight, careful defense with masterful *ethopoeia*, but still the only witnesses to the adultery charge are friends of Euphiletos, and through a few minor cracks on the surface the careful reader might start questioning the details of the narrative on the fateful night when Eratosthenes was killed and become more suspicious. Euphiletos might not have been the inexorable avenger of his honor, but a cold-blooded, calculating killer using the pretense of adultery to escape punishment.

83 We do not know of any case ever tried in this court, and one would imagine that such trials were extremely rare.

84 See Lysias 13 *Against Agoratos*. See also Paoli 1932: 289–308;

85 For the use of *apagoge*, *endeixis*, or *ephegesis* for homicide cases see Gagarin 1979: 301–23; Hansen 1976 and 1981: 11–30 (a response to Gagarin); Volonaki 2000: 147–76; Bianchetti 1983: 91–104; Evjen 1970: 403–15; Zajonz 2014: 251–71.

86 On the tetralogies see Carawan 1993: 235–70.

87 See Apostolakis 2007: 179–92.

9 The safety net

Protecting those in need

9.1 Sources

1 The primary law requiring of the *archon* to protect the weaker members of society

> ΝΟΜΟΣ: Ὁ ἄρχων ἐπιμελείσθω τῶν ὀρφανῶν καὶ τῶν ἐπικλήρων καὶ τῶν οἴκων τῶν ἐξερημουμένων καὶ τῶν γυναικῶν, ὅσαι μένουσιν ἐν τοῖς οἴκοις τῶν ἀνδρῶν τῶν τεθνηκότων φάσκουσαι κυεῖν. τούτων ἐπιμελείσθω καὶ μὴ ἐάτω ὑβρίζειν μηδένα περὶ τούτους. ἐὰν δέ τις ὑβρίζῃ ἢ ποιῇ τι παράνομον, κύριος ἔστω ἐπιβάλλειν κατὰ τὸ τέλος. ἐὰν δὲ μείζονος ζημίας δοκῇ ἄξιος εἶναι, προσκαλεσάμενος πρόπεμπτα καὶ τίμημα ἐπιγραψάμενος, ὅ τι ἂν δοκῇ αὐτῷ, εἰσαγέτω εἰς τὴν ἡλιαίαν. ἐὰν δ᾽ ἁλῷ, τιμάτω ἡ ἡλιαία περὶ τοῦ ἁλόντος, ὅ τι χρὴ αὐτὸν παθεῖν ἢ ἀποτεῖσαι.
>
> (D. 43.75)
>
> LAW: Let the *archon* take charge of orphans and of heiresses and of families that are becoming extinct, and of all women who remain in the houses of their deceased husbands, declaring that they are pregnant. Let him take charge of these, and not suffer anyone to do any outrage to them. And if anyone shall commit any outrage or any lawless act against them, he shall have power to impose a fine upon such person up to the limit fixed by law. And if the offender shall seem to him to be deserving of a more severe punishment, let him summon such a person, giving him five days' notice, and bring him before the court of Heliaea, writing upon the indictment the penalty which he thinks is deserved. And if there be a conviction, let the court of Heliaea appoint for the one convicted what penalty he ought to suffer or pay.[1]

2 Social protection network and the responsibilities of the *archon*

> γραφαὶ δ[ὲ καὶ δ]ίκαι λαγχάνονται πρὸς αὐτόν, ἃς ἀνακρίνας εἰς τὸ δικαστήριον εἰσάγει,[γο]νέων κακώσεως (αὗται δ᾽ εἰσὶν ἀζήμιοι τῷ βουλο-μένῳ δ[ι]ώκειν), ὀρφανῶν κ[ακώ]σεως (αὗται δ᾽ εἰσὶ κατὰ τῶν ἐπιτρόπων), ἐπικλήρου κακώσε[ως (αὗτ]αι δ᾽ εἰσὶ κατὰ [τῶν] ἐπιτρόπων

καὶ τῶν συνοικούντων), οἴκου ὀρφανικοῦ κακώσεως (εἰσὶ δὲ καὶ [αὗται κατὰ τῶν] ἐπιτρόπων), παρανοίας, ἐάν τις αἰτιᾶταί τινα παρανοοῦντα τὰ[ὑπάρχοντα ἀ]πολλύν[αι], εἰς δατητῶν αἵρεσιν, ἐάν τις μὴ θέλῃ κοινὰ [τὰ ὄντα νέμεσθ]αι, εἰς ἐπι[τρ]οπῆς κατάστασιν, εἰς ἐπιτροπῆς διαδικασίαν, εἰς [ἐμφανῶν κατάστας]ιν, ἐπίτρ[οπ]ον αὑτὸν ἐγγράψαι, κλήρων καὶ ἐπικλήρων ἐπι[δικασίαι. ἐπιμελεῖτ]αι δὲ καὶ τῶν [ὀρφ]ανῶν καὶ τῶν ἐπικλήρων, καὶ τῶν γυναικῶν ὅσαι ἂν τελευτή[σαντος τοῦ ἀνδρ]ὸς σκή[πτω]νται κύειν. καὶ κύριός ἐστι τοῖς ἀδικοῦσιν ἐπιβάλ[λειν ἢ εἰσάγειν εἰς] τὸ δικα[στή]ριον. μισθοῖ δὲ καὶ τοὺς οἴκους τῶν ὀρφανῶν καὶ τῶν ἐπικλ[ήρων, ἕως ἄν τις τετταρ]ακαιδε[κέ]τις γένηται, καὶ τὰ ἀποτιμήματα λαμβάν[ει, καὶ τοὺς ἐπιτρόπους], ἐὰν μὴ [δι]δῶσι τοῖς παισὶ τὸν σῖτον, οὗτος εἰσπράττει.

(Arist. *Ath. Pol.* 56)

Criminal and civil law-suits are instituted before him, and after a preliminary trial he brings them in before the Jury-court: actions for ill-usage of parents (in which anybody who wishes may act as prosecutor without liability to penalty); for ill-usage of orphans (which lie against their guardians); for ill-usage of an heiress (which lie against the guardians or the relations that they live with); for injury to an orphan's estate (these also lie against the guardians); prosecutions for insanity, when one man accuses another of wasting his property when insane; actions for the appointment of liquidators, when a man is unwilling for property to be administered in partnership; actions for the institution of guardianship; actions for deciding rival claims to guardianship; actions for the production of goods or documents; actions for enrollment as trustee; claims to estates and to heiresses. [7] He also supervises orphans and heiresses and women professing to be with child after the husband's death, and he has absolute power to fine offenders against them or to bring them before the Jury-court. He grants leases of houses belonging to orphans and heiresses until they are fourteen years of age, and receives the rents, and he exacts maintenance for children from guardians who fail to supply it.[2]

3 There was no risk or administrative fee for prosecuting maltreatment of orphans and heiresses

Καὶ οὐκ [ἂν] εἰσήγγειλας πρὸς τὸν ἄρχοντα κακοῦσθαι τὴν ἐπίκληρον ὑπὸ τοῦ εἰσποιήτου οὕτως ὑβριζομένην καὶ ἄκληρον τῶν ἑαυτῆς πατρῴων καθισταμένην, ἄλλως τε καὶ μόνων τούτων τῶν δικῶν ἀκινδύνων τοῖς διώκουσιν οὐσῶν καὶ ἐξὸν τῷ βουλομένῳ βοηθεῖν ταῖς ἐπικλήροις; Οὔτε γὰρ ἐπιτίμιον ταῖς πρὸς τὸν ἄρχοντα εἰσαγγελίαις ἔπεστιν, οὐδὲ ἐὰν μηδεμίαν τῶν ψήφων οἱ εἰσαγγείλαντες μεταλάβωσιν, οὔτε πρυτανεῖα οὔτε παράστασις οὐδεμία τίθεται τῶν εἰσαγγελιῶν· ἀλλὰ τοῖς μὲν διώκουσιν ἀκινδύνως εἰσαγγέλλειν ἔξεστι, τῷ βουλομένῳ, τοῖς δ᾽ ἁλισκομένοις <αἱ> ἔσχαται τιμωρίαι ἐπὶ ταῖς εἰσαγγελίαις ἔπεισιν.

(Is. 3.46)

And did you fail to bring a denunciation in the *archon*'s court for injury to the heiress thus maltreated by the adopted son and despoiled of her paternal inheritance, especially as this is the only class of public actions which involves no risk to the party who brings it, and anyone who wishes is allowed to defend the rights of heiresses? For no fine can be inflicted for denunciations made to the *archon*, even if the informants fail to receive a single vote,[1] and there are no deposits or court fees[2] paid in any impeachments; but while the prosecutors may bring an impeachment without running any risk, extreme penalties are inflicted on those who are convicted in such impeachments.[3]

4 Athenian men are responsible for the maintenance of their elderly parents and their patrimony

Δοκεῖ δὲ καὶ κάλλιστα νομοθετῆσαι· ἐάν τις μὴ τρέφῃ τοὺς γονέας, ἄτιμος ἔστω· ἀλλὰ καὶ ὁ τὰ πατρῷα κατεδηδοκὼς ὁμοίως.

(Diogenes Laertios 1.55)

It appears that [Solon] introduced an excellent law: if one does not provide for his parents, he is to be disfranchised; likewise, the man who squanders his patrimony is to suffer the same punishment.

5 Legal definition of the term "parent"

Οὐ τοίνυν ἐκ τούτου μόνον, ἀλλὰ καὶ ἐκ τοῦ περὶ τῆς κακώσεως νόμου δῆλόν ἐστιν . . . . Κελεύει γὰρ τρέφειν τοὺς γονέας· γονεῖς δ' εἰσὶ μήτηρ καὶ πατὴρ καὶ πάππος καὶ τήθη καὶ τούτων μήτηρ καὶ πατήρ, ἐὰν ἔτι ζῶσιν· ἐκεῖνοι γὰρ ἀρχὴ τοῦ γένους εἰσὶ καὶ τὰ ἐκεί-νων παραδίδοται τοῖς ἐγγόνοις· διόπερ ἀνάγκη τρέφειν αὐτούς ἐστι, κἂν μηδὲν καταλίπωσι.

(Isaios 8.32)

This is the clear intention not only of this law but also of that dealing with the neglect of parents. . . . For the law enjoins us to support our parents, meaning by "parents" father, mother, grandfather, and grandmother, and their father and mother, if they are still alive; for they are the source of the family, and their property is transmitted to their descendants, and so the latter are bound to support them even if they have nothing to bequeath to them.[4]

6 Provisions for disabled citizens

δοκιμάζει δὲ καὶ τοὺς ἀδυνάτους ἡ βουλή· νόμος γάρ ἐστιν, ὃς κελεύει τοὺς ἐντὸς τριῶν μνῶν κεκτημένους καὶ τὸ σῶμα πεπηρωμένους, ὥστε μὴ δύνασθαι μηδὲν ἔργον ἐργάζεσθαι, δοκιμάζειν μὲν τὴν βουλήν, διδόναι δὲ δημοσίᾳ τροφὴν δύο ὀβολοὺς ἑκάστῳ τῆς ἡμέρας. καὶ ταμίας ἐστὶν αὐτοῖς κληρωτός.

(Arist. *Ath. Pol.* 49.4)

The Boule scrutinizes disabled men, for the law states that those who possess property less than three mine and have a physical disability, and as a result they cannot do any work, are to be scrutinized by the Boule, and given from the public purse two obols a day, so as to be able to feed themselves, and the treasurer in charge of this is to be appointed by lot.

7 Who qualifies for disability, and level of income support

> ἀδύνατοι· οἱ μέρος τι βεβλαμμένοι τοῦ σώματος ὡς μηδὲ<ν ἔργον> ἐργάζεσθαι, οἳ καὶ ἐχορηγοῦντο τὰ πρὸς τὸ ζῆν παρὰ τῆς πόλεως, μισθοφορούντων [αὐτοῖς] τῶν ἐντὸς τριῶν μνῶν περιουσίαν κεκτημένων. ἐδοκιμάζοντο δὲ οἱ ἀδύνατοι ὑπὸ τῆς τῶν <φ> βουλῆς, καὶ ἐλάμβανον τῆς ἡμέρας, ὡς μὲν Λυσίας λέγει, ὀβολὸν ἕνα, <ὡς δὲ Φιλόχορος † πέντε·> Ἀριστοτέλης δὲ δύο ἔφη.
>
> (Philochoros *FGrH* 328 F 197 b)

Disabled out those who have a damaged part on their body and as a result of they cannot do any work. They were offered what was necessary for their maintenance from the public treasury, if the process property lower than three minae. Disabled people were scrutinized by the Council of the 500, and received a stipend of one obol, as Lysias says, <five obols † as Philochoros says>, or two obols as Aristotle says.

8 The law absolving doctors from liability during the performance of their duties

> Εἰ δέ τοι καὶ ὑπὸ τοῦ ἰατροῦ ἀπέθανεν, ὡς οὐκ ἀπέθανεν, ὁ μὲν ἰατρὸς οὐ φονεὺς αὐτοῦ ἐστιν, ὁ γὰρ νόμος ἀπολύει αὐτόν, διὰ δὲ τὰς τούτου πληγὰς ἐπιτρεψάντων ἡμῶναὐτῷ, πῶς ἂν ἄλλος τις ἢ ὁ βιασάμενος ἡμᾶς χρῆσθαι αὐτῷ φονεὺς εἴη ἄν;
>
> (Antiphon *Tetralogy* 3.5)

But even if his death was due to the physician, which it was not, the physician is not his murderer, because the law absolves him from blame. On the other hand, as it was only owing to the blows given by the defendant that we placed the dead man under medical care at all, can the murderer be anyone save him who forced us to call in the physician?[5]

9.2 Protecting legal minors and the elderly from abuse

It is a testament to Solon's wisdom and humanity that when he tried to curb the excesses of the aristocratic state and alleviate the suffering of the lower classes, he did not leave out of the picture those who were unable to protect themselves and their own rights before the courts, like children, widows, orphans, the elderly and the infirm. Several authentic Solonean laws actually were intended to safeguard the legal rights of these groups among the population, primarily but not exclusively from abusive or negligent family members and legal guardians. Some of these laws were an integral part of his legislation on inheritance and intestate succession, and as such they remained enshrined at the core of Athenian family law for centuries (S 1–3). Others were specific provisions for a certain group, like the laws defining one's duties to his elderly parents (S 4–5), as well as exemptions from responsibility, like the provision that a man was not under any obligation to provide for his father if the latter had prostituted him.[6] Other Solonean laws on procurement, which had fallen into disuse in the classical period, meted out severe punishments to family members or outsiders trafficking free children.[7] The centerpiece of the Solonean legislation for the protection of legal minors who could not protect themselves is a law quoted in the speech *Against Makaratos* (S 1). This law placed in the hands of the *archon* the responsibility to look after orphans, heiresses and widows, including those who had remained in their deceased husband's *oikos* claiming that they were pregnant. By the time of Aristotle this law had been incorporated into a much broader network of legal provisions intended to safeguard the financial position and personal welfare of legal minors in the family and the wider community (S 2).[8]

The original law of Solon was a very straight-forward piece of legislation, and in some ways it seems to be an extension of the Solonean legislation on inheritance and the continuation of the *oikos*. It places under the responsibility of the *archon* the care of legal minors in households left without a *kyrios*, such as orphans, heiresses and widows claiming to be carrying the dead husband's child. These women no longer were under the authority of their father or original *kyrios* but were residing in a household without a living *kyrios*, with the hope that they would produce an heir to continue their deceased husband's *oikos*. It seems that the primary objective of this law was to ensure the lawful and uneventful transfer of property and the continuation of the *oikos*, and to safeguard the legal rights of the lawful heirs. This primary purpose of the law was strengthened by another Solonean law which made the *epidikasia* of an *epikleros* mandatory, taking away from families the discretion to arrange matters among themselves.[9]

However, this law was not concerned solely with property, inheritance and the continuation of the *oikos*. The actual wording of the law confirms beyond reasonable doubt that the welfare of the persons involved was a primary concern of the lawgiver. The *archon* was not only expected to oversee the lawful transfer of property in the best interests of the *oikos*, but also to protect persons from abuse or wrong-doing of any kind. It was his duty to intervene if anyone tried to treat them contemptuously or commit a crime against them. The Solonean text does not actually name any specific target; anyone committing a crime against legal minors was to be punished. However, the author of the *Athenaion Politeia* in his interpretation of this legislation explicitly mentions close family members and guardians as the prime targets. It seems that, as with the laws on trafficking, Solon tried to protect the weaker members of the *oikos* from unscrupulous family members.

Solon gave the *archon* the power to punish offenders on his own authority up to a certain point. The Solonean text does not circumscribe the limits of the *archon*'s powers, but if the practice of the classical period, when all magistrates could impose a fine up to 50 drachmas without referral to court, had its origins in the time of Solon, then probably the punitive powers of the *archon*, like those of other magistrates, were limited to a certain sum. If the *archon* felt that the transgression deserved a more severe punishment he had the authority to refer the offenders to court, explaining the reason for the referral and proposing the monetary or physical penalty which he thought that the offender deserved. In the time of Solon the *archon* had more extensive powers, but in the classical period his role was that of the introducing authority who accepted and processed lawsuits, and sometimes that of a consultant who heard the parties, discussed matters with them and offered advice. If necessary, he could also serve as a facilitator of contracts or as the authority collecting money on behalf of orphans and *epikleroi*.[10] Although theoretically he still had the authority to refer serious offenders to court for a heavier penalty, in practice it seems that he acted more as a legal advisor or intercessor in such cases, one would imagine because complicated and messy family affairs rarely were a clear-cut case of crime and punishment. Particularly significant is a passage from the first speech *Against Onetor*, where Demosthenes asserts that many people had noticed how badly his guardians were conducting themselves and there were repeated consultations and discussions with the *archon*.[11] However, instead of taking legal action it seems that the *archon* and all those concerned were waiting for the young Demosthenes to come of age and himself pursue his guardians. If there is any truth in this assertion, it seems clear that the *archon* and other citizens chose not to get directly involved in the affairs of the family of Demosthenes, but rather to wait for the male heir of the *oikos* to handle matters himself when he came of age. This provides us with a useful insight into the actual role of the *archon* in the 4th century Just as the *Athenaion Politeia* suggests, he would lend a sympathetic ear, advise, help with practical matters such as leases or collections, and exert pressure upon those who were mistreating an orphan or an *epikleros*, but typically he would not take the initiative and bring those responsible to justice unless someone stepped in and submitted a lawsuit, like an *eisangelia*, a *dike* or a *graphe*.

The scope and processes of the Solonean law appear to be substantially expanded in the classical period. The *Athenaion Politeia* mentions a whole array of lawsuits for maltreatment (κάκωσις) of parents, orphans, or heiresses and even of an orphaned *oikos*. It also mentions a number of procedures intended to safeguard the best interests of legal minors such as the appointment of guardians or magistrates who had the authority to decide on property distribution (δατηταί), or a lawsuit to decide someone's mental competence, in order to make sure that he is not unwittingly squandering property destined for his heirs.[12] Interestingly in the end of this list the *Athenaion Politeia* quotes almost verbatim the aforementioned law of Solon (S 1). We should take this as an indication that although the Solonean law was still valid in the 4th century and formed the core of the legislation intended to protect the property, personal and legal rights of persons who were unable to protect themselves, the processes through which this legislation was implemented had become much more complicated and aligned with standard legal procedures of the radical democracy. Although the nobler objectives of this legislation had not changed, they had been reinterpreted in the language of the Democratic Constitution and required collective responsibility from the entire citizen body. Looking after those in need and protecting those who could not protect themselves was no longer the sole duty of a lone magistrate, but the moral obligation of the entire community and every citizen who was in the position to do something about it. While the *archon* would remain the focal point of reference for all efforts to protect someone in need, he would listen to complaints, complete the preliminary *anakrisis* and introduce cases to court, in the classical democracy he did not have to shoulder this responsibility alone and unaided; he had the entire citizen body to support his work and could rely upon volunteer prosecutors to take the cases to court.[13]

The actual legal procedures which needed to be followed in such cases are somewhat unclear, because our most important source, *the Athenaion Politeia*, is vague, mentioning both public and private lawsuits for maltreatment (γραφαὶ δ[ὲ καὶ δ]ίκαι) but not specifying which was to be followed when. Other sources do not help much either: In the speech *Against Theokrines* a γραφὴ κακώσεως is mentioned, while Haprocration presents additional evidence from several orators proving that anyone could introduce a *graphe kakoseos*.[14] However, in the same entry Harpocration also presents specific evidence on several *dikai kakoseos*. The entry of Pollux mentions a *dike kakoseos* among a series of other *dikai*, like the *dike proikos*, or the *dike sitou*.[15] Other lexico*graphe*rs also mention a *dike kakoseos*.[16] It is unlikely that all these sources are using imprecise terminology; in particular Harpocration, like the *Athenaion Politeia*, is quite specific that both a *graphe* and a *dike kakoseos*, were legal options. It seems that a relative could introduce a *dike*, while someone else, like a neighbor or someone's enemy, could introduce a *graphe kakoseos*. In this case duplication would be unimportant since both procedures, public or private, were risk free. The state wanted to encourage people to prosecute abusers, and in order to do so, it was willing to enable different avenues for potential prosecutors, and to forego any administrative fees and, exceptionally for this case, the risk of 1000 drachmas for a *graphe* that did not secure 1/5th of the votes.[17]

We are better informed about *eisangelia* available for cases of maltreatment. *Eisangelia* as a legal procedure is sparsely mentioned in 5th century sources, although it is certain that it existed as a legal option and was famously employed to denounce to the Boule and the Assembly the alleged violations related to the scandal of the Hermocopids in 415, and also a case of corruption of public officials in Antiphon *On the Chorister*.[18] On the basis of a couple of passages from the *Athenaion Politeia* scholars have argued that the procedure was truly ancient, because the Areopagos accepted *eisangelia* against magistrates who were violating the law, and a law of Solon allowed *eisangelia* against persons who were conspiring against the democratic constitution (ἐπὶ καταλύσει τοῦ δήμου).[19] However, the evidence is tenuous, and I share the concerns of P.J. Rhodes about the slippery boundaries between the technical and non-technical usages of εἰσαγγελία and εἰσαγγέλω in classical authors.[20] Moreover, even if the author of the *Athenaion Politeia* employed the term in a technical sense, it is quite possible that he was retroactively using 4th century terminology. On account of these considerations, and since the term is not encountered in any source which dates before the last quarter of the 5th century, it is very difficult to confidently argue that *eisangelia* was in use before the classical period.[21] Most likely it was introduced in the years of the Peloponnesian war to ward against inside threats to the state and the democratic constitution, brought about by those perilous times.

A passage of Isocrates which separates public lawsuits into *graphai*, *eisangeliai* and *probolai*, depending on whether they are submitted to the *thesmothetai*, the boule or the assembly probably stands on firmer grounds.[22] This seems to be the proper technical distinction for pubic lawsuits, even though sometimes authors use the terms loosely to indicate denunciations and accusations that were not part of formal legal proceedings. In its technical sense as a legal procedure an *eisangelia* began with a denunciation before the boule, and occasionally the Assembly. The Council had the authority to punish someone with a fine up to 500 drachmas, with the possibility of an appeal to the courts. If, on the other hand, the boule considered that the offense deserved greater punishment, it could refer the matter to the courts, and the person who had made the denunciation became the prosecutor. In order to ensure that persons with knowledge of subversive activities against the state and the constitution could come forward without fear there was no risk for the person who made the denunciation.

The *eisangelia*, like the *probole*, was initially envisaged as a risk-free, two-tier process, where the first vote in the Boule or the Assembly functioned as a vetting process, and only cases which had substantial support and were deemed to be sufficiently serious could proceed to a trial by court.[23] However, the no-risk factor, compared with the serious dangers of a *graphe*, made the *eisangelia* a very attractive option for settling scores in public life. This compounded with the very broad definition of what constituted an offense under the *eisangelia* law created the ideal conditions for this procedure to be used and abused in the 4th century to the point that the Athenian state was forced eventually, probably in the 330s, to bring it in line with the *graphe* and introduce a risk of 1000 drachmas for the prosecutor who did not secure 1/5 of the votes in an *eisangelia* trial. This move undoubtedly was intended to correct the imbalance and discourage the widespread misuse of *eisangelia*.[24]

An important passage of Harpocration which summarizes the uses of *eisangelia* as a legal procedure in the classical period explicitly states that denunciations for maltreatment of persons who could not defend themselves by taking the offender to court, such as women, children and the elderly, were different from other cases of *eisangelia*.[25] Harpocration is right: other than the term εἰσαγγελία (denunciation) there is little similarity between prosecution of persons deemed to be dangerous for the safety of the state and the constitution, with the prosecution of persons who had mistreated someone under their care at home. The former were submitted to the Council and were concerned with important matters in public life, while the latter were submitted to the *archon* and had to do with families and the private sphere.

There is no mention of *eisangelia* for maltreatment in 5th century sources. Our earliest references come from the speeches of Isaios (after the 380s) which may signify that this form of *eisangelia* was introduced in the 380s with the specific purpose of addressing cases of maltreatment. Whether it was intentionally modelled on the *eisangelia* procedure for public cases, or the employment of the term εἰσαγγελία was nothing more than broad usage of a term with a sufficiently wide semantic field to encompass any kind of denunciation is difficult to tell; my instincts would side with the latter option. Unlike the widespread use and abuse of *eisangelia* in public life in the 4th century, this kind of *eisangelia* remained limited to the private sphere, and we only hear about it occasionally. This, along with other significant differences from *eisangelia* in public life may explain why it remained risk free for the prosecutor who did not secure 1/5th of the votes, even when *eisangelia* in public life was reformed and aligned with other public procedures in the 330s.[26] The state continued to encourage private citizens to come forward and prosecute abuses of children, widows and orphans, even after it tried to put the brakes on the misuse of *eisangelia* to settle political scores in public life (S 3). This form of *eisangelia* most likely was introduced in order to modernize the old Solonean laws on maltreatment and bring them in line with the procedures of the reorganized 4th century democracy.

Several sources suggest that the penalties in an *eisangelia* case for maltreatment could be severe (see S 3). The case was an *agon timetos*. The law did not fix the penalty but it was left up to the jury to decide how to punish the convicted offender. A passage of Isaios implies that the death penalty and confiscation of property were a possibility, but we need to be cautious in this case because the speaker had good reasons to exaggerate the potential dangers of an *eisangelia* for maltreatment.[27] There is only one extant speech delivered in such a case. The speech of Isaios *On the Estate of Hagnias*, which undoubtedly was delivered by the defendant in an *eisangelia* trial,[28] belongs to the same arc of intricate suits and countersuits that went on for years, as the pseudo-Demosthenic speech *Against Makaratos*. It is clear that in this case the lawsuit was not about the best interests of a young orphan boy, as it claims to be, but about property and inheritance, and understandably Isaios builds the case as if it were nothing more than an inheritance dispute. As Wyse points out in his introduction to the speech,[29] the development of the argument has much to do with the facts of the case and the property rights of the claimants, and virtually nothing to do with the mistreatment of an orphan.

Isaios in the speech *On the Estate of Pyrrhos* refers to *eisangelia* along the same lines. The brother of Endios, who is claiming the estate of Pyrrhos from Phile, the daughter of Pyrrhos, is arguing that Phile was illegitimate because if Endios, her adopted brother, had given her away in marriage without a dowry, he should be liable to an *eisangelia* for maltreatment. The argument is of course completely hypothetical. Endios was adopted in the house of Pyrrhos while the latter was still alive, and consequently Phile was not an *epikleros* after her father's death. Her adopted brother eventually arranged the marriage of Phile to a man named Xenokles from the deme of Kopros,[30] and when Endios died childless she rightfully claimed the entire estate. There was nothing unusual in such arrangements when a male heir was adopted into a household with only female issue *inter vivos*. It appears that in both cases where Isaios mentions an *eisangelia* for maltreatment, the procedure is little more than a thin disguise for property claims. It is unfortunate that we do not have more evidence from other orators, which could help us decide whether this line of argumentation was characteristic of Isaios, or altogether *eisangelia* for maltreatment was for the most part yet another weapon in acrimonious property disputes. We do not need to assume a uniform application of the procedure: while it appears that the intention of the lawgiver was to protect children, women and the elderly from all kinds of abuse in the hands of cruel and unscrupulous relatives, sometimes the process could be misused as a weapon during inheritance disputes.

An unusual case is reported by Aeschines,[31] where a youth named Diophantos appeared before the *paredros* of the *archon* to report that a foreign man had defrauded him of four drachmas, as a fee for sexual services. It appears that young Diophantos, who was an orphan and did not have a family to look after him, was practicing prostitution in order to survive, and when he was wronged he sought the help of the *archon* in his capacity as the magistrate looking after orphans. The case is highly unusual but nonetheless confirms that minors, women and the elderly could always ask for the protection of the *archon* when their rights were violated. The role of the *archon* remained central in such proceedings from the time of Solon to the 4th century. Families did not have the discretion to settle such matters among themselves; everything had to be done through the *archon*. His authorization and final adjudication was necessary before someone could claim an *epikleros* and her property,[32] even when there was a single claimant without other contestants. Undoubtedly the purpose of such arrangements was to make sure that families did not conspire to defraud an heiress of her property. His role was also indispensable in the case of a divorce initiated by the woman. In this case his role was to register the proceedings and make sure that interest would be paid on a withheld dowry from the moment that the woman officially declared her intention to abandon her husband. Again, the role of the *archon* was to make sure that the woman was not defrauded from the maintenance money (σῖτος) which was rightfully owed to her.[33]

The *Athenaion Politeia* contains a long list of routine duties and activities of the *archon* intended to safeguard the rights of orphans and heiresses. Although for several of them there is no confirmation from other sources, they all serve similar purposes and we have no reason to doubt the reliability of this evidence. Such routine duties included the appointment of guardians for orphaned children, and the possibility to take legal action in order to protect their property from unscrupulous guardians. While it appears that families often chose the guardians themselves,[34] still the *archon* needed to be notified and to make the appointment official. When someone could see the end of his life he might wish to make arrangements in a will which included the appointment of guardians for his children. Although Athenian law did not allow him to dispose his property as she wished, especially if he had legitimate sons, who by right inherited their father in equal shares, a man could still make his wishes known on other matters such as the care and welfare of his loved ones after his death.[35] The role of the *archon* in such cases was to ensure that guardians had been properly appointed taking into account the wishes of the family.

If the guardians proved incompetent or malicious and did not support the children in their charge the *archon* had the authority to intervene and collect the fees for the maintenance of the children on their behalf (S 2). He also had the authority to lease the property of orphans and heiresses and collect the proceeds from the lease for them. In the case of an *epikleros* this duty ended once she reached her 14th year of age and could move in with the husband chosen for her through the *epidikasia* process (S 2). The author of the *Athenaion Politeia* did not mean here that the *archon* was under obligation to lease all properties of orphans and *epikleroi* in Attica; he only meant that the *archon* had the authority to do so when asked, or when the appointed guardians had failed in their duty to look after the property of the children under their care. One would imagine that such cases were rather rare, especially since investing the property of the orphan in their charge could be profitable for the guardians too.[36] Moreover, it seems that the *archon* had the authority to initiate a more comprehensive, and probably more serious lawsuit for the mistreatment of an orphaned *oikos* (S 2: οἴκου ὀρφανικοῦ κακώσεως). We do not know exactly what this meant, but it would be a fair guess that such a lawsuit could be concerned with the mistreatment of orphaned children as well as the squandering of the property of the *oikos* by the guardians. Such a lawsuit could perhaps be initiated through an *eisangelia*, and if so, it could carry more severe penalties than private cases brought against guardians. Finally, the *archon* could help with the distribution of property by appointing a panel of distributors (δατηταί)[37] in charge of helping with the task when the beneficiaries were unwilling or unable to split everything in half (S 2).

The *Athenaion Politeia* also informs us that the *archon* was in charge of cases of *paranoia*, a procedure well attested in other sources.[38] When family members were claiming that someone because of old age or mental illness had lost the capacity to manage the property of the *oikos*, they could sue in order to declare him mentally incompetent, and then assume control of the property. In a story told by late antiquity authors the nonagenarian Sophocles was challenged by his sons because he was spending the property of the family on expensive *hetairai*.[39] During the trial he proved that he was *compos mentis* by reciting to the jury the lyrics from his latest play *Oedipous Coloneus*. Although this particular story is almost certainly a fabrication from the period of the second sophistic, it still provides us with an insight into such cases. This passage of the *Athenaion Politeia* completes the picture by telling us how this law could be enforced through an indictment to the *archon*. His role again was to protect the interests of persons whose property and inheritance rights had been violated.

This very long list of responsibilities in the hands of the most senior civil servant in Athens, the *archon* who gave his name to the year, had much to do with the smooth and lawful transfer of properties from one generation to the next, but it was not limited to financial concerns. The language of the laws themselves makes clear that the responsibilities of the *archon* were much more extensive and encompassed the entire well-being of orphaned children, *epikleroi*, widowed women, the elderly and in the infirm. However, how much he could do beyond his regular duties as a civil servant and as the introducing authority in cases of maltreatment probably was limited by the procedures of the radical democracy, and perhaps to some extent depended on his personal temperament.

9.3 Providing for disabled citizens

Modern histories of disability rarely go back in time before the 18th century, and when they do they are more likely to focus on mythologies like the one about the exposure of disabled infants in Sparta, while ignoring important realities about the ancient city-states, such as the fact that the most towering personality in the history of 4th century Sparta, king Agesilaos II, was a disabled man.[40] The humane record of the First Democracy on treating its disabled citizens with respect, recognizing their rights and providing disability benefits for those who were not able to work, has been surprisingly ignored. The Athenian state did not bar disabled persons from full citizenship. They had the same rights as every other citizen to participate in the political process, to vote or be appointed into office, and had full access to the justice system.[41] Since most offices were filled by lot, the possibility of disabled citizens to be selected was equal to that of any other citizen. This possibility dictated some exceptions based on religious considerations. As an important passage of Lysias suggests, disabled people could not be appointed to offices which had religious duties, like priesthoods or the nine *archon*s, because physical imperfection was incompatible with religious duties.[42] The *archon*s had extensive religious duties which should not be performed by individuals with bodily defects.[43] This perspective should not surprise us. Repeatedly we hear in the sources that only perfect animals could be used for sacrifice, because clearly the gods deserved nothing less and imperfection in the ritual might offend them.[44]

Religious observance motivated by similar factors excluded other groups from offices with religious duties. Naturalized citizens were barred from priesthoods, and, in their case, we can be absolutely certain that the motive was religious observance, and not any desire to marginalize exceptional persons who had just been admitted into the Athenian citizen body because of ἀνδραγαθία, namely outstanding services to the city.[45] Another such exception was the rule that the wife of the *basileus* needed to be in her first marriage and of citizen stock. Again, the law did not intend to discriminate against women who had been married more than once; it was simply aiming at ritual correctness, since in a mock-marriage ceremony, the wife of the *basileus* would be offered as a bride to Dionysos during the festival of the Anthesteria.[46]

The most important source for our understanding of disability and the law in the early 4th century is a speech of Lysias where a disabled man is defending his benefit before the Boule.[47] A middle-aged man, who seemingly has been receiving the benefit for several years, has been accused of benefit fraud, and with a masterfully composed speech he is claiming that he needs to continue receiving the benefit of one obol per day. His opponent had accused him of fraud, on account of the fact that he owned a profitable workshop in the marketplace, and therefore he did not qualify for the benefit. Moreover, the opponent alleged that his disability was not severe enough, because he could ride horses. The disabled man replies that his workshop makes so little profit that he cannot even take an apprentice, and also that he needs two sticks to walk, and he only rides borrowed horses from time to time because of his limited mobility. His opponent had also alleged that the disabled man had rich friends of questionable character.[48] Admittedly, there is something suspicious in these associations. An aging disabled man who could barely make ends meet was not the typical companion of rich men, nor the typical client of Lysias, one of the most expensive litigators in the city. Nonetheless, Lysias has successfully created the portrait of a poor, disabled man fighting for his small benefit of one obol a day with good humor.

It is likely that cases like the one in Lysias led to some tightening of the laws by the time of the *Athenaion Politeia*. We are informed that by the 330s any kind of work would disqualify someone from receiving disability benefits. In order to qualify a citizen needed to be incapable of profitable employment, and also any property in his possession should not exceed the sum of three mine (S 2). On the other hand, it appears that the meager benefit of one obol a day in the time of Lysias had been increased to two obols a day.[49] The process for claiming the benefit was relatively straightforward. The disabled citizen needed to appear before the Boule once in every *prytany* (namely ten times a year) in order to claim his benefit.[50] In most cases the procedure probably was a simple case of renewal, but if someone questioned the right of a citizen to the benefit then a hearing followed before the Boule, like the one in which Lys. 24 was delivered, where he needed to defend his right to claim.

The narrative of Aeschines *Against Timarchos* suggests that failure to appear before the *prytaneis* resulted in loss of the benefit for that *prytany*. Aeschines informs us that an uncle of Timarchos named Arignotos, who was blind from birth, failed to appear one month when his nephew was one of the *prytaneis*. He turned up later as a suppliant to plead for his benefit, but he was unsuccessful. He then angrily blamed his nephew and appeared as a hostile witness during the trial of Timarchos, quite possibly with a devastating effect. The narrative of Aeschines raises some important questions, like, for example, how Arignotos was able to bypass the three minae property requirement when in fact he was born into a well-off family, which certainly owned properties well above this limit. Unless we are prepared to assume that this rule had not been introduced in the early 340s, when the incident occurred, we need to consider the possibility that Aeschines may be misrepresenting these events. In any case, even if Aeschines has misrepresented this incident and the subsequent testimony of Arignotos against his nephew, the information which he provides about the claiming process, the scrutiny before the *prytaneis*, the frequency of the *dokimasia*, and the process of an appeal through a supplication if someone missed his *dokimasia* because of illness or other eventuality, should be considered reliable and an important contribution to our understanding of disability benefit claims.

9.4 Caring for the elderly

Care for the elderly rested primarily with families almost everywhere throughout history, and only when family was absent other state, religious or communal organizations and help groups could step in to fill the void. The concept of homes or hospices caring for the elderly did not come around before significant changes in the structures of the traditional family in the second half of the 20th century. In classical Athens, as in the rest of the ancient Greek world, the elderly would normally stay in the family home until the end of their lives. In families with male heirs the family home and *oikos* would accommodate several generations, including children, their parents, grandparents, and great-grandparents. A law quoted by Isaios recognized this fact of life, and legally defined the term "parents" (γονεῖς) as someone's parents, grandparents, and great grandparents (S 4). For as long as they were alive any of these people expected to be under the legal protection of the *kyrios* of the *oikos*. While older citizen men would remain legally independent and retained full citizenship rights until the end of their lives, as they got older and more infirm, they might need to rely on the *kyrios* to represent their interests, just as the female members of the household always did.

A law of Solon made it mandatory for a man to provide for his parents (S 4 and 5).[51] The law of Solon threatened a delinquent son with disfranchisement (ἀτιμία), and a passage of Andocides confirms that ἀτιμία could still be the penalty in the classical period.[52] Andocides clarifies that a person convicted of maltreatment of his parents would be personally *atimos*, but he could still keep his property, and his disfranchisement would not be passed down to his descendants. The process by which one could be disfranchised for mistreating or neglecting his parents was a standard *graphe* (or *dike*) *kakoseos*, while the more serious process of *eisangelia*, which was an *agon timetos* and could potentially lead to the death penalty, was always an option after the years of the Peloponnesian war. Moreover, failure to look after one's parents would result in disqualification from public office in the classical period, since a standard question during the scrutiny of incoming officials was whether they were looking after their parents.[53]

Aeschines while quoting the law on the *dokimasia* of the orators, which mirrored questions typically asked in the scrutiny of public officials, mentions three specific points, which would constitute maltreatment of one's parents: hitting his father or mother,[54] not providing for their maintenance, and not providing a roof for them.[55] While it is difficult to tell precisely how the question addressed to incoming officials was phrased (and it is possible that it took various forms), the main points as outlined by Aeschines were at the heart of the matter. Any person who engaged in one or more of these behaviors could be prosecuted for parent abuse.

The impact of a simple question included in the scrutiny of all incoming magistrates was certainly much deeper than any threat of prosecution for maltreatment of one's parents. While the possibility of a prosecution was very real and the penalties were severe, volunteer prosecutors did not come easily. Prosecuting someone for abusing his parents was a massive interference into the affairs of someone else's *oikos* and would require a lot of energy and time over a long period of time. This is why such cases were probably rare, and in the extant literature there is not a single attested case. It appears that this law was nothing more than a threat which rarely if ever materialized in real prosecutions. This is why the inclusion of the question about maltreatment of one's parents in the scrutiny of incoming magistrates was so significant. This simple question ensured that anyone with any kind of political ambition, and anyone who was even vaguely considering entering public office in the Athenian Democracy, needed to be able to answer that he was providing for his parents and he was treating them well. If he had not, one of his enemies could oppose his appointment on these grounds, and in a subsequent court case a citizen's reputation could be badly damaged if it became apparent that he was not looking after his parents. This is how the laws of Athens made sure that elderly people were cared for by their families, had their basic needs met, and were treated with appropriate respect.

It appears that the law did not hold women responsible for the maintenance and well-being of their parents, even in the absence of a male heir, one would think because their property was under the control of their *kyrios*. Apparently, the need for someone to look after them in their old age was a major consideration in cases where Athenian men adopted a male heir into the *oikos*, even when they had legitimate daughters, as Pyrrhos does in Isaios 3. When such arrangements had not been made it is reasonable to extrapolate that two different models suggested themselves. One would be the model of Polyeuktos and his family (D. 41), where once the daughters had been given in marriage through *engye* by their father while he was still alive, the bulk of the estate would remain undivided and provide for the elderly parents. After their death, the remaining property would be equally divided among the daughters (assuming that they already had children, and therefore were not *epikleroi*). The alternative model would be that of Epilykos in Andocides 1.[56] Since he had not made any arrangements for his daughters when he died they became *epikleroi*. His property would go to the person who won the *epidikasia* along with the *epikleros*, and the winner would be obligated to provide for the maintenance of any elderly people still alive, since he had in his possession the property of the *oikos*. In the event that the property was worthless, as in the case of Epilykos, who left two talents of property and five talents of debts, one would imagine that whoever was under legal obligation to provide for the poor *epikleros*, he would also be responsible for her elderly mother or grandparents, if still alive. Although to my knowledge there is no recorded instance of this, it would be consonant with the processes of Athenian inheritance law, and the moral thing to do for impoverished elderly relatives.

9.5 Income support for the poor and the needy

In a direct democracy like classical Athens how does one ensure that the most important decisions of the state are not taken by a minority of affluent citizens who have the leisure to attend the meetings of the Assembly regularly, while the will of the working classes is ignored, since they cannot afford to stay away from their occupations for a whole day every week? Perhaps such considerations added legitimacy to the demagogic plans of politicians and led to the introduction of compensation for attendance of the Assembly, probably in the later part of the 5th century. The dangers of such a measure are summarized, somewhat dramatically, by Augustus Boeckh as following:

> The citizens must have become not only eager for fees, and averse to all useful employment, but also disputatious and sophistical, and the whole city full of pettifoggers and chicaners, without a profound knowledge of the law, but the bolder for that reason, and the more reckless.[57]

The inherent dangers of the citizens of the democracy paying themselves in order to participate were already noted in the *Athenaion Politeia*:

> εὐδιαφθορώτεροι γὰρ ὀλίγοι τῶν πολλῶν εἰσιν καὶ κέρδει καὶ χάρισιν. μισθοφόρον δ' ἐκκλησίαν τὸ μὲν πρῶτον ἀπέγνωσαν ποιεῖν· οὐ συλλεγομένων δ' εἰς τὴν ἐκκλησίαν, ἀλλὰ πολλὰ σοφιζομένων τῶν πρυτάνεων, ὅπως προσιστῆται τὸ πλῆθος πρὸς τὴν ἐπικύρωσιν τῆς χειροτονίας, πρῶτον μὲν Ἀγύρριος ὀβολὸν ἐπόρισεν, μετὰ δὲ τοῦτον Ἡρακλείδης ὁ Κλαζομένιος ὁ βασιλεὺς ἐπικαλούμενος διώβολον, πάλιν δ' Ἀγύρριος τριώβολον.[58]
>
> It is easier to corrupt the many than the few with money and favors. This is why at first they decided not to introduce payment for the Assembly. However, since the people did not attend the Assembly, even though the prytaneis had used many tricks to make sure that the crowd was present for the vote, at first Agyrrios introduced compensation of an obol, after that Herakleides of Klazomenai, the so-called "king", increased it to two obols, and later again Agyrrios to three obols.

While scholars are sometimes quick to agree on the detrimental effects of the Assembly pay upon the institutions of the Athenian Democracy, the positive contribution of this measure towards creating a more stable and sustainable society has largely been ignored. Vast inequalities of wealth, which had resulted in a very imbalanced society and had torn apart Solonean Athens, could have created similar problems, even if not on the same scale, in 5th century Athens. The capital city of a prosperous empire offered many opportunities for enrichment, and many took advantage of such opportunities. But at the same time Attica also had large populations living in poverty, but with full voting rights and the confident belief that they deserved no less than full equality before the law (ἰσονομία). One can see in this combination an explosive potential for unrest and endless social problems. The ecclesiastic pay, modest and insufficient as it was, could guarantee that at least once a week there would be a decent meal on the table for those among the poorest citizens who were willing to participate in public life.

More reliable would be the income from the dicastic pay, the compensation of three obols for service in one of the courts of Athens, but also more demanding, since a citizen would need to spend many days of the year in court. Unlike the ecclesiastic pay, the dicastic pay has raised much less controversy, one would imagine because no one could expect of a citizen to devote so much of his time, day after day throughout the year, without some form of remuneration. The amount of the remuneration was equal to the standard pay of an unskilled worker for much of the classical period. In this respect, the payment was not extravagant, but only the bare minimum the state could offer as compensation for persons who needed to drop their duties and activities to be in the courts for as many as 200 days a year.[59]

We are told that Pericles established the dicastic pay as a measure to counter the largesse of Cimon. While the latter was spending generous sums of money from his own estates in order to gain favor with the people, Pericles instead used the resources of the state. If the author of the *Athenaion Politeia* is correct in his interpretation of the motives of Pericles, then it seems that the remuneration of dicasts was motivated by political antagonisms and initially was a demagogic measure. Nonetheless, its impact was going to far outlast the political careers of Pericles and Cimon, as it established a very different welfare model, one which no longer relied on the good will, generosity and whims of rich men; this model incorporated concepts of rights and entitlements using the machinery of the state to consistently offer much-needed income support to the poorest of the Athenians. How important this safety network was is reflected with abundant clarity in the chorus of old men in the *Wasps* of Aristophanes. They get up in the middle of the night (ἀπὸ μέσων νυκτῶν)[60] to get to the courts, and we get to hear why:

> {Χο.} ἀπὸ γὰρ τοῦδέ με τοῦ μισθαρίου
> τρίτον αὐτὸν ἔχειν ἄλφιτα δεῖ καὶ ξύλα κὤψον·
> σὺ δὲ σῦκά μ' αἰτεῖς.
> {Πα.} ἄγε νυν, ὦ πάτερ, ἢν μὴ {ἀντ.}
> τὸ δικαστήριον ἄρχων
> καθίσῃ νῦν, πόθεν ὠνη-
> σόμεθ' ἄριστον; ἔχεις ἐλ-
> πίδα χρηστήν τινα νῷν ἢ
> πόρον Ἕλλας ἱερόν;
> {Χο.} ἀπαπαῖ φεῦ. μὰ Δί' οὐκ ἔγωγε νῷν οἶδ'
> ὁπόθεν γε δεῖπνον ἔσται.
> {Πα.} τί με δῆτ', ὦ μελέα μῆτερ, ἔτικτες;
> {Χο.} ἵν' ἐμοὶ πράγματα βόσκειν παρέχῃς.
> {Πα.} ἀνόνητον ἄρα σ', ὦ θυλάκιον, γ' εἶχον ἄγαλμα.[61]

> **Chorus**: With my small pay, I am obliged to buy bread, wood, and stew; and now you ask me for figs!
> **Boy**: But, father, if the Archon should not form a court today,
> how are we to buy our dinner?
> Have you some good hope to offer us or only
> "Helle's sacred waves"?
> **Chorus**: Alas! alas! I have not a notion how we shall dine.
> **Boy**: Oh! my poor mother! why did you let me see this day?
> **Chorus**: So that you might give me troubles to feed on.
> **Boy**: Little wallet, you seem like to be a mere useless ornament!

This text is significant for our understanding of the important role which such benefits played in the daily battle for survival among the poorest members of

Athenian society. The dicastic salary could buy the basic necessities of life, such as bread and stew, and some wood for the fire in the winter months, while the young boy could be occasionally dreaming of some dried figs. Even more significant is the answer to the question what would happen if there was no court on that day. The old man replies that he has no plan B, and simply they would have to do without food. This passage very clearly indicates that the meager income from the dicastic pay could make the difference between survival or complete destitution and starvation for the poorest citizens of Athens, and this is why the Athenian *demos* was so protective of such benefits.

A more coveted boon would be an appointment to the Boule of the Five Hundred. Pay was higher (1 drachma, equal to the daily pay of a skilled worker), the Boule met many days of the year, and for one *prytany* (1/10th of the year), when one's tribe was holding the presidency, the deal also included daily free meals in the Tholos. Considering that these meals were prepared for honored guests of the city, they were probably much richer than the meal which an ordinary Athenian family would eat at home. This is why we can imagine that for a poor Athenian an appointment to the Boule was probably a stroke of good fortune for the year. However, unlike service in the *dikasteria* which was available more or less to anyone who wanted it and cared to get up early enough to take part in the selection process, an appointment to the Boule with all its perks was a rare opportunity. Only 500 citizens were selected by lot every year, and a man could not serve more than twice in his lifetime, and never in two successive years. Statistically this meant that most Athenians would serve in the Boule at least once in their lives. Service in the boule was demanding on someone's time, but it was adequately compensated, and with perks like dining for free with prominent guests and foreign dignitaries, influencing the agenda of the Assembly, and for a year being an important part of public life, we can understand why even rich men like Apollodoros, the son of Pasion, were happy to serve.[62]

Additional opportunities for extra income were presented through embassies, and these could be quite profitable in the long run. Ambassadors could be away for months and were offered a lump sum for their maintenance and expenses during their absence (ἐφόδια) at a rate of two to three drachmas a day.[63] Considering that ambassadors would often receive hospitality, free meals and accommodations in the cities they visited, a fair part of that money would not be used for the needs of the trip. If one were to add underhanded ways of maximizing the benefits of the trip, such as the bribes from foreign powers and individuals so frequently mentioned in the orators,[64] an embassy could be a good way of supplementing someone's income. The only problem in this case would be that ambassadors were typically elected with a show of hands (χειροτονεῖν) from experienced public figures, not from destitute citizens with an eye on the perks of the office.[65]

Finally, the poorest citizens of Athens were receiving subsidized seats in the theater and later on in other festivals through the theoric fund. These subsidies were originally set up by Pericles, according to some evidence from later antiquity authors, which Peter Rhodes questions,[66] but organized into a theoric fund and expanded by Agyrrios. It seems that at some point the state decided to start charging for entry to the theater during the dramatic festivals, but in order to include those who could not afford to pay, the state offered to the poorest citizens the admission fee of two obols for each day of the festival (διωβελία), a total of one drachma.[67] In the 4th century, under the influence of populist politicians, the theoric fund came to include payments for other festivals and public works, and from time to time direct distribution of cash. Its manager, the secretary of the theoric fund (ἡ ἐπὶ τῶν θεωρικῶν ἀρχή), was directly elected from the Assembly. In the middle of the 4th century, under the capable leadership of Euboulos, the theoric fund became the centerpiece of prosperity in the city and a visible way by which the Athenian Democracy routinely redistributed funds from the richer to the poorer citizens. This is why the theoric fund was entrenched in public perception as the "glue of democracy," in the words of Demades,[68] and when the threat of Philip demanded more moneys to be directed towards military purposes, Athenian politicians found it very difficult to convince the Assembly to redirect the necessary resources away from the theoric fund.[69]

The willingness of Athenian politicians to redistribute some of the city's wealth through a number of different measures and offer the lowest classes a basic safety net and the proud sense of belonging to the leading city of the Greek world, functioned as a steam valve and relieved the pressures created by social injustice on the institutions of the democracy thus establishing a more stable and unified society despite its continuing inequalities of wealth or ideological divisions. However, the Athenian Democracy wisely did not bruise the dignity of the lower classes and turn them into beggars through free handouts. Citizens had to earn the support they received from the state by participating in the institutions of the democracy, the Assembly, the Boule, the courts and public offices. This kind of support was essential for the elimination of extreme socio-economic problems which Athens had experienced before the times of democracy, and a major factor which helped consolidate the rule of the people.

This pattern was upset in the years of the Peloponnesian war, when a series of major disasters emboldened and empowered extremist elements and led to two debilitating but ultimately unsuccessful attempts against the democratic constitution. After the restoration of democracy in 403 it can be argued that an even more cohesive and stable society would be created in the 4th century at the time when every other major power in the Greek world was experiencing massive changes, dizzying heights for a brief period of time and abysmal lows which had led to their sharp decline by the middle of the 4th century, leaving Athens still standing alone as a great power until the end of the Greek *polis*, and securing for herself a very special place in history through major cultural accomplishments in literature and art.

9.6 The Athenian healthcare system: medical care and the law

While medical care in the Greek city-states was in private hands for the most part, there is ample evidence suggesting that that from early times many cities operated an elementary public health-care service. This included public physicians paid by the state to offer their services to anyone who needed them at no cost to the patient, as well as sanctuaries which offered some rational medical care in addition to a faith-based promise of healing. The presence of public physicians in the Greek city-states is well attested from early times, and if there is any truth in the relevant narrative of Diodoros of Sicily, it even preceded the legendary lawgiver Charondas, who lived probably in the 6th century.[70] Herodotos offers concrete evidence on public physicians in the Greek cities in the story of Demokedes of Kroton, who reached the peak of his fame in the early 5th century. We're told that Demokedes could not stand his domineering father and moved away to Aigina, where he privately practiced medicine for a year in adverse circumstances. As he was far superior to all other physicians on the island the city hired him as a public physician with the substantial salary of one talent. The Athenians stole him away with a salary of 100 minae, and finally Polykrates of Samos hired him for two talents. The gifted doctor subsequently served as a royal physician to Darius I, and on account of his superior skills doctors from Kroton came to enjoy a high reputation, while the Persian court regularly employed Greek physicians.[71]

The practice of appointing public physicians was widespread in the Greek world and continued all the way into the Byzantine period.[72] Plato implies that there were more than one public physicians in Athens, and considering the population of the city, this should not surprise us.[73] Aristophanes mentions public physicians several times. One of them named Pittalos features in several jokes.[74] The scholiast of Aristophanes informs us that they were appointed by show of hands in the Assembly (χειροτονούμενοι). This method of appointment would be in accordance with procedures for the appointment of other magistrates where competence or honesty were of paramount importance, such as the generals and the treasurers.[75] Several sources suggest that private practice was not incompatible with the office of public physician.[76] Intriguingly an inscription from the late 4th century suggests that the physician Pheidias, the son of Apollonios from Rhodes, who was living in Athens, offered his services as public physician for free in order to carry favor with the Athenian *demos* (perhaps with an eye to a tax exemption or even naturalization).[77]

A passage of the philosopher Teles, as well as the narrative of Herodotos mentioned above, and other sources suggest that distinction in the practice of medicine was the primary criterion for the appointment of a public physician.[78] Lucian mentions public honors, tax exemptions, public offices and other privileges offered to physicians, and this evidence is supported by a number of honorary decrees preserved on inscriptions throughout the Greek world.[79] The evidence on the system of public physicians in the Greek world from the archaic period to the Byzantine era is considerable and a thorough discussion of it is beyond the purposes of this study.[80] All things considered, the conclusion that Greek city-states paid substantial amounts of money out of the public purse to secure the services of competent physicians for the benefit of the people, especially persons who could not afford private healthcare, seems safe.

Side by side with the public health care network, private practice also flourished in classical Athens, and there are several references in the orators attesting to the widespread employment of family physicians. When, for example, Euergos and Mnesiboulos injured the old servant of Theophemos, during the infamous incident when they invaded his home, he invited them to bring their own physicians to treat her. When they did not, he brought in his own family physician, who diagnosed that the woman was critically injured and she would not survive. The implication here is that since they were legally responsible for the assault as the ones who started it, they should have the opportunity to do their best to prevent the death of the woman and the homicide charges, which they might face if she died. In this case they did nothing, the woman died, and they were not prosecuted on account of an important technicality.[81] However, by bringing up this incident in court, the speaker is inviting the jury to treat his opponents not only as liars and cheats, but as murderers who deserve to be punished for their crimes against gods and men with the utmost severity.

There are several more instances in the orators suggesting that family doctors and attending physicians were routinely summoned to testify in court.[82] The family physician who tended to the wounds of the injured Ariston, in the speech *Against Konon*, was invited to testify during the trial.[83] The physician in this case appeared as a supporting witness for Ariston, and his role was to inform the court on the extent of the injuries as a result of the attack (see also the discussion in Chapter 7.2). By contrast, in the speech *Against Boiotos, On the Dowry* the physician appears as a hostile witness to confirm that the injuries of Boiotos were not genuine, and that he had not been assaulted. In this case it appears that the testimony of the physician had a decisive impact upon the verdict, and Boiotos lost that trial.[84] Aeschines appears to be using a physician who was also a family member to excuse his absence from an embassy, allegedly because he had been bribed by Philip.[85]

Most interesting is the presence of some physicians as expert witnesses in a very unusual trial, which is only attested in a few scant fragments from the defense speech. It appears that a man named Antigenes prosecuted his wife for homicide, because he suspected that she had an abortion without his knowledge. During the trial the expert testimony of doctors and midwives was presented in court, very likely testifying that the aborted fetus was not yet formed, and therefore not animated. Consequently, the interruption of the pregnancy, whether deliberate or spontaneous, did not amount to homicide. This was the prevailing medical opinion on the human status of the unborn in Hippocratic medicine.[86] It is almost certain that jury accepted the testimony of the physicians and the woman in question was acquitted; abortion would not be criminalized anywhere in the Greco-Roman world for another 600 years.[87]

Although many of the physicians who worked in Athens were not citizens, they were not impeded from giving evidence in court since they were free men, mostly Greeks from other city-states, like Diocles of Karystos and Hippocrates of Kos, just to mention two very prominent names. Some of those aliens would be settled metics, while others were travelling physicians, like the author of the *Epidemics*, who clearly was practicing medicine traveling to several cities.

Medical care was a time-honored practice throughout the ancient Mediterranean, and there is good evidence to suggest that it was practiced in Egypt, as well as the other lands which in the classical period were ruled by the Great King of Persia, centuries before the advent of rational medicine in the Greek word. However, medicine in these lands was entangled with religion and magic as much as it seems to be in the Greek world before the time of Hippocrates. This was about to change in the cosmopolitan fringes of the Greek world, in places like Ionia, the islands of the Eastern Aegean, and southern Italy. As James Longrigg explains, in these parts of the Greek world traditional religions had lost some of their grip on these multicultural societies, and the inhabitants of these cities were prepared to accept a more open-minded and self-confident view of the world. Medical treatment gradually changed direction in these places, diverging away from traditional religion, ritual and magic and moving towards rational explanations of health and disease, which would result in a never-ending quest for better cures, better treatments, and improved methods to be procured by humans based on their own ability to reason, and invented for the benefit of humanity as a whole. Thus, a major shift occurs in the late 6th century, which was going to generate a medical science and a health care system based on rational inquiry.

This revolution in the development of the human spirit, where people came to rely on their own resources in order to tackle some of their worst fears and anxieties, such as disease, insanity and death, was going to result in a more confident humanity ready to forge ahead towards a more enlightened future and benefited greatly from another development which coincidentally took place around that time in the political arena. When Demokedes was impressing the Greek World and the Persian Empire alike with his remarkable skills as a physician, an Athenian aristocrat named Kleisthenes would break down barriers that had stood from time immemorial and he would introduce Democracy. This new constitutional form by guaranteeing the rights of free speech and free thought encouraged that restless spirit of the early scientists, physicians and natural philosophers to seek out the great mysteries in the natural world and in the human body. By doing so, it provided fertile ground for scientific inquiry and the nascent medical *techne* to flourish and with enhanced confidence to seek out not only treatments for human pain and suffering but also intellectual endeavors aiming at a better understanding of the surrounding world as a whole.

Medical care advanced with leaps and bounds from the late 6th century, when the link between medicine and irrational factors weakened in favor of natural explanations of disease. This resulted in an unending quest for ever better methods, drugs and techniques of treating disease, and to a concept of healthcare where hope of a supernatural intervention was going to become optional and typically marginal. However, while such advances were major steps in the right direction ancient science was still too young and too limited to be able to guarantee the outcomes of its treatments with a high level of probability.[88] The Greeks trusted their physicians and were willing to submit to their painful treatments, but they understood that physicians could never guarantee a cure. All they could do was try to help, and often they succeeded, but success or failure was contingent upon factors which they did not understand well, and this is why they could not be held responsible for the outcomes of their efforts. A law mentioned by Antiphon exonerated the physician from any harm which a patient suffered during the course of treatment, including the death of the patient. Without such guarantees no one could safely practice medicine the ancient world. Those physicians who swore the Hippocratic oath pledged to do no harm intentionally, and the law in return offered them unconditional immunity, and allowed them to help their patients as best as they could without fear of legal repercussions.

9.7 Conclusions

Never before in history any state or political entity had considered itself responsible to look after its poorest citizens. But Athens was unlike any state that had existed until then; it was a democracy based on the concept of equality of all citizens before the law, and the right of every citizen to express his opinion on the affairs of the state. These concepts of equality and equal share in the Athenian *polis* could be totally undermined by vast inequalities of wealth and privilege. However, the nascent democracy took itself seriously, believed in itself and sincerely believed in its principles, which is why some of its most vocal critics, like the *Old Oligarch*, Plato or Xenophon, disapproved of democracy in its entirety, and not of specific parts of it. It would be a vote of no-confidence in the new constitutional form if only its better-off citizens could take their place in the theater or in the festivals, since they alone had the means to pay the admission fee, as it would sound hollow and hypocritical to tell homeless and starving citizens that they have an equal share in the *polis* as wealthy people.

It seems that Pericles, like Solon had done more than a century before him, did not set out to eliminate inequalities of wealth and privilege. He only tried to improve, even if slightly, the lives of those at the bottom of the pile. Infrequent distributions of grain or money where extraordinary events, often necessitated by the circumstances, like for example the distributions in the Peloponnesian war, which were meant to alleviate immediate situations of crisis. In this respect, they should probably be considered emergency measures to address urgent needs, and occasionally to boost the popularity of political leaders. The measures of Pericles which have cosmic significance are the institution of the theoric pay and the compensation of citizens for participating in the institutions of the democracy, like the assembly and the courts. These measures were designed to offer to the poorest citizens a modest amount of financial support, just enough to save them from complete destitution, and to use the mechanisms of the state for a limited redistribution of wealth. Rich citizens could keep and enhance their fortunes, but they needed to give something back to the state in the form of liturgies and trierarchies, while poor citizens would be sharing in the enjoyment of the public spectacles and benefiting from the safety which the fleet guaranteed. The state would also distribute funds collected from taxation, court fees, property confiscations following court decisions, and the use of the city's natural resources like mines. The Athenian state has often been criticized for wantonly throwing public money on the poor, but perhaps it should be praised for the ingenuity of a system which allowed the state to support its poorer citizens, but not for nothing in return. The poorest Athenians needed to work for their income support, by dedicating much time and energy to service as dicasts or *bouleutai*, and by actively participating in public life through regular attendance of the assembly meetings. Athens supported its citizens, but required of them to be good, active participants in return.

Notes

1 English translation by A.T. Murray.
2 Translation by H. Rackham.
3 Translation by Edward Seymour Forster.
4 Translation by Edward Seymour Forster.
5 Translation K.J. Maidment.
6 Aesch. 1.13. The exemption applied only to the father not to the mother, since the law did not consider her responsible for the procurement of her son. After the death of the father the son was still under obligation to bury him and perform the traditional religious rites. Aeschines explains that while the father was alive the law removed from him the benefit of having children, but when he was dead and could not feel anything, then the law required the divine rites to be honored. See also my discussion in Kapparis 2017: 156–8.
7 See the discussion in Chapter 6.4.
8 See also Rhodes 1981: 629–36; Leão and Rhodes 2016: 85–91.
9 See the law quoted in D. 46.22: ἀνεπίδικον δὲ κλῆρον μὴ ἔχειν [it is not permitted to have an inheritance without *epidikasia*], and the paraphrase of the orator above ἀνεπίδικον μὴ ἐξεῖναι ἔχειν μήτε κλῆρον μήτε ἐπίκληρον [it is not permitted to have the inheritance and the *epikleros* without *epidikasia*].
10 See for example Is. 3.46–7; Is. 11.33–4; D. 37.46; 43.7, 16, 31; 44.1, 11, 29, 34, 39,52; 46.22–3; 48.23.
11 See D. 30.6–7: Ἐγὼ γάρ, ὦ ἄνδρες δικασταί, πολλούς τ' ἄλλους Ἀθηναίων καὶ τοῦτον οὐκ ἐλάνθανον κακῶς ἐπιτροπευόμενος, ἀλλ' ἦν καταφανὴς εὐθὺς ἀδικούμενος· τοσαῦται πραγματεῖαι καὶ λόγοι καὶ παρὰ τῷ ἄρχοντι καὶ παρὰ τοῖς ἄλλοις ἐγίγνονθ' ὑπὲρ τῶν ἐμῶν. τό τε γὰρ πλῆθος τῶν κατα- λειφθέντων ἦν φανερόν, ὅτι τ' ἀμίσθωτον τὸν οἶκον ἐποίουν οἱ διαχειρίζοντες, ἵν' αὐτοὶ τὰ χρήματα καρποῖντο, οὐκ ἄδηλον ἦν. ὥστ' ἐκ τῶν γιγνομένων οὐκ ἔσθ' ὅστις οὐχ ἡγεῖτο τῶν εἰδότων δίκην με λήψεσθαι παρ' αὐτῶν, ἐπειδὴ τάχιστ' ἀνὴρ εἶναι δοκιμασθείην. [In common with many others of the Athenians, men of the jury, this man was well aware that my guardians were proving false to their trust. Indeed, it became clear very early that I was being wronged, so many were the discussions and arguments regarding my affairs held before the *archon* and before other officials. For the value of the property left me was well known, and it was pretty clear that the administrators were leaving it unlet in order that they might have the use of the money themselves. There was not a single one, therefore, among those who realized what was going on, who did not expect that I should obtain a judgement for damages from these men, as soon as I should attain my majority.] (Translation by A.T. Murray).
12 See Phillips 2013: 207–15 for the most important sources on *kakosis* cases.
13 See also Rhodes 1981: 633–4.
14 D. 58.32; Hyp. Fr. 160 Jensen; Harp. s.v. κακώσεως.
15 Pol. 3.47; for the *dike proikos* and the *dike sitou* see Chapter 6.2.
16 Phot. s.v.; Suda κ 178; *Lex. Seg.* s.v; see also Sch. Ar. Eq. 400a; Sch. Dem. 10.15 Dilts; Sch. Luc. 29.29 Rabe.
17 P.J. Rhodes correctly emphasizes the slippery usage of the terminology in the *Athenaion Politeia* (1981: 629–35).
18 See Andoc. 1.14, 37, 43; Ant. 6.14, 35; see also Lys. 12.48, about *eisangelia* under the Thirty, 16.12. Important studies on *eisangelia* in public life, and the νόμος

εἰσαγγελτικός are Hansen 1975 and 1980: 89–95; Carawan 1987: 176–208 and 1985: 115–40; Pecorella Longo 2002: 222–8; Piccirilli 1983: 333–63; Rhodes 1979: 103–14; Sealey 1981: 125–34.

19 Arist. *Ath. Pol.* 4.4, 8.5.

20 Rhodes 1979: 103–4

21 For the relevant discussion see Hansen 1975 and 1980: 89–95; Rhodes 1979: 103–14; Carawan 1985: 115–40 and 1987: 167–208; Piccirilli 1983: 333–63; Pecorella Longo 2002: 222–8.

22 Isoc. 15.314: Τοῖς μὲν γὰρ μεγίστοις τῶν ἀδικημάτων ἐν ἑνὶ τῶν δικαστηρίων τὴν κρίσιν ἐποίησαν, κατὰ δὲ τούτων γραφὰς μὲν πρὸς τοὺς θεσμοθέτας, εἰσαγγελίας δ' εἰς τὴν βουλήν, προβολὰς δ' ἐν τῷ δήμῳ. [For the most serious crimes, although the trials are to be held in the same court, the *graphai* are to be introduced to the *thesmothetai*, the *eisangelia*i to the boule, and the *probolai* to the people.]

23 See also Chapter 8.4 on *probole* as a two-tier process.

24 See D. 18.250; Harp. s.v. εἰσαγγελία, and the discussion in Phillips 2006: 376–81; Hansen 1975: 30–2; Carawan 1985: 131–2.

25 ἑτέρα δὲ εἰσαγγελία λέγεται ἐπὶ ταῖς κακώσεσιν· αὗται δ' εἰσὶ πρὸς τὸν ἄρχοντα, καὶ τῷ διώκοντι ἀζήμιοι, κἂν μὴ μεταλάβῃ τὸ ε' μέρος τῶν ψήφων. [Another kind of *eisangelia* is employed for maltreatment; these cases are introduced to the *archon*, and there is no penalty for the prosecutor, even if he does not receive the 1/5 of the votes.]

26 Harp. s.v. εἰσαγγελία; Is. 3.47.

27 Is. 3.62: δημοσίᾳ εἰσαγγελθεὶς πρὸς τὸν ἄρχοντα ἐκινδύνευεν ἂν περὶ τοῦ σώματος καὶ τῆς οὐσίας ἁπάσης τῆς ἑαυτοῦ [after a denunciation to the *archon* he would be in danger for his life and his entire property].

28 Is. 11.6 and 15.

29 Wyse 1904: 673–7.

30 This should settle for us the question on Phile's legitimacy. She could not be married to a citizen after the 380s, unless she was a citizen herself. And even if she had been the daughter of Pyrrhos and an alien *hetaira* born before 403, and citizen on account of this, she would still have full inheritance rights, because all *nothoi* born before 403 had full citizen and inheritance rights. There is no conceivable scenario where Phile could be a νόθη non-citizen woman married to a citizen man at the time when this case came to trial (Blass 1892: 537–538 was convinced that this is one of the later speeches of Isaios). It is a tribute to the supreme skill of Isaios as a litigator that he has created a case against her out of thin air.

31 Aesch. 1.158; see also Fisher 2001: 302–5.

32 D. 46.22: ἀνεπίδικον μὴ ἐξεῖναι ἔχειν μήτε κλῆρον μήτε ἐπίκληρον

33 See also the discussion in Chapter 6.2.

34 See for example the arrangements of the elder Demosthenes in D. 27, and those of Diodotos in Lys. 32.

35 See the discussion in Chapter 5.6.

36 Although the law required that the property of the orphan with all earnings should be returned to him or her in due course, the guardian who made substantial profit for himself by investing the property of the orphan might not consider himself under any obligation to return everything. The guardian who simply handed over the property which the orphan had inherited would be beyond reproach before the law. All cases of mismanagement brought against guardians in the extant corpus of the Attic orators are built upon the assumption that the guardians handed over only a fraction of the property which the orphan had inherited from his or her father. See also the discussion in Chapter 5.

37 δατηταί from δαίω literally means «distributors». See also Rhodes 1981: 631.

38

{Φε.} οἴμοι· τί δράσω παραφρονοῦντος τοῦ πατρός;
πότερον παρανοίας αὐτὸν εἰσαγαγὼν ἕλω,
ἢ τοῖς σοροπηγοῖς τὴν μανίαν αὐτοῦ φράσω;

(Ar. *Nu.* 844–6)

What should I do if my father goes mad?
Should I prosecute and have him convicted of *paranoia*
Or should I mention his madness to the coffin makers?

See also Is. 1.19, 50; 9.36; X. Mem. 1.2.49; 3.9.7; Pl. *Lg.* 928 e; Aesch. 3.251, and Rhodes 1981: 631.

39 Plu. 785 a; Cic. *Sen.* 22; Apuleius *Apol.* 37; Luc. *Marc.* 24; *Vita Sophoclis* 13.

40 A good example of this sensationalist approach to the history of disability is Robert Garland's *Eye of the Beholder*. While it contains many striking discussions of attitudes to disability, it shows no interest in the political, legal and economic protections for disabled persons in the Athenian Democracy. Equally absent is a proper study of Athenian institutions from the more sober-minded collection of essays *The Body and Physical Difference: Discourses of Disability*, edited by David T. Mitchell and Sharon L. Snyder. Several more studies explore aspects of disability in ancient Greek life and culture; see Penrose 2015: 499–523; Edwards 1995 and 1998: 3–9; Macfarlane and Polansky 2004: 25–41.

41 See for example Aesch. 1.104, where a blind man takes the stand to testify against his nephew.

42 Lys. 24.13. Stephen Todd has suggested that the disqualification of disabled citizens from the archonships was related to their inability for military service. Since they could not serve in the army, they could not perform properly the duties of a citizen (1993: 183). However, if this were the reason then disabled citizens should have been barred from all offices, and this does not seem to be the case, since Lysias only mentions the office of the nine *archons*.

43 See, for example, the strenuous objections raised against the possibility that Andocides might be selected as one of the nine *archons* despite his grave offenses against the gods (Lys. 6.4–6).

44 See, for example, *Oracula Sibyllina* 3.577; And. 1.97; D. 59.60.

45 See the discussion in Chapter 2.3.

46 D. 59.76; see also my previous discussion of this law in Kapparis 1999: 335–339, and the discussion in Chapter 8.3.

47 Lysias 24, *Ὑπὲρ τοῦ ἀδυνάτου*. For a brief discussion of the speech with some bibliography see Wolpert and Kapparis 2011: 65–72.

48 This may be a reference to men of oligarchic sympathies, which the disabled man is trying to brush aside.

49 Even the increased benefit of two obols was still lower than the wage of an unskilled worker, which was three obols. This suggests that a person on benefit could scrape a living at the most basic level, but the benefit was never a substitute even for the most basic wage of an unskilled worker, and this in itself should discourage fraudulent claims. The sarcastic comment of the defendant in Lysias 24 comes to mind, when he reminds the jury that this entire hearing was over a single obol, and not some wealthy *epikleros* (Lys. 24.14 and 27).

50 Aesch. 1.104.

51 See also Arist. *Ath. Pol.* 55.3–4; X. *Mem.* 2.2.13; D. 24.103–4; 57.70; And. 1.74; Din. *In Aristogitonem* 17.

52 Andocides 1.74; see also D. 24.104, where it is suggested that a man who had mistreated his parents and still entered the agora could be imprisoned. But, this penalty would be imposed on any *atimos* who did not observe the restrictions of ἀτιμία, and it was not specific to parent abusers.

53 For example, D. 57.70; Din. *In Aristogitonem* 17.

54 The closing scene in the *Clouds* of Aristophanes, where Pheidippides is giving his father Strepsiades a good beating, and then convinces him that it was for his own good, is a memorable comic account of this theme. This shocking scene provides the justification for the burning of the school of Socrates.

55 See Aesch. 1.28.

56 Andoc. 1.117–28.

57 Boeckh 1857 (trsl. A. Lamb): 315. The classic study of Boeckh, now readily available online, remains a goldmine of information. For an informative overview of Athenian public finances see Rhodes 2013: 203–31. Important information about the mechanisms of the Athenian economy especially in the 4th century can be found in Cohen 1997.

58 Arist. *Ath. Pol.* 41.3

59 See Hansen 1979: 243–246.

60 Ar. *V.* 218.

61 Ar. *V.* 300–314 (Trsl. by Eugene O'Neill, Jr.).

62 D. 59.3.

63 In D. 19.158 ten ambassadors received 1000 drachmas as ἐφόδιον for an embassy which lasted three months. This amounts to slightly more than three drachmas a day per person. Demosthenes considers this sum extravagant, but he has reasons to downplay the value which the *demos* received for their money. Surely the assembly approved what was considered a reasonable amount for the duration of the trip. For details on the remuneration of public officials in Athens see Gabrielsen 1981.

64 For example, D. 19.124 compared with Aesch. 2.94; Plu. *Pelop.* 30.4; see Perlman 1976: 223–33. The main thesis of Perlman that bribes are always mentioned in connection with foreign states like Macedonia or Persia, but not with Greek cities is incorrect, first because Macedonia was not a foreign state, and second because the impoverished Greek cities in the middle of the 4th century had far fewer resources to spend on bribery than the rich states of Phillip II or the Persian court. This does not mean that bribery within the Greek city-states did not exist. Such objections aside, Perlman's discussion on bribery and the presentation of the available evidence is remains useful.

65 See, for example, Aesch. 2.18, 3.63. On embassies in the Greek world see Dimakis 1997: 87–91; Mosley 1962: 26–7.

66 Plu. *Per.* 9.1, 34.2; Sch. D. 1.1; Rhodes 1981: 514. While it is true that the evidence is later, and there is no sign of theoric funds in 5th century sources, literary or epigraphical, it is not impossible that Pericles instituted this pay. If we believe that he also introduced the dicastic pay in order to compete with Cimon's largess, then we may be able to see a pattern, where Pericles was seeking to consolidate his popularity through measures like these.

67 Plu. *Per.* 9.1

68 Demades fr. 36 De Falco.

69 See D. 3.11, 10.46, 59.3–8; 19.291; Philochoros 328 F 33; Harp. s.v. θεωρικὰ; Hesychios s.v. δραχμὴ χαλαζῶσα. See also Hansen 1976: 235–46; Roselli 2009: 5–30; Rhodes 2013: 203–31.

70 Diodoros of Sicily, while praising Charondas for establishing universal education, says that the wise lawgiver did a lot more good than those who hire public physicians to look after the sick, because the latter take care of the body, while he took care of the soul. D. S. 12.13.4–12.14.1: τοσοῦτον ὑπερεβάλετο τοὺς πρότερον νομοθετήσαντας δημοσίῳ μισθῷ τοὺς νοσοῦντας τῶν ἰδιωτῶν ὑπὸ ἰατρῶν θεραπεύεσθαι, ὥσθ' οἱ μὲν τὰ σώματα θεραπείας ἠξίωσαν, ὁ δὲ τὰς ψυχὰς τὰς ὑπ' ἀπαιδευσίας ἐνοχλουμένας ἐθεράπευσε, κἀκείνων μὲν τῶν ἰατρῶν εὐχόμεθα μηδέποτε χρείαν ἔχειν, τοῖς δὲ τῆς παιδείας διδασκάλοις ἐπιθυμοῦμεν ἅπαντα τὸν χρόνον συνδιατρίβειν. "[He so far exceeded previous lawgivers who had established that private citizens who were sick could be treated by doctors paid by the state. They sought to heal the bodies, while he healed the souls burdened by ignorance. We hope that we will never need one of those doctors, but we like to be in the company of learned teachers all the time.]

71 Hdt. 3.131. Ktesias of Knidos is the best known among Greek physicians in the Persian court. He tended the wound of Artaxerxes II as his royal physician during the battle of Cunaxa (1.8.27), and in his spare time he collected materials for his valuable histories of ancient Persia and India, the first ever to be written by a European historian on the subject. On Ktesias and his works see Lenfant 2011; Nichols 2013.

72 See Str. 4.1.5; *ICS* 217 (an early 5th century syllabic Cypriot inscription, where the physician Onasilos is honored for healing those injured in battle free of charge with an appointment as public physician with a salary of one talent.) Procop. *Anecd.* 26.7; The Byzantines took public healthcare to a higher level by establishing hospitals organized around monasteries and offering free care for the sick. See Miller 1997; Sipsas 1993.

73 Ar. *Ach.* 1030; Pl. *Grg.* 514 d.

74 See Ar. *Ach.* 1032, 1222 (where the injured Lamachos is asking to be taken to the doctor's practice), *V.* 1432.

75 Sch. Ar. Ach. 1030. The same information seems to be drawn from a passage from the philosopher Teles (*De Fuga* 26).

76 Pl. *Plt.* 259 a; *IG* ii^2 483; Damascius *Life of Isidore* 123.

77 *IG* ii^2 483.

78 Teles, *De Fuga* 26.

79 Luc. *Abd.* 23. For the inscriptions see Pohl 1905; Cohn-Haft 1956; Nutton 1977: 191–226.

80 The most valuable study for the classical period still is the German dissertation of Rudolf Pohl (1905), which contains much of the available evidence, and a brief, sober account of the subject. Some inscriptions published in later years have been discussed by subsequent studies. The monograph of Louis Cohn-Haft (1956) was rather disappointing, as it promoted some unorthodox (and almost certainly wrong) views, such as the prospect that public physicians were not treating their patients free of charge, despite ample evidence to the contrary. One wonders why cities would pay them hefty salaries from the public treasury, if not for the purpose of treating the sick. The style, methodology and unsafe conclusions of this study were extensively criticized in subsequent years. Later Vivian Nutton (1977: 191–226) published a study on the public physicians in Roman times.

81 Theophemos was not the owner of the woman, since she had been freed by his father, and he was not a blood relative either, so he had no authority to prosecute her killers. The woman was essentially an employee living in his household. The case is extensively discussed in Tulin 1996; see also Gagarin's objections in *BMCR* 97.4.17, and my previous discussion of the incident in Kapparis 2017: 293–300.

82 The main study of the topic is Amundsen and Ferngren 1977: 202–3; see also Amundsen and Ferngren 1979: 39–56 for Roman law, and also Watson 2010 for a broader overview of forensic medicine in the western world.

83 D. 54.9–12.

84 The physician was invited by the opponent of Boiotos, his half-brother Mantitheos, to testify that Boiotos had asked him to inflict cuts and bruises on his head intentionally. He would then accuse Manthitheos for deliberate wounding (τραῦμα ἐκ προνοίας). His ultimate goal was to have Mantitheos permanently exiled. The physician refused to injure Boiotos, but testified for Mantitheos in the trial (D. 40.33). The jury believed the doctor, Boiotos was discredited and lost the case (see also the discussion in Chapter 7.2).

85 For the two sides of the story see D. 19.124 and Aesch. 2.94. The physician went to the Boule and testified in order to excuse his patient.

86 See Kapparis 2002: 44–52.

87 See Lys. Fr. 19–24 Carey, my discussion in Kapparis 2002: 185–94, and Carey's comments in pp. 319–21.

88 Internal pathology was tied to the theory of the four humors, and would remain so until the 19th century, when Louis Pasteur was able to fully understand the role of microbes

in health and disease and develop immunizations which changed the face of medicine. Before that, health and disease were viewed as the result of humoral imbalance. When one of the four humors in the body (blood, phlegm, yellow bile, black bile) existed in excess, was absent or was not properly mixed with the rest, the body developed disease, which needed to be addressed with attempts to restore the humoral balance. The classic study on the theory of the four humors is the Hippocratic work *Places in Man*, edited with introduction and informative commentary by Elizabeth Craik (1998).

Epilogue

Athenian law as the voice of the democratic *polis*

The authors of the classical period only offer a few hints on the administration of law in archaic Athens, sometimes just lexicographic clues, like for example the name of the *Thesmothetai*, which literally means "those who set laws", or the actual word for "law" in the archaic period which is θεσμός, and implies a long-standing, sanctified custom, which society had accepted as an established rule, rather than a statute as we understand it from later times. It is not always easy to decide how much we should read in such lexicographic clues. While these terms could be pregnant with meaning, and telling us something important, there is always the impending danger to go too far and start projecting our own theories on them. On other occasions, classical authors have preserved historical memories in the form of legends, stories, tales from the past, and again these could contain valuable information, or they could be misleading inventions of later times. This is why it is difficult to envisage how the aristocratic state operated, how it maintained order, and how it dealt with offenses, especially those committed by the members of the aristocracy. We can make reasonable suggestions and extrapolations, and this is what scholars have done, but we will never go past the level of hazy and tentative conclusions. This is why we cannot be certain why the Athenians decided in the late 7th century (621) to follow the example of other Greek city-states and have their first law code, written in blood, not ink, according to the orator Demades.[1]

One obvious reason why the aristocracy might become willing to curb its own power suggests itself: anxiety over developments in other city-states, where widespread resentment against the rule of aristocracy had supported a power grab by tyrants. Perhaps there were additional problems, social and economic. It would be reasonable to assume that the socioeconomic problems which compelled the Athenians to appoint Solon as lawgiver a quarter of a century later were already present and festering in the time of Drakon too. It seems that most of Drakon's laws were repealed and replaced by Solon, but if the small part of his laws which the Athenians retained in later centuries is any indication, his laws appear to have been inspired by very traditional principles, such as a prominent role for religion, and the direct participation of entire families in the legislative process. Since it is not likely that Drakon invented such processes, we may reasonably conclude that he incorporated existing practices and principles in his law code. The laws of Drakon were probably designed to serve as a valve that would let out some steam and reduce the pressure, but if we can judge by the fact that they only stood for a short period of time, they probably failed to improve things in every other respect, except perhaps in homicide, where some highly effective precepts were in operation, like inviting the family of the victim to become the inexorable prosecutors of the killer, and allowing self-help for the ordinary person by giving him the right to avenge his honor and protect his family if he had caught someone seducing or violating the women of his household. Perhaps this is why Solon, recognizing the effectiveness of the homicide laws of Drakon, could not offer a better alternative and decided to retain them. Some religious conservatism may also have played a role in the decision, but perhaps religious conservatism alone is not a sufficient reason why an inspired and creative lawgiver like Solon would be content to accept the laws of his predecessor without attempting any changes or improvements.

The laws of Solon endured in later centuries even though the constitution, politics, ethics, economics, cultural values and social institutions of Athens had already changed dramatically in less than a century after his legislation was introduced. It seems very strange that the Athenians in later centuries would be willing to attribute to him laws created under very different circumstances and for very different purposes. His legislative activity had been sanctified in the collective memory of the Athenians, and when in 403, during a large-scale reorganization of public life, it was proposed that the laws of Solon should be repealed, in the end the Athenians were not willing to go with this plan all the way. They settled for a compromise solution and repealed only obsolete or unsuitable laws, while the laws of Solon remained the basic Athenian law-code. But, of course, the citizens of the Athenian Democracy also had a practical mind. They were only able to retain the laws of Solon by making additions and expansions to the original core, and also by not enforcing the parts of the Solonean legislation which were out of sync with the times, like for example his law that a woman could not own property worth more than a *medimnos* of barley, namely the amount of income necessary to support the household for one week.[2] In the classical period most women in Athens, as members of an *oikos* or as independent women, would own jewelry and servants worth a lot more than a *medimnos* of barley, and several, like the *hetaira* Phryne, would become quite wealthy in their own right. Nonetheless, the laws of Solon formed the core code of Athenian law, and although they were not beyond critique and change, they had been consecrated in the collective memory of the Athenians as the foundation of democratic rule.

The laws of Solon were introduced at the time of crisis. The aristocrats owned most of the wealth of the city, and they were not willing to share. The rest of the population (δῆμος) was living in difficult conditions, to the point that people were forced to pawn their own freedom in order to be able to survive. This is why it is not surprising to see that Solon tried to correct the situation with some measures which were intended to alleviate the suffering of the poorer classes, without upsetting too much the established order and the privileges of the ruling class. He freed those who had been turned into slaves for debts and prohibited borrowing in future with one's freedom as collateral, he protected the children of destitute families from exploitation by family members and outsiders, and encouraged alternative income sources by encouraging his compatriots to take up trades, manufacturing and commerce.

However, as it often happens with compromise solutions, no one was satisfied. The disparities remained large, and this is why three decades later the disaffected found a new champion in Peisistratos, the popular tyrant who intermittently ruled Athens between 561 and 527. Peisistratos did not abolish the established laws and Constitution, nor did he confront the aristocracy directly. The leading aristocratic families continued to occupy the *archon*ships and to populate the Areopagos. Peisistratos appeared to respect the Constitution and laws of Athens, like Augustus did in Rome six centuries later, but, like Augustus, he gradually introduced targeted reforms, like for example the tribal judges, and enfranchised large numbers of new citizens loyal to him, thus eroding the power of the aristocracy. The changes which were brewing in Athens during the rule of Peisistratos made it possible for Kleisthenes to introduce the Democratic Constitution in the end of the century.

The laws of Solon remained in place during the rule of the Peisistratids, while Kleisthenes, too, did not feel the need to introduce a new code of laws when the new Constitution was established. The corpus of Solon was simply adopted as the law code of the Athenian Democracy, to which the assembly could add new laws as the need arose in subsequent years. Matters changed a lot in public life, as expected. Numerous offices were created in the course of the 5th century, power and responsibility kept shifting, the very definition of Athenian citizenship changed in 451 with the Periclean citizenship law, the popular law-courts took over the administration of justice, and even when individual magistrates retained some of their traditional punitive powers, these were capped, while the courts had the final say for most legal disputes in the city. On the other hand, changes in the family laws were very slow and incremental. The laws of Solon continued to dominate inheritance, marriage, the affairs of the *oikos* and the roles of men and women in it, the rights and responsibilities of families towards widows, orphans and heiresses, and a series of other matters related to private life. It seems that in private affairs Athenian families were set in their ways and were not keen in sweeping legal changes, even if this meant that they needed to use a body of laws that had been instituted under the aristocratic state a quarter of a millennium before their time.

The 4th century brought about some changes deep in the structures of the Athenian Democracy. From now on only written laws could be used as the basis for prosecutions or legal disputes, substantial procedural safeguards were put in place to make sure that citizens and magistrates took the legislative process seriously, and those who proposed new laws and decrees were willing to take personal responsibility for their actions. The magistrates of the state were under constant scrutiny to make sure that they fulfilled their duties responsibly and within the bounds of the law, while legal processes were often streamlined for greater efficiency and speedier resolution, especially when substantial financial interests were at stake, as for example in the case of commercial and trading disputes. The Athenians compensated for the loss of income from the dissolution of their Empire in 404 by creating the world's first banking system, which provided capital for enterprising projects. The renewed economic activity in the course of the 4th century contributed to the general prosperity of the city and allowed her to retain a leading role in the Greek world especially after the dissolution of Spartan power in 371, after the battle of Leuctra. In the 4th century Isocrates would boast about the contribution and achievements of the his city with the following words:

> For, finding the Hellenes living without laws and in scattered abodes, some oppressed by tyrannies, others perishing through anarchy, she (Athens) delivered them from these evils by taking some under her protection and by setting to others her own example; for she was the first to lay down laws and establish a polity. This is apparent from the fact that those who in the beginning brought charges of homicide, and desired to settle their mutual differences by reason and not by violence, tried their cases under our laws. Yes, and the arts also, both those which are useful in producing the necessities of life and those which have been devised to give us pleasure, she has either invented or stamped with her approval, and has then presented them to the rest of the world to enjoy. Moreover, she has established her polity in general in such a spirit of welcome to strangers and friendliness to all men, that it adapts itself both to those who lack means and to those who wish to enjoy the means which they possess, and that it fails to be of service neither to those who are prosperous nor to those who are unfortunate in their own cities; nay, both classes find with us what they desire, the former the most delightful pastimes, the latter the securest refuge. Again, since the different populations did not in any case possess a country that was self-sufficing, each lacking in some things and producing others in excess of their needs, and since they were greatly at a loss where they should dispose of their surplus and whence they should import what they lacked, in these difficulties also our city came to the rescue; for she established Piraeus as a market in the center of Hellas – a market of such abundance that the articles which it is difficult to get, one here, one there, from the rest of the world, all these it is easy to procure from Athens.[3]

What is astonishing in this lavishly flattering account is that every word is true. The accomplishments of this extraordinary society in the arts, the good life and the pursuit of pleasure, the elevation of the human spirit, the culturally open and diverse society, the bright example of a democratic government, the enterprising spirit and economic success of the city, its key place as the trading center of the Greek world and a major trading center for the whole of the eastern Mediterranean, the Near East and North Africa, all these are facts, and part of the legacy of classical Athens which we still admire two and a half millennia after this shining moment in human history came to an end. The wholly true statement of Isocrates that Athens was a welcoming place not only for the affluent and the talented but also for those in need who fled misfortune and danger to find refuge, a safe haven and a new life in the city underlines the humanitarian spirit and principled outlook of the Athenians. However, what is more striking in the account of Isocrates is his belief that none of these accomplishments would have been possible without democracy and good laws.

As Isocrates puts it, the moment when people decided to resolve their differences through the justice system, instead of killing each other, was a pivotal one in their evolution. The Athenians, like the rest of the Greeks, believed in the rule of law, and considered it the primary differentiating characteristic between civilization and barbarism. They felt superior to the Persians because the latter, instead of being governed by laws, they were abused by their rulers (ὑπὸ δυναστειῶν ὑβριζομένους), and they also felt superior to savages who lived in lawlessness (τοὺς δὲ δι' ἀναρχίαν ἀπολλυμένους). Isocrates is claiming for Athens the privilege of being the first Greek *polis* to introduce laws and a constitution. Even if, strictly speaking, this may not be true, it matters little. Athens was one of the first Greek cities to introduce a body of laws, followed by a more ambitious legislative program introduced by Solon a quarter of a century later, and then its citizens kept revising, adding, modifying and codifying their laws to keep up with political, social, economic and cultural developments. Although the orators complain about the frequency with which the Athenians were changing their laws,[4] it is certainly to their credit that the citizens of the First Democracy saw their laws as a living, ever-changing body, rather than something static, fossilized and incapable of meeting the evolving needs of their society, like the Spartans did with the laws they attributed to Lycurgus, to their detriment

For almost three centuries the Athenians continued to work on their laws, because they believed in their importance as the basis for civilization, and as the fundamental precondition upon which all other freedoms, rights, privileges and daily comforts rested. And yet, in all that time the entire body of their laws remained slim, intentionally simple in language, style and content, and easily accessible not only to professional speech-writers and legal advisers, but also to the ordinary person with no legal expertise. Athenian culture certainly had the political and intellectual maturity to develop complex jurisprudence; it simply chose not to, for an important reason. By keeping the law accessible to the ordinary person the Athenian state not only recognized that it is the right of every citizen to have equal access to the legal system, but also that it is a duty of every citizen to obey, implement and enforce the laws. The Athenian Democracy was perhaps unique in history in this respect: the statement that the ordinary citizen had a duty to come to the aid of the laws (τοῖς νόμοις βοηθεῖν) was not just empty propaganda. The magistrates of the state and the individual citizen were meant to work together to make sure that the laws of the city are obeyed. Both sides had the authority to bring offenders to court, and ordinary citizens were meant to apply these laws and in accordance with them reach verdicts as arbitrators, or as judges in the various courts of the city.

The Athenians chose not to make their laws the privileged domain of a few professionals, as it happened later in history and still happens today; they never detached them from the daily lives of ordinary citizens, and always expected everyone to have a share in the writing, interpretation and implementation of the laws. Perhaps in this there is a valuable lesson which they can still teach us. It is not a paradox that classical Athens was a law-abiding society, even though it never developed a complex legal system. This is the reason why it was so. Every citizen was having a stake in the legislative and judicial processes motivated by the belief that the rule of law amounted to civilization, progress and prosperity, Athenian society was peaceful and law-abiding not only because its citizens feared the law, but also because they felt that they had a duty of care for this cornerstone upon which their democracy, freedoms and fundamental rights rested.

Notes

1 Plu. *Sol.* 17.3
2 Is. 10.10.
3 Isoc. 11.39–42.
4 For example, D. 24.139

Bibliography

Adam-Magnissali, S. and R. Cudjoe. 2010. "Family law in [Demosthenes] 43: Against Makartatos, 75." *EHHD* 42: 67–93.

Adamidis, Vasileios. 2016. *Character Evidence in the Courts of Classical Athens: Rhetoric, Relevance and the Rule of Law*. Taylor and Francis.

Adamidis, Vasileios. 2017. "The Relevance of Liturgies in the Courts of Classical Athens." *Athens Journal of History* 3 (2): 85–96.

Adeleye, Gabriel. 1983. "The Purpose of 'Dokimasia'." *Greek, Roman and Byzantine Studies* 24 (4): 295–306.

Aka, Adou Marcel. 2015. "The Rhetorical Use of the Argument of the Non-Citizenship of the Opponent in the Trials of the Fourth Century in Athens." *Dialogues d'histoire ancienne* 41 (2): 41–69.

Akrigg, Ben. 2015. "Metics in Athens." In Vlassopoulos, C.I. and Taylor, K. (eds,) *Communities and Networks in the Ancient Greek World* (pp. 155–76). Oxford: Oxford University Press.

Akrigg, Ben and Robert Tordoff. 2013. *Slaves and Slavery in Ancient Greek Comic Drama*. Cambridge and New York: Cambridge University Press.

Albertoni, Aldo. 1923. *L'apokeryxis: contributo alla storia della famiglia*: Seminario Giuridico della R. Università di Bologna.

Alcock, J.P. 2006. *Food in the Ancient World.* Westport, CT: Greenwood Press.

Alexandrakis, Dimitris S. 1987. "The education of children from birth to age fourteen in classical Athens (500–300 BC)." Diss. Boston College.

Alwine, Andrew T. 2015. *Enmity and Feuding in Classical Athens*. Austin, TX: University of Texas Press.

Ambler, Wayne. 1987. "Aristotle on nature and politics: The case of slavery." *Political Theory* 15 (3): 390–410.

Amundsen, D.W. and G.B. Ferngren. 1976. "The physician as an expert witness in Athenian law." *Bulletin of the History of Medicine* 51 (2): 202–13.

Amundsen, Darrel W. and Garry B. Ferngren. 1979. "The forensic role of physicians in Roman law." *Bulletin of the History of Medicine* 53 (1): 39–56.

Anaoutoglou, Ilias. 2007. "Fear of Slaves in Ancient Greek Legal Texts." In Serghidou, Anastasia (ed.), (pp. 133–44). Besançon: Pr. Universitaires de Franche-Comté.

Anderson, Greg. 2003. *The Athenian Experiment: Building an Imagined Political Community in Ancient Attica, 508–490 BC*. University of Michigan Press.

Anderson, Gregor William. 2000. "Alkmeonid 'homelands', political exile, and the unification of Attica." *Historia: Zeitschrift für Alte Geschichte = revue d'histoire ancienne* 49 (4) 387–412.

Andreassi, Mario. 2013. "'Adultery mime': da pratica scenica a modello ermeneutico." *Rheinisches Museum für Philologie* 156 (3–4): 293–313.

Andrewes, Antony. 1977. "Kleisthenes' reform bill." *Classical Quarterly* XXVII: 241–8.

Andriolo, N. 1995–6. "Eisangelia." *Atti dell' Istituto Veneto di Scienze, Lettere ed Arti (Classe di scienze morali)* 154: 173–95.

Apostolakis, Kostas E. 2007. "Tragic Patterns in Forensic Speeches: Antiphon 1 Against the Stepmother." *Classica et mediaevalia* 58: 179–92.

Armstrong, James I. 1949. *The Trierarchy and the Tribal Organization of the Athenian Navy*. Princeton: Princeton University.

Arnaoutoglou, Ilias N. 1993. "Pollution in the Athenian homicide law." *Revue Internationale des Droits de l'Antiquité* 3e sér. (4040): 109–37.

Arnaoutoglou, Ilias N. 2009. "Dispute settlement between 'poleis'-members of the Achaean League: a new source." *Dike: Rivista di Storia del Diritto Greco ed Ellenistico* 12–13: 181–201.

Arnason, Johann P., Kurt A. Raaflaub and Peter Wagner. 2013. *The Greek Polis and the Invention of Democracy: A Politico-Cultural Transformation and its Interpretations*. Vol. 25: John Wiley and Sons.

Asheri, David. 1963. "Laws of inheritance, distribution of land and political constitutions in ancient Greece." *Historia: Zeitschrift für Alte Geschichte* (H. 1): 1–21.

Avagianou, Aphrodite A. 1991. *Sacred Marriage in the Rituals of Greek Religion, Europ. University stud. ser. 15; 54*. Bern; Frankfurt am Main: Lang.

Avezzù, Guido. 1985. *Apologia per l'uccisione di Eratostene; Epitafio*. Vol. 3: Antenore.

Aviles, Domingo. 2011. "Slaves, non-citizens and written law in ancient Greece." *The Ancient History Bulletin* 25 (1–2): 1–8.

Avramovic, Sima. 2005. "The Rhetra of Epitadeus and Testament in Spartan Law." *Vorträge zur Griechischen und Hellenistischen Rechtsgeschichte, Österreichische Akademie der Wissenschaften*: 175–86.

Avramović, Sima. 2010. "Katoikodomeō in Isaeus, VIII 41: imprisonment, hybris and atimia in Athenian law." *Zeitschrift der Savigny-Stiftung für Rechtsgeschichte. Romanistische Abteilung* 127: 261–74.

Ayres, Ian and Richard Luedman. 2013. "Tops, Bottoms and Versatiles: What Straight Views of Penetrative Preferences Could Mean for Sexuality Claims under Price Waterhouse." *Yale LJ* 123: 714.

Bach, Amy. 2010. *Ordinary Injustice: How America Holds Court*. Metropolitan Books.

Bakewell, Geoff. 1999. "Lysias 12 and Lysias 31: metics and Athenian citizenship in the aftermath of the Thirty." *Greek, Roman and Byzantine Studies* 40 (1): 5–22.

Bakewell, Geoffrey W. 2008. "Forbidding marriage: Neaira 16 and metic spouses at Athens." *The Classical Journal* 104 (2): 97–109.

Balcer, Jack Martin. 1964. *From confederate freedom to imperial tyranny. A study of the restrictions imposed by Athens on the political self-determination of the member States of the Delian confederacy 478–31 BC*. University of Michigan.

Balogh, Elemer. 1953. "Some Notes on Adultery and the Epikleros According to Ancient Athenian Law." In *Studi in memoria di Emilio Albertario, Vol I-II*.", 683–719. A. Giuffrè.

Bandes, Susan. 2000. *The Passions of Law*. NYU Press.

Baragwanath, Emily. 2012. "The wonder of freedom: Xenophon on slavery." In Hobden, Fiona and Tuplin, Christopher J. (eds), *Xenophon: Ethical Principles and Historical Enquiry* (pp. 631–63). Leiden; Boston, MA: Brill.

Beckett, Katherine and Theodore Sasson. 2003. *The Politics of Injustice: Crime and Punishment in America*: Sage Publications.

Bentley, Russell. 1999. "Loving freedom: Aristotle on slavery and the good life." *Political Studies* 47 (1): 100–13.

Berent, Moshe. 2000. "Sovereignty: ancient and modern." *Polis: The Journal of the Society for Greek Political Thought* 17 (1–2): 2–34.

Bianchetti, Serena. 1981. "La normativa ateniese relativa al κακῶς λέγειν da Solone al IV secolo." *Studi e Ricerche dell'Istituto di Storia, Università di Firenze* I: 65–87.

Bianchetti, Serena. 1983. "Osservazioni sull' 'apagoge' in caso di omicidio." *Sileno*: 91–104.

Bingham, Dennis. 2010. *Whose Lives Are They Anyway?: The Biopic as Contemporary Film Genre*. New Brunswick, NJ: Rutgers University Press.

Biscardi, Arnaldo. 1988. "Sulla cosiddetta consensualità del contratto dotale in diritto attico." *Bullettino dell'Istituto di Diritto Romano "Vittorio Scialoja"* (30): 225–35.

Blass, Friedrich. 1874. *Die attische Beredsamkeit: Abth. Isokrates und Isaios*. Vol. 2: BG Teubner.

Blickman, Daniel R. 1986. "The Myth of Ixion and Pollution for Homicide in Archaic Greece." *The Classical Journal* 81 (3): 193–208.

Bloch, Herbert. 1953. "The Exegetes of Athens and the Prytaneion Decree." *The American Journal of Philology* 74 (4): 407–18.

Blok, Josine. 2017. *Citizenship in classical Athens*. Cambridge: Cambridge University Press.

Blok, Josine H. 2005. "Becoming citizens: some notes on the semantics of 'citizen' in Archaic Greece and Classical Athens." *Klio: Beiträge zur Alten Geschichte* 87 (1): 7–40.

Blok, Josine H. 2009. "Gentrifying genealogy: on the genesis of the Athenian autochthony myth." In Dill, Ueli and Walde, Christine (eds), *Antike Mythen: Medien, Transformationen und Konstruktionen* (pp. 251–75). Berlin; New York: De Gruyter.

Blok, Josine H. 2009. "Perikles' Citizenship Law: a new perspective." *Historia: Zeitschrift für Alte Geschichte* (H. 2): 141–70.

Blok, Josine H. and Lardinois, André Pierre M.H. (eds). 2006. Leiden; Boston, MA: Brill.

Blundell, Sue. 1995. *Women in Ancient Greece*. Cambridge, MA: Harvard University Press.

Blundell, Sue and Lloyd Llewellyn-Jones (eds). 2002. *Women's Dress in the Ancient Greek World*. Swansea: Classical Press of Wales.

Blundell, Sue and Margaret Williamson (eds). 1998. *The sacred and the feminine in ancient Greece*. London: Routledge.

Bodenhausen, Galen V., Lori A. Sheppard and Geoffrey P. Kramer. 1994. "Negative affect and social judgment: The differential impact of anger and sadness." *European Journal of Social Psychology* 24 (1): 45–62.

Boeckh, August. 1842. *The public economy of Athens*. London: John W. Parker.

Boegehold, Alan L. 1994. "Perikles' citizenship law of 451/0 BC." *Athenian Identity and Civic Ideology*: 57–66.

Boegehold, Alan L. 1996. "Group and single competitions at the Panathenaia." In Neils, Jenifer (ed.), *Worshipping Athena: Panathenaia and Parthenon* (pp. 95–105). Madison, WI: University of Wisconsin Press.

Boegehold, Alan L. and John McKesson Camp. 1995. Princeton, NJ: American School of Classical Studies at Athens.

Boegehold, Alan L. and Adele C. Scafuro (eds). 2002. *Athenian Identity and Civic Ideology*. JHU Press.

Bogaert, R. 1962. "A propos de la phasis (Isocrate, Trapézitique, 42). Contribution à l'histoire du droit athénien." *RIDA* 9: 157–68.

Bolkestein, H. 1922. "The exposure of children at Athens and the *enchytrestriai*." *Classical Philology* 17 (3): 222–39.

Bonnechère, Pierre. 2013. "The religious management of the polis: oracles and political decision-making." In Beck, Hans (ed.), (pp. 366–81). Chichester: Wiley-Blackwell.

Bonnechère, Pierre and Gabriela Cursaru (eds). 2015. *'Katábasis' dans la tradition littéraire et religieuse de la Grèce ancienne. 1,: Actes du colloque de Montréal et de Québec (2–5 mai 2014)*. Namur: Société des études classiques.

Bonner, Stanley. 2011. *Education in Ancient Rome: From the Elder Cato to the Younger Pliny*. London: Routledge.

Bouricius, Terrill G. 2013. "Democracy through multi-body sortition: Athenian lessons for the modern day." *Journal of Public Deliberation* 9 (1). Without pagination.

Bowden, Hugh. 2015. "Impiety." In Eidinow, Esther and Kindt, Julia (eds). Oxford: Oxford University Press.

Bradley, Mark. 2015. "Foul bodies in ancient Rome." In Bradley, Mark (ed.), (pp. 133–45). London; New York: Routledge.

Bratkin, Dimitri A. 2013. "The trial scenes in the 'Acts of the Apostles', in Chariton's 'Callirhoe' and in the Roman forensic papyri." In Kazansky, Nikolai N. (ed.), *Indo-European linguistics and Classical philology. 17: Proceedings of the 17th conference in memory of Professor Joseph M. Tronsky: June 24–6, 2013* (pp. 107–18). Sankt-Peterburg: Nauka.

Braund, David. 2006. "In Search of the Creator of Athens' Scythian Archer-Police: Speusis and the 'Eurymedon Vase'." *Zeitschrift für Papyrologie und Epigraphik*: 109–13.

Bremmer, Jan Nicolaas (ed.). 1987. *Interpretations of Greek Mythology*. London: Croom Helm.

Brickhouse, Thomas C. and Nicholas D. Smith. 1989. *Socrates on Trial*. Clarendon Paperbacks.

Bright, David A. and Jane Goodman-Delahunty. 2006. "Gruesome evidence and emotion: anger, blame, and jury decision-making." *Law and Human Behavior* 30 (2): 183–202.

Brock, Roger. 2010. "Citizens and non-citizens in Athenian tragedy." In Harris, Edward Monroe, Leão, Delfim Ferreira and Rhodes, Peter John (eds), (pp. 94–107). London: Duckworth.

Brock, Roger. 2014. "Priestesses and citizens." In Bultrighini, Umberto and Dimauro, Elisabetta (eds), (pp. 93–107). Lanciano: Carabba.

Broneer, Oscar. 1942. "The Thesmophorion in Athens." *Hesperia: The Journal of the American School of Classical Studies at Athens* 11 (3): 250–74. doi: 10.2307/146735.

Brown, Peter G. McC. 1991. "Athenian attitudes to rape and seduction: the evidence of Menander, Dyskolos 289–93." *Classical Quarterly* 41: 533–4.

Bruce, Iain A.F. 1968. "Plataea and the fifth-century Boeotian confederacy." *Phoenix* 22: 190–9.

Brumfield, Allaire Chandor. 1981. *The Attic Festivals of Demeter and their Relation to the Agricultural Year*. New York: Arno Press.

Brunt, Peter A. 1993. "Aristotle and slavery." In Brunt, Peter A. (ed.). 1996. 343–88. Oxford: Clarendon Press.

Buckler, John. 2000. "The phantom 'synedrion' of the Boiotian Confederacy (378–35 BC)." In Flensted-Jensen, Pernille, Heine Nielsen, Thomas and Rubinstein, Lene (eds), (pp. 431–46). Copenhagen: Museum Tusculanum Press.

Burger, Friedrich. 1892. *Stichometrische Untersuchungen zu Demosthenes und Herodot: ein Beitrag zur Kenntnis des antiken Buchwesens*. Munich: Lindl.

Burkert, W. 1996. "Isonomia und Polisreligion im kleisthenischen Athen." In Adrados, Francisco R. and Sakellariou, Michel B. (eds), (pp. 51–65). Athens: Academy of Athens.

Burkert, Walter. 1985. *Greek Religion*. Cambridge, MA: Harvard University Press. (transl. by Raffan J.)

Burns, Tony. 2003. "The tragedy of slavery: Aristotle's Rhetoric and the history of the concept of natural law." *History of Political Thought* 24 (1): 16–36.

Bushala, E.W. 1968. "Torture of non-citizens in homicide investigations." *Greek, Roman and Byzantine Studies* 9: 61–8.

Cairns, Douglas L. 1996. "Hybris, dishonour, and thinking big." *The Journal of Hellenic Studies* 116: 1–32.

Cairns, Douglas L. and Stephen D. Lambert (eds). 2011. *Sociable Man: Essays on Ancient Greek Social Behaviour in Honour of Nick Fisher*. Swansea: Classical Press of Wales.

Calabi Limentani, I. 1982. "Demosthene XX, 137: A proposito della graphe nomon me epitedeion theinai." In Pastori, F. et al. (eds), *Studi in onore di Arnaldo Biscardi* (357–68). Milan: Istituto editoriale cisalpino, La Goliardica.

Calame, Claude. 2011. "Myth and performance on the Athenian stage: Praxithea, Erechtheus, their daughters, and the etiology of autochthony." *Classical Philology: A Journal Devoted to Research in Classical Antiquity* 106 (1): 1–19.

Cambiano, Giuseppe. 1987. "Aristotle and the anonymous opponents of slavery." *Slavery and Abolition* 8 (1): 22–41.

Cameron, A. 1932. "The exposure of children and Greek ethics." *Classical Review*: 105–14.

Canawan, Edwin. 1993. "The Tetralogies and the Athenian homicide trials." *American Journal of Philology* 114: 235–70.

Canevaro, Mirko. 2010. "The decree awarding citizenship to the Plataeans ([Dem.] 59.104)." *Greek, Roman, and Byzantine Studies* 50 (3): 337–69.

Canevaro, Mirko and Edward Monroe Harris. 2013. *The Documents in the Attic Orators: Laws and Decrees in the Public Speeches of the Demosthenic Corpus*. Oxford: Oxford University Press.

Cantarella, Eva. 1972. "Moicheia e omicidio legittimo in diritto attico." *Labeo: rassegna di diritto romano* 18: 78–88.

Cantarella, Eva. 1991. "Moicheia. Reconsidering a problem." In Gagarin, M. (ed.), *Symposion 1990*: 289–96.

Cantarella, Eva. 2002. *Bisexuality in the Ancient World*. Yale University Press.

Carawan, E. 1990. "Trial of Exiled Homicides and the Court at Phreatto." *Revue internationale des droits de l'antiquité* 37: 47–67.

Carawan, Edwin. 1987. "Eisangelia and euthyna. The trials of Miltiades, Themistocles, and Cimon." *Greek, Roman and Byzantine Studies* XXVIII: 167–208.

Carawan, Edwin. 1991. "EØETAI and Athenian courts for homicide in the age of orators." *Classical Philology: A Journal Devoted to Research in Classical Antiquity* LXXXVI: 1–16.

Carawan, Edwin. 1998. *Rhetoric and the Law of Draco*. Oxford: Clarendon.

Carawan, Edwin. 2008. "Pericles the Younger and the citizenship law." *The Classical Journal*: 383–406.

Carawan, Edwin. 2010. "Diadikasiai and the Demotionid problem." *The Classical Quarterly* (New Series) 60 (2): 381–400.

Carawan, Edwin M. 1985. "'Apophasis' and 'Eisangelia': The Rôle of the Areopagus in Athenian Political Trials." *Greek, Roman and Byzantine Studies* 26 (2): 115–40.

Carcieri, Martin D. 2002. *Democracy and Education in Classical Athens and the American Founding, Major Concepts in Politics and Political Theory; 20*. Bern and Frankfurt am Main: Lang.

Carey, Christopher. 1988. "A note on torture in Athenian homicide cases." *Historia: Zeitschrift für Alte Geschichte = revue d'histoire ancienne* XXXVII: 241–5.

Carey, Christopher. 1991. "Apollodoros' mother: The wives of enfranchised aliens in Athens." *The Classical Quarterly* (New Series) 41 (01): 84–9.

Carey, Christopher. 1995. "Rape and adultery in Athenian law." *Classical Quarterly* 45 (2): 407–17.

Carnes, Jeffrey S. 1990. "The Aiginetan Genesis of the Myrmidons: A Note on 'Nemean' 3.13–16." *The Classical World* 84 (1): 41–4.

Carrara, Laura. 2007. "Il processo areopagitico di Oreste: le Eumenidi di Eschilo e la tradizione attica." *Philologus* 151 (1): 3–16.

Cartledge, Paul. 1987. *Agesilaos and the Crisis of Sparta*. London: Duckworth.

Cartledge, Paul. 2002. "Greek civilization and slavery." In Wiseman, Timothy Peter (ed.), (pp. 247–62). Oxford; New York: Oxford University Press.

Cartledge, Paul. 2003. "Raising Hell? The Helot Mirage: A Personal Re-View." In N. Luraghi and S. Alcock (eds), *Helots and their Masters in Laconia and Messenia: Histories, Ideologies, Structures*: 12–30.

Cartledge, Paul. 2013. *Sparta and Lakonia: A Regional History 1300–362 BC*. Routledge.

Carusi, U. and C. Fantasia. 2004. "Revisioni e controlli delle liste dei cittadini: la diapsephisis ateniese del 346/5 aC." In *Poleis e politeiai: esperienze politiche, tradizioni letterarie, progetti costituzionali: atti del convegno internazionale di storia greca, Torino, 29–31 maggio 2002*, edited by Silvio Cataldi, 187–216. Torino: Edizioni dell' Orso.

Casanova, A. 1962. *Nel mondo delle etere. Il processo di Frine*, Diadosis, Voci presenza classica (Tortona).

Casson, Lionel. 1990. "New light on maritime loans: P. Vindob G 40822." *Zeitschrift für Papyrologie und Epigraphik*: 195–206.

Chlup, Radek. 2007. "The semantics of fertility: levels of meaning in the Thesmophoria." *Kernos: Revue Internationale Et Pluridisciplinaire De Religion Grecque Antique* 20: 69–95.

Christ, Matthew R. 1990. "Liturgy avoidance and antidosis in classical Athens." *Transactions of the American Philological Association* CXX: 147–69.

Christ, Matthew R. 1998. *The Litigious Athenian*. Baltimore: Johns Hopkins University Press.

Christ, Matthew R. 2006. *The Bad Citizen in Classical Athens*. Cambridge and New York: Cambridge University Press

Christ, Matthew Robert. 2012. *The Limits of Altruism in Democratic Athens*. Cambridge and New York: Cambridge University Press.

Christensen, Kerry A. 1984. "The Theseion: A slave refuge at Athens." *American Journal of Ancient History* 9 (1): 23–32.

Christien, Jacqueline. 1974. "La loi d'Épitadeus. Un aspect de l'histoire économique et sociale à Sparte." *Revue Historique De Droit Français Et Étranger* LII: 197–221.

Clark, Donald Lemen. 1957. *Rhetoric in Greco-Roman Education*. New York: Columbia University Press.

Cleland, Liza, Mary Harlow and Lloyd Llewellyn-Jones (eds). 2005. *The Clothed Body in the Ancient World*. Oxford: Oxbow Books.

Clinton, Kevin. 1974. *The sacred officials of the Eleusinian mysteries*, *TAPhS*; 44, 3.

Clinton, Kevin. 1996. "The 'Thesmophorion' in central Athens and the celebration of the 'Thesmophoria' in Attica." In Hägg, Robin (ed.), (pp. 111–25). Jonsered: Åströms Förl.

Closterman, Wendy Elizabeth. 2006. "Family members and citizens: Athenian identity and the peribolos tomb setting." *Helios* 33 (Supplement): 49–78.

Cobetto Ghiggia, P. 2008. "Il tentativo di apokeryxis contro Alcibiade." In *Studi in onore di Remo Martini*. Milan: Giuffré Editore.

Cohen, David. 1987. "Law, society and homosexuality in classical Athens." *Past and Present* (117): 3–21.

Cohen, David. 1988. "The prosecution of impiety in Athenian law." *Zeitschrift der Savigny-Stiftung für Rechtsgeschichte: Romanistische Abteilung* 105 (1): 695–701.

Cohen, David J. 1983. *Theft in Athenian law, Münchener Beitr. zur Papyrusforsch. and antiken Rechtsgesch.* 74. München: Beck.

Cohen, David J. 1984. "The Athenian law of adultery." *Revue Internationale Des Droits De l'Antiquité* 31: 147–65.

Cohen, David J. 1989. "The prosecution of impiety in Athenian law." In Thür, Gerhard (ed.), (pp. 99–107). Köln: Böhlau.

Cohen, David J. 1990. "The social context of adultery at Athens." In Cartledge, Paul, Millett, Paul and Todd, Stephen Randolph (eds), (pp. 147–65). Cambridge: Cambridge University Press.

Cohen, David J. 1993. "Consent and sexual relations in classical Athens." In Laiou, Angeliki E. (ed.), (pp. 5–16). Washington, DC: Dumbarton Oaks Research Library and Collection.

Cohen, David J. 1995. *Law, Violence, and Community in Classical Athens, Key themes in ancient history*. Cambridge and New York: Cambridge University Press

Cohen, Edward. 1997. *Athenian Economy and Society: A Banking Perspective*. Princeton University Press.

Cohen, E.E. (ed.). 2000. *Written Contracts of Prostitution in Fourth-Century Athens, Timai Iohannou Triantaphyllopoulou*. Athens: Sakkoula.

Cohen, Edward E. 1963. *The dikai emporikai. A Study of the Commercial Maritime Courts at Athens in the Fourth Century BC*. Princeton: Princeton University

Cohen, Edward E. 1973. *Ancient Athenian Maritime Courts*. Princeton: Princeton University Press

Cohen, Edward E. 1990. "A Study in Contrast: 'Maritime Loans' and 'Landed Loans' at Athens." In Nenci, Giuseppe and Thür, Gerhard (eds), (pp. 57–79). Köln: Böhlau.

Cohen, Edward E. 1998. "The wealthy slaves of Athens: legal rights, economic obligations." In Jones, Huguette (ed.), *Le monde antique et les droits de l'homme: actes de la 50e session de la Société internationale Fernand De Visscher pour l'histoire des droits de l'antiquité: Bruxelles, 16–19 septembre 1996* (pp. 105–29). Bruxelles: Université libre de Bruxelles.

Cohen, Edward E. 2000. "Whoring Under Contract: The Legal Context of Prostitution in Fourth-Century Athens." In Hunter, Virginia and Edmondson, Jonathan (eds), *Law and Social Status in Classical Athens* (pp. 113–48). Oxford: Oxford University Press.

Cohen, Edward E. 2007. "Laws affecting prostitution at Athens." In Cantarella, Eva (ed.), *Symposion 2005: Vortra ̈ge zur griechischen und hellenistischen Rechtsgeschichte* (pp. 201–24). Verlag der Österreichischen Akademie der Wissenschaften.

Cohen, Edward E. 2015. *Athenian Prostitution: The Business of Sex*. Oxford University Press.

Cohen, Edward E. 2015. "Maritime profiteering in fourth-century Athens." In Matthaiou, Angelos P. and Papazarkadas, Nikolaos (eds). 2015. 393–424. Athens: Greek Epigraphic Society.

Cohen, Edward E. 2014. "Sexual abuse and sexual rights: slaves' erotic experience at Athens and Rome." In Hubbard, Thomas K. (ed.), (pp. 184–98). Oxford: Blackwell.

Cohn, Norman. 1956. Northampton, MA.

Cohn-Haft, Louis. 1995. "Divorce in classical Athens." *The Journal of Hellenic Studies* 115: 1–14.

Coker, Donna. 2002. "Foreword: Addressing the real world of racial injustice in the criminal justice system." *J. Crim. L. and Criminology* 93: 827–79.

Cole, David. 1999. *No Equal Justice: Race and Class in the American Criminal Justice System*. Vol. 1: New York: New Press.

Cole, Susan Guettel. 1984. "Greek sanctions against sexual assault." *Classical Philology: A Journal Devoted to Research in Classical Antiquity* LXXIX: 97–113.

Colombatto, Enrico. 2007. "It Was the Rule of Law: Will It Be the Rule of Judges?" *Revue Économique* 58 (6): 1163–80.

Connor, W. Robert. 1990. "City Dionysia and Athenian democracy." In Fears, J. Rufus (ed.), (pp. 7–32). Copenhagen: Museum Tusculanum Press.

Connor, W. Robert. 1991. "The other 399: Religion and the trial of Socrates." *Bulletin of the Institute of Classical Studies* 37 (S58): 49–56.

Cook, Brad L. 2012. "Swift-boating in antiquity: rhetorical framing of the good citizen in fourth-century Athens." *Rhetorica: A Journal of the History of Rhetoric* 30 (3): 219–51.

Cook, Brad L. and Farid Abdel-Nour. 2014. "'As if' they could be brought to account: how Athenians managed the political unaccountability of citizens." *History of Political Thought* 35 (3): 436–57.

Cooper, Craig. 1995. "Hyperides and the trial of Phryne." *Phoenix: Journal of the Classical Association of Canada = revue de la Société canadienne des études classiques* 49 (4): 303–18.

Corner, Sean. 2012. "Did 'respectable' women attend symposia?" *Greece and Rome* Ser. 2 (59 (1)59 1): 34–45.

Cox, Cheryl Anne. 1989. "Incest, inheritance and the political forum in fifth-century Athens." *The Classical Journal* LXXXV: 34–46.

Cox, Cheryl Anne. 1992. "On Roger Just's Women in Athenian law and life." *The Ancient History Bulletin* VI: 177–86.

Cox, Cheryl Anne. 1998. *Household Interests: Property, Marriage Strategies, and Family Dynamics in Ancient Athens*. Princeton, NJ: Princeton University Press

Cox, Cheryl Anne. 2001. "Is Sostratus' family urban in Menander's 'Dyskolos'?" *The Classical Journal* 97 (4): 351–8.

Cox, Cheryl A. 2012. "Women and Family in Menander." *A Companion to Women in the Ancient World*: 278–87.

Craik, Elizabeth M. 1987. "One for the pot. Aristophanes' *Birds* and the Anthesteria." *Eranos: Acta Philologica Suecana* LXXXV: 25–34.

Crane, Gregory. 1997. "Oikos and agora: mapping the polis in Aristophanes' 'Wasps'." In Dobrov, Gregory W. (ed.), (pp. 198–229). Chapel Hill, NC: University of North Carolina Press.

Crawford, Michael H. 2010. "From Alcibiades to Diocletian: slavery and the economy in the 'longue durée'." In Roth, Ulrike (ed.), (pp. 61–73). London: Institute of Classical Studies, University of London.

Cromey, Robert. 2006. "Apollo Patroos and the phratries." *L'Antiquité Classique* 75: 41–69.

Cudjoe, Richard V. 2005. "The purpose of the 'epidikasia' for an 'epikleros' in classical Athens." *Dike: Rivista di Storia del Diritto Greco ed Ellenistico* 8: 55–88.

Cudjoe, Richard V. 2010. *The social and legal position of widows and orphans in classical Athens, Symboles. Contributions to the research of ancient Greek and Hellenistic law; 3*. Athens: Centre for Ancient Greek and Hellenistic Law, Panteion University.

Cuniberti, Gianluca. 2011. "Solone e la riforma religiosa della polis: il popolo, le donne e gli dei." *Mythos* 5 (5): 45–58.

Daude, Cécile. 2001. "Le personnage d'Artaxerxès dans le roman de Chariton, 'Chairéas et Callirhoé': fiction et histoire." In Pouderon, Bernard, Hunzinger, Christine and Kasprzyk, Dimitri (eds), (pp. 137–48). Lyon: Maison de l'Orient Méditerranéen.

Davidson, James. 1995. "Opsophagia: revolutionary eating at Athens." In Davidson, Alan, Harvey, David, Wilkins, John B. and Dobson, Michael J. (eds), *Food in antiquity* (pp. 204–13). Exeter: University of Exeter Press

Davidson, James. 2001. "Dover, Foucault and Greek Homosexuality: Penetration and the Truth of Sex " *Past and Present* 170: 3–51.

Davidson, James. 2007. *The Greeks and Greek Love: A Radical Reappraisal of Homosexuality in Ancient Greece*. Weidenfeld and Nicolson.

Davidson, James N. 1997. *Courtesans and Fishcakes: The Consuming Passions of Classical Athens*: Macmillan.

Davies, John K. 1977. "Athenian citizenship: the descent group and the alternatives." *The Classical Journal* 73 (2): 105–21.

De Brauw, Michael. 2001. "'Listen to the Laws Themselves': Citations of Laws and Portrayal of Character in Attic Oratory." *The Classical Journal* 97 (2): 161–76.

De Bruyn, Odile. 1995. *La compétence de l'Aréopage en matière de procès publics: des origines de la Polis athénienne à la conquête romaine de la Grèce (vers 700–146 avant J.-C.)*. Franz Steiner Verlag.

De Laix, Roger Alain. 1973. *Probouleusis at Athens: A Study of Political Decision-Making*. University of California Press.

De Rossi, F. Canali. 1999. "Proprietà privata, religione e politica nell'orazione VII di Lisia." *Per l'olivo sacro, ARF*: 27–34.

de Ste Croix, Geoffrey E.M. 1974. "Ancient Greek and Roman maritime loans." In Edey, H.C. and Yamey, B.S. *Debits, Credits, Finance and Profits* (pp. 41–59). London: Sweet and Maxwell.

Deacy, Susan and Karen F. Peirce (eds). 1997. *Rape in Antiquity: Sexual Violence in the Greek and Roman Worlds*. Swansea: Classical Press of Wales.

Deene, Marloes. 2011. "Naturalized citizens and social mobility in classical Athens: the case of Apollodorus." *Greece and Rome* Ser. 2 58 (2): 159–75.

Delannoi, Gil and Oliver Dowlen. 2010. *Sortition: Theory and Practice*. Exeter: Imprint Academic.

Detienne, Marcel. 2001. "The art of founding autochthony: Thebes, Athens, and old-stock French." *Arion* 9 (1): 46–55.

Develin, Robert. 1973. "The good man and the good citizen in Aristotle's 'Politics'." *Phronesis*: 71–9.

Develin, Robert. 1991. "Euboulides' office and the diapsephisis of 346/5 B.C." *Classica et Mediaevalia* 42: 75–9.

Devine, Dennis J, Laura D. Clayton, Benjamin B. Dunford, Rasmy Seying and Jennifer Pryce. 2001. "Jury decision making: 45 years of empirical research on deliberating groups." *Psychology, Public Policy, and Law* 7 (3): 622–727.

Diamant, Steven. 1982. "Theseus and the unification of Attica." *Hesperia Supplements* 19: 38–47.

Dillon, Matthew. 2002. *Girls and Women in Classical Greek Religion*. London: Routledge.

Dimakis, Panayotis D. 1997. "Les ambassadeurs dans la Grèce antique." *Bullettino dell'Istituto di Diritto Romano* 3a ser. (3939): 87–91.

Dimopoulou-Piliouni, Athina. 2008. "Apeleutheroi: Metics or Foreigners?" *Dike* 11: 27–50.

Dmitriev, Sviatoslav. 2014. "Posthumous adoption in classical Athens." *Chiron* 44: 67–85.

Dmitriev, Sviatoslav. 2016. "The Protection of Slaves in the Athenian Law against hubris." *Phoenix* 70 (1/2): 64–76.

Doulamis, Konstantin. 2011. "Forensic oratory and rhetorical theory in Chariton book 5." In Doulamis, Konstantin (ed.), (pp. 21–48). Eelde: Barkhuis.

Dover, Kenneth James. 1975. "The freedom of the intellectual in Greek society." *Talanta* 7: 24–54.

Dowlen, Oliver. 2008. *The Political Potential of Sortition: A Study of the Random Selection of Citizens for Public Office*. Exeter: Imprint Academic, 2009.

Dowlen, Oliver. 2009. "Sorting out sortition: A perspective on the random selection of political officers." *Political Studies* 57 (2): 298–315.

Drerup, Engelbert. 1898. "Uber die bei den attischen Rednern eingelegten Urkunden." *Jb. Cl.Ph.* (Suppl. 24): 221–366.

Drews, Robert. 1983. *Basileus: The Evidence for Kingship in Geometric Greece*. Yale University Press.

Droysen, Johann Gustav. 1893. *Kleine Schriften zur alten Geschichte*. Vol. 1. Veit.

Eagly, Alice H. 1995. "The science and politics of comparing women and men." *American Psychologist* 50 (3): 145.

Edmondson, Jonathan C. and Virginia J. Hunter (eds). 2000. *Law and Social Status in Classical Athens*. Oxford and New York: Oxford University Press

Edwards, Martha Lynn. 1995. "Physical disability in the ancient Greek world." Ph.D., University of Minnessota.

Edwards, Martha Lynn. 1998. "Women and physical disability in ancient Greece." *The Ancient World* 29 (1): 3–9.

Efstathiou, Athanasios. 2007. "Euthyna procedure in 4th century: Athens and the case on the false embassy." *Dike* 10: 113–35.

Ehrenberg, Victor. 2010 (first edition 1968). *From Solon to Socrates: Greek History and Civilization during the 6th and 5th Centuries BC*. London: Routledge.

Eidinow, Esther. 2010. "Patterns of Persecution: 'Witchcraft'Trials in Classical Athens." *Past and Present* 208 (1): 9–35.

Eidinow, Esther. 2015. *Envy, Poison, and Death: Women on Trial in Classical Athens*. Oxford: Oxford University Press.

Eidinow, Esther and Julia Kindt. 2015. *The Oxford Handbook of Ancient Greek Religion*. Oxford: Oxford University Press.

Eliot, C.W.J. 1962. *Coastal Demes of Attica. A Study of the Policy of Kleisthenes, Phoenix Suppl.; V*. Toronto: University of Toronto Press

Engels, Donald W. 1980. "The problem of female infanticide in the Greco-Roman world.", 75, 112–20

Erbse, Hartmut. 1977. "Antiphons Rede (Or. 5) über die Ermordung des Herodes." *Rheinisches Museum für Philologie* 120 (H. 3/4): 209–27.

Erez, Edna and Linda Rogers. 1999. "Victim impact statements and sentencing outcomes and processes. The perspectives of legal professionals." *British Journal of Criminology* 39 (2): 216–39.

Evans, Nancy. 2010. *Civic Rites: Democracy and Religion in Ancient Athens*. University of California Press.

Evans, Nancy A. 2002. "Sanctuaries, sacrifices, and the Eleusinian mysteries." *Numen: International Review for the History of Religions* 49 (3): 227–54.

Evans, Nancy A. 2004. "Feasts, citizens, and cultic democracy in Classical Athens." *Ancient Society* 34: 1–25.

Evjen, Harold D. 1962. *An Institutional Study of the Athenian Law of Homicide during the Fourth Century BC*. Madison: University of Wisconsin.

Evjen, Harold D. 1970. "Ἀπαγωγή and Athenian homicide procedures." *Tijdschrift voor Rechtsgeschiedenis = revue d'histoire du droit* 38: 403–15.

Eyben, Emiel. 1980. "Family Planning in Graeco-Roman Antiquity." *Ancient Society* (11): 5–82.

Fabbri, L. 2014. "Considerazioni sulla Krokōnidōn diadikasia." *Dike* 17: 35–44.

Farenga, Vincent. 2006. *Citizen and Self in Ancient Greece: Individuals Performing Justice and the Law*. Cambridge and New York: Cambridge University Press.

Farina, Antonio. 1969. *Il processo di Frine*. Vol. 32: Libreria scientifica editrice.

Fartzoff, Michel. 1984. "Oikos et polis dans l'Orestie. Quelques considérations." *Ktèma* IX: 171–84.

Fehr, Burkhard. 2009. "'Pornos' and the pleasure of rest: some thoughts on body language in ancient Greek art and life." In Yatromanolakis, Dimitiros (ed.), (pp. 128–58). Athina: Kardamitsas.

Ferrucci, Stefano. 2002. "Gli schiavi nell' 'oikos' ad Atene: la testimonianza delle orazioni di Iseo." In Garrido-Hory, Marguerite (ed.), (pp. 29–50). Besançon: Pr. Universitaires Franc-Comtoises.

Ferrucci, Stefano. 2006. "L''oikos' nel diritto attico: pubblico, privato e individuale nella democrazia ateniese classica." *Dike: Rivista di Storia del Diritto Greco ed Ellenistico* 9: 183–210.

Ferrucci, Stefano. 2013. "L' 'oikos' alla sbarra: la rappresentazione dei rapporti familiari nello spazio giuridico ateniese." *Seminari Romani di Cultura Greca* N.S. 2 (2): 263–84.

Feyel, Christophe. 2007. "La 'dokimasia' des nouveaux citoyens dans les cités grecques." *Revue des Études Grecques* 120 (1): 19–49.

Feyel, Christophe. 2009. *Dokimasía: la place et le rôle de l'examen préliminaire dans les institutions des cités grecques, études anciennes; 36*. Paris: de Boccard.

Fialho, Maria do Céu Zambujo. 2010. "Clitemnestra en su 'oikos' vacío." In De Martino, Francesco and Morenilla, Carmen (eds), (pp. 113–21). Bari: Levante Ed..

Figueira, Thomas J. 2003. "The demography of the Spartan helots." In Luraghi, Nino and Alcock, Susan E. (eds), (pp. 193–239). Cambridge, MA: Harvard University Press.

Filonik, Jakub. 2013. "Athenian impiety trials: a reappraisal." *Dike* 16: 11–96.

Finkelberg, Margalit. 2006. "The City Dionysia and the social space of Attic tragedy." In Davidson, John F., Muecke, Frances and Wilson, Peter J. (eds), (pp. 17–26). London: Institute of Classical Studies, University of London.

Finley, Moses I. 1960. Cambridge: Heffer.

Finley, Moses I. 1981. "The Elderly in Classical Antiquity." *Greece and Rome* 28 (2): 156–71.

Fisher, N.R.E. 2001. *Aeschines, Against Timarchos*. Oxford: Oxford University Press.

Fisher, N.R.E. 2005. "Body-Abuse: The Rhetoric of Hybris in Aechines' Against Timarchos." In Bertrand, Jean-Marie (ed.), *La violence dans les mondes grec et romain: actes du colloque international Paris, 2–4 mai 2002*, 67–89.

Fisher, Nicolas Ralph Edmund. 1992. *Hybris: A Study in the Values of Honour and Shame in Ancient Greece*. Warminster: Aris and Phillips.

Fisher, Nicolas Ralph Edmund. 1993. *Slavery in Classical Greece*. London: Bristol Classical Press.

Fisher, Nicolas Ralph Edmund. 1997. "'Hybris', status and slavery." In Powell, Anton (ed.), (pp. 44–84). London: Routledge.

Fisher, Nicolas Ralph Edmund. 1998. "Violence, masculinity and the law in classical Athens." In Foxhall, Lin and Salmon, John (eds), (pp. 68–97). London: Routledge.

Fisher, Nicolas Ralph Edmund. 2003. "'Let envy be absent': envy, liturgies and reciprocity in Athens." In Konstan, David and Rutter, N. Keith (eds), (pp. 181–215). Edinburgh: Edinburgh University Press.

Fisher, Nicolas Ralph Edmund. 2005. "Body-abuse: the rhetoric of 'hybris' in Aeschines' 'Against Timarchos'." In Bertrand, Jean-Marie (ed.), (pp. 67–89). Paris: Publ. de la Sorbonne.

Flament, Christophe. 2011. "'Basileús"-archonte, 'filobasileis' et 'basileis': tous 'rois' d'Athènes? Recherches sur la nature et les fonctions des 'basileis' dans l'Athènes préclisthénienne." *Etudes Classiques* 79 (3): 285–308.

Fletcher, Judith. 1999. "Sacrificial bodies and the body of the text in Aristophanes' Lysistrata." *Ramus* 28 (2): 108.

Florence, Monica. 2014. "The body politic: sexuality in Greek and Roman comedy and mime." In Hubbard, Thomas K. (ed.), (pp. 366–80). Oxford: Blackwell.

Flower, Michael Attyah. 1985. "IG II FD.2344 and the size of phratries in classical Athens." *Classical Quarterly* XXXV: 232–5.

Foley, Helene P. 1982. "The 'Female Intruder' Reconsidered: Women in Aristophanes' Lysistrata and Ecclesiazusae." *Classical Philology* 77 (1): 1–21.

Fornara, Charles W. 1971. *The Athenian Board of Generals from 501 to 404, Historia Einzelschr. XVI*. Stuttgart: Steiner.

Foxhall, Lin. 1989. "Household, gender and property in classical Athens." *The Classical Quarterly* (New Series) 39 (01): 22–44.

Foxhall, Lin. 1991. "Response to Eva Cantarella." In Gagarin, M. (ed.), *Symposion 1990*: 297–304.

Foxhall, Lin. 1995. "Women's ritual and men's work in ancient Athens." In Hawley, Richard and Levick, Barbara Mary (eds), (pp. 97–110). London: Routledge.

Foxhall, Lin. 1996. "The law and the lady: women and legal proceedings in classical Athens." In Foxhall, Lin and Lewis, Andrew D.E. (eds), (pp. 133–52). Oxford; New York: Oxford University Press.

Foxhall, Lin and Andrew D.E. Lewis. 1996. *Greek Law in its Political Setting: Justifications not Justice*. Oxford University Press.

French, Alfred. 1994. "Pericles' citizenship law." *Ancient History Bulletin* 8: 71–5.

Frost, Frank. 2002. "Solon Pornoboskos and Aphrodite Pandemos." *Syllecta Classica* 13 (1): 34–46.

Frost, Frank J. 1990. "Peisistratos, the Cults, and the Unification of Attica." *Ancient World* 21 (1–2): 3–9.

Gabrielsen, V. 1981. *Remuneration of State Officials in Fourth Century BC Athens* (Vol. 11). Odense University Press.

Gabrielsen, Vincent. 1987. "The antidosis procedure in classical Athens." *Classica et Mediaevalia: Revue Danoise de Philologie et D'histoire* XXXVIII: 7–38.

Gagarin, M. 1989. *The Murder of Herodes: A Study of Antiphon 5*. Frankfurt am Mein: P. Lang.

Gagarin, Michael. 1978. "Self-defense in Athenian homicide law." *Greek, Roman and Byzantine Studies* 19: 111–20.

Gagarin, Michael. 1979. "The Athenian law against hybris." In Bowersock, Glen Warren, Burkert, Walter and Putnam, Michael C.J. (eds), (pp. 229–36). Berlin: De Gruyter.

Gagarin, Michael. 1979. "The prosecution of homicide in Athens." *Greek, Roman and Byzantine Studies* 20 (4): 301–23.

Gagarin, Michael. 1981. *Drakon and Early Athenian Homicide Law, Yale Class. Monogr.*. New Haven, CT: Yale University Press.

Gagarin, Michael. 1981. "The thesmothetai and the earliest Athenian tyranny law." *Transactions of the American Philological Association* 111: 71–7.

Gagarin, Michael. 1982. "The Organization of the Gortyn Law Code." *Greek, Roman and Byzantine Studies* 23 (2): 129–46.

Gagarin, Michael. 1990. "Bouleusis in Athenian homicide law." In Nenci, Giuseppe and Thür, Gerhard (eds), (pp. 81–99). Köln: Böhlau.

Gagarin, Michael. 1990. "The nature of proofs in Antiphon." *Classical Philology* 85 (1): 22–32.

Gagarin, Michael. 1996. "The torture of slaves in Athenian law." *Classical Philology: A Journal Devoted to Research in Classical Antiquity* 91 (1): 1–18.

Gagarin, Michael. 1998. "Women in Athenian courts." *Dike* 1: 39–51.

Gagarin, Michael. 2000. "The 'basileus' in Athenian homicide law." In Flensted-Jensen, Pernille, Heine Nielsen, Thomas and Rubinstein, Lene (eds), (pp. 569–79). Copenhagen: Museum Tusculanum Press.

Gagarin, Michael. 2001. "Women's voices in Attic oratory." In Lardinois, André Pierre M.H. and McClure, Laura K. (eds), (pp. 161–76). Princeton, NJ: Princeton University Press.

Gagarin, Michael. 2005. "La violence dans les plaidoyers attiques." In Bertrand, Jean-Marie (ed.), *La violence dans les mondes grec et romain: actes du colloque international (Paris, 2–4 mai 2002)* (pp. 365–76). Paris: Publ. de la Sorbonne.

Gagarin, Michael. 2011. "Writing sacred laws in archaic and classical Crete." In Lardinois, André Pierre M.H., Blok, Josine H. and Van der Poel, Marc G.M. (eds), (pp. 101–11). Leiden; Boston, MA: Brill; Leiden: Brill.

Gagliardi, Lorenzo. 2002. "Per un'interpretazione della legge di Solone in materia successoria." *Dike* 5: 5–59.

Gambón, Lidia. 2009. *La institución imaginaria del 'oikos' en la tragedia de Eurípides, Extensión*. Bahía Blanca: Universidad Nacional del Sur.

Gardner, Jane F. 1989. "Aristophanes and male anxiety, the defense of the oikos." *Greece and Rome* 36: 51–62.

Garlan, Yvon. 1988. *Slavery in Ancient Greece*. Ithaca: Cornell University Press

Garland, Robert. 2010. *The Eye of the Beholder: Deformity and Disability in the Graeco-Roman World*. London: Bristol Classical Press

Garnsey, Peter. 1996. *Ideas of Slavery from Aristotle to Augustine*. Cambridge: Cambridge University Press.

Garnsey, Peter, Keith Hopkins and Charles Richard Whittaker. 1983. *Trade in the Ancient Economy*. University of California Press.

Gauthier, Philippe. 1972. *Symbola. Les étrangers et la justice dans les cités grecques, Annales de l'Est publ. par l'University de Nancy; II*. Nancy.

Gauthier, Philippe. 1999. "'Symbola' athéniens et tribunaux étrangers à l'époque hellénistique." *Bulletin de Correspondance Hellénique* 123 (1): 157–74.

Gernet, L. 1921. "Sur L'epiclérat." *REG* 34: 337–79.

Gernet, Louis. 1955. *Droit et société dans la Grèce ancienne*. Vol. 13. Recueil Sirey.

Geschiere, Peter. 2009. *The Perils of Belonging: Autochthony, Citizenship, and Exclusion in Africa and Europe*. University of Chicago Press.

Gherchanoc, Florence. 2012. *L'oikos en fête: célébrations familiales et sociabilité en Grèce ancienne, Publications de la Sorbonne; 111*. Paris: Publications de la Sorbonne.

Giannadaki, Ifigeneia. 2014. "The time limit ('prothesmia') in the 'graphe paranomon'." *Dike: rivista di storia del diritto greco ed ellenistico* 17: 15–33.

Gilhuly, Kate. 2006. "The phallic lesbian: philosophy, comedy, and social inversion in Lucian's Dialogues of the courtesans." In McClure, C.A. and Faraone L.K. (eds), *Prostitutes and Courtesans in the Ancient World*. Madison, WI: University of Wisconsin Press.

Gilmore, D.D. 1990. *Manhood in the Making: Cultural Concepts of Masculinity*. Yale University Press.

Giordano, Manuela. 2014. "Contamination et vengeance: pour une diachronie du miasma." *Mètis*: 291–310.

Gish, Dustin A. 2012. "Defending dēmokratia: Athenian justice and the trial of the Arginusae generals in Xenophon's 'Hellenica'." In Hobden, Fiona and Tuplin, Christopher J. (eds), (pp. 161–212). Leiden; Boston, MA: Brill.

Glancy, Jennifer A. and Stephen D. Moore. 2011. "How Typical a Roman Prostitute Is Revelation's 'Great Whore'?" *Journal of Biblical Literature* 130 (3): 551–69.

Glazebrook, Allison Mary Jane. 2006. "The bad girls of Athens: the image and function of hetairai in judicial oratory." In Faraone, Christopher A. and McClure, Laura K. (eds), (pp. 125–38). Madison, WI: University of Wisconsin Press.

Gleba, Margarita. 2008. "You Are What You Wear: Scythian Costume as Identity." *Dressing the Past* 3: 13.

Godoy, Angelina Snodgrass. 2006. *Popular Injustice: Violence, Community, and Law in Latin America*. Stanford University Press.

Gofas, Dimitri C. 1979. "Les emmenoi dikai à Thasos." In Biscardi, Arnaldo (ed.), (pp. 175–86). Athen: Panteios-Hochschule; Köln: Böhlau.

Goff, Barbara. 2004. *Citizen Bacchae: Women's Ritual Practice in Ancient Greece*. Berkeley, CA: University of California Press.

Goldberg, Julie H., Jennifer S. Lerner and Philip E. Tetlock. 1999. "Rage and reason: The psychology of the intuitive prosecutor." *European Journal of Social Psychology* 29 (56): 781–95.

Golden, Mark. 1981. "Demography and the Exposure of Girls at Athens." *Phoenix* 35 (4): 316–31.

Goldhill, Simon. 1990. "The Great Dionysia and civic ideology." In Winkler, John J. and Zeitlin, Froma I. (eds), (pp. 97–129). Princeton: Princeton University Press.

Gomme, A.W. 1933. Oxford: Blackwell.

Görgemanns, Herwig. 2001. "Sokratischer Eros in Platons 'Symposion' und die Krisis der attischen Knabenliebe." In Kessler, Herbert L. (ed.), (pp. 135–66). Zug: Die Graue Edition.

Grafton, Antony. 1990. Princeton: Princeton University Press.

Greene, Judith A. 1999. "Zero tolerance: A case study of police policies and practices in New York City." *Crime and Delinquency* 45 (2): 171–87.

Griffith, Mark. 2011. "Extended families, marriage, and inter-city relations in (later) Athenian tragedy: dynasts II." In Carter, David M. (ed.), (pp. 175–208). Oxford; New York: Oxford University Press.

Griffith-Williams, Brenda. 2012. "Oikos, family feuds and funerals: argumentation and evidence in Athenian inheritance disputes." *Classical Quarterly* N.S. 62 (1): 145–62.

Griffith-Williams, Brenda. 2013. "Violence in court: law and rhetoric in Athenian and English assault cases." *Greece and Rome* Ser. 2 60 (1): 89–100.

Griffith-Williams, Brenda. 2016. "Rational and emotional persuasion in Athenian inheritance cases." In Johncock, E. and Sanders, M. (eds), *Emotion and Persuasion in Classical Antiquity* (pp. 41–55). Stuttgart: Steiner.

Grzybek, Erhard. 1989. "Die griechische Konkubine und ihre 'Mitgift' (P. Eleph. 3 und 4)." *Zeitschrift für Papyrologie und Epigraphik* 76: 206–12.

Günther, Linda-Marie. 1993. "Witwen in der griechischen Antike: zwischen Oikos und Polis." *Historia: Zeitschrift für Alte Geschichte = revue d'histoire ancienne* 42 (3): 308–25.

Gutzwiller, Kathryn J. 2012. "All in the family: forgiveness and reconciliation in New Comedy." In Griswold, Charles L. and Konstan, David (eds), (pp. 48–75). Cambridge; New York: Cambridge University Press.

Hagan, John and Celesta Albonetti. 1982. "Race, class, and the perception of criminal injustice in America." *American Journal of Sociology* 88 (2): 329–55.

Hägg, Robin (ed.). 1996. *The role of religion in the early Greek polis: proceedings of the third international seminar on ancient Greek cult, organized by the Swedish Institute at Athens, 16–18 October 1992*. Edited by Robin Hägg, *Skrifter utgivna av Svenska Institutet i Athen. 8°; 14*. Sävedalen: Åström.

Hamel, Debra Louise. 1998. *Athenian generals: military authority in the classical period, Mnemosyne. Supplementum 182*. Leiden: Brill.

Hamilton, Charles Daniel. 1993. "Cleisthenes and the demos." In Cherf, William J. (ed.), *Alpha to Omega: Studies in Honor of George John Szemler on his Sixty-Fifth Birthday* (pp. 69–930). Chicago: Ares.

Hamilton, Richard. 1984. "Sources for the Athenian Amphidromia." *Greek, Roman and Byzantine Studies* 25 (3): 243–51.

Hamilton, Richard. 1992. *Choes and Anthesteria: Athenian Iconography and Ritual*. Ann Arbor, MI: University of Michigan Press.

Hammond, N.G.L. 1985. "Arbitration in Ancient Greece." *Arbitration International* 1 (2): 188–90.

Hanafi, Alia. 2001. "Two contracts of marriage of papyrus collections in Cairo and Copenhagen." In Andorlini, Isabella (ed.), (pp. 571–84). Firenze: Istituto Papirologico G. Vitelli.

Handy, Markus. 2005. "Bemerkungen zur spartanischen 'krypteía'." In Strobel, Karl (ed.), *Die Geschichte der Antike actuell: Methoden, Ergebnisse und Rezeption* (pp. 99–120). Klagenfurt.

Hansen, Mogens Herman. 1974. *The Sovereignty of the People's Court in Athens in the Fourth Century BC and the Public Action against Unconstitutional Proposals*. Vol. 4: University Press of Southern Denmark.

Hansen, Mogens Herman. 1975. *Eisangelia. The Sovereignty of the People's Court in Athens in the Fourth Century B.C. and the Impeachment of Generals and Politicians*. Vol 6. Odense: Odense University Press

Hansen, Mogens Herman. 1976. "The Theoric Fund and the 'graphe paranomon'" against Apollodorus." *Greek, Roman and Byzantine Studies* 17 (3): 235–46.

Hansen, Mogens Herman. 1976. *Apagoge, Endeixis and Ephegesis against Kakourgoi, Atimoi and Pheugontes: A Study in the Athenian Administration of Justice in the Fourth Century BC*. Vol. 8: University Press of Southern Denmark.

Hansen, Mogens Herman. 1979. "How often did the Athenian dicasteria meet." *Greek, Roman, and Byzantine Studies* 20 (3): 243–6.

Hansen, Mogens Herman. 1980. "Eisangelia in Athens. A reply." *The Journal of Hellenic Studies* C: 89–95.

Hansen, Mogens Herman. 1981. "The prosecution of homicide in Athens." *Greek, Roman and Byzantine Studies* 22: 11–30.

Hansen, Mogens Herman. 1983. ""Graphe" or" Dike Traumatos"?" *Greek, Roman and Byzantine Studies* 24 (4): 307–20.

Hansen, Mogens Herman. 1985. "Athenian 'Nomothesia'." *Greek, Roman and Byzantine Studies* 26 (4): 345–71.

Hansen, Mogens Herman. 1986. "Demography and democracy. The number of citizens in fourth century Athens." *Proceedings of the Classical Association* 83: 16–17.

Hansen, Mogens Herman. 2006. *Polis: An Introduction to the Ancient Greek City-State*. Oxford University Press.

Hanson, Jon and Kathleen Hanson. 2006. "The blame frame: Justifying (racial) injustice in America." *Harvard Civil Rights-Civil Liberties Law Review* 41: 413–80.

Harrell, H.C. 1936. *Public Arbitration in Athenian Law*. Columbia: University of Missouri.

Harris, Edward M. 2006. *Democracy and the Rule of Law in Classical Athens: Essays on Law, Society, and Politics*. Cambridge: Cambridge University Press.

Harris, Edward M. 2008. "Demosthenes, Speeches 20–2 Translated by Edward M. Harris." In *The Oratory of Classical Greece*, edited by M. Gagarin. Austin: University of Texas Press.

Harris, Edward M. 2013. *The Rule of Law in Action in Democratic Athens*. Oxford University Press.

Harris, Edward M. 2015. "The Family, the Community and Murder: the role of pollution in Athenian homicide law." In Ando, Clifford and Rüpke, J. (eds), *Public and private in ancient Mediterranean law and religion* (pp. 11–35). Berlin: De Gruyter.

Harris, Edward M. 2017. "How to 'Act' in an Athenian Court: Emotions and Forensic Performance." In Papaioannou, S., Serafim, A. and da Vela, B. (eds), *The Theatre of Justice. Aspects of Performance in Greco-Roman Oratory and Rhetoric* (pp. 223–42). Leiden: Brill.

Harris, Edward Monroe. 1990. "Did the Athenians regard seduction as a worse crime than rape?" *Classical Quarterly* XL: 370–7.

Harris, Edward Monroe. 1992. "Women and lending in Athenian society: a horos re-examined." *Phoenix* 46: 309–21.

Harris, Edward Monroe. 2004. "Did rape exist in classical Athens?: Further reflections on the laws about sexual violence." *Dike: Rivista di Storia del Diritto Greco ed Ellenistico* 7: 41–83.

Harris, Edward Monroe. 2010. "Is Oedipus guilty?: Sophocles and Athenian homicide law." In Harris, Edward Monroe, Leão, Delfim Ferreira and Rhodes, Peter John (eds), (pp. 122–46). London: Duckworth.

Harris, Edward Monroe. 2015. "Toward a typology of Greek regulations about religious matters: a legal approach." *Kernos: Revue Internationale et Pluridisciplinaire de Religion Grecque Antique* 28: 53–83.

Harris, Edward Monroe and Lene Rubinstein. 2004. *The Law and the Courts in Ancient Greece*. Bristol Classical Press.

Harter-Uibopuu, Kaja. 2002. "Ancient Greek Approaches Toward Alternative Dispute Resolution." *Willamette Journal of International Law and Dispute Resolution* 10: 47–69.

Hartmann, Elke. 2000. "Heirat und Bürgerstatus in Athen." In Späth, Thomas and Wagner-Hasel, Beate (eds), (pp. 16–31). Stuttgart: Metzler.

Harvey, F.D. 1984. "The wicked wife of Ischomachos." *Échos du monde classique = Classical views* 28: 68–70.

Hasegawa, Takeo. 1994. "The political organizations of the Achaian confederacy." *Journal of Classical Studies* 42: 79–89.

Hashiba, Yuzuru. 1997. "'Dokimasia' reconsidered: what was its purpose." *Kodai: Journal of Ancient History* 8/9: 1–10.

Healey, R.F. 1962. "Eleusinian sacrifices in the Athenian law code." *Harvard Studies in Classical Philology* LXVI: 256–9.

Heath, Malcolm. 2008. "Aristotle on natural slavery." *Phronesis: A Journal for Ancient Philosophy* 53 (3): 243–70.

Hedrick, Charles W. 1984. *The Attic Phratry*. University of Pennsylvania Philadelphia.

Hedrick, Charles W. 1991. "Phratry shrines of Attica and Athens." *Hesperia: the journal of the American School of Classical Studies at Athens* LX: 241–68.

Heftner, Herbert. 2012. "Rechts- und Verfassungsinstrumente als Mittel der Konfliktbewältigung in der athenischen Demokratie: Stasisgesetze, Ostrakismos und Graphe paranomon." *Dike: Rivista di Storia del Diritto Greco ed Ellenistico* 15: 1–32.

Henry, Madeleine Mary. 1995. *Prisoner of History: Aspasia of Miletus and her Biographical Tradition*. Oxford: Oxford University Press.

Henry, Madeleine Mary. 2011. "The traffic in women: from Homer to Hipponax, from war to commerce." In Glazebrook, Allison Mary Jane and Henry, Madeleine Mary (eds), (pp. 14–33). Madison, WI; London: University of Wisconsin Press.

Herman, G. 2006. *Morality and Behaviour in Democratic Athens: A Social History*. Cambridge University Press.

Hernández Lara, Carlos. 1990. "Rhetorical aspects of Chariton of Aphrodisias." *Giornale Italiano di Filologia* 42: 267–74.

Hernández Lara, Carlos. 1994. *Estudios sobre et aticismo de Caritón de Afrodisias, Classical and Byzantine monographs; 29*. Amsterdam: Hakkert.

Herz, Peter. 2009. "Oikonomia und Politik bei Aristoteles: der oikos als Grundlage des staatlichen Lebens." *Jahrbuch für Wirtschaftsgeschichte* (1): 177–94.

Hodkinson, Stephen. 1986. "Land tenure and inheritance in classical Sparta." *Classical Quarterly* 36: 378–406.

Hodkinson, Stephen. 1989. "Inheritance, marriage and demography: perspectives upon the success and decline of classical Sparta." In Powell, Anton and Cartledge, Paul (eds), (pp. 79–121). London: Routledge.

Hodkinson, Stephen. 2008. "Spartiates, helots and the direction of the agrarian economy: toward an understanding of helotage in comparative perspective." In Katsari, Constantina and Dal Lago, Enrico (eds), *Slave Systems: Ancient and Modern* (pp. 285–320). Cambridge: Cambridge University Press.

Hodkinson, Stephen and Timothy D. Barnes (eds). 2009. *Sparta: Comparative Approaches*. Swansea: Classical Press of Wales.

Hodkinson, Stephen and Powell, Anton (eds). 1999. London: Duckworth.

Hoernes, Matthias. 2012. "Bilder und Konstruktionen einer Hetäre: 'Und Phryne soll nicht durch die Gerichtsrede des Hypereides, sondern durch den Anblick ihres Körpers gerettet worden sein'." In Müller, Florian Martin, Sossau, Veronika and El-Nagashi, Faika A. (eds), (pp. 55–70). Innsbruck: Innsbruck University Press.

Hoff, Ralf von den. 2009. "Die Bildnisstatue des Demosthenes als öffentliche Ehrung eines Bürgers in Athen." In Mann, Christian, Haake, Matthias and Hoff, Ralf von den (eds), (pp. 193–220). Wiesbaden: Reichert.

Hopwood, Keith, (Ed.). 1999. *Organised Crime in Antiquity*. Swansea: Classical Press of Wales.

Hubbard, Thomas K. 2003. *Homosexuality in Greece and Rome: A Sourcebook of Basic Documents*. University of California Press.

Humphreys, S.C. 1989. "Family quarrels." *JHS* 109: 182–5.

Humphreys, Sally C. 1977. "Public and private interests in classical Athens." *The Classical Journal* 73: 97–104.

Humphreys, Sally C. 2002. "Solon on adoption and wills." *Zeitschrift der Savigny-Stiftung für Rechtsgeschichte. Romanistische Abteilung* 119: 340–7.

Hunter, Virginia. 1993. "Agnatic Kinship in Athenian Law and Athenian Family Practice: Its Implications for Women." In Halpern, Baruch and Hobson, Deborah W. (eds), (pp. 100–21). Sheffield: Sheffield Academic Press.

Hunter, Virginia J. 1994. *Policing Athens: Social Control in the Attic Lawsuits, 420–320 BC*. Princeton: Princeton University Press.

Iddeng, Jon W. and J. Rasmus Brandt (eds). 2012. *Greek and Roman Festivals: Content, Meaning and Practice*. Oxford and New York: Oxford University Press

Ingalls, Wayne B. 2002. "Demography and dowries: perspectives on female infanticide in classical Greece." *Phoenix: Journal of the Classical Association of Canada = revue de la Société canadienne des études classiques* 56 (3–4): 246–54.

Irigoyen Troconis, Martha Patricia. 2004. "'Oikos'." In Leão, Delfim Ferreira, Rossetti, Livio and Fialho, Maria do Céu Zambujo (eds), (pp. 141–51). Madrid: Ed. Clásicas.

Isager, Signe. 1981. "The marriage pattern in classical Athens. Men and women in Isaios." *Classica et Mediaevalia: Revue Danoise de Philologie et D'histoire* XXXIII: 81–96.

Isager, Signe and Mogens Herman Hansen. 1975. *Aspects of Athenian Society in the Fourth Century BC: A Historical Introduction to and Commentary on the Paragraphe Speeches and the Speech Against Dionysodorus in the Corpus Demosthenicum (XXXII-XXXVIII and LVI)*. Vol. 5: Odense University Press.

Ivantchik, Askold I. 2006. "'Scythian' Archers on Archaic Attic Vases: Problems of Interpretation." *Ancient Civilizations from Scythia to Siberia* 12 (3): 197–271.

James, Sharon L. 1998. "From boys to men: rape and developing masculinity in Terence's Hecyra and Eunuchus." *Helios* 25 (1): 31–47.

Jameson, Michael Hamilton. 1997. "Women and democracy in fourth-century Athens." In Brulé, Pierre and Oulhen, Jacques (eds), (pp. 95–107). Rennes: Pr. universitaires de Rennes.

Jameson, Michael Hamilton. 2014. *Cults and Rites in Ancient Greece: Essays on Religion and Society*. Cambridge and New York: Cambridge University Press

Johnstone, Steven. 1998. "Cracking the code of silence: Athenian legal oratory and the histories of slaves and women." In Joshel, Sandra R. and Murnaghan, Sheila (eds), (pp. 221–35). London: Routledge.

Jones, Meriel. 2007. "'Andreia' and gender in the Greek novels." In Morgan, John R. and Jones, Meriel (eds), (pp. 111–35). Groningen: Barkhuis.

Jones, Nicholas F. 1991. "Enrollment Clauses in Greek Citizenship Decrees." *Zeitschrift für Papyrologie und Epigraphik*: 79–102.

Jones, Nicholas F. 1999. *The associations of Classical Athens: The Response to Democracy*. Oxford University Press.

Jones, W.H.S. 1957. "Ancient Roman folk medicine." *Journal of the History of Medicine and allied Sciences* XII: 459–72.

Jorquera Nieto, José Miguel. 1994. "Productividad y 'kalokagathia' en el 'oikos' de Iscómaco." In (pp. 213–18). Madrid: Ed. Clásicas.

Just, Roger. 1989. *Women in Athenian Law and Life*. London: Routledge.

Kapparis, K. 1998. "The Law on the Age of the Speakers in the Athenian Assembly." *Rheinisches Museum für Philologie* 141 (H. 3/4): 255–9.

Kapparis, Kostantinos. 1995. "The Athenian decree for the naturalisation of the Plataeans." *Greek, Roman and Byzantine Studies* 36 (4): 359.

Kapparis, Konstantinos. 1999. *Apollodoros, Against Neaira [D. 59]*. Berlin: DeGruyter.

Kapparis, K.A. 1998. "Assessors of magistrates (paredroi) in classical Athens." *Historia: Zeitschrift fur Alte Geschichte*: 383–93.

Kapparis, K.A. 2017. "Rhetoric and performance in the speeches of Apollodoros." In Andreas Seraphim, Papaioannou, Sophia, de Vela, Beatrice (eds), *A Theatre of Justice: aspects of performance in Greco-Roman Oratory and Rhetoric* (pp. 283–303). Leiden: Brill.

Kapparis, Konstantinos A. 1995. "When were the Athenian adultery laws introduced?" *Revue internationale des droits de l'Antiquité* 3e sér. (42): 97–122.

Kapparis, Konstantinos A. 2015. "Mirko Canevaro: The Documents in the Attic Orators. Laws and Decrees in the Public Speeches of the Demosthenic Corpus. With a chapter by EM Harris." *Gnomon* 87 (1): 40–3.

Karabelias, E. 1979. "Contribution a l'étude de L'epidikasia attique." *Symposion 1974*: 201–23.

Karakantza, E.D. 2004. "Literary rapes revisited: a study in literary conventions and political ideology." *Métis: revue d'anthropologie du monde grec ancien: philologie, histoire, archéologie* N.S. (22): 29–45.

Karbowski, Joseph Anthony. 2013. "Aristotle's scientific inquiry into natural slavery." *Journal of the History of Philosophy* 51 (3): 331–53.

Karnezis, I.E. 1979. "The non-aphairesis of the epikleros and the testamentary engyetè woman in classical Athens." *Athina: Syngramma Periodikon tis en Athinais Epistimonikis Etaireias* LXXVII: 145–71.

Katsari, Constantina and Enrico Dal Lago (eds). 2008. *Slave Systems: Ancient and Modern*. Cambridge and New York: Cambridge University Press.

Katz, Marylin A. 1992. "Patriarchy, ideology and the epikleros." *Studi Italiani di Filologia Classica* 10: 692–708.

Katzoff, Ranon. 1996. "Greek and Jewish marriage formulas." In (pp. 223–34). Ramat-Gan: Bar-Ilan University Press.

Kavoulaki, Athina. 1997. "Staging the wedding: the nuptial 'pompe' in Greek tragedy." In Papademetriou, Joannes-Theofanes A. (ed.), (pp. 351–71). Αθήνα: Ελληνική Ανθρωπιστική Εταιρεία.

Kennedy, Rebecca Futo. 2009. *Athena's Justice: Athena, Athens and the Concept of Justice in Greek Tragedy*. Vol. 16.: Peter Lang.

Kennedy, Rebecca Futo. 2014. *Immigrant Women in Athens: Gender, Ethnicity, and Citizenship in the Classical City*. London: Routledge.

Kennell, Nigel Martin. 2006. *Ephebeia: A Register of Greek Cities with Citizen Training Systems in the Hellenistic and Roman periods, Nikephoros. Beihefte; 12*. Hildesheim: Weidmann.

Keuls, Eva C. 1983. "The hetaera and the housewife. The splitting of the female psyche in Greek art." *Mededelingen van het Nederlands Instituut te Rome = Papers of the Netherlands Institute in Rome. Antiquity* 44–5: 23–40.

Keuls, Eva C. 1985. *The Reign of the Phallus. Sexual Politics in Ancient Athens*. New York: Harper and Row.

Kienast, Dietmar. 2005. "Die Funktion der attischen Demen von Solon bis Kleisthenes." *Chiron: Mitteilungen der Kommission für Alte Geschichte und Epigraphik des Deutschen Archäologischen Instituts* 35: 69–100.

Kilmer, Martin F. 1990. "Sexual violence: archaic Athens and the recent past." In Craik, Elizabeth M. (ed.), (pp. 261–77). Oxford: Clarendon Press.

Kilmer, Martin F. 1993. *Greek Erotica on Attic Red-Figure Vases*. London: Duckworth.

King, H.T. and Marc A. LeForestier. 1994. "ARBITRATION IN ANCIENT-GREECE." *Dispute Resolution Journal* 49 (3): 38–46.

Kirchner, John E. 1885. "Zur Glaubwürdigkeit der in die [Demosthenische] Rede wider Neaira eingelegten Zeugenaussagen." *Rheinisches Museum für Philologie*: 377–86.

Koch-Harnack, Gundel. 1983. *Knabenliebe und Tiergeschenke; ihre Bedeutung im päderastischen Erziehungssystem Athens, Gebr.-Mann-Studio-R*. Berlin: Mann.

Konaris, Michael. 2016. *The Greek Gods in Modern Scholarship: Interpretation and Belief in Nineteenth and Early Twentieth Century Germany and Britain, Oxford Classical Monographs*. Oxford: Oxford University Press

Koršunkov, V.A. 1989. *L'Aréopage d'Athènes: une assemblée aristocratique dans une cité démocratique*. Leningrad: Leningrad University

Kowalski, G. 1947. "De Phrynes pectore nudato." *Eos: commentarii Societatis Philologae Polonorum* 42: 50–62.

Kratz, Reinhard Gregor and Anselm C. Hagedorn (eds). 2013. *Law and Religion in the Eastern Mediterranean: From Antiquity to Early Islam*. Oxford: Oxford University Press

Kremmydas, Christos. 2012. *Commentary on Demosthenes Against Leptines: With Introduction, Text, and Translation*. Oxford: Oxford University Press.

Kremmydas, Christos. 2013. "The Discourse of Deception and Characterization in Attic Oratory." *Greek, Roman, and Byzantine Studies* 53 (1): 51–89.

Kuenen-Janssens, L.J.Th. 1941. "Some notes upon the competence of the Athenian woman to conduct a transaction." *Mnemosyne* 19: 199–214.

Lacey, Walter Kirkpatrick. 1968. Ithaca, NY: Cornell University Press.

Lambert, Stephen D. 1998. *The Phratries of Attica*. University of Michigan Press.

Lambert, Stephen D. 2005. "Athenian state laws and decrees 352/1–322/1. 2,: Religious regulations." *Zeitschrift für Papyrologie und Epigraphik* 154: 125–59.

Lambert, Stephen D. 2010. "A polis and its priests: Athenian priesthoods before and after Pericles' citizenship law." *Historia* 59 (2): 143–75.

Lambert, Stephen D. 2012. *Inscribed Athenian Laws and Decrees 352/1–322/1 BC: Epigraphical Essays*. Leiden: Brill.

Lang, Mabel L. 2004. Athens: American School of Classical Studies at Athens.

Lanni, Adriaan. 2005. "Relevance in Athenian Courts." In Cohen, M. and Gagarin, D. (eds), *Cambridge Companion to Ancient Greek Law* (pp. 112–28). Cambridge: Cambridge University Press.

Lanni, Adriaan. 2006. *Law and Justice in the Courts of Classical Athens*. Cambridge University Press.

Lanni, Adriaan. 2010. "The Expressive Effect of the Athenian Prostitution Laws." *Classical Antiquity* 29 (1): 45–67.

Lanni, Adriaan. 2012. "Publicity and the Courts of Classical Athens." *Yale Journal of Law and the Humanities* 24: 119–35.

Lanni, Adriaan. 2016. *Law and Order in Ancient Athens*. Cambridge University Press.

Lape, Susan. 2001. "Democratic ideology and the poetics of rape in Menandrian comedy." *Classical Antiquity* 20 (1): 79–119.

Lape, Susan. 2002. "Solon and the Institution of the 'Democratic' Family Form." *The Classical Journal* 98 (2): 117–39.

Lape, Susan. 2010. *Race and Citizen Identity in the Classical Athenian Democracy*. Cambridge University Press.

Laplace, Marie Marcelle Jeanine. 1997. "Le roman de Chariton et la tradition de l'éloquence et de la rhétorique: constitution d'un discours panégyrique." *Rheinisches Museum für Philologie* 140 (1): 38–71.

Larsen, J.A.O. 1955. "The Boeotian confederacy and fifth-century oligarchic theory." *Transactions of the American Philological Association* LXXXVI: 40–50.

Larsen, J.A.O. 1971. "The rights of cities within the Achaean confederacy." *Classical Philology: A Journal Devoted to Research in Classical Antiquity* LXVI: 81–6.

Lattimore, Steven. 1987. "Two men in a boat: Antiphon, On the murder of Herodes 42." *The Classical Quarterly* 37 (2): 502–4.

Leão, Delfim. 2005. "Sólon e a legislação em matéria de direito familiar." *Dike: Rivista di Storia del Diritto Greco ed Ellenistico* 8: 5–31.

Leão, Delfim and Peter Rhodes. 2015. *The Laws of Solon. A New Edition with Introduction, Translation and Commentary*. IB Tauris.

Leão, D.F. 2006. "Dikai emporikai. Processos relativos a comerciantes maritimos na Grecia antiga." In de Oliveira, Francisco, Thiercy, Pascal and Vilaça, Raquel (eds), *Mar Greco-Latino* (pp. 127–38). Coimbra: Imprensa da Universidade de Coimbra/Coimbra University Press.

Leão, Delfim F. 2012. "The Myth of Autochthony, Athenian Citizenship and the Right of Enktesis: A Legal Approach to Euripides' Ion." In *Symposion 2011*, pp. 135–52. Verlag der Österreichischen Akademie der Wissenschaften.

Leão, Delfim Ferreira, Edward Monroe Harris and Peter John Rhodes. 2010. *Law and Drama in Ancient Greece*. London: Duckworth.

Leão, Delfim Ferreira. 2004. Matéria religiosa: processos de impiedade ("asebeia"). In Leão, Delfim Ferreira, Rossetti, Livio and Fialho, Maria do Céu Zambujo (eds), (pp. 201–26). Madrid: Ed. Clásicas.

Ledl, Artur. 1907. *Studien zum attischen Epiklerenrechte*. Vol. 1., Graz.

Leduc, Claudine. 1998. "L'adoption dans la cité des Athéniens, VIe siècle – IVe siècle av. J.-C." *Pallas: revue d'études antiques* 48: 175–202.

Lee, Mireille Michelle. 2005. "Constru(ct)ing gender in the feminine Greek 'peplos'." In Cleland, Liza, Harlow, Mary and Llewellyn-Jones, Lloyd (eds), (pp. 55–64). Oxford: Oxbow Books.

Lee, Mireille Michelle. 2015. *Body, Dress, and Identity in Ancient Greece*. Cambridge and New York: Cambridge University Press

Lenfant, Dominique. 2011. Paris: Colin.

Lengauer, Wlodzimierz. 2006. "Eros among citizens." *Palamedes: A Journal of Ancient History* 1: 67–83.

Lepri Sorge, Luisa. 1987. "Ancora in terma di ephesis. La dokimasia degli arconti, VI." In Pastori, F. et al. (eds), *Studi in onore di Arnaldo Biscardi, VI* (pp. 427–34). Milan: Istituto editoriale cisalpino, La Goliardica.

Levick, Barbara. 2012. "Women and law." In James, Sharon L. and Dillon, Sheila (eds), Chichester; Malden, MA: Wiley-Blackwell.

Lewis, David M. 1959. "Law on the lesser Panathenaia." *Hesperia: The Journal of the American School of Classical Studies at Athens* XXVIII: 239–47.

Lewis, John. 2004. "Slavery and lawlessness in Solonian Athens." *Dike* 7: 19–40.

Link, Stefan. 2006. "Zur Entstehungsgeschichte der spartanischen Krypteia." *Klio* 88 (1): 34–43.

Long, Anthony A. 2012. "Slavery as a philosophical metaphor in Plato and Xenophon." In Patterson, Richard, Karasmanis, Vassilis and Hermann, Arnold (eds), (pp. 351–65). Las Vegas (Nev.): Parmenides Publications.

Loomis, William T. 1972. "The Nature of Premeditation in Athenian Homicide Law." *The Journal of Hellenic Studies* 92: 86–95.

Loomis, William T. 1998. *Wages, Welfare Costs, and Inflation in classical Athens*. University of Michigan Press.

Lowe, Nicholas John. 1998. "Thesmophoria and Haloa: myth, physics and mysteries." In Blundell, Sue and Williamson, Margaret (eds), (pp. 149–73). London: Routledge.

Lupu, Eran (ed.). 2005. *Greek Sacred Law: A Collection of New Documents (NGSL), Religions in the Graeco-Roman world; 152*. Leiden: Brill.

Luraghi, Nino. 2003. "The imaginary conquest of the helots." In Luraghi, Nino and Alcock, Susan E. (eds), *Helots and their Masters in Laconia and Messenia: Histories, Ideologies, Structures* (pp. 109–41). Cambridge, MA: Harvard University Press.

Luraghi, Nino. 2014. "Ephorus in context: the return of the Heraclidae and fourth-century Peloponnesian politics." In Parmeggiani, Giovanni (ed.), (pp. 133–51). Cambridge, MA: Harvard University Press.

Luraghi, Nino and Susan E. Alcock (eds). 2003. *Helots and their Masters in Laconia and Messenia: Histories, Ideologies, Structures, Hellenic Studies; 4*. Cambridge, MA: Harvard University Press.

Luraghi, Nino and Timothy Gordon Barnes. 2009. "The helots: comparative approaches, ancient and modern." In *Sparta: Comparative Approaches* (pp. 261–304). Swansea: Classical Press of Wales.

Luschnig, Celia A.E. 1990. "Euripides' Alcestis and the Athenian oikos." *Dioniso: rivista trimestrale di studi sul teatro antico* 60: 9–39.

MacDowell, Douglas M. 1963. *Athenian Homicide Law in the Age of the Orators, Publ. Fac. of Arts University of Manchester; XV*. Manchester: Manchester University Press

MacDowell, Douglas M. 1976. "Hybris in Athens." *Greece and Rome* 23: 14–31.

MacDowell, Douglas M. 1976. "Bastards as Athenian citizens." *The Classical Quarterly* 26: 88–91.

MacDowell, Douglas M. 1978. *The Law in Classical Athens*. London:

MacDowell, Douglas M. 1986. *Spartan Law, Scottish Class. Stud.; I*. Edinburgh: Scott. Acad. Press.

MacDowell, Douglas M. 1989. "The oikos in Athenian law." *The Classical Quarterly* 39 (01): 10–21.

MacDowell, Douglas M. 1990. *Demosthenes, Against Meidias (Oration 21)*. Oxford: Oxford University Press.

MacDowell, Douglas M. 1990. "The Athenian procedure of phasis." *Symposion*: 187–98 = Arnaoutoglou, I. Kapparis, K. and D. Spatharas (eds), *Studies on Greek Law, Oratory and Comedy*, 159–70, London: Routledge.

MacDowell, Douglas M. 2000. "Athenian laws about homosexuality." *Revue Internationale des Droits de L'antiquité* 42: 13–27.

MacDowell, Douglas M. 2000. "The length of trials for public offenses in Athens." In Camp, John M. (ed.), *Polis and Politics: Studies in Ancient Greek History* (pp. 536–8). Copenhagen (= Arnaoutoglou, I. Kapparis, K. and D. Spatharas (eds), *Studies on Greek law, oratory and comedy*, 144–8, London): Museum Tusculanum Press.

MacEwen, Sally. 1990. "Oikos, polis and the question of Clytemnestra." In MacEwen, Sally (ed.), (pp. 16–34). Lewiston, NY: Edwin Mellen Press.

MacEwen, Sally (ed.). 1990. Lewiston, NY: Edwin Mellen Press.

Macfarlane, Patrick and Ronald M. Polansky. 2004. "Physical disability in earlier Greek philosophy." *Σκέψις: περιοδικὴ ἔκδοση φιλοσοφίας καὶ διεπιστημονικῆς ἔρευνας = a journal for philosophy and inter-disciplinary research* 15 (2): 25–41.

Maffi, A. 2007. "L'Onomasticon di Polluce come fonte di diritto attico." In Bearzot, C., Landucci, F. and Zecchini, G. (eds), *L'Onomasticon di Giulio Polluce. Tra lessicografia e antiquaria* (pp. 29–42). Vita E Pensiero.

Maffi, Alberto. 1973. "Strateuesthai meta Athenaion. Contributo allo studio dell'isoteleia." *RIL* 107: 939–64.

Maffi, Alberto. 1982. "Τα ἱερα και τα ὅσια. Contributo allo studio della terminologia giuridicosacrale greca." In Mélèze-Modrzejewski, Joseph and Liebs, Detlef (eds), (pp. 33–53). Köln: Böhlau Verl.

Maffi, Alberto. 1985. "Matrimonio, concubinato e filiazione illegitima nell'Atene degli oratori." *Symposion 1985*: 177–214.

Maffi, Alberto. 1990. "E' esistita l'aferesi dell' epikleros?" In Nenci, Giuseppe and Thür, Gerhard (eds), (pp. 21–36). Köln: Böhlau.

Manuwald, Bernd. 2014. "Bürger als polistische Akteure: Überlegungen zur allgemeinen Politikkompetenz bei Platon und Aristoteles." *Hyperboreus: Studia Classica* 20 (1–2): 225–43.

Marasco, Gabriele. 1980. "La retra di Epitadeo e la situazione sociale di Sparta nel IV secolo." *L'antiquité Classique*: 131–45.

Margaret Mary, Sister. 1953. "Slavery in the writings of St. Augustine." *The Classical Journal* XLIX: 363–9.

Marr, J.L. 1971. "Andocides' part in the mysteries and hermae affairs 415 BC." *Classical Quarterly* XXI: 326–38.

Marr, J.L. 1990. "The Athenian archons and the Areopagus." *Liverpool Classical Monthly* XV: 44–5.

Marshall, Christopher W. 2013. "Sex slaves in New Comedy." In Akrigg, Ben and Tordoff, Rob (eds), (pp. 173–96). Cambridge; New York: Cambridge University Press.

Martin, Jochen. 1974. "Von Kleisthenes zu Ephialtes. Zur Entstehung der athenischen Demokratie." *Chiron: Mitteilungen der Kommission für Alte Geschichte und Epigraphik des Deutschen Archäologischen Instituts* IV: 5–42.

Martínez García, Francisco Javier (ed.). 2014. Leiden; Boston, MA: Brill.

Maurizio, Lisa. 2001. "Performance, hysteria, and democratic identities in the Anthesteria." *Helios* 28 (1): 29–41.

McGlew, James F. 1999. "Politics on the margins: the Athenian hetaireiai in 415 B.." *Historia* 48 (1): 1–22.

McGowan Tress, Daryl. 1997. "Aristotle's child: development through genesis, oikos, and polis." *Ancient Philosophy* 17 (1): 63–84.

McPherran, Mark L. 2002. "Justice and Pollution in the Euthyphro." *Apeiron* 35 (2): 105–30.

Mélèze-Modrzejewski, Joseph. 1981. "La structure juridique du mariage grec." In Bresciani, Edda (ed.), *Scritti in onore di Orsolina Montevecchi (reprint of the original publication in Symposion 1979, 37–72)* (pp. 231–68). Bologna: Clueb.

Meritt, Benjamin D. 1970. "The election of Athenian generals." *Klio: Beiträge zur Alten Geschichte* LII: 277–82.

Métraux, Guy P.R. 1999. "Ancient housing: oikos and domus in Greece and Rome." *Journal of the Society of Architectural Historians* 58 (3): 392–405.

Meyer, Elizabeth A. 2010. *Metics and the Athenian Phialai-inscriptions: A Study in Athenian Epigraphy and Law*. Vol. 208, *Historia Einzelschriften*. Stuttgart.

Migeotte, Léopold. 1992. "Citoyens, femmes et étrangers dans les souscriptions publiques des cités grecques." *Échos du monde classique = Classical Views* 36: 293–308.

Migeotte, Léopold. 2002. "La cité grecque, les citoyens et les finances publiques." *Les Études Classiques* 70 (1–2): 13–26.

Mikalson, Jon. 2016. *New Aspects of Religion in Ancient Athens: Honors, Authorities, Esthetics, and Society*. Brill.

Miles, J.C. 1950. "The Court in Phreatto." *RIDA* 1: 219–24.

Miller, Margaret Christina. 2010. "I am Eurymedon: tensions and ambiguities in Athenian war imagery." In Pritchard, David M. (ed.), (pp. 304–38). Cambridge; New York: Cambridge University Press.

Miller, S.G. and Miller, S.G., 1978. *The Prytaneion: Its Function and Architectural Form*. University of California Press.

Miller, T. 1997. *The Birth of the Hospital in the Byzantine Empire*. Baltimore.

Millett, Paul. 1983. "Maritime loans and the structure of credit in fourth-century Athens." *Trade in the Ancient Economy*: 36–52.

Millett, Paul. 1991. *Lending and Borrowing in Ancient Athens*. Cambridge University Press.

Millett, Paul. 2007. "Aristotle and slavery in Athens." *Greece and Rome* Ser. 2 54 (2): 178–209.

Mirhady, David Cyrus. 1996. "Torture and rhetoric in Athens." *The Journal of Hellenic Studies* 116: 119–31.

Mirhady, David Cyrus. 2000. "The Athenian rationale for torture." In Hunter, Virginia J. and Edmondson, Jonathan C. (eds), (pp. 53–74). Oxford; New York: Oxford University Press.

Mirón Pérez, María Dolores. 2004. "'Oikos' y 'oikonomia': el análisis de las unidades domésticas de producción y reproducción en el estudio de la economía antigua." *Gerión* 22 (1): 61–79.

Mitchell, David T. and Sharon L. Snyder. 1997. *The Body and Physical Difference: Discourses of Disability*: University of Michigan Press.

Miyazaki, Makoto. 1996. "On public arbitration in Athens." *Journal of Classical Studies* 44: 73–83.

Morales, Helen L. 2011. "Fantasising Phryne: the psychology and ethics of ekphrasis." *Cambridge Classical Journal: Proceedings of the Cambridge Philological Society* 57: 71–104.

Morales, Kelly. 2004. "'Et in Arcadia ego': understanding autochthony, geography and the other in Herodotus." *Ancient History* 34 (1): 22–37.

Morenilla Taléns, Carmen. 2009. "'Andrómaca' y 'Helena': sobre el amor en el 'oíkos'." In Benoit, Claude (ed.), (pp. 195–206). València: Universitat de València.

Moreno, Alfonso. 2007. *Feeding the Democracy: The Athenian Grain Supply in the Fifth and Fourth Centuries BC, Oxford classical monographs*. Oxford and New York: Oxford University Press

Morgan, Kathryn A. 2004. "The education of Athens: politics and rhetoric in Isocrates and Plato." In Pulakos and Depew (eds), *Isocrates and Civil Education* (pp. 125–54).

Morgan, Teresa J. 1999. "Literate education in classical Athens." *Classical Quarterly* 49: 46–61.

Morley, Neville. 2007. *Trade in CLASSICAL ANTIQuity*. Cambridge University Press.

Mosley, Derek J. 1962. "An Athenian law on ambassadors?" *Proceedings of the African Classical Association* V: 26–7.

Mossé, Claude. 1993. *Le citoyen dans la Grèce antique, Collection 128; 35*. Paris: Nathan.

Mylonas, G.E. 1961. *Eleusis and the Eleusinian mysteries*. Princeton: Princeton University Press

Nadareishvili, Ketevan. 2015. "Women in the law of democratic Athens." *Journal Phasis-Greek and Roman Studies* 5 (19).

Napolitano, Michele (ed.). 2014. *"Oikos": spazio architettonico, sociale, letterario*. Roma: Quasar.

Nehamas, Alexander. 2007. "Beauty of body, nobility of soul: the pursuit of love in Plato's 'Symposium'." In Scott, Dominic (ed.), (pp. 97–135). Oxford; New York: Oxford University Press.

Neils, Jenifer. 1996. *Worshipping Athena: Panathenaia and Parthenon, Wisconsin Studies in Classics*. Madison: University of Wisconsin Press

Nemeth, Gy. 2001. "Metics in Athens." *AAntHung* 41: 331–48.

Nichols, Andrew. 2013. *Ctesias: On India*. AandC Black.

Nichols, Andrew (ed.). 2011. London: Bristol Classical Press.

Nilsson, Martin P. 1986. *Cults, Myths, Oracles, and Politics in Ancient Greece: The Ionian Phylae. The Phratries, Stud. in Mediterranean Archeol. and Liter. Pocket-books; 44*. Sävedalen: Åström.

Nilsson, Martin P. 1949. Oxford: Clarendon Press.

Nimis, Stephen A. 2007. "Autochthony, misogyny, and harmony: Medea 824–45." *Arethusa* 40 (3): 397–420.

Nissinen, Martti and Risto Uro (eds). 2008. *Sacred Marriages: The Divine-Human Sexual Metaphor from Sumer to early Christianity*. Winona Lake, IN: Eisenbrauns.

Noreña, Carlos F. 2008. "Divorce in classical Athenian society: law, practice and power." *Past Imperfect* 7: (not paginated).

Nutton, Vivian. 1977. "Archiatri and the Medical Profession in Antiquity." *Papers of the British School at Rome* 45: 191–226.

Nutton, Vivian. 1986. "'The birth of the hospital in the Byzantine Empire'. By Timothy S. Miller. Essay review." *Medical History* 30 (2): 218.

O'Connell, Peter A. 2017. *The Rhetoric of Seeing in Attic Forensic Oratory*. University of Texas Press.

O'Connell, Peter Alfred. 2013. "Hyperides and 'epopteia': a new fragment of the 'Defense of Phryne'." *Greek, Roman and Byzantine Studies* 53 (1): 90–116.

O'Sullivan, Patrick. 2011. "Sophistic ethics, Old Atheism, and 'Critias' on religion." *The Classical World* 105 (2): 167–85.

Oakley, John Howard and Rebecca H Sinos. 1993. *The Wedding in Ancient Athens*. Madison: University of Wisconsin Press.

Ober, Josiah. 2001. "The debate over civic education in classical Athens." In Too, Yun Lee (ed.), (pp. 175–207). Leiden; Boston, MA: Brill.

Ober, Josiah. 2009. *Mass and Elite in Democratic Athens: Rhetoric, Ideology, and the Power of the People*. Princeton University Press.

Ogden, Daniel. 1996. *Greek Bastardy in the Classical and Hellenistic Periods*. Oxford University Press.

Ogden, Daniel. 1997. "Rape, adultery and the protection of bloodlines in classical Athens." In Deacy, Susan and Peirce, Karen F. (eds), (pp. 25–41). Swansea: Classical Pr. of Wales.

Oliver, James H. 1950. *The Athenian Expounders of the Sacred and Ancestral Law*. Baltimore: Hopkins Press

Omitowoju, Rosanna. 1997. "Regulating rape: soap operas and self-interest in the Athenian courts." In Deacy, Susan and Peirce, Karen F. (eds), (pp. 1–24). Swansea: Classical Pr. of Wales..

Omitowoju, Rosanna. 2002. *Rape and the Politics of Consent in Classical Athens, Cambridge Classical Studies*. Cambridge and New York: Cambridge University Press

Oranges, A. 2016. "L'accusa di corruzione nel contesto di euthyna: Verifica delle finanze e della fedeltà democratica dei magistrate." *Anthesteria* (5): 81–97.

Osborne, Michael J. 1981. *Naturalization in Athens, Verh. Koninkl. Acad. Wet. Lett. and Schone Kunste van België Kl. der Lett.; XLIII,98*. Brussels: Palais des Acad.

Osborne, Michael J. 1982. *Naturalization in Athens, II, Verh. Koninkl. Acad. Wet. Lett. and Schone Kunste van België Kl. der Lett.; XLIV, 101*. Brussels: Paleis der Academien.

Osborne, Michael J. 1983. *Naturalization in Athens, III: The testimonia for grants of citizenship, Verh. Koninkl. Acad. Wet. Lett. and Schone Kunste van België Kl. der Lett.; XLV, 109*. Brussels.

Osborne, Michael J. 1983. *Naturalization in Athens, IV: The law and practice of naturalization in Athens from the origins to the Roman period, Verh. Koninkl. Acad. Wet. Lett. and Schone Kunste van België Kl. der Lett.; XLV, 109*. Brussels.

Osborne, Robin. 1985. "Law in action in classical Athens." *The Journal of Hellenic Studies* 105: 40–58.

Osborne, Robin. 1997. "Law, the democratic citizen and the representation of women in classical Athens." *Past and Present: A Journal of Historical Studies* 155: 3–33.

Osborne, Robin. 2008. "Law and religion in classical Athens: the case of the dead." In Langenfeld, C. and Schneider, I. (eds), *Recht und Religion in Europa* (pp. 46–58). Göttingen: Universitätsverlag.

Osborne, Robin. 2011. *The History Written on the Classical Greek Body*. Cambridge and New York: Cambridge University Press

Osborne, Robin. 2011. "Local environment, memory, and the formation of the citizen in classical Attica." In Lambert, Stephen D. and Cairns, Douglas L. (eds), (pp. 25–43). Swansea: Classical Pr. of Wales.

Ostwald, Martin. 1987. *From Popular Sovereignty to the Sovereignty of Law: Law, Society, and Politics in Fifth-Century Athens*: University of California Press.

Owens, Ron. 2010. *Solon of Athens: Poet, Philosopher, Soldier, Statesman*. Eastbourne, Sussex: Sussex Academic Press.

Paoli, U.E. 1976. "La legittima aferesi dell'epikleros nel diritto attico, in 'Miscellanea Mercan', Città del Vaticano 1946, V." *Altri studi di diritto greco e romano*: 363–76.

Paoli, Ugo Enrico. 1932. "Il processo di Agorato." *RFIC* 10: 289–308.

Paoli, Ugo Enrico. 1946. "La legittima aferesi della epikleros nel diritto attico." In . Città del Vaticano: Bibl. Apostolica.

Papadimitriou, Ioannis-Theofanis A. (ed.). 1997. *ΠΡΑΚΤΙΚΑ: ΠΡΩΤΑ ΠΑΝΕΛΛΗΝΙΟ ΚΑΙ ΔΙΕΘΝΕΣ ΣΥΝΕΔΡΙΟ ΑΡΧΑΙΑΣ ΕΛΛΗΝΙΚΗΣ ΦΙΛΟΛΟΓΙΑΣ, 23–6 ΜΑΪΟΥ 1994*. Edited by Ioannis-Theofanis A. Papadimitriou, *Meletes kai erevnes / Elliniki Anthropistiki Etaireia; 38*. Athina: Elliniki anthropistiki etaireia.

Paradiso, Annalisa. 1995. "Violenza sessuale, 'hybris' e consenso nelle fonti greche." In Raffaelli, Renato (ed.), (pp. 93–109). Ancona: Commissione per le pari opportunità tra uomo e donna della Regione Marche.

Parca, Maryline G. and Tzanetou, Angeliki (eds). 2007. *Finding Persephone: Women's Rituals in the Ancient Mediterranean, Studies in Ancient Folklore and Popular Culture*. Bloomington, IN: Indiana University Press.

Parke, Catherine Neal. 1996. *Biography: Writing Lives*. Vol. 11. Psychology Press.

Parke, Herbert William. 1977. *Festivals of the Athenians*: Ithaca, NY: Cornell University Press.

Parker, R. 1983. Oxford: Clarendon Press.

Parker, Richard Guy, Regina Maria Barbosa and Peter Aggleton. 2000. *Framing the Sexual Subject: The Politics of Gender, Sexuality, and Power*. University of California Press.

Parker, Robert. 1997. *Athenian Religion: A History*. Oxford University Press.

Parker, Robert C.T. 1979. "Dionysos at the Haloa." *Hermes: Zeitschrift für klassische Philologie* CVII: 256–7.

Parker, Robert C.T. 1987. "Myths of early Athens." In Bremmer, Jan Nicolaas (ed.), *Interpretations of Greek Mythology* (pp. 187–214). London: Croom Helm.

Parker, Robert C.T. 2004. "What are sacred laws?" In Harris, Edward Monroe and Rubinstein, Lene (eds), *The Law and the Courts in Ancient Greece* (pp. 57–70). Bristol Classical Press.

Parker, Robert C.T. 2005. "Law and religion." In Gagarin, Michael and Cohen, David J. (eds), (pp. 61–81). Cambridge; New York: Cambridge University Press.

Pascual González, José. 2006. "Poleis and confederacy in Boiotia in the early fourth century BC." *The Ancient World: A Scholarly Journal for the Study of Antiquity* 37 (1): 22–45.

Patterson, Cynthia. 1985. "'Not Worth the Rearing': The Causes of Infant Exposure in Ancient Greece." *Transactions of the American Philological Association (1974–)* 115: 103–23.

Patterson, Cynthia. 1987. "Hai-attikai – the other Athenians." *Helios* 13 (2): 49–67.

Patterson, Cynthia. 2000. "The hospitality of Athenian justice: the metic in court." In Edmondson, V.J. and Hunter, J.C. (eds), *Law and Social Status in Classical Athens* (pp. 93–112). Oxford: Oxford University Press.

Patterson, C.B. 1981. *Pericles' Citizenship Law of 451–50 B.C.* Salem, NH: Arno Press.

Patterson, Cynthia B. 2007. "Other sorts: slaves, foreigners, and women in Periclean Athens." In Samons, Loren J. (ed.), (pp. 153–78). Cambridge; New York: Cambridge University Press.

Patterson, Cynthia B. 1990. "Those Athenian Bastards." *Classical Antiquity* 9 (1): 40–73.

Patterson, Cynthia B. 1991. "Marriage and the married woman in Athenian law." *Women's History and Ancient History*: 48–72.

Patterson, Cynthia B. 2006. "'Citizen cemeteries' in classical Athens?" *Classical Quarterly* N.S. 56 (1): 48–56.

Patterson, Cynthia B. 2009. *The Family in Greek History*. Harvard University Press.

Patterson, Cynthia B. 1981. New York: Arno Press.

Pečírka, Jan. 1966. *The Formula for the Grant of Enktesis in Attic Inscriptions*. University Karlova.

Pecorella Longo, Chiara. 1981. "γραφὴ τραύματος ο δίκη τραύματος." *Studi italiani di filologia classica* 53: 246–61.

Pecorella Longo, Chiara. 2002. "Aristofane e la legge sull' 'eisangelia'." *Prometheus: Rivista Quadrimestrale di Studi Classici* 28 (3): 222–8.

Pedersen, Lars and Mogens Herman Hansen. 1990. "The size of the Council of the Areopagos and its social composition in the fourth century B.C." *Classica et mediaevalia: revue danoise de philologie et d'histoire* XLI: 73–8.

Pelling, Christopher B.R. 2008. "Bringing autochthony up-to-date: Herodotus and Thucydides." *The Classical World* 102 (4): 471–83.

Penrose, Walter, D. 2015. "The Discourse of Disability in Ancient Greece." *Classical World* 108 (4): 499–523. doi: 10.1353/clw.2015.0068.

Perlman, Paula J. and Michael Gagarin. 2016. *The Laws of Ancient Crete: c. 650–400 BCE*. Oxford: Oxford University Press

Perlman, Shalom. 1976. "On bribing Athenian ambassadors." *Greek, Roman and Byzantine Studies* 17 (3): 223.

Pesando, Fabrizio. 1987. *Oikos e ktesis. La casa greca in età classica, Pubbl. dell'Ist. di storia della Fac. di lett. e filos. di Perugia*. Roma: Quasar.

Pettinato, Maria, Mauro Moggi and Giuseppe Cordiano (eds). 1997. *Schiavi e dipendenti nell'ambito dell''oikos' e della 'familia': atti del XXII Colloquio GIREA, Pontignano (Siena), 19–20 novembre 1995, Studi e testi di storia antica; 8*. Pisa: ETS.

Phillips, David D. 2006. "Why was Lycophron prosecuted by eisangelia?" *Greek, Roman, and Byzantine Studies* 46 (4): 375–94.

Phillips, David D. 2007. "Trauma ek pronoias in Athenian Law." *The Journal of Hellenic Studies* 127: 74–105.

Phillips, David D. 2013. *The Law of Ancient Athens*: University of Michigan Press.

Phillips, David D. 2014. "Hubris and the Unity of Greek Law." In Gagarin, M. and Lanni A. (eds), *Symposion 2013. Vortraege zur griechischen und hellenistischen Rechtsgeschichte (Cambridge MA, 26. – 29. August 2013)* (pp. 75–97). Vienna: Verlag der Oesterreichischen Akademie der Wissenschaften/Austrian Academy of Sciences Press.

Phillips, David Daniel. 2000. *Homicide, Wounding, and Battery in the Fourth-Century Attic Orators*. [S. l.]: [s. n.].

Phillips, David Daniel. 2008. *Avengers of Blood: Homicide in Athenian Law and Custom from Draco to Demosthenes, Historia. Einzelschriften; 202.* Stuttgart: Steiner.

Photiades, P.S. 1925. *Ἡ ἀποκήρυξις ἐν τῷ ἀρχαίῳ Ἑλληνικῷ δικαίῳ.* Athens.

Piccirilli, Luigi. 1983. "Eisangelia e condanna di Temistocle." *Civiltà classica e cristiana* 4: 333–63.

Piérat, M. 1971. "Les euthynoi atheniens." *AC* 40: 526–73.

Pierce, Karen F. 1997. "The portrayal of rape in New Comedy." In Deacy, Susan and Peirce, Karen F. (eds), (pp. 163–84). Swansea: Classical Pr. of Wales.

Pilitsis, G. 1981. *The Drama of Euripides. A study in the Institution of Marriage and a Reconstruction of Marriage Customs in Fifth Century B.C. Athens.* New Brunswick, NJ: Rutgers University.

Pinto, L.B. 1973. "The folk practice of gynecology and obstetrics in the Middle Ages." *Bulletin of the History of Medicine* LXVII: 513–22.

Pohl, Rudolf. 1905. *De Graecorum medicis publicis.* Berlin: Georgius Reimer.

Pomeroy, Sarah. 2011. *Goddesses, Whores, Wives, and Slaves: Women in Classical Antiquity.* Schocken.

Pomeroy, Sarah B. 1983. "Infanticide in Hellenistic Greece." In Cameron, Averil and Kuhrt, Amélie (eds), *Images of Women in Antiquity* (pp. 207–22). Wayne State University Press.

Pomeroy, Sarah B. 1994. *Xenophon, Oeconomicus: A Social and Historical Commentary.* Oxford: Oxford University Press.

Pomeroy, Sarah B. 1998. *Families in Classical and Hellenistic Greece: Representations and Realities.* Peterson's.

Porter, John R. 2003. "Chariton and Lysias 1: further considerations." *Hermes: Zeitschrift für klassische Philologie* 131 (4): 433–40.

Porter, John Roberts. 1997. "Adultery by the book: Lysias I (On the murder of Eratosthenes) and comic diegesis." *Échos du monde classique = Classical views* N.S. (16 (3)16 3): 421–53.

Poulakos, Takis and David J. Depew (eds). 2004. *Isocrates and Civic Education.* Austin, TX: University of Texas Press

Powell, Anton and Stephen Hodkinson (eds). 1997. *The Shadow of Sparta.* Swansea; New York: The Classical Press of Wales and Routledge.

Prandi, Luisa. 1996. "I tempi del processo di Alcibiade nel 415 a. C." In Sordi, Marta (ed.), (pp. 65–70). Milano: Vita e Pensiero.

Pretzler, Maria. 2009. "Arcadia: Ethnicity and Politics in the Fifth and Fourth Centuries BCE." In Funke, Peter and Luraghi, Nino (eds). Cambridge, MA: Harvard University Press.

Prichett, W. Kendrick. 1986. "The Παννυχίς of the Panathenaia, II." In (pp. 179–88). Βιβλιοθήκη τῆς ἐν Ἀθήναις ἀρχαιολογικῆς Ἑταιρείας. Athens.

Pritchard, David. 2003. "Athletics, education and participation in Classical Athens." In Phillips, D.J and Pritchard, D (eds), *Sport and Festival in the Ancient Greek World* (pp. 293–349). Swansea: Classical Press of Wales.

Proffitt, Laura. 2011. "Family, Slavery and Subversion in Menander's Epitrepontes." In Alston, Richard, Hall, Edith and Proffitt, Laura (eds), (pp. 152–74). London: Bristol Classical Press.

Prytz Johansen, J. 1975. "The Thesmophoria as a women's festival." *Temenos: Studies in Comparative Religion Presented by Scholars in Denmark, Finland, Norway and Sweden* 11: 78–87.

Purves, Alex. 1997. "Empowerment for the Athenian citizen: Philocleon as actor and spectator in Aristophanes' *Wasps*." In Zimmermann, Bernhard (ed.), (pp. 5–22). Stuttgart: M und P.

Raaflaub, K. 1998. "The transformation of Athens in the fifth century." In Boedeker, D. and Raaflaub, K.A. (eds), *Democracy, Empire, and the Arts in fifth-century Athens*. Cambridge, MA; London.

Reed, Charles M. 2003. *Maritime Traders in the Ancient Greek World*. Cambridge University Press.

Rehm, Rush. 1994. *Marriage to Death: The Conflation of Wedding and Funeral Rituals in Greek Tragedy*. Princeton: Princeton University Press.

Reuben, Richard C. 2004. "Democracy and Dispute Resolution: The Problem of Arbitration." *Law and Contemporary Problems* 67 (1/2): 279–320.

Rhodes, P.J. 1972. *The Athenian Boule*. Oxford: Clarendon Press.

Rhodes, P.J. 1978. "Bastards as Athenian citizens." *The Classical Quarterly* 28 (1): 89–92.

Rhodes, P.J. 1979. "Eisangelia in Athens." *JHS* 99: 103–14.

Rhodes, P.J. 1981. *A Commentary on the Aristotelian Athenaion Politeia*. Oxford: Clarendon Press.

Rhodes, P.J. 2013. "The Organization of Athenian Public Finance." *Greece and Rome* 60 (2): 203–31. doi: 10.1017/S0017383513000053.

Rhodes, Peter J. 2009. "State and religion in Athenian inscriptions." *Greece and Rome* 56 (1): 1–13.

Rhodes, Peter John. 1981. *A Commentary on the Aristotelian Athenaion Politeia*. Oxford University Press.

Rhodes, Peter John. 1985. "Nomothesia in fourth-century Athens."*Classical Quarterly* 35 (1): 55–60.

Rhodes, Peter John. 2003. "Sessions of 'nomothetai' in fourth-century Athens." *Classical Quarterly* N.S. (53 (1)53 1): 124–9.

Rhodes, Peter John. 2011. "The Dionysia and democracy again." *Classical Quarterly* 61 (1): 71–4.

Richarz, Irmintraut. 1991. *Oikos, haus und haushalt: ursprung und geschichte der haushaltsökonomik*. Göttingen: Vandenhoeck and Ruprecht.

Riddle, John M. 1987. "Folk tradition and folk medicine. Recognitions of drugs in classical antiquity." In Scarborough, John (ed.), (pp. 33–61). Madison, WI: Amer. Inst. of the history of pharmacy.

Riess, Werner. 2008. "Private violence and state control: the prosecution of homicide and its symbolic meanings in fourth-century BC Athens." In Van Wees, Hans, Ducrey, Pierre and Brélaz, Cédric (eds), (pp. 49–94). Genève-Vandœuvres: Fondation Hardt.

Riess, Werner. 2012. *Performing interpersonal violence: court, curse, and comedy in fourth-century BCE Athens, MythosEikonPoiesis; 4*. Berlin; New York: de Gruyter.

Robertson, Bruce G. 2000. "The scrutiny of new citizens at Athens." In Hunter, Virginia J. and Edmondson, Jonathan C. (eds), (pp. 149–74). Oxford; New York: Oxford University Press.

Robertson, Bruce G. 2008. "The slave-names of IG I³ 1032 and the ideology of slavery at Athens." In Cooper, Craig Richard (ed.), (pp. 79–116). Toronto: University of Toronto Press.

Robertson, D.S. 1927. "The duration of a trierarchy." *Classical Review* XLI: 114–16.

Robertson, Noel. 1998. "Phratries and τρίττυες: the early organization of Attica." In Hillard, Tom W. (ed.), (pp. 111–20). North Ryde (N.S.W.): Ancient history documentary research centre, Macquarie University.

Robertson, Noel. 2013. "The concept of purity in Greek sacred laws." In Frevel, Ch. and Nihan, Ch. (eds), *Purity and the Forming of Religious Traditions in the Ancient Mediterranean and Ancient Judaism* (pp. 195–244). Leiden; Boston.

Rodríguez Adrados, Francisco and Michail V. Sakellariou (eds). 1996. *Colloque international 'Démocratie athénienne et culture' organisé par l'Académie d'Athènes en coopération avec l'UNESCO (23, 24 et 25 novembre 1992)*. Athina: Akadimia Athinon.

Roebuck, Derek. 2000. "Best to Reconcile: Mediation and Arbitration in the Ancient Greek World." *Arbitration: the Journal of the Chartered Institute of Arbitrators* 66 (4): 275–87.

Roebuck, Derek. 2001. *Ancient Greek Arbitration*. Oxford: Holo Books.

Roisman, Joseph and Ian Worthington. 2015. *Lives of the Attic Orators: Texts from Pseudo-Plutarch, Photius, and the Suda*. Clarendon Ancient History Series.

Roselli, David Kawalko. 2009. "Theorika in fifth-century Athens." *Greek, Roman, and Byzantine Studies* 49 (1): 5–30.

Rosivach, Vincent J. 1984. "Aphairesis and apoleipsis: a study of the sources." *Revue internationale des droits de l'Antiquité* 31: 193–230.

Rosivach, Vincent J. 1987. "Autochthony and the Athenians." *Classical Quarterly* 37: 294–306.

Rosivach, Vincent J. 1995. "Solon's Brothels." *Liverpool Classical Monthly* 20: 2–3.

Rosivach, Vincent J. 1999. "Enslaving" Barbaroi" and the Athenian Ideology of Slavery." *Historia* 129–57.

Ross, Donald L. 2008. "Aristotle's ambivalence on slavery." *Hermathena* 184: 53–67.

Rowe, Galen O. 1993. "The many facets of hybris in Demosthenes' Against Meidias." *American Journal of Philology* 114: 397–406.

Roy, J. 1999. "Polis and oikos in classical Athens." *Greece and Rome* 46 (1): 1–17.

Roy, James. 2000. "Problems of democracy in the Arcadian confederacy 370–62 B.C." In Brock, Roger and Hodkinson, Stephen (eds), (pp. 308–26). Oxford; New York: Oxford University Press.

Rubinstein, Lene. 1993. *Adoption in IV. century Athens, Opuscula Graecolatina; 34*. Copenhagen: Museum Tusculanum Press

Rubinstein, Lene. 2009. "Ateleia grants and their enforcement in the classical and early Hellenistic periods." In Rubinstein, L. and Mitchell, L. (eds), *Greek History and Epigraphy: Essays in Honour of PJ Rhodes. Swansea: Classical Press of Wales* (pp. 115–43). Swansea: Classical Press of Wales.

Rubinstein, Lene. 2016. "Communal revenge and appeals to dicastic emotions." In Tiersch, C. (ed.), *Die athenische Demokratie im 4. Jahrhundert zwischen Modernisierung und Tradition* (pp. 55–72). Stuttgart: Steiner.

Rubinstein, Lene. 2018. "Immigration and Refugee Crises in Fourth-Century Greece: An Athenian Perspective." *The European Legacy* 23 (1–2): 5–24.

Rücker, Michaela. 2014. *'Pharmakeía und crimen magiae': frauen und magie in der griechisch-römischen Antike, Philippika; 78*. Wiesbaden: Harrassowitz.

Ruiz, Florinda. 1994. *Use and Control of violence in Classical Athens*.

Rüpke, Jörg and Clifford Ando (eds). 2015. *Public and Private in Ancient Mediterranean Law and Religion, Religionsgeschichtliche Versuche und Vorarbeiten; 65*. Berlin; Boston, MA: de Gruyter.

Ruschenbusch, Eberhard. 1962. "ΔΙΑΤΙΘΕΣΘΑΙ ΤΑ ΕΑΥΤΟΥ." *Zeitschrift der Savigny-Stiftung für Rechtsgeschichte. Romanistische Abteilung* 79 (1): 307–11.

Ruschenbusch, Eberhard. 1966. *Σόλωνος νόμοι, Die Fragmente des solonischen Gesetzeswerkes mit einer Text-und Überlieferungsgeschichte*. Wiesbaden: F. Steiner.

Salmenkivi, Erja. 1997. "Family life in the comedies of Menander." In Brock, Roger and Hodkinson, Stephen (eds), (pp. 308–26). Oxford; New York: Oxford University Press.

Salmon, John and Lin Foxhall (eds). 1998. *When Men Were Men: Masculinity, Power and Identity in Classical Antiquity, Leicester-Nottingham Studies in Ancient Society; 8*. London: Routledge.

Samaras, Thanassis. 2007. "Who Believes in Socrates' Innocence? The Religious charges against Socrates and the Intended Audience of Plato's Apology." *Polis: The Journal for Ancient Greek Political Thought* 24 (1): 1–11.

Sanders, Ed and Matthew Johncock. 2016. *Emotion and Persuasion in Classical Antiquity*. Franz Steiner Verlag.

Saunders, Trevor J. 1990. "Plato and the Athenian law of theft." In Powell, Anton (ed.), (pp. 591–609). London: Routledge.

Saunders, Trevor J. 1997. "Plato on women in the 'Laws'." In Powell, Anton (ed.), (pp. 591–609). London: Routledge.

Saxonhouse, Arlene W. 1986. "Myths and the origins of cities: reflections in the autochthony theme in Euripides' Ion." In Euben, J. Peter (ed.), (pp. 252–73). Berkeley, CA: University of California Press.

Scarborough, John. 1987. "Adaptation of folk medicines in the formal materia medica of classical antiquity." In Scarborough, John (ed.), (pp. 21–32). Madison, WI: Amer. Inst. of the history of pharmacy.

Schaps, David M. 1975. "Women in Greek inheritance law." *Classical Quarterly* 25: 53–7.

Schaps, David M. 1979.*Economic rights of women in ancient Greece*. Edinburgh University Press.

Schaps, David M. 1998. "What was free about a free Athenian woman?" *Transactions of the American Philological Association* 128: 161–88.

Schlaifer, Robert. 1936. "Greek theories of slavery from Homer to Aristotle." *Harvard Studies in Classical Philology* 47: 165–204.

Schmid, W. 1917. "Die Datierung der gefälschten Urkunden in der Kranzrede des Demosthenes." *Berl. philol. Vochen* 37: 1538–40.

Schmidt-Lawrenz, Stefan and Ralf von den Hoff (eds). 2001. *Konstruktionen von Wirklichkeit: Bilder im Griechenland des 5. und 4. Jahrhunderts v. Chr*. Stuttgart: Steiner.

Schmitter, Peter. 1975. "Compulsory schooling at Athens and Rome? A contribution to the history of Hellenistic education." *American Journal of Philology* 96: 276–89.

Schmitz, Winfried. 1997. "Der nomos moicheias: das athenische Gesetz über den Ehebruch." *Zeitschrift der Savigny-Stiftung für Rechtsgeschichte. Romanistische Abteilung* 114: 45–140.

Scholz, Peter. 2009. "Der 'gute' Bürger in Lykurgs Rede gegen Leokrates." In Mann, Christian, Haake, Matthias and Hoff, Ralf von den (eds), (pp. 171–92). Wiesbaden: Reichert.

Schönbauer, Ernst. 1964. "Paragraphe, diamartyria, exceptio, praescriptio: zur antiken Einrede der Unzulässigkeit des Streitverfahrens." *AAWW* 101: 203–31.

Schütrumpf, Eckart E. 1987. "The rhetra of Epitadeus. A Platonist's fiction." *Greek, Roman and Byzantine Studies* 28: 441–57.

Schwartzberg, Melissa. 2012. "Was the Graphe Paranomon a Form of Judicial Review." *Cardozo Law Review* 34: 1049–62.

Scodel, Ruth. 1998. "Meditations on Lysias 1 and Athenian adultery." *Études de lettres: revue de la Faculté des Lettres de l'Université de Lausanne* 1 (1).

Scodel, Ruth. 2006. "Aetiology, autochthony, and Athenian identity in 'Ajax' and 'Oedipus Coloneus'." In Davidson, John F., Muecke, Frances and Wilson, Peter J. (eds), (pp. 65–78). London: Institute of Classical Studies, University of London.

Scourfield, John H.D. 2003. "Anger and gender in Chariton's 'Chaereas and Callirhoe'." *Yale Classical Studies* 32: 163–84.

Scullion, John Scott. 2012. "Talking of festivals: the status of choruses and choregia." In Brandt, J. Rasmus and Iddeng, Jon W. (eds), (pp. 217–46). Oxford: Oxford University Press.

Sealey, Raphael. 1969. "Probouleusis and the sovereign assembly." *California Studies in Classical Antiquity* 2: 247–69.

Sealey, Raphael. 1981. "Ephialtes, eisangelia and the council." In Shrimpton, Gordon S. and McCargar D.J. (eds), (pp. 125–34). Locust Valley, NY: Augustin.

Sealey, Raphael. 1983. "The Athenian courts for homicide." *Classical Philology: A Journal Devoted to Research in Classical Antiquity* LXXVIII: 275–96.

Sealey, Raphael. 1984. "On lawful concubinage in Athens." *Classical Antiquity* 3 (1): 111–33.

Sealey, Raphael. 1990. *Women and Law in Classical Greece*: University of North Carolina Press.

Seifert, Martina. 2011. Stuttgart: Steiner.

Serafim, Andreas. 2017. *Attic Oratory and Performance*. London: Routledge.

Sfameni-Gasparo, Giulia. 1986. *Misteri e culti mistici di Demetra*. Roma: L'Erma di Bretschneider.

Shapiro, H. Alan. 1998. "Autochthony and the visual arts in fifth-century Athens." In Boedeker, Deborah Dickmann and Raaflaub, Kurt, A. (eds), *Democracy, Empire, and the Arts in Fifth-Century Athens*. Cambridge: Harvard University Press, 127–51.

Shapiro, Harvey Alan. 1996. "Democracy and imperialism: the Panathenaia in the age of Perikles." In Neils, Jenifer (ed.), (pp. 215–25). Madison, WI: University of Wisconsin Press.

Shaw, Michael. 1975. "The female intruder: women in Fifth-Century drama." *Classical Philology* 70 (4): 255–66.

Shear, Julia L. 2001. *Polis and Panathenaia: The History and Development of Athena's Festival*. Diss. University of Pennsylvania.

Shiffrin, Steven H. 2000. *Dissent, Injustice, and the Meanings of America*. Princeton University Press.

Sickinger, James P. 1999. *Public Records and Archives in classical Athens*. UNC Press Books.

Silverman, David Leopold. *The Trierarchy and Athenian Civic Identity*. [Diss. University of California, 1994 264 p.]

Simon, Erika. 1983. *Festivals of Attica. An Archaeological Commentary, Wisconsin Stud. in Class*. Madison: University of Wisconsin Press

Simon, Erika. 2002. *Festivals of Attica: An Archaeological Commentary*. Univ of Wisconsin Press.

Sinos, Rebecca Hague and John Howard Oakley. 1993. *The Wedding in Ancient Athens, Wisconsin Studies in Classics*. Madison: University of Wisconsin Press

Sipsas, Nikolas. 1993. *The Pantokrator Xenon: A Byzantine Hospital of the 12th Century*.

Skov, G.E. 1975. "The priestess of Demeter and Kore and her role in the initiation of women at the festival of the Haloa at Eleusis." *Temenos: Studies in Comparative Religion Presented by Scholars in Denmark, Finland, Norway and Sweden* 11: 136–47.

Smith, Amy Claire. 1999. "Eurymedon and the evolution of political personifications in the early classical period." *The Journal of Hellenic Studies* 119: 128–41.

Smith, Amy Claire. 2005. "The politics of weddings at Athens: an iconographic assessment." *Leeds International Classical Studies* 4 (1). doi: http://arts.leeds.ac.uk/lics/2005/200501.pdf

Smith, Nicholas D. 1983. "Aristotle's theory of natural slavery." *Phoenix* 37 (2): 109–22.

Smith, Steven D. 2007. *Greek Identity and the Athenian Past in Chariton: The Romance of Empire, Ancient Narrative. Supplementum; 9*. Eelde: Barkhuis.

Sokolowski, Franciszek. 1969. *Lois sacrées cités grecques, [publiées]*. E. de Boccard.

Sommerstein, Alan Herbert. 1998. "Rape and young manhood in Athenian comedy." In Foxhall, Lin and Salmon, John (eds), (pp. 100–14). London: Routledge.

Sommerstein, Alan Herbert. 2009. "Slave and citizen in Aristophanic comedy." In Sommerstein, Alan H. (ed.), (pp. 136–54). Oxford; New York: Oxford University Press.

Sommerstein, Alan Herbert. 2010. "Orestes' trial and Athenian homicide procedure." In Harris, Edward Monroe, Leão, Delfim Ferreira and Rhodes, Peter John (eds), (pp. 25–38). London: Duckworth.

Sommerstein, Alan Herbert and Andrew J. Bayliss. 2013. *Oath and State in ancient Greece, Beiträge zur Altertumskunde; 306*. Berlin and New York: de Gruyter.

Sosin, Joshua D. 2016. "A Metic was a Metic." *Historia* 65 (1): 2–13.

Sossau, Veronika, Faika A. El-Nagashi and Florian Martin Müller (eds). 2012. *Gefährtinnen: vom Umgang mit Prostitution in der griechischen Antike und heute, Spectanda: Schriften des Archäologischen Museums Innsbruck; 1*. Innsbruck: Innsbruck University Press

Sourvinou-Inwood, Christiane. 2003. "Festival and mysteries: aspects of the Eleusinian cult." In Cosmopoulos, Michael B. (ed.), (pp. 25–49). London: Routledge.

Sourvinou-Inwood, Christiane. 2011. *Athenian Myths and Festivals: Aglauros, Erechtheus, Plynteria, Panathenaia, Dionysia*. Oxford; New York: Oxford University Press

Späth, Thoma and Beate Wagner-Hasel (eds). 2000. *Frauenwelten in der Antike: Geschlechterordnung und weibliche Lebenspraxis*. Stuttgart: Metzler.

Spatharas, Dimos. 2006. "Wounding, Rhetoric and the Law in Lysias IV." *Revue internationale des droits de l'antiquité* (52): 87–106.

Spatharas, Dimos. 2009. *Ισοκράτης, Κατὰ Λοχίτου: Εισαγωγή, κείμενο, μετάφραση, ερμηνευτικό υπόμνημα*. Athens: Σμίλη.

Spetsieri-Choremi, Alkistis and Olga Palagia (eds). 2007. *The Panathenaic Games: proceedings of an international conference held at the University of Athens, May 11–12, 2004*. Oxford: Oxbow Books.

Stallsmith, Allaire B. 2008. "Interpreting the Athenian Thesmophoria." *The Classical Bulletin* 84 (1): 28–45.

Stanton, Greg R. 1994. "The trittyes of Kleisthenes." *Chiron* 24: 161–207.

Stehle, Eva M. 2007. "Thesmophoria and Eleusinian mysteries: the fascination of women's secret ritual." In Parca, Maryline G. and Tzanetou, Angeliki (eds), (pp. 165–85). Bloomington, in: Indiana University Press.

Steinbock, Bernd. 2011. "A Lesson in Patriotism: Lycurgus' Against Leocrates, the Ideology of the Ephebeia, and Athenian Social Memory." *Classical Antiquity* 30 (2): 279–317.

Strauss, Barry. 2002. *Fathers and Sons in Athens: Ideology and Society in the Era of the Peloponnesian War*. London: Routledge.

Stroud, Ronald S. 1968. *Drakon's Law on Homicide*. University of California Press.

Stroud, Ronald S. 1979. *The Axones and Kyrbeis of Drakon and Solon, University of California Publ. Class. Stud.; XIX*. Berkeley: University of California Press.

Stroud, Ronald S. 1993. "Aristotle and the Athenians homicide." In Piérart, Marcel (ed.), (pp. 203–21). Fribourg: Séminaire d'histoire ancienne de l'université de Fribourg; Paris: De Boccard.

Sullivan, Janet. 2003. "Demosthenes' Areopagus Legislation: Yet Again." *The Classical Quarterly* 53 (1): 130–4.

Sundahl, Mark Jefferson. 2000. "The use of statutes in the seven extant 'graphe paranomon' and 'graphe nomon me epitedeion theinai' speeches." Diss. Brown University

Sutton, Dana Ferrin. 1981. "Critias and atheism." *Classical Quarterly* 31: 33–6.

Sutton, Robert F. 1981. *The Interaction between Men and Women Portrayed on Attic Red-Figure Pottery*. Chapel Hill: University of North Carolina.

Sutton, Robert F. 1987. "Pornography and Peitho on Attic pottery." *AAPhA*: 28–8.

Sutton, Robert F. 1991. "Pornography and persuasion on Attic pottery." In Richlin, Amy (ed.), (pp. 3–35). Oxford: Oxford University Press.

Sutton, Robert F. 1997. "Nuptial Eros: the visual discourse of marriage in Classical Athens." *Journal of the Walters Art Gallery* 55–6: 27–48.

Sutton, Robert F. 2000. "The good, the base, and the ugly: the drunken orgy in Attic vase painting and the Athenian self." In Cohen, Beth (ed.), (pp. 180–202). Leiden: Brill.

Sutton, Robert F. 2004. "Family portraits: recognizing the oikos on Attic red-figure pottery." In Chapin, Anne Proctor (ed.), (pp. 327–50). Princeton, NJ: American School of Classical Studies at Athens.

Sutton, Robert F. 2009. "Female bathers and the emergence of the female nude in Greek art." In Kosso, Cynthia and Scott, Anne (eds), (pp. 61–86). Leiden; Boston, MA: Brill.

Sutton, Robert F. 2009. "Lovemaking on Attic black-figure pottery: corpus with some conclusions." In Schmidt, Stefan and Oakley, John Howard (eds), (pp. 77–91). München: Beck.

Syropoulos, Spiridon D. 2001. "An exemplary Oikos: domestic role-models in Euripides' 'Alcestis'." *Eirene: Studia Graeca et Latina* 37: 5–18.

Taylor, Claire. 2007. "From the whole citizen body?: the sociology of election and lot in the Athenian democracy." *Hesperia: The Journal of the American School of Classical Studies at Athens* 76 (2): 323–45.

Tetlow, Elisabeth Meier. 2004. *Women, Crime, and Punishment in Ancient Law and Society. 2: Ancient Greece*. London: Continuum.

Thompson, Wesley E. 1971. "The deme in Kleisthenes' reforms." *Symbolae Osloenses: Norwegian Journal of Greek and Latin Studies* 46: 72–9.

Thompson, Wesley E. 1976. *De Hagniae hereditate. An Athenian inheritance case, Mnemosyne Suppl.* 44. Leiden: Brill.

Threatt, Tiffany. 2009. "Legally speaking: rape and seduction in Athenian law." *Rhetoric Review* 28 (1): 87–8.

Thür, Gerhard. 1996. "Reply to D.C. Mirhady: torture and rhetoric in Athens." *The Journal of Hellenic Studies* 116: 132–4.

Tilg, Stefan. 2010. *Chariton of Aphrodisias and the Invention of the Greek Love Novel*. Oxford and New York: Oxford University Press.

Todd, Stephen. 1990. "The purpose of evidence in Athenian courts." In Cartledge, Paul et al. (eds), *NOMOS: Essays in Athenian Law, Politics and Society* (pp. 19–40). Cambridge: Cambridge University Press.

Todd, Stephen. 1993. *The Shape of Athenian Law*. Oxford: Oxford University Press.

Todd, S.C. 2017. "Death and Religion in Athenian Law: Identifying Pollution?" In Thür, D.F. and Leão, G. (eds), *Symposion 2015. Vorträge zur griechischen und hellenistischen Rechtsgeschichte* (pp. 325–64). Wien.

Todd, Stephen C. 2011. "The Athenian Procedure (s) of dokimasia." In *Symposion 2009*, 73–108. Verlag der Österreichischen Akademie der Wissenschaften.

Todd, Stephen Charles. 2007. *A Commentary on Lysias, Speeches 1–11*. Oxford: Oxford University Press.

Too, Yun Lee (ed.). 2001. *Education in Greek and Roman Antiquity*. Leiden: Brill.

Too, Yun Lee. 2001. "Legal instructions in classical Athens." In Too, Yun Lee (ed.), (pp. 111–32). Leiden; Boston, MA: Brill.

Torrance, Isabelle and Alan Herbert Sommerstein. 2014. *Oaths and swearing in ancient Greece, Beiträge zur Altertumskunde; 307*. Berlin; Boston, MA: de Gruyter.

Traill, Ariana E. 2008. *Women and the comic plot in Menander*. Cambridge; New York: Cambridge University Press.

Traill, John S. 1986. *Demos and Trittys: Epigraphical and topographical studies in the organization of Attica*: Athenians, Victoria College.

Travlos, J. 1974. "The lawcourt *epi Palladioi*." *Hesperia* 43: 500–11.

Trümpy, Catherine. 2004. "Die Thesmophoria, Brimo, Deo und das Anaktoron: Beobachtungen zur Vorgeschichte des Demeterkults." *Kernos* 17: 13–42.

Tsouyopoulou-Saveriadou, Nelly. 1994. "Oikos, Oikonomia und die Stellung der Frau in der griechischen Antike bei Xenophon und Aristoteles." In Richarz, Irmintraut (ed.), (pp. 41–9). Göttingen: Vandenhoeck und Ruprecht.

Tulin, Alexander. 1996. *Dike phonou: the right of prosecution and Attic homicide procedure*. Vol. 76. Berlin: Walter de Gruyter.

Turner, Victoria and Ian Jenkins. 2009. *The Greek Body*. Malibu, CA: J. Paul Getty Museum.

Ustinova, Yulia. 1996. "Orgeones in phratries: a mechanism of social integration in Attica." *Kernos* 9: 227–42.

Van Wees, Hans. 2003. "Conquerors and serfs: wars of conquest and forced labor in archaic Greece." In Luraghi, Nino and Alcock, Susan E. (eds), (pp. 33–80). Cambridge, MA: Harvard University Press.

Vatin, Claude. 1984. *Citoyens et non-citoyens dans le monde grec, Regards sur l'histoire*. Paris: SEDES.

Velissaropoulou-Karakosta, Ioulia. 1993. *Λόγοι Εὐθύνης*. Athens: A.N. Sakkoulas.

Vester, Christina. 2004. *Citizen Production, Citizen Identity: The Role of the Mother in Euripides and Menander*. Diss. University of Washington, Seattle.

Viljoen, G. van N. 1959. "Plato and Aristotle on the exposure of infants at Athens." *Acta Classica* 2: 58–69.

Visser, Margaret. 1984. "Vengeance and pollution in Classical Athens." *Journal of the History of Ideas* 45 (2): 193–206.

Vlachakis, Ilias. 1998. *Engye in classical Athens*. M.Litt, Classics, University of Glasgow.

Volonaki, Eleni. 2000. "Apagoge in Homicide Cases." *Dike* 3: 147–76.

Von Reden, Sitta. 1995. "The Piraeus – a world apart." *Greece and Rome* 42 (01): 24–37.

Wagner-Hasel, Beate. 2009. "Brautgut oder Mitgift?: das textile Heiratsgut in den Solonischen Aufwandbestimmungen." In Hildebrandt, Berit and Veit, Caroline (eds), (pp. 143–81). München: Utz.

Wallace, Robert. 1997. "On not legislating sexual conduct in fourth-century Athens." *Symposion 1995: Vorträge zur grieschischen und hellenistischen Rechsgeschichte*: 151–66.

Wallace, Robert W. 1984. *The Areopagus, from the Origins to 307 BC*. Cambridge, MA: Harvard University.

Wallace, Robert W. 1994. "Private lives and public enemies: freedom of thought in classical Athens." In Scafuro, A.L. and Boegehold, A.C. (eds), *Athenian Identity and Civic Ideology* (pp. 127–55). Baltimore: JHU Press.

Wallace, Robert W. 1996. "Book Burning in Ancient Athens." In Harris, R.W. and Wallace, E.M. (eds), *Transitions to Empire: Essays in Greco-Roman History* (pp. 226–40). Norman and London: University of Oklahoma Press.

Walters, Kenneth R. 1983. "Perikles' citizenship law." *Classical Antiquity* 2 (2): 314–36.

Walters, Kenneth R. 1993. "Women and power in classical Athens." In Deklavon, David Raymond (ed.), (pp. 194–214). Wauconda, Ill: Bolchazy-Carducci.

Wankel, Hermann. 1976. Heidelberg: Winter.

Wannagat, Detlev. 2001. "'Eurymedon eimi': Zeichen ethnischer, sozialer und physischer Differenz in der Vasenmalerei des 5. Jahrhunderts v. Chr." In Hoff, Ralf von den and Schmidt, Stefan (eds), (pp. 51–71). Stuttgart: Steiner.

Watson, James. 2010. "The origin of metic status at Athens." *The Cambridge Classical Journal* 56: 259–78.

Watson, Katherine D. 2010. *Forensic Medicine in Western Society: A History*. London: Routledge.

Weissenberger, Michael. 1987. *Die Dokimasiereden des Lysias: (orr. 16, 25, 26, 31)*. Vol. 182. Frankfurt: Athenäum.

Welwei, Karl-Wilhelm. 2004. "War die Krypteia ein grausames Terrorinstrument ?: zur Entstehung einer Fiktion." *Laverna: Beiträge zur Wirtschafts- und Sozialgeschichte der Alten Welt* 15: 33–46.

Westermann, Anton. 1850. *Untersuchungen über die in die attischen Redner eingelegten Urkunden*. Vol. 1. Leipzig: Weidmann.

Westra, Haijo Jan. 2006. "The irreducibility of autochthony: Euripides' 'Ion' and Lévi-Strauss' interpretation of the Oedipus myth." In Davidson, John F., Muecke, Frances and Wilson, Peter J. (eds), (pp. 273–9). London: Institute of Classical Studies, University of London.

Whitby, Michael, (Ed.) 2013. *Sparta*. London: Routledge.

Whitehead, D. 1986. "Women and naturalisation in fourth-century Athens. The case of Archippe." *Classical Quarterly* 36: 109–14.

Whitehead, David. 1977. *The ideology of the Athenian metic*. Cambridge: Cambridge Philological Society.

Whitehead, David. 1986. "The ideology of the Athenian metic: some pendants and a reappraisal." *The Cambridge Classical Journal* 32: 145–58.

Whitehead, David. 1991. "Norms of citizenship in ancient Greece." In Molho, Anthony, Raaflaub, Kurt A. and Emlen, Julia (eds), (pp. 135–54). Stuttgart: Steiner.

Whitehead, David. 2000. *Hypereides: The Forensic Speeches*. Oxford University Press.

Whitehead, David. 2007. "'Theft' in Greek oratory." *Classical Quarterly* 57 (1): 70–6.

Whitehead, David. 2014 (original edition 1986). *The demes of Attica, 508/7 – ca. 250 BC: A political and social study*. Princeton University Press.

Whitmarsh, Tim. 2015. *Battling the Gods: Atheism in the Ancient World*. New York: Knopf.

Wickkiser, Bronwen L. 2008. *Asklepios, Medicine, and the Politics of Healing in Fifth-Century Greece: Between Craft and Cult*. Baltimore: Johns Hopkins University Press.

Will, Édouard. 1977. "Les groupes d'Alcibiade, de Léogoras et de Teucros. Remarques sur la vie politique athénienne en 415 avant J.C." *Revue de Philologie, de Littérature et D'histoire Anciennes* 51: 92–6.

Willetts, Ronald F. 1967. *The Law Code of Gortyn*. Berlin: Walter de Gruyter.

Wilson, Peter J. 2009. "Tragic honours and democracy: neglected evidence for the politics of the Athenian Dionysia." *Classical Quarterly* N.S. 59 (1): 8–29.

Wolff, H.J. 1970. *Normenkontrolle und Gesetzesbegriff in der athenischen Demokratie. Untersuchungen zur graphe paranomon, Sitzungsberichte der Heidelberger Akademie der Wissenschaften, Philos.-Histor. Klasse 2*. Heidelberg.

Wolff, Hans Julius. 1944. "Marriage law and family organization in ancient Athens. A study on the interrelation of public and private law in the Greek city." *Traditio: Studies In Ancient and Medieval History, Thought and Religion* 2: 43–95.

Wolff, Hans Julius. 1946. "The origin of judicial litigation among the Greeks." *Traditio*: 31–87.

Wolff, Hans Julius. 1966. *Die attische Paragraphe*. Weimar: Böhlau.

Wolpert, Andrew. 2001a. "Lysias 1 and the Politics of the Oikos." *The Classical Journal* 96 (4): 415–24.

Wolpert, Andrew. 2001b. *Remembering Defeat: Civil War and Civic Memory in Ancient Athens*: Baltimore: Johns Hopkins University Press.

Wolpert, Andrew. 2002. "Lysias 18 and Athenian memory of the civil war." *Transactions of the American Philological Association*, 132, 109–26.

Wolpert, Andrew and Konstantinos Kapparis. 2011. *Legal Speeches of Democratic Athens: Sources for Athenian History*. Indianapolis: Hackett Publishing.

Woodhouse, William John. 1938. *Solon the Liberator: A Study of the Agrarian Problem in Attica in the Seventh Century*. Oxford: Oxford University Press.

Worthington, Ian. 2003. "The length of an Athenian public trial: A reply to professor MacDowell." *Hermes* 131 (H. 3): 364–71.

Wyse, W. (ed.). 1904. *The Speeches of Isaeus*. Cambridge University Press.

Yunis, Harvey Evan. 1988. "Law, politics and the graphe paranomon in fourth-century Athens." *Greek, Roman and Byzantine Studies* 29: 361–82.

Zajonz, Sandra. 2014. "APAGOGE BEI TÖTUNGSVORWURF Ein neuer Vorschlag zum Verständnis von Dem. 23, 80." *Rheinisches Museum für Philologie* 157: 251–71.

Zeitlin, Froma I. 1981. "Travesties of Gender and Genre in Aristophanes' 'Thesmophoriazousae'." *Critical Inquiry* 8 (2): 301–27.

Index

Abortion in the Ancient Greek World 14
Adamidis, Vasileios 36, 45, 53
The Administration of Justice from Homer to Aristotle 10
adulterer, bodily humiliations 182
adultery 154, 182–206; false accusations of 183; laws 84; mandatory divorce after 183; public prosecution for 183–4
adversity 129
Aeschinean "master plan" 199
Aeschines 37, 38, 41, 52, 53, 105, 121, 128, 193, 197–200, 289, 292
age of consent 151
agon timetos 37, 288, 293
Agora 247
agoranomoi 29
Aigos Potamoi 60
Akastos 54
Alcibiades 59, 249, 254
amateurism 46–9
Amphis 14
Andocides 27, 35, 81, 293
andragathia 94
Anthesteria 56, 291
Antiphon 219, 220, 272, 301
apagoge 41, 230
Apatouria 80, 122, 256
aphairesis of Neaira 106
apographe 41
Apollodoros 38, 48, 53, 77, 81, 92, 94, 126, 146, 148, 175–6, 201, 223, 224, 256, 267
Apology 262
arbitration 225–7
Archilochus 60
Archinos 46
archon 284–6, 289–91; primary law requiring of 280; social protection network and responsibilities 280–1
archonship of Antidotos 139
archonship of Eucleides 140, 165
archonship of Eukleides 145
Areopagos Council 21, 44, 52, 220, 270; in homicide cases 246
Aristagora 102, 103
aristocracy 309
Aristogeiton 55, 56, 199
Ariston 215, 220
Aristophanes 7, 26, 37, 126, 142, 229, 259, 263
Aristophon 83, 144, 145, 171
Aristotle 6, 51, 55, 77, 89, 119, 124, 127, 143, 173, 176, 177
Armodios 55
Arnaoutoglou, Ilias 11
Artemis 55
assault 214–22; definition of 208–9
astynomoi 28, 29
Athenaion Politeia 6, 8, 54, 55, 57, 58, 83, 91, 192, 195, 232, 284–6, 289–90, 292, 295, 296
Athenaios 196
Athenian arbitration 43; *see also* arbitration
Athenian citizen men: privileges of 86–8; rights of 86–8
Athenian citizenship 75, 82, 94, 176, 198, 311
Athenian Democracy 1, 4, 10, 24, 34, 36, 39, 47, 50, 60, 61, 87, 88, 118, 144, 170, 195, 214, 223, 225, 255, 258, 261, 267, 268, 294, 295, 298, 310, 313; division of powers 20–2; open government in 36–40; rule of law, question 22–4
Athenian economy 93, 232
Athenian healthcare system 298–302
Athenian homicide law 269
Athenian immigration model 89
Athenian justice system 30

Athenian law: amateurism of 46–9; citizens in 70–115; core human rights, protections 30–6; definition of intent in 209; metics in 70–115; scholarship 9–15; slaves in 70–115; sources of 4–9; voice of democratic *polis* 309–14
Athenian legal system 37, 44, 45, 48–9
Athenian mercantile law 231
Athenian military service 72–3, 83
Athenian *oikos* 116–37; definition of 116; and members 119–32; *polis,* nucleus 116; and *polis* 117–19; purpose of 117; sources 116–17
Atheniensium 19
Attica 56, 78, 82, 90, 131, 222, 252, 255, 257, 271, 295
attic comedy 7
Attic Orators 3, 4, 29, 51, 53, 81, 148, 215, 223, 224, 231, 251, 252, 265
authentic legal citations 4
authoritarian monarchies 20
autochthony 77

Bacchides 201
Bacchis 145
Bakewell, Geoffrey 147
basileus 44, 55, 56, 250, 256, 268, 271, 291; religion 241–2
Battaros 97
Bauchet, L. 10
Baughman, Elizabeth 28
bemusement 1
biaion 208
Birds 267
Bisexuality in the Ancient World 13
Blok, Josine 77
Blundell, Sue 13
board of 11 magistrates (Eleven) 27
Bocchoris 197
Boeckh, Augustus 253, 294
Boeotian League 79
Boeotians 96
Bonner, Robert 10
Boulai 26
Boule 34, 37, 38, 41, 55, 83, 94, 260, 297
Brandt, Paul 12
bribery 19–20
brothel keeper 97
Burger, Friedrich 5

Cameron, Averil 169
Cantarella, Eva 12
Carawan, Edwin 82, 144
Carey, Christopher 228
Christianity 249, 250
Chrysilla 81
citizen body 80–6
classical Athens 29, 58, 92
Cleomenes III 78
Clouds of Aristophanes 122, 267
Cohen, David 214
Cohen, Edward 14, 194, 197, 232
Cohn-Haft, Louis 186
common law systems 49
concubines 138–62; of Euktemon 154; illegitimate children 154; of Philoneos 153; unions and 152–5
confiscation, of property 32
The Constraints of Desire 13
Contraception and Abortion from the Ancient World to the Renaissance 14
Corpus Iuris Civilis 60
corpus of Athenian laws 36
Cox, Cheryl 13, 119
criminal justice 207–40
Cudjoe, Richard 151

Das attische Recht und Rechtsverfahren 10
Davidson, James 13, 14
Dean-Jones, Lesley 14
death penalty 216
deep emotional bonds 7
Deinarchos 102
Delian League 253
Demades 298
democracy 33, 35, 37, 44, 50, 56, 59, 70, 131, 225, 254; *see also* Athenian Democracy
Democratic Athenian Constitution 58
democratic Athenian law 2
Democratic Constitution 2, 261, 268, 311
democratic political thought 2
Demokedes of Kroton 299
Demophilos 104, 105
Demosthenes 29, 30, 37, 38, 46, 48, 59, 121, 167, 175, 198, 201, 216, 217, 221, 230, 254, 260, 265, 285
Demosthenic Corpus 39
Detienne, Marcel 76
deuterology 43
diamartyria 46
diapsephisis 105
Dieaneira 77
dikasteria 22
dike apostasiou 91
dike pseudomartyrion 46, 101

Dinarchos 265
Diocles of Karystos 300
Diodotos 175
Dionysia, Lenaean 242
Dionysios 272
Dionysios Halicarnassus 102
Dionysos 256, 263
Dionysus 253
Diopeithes 259, 261
Diophantos 128
Diotima 11
disabled citizens 291–2; provisions 282–3
disabled persons 200
disbelief 1
dispute resolution 40–5
divorce 155, 182–206; primary law on 182
Dover, Kenneth 13
dowry 186; return of 182
Drakon 31, 32; homicide law of 2, 5, 6, 244–5, 247; law of 154, 182, 191, 193; laws of 34–6
Drerup, Engelbert 5
Droit et société dans la Grèce ancienne 10

education 32–4, 36, 189
Eidinow, Esther 266, 267
eisangelia 40, 41, 170, 259–61, 286–9
eisangelia xenias 102
elderly, caring for 292–4
elderly, protecting from abuse 283–90
Eleusinean Mysteries 249, 254, 266
Eleusis 255
emotional arguments 51
emotions 51, 52, 214, 267
employment opportunities 93
endeixis 41
Engels, D. 169
Enyalios 55
epangelia 198
ephegesis 41
ephetai 47, 271
epicleros 130
Epidemics 300
epidikasia 149–51
epikleros 1, 149–51, 164, 165–6, 169–71, 187, 189
Epitadeus 176
Epitaphios of Pericles 118, 199
erastes 14
Eratosthenes 53, 190, 272
eromenos 14
ethopoeia 53
Euboulos 59, 131
Eucleides 18
Eukleides 35
Euktemon 81, 154
Eumolpidai 55
eunomie 31
Euphiletos 53, 104, 127, 190
Euripides 43, 77
Eurystheus 77
euthyna 25, 26, 43
euthynoi 26
Euxitheos 52, 92
Evidence in Athenian Courts 10
executive officers, Athenian state 54–61
extra-judicial tactics 52

Fantham, E. 12
fatherhood 85
father of Lysias 93
festivals 252–7
Filonik, Jakub 259, 261
financial compensation 191
financial gain 44
First Democracy 227, 291, 313
Fisher, Nick 214
Foley, H.P. 12
foreign woman fraudulent betrothal, law prohibiting 140
Foucault, Michael 13
Foxhall, Lin 169
Frauen im klassischen Athen: sozialer Raum und reale Bewegungsfreiheit 13
Frazer, James George 252
Frost, Frank 194
Funeral Speech of Pericles 33

Gagarin, Michael 2, 11
gender imbalance 127
Gernet, Louis 10, 46
Glazebrook, Allison 194
Goddesses, Whores, Wives and Slaves 12
Golden, Mark 169
The Golden Bough 252
Gomme, A.W. 12, 169
grammarians 9
grape stomping 125
graphai asebeias 262
graphe apostasiou 91
graphe aprostasiou 57, 90, 91
graphe asebeias 57, 259, 261, 264
graphe doroxenias 56, 102
graphe hybreos 92, 97, 217, 223–5, 227, 228
graphe kakoseos 286
graphe moicheias 193

graphe paranomon 37–40, 42, 95
graphe traumatos ek pronoias 221
graphe xenias 56, 74, 92, 101, 103
Great Dionysia 253
Greek Bastardy in the Classical and Hellenistic periods 14
Greek medical theory 152

Haloa 255
Halperin, David 13
Hansen, H. 39, 221
hard-working metics 94
Harmodios 56, 199
Harpocration 9, 91, 142, 286, 287
Harris, Edward 50, 223, 227, 228
Harrison, A.R.W. 10
heautontimorumenos 120
Heirat, Hetaerentum und Konkubinat im klassischen Athen 13
Heliaia 21
Hellenistic period 5
Heracles 77
Heraclidae 77
Herman, Gabriel 214
Herodotos 77, 299
Heroines and Hysterics 12
Hesiod 119
hetairai 7, 34
Hippias 20, 21
Hippocrates of Kos 300
Hippocrates' Woman: Reading the Female Body in Ancient Greece 14
Hipponikos 224
History of Contraception: From Antiquity to the Present Day 14
History of Sexuality 13
History of Thucydides 8
homicide 268–73; trial, procedures and oaths 248
honorary decrees 7
Humphreys, S.C. 118
hybris 223–5, 228; law of 209–10
Hypereides 103, 128, 196, 224

illegitimate children 171–2
income support 283; for poor and needy 294–8
In Defense of Euphiletos 104
Ingalls, Wayne 169
inheritance 163–81; law, statutory time-limit 165; law regulating 163
Isaios 167, 224
Ischomachos 123–6
Isocrates 46, 122, 216, 287, 312, 313
isonomia 31, 48
isopoliteia 31
isoteleia 93

Just, Roger 13
justice, administration 18–69; Athenian Democracy 20–4; dispute resolution 40–5; officials and individuals, accountability 24–30; sources 18–20

Kallias 81, 121
Kallimachos 56
Kallistratos 196
Kekropid dynasty 54
Kenyon, F.G. 10
Kephalos, Syracusan 89
Kerameikos 86
Kimon 37
King, Helen 14
Kleisthenes 2, 20, 21, 31, 82, 268, 301
Kleon 58
Kodros 54
koureotis 80
Ktesiphon 37
kyrbeis 35
kyria ekklesia 95
kyrios 87, 88, 119–23, 129, 148, 149, 166, 176, 182, 188, 190, 193, 284, 293, 294

Laconia 79
Lape, Susan 77
lawful marriage 147–52
The Law in Classical Athens 10
The Law of Ancient Athens 11
law of Athens 4
The Law of Athens 10
law on *hetairesis* 184
Laws 52
lawsuits: blocking 46; processes and types 40–5
Leduc, Claudine 172
Lefkowitz, Mary 12
legal compensation 207
legal minors, protecting 283–90
legitimate daughters 167–9
Lenaia 55
Leocrates 174
Lewis, D.M. 253
Lexica Segueriana 102
lexicographers 9
Life of Solon 8
Lipsius, Justus Hermann 10

litigation 18, 92, 106, 122, 141, 167
logistai 25
Longo, Chiara Pecorella 221
Lycurgus 177
Lykophron 192
Lykourgos 52, 77
Lysias 25, 292

MacDowell, D.M. 3, 5, 10, 11, 15, 21, 37, 83, 119, 141, 143, 171, 186, 221, 223, 225, 231, 232, 269
Macedon 38
magistrates, scrutiny of 18
Mantitheos 81
marriage 117, 122, 123, 186; ever-shifting definition of 140–7; formation and purposes 138–62; primary law on 138; primary purposes of 148; sources 138–40
McLaren, Angus 14
Medea of Euripides 8
medical care 298–302
Medon 54
meidias 26, 208, 216, 217
Messenia 79
metics 88–96
metoikion 90, 93
metronomoi 29
Metroon 35
miasma 44, 123
Mirhady, David 11
Misgolas 84
Misoumenos 146
mixed marriages 145, 146; law prohibiting 139
modern jurisprudence 4
Modrzejewski, Joseph 187
monogamous heterosexual relations 85
Montesqieu 20
murder prosecution 246

naturalization 75; laws and procedures 73–4
Nephelokokkygia 38
Nikias 59
Nikocles 144
Nikomenes 144, 145, 171
Ninos 267
nomon me epitedeion thenai 40
nomothesia 38
nomothetai 3
non-monetary items 149
non-violent conflict resolution 225–7
Noreña, Carlos 187

O'Connell, Peter 51, 265
Odeon of Pericles 188, 233
Oedipous Coloneus 290
Oedipus Tyrannus 269
Ogden, Daniel 14, 82, 144
oikos 33, 34, 85; *see also* Athenian *oikos*; continuation of 163–81; legal protections of 131; in peril 182–206
Olympiodoros 84, 153
Omitowoju, Roseanna 228
One Hundred Years of Homosexuality 13
On the Estate of Hagnias 288
On the Estate of Menekles 148
On the Estate of Pyrrhos 288
On the False Embassy 59
On the murder of Eratosthenes 126
On the Murder of Eratosthenes 228
On the Stepmother 153

paganism 33
paidagogos 151
Paleologean period 9
Panathenaia 252
Pandora's Daughters: The Role and Status of Women in Greek and Roman Antiquity 12–13
parent, legal definition 282
patrimony 282
Patterson, Cynthia 13, 83, 118, 144
Peisistratids 2, 20, 31
Peisistratos 31, 78, 311
Peloponnesian war 25, 35, 39, 58, 59, 82, 87, 94, 143, 171, 172, 267, 287, 298, 302
Periclean citizenship law 8, 78, 82, 139, 141–5, 152, 171, 173, 191, 192, 256, 311
Periclean law reinstated 139
Pericles 30, 37, 58, 89, 144, 296, 297, 302
Perikeiromene 146
Perioikoi 78
phasis 41
Pherekydes 76
Phillips, David 11, 221
Philodades 105
Philoneos 153
Phokion 59
Phormion 48
Photios 91
phratry 122
Phryne 264, 265, 267, 268
Phrynion 106
Phyle 36
Piraeus 72
Pittalakos 89

Plato 52, 87
Plautus 7, 201
Plutarch 8, 25, 32, 59, 144, 196, 215, 259
polemarch 54, 231; religious and judicial duties 74
Polemon 196
Policing Athens 27
polis 18–69, 189; citizenship in 70–1, 75–80
Politics 143
Polykrates of Samos 299
Pomeroy, Sarah 12, 13, 169
Praxiteles 266
private arbitration 211; description of 211–12; law on 211
private arbitrators 44
private lawsuits 42–5, 57, 216
probole: law on 243; sykophants 244
probouleuma 2
property crimes 207–40
property disputes 229–33
prostitution 182–206
pseudo-hetaira 146
pseudomartyrion 43, 74
public lawsuits 45
public prosecutor 27
Pythias 196

quasi-mythical lawgiver Lycurgus 2

rape 208
Reflections of Women in Antiquity 12
religion 241–79; basileus 241–2; intersection of law 248–52; prosecutions on 257–68
Rhetoric 77
rhetra of Epitadeus 176, 177
Rhodes, Peter 42, 83, 259, 286, 297
Riddle, John 14
Riess, Werner 214
right to privacy 33
Roebuck, Derek 225
Rosivach, Vincent 194
Rowe, G. 223
Roy, J. 118
rule of law 49–54
rules of evidence 49–54

safety net 280–308
Samians 96
Schaps, David 13
Schnurr-Redford, Christine 13
scholarship 9–15
scrutiny, law on 185
Scythia 99
Scythian archers 27, 28, 99
Sealey, Rafael 13
self-defense 247, 269
sexual assault 208
sexual maturity 152
sexual violence 227–9
Sicily 60, 249, 258, 299
sitophylakes 29
Skamandrios 32, 35, 38
slander 214–22; penalty for 211; primary law on 210–11; Solon's law on 210
slave labor 101
slaves 96–101
Smith, Gertrud 10
Socrates 123, 124, 259, 262–4, 267
Solon, laws of 34, 36, 310
Solonean Athens 32
Solonean corpus of laws 2
Solonean laws 118
Spartan educational system 33
state religion 252–7
state-sponsored killings 32
status disputes, legal procedures 101–7
Stephanos 73, 92
Stephanos of Eroiadai 153
stereotypes 127
Strepsiades 122
Studies in Greek Law, Oratory and Comedy 11
succession 163–81; by adopted children 172–7; law, legitimate daughters 163–4; law regulating 163; by natural legitimate sons 166–7
Sundahl, Mark J. 11
supernatural infection 269
Syracusan Kephalos 93
Syracuse Dionysios I 94

tactics 51
Terence 7, 120
Thebes 79
theft, law on 212–13
Theomnestos 92
Theophemos 218
Theophrastos 173
Theramenes 59
Thermopylae 78
Thesmophoria 250
Thesmophoriazousai of Aristophanes 128
thesmothetai 2, 55–7, 191
Thucydides 30, 77

Timarchos 200
Todd, Stephen 11, 49, 90–1, 143, 186, 228
Trachiniae of Sophocles 8
tyrannicides 56
Tyrtaios 77

United States Federal Rule of Evidence 404 53

violence 207–40; in Athenian law and life 214–22; law on 208
Vitruvius 32

Wallace, R. 118
wasps of Aristophanes 88, 296
Watson, James 89
wealthier metics 87
wills: by adopted children 172–7
Winkler, Jack 13
wives 138–62
Wolff, Hans Julius 10
Wolpert, Andrew 217
women 7, 11–14, 33, 34, 43, 47, 53, 56, 78, 81, 82, 84, 85, 123, 192, 229, 310, 311
Women in Ancient Greece 13
Women in the Classical World 12
Women's bodies in classical Greek Science 14

Xanthins 98
Xenophon 8, 126, 127, 148, 152, 231, 263

Zeus 128, 185, 199, 262